Springer Series in Transitional Justice

Series Editor
Olivera Simic, Law School, Griffith University,
Nathan, QLD, Australia

Transitional justice is a field of study that focuses on mechanisms developed to uncover crimes of the past, and to find ways to deal with them in the present. |This global, interdisciplinary field of study critically analyses forms of intervention that follow civil wars and political repression. It is an ever-growing field with its own concepts, perspectives and methodologies that have been developed in response to dilemmas arising from how successor regimes should deal with the human rights abuses of their authoritarian predecessors. Transitional justice includes the mechanisms and processes associated with a society's attempts to come to terms with large-scale past abuses not only to ensure accountability and serve justice, but also to achieve healing, reconciliation, truth, conflict resolution, democracy and peace. These mechanisms include, among others, criminal justice, institutional and rule-of-law reform, truth-telling and reparations. As an interdisciplinary field, transitional justice takes place across a range of disciplines such as law, anthropology, international relations, political science, history, ethics, development studies, cultural studies, sociology, psychology, theology and education. The aim of the Springer Series in Transitional Justice is to address the legal, moral, social, and political issues that arise in countries emerging from war, dictatorships or other repressive regimes. It will focus on the strategies available to societies pursuing accountability for mass atrocities or human rights abuses. The strategies may be local, regional or global, and led by either state officials or civil societies who often pursue either judicial and non-judicial responses to human rights abuses, or both. While the series will encourage both top-down and bottom-up theoretical and qualitative inquiries, it will also emphasize relatively unexplored and under-researched role of civil society groups and social movements, such as local women's groups, the role of art, theater and media and other grass-roots transitional justice mechanisms and initiatives.

More information about this series at https://link.springer.com/bookseries/11233

Jeremie Bracka

Transitional Justice for Israel/Palestine

Truth-Telling and Empathy in Ongoing Conflict

Springer

Jeremie Bracka
Minerva Centre for Human Rights
Hebrew University of Jerusalem
Jerusalem, Israel

Springer Series in Transitional Justice
ISBN 978-3-030-89434-4 ISBN 978-3-030-89435-1 (eBook)
https://doi.org/10.1007/978-3-030-89435-1

This Springer imprint is published by the registered company Springer Nature Switzerland AG
The registered company address is: Gewerbestrasse 11, 6330 Cham, Switzerland

Preface

In 1993, the Israelis and the Palestinians signed a Declaration of Principles initiating a peace process, which promised to deliver a solution to their historical conflict within 5 years. Almost three decades later, the Oslo Accords are in tatters, and the prospects of a peace agreement have never seemed more elusive. The failure of historical efforts in the Israeli–Palestinian context to reach a political settlement raises questions about the merits of top-down peacebuilding, the sidelining of civil society, and the exclusion of international human rights law from the conflict's resolution. In this light, an understanding of transitional justice in the region is instrumental to reframing our understanding of the current political impasse, and more generally developing new frameworks for transitional justice in active conflict. Whether used as a post-conflict tool, creative diplomacy, or a game-changing civil society initiative, the transitional justice paradigm has the potential to inform the current political and social landscape.

Notably, as explored in Chap. 4, most political leaders outrightly dismiss transitional justice for Israelis and Palestinians. Others protest that any mechanism contending with the past is premature, naïve, and fraught with perils. Although the Oslo Accords marked a significant milestone towards peace, transitional justice has been all but absent in conflict resolution efforts between the two nations.[1] Until today, the political landscape frames peacebuilding in practical and material terms, deliberately avoiding thorny issues of the past, like questions of legitimacy, narratives, justice, collective memory, and human rights abuse.

As discussed in Chap. 7, mainstream non-governmental organisations (NGOs) in the region have also avoided the language of transitional justice and 1948. On the Israeli side, human rights work is commonly confined to individual 'apolitical' legal campaigns divorced from historical context. For Palestinians, NGOs tend to be

[1] The term 'nation' will be used to refer to Israeli and Palestinian societies as a community of people based on a common language, territory, history, ethnicity, or religion. It will also be used subjectively to describe 'an imagined political community [that is] imagined as both inherently limited and sovereign'. See Benedict R. Anderson, *Imagined Communities: Reflections on the Origin and Spread of Nationalism* (Verso, 1991). 224.

driven by highly politicised notions of absolute justice and national resistance. Overall, the desirability of transitional justice discourse has not entered the lexicon of human rights groups, peacebuilders, or the public.

Nevertheless, somewhere between lofty transitional justice ideals and prevailing wisdom lies the viability of an alternative theoretical and discursive paradigm. This research project is therefore both timely and innovative in exploring the potential role of the past, truth-telling, restorative justice, and notions of empathy as reconciliation in long-term conflict resolution. Specifically, it is worth challenging state-centred paradigms and legal mechanisms in the Israeli–Palestinian context to meaningfully transform a culture of conflict to one of peaceful coexistence.

Structure

The book begins by examining the centrality of history and narratives to both nations (Chap. 1) and the international legal dimensions of the dispute (Chap. 2). Both Israelis and Palestinians buttress their respective histories and narratives by recourse to international law. The first two chapters are thus devoted to the theoretical, historical, and legal implications of the Israeli–Palestinian past. They address the key divisive issues comprising the conflict, namely the significance of 1948 and the Palestinian right of return, 1967, the Israeli occupation and the Jewish settlements, as well as the Second Intifada, with its legacy of human rights abuse and political violence (2000–2005). It is contended that the emotional orientation of fear, and ethos of conflict, borne out by these events, continue to dominate and define both societies. The historical and legal frameworks outlined in Chaps. 1 and 2 will be used to guide the design of an IPTEC in addressing the unlawful conduct of Israelis and Palestinians across the conflict.

Given the Israeli–Palestinian struggle is one characterised by antagonistic belief systems and national identities, it is argued that alternate models of conflict resolution beyond the current one are particularly relevant to the Middle East. A growing interest exists around the desirability of transitional justice and international human rights law to conflict resolution (Chap. 3). This chapter highlights the value of the transitional justice paradigm to conflict resolution and peace-building efforts around the globe. Specifically, it demonstrates how transitional justice may serve as a relevant tool to foster truth-telling, historical justice, and grassroots reconciliation in ethno-national conflict.

From this standpoint, the transitional justice paradigm, as defined in Chap. 3, is particularly desirable for both Israeli and Palestinian societies at present. Chapter 4 addresses the desirability of engaging the historical record and human rights law to reframe the polarised narratives of 'justice' that fuel the conflict. Notwithstanding prevailing political wisdom to marginalise the Israeli–Palestinian past, both nations should address the central events of the conflict (1948, 1967, and the Second Intifada) if they are to meaningfully transform a culture of conflict to one of sustainable peace. Ultimately, reconciliation for Israelis and Palestinians will first necessitate reshaping collective memory and engaging empathy between the two communities.

As discussed in Chap. 3, a range of mechanisms exist to pursue accountability for the past. However, criminal trials and truth commissions remain the flagship tools of transitional justice. Given their primacy in the field, and the current ICC situation in Palestine, the potential contribution of international criminal justice (ICJ) (Chap. 5) and a truth commission for the Middle East (Chap. 6) are evaluated in these two chapters. Arguably, meaningful and legitimate transitional justice measures must address the patterns of systematic abuses committed by both nations against each other's civilians. Given the systemic and complex nature of the Israeli–Palestinian conflict, it is concluded that ICJ, as represented by an ICC intervention, is a relatively impractical and undesirable means of addressing the Israeli–Palestinian past at present (Chap. 5). From this standpoint, the applicability of truth commissions and restorative justice theory is considered for Israelis and Palestinians (Chap. 6). This chapter evaluates the possibilities of the truth commission model based on the three normative pillars of transitional justice as defined in Chap. 3.

Given the centrality of civil society to transitional justice, and its growing role in conflict resolution, this thesis also explores how a nation's non-state actors can devise and prioritise the goals of transitional justice during ongoing hostilities (Chap. 7). In cases like the Israeli–Palestinian one, civil society occupies a particularly important role given the reluctance of state actors to pursue transitional justice. Chapter 7 also focuses on the existing landscape of Israeli and Palestinian civil society and describes two types of unofficial transitional justice measures that Israeli Jews and Palestinians have been using to negotiate the conflict. Many scholars have lauded the capacity of such projects to reconfigure the social and psychological dynamics of the conflict.

Finally, building on this framework, an unofficial Israeli-Palestinian Truth and Empathy Commission (IPTEC) is conceived for Israelis and Palestinians to promote the goals of transitional justice and long-term conflict resolution (Chap. 8). This final chapter explores various debates around the institutional design of an IPTEC, the scope of historical inquiry and its legal mandate. The chapter will also consider the extent to which an IPTEC may forge an authoritative bridging narrative for Israelis and Palestinians at present, as well as cultivate a more informed moral conversation about the past.

Notably, a small chorus of Israeli and Palestinian academics has already championed a truth commission.[2] However, with few exceptions, there has been scant attention devoted to the actual infrastructure of such a body, let alone an unofficial one, created during conflict, or one seeking to investigate events beyond 1948, as

[2]Zinaida Miller, 'Settling with History: A Hybrid Commission of Inquiry for Israel/Palestine' (2007) 20 *Harvard Human Rights Journal* 293; See also Adrien Wing, 'A Truth and Reconciliation Commission for Palestine/Israel: Healing Spirit Injuries?' (2008) 17(1) *Transnational Law & Contemporary Problems* 139; Ariel Meyerstein, 'On the Advantage and Disadvantage of Truth Commission for Life: Dreaming an Israeli-Palestinian Truth Commission' (2003) 45 *Journal of Church and State* 457 ('Dreaming an Israeli-Palestinian Truth Commission').

well as Palestinian abuses. Indeed, there has been virtually no scholarship on the truth commission model for the Israeli–Palestinian conflict over the past decade. This book therefore seeks to expand the existing truth commission proposals for the region based on present realities and current theoretical and practical considerations. Ultimately, the final chapter innovatively designs a grassroots bilateral project to involve local academics, lawyers, historians, and moderate religious and political leaders on both sides. This thesis uniquely adopts the notion of 'empathy' into the central goal of an unofficial truth commission designed for ongoing conflict.

Jerusalem, Israel Jeremie Bracka

Acknowledgements

I once heard about an old Arab Mufti who made peace with his neighbouring village after years of bloodshed. He was asked, why he shook hands with the man who killed his son? The Mufti replied: because I have another son, and I don't want to lose him too. (Marc Joseph Bracka (1934–1996))

My passion for Middle East peacebuilding was inspired by my family's experiences as displaced Jews from Egypt and Poland. My parents' capacity to transcend their own narratives of persecution and prejudice enabled me to ask the questions that led to this book. I am indebted to the indomitable spirit of my late father Marc, whose love and presence hover over me. His guidance paves the ground beneath my feet. I am deeply grateful to my extraordinary mother and emotional mentor, *Faygaleh*. My Mamma bird has given unconditionally of her heart to make all this possible. Her unwavering faith and nurture lend me courage to claim the most authentic parts of myself.

Writing this monograph meant taking the road less travelled. This subject matter demanded great leaps of faith against the currents of violence and hopelessness. I was often asked why bother spilling more ink on such a politicised and intractable dispute? Are attempts to address the past not fruitless ones teetering on irrelevance? Few conflicts so test the expertise of scholars and deplete the hope of human rights practitioners. Over the course of my research however, I grew emboldened by the work of various transitional justice and conflict resolution experts. I was particularly encouraged by tireless Israeli and Palestinian activists resisting the tide. Their projects defy the polarity that fuels the violence. My book pays tribute to them and to their vivid moral imagination. I am humbled to join a more nuanced conversation about the Israeli–Palestinian past. It is my hope that this might even allow us to envision a post-conflict reality.

In researching and drafting this book, I was supported by three remarkable women. The inimitable Professor Sarah Joseph, who first taught me human rights law in 2001, has been a guiding light. Her mentorship, prompt feedback, and outstanding supervision helped me to believe that conceiving an IPTEC was a subject worthy of inquiry. The ever-insightful Dr. Joanna Kyriakakis lent an expert eye to many complex parts of this work. In addition to caring for her own infant, she remained committed to midwifing my project from start to finish. Associate Professor Melissa Castan was a bulwark of support and friendship. Over the past two decades, not a drop of her kindness has left my cup. My gratitude also extends to Professor Aeyal Gross who reviewed each chapter and gave generously of his time and resources at Tel Aviv University.

To my Bracka and Berman families, thank you for being loving passengers on the ride. I am blessed to be the beneficiary of such deep connections. Special love to a small circle of sisters, who initiate me daily into meaningful friendship. You give me courage and wisdom for the journeys I travel ahead and within. Finally, I dedicate this book to my husband and life partner Ronen, who lightens and enlivens my heart. You bore patient witness to the process. It is no small thing to be lovingly shadowed in the world. I do not take one breathe with you and our beautiful son Matteo Joseph for granted.

Contents

About the Author

Jeremie M. Bracka is an Australian-Israeli human rights lawyer and academic at Hebrew University, Minerva Center for Human Rights (Jerusalem), and the Max Planck Institute for Comparative Public Law (Heidelberg). He lectures in constitutional law, human rights law, international criminal law, and transitional justice. His PhD from Monash University (2020) focused on transitional justice in ongoing conflict and specifically Israel/Palestine. Jeremie has published with Oxford University Press, the *Vanderbilt Journal of Transnational Law*, and the *Melbourne Journal of International Law*. In 2018, Jeremie won the Monash University Law Publication Award for his chapter in *Law and Memory: Towards Legal Governance of History* (Cambridge University Press, 2017). He has worked as a legal advisor at the International Criminal Tribunal for Rwanda (2004), Israel's Permanent Mission to the U.N (2009), Israel's Supreme Court (2010), and the Israeli Ministry of Foreign Affairs (2011–2013).

Chapter 1
The Historical Framework: The Struggle over Narrative, Memory, and Identity

1.1 Introduction

> *...Like the invisible 'dark matter'... the intangibles in the conflict, largely based on history that is 'remembered, recovered, invented' profoundly influence the willingness of the two sides to make peace or continue with war.*[1]

To fully appreciate transitional justice and the Israeli–Palestinian conflict, it is essential to outline the historical dimensions of the dispute. Through sub-cultures of suffering, and repertoires of victimhood, each nation has developed its own cognitive schema of the past that merits close review. This is not only because it informs their self-conception, and the intractability of the conflict, but also because it is crucial to assessing the role of 'truth-telling', 'justice', and 'reconciliation' in the dispute's resolution. Appropriately framing narratives around key historic experiences helps to identify the hurdles facing transitional justice.[2] It could also shed light on how practitioners might best apply human rights norms and conflict resolution theory to this unique context.

At its core, the Israeli–Palestinian struggle is one waged over contested territory known historically as Palestine, which two national movements claim as their homeland. For more than half a century, Palestinian nationalism and Zionism, the Jewish national movement, have collided over the right to self-determination, statehood, and justice. Beyond geography and borders, Israelis and Palestinians are also divided conceptually by a gulf mediated through historical experience. The central premise of this chapter is that the conflict is primarily driven by history. This discussion does not attempt however to provide an exhaustive chronology of Arab–Israeli

[1] Walid Salem,Benjamin Pogrund and Paul Scham (eds), *Shared Histories: A Palestinian-Israeli Dialogue* (Left Coast Press, 2005) 1.

[2] The term 'transitional justice' will be used throughout the thesis to refer to the field of transitional justice, namely its practitioners, academics, and mechanisms.

J. Bracka, *Transitional Justice for Israel/Palestine*, Springer Series in Transitional Justice, https://doi.org/10.1007/978-3-030-89435-1_1

relations, but rather focuses on three transformative events crucial to discursive mapping of the conflict. Namely, it examines the Palestinian right of return (1948), the Israeli occupation and the Jewish settlements (1967), and the Second Intifada, with its legacy of bloodshed and political radicalisation (2000–2005). It is contended that the emotional orientation of fear and ethos of conflict created by these three events continue to dominate and define both societies.

The following discussion will sketch out the 'grand narratives' of these key historical incidents through each nation's rhetorical prism. Israeli and Palestinian accounts need to be examined side by side because they shape the parties as well as their understanding, and/or misunderstanding of each other. To properly conceive the role for transitional justice, it is essential to appreciate the extent to which each national narrative is oppositional, and in a sense, based on a fundamental negation of the other's. In truth, these mirrors of mistrust or 'dialogues of the Deaf'[3] fuel the struggle over memory, power, and legitimacy for both the nations.[4] Moreover, historical narratives are significant because '…many facets of society do not necessarily see these stories as myth, incorporating them instead into their fundamental beliefs about the group's past'.[5]

It is worth noting that accepting the existence of competing narratives does not mean to obscure history or gloss over the past with naive relativism. Rather, building on the notion of 'constructed memory'[6]—this chapter seeks to frame discussion around the points of friction within dominant national discourse. So, while many individual Israeli Jews and Palestinians might dismiss particular elements of their collective repertoire, '…the telling and re-telling of that narrative has marked them, and made it difficult to accept a contrary story'.[7] By definition, it is acknowledged that narratives 'narrate' and are multi-layered, politically tainted[8] and thus liable to factual distortions and denials.[9] Ultimately, this chapter attempts to soberly unravel the struggle, by shedding light on history, in the hope of changing the historical record. The events and narratives discussed below provide the basis for understanding the national claims and legacies of human rights abuse arising from the conflict. They also directly inform the historical mandate and temporal scope of the transitional justice mechanism designed for Israelis and Palestinians in the final chapter.

---

[3] Adina Friedman, 'Unraveling the Right of Return' (2003) 21(2) *Refuge* 63.

[4] Edward Said, *Orientalism* (Vintage Books, 1979) 'Afterword' (1995) 329, 332.

[5] Barbara Tint, 'History, Memory and Intractable Conflict' (2010) 27(3) (Spring) *Conflict Resolution Quarterly* 239, 243.

[6] Benedict Anderson's characterisation of the nation as an 'imagined community', and Eric Hobsbawn's reference to the 'invention of tradition' has become essential to understanding nationalism and history. See Dov Waxman, *The Pursuit of Peace and the Crisis of Israeli Identity* (Palgrave Macmillan, 2006) 22.

[7] Salem, Pogrund and Scham, above n 1, 6.

[8] Tint, above n 5, 243.

[9] Uri Ram, *Israeli Nationalism: Social Conflicts and the Politics of Knowledge* (Routledge, 2010), 33 ('*Israeli Nationalism*').

1.2 Part One: '1948'

Historical Outline

Outlining the historical genesis of the Israeli–Palestinian conflict is an undertaking fraught with perils. The essentially contentious character of the struggle flows from the fact that the original cause of the Palestinian refugee problem, rooted in the 1948–1949 Arab–Israeli war, remains largely unresolved. More often than not, it is a question considered through the prisms of irreconcilable political and ideological narratives. Nevertheless, what is incontrovertible is that the 1948 hostilities, which began in the wake of the United Nations (UN) partition of Palestine in November 1947[10] and erupted into full-scale war between Israel and several Arab states after the Declaration of Israeli Independence in May 1948,[11] resulted in the exile of much of Palestine's Arab inhabitants. Between December 1947 and September 1949, some 600,000–760,000 Palestinians departed, fled, or were expelled from those regions in Palestine which are now territories within the State of Israel.[12]

The massive exodus of roughly half of the territory's population profoundly altered the demographics of Jews and Arabs within the new borders.[13] Only 150,000 of the Arab population of pre-1948 Palestine remained behind, most of whom ultimately became Israeli citizens in the nascent Jewish State.[14] By the war's end with the Armistice Agreements of 1949,[15] the vast majority of Palestinians were plunged into makeshift refugee camps under Egyptian or Jordanian control. The United

---

[10] *Future Government of Palestine,* GA Res 181(II), UN Doc A/519 (29 November 1947) [131] adopted a plan to partition Palestine into separate states, one Jewish and the other Arab.

[11] On 14 May 1948, the Jewish leaders declared the establishment of the State of Israel on the heels of the final withdrawal of British troops from Palestine. On the following day, the armies of Transjordan, Syria, Lebanon, Egypt, and Iraq invaded the newly declared State. After several successful Israeli military campaigns, Israel assured its existence.

[12] Yoav Tadmor, 'The Palestinian Refugees of 1948: The Right to Compensation and Return' (1994) 8 *Temple International and Comparative Law Journal* 403 ('The Palestinian Refugees of 1948'); See also Kurt Renee Radley, 'The Palestinian Refugees: The Right to Return in International Law' (1978) 72 *American Journal of International Law* 587, 595; Donna E Arzt and Karen Zughaib 'Return to the Negotiated Lands: The Likelihood and Legality of a Population Transfer Between Israel and a Future Palestinian State' (1991–2) 24 *New York University Journal of International Law and Politics* 1399, 1420–22.

[13] Eyal Benvenisti and Eyal Zamir, 'Private Claims to Property Rights in the Future Israeli-Palestinian Settlement' (1995) 89 *American Journal of International Law* 295, 297.

[14] Lex Takkenberg, *The Status of Palestinian Refugees in International Law* (Clarenden Press, 1998) 14.

[15] The 1949 Armistice Agreements are a set of armistice agreements signed during 1949 between Israel and neighbouring Egypt, Lebanon, Jordan, and Syria to formally end the official hostilities of the 1948 Arab–Israeli War and establish armistice lines between Israeli forces and Jordanian–Iraqi forces, also known as the Green Line. The complete texts of the Armistice Agreements can be found at The Avalon Project at Yale Law School https://avalon.law.yale.edu/20th_century/arm03.asp.

Nations Relief and Works Agency for Palestine Refugees in the Near East (UNRWA) was subsequently created to take care of needy Palestinians.[16] Many of these refugees, whose numbers have increased considerably over the decades due to natural growth, continue to live in squalid camps where they first relocated and are dependent on help from the UNRWA.[17] In this regard, the creation and continuing unresolved status of the Palestinian refugees from 1948 is pivotal to understanding the conflict.

There presently exists a wide spectrum of figures for the total Palestinian refugee population since 1948. Conflicts over its demographic dimension and the precise definition of 'refugee' carry critical implications on the Palestinian right of return issue as discussed and defined in Chap. 2. In 2001, the UNRWA registered over 3.6 million Palestinians[18] as refugees, a figure that includes the descendants of those originally displaced in 1948.[19] Prima facie, they would be the potential beneficiaries of any Palestinian right of return, which poses a demographic challenge to Israel as a Jewish-majority State.

The '1948' Blame-Game

As with any intractable ethno-national conflict, there is no authoritative and legitimated determination of the immediate causes or motivations for the Palestinian exodus. Rather, both sides, Israeli and Arab, traditionally ascribe responsibility for the mass displacement entirely to the other and maintain conflicting factual assessments in what might best be termed 'official history'.[20] It is worth pointing out that propagating a reductive version of the 1948 war has been integral in pursuing political and moral leverage. In Israel, nationalist historians conventionally claim that the Palestinians either voluntarily fled free from Jewish compulsion, due to a 'general sense of fear and confusion',[21] or that they were prompted or ordered to evacuate by leaders of the Arab States bent on Israel's destruction.[22] Israeli government sources

---

[16] UNRWA was established in 1949 by the U.N's General Assembly and provides essential services to Palestine refugees until today. For more information, see https://www.unrwa.org/.

[17] Ruth Lapidoth, 'Legal Aspects of the Palestinian Refugee Question' 485 *Jerusalem Viewpoints* (Jerusalem Centre for Public Affairs, 1 September 2002) 2 www.jcpa.org/jl/vp485.htm ('Legal Aspects').

[18] The figures on UNRWA registered Palestine refugees are not to be regarded as comprehensive demographic data.

[19] Lapidoth, 'Legal Aspects', above n 16, 2.

[20] Eugene Rogan and Avi Shlaim (eds), *The War for Palestine: Rewriting the History of 1948* (Cambridge University Press, 2007) 79–103.

[21] Laurence J. Silberstein, *The Post Zionism Debates: Knowledge and Power in Israeli Culture* (Routledge, 1999) 88.

[22] See Ibid 97–8; Israel Office of Information, The Arab Refugees (1953) 11, as cited in Tanya Kramer, 'The Controversy of a Palestinian "Right of Return" to Israel' (2001) 18 *Arizona Journal of International and Comparative Law* 979, 998; See also Rashid Khalidi, 'The Palestinians and 1948: The Underlying Causes of Failure' in Rogan and Shlaim, above n 20, 12, 14 ('The Palestinians and 1948'); Christopher Sykes, *Crossroads to Israel* (World Publishing Company, 1965) 353–4.

also stress that hundreds of thousands of Jewish refugees simultaneously fled their homes in Arab countries to Israel as a direct consequence of the 1948 hostilities.[23] Accordingly, Israel contends that it was the Arabs who caused the Palestinian refugee problem by rejecting the creation of the State of Israel and declaring war upon it—'a war, which, like most wars created refugee problems, including a Jewish one'.[24]

Conversely, Palestinian and Arab accounts insist that the Israelis forcibly expelled the Palestinians as a part of a premeditated and prearranged 'grand political-military design'.[25] Palestinian historians[26] highlight Deir Yassin[27] and other massacres[28] as indicative of a Jewish conspiracy to rid Palestine of its Arab inhabitants.[29] Upon this historical construction, the Palestinians insist on the right of the refugees to return to their homes and demand that Israel unilaterally acknowledge complete moral responsibility for the injustice of their expulsion and present refugee status.[30] In sum, both evaluations of 1948 subscribe to an uncritically nationalist account of the Palestinian displacement, and accordingly 'the pretence of objectivity is particularly misplaced, if not totally unfounded'.[31]

Historical Reappraisal of '1948'

Nevertheless, in recent decades, new scholarship has subverted the foundational premises of these dominant narratives. The most significant reappraisals have emerged from mostly Israeli historians relying on newly discovered archival

---

[23] State of Israel, 'The Refugee issue: A Background Paper, Government Press office' (October 1994) 3, cited in Takkenberg, above n 14, 14.

[24] Yossi Alpher and Khalil Shikaki, 'Concept Paper: The Palestinian Refugee Problem and the Right of Return' (1999) 6(3) *Middle East Policy* 172.

[25] Tadmor, 'The Palestinian Refugees of 1948', above n 12, 403; See also Wadie E. Said, 'Palestinian Refugees: Host Countries, Legal Status and the Right of Return' (2003) 21(2) *Refuge* 89, citing Nur Masalha, *A Land without a People: Israel, Transfer and the Palestinians 1949–96* (Faber and Faber, 1997) xi.

[26] On the early Palestinian historiography, see Beshara B. Doumani, 'Rediscovering Ottoman Palestine: Writing Palestinians into History' (1992) 21(2) *Journal of Palestine Studies* 5 13–17.

[27] On 9 April 1948, Jewish members of the Irgun and Stern militias (Jewish fringe militant factions) attacked Deir Yassin, an Arab village located next to a major thoroughfare connecting Jerusalem to the coast. The attack resulted in the deaths of around 250 Arab civilians.

[28] Palestinian historian Saleh Abdel Jawad lists around 20 villages where indiscriminate killings of Palestinian civilians occurred. Saleh Abdel Jawad, 'Zionist Massacres: The Creation of the Palestinian Refugee Problem in the 1948 War' in Eyal Benvenisti et al. (eds), *Israel and the Palestinian Refugees*, (Berlin Springer, 2007) 59–127.

[29] Justus R Weiner, 'The Palestinian Refugees Right to Return and the Peace Process' (1997) 20(1) *Boston College International and Comparative Law Review* 1, 16.

[30] Alpher and Shikaki, above n 23, 171.

[31] Ilan Pappe, 'Humanising the text: Israeli 'New History' and the Trajectory of 1948 Historiography' (2003) 86 *Radical History Review* 102, 103.

evidence.[32] Dubbed the 'New Historians',[33] they depict the 1948 war as something other than '…a miraculous victory of beleaguered underdogs'.[34] Indeed, Morris[35] was the first Israeli historian to admit that mass expulsions of Palestinians occurred in 1948 and decisively refute the claim that Arab leaders ordered the Palestinians to flee and clear the way for impending armies.[36] Most shocking was the disclosure that Zionist leaders had actively driven out the Arab inhabitants of Palestine.[37] Morris determined however that neither the expulsions nor the subsequent refugee problem was the result of a Jewish blueprint or 'master plan', but rather the consequence of war and associated circumstances.[38]

More generally, revisionist scholarship challenged mobilising myths of official history with a 'post-Zionist' conflict narrative.[39] Segev, for example, refuted the notion that Palestinians lacked a collective identity distinct from Arabs in neighbouring states.[40] Some historians, like Kimmerling, examined Zionism through a colonial prism.[41] During the 1990s, the Oslo peace process fanned debates about 1948.[42] This trend also provoked a nationalist backlash.[43] Many 'old guard'

---

[32] As a result of Israel's 5715–1955 *Archives Law* and its attending regulations, hundreds of thousands of previously closed State papers became available to researchers in the early 1980s. PA Alsberg, 'The Israel Archives Law, History and Implementation', Arkhyon: Reader in Archives Studies and Documentation 1 (1987) 7–29 (Hebrew).

[33] Avi Shlaim, *Collusion across the Jordan: King Abdullah, the Zionist Movement and the Partition of Palestine* (Clarendon Press, 1988). See also Simon Flapan, *The Birth of Israel, Myths and Realities* (Pantheon Books, 1987); Ilan Pappe, *Britain and the Arab-Israeli conflict, 1948–51* (Macmillan Press, 1988).

[34] Takkenberg, above n 14, 15, citing Neil Caplan, 'The New Historians' (1994/95) 24(4) *Journal of Palestine Studies* 96.

[35] Benny Morris, *The Birth of the Palestinian Refugee Problem 1947–1949* (Cambridge University Press, 1987). Morris has written critically, for example, about the expulsion of 60,000 Arab residents from the towns of Lydda and Ramle.

[36] Flapan, above n 32, 85 also dismisses this contention as illogical, cited in Arzt and Zughaib, above n 12, 1421.

[37] See both Morris, above n 34, and Pappe, *The Ethnic Cleansing of Palestine* (Oneworld Publications, 2006) for clashing interpretations of how this flight unfolded.

[38] Morris, above n 34, 286.

[39] Generally, the post-Zionist narrative criticises the Zionist narrative. Some of the post-Zionists associate themselves with post-modernism. See Uri Ram, 'Post Nationalist Pasts-The Case of Israel' (1998) 24(4) *Social Science History* 515–23. See also David Ohana and Robert Wistrich, *Myth and Memory: Genealogy of the Israeli Consciousness* (Ha Kibbutz Hamehoohad and Van-Leer Institute, 1996) 21–32.

[40] Tom Segev, *One Palestine, Complete: Jews and Arabs Under the British Mandate* (Metropolitan Books, 2000).

[41] Baruch Kimmerling, *Zionism and Territory: The Socio-Territorial Dimensions of Zionist Politics* (University of California Press, 1983) and Gershon Shafir, *Land, Labor and the Origins of the Israeli-Palestinian Conflict, 1882–1914* (Cambridge University Press, 1989).

[42] Anita Shapira and Ora Wiskind-Elper, 'Politics and Collective Memory: The Debate over the "New Historians' in Israel"'(1995) 7 *History and Memory* 9, 55.

[43] See Ram, *Israeli Nationalism*, above n 9, 30.

historians challenged the new historiography.[44] Nevertheless, the central critiques withstood a torrent of Zionist outrage, disclaimers, and apologetics.[45] Ultimately, they provoked a wide-ranging debate that spilled over from scholarly journals and academic conferences into the public domain. In the words of Ram: 'One way or another, the new historians have radically transformed the historical consciousness…in Israel'.[46] Consequently, there is at present an increasing academic recognition of Israel's shared accountability for 1948.

In a similar vein, Palestinian writers have challenged Arab world histories of 1948. Palestinian historian Sayigh confirms the 'necessity of re-thinking, decoupling and reclaiming 1948…'[47] beyond its ideological encasing. This approach, it is argued, should include re-visiting the causes of Palestinian dislocation and Arab policies without absolving Palestinian individuals and groups '…of moral and legal responsibility for their own acts'.[48] Thus, Kalaf examines factionalism and social disintegration as causes of the Palestinian tragedy,[49] and Mattar calls the Mufti's policies 'a failure' which 'contributed to the dispossession of the Palestinian people'.[50]

Notably, Palestinian historiography lacks the robust revisionism and self-criticism of its Israeli counterpart. However, Jawad highlights the extent to which practical obstacles of access, Arab censorship,[51] and documents destroyed in 1948 contributed to this deficit.[52] According to Jawad, Arab archives are typically closed to independent researchers. Not a single Arab states that participated in the war of 1948 has opened up the archives of the relevant time period to the public. Even archives in Israel (and documents in the Palestinian territories) are often inaccessible

---

[44] These critics argued that the New Historians isolated events and processes; that their conclusions are detached from the distress of the Jewish people at large and ignore the existential motives at the time. See Shapira and Wiskind-Elper, above n 41, 17–18; See also Michal Hirsch Ben-Josef, 'From Taboo to the Negotiable: The Israeli New Historians and Changing Representations of Palestinian Refugees' (2007) 5(2) *Perspectives on Politics* 241, 245, citing Shabtai Teveth, 'Charging Israel with Original Sin' (1989) 88 (3) *Commentary* 24–33 and Efraim Karsh, *Fabricating Israeli History 'The New Historians'* (Cass, 1997) (second ed., 2000).

[45] Despite the lack of historical unanimity on 1948, '…there is today a far more complete, credible, and documented historical picture of why the Palestinians left and of the significance of Israel's role in the process'. See Rashid Khalidi, 'Attainable Justice: Elements of a Solution to the Palestinian Refugee Issue' (1998) 33(2) (Spring) *International Journal* 233, 239 ('Attainable Justice').

[46] Ram, *Israeli Nationalism,* above n 9, 34.

[47] Yezid Sayigh et al., 'Reflections on al-Nakba' (1998) 28(1) *Journal of Palestine Studies* 5, 23.

[48] Ibid 21.

[49] Issa Kalaf, *Politics in Palestine Arab Factionalism and Social Disintegration, 1939–1948* (SUNY Press, 1991).

[50] Phillip Matar, *The Mufti of Jerusalem and the Palestinian National Movement* (Columbia University Press, 1988).

[51] Saleh Abdel Jawad, 'The Arab and Palestinian Narratives of the 1948 war' in Robert Rotberg (ed), *Israeli-Palestinian Narratives of Conflict: History's Double Helix* (Indiana University Press, 2006) 100.

[52] Ibid.

to Palestinians.[53] Notwithstanding this academic asymmetry, the mixture of historical developments and epistemological shifts in both camps has paved the ground for re-conceiving Palestinian displacement.

Multidimensional Causes

There are certain key historical issues that continue to complicate any single dimensional allocation of responsibility for the 1948 displacement. Firstly, Israeli national survival was a pervasive concern.[54] Given the Arab League's overt opposition to any form of Jewish sovereignty[55] and the ensuing hostilities, the Arab inhabitants of Palestine inevitably came to be seen by the Israelis as a 'fifth column' in the war.[56] Khalidi affirms: '[i]f some Jews in Palestine perceived themselves as facing an uphill fight against the Arabs, this was certainly understandable'.[57]

Secondly, there were indirect causes connected to the flight. Although its extent has been exaggerated, the impact of the first stage of the Arab exodus 'when an estimated 30,000 upper- and middle-class Arabs left [voluntarily]...'[58] remains uncontroverted. The loss of so many key leaders led to a serious breakdown in communications and political institutions 'so that those remaining behind were invariably left to the mercy of rumor, anxiety and fear'.[59] Finally, scare propaganda directed at the Arab population came not only from the Zionists[60] but also from the Arabs themselves.[61] Since 1948, the Arab countries' contribution to the refugee problem is also significant. The former Director of UNRWA, Ralph Galloway, was so outraged by Arab state's refusal to absorb Palestinians; he declared in 1958: '[t]he Arab states do not want to solve the refugee problem. They want to keep it as an open sore, as an affront to the UN and as a weapon against Israel ...'.[62] Such

---

[53] Ibid 94–97.

[54] According to Shapira and Wiskind-Elper: 'The borders established in the war's wake were considered the absolute minimum for the existence of a viable state'. See Shapira and Wiskind-Elper, above n 41, 15.

[55] Sabel, for example, highlights the open admission by Arab states that their armies were sent to Palestine 'to prevent the creation of the proposed Jewish State': Robbie Sabel, 'The Palestinian Refugees, International Law and the Peace Process' (2003) 21(2) *Refuge* 52, 53. On this point, see *Cable of 15 May 1948 from the Secretary-General of the League of Arab States to the Secretary-General of the UN*, UN SCOR, Supp, 83, UN Doc S/745 (May 1948).

[56] Hillel Cohen, 'Land, Memory and Identity: The Palestinian Internal Refugees in Israel' (2003) 21(2) *Refuge* 7.

[57] Rashid Khalidi, 'The Palestinians and 1948', above n 21, 16.

[58] Radley, above n 12, 592.

[59] Ibid.

[60] Various accounts attest to the Haganah's use of 'psychological warfare' against the Arabs. See generally Silberstein, above n 21; Cohen, above n 56; Radley, above n 12, 594.

[61] Radley, above n 12, 593.

[62] Ralph Galloway, as quoted in Justus R Weiner, above n 29, 32. For example, in 1955 the Arab states dismissed outright the US-led 'Johnston plan' which pioneered a joint immigration initiative between Israel, Syria, Jordan, and Lebanon.

factors problematise blanket calls for a Palestinian right of return based on exclusive Israeli accountability.

Collective Memory and National Narratives

> *For Jews, the word is galut; for Palestinians, it is ghurba. For both it means exile, a condition from which one returns to the Promised Land. Like the Jewish dream of return to Zion, 'Palestine has [also] become an idyllic place of return, a force of national hope blessed with perfection'.*[63]

Historical inquiry aside, the ostensible intractability of 1948 cannot be understood without outlining its ideological roots. According to Shapira, 'the debate is less about historiography than it is about collective memory'.[64] Indeed, this event is deeply embedded into each nation's meta-narratives of entitlement, villain, and victimhood. Both Israelis and Palestinians have drawn on 1948 to cope with the conflict and enable its members to contribute to the ongoing struggle.[65] The meanings and implications, derived from 1948, strike at the very heart of both parties' legitimacy obstructing even partial acceptance, of either side's discourse. What for Palestinians is a historic sacred right to return is for Israeli Jews a frontal attack on the Jewish state's legitimacy. In short, the conflict over 1948 is as much about a clash of constructed discourses, as it is a factual debate over entitlement to land.

Broadly defined, collective memory is how social groups recall and interpret historical events.[66] According to Halbwachs, collective memory is consciously selective, socially constructed, and contextual.[67] Moreover, it serves current political beliefs and needs.[68] In the words of Osiel: 'The real question…is not whether collective memory of national history can be constructed, but whether it ever cannot'.[69] In this way, memory is a mobilising, myth-making tool, and how it is

---

[63] Arzt and Zughaib, above n 12, 1427, citing David Shipler, *Arab and Jew: Wounded Spirits in a Promised Land* (Broadway Books, 1986) 59.

[64] Shapira and Wiskind-Elper, above n 41, 12.

[65] Rafi Nets-Zehngut, 'The Israeli National Information Center and Collective Memory of the Israeli-Arab Conflict' (2008) 62(4) (Autumn) Middle East Journal 653, 669.

[66] Meir Litvak (ed), *Palestinian Collective Memory and National Identity* (Palgrave Macmillan, 2009), 12.

[67] Maurice Halbwachs' work is considered the foundational framework for the study of societal remembrance. See Maurice Halbwachs, *On Collective Memory* (University of Chicago Press, 1992). See also Tint, above n 5; Daniel Bar-Tal, 'Socio-sychological Foundations of Intractable Conflicts' (2007) 50 *American Behavioural Scientist* 1430, 1436 ('Socio-psychological Foundations'); Litvak, Ibid, 12–14.

[68] Social constructions of the past are influenced by the needs of the present. See generally Tint, above n 5, 243.

[69] Mark Osiel, 'Ever Again: Legal Remembrance of Administrative Massacre' (1995–6) 144 University of Pennsylvania Law Review 463, 646.

forged and mediated becomes vitally important to examining societies in conflict.[70] The images and myths arising from 1948 have most conspicuously shaped modern Palestinian and Israeli identities and their 'returning' to the Promised Land. These strong and interdependent links between history, nationalism, identity, and memory materialise in the narratives below.

Palestinian 'Nakba' Narrative

Record!
I am an Arab
You have stolen the orchards of my ancestors
And the land which I cultivated
Along with my children
And you left nothing for us
Except for these rocks...
So will the State take them [also]
As it has been said?!...[71]

'Palestine' is more than nostalgic remembrance. For over 70 years, the Palestinian displacement in 1948 and the right of return have been the central constituent of the Palestinian national narrative, 'the cornerstone of [their] political struggle'[72] for recognition and defiance of Israel. Ever since 1948, Palestinians have continuously voiced their demand to return to their villages, and Palestinian 'refugee' identity remains firmly anchored in collective experiences of dispossession and exile [*Ghurba*], homelessness, insecurity, and uprootedness.[73]

Khalidi insists: '[o]nly by understanding the centrality of the 1948 politicide and expulsion that befell the Palestinian people—*al nakba* (the "catastrophe" in Arabic)—is it possible to understand the Palestinian sense of the right of return'.[74] Indeed, the continued existence of the refugee crisis symbolises for Palestinians a profound sense of historical injustice, that which 'only a return to their original homes could remedy'.[75] Israel's prolonged unwillingness to even recognise the Palestinian right strengthened 'a holy principle of return, which [has] united the

70 Bar-Tal notes four ways in which collective memory serves conflict societies. It justifies the outbreak of the conflict; presents a positive-image of the in-group; delegitimizes the opponent and presents one's own society as the victim of the opponent. See Bar-Tal, 'Socio-psychological Foundations', above n 66, 1436–7.

71 Mahmoud Darwish, 'Identity Card', as quoted in Ahmad Sa'di, 'Catastrophe, Memory and Identity: Al Nakbah as a Component of Palestinian Identity' (2002) 7(2) *Israel Studies* 175, 185.

72 Justus R Weiner, above n 28, 1.

73 Helena Lindholm, 'Palestinian National Identities: Change and Continuity of the Palestinian as a Struggler' in Helena Lindholm (ed), *Ethnicity, Nationalism, Formation of Identity and Dynamics of Conflict in the 1990s* (1993), as cited in Friedman, above n 3, 65–66.

74 Rashid Khalidi, 'Observations on the Right of Return' (1992) 21(2) *Journal of Palestine Studies* 29, 30 ('Observations').

75 Alpher and Shikaki, above n 23, 176.

refugees and preserved their identity'.[76] Consequently, 1948 not only carries moral connotations, but also is intimately connected with a sense of national and historical legitimacy.

Israeli–Jewish 'Return'

By the Rivers of Babylon, there we sat down, yea we wept when we remembered Zion...
If I forget thee, O Jerusalem, let my right hand forget her cunning.[77]

Akin to the Palestinians, the historical Jewish right of return, institutionalised through Israel's Law of Return, is a crucial component of the Jewish national ethos, the kernel of Zionism and a cardinal tenet upon which Israel was created. The departure point of any discussion of 1948 and Jewish return is the central location of Zion 'in the thoughts, prayers and dreams of the Jews in their dispersions'[78] and the concept of *Kibbutz Galuiot*—'the ingathering of the exiles'. Following two millennia of homelessness, the Jewish Return to their ancient birthplace, 'Eretz Israel', was 'thought to heal a deformative rupture produced by exilic existence'.[79]

Indeed, Zionism transformed the messianic conception of 'Return' into a secular notion of Jewish salvation on earth through state-building and reclaiming the ancestral land.[80] Legally, Jewish return is embodied in the *Israeli Declaration of Independence*, *the Law of Return*[81]and the *Nationality Law* (1952),[82] which guarantees all Jews a virtually automatic right to Israeli citizenship. A corollary of Jewish return is the staunch resistance to the notion of Palestinian return. Indeed, the *Nationality Law* was arguably expressly drafted to render the Palestinians displaced in 1948 ineligible for citizenship.[83] Israel has consistently rejected proposals that advocate the repatriation of Palestinian refugees except for small numbers within the context of family reunification.

---

[76] Cohen, above n 55, 10. See also Dan Rabinowitz, 'Israel and the Palestinian Refugees: Postpragmatic Reflections on Historical Narratives, Closure, Transitional Justice, and Palestinian Refugees' Right to Refuse' in Barbara Rose Johnston and Susan Slyomovics (eds), *Waging War, Making Peace: Reparations and Human Rights* (Left Coast Press, 2009) 225–39, 227.

[77] Psalm 137, in A Cohen (ed), *The Psalms* (1945) 448.

[78] Walter Laqueur, *A History of Zionism* (Holt, Rinehart and Winston, 1972) 40.

[79] Ella Shohat, 'Rupture and Return: Zionist Discourse and the Study of Arab Jews' (2003) 21(2) *Social Text* 49, 49.

[80] Alfred de Zayas, 'The Illegality of Population Transfers and the Application of Emerging International Norms in the Palestinian Context' (1990–91) VI *The Palestine Yearbook of International Law* 17, 42.

[81] Law of Return, 4 Laws of the State of Israel, 114 (1950).

[82] Nationality Law, 6 Laws of the State of Israel, 50 (1952).

[83] s 3 *Nationality Law* (1952) provides that '[a] person who resided in Palestine immediately prior to the establishment of the state is only automatically regarded as a resident if they were registered as a resident prior to the enactment' of the *Nationality Law*. See Kramer, above n 22, 998; See Ram, *Israeli Nationalism*, above n 9, 38.

In Israeli eyes, the basis for the obstruction is deeply rooted. Firstly, the Palestinian refugee problem is perceived first and foremost as an existential security issue. Israelis have not had difficulty concluding from the successive Arab–Israeli wars and the rhetoric of Palestinian leaders that the Palestinian Liberation Organisation (PLO), if not the Palestinians in general, intends the total annihilation of the Israeli population.[84] Until today, such fears have not abated.[85] Secondly, Israel has sought to preserve the demographic character of the Jewish State. Indeed, it is believed that some 360,000 persons consider themselves Palestinian refugees and potential claimants of the right of return.[86] Finally, the acceptance of any Israeli responsibility for the suffering of the refugees and the recognition of a right of return would cast doubt on the state's legitimacy.[87] Israel therefore refuses to accept the Palestinian narrative of an Israeli 'original' sin and denies moral culpability in creating the problem.[88] Ultimately, the notion of Palestinian return is antithetical to Zionist discourse.

Competing Victimhood

Within this 1948 dialectic, each side perceives itself as the exclusive victim of the conflict. Whilst the Palestinians recount a story of dispossession and catastrophe based on the Nakba, the Israelis recall the War of Independence and its symbolic compensation for the Holocaust. Both nations have their own cosmic catastrophes, and both draw on a strong memory of victimhood in what is perceived as an existential struggle.

> *Every IDF soldier must see himself as a survivor of Auschwitz....* (Israel Defense Forces (IDF), Chief Educational Officer)[89]

For Israelis, the trauma of Nazi genocide makes Arab threats of destruction credible '...casting the conflict as one of basic survival, aimed at preventing a second Holocaust'.[90] It has assumed 'meta-physical proportions' in the Jewish Israeli

[84] Arzt and Zughaib, above n 121,432.

[85] Justus R Weiner, above n 28, 19.

[86] Sabel, above n 54, 54.

[87] Jeffrey Ghannam, 'Where Will They Go?' (2000) 86 *American Bar Association Journal* 40, 43, discussing the approach of Gershon Baskin, then co-director of the Israel/Palestine Center for Research and Information.

[88] Alpher and Shikaki, above n 23, 176.

[89] Brigadier-General Stern, *Kol Israel,* Radio Network B, 'In the Afternoon' (6 December, 2004) (Hebrew) as quoted in Dan Zakay and Dida Fleisig, 'The Time Factor As a Barrier to Resolution of the Israeli-Palestinian Conflict' in Yaacov Bar-Siman-Tov (ed), *Barriers to Peace in the Israeli Palestinian Conflict* (Jerusalem Institute for Israel Studies, 2010) 264–299, 280 ('*Barriers to Peace*').

[90] Waxman, above n 6, 49.

psyche.[91] To varying degrees, this legacy has served to justify the primacy of national security in Israeli foreign policy.[92] Since 1948, Israel maintains an endless state of emergency, whereby legal norms are suspended. Thus, 'It is not a formidable army that penetrates Lebanon…but a handful of survivors that go out to avenge Auschwitz...'.[93] This motif is woven into the conflict with the Palestinians, by drawing comparisons between Yasser Arafat and Hitler, the PLO and the Nazi party '…or responding to a picture of an Arab girl killed in the 1982 Lebanon war with that of a boy from the Warsaw ghetto'.[94] On the global stage, current Israeli PM Benjamin Netanyahu frequently refers to the Nazi genocide of Jews in his speeches at the UN General Assembly (UNGA).[95]

Thus, we [Palestinians] are the victims of the victims, the refugees of the refugees.[96] (Edward Said, 1999)

For Palestinians, the Nakba has become a hallowed symbol of identity.[97] Mirroring Holocaust discourse, Palestinians regard themselves as casualties of a colossal tragedy.[98] Striking similarities exist therefore in how both communities cultivate an ethos of victimhood through tradition,[99] historiography,[100] and commemoration. For example, the attacks at Deir Yassin noted above evolved into a

---

[91] Ibid.

[92] Ibid 188. See generally Idit Zertal *Israel's Holocaust and the Politics of Nationhood* (Cambridge University Press, 2010).

[93] Idit Zertal, 'Du bon usage du souvenir: Les Israéliens et le Shoa' (1990) 11(58) *Le Debat* 92, 101, as cited in Scott Atran, 'Stones Against the Iron Fist, Terror within the Nation: Alternating Structures of Violence and Cultural Identity in the Israeli-Palestinian Conflict' (1990) 18(4) *Politics and Society* 484, 498.

[94] See Shapira and Wiskind-Elper, above n 41, 19.

[95] On 24 September 2009, Israeli PM Benjamin Netanyahu displayed original construction plans for the Auschwitz-Birkenau concentration camp during his speech to the UN General Assembly.

[96] Edward Said, 'The One State Solution', *The New York Times* (New York, January 10 1999). Many Palestinians claim that the *Nakba* has brought about an exchange of historical roles, and the Palestinians have been transformed into the 'victims of the victims'. See Michael Milshtein, 'The Memory that Never Dies: The Nakba Memory and the Palestinian National Movement' in Litvak, above n 65, 50. See also generally Rashid Khalidi, *Palestinian Identity: The Construction of Modern National Consciousness* (Columbia University Press, 1997) ('*Palestinian Identity*').

[97] Al Quds, 15 May 1998, cited in Esther Webman 'The Evolution of a Founding Myth: The Nakba and Its Fluctuating Meaning' in Litvak, above n 65, 35. See Rashid Khalidi, 'Attainable Justice', above n 44, 245.

[98] Webman, above n 96, 35–36. See Ata Qaymari 'The Holocaust in the Palestinian Perspective' in Salem, Pogrund and Scham, above n 1, 151.

[99] For example, Palestinian refugees preserve keys of their original houses and commonly refer to themselves by their villages of origin and not the refugee camps where they live in. See Ata Qaymari, above n 97, 151.

[100] Collecting oral testimony from 1948 is a popular historiographical approach among Palestinian researchers and historians. See ibid.

symbol of memorialisation[101] like Auschwitz. Established in 1999, the Palestinian state Nakba Museum Dar al Dahkira[102] resembles Israel's Yad Vashem, and akin to Holocaust Memorial day, Palestinians officially mark 'Nakba' day through national ceremony and siren sounding.[103] Until today, 1948 serves as a powerful political tool for mobilising Palestinians in their national struggle. The Palestinian National Authority (PA) has consciously cultivated the Nakba memory in schools[104] and demonstrations.[105] Like the Holocaust, the Nakba is not merely a passing historical event, but an ongoing process of victimisation[106] that heightens threat perceptions and bolsters political and legal claims.

Ultimately, the Israeli–Palestinian conflict is not a conventional one for power and territory, but an existential one drawn from the collective memories of catastrophic events. These founding myths significantly mould the political behaviour of both the people, and each side negates the victim narrative of the other. 'For many Palestinians, the Holocaust seems an excuse and a camouflage for the atrocities…which Israel thrusts upon them'.[107] In Israel, the incomparable trauma of the Holocaust appears to blind Israelis to the plight of Palestinians,[108] whilst the notion of return is understood as a euphemism for Israel's destruction. Tragically, there is an ironic symmetry to each nation's exclusive claim to victimhood and refusals to acknowledge the national trauma of the other.

Conclusion

As the present discussion demonstrates, many of the anxieties and fears permeating Israeli and Palestinian societies are traceable to the conflict's genesis. Most practitioners in this field would likely acknowledge the centrality of 1948 to both the nations' identity. It is also contended that an ethos of victimhood, cultivated on both

---

[101] Deir Yassin has become a key element in the Palestinian transformation of the events of 1947–1949 into a 'cosmic injustice'. See generally Walid Khalidi, 'Deir Yassine: Autopsie d'un Massacre' (1998) 17 (69) *Revue d'etudes Palestiniennes* 20–58.

[102] The site located at Kafr Ayn Siniya near Ramallah exhibits numerous data based on the *Nakba* in general and destroyed villages. See Milshtein, above n 95, 55.

[103] In 1998, the PNA set up 15 May as the official Nakba day, marking the date on which the State of Israel was established.

[104] For example, in textbooks and teacher's guides published by the Palestinian Ministry of Education the Nakba and its aftermath receive comprehensive treatment, while the existence of Israel is patently ignored. See Milshtein, above n 95, 55.

[105] Yasser Arafat's address to the 'March of Millions' on 14 May 1998 connected the *Nakba* with the creation of a Palestinian state and the right of return. Yasser Arafat quoted in Webman, above n 96, 34.

[106] For a detailed discussion on the seminal role of the holocaust and Jewish persecution on Israeli identity and politics see Idit Zertal *Israel's Holocaust and the Politics of Nationhood* (Cambridge University Press, 2010).

[107] Ata Qaymari, above n 97, 150.

[108] See Rashid Khalidi, *Palestinian Identity,* above n 95, xxvi.

the sides, contributes to the formation and sustenance of the conditions and experiences of intractable conflict.[109] Thus, it is important to find ways to engage the psychological repertoires of 1948 so as to assist in the reduction, de-escalation, and potential resolution of the conflict. As will be explored in Chap. 2, the historical controversies around 1948 also inform the international legal dimensions of the Israeli–Palestinian conflict. The singular most important legal question triggered by 1948 is the Palestinian right of return which remains contested and unresolved.

1.3 Part Two: '1967'

Historical Outline

Following 1948, the Six-Day War of 1967 similarly transformed the geo-political landscape of the conflict. Among the Israeli–Arab wars, the 1967 war is particularly significant as it led to Israel's seizure of the West Bank, Gaza Strip, East Jerusalem,[110] Golan Heights,[111] and the Sinai Peninsula.[112] As a result of Israel's decisive victory,[113] its territory grew by a factor of 3, and approximately one million Arab inhabitants (including a significant number of the 1948 Palestinian refugees) were placed under Israel's direct control.[114] Although immediately following the war, Israel offered to return all of the acquired territories (aside from East Jerusalem) in exchange for full peace accords,[115] the Arab nations rejected this plan.[116] By the late 1960s, Israel had

[109] See Bar-Tal, 'Socio-psychological Foundations', above n 66, 1443. See also Tint, above n 5, 242.

[110] In 1967, only 8 weeks after the end of the war, the Knesset extended its law, jurisdiction, and administration to East Jerusalem. Unlike the Golan Heights, and despite harsh criticism by the international community, including the UNGA, UNSC, and the ICJ, East Jerusalem was officially annexed when the Knesset adopted the Basic Law: Jerusalem, Capital of Israel (1980). See Eyal Benvenisti, *The International Law of Occupation* (Oxford University Press, 2012) 204–206.

[111] The Golan Heights was seized from Syria and remains under Israeli control until this day. In 1981 Israel passed a law extending its law, jurisdiction, and administration to the Golan.

[112] The Sinai Peninsula was returned to Egypt as part of the 1979 Peace Agreement between Egypt and Israel.

[113] Israel launched a pre-emptive strike that destroyed most of the Egyptian army's planes while they were still on the ground. The international community generally saw Israel's actions as a legitimate use of defensive force after its neighbouring countries were moving troops, removing UN peacekeeping forces, and closing the Straits of Tiran to Israeli vessels, clearly preparing to attack Israel. See Stephen Schwebel, 'What Weight to Conquest' (1970) 64 *American Journal of International Law* 344, 346.

[114] Baruch Kimmerling, *Clash of Identities: Explorations in Israeli and Palestinian Societies* (Columbia University Press, 2013) 169 ('*Clash of Identities*').

[115] On 19 June 1967, the National Unity Government of Israel voted unanimously to return the Sinai to Egypt and the Golan Heights to Syria in return for peace agreements. The government also resolved to open negotiations with King Hussein of Jordan regarding the Eastern border.

[116] See Jill Alisson Weiner, 'Israel, Palestine and the Oslo Accords' (1999–2000) 23 *Fordham International Law Journal* 230, 236.

established full control over the remainder of what was once British mandatory Palestine.[117] The new territory acquired by Israel comprised the other 20% of what was British-occupied Palestine.

Until today, Israel retains a military administration in the West Bank, with more than half a million of its own citizens living in these territories (including East Jerusalem).[118] Since the Declaration of Principles on Interim Self-Government Arrangements (1993) (Oslo 1),[119] most of the Palestinian population has come under the jurisdiction of the PA. Nevertheless, Israel frequently redeploys its troops and has reinstated full military administration in various parts of the Palestinian territories.

In 2005, Israel unilaterally withdrew its entire military and civilian presence from the Gaza Strip. Following that disengagement, the Hamas party won the 2006 Palestinian elections in Gaza, and internal conflict began between Hamas and Fatah, the political party controlling the PA.[120] Hamas then violently eliminated Fatah elements from Gaza and gained exclusive control over the strip, thus creating two separate regions of the Palestinian territories. Despite Israel's claim that the occupation of the Gaza Strip ended with the disengagement, Gaza remains dependent on Israel for fuel and electricity, and the IDF continues to control the airspace, as well as access to the strip through land and sea.[121] Thus, the geographic and political realities engendered by 1967 continue to shadow Israeli–Palestinian relations.

National Narratives

Akin to 1948, 1967 has made a lasting discursive footprint on the conflict. It is therefore worth investigating the socio-psychological infrastructure of this event and the Israeli and Palestinian narratives around occupation and settlements.

[117] Ibid.

[118] From 1967 through 2017, over 200 Israeli settlements were established in the West Bank (including East Jerusalem); their current population is almost 620,000. See B'Tselem, *Settlements* https://www.btselem.org/topic/settlements.

[119] Signed 13 September 1993, Israel-PLO, 32 ILM 1525 (entered into force 13 October 1993).

[120] Hamas's strong electoral showing was arguably more due to the widespread perception that Hamas would end corruption rather than on its Islamist agenda. Hamas has a reputation for being non-corrupt and also provides basic services, such as schools and medical clinics, in areas where the PA does not. See Palestinian Centre for Policy and Survey Research, 'Special Gaza War Poll-Press release', 2 September 2014 https://www.pcpsr.org/en/node/489.

[121] Benjamin Rubin, 'Israel, Occupied Territories' in *Max Planck Encyclopedia of Public International Law*, online edition (2009) ¶ 2 http://www.mpepil.com.

Israeli Narratives: 'Greater Israel' and National Defence

We have returned to you Shilo and Anatot [the ancient cities of the Hebrew prophets near Jerusalem] in order never to leave you.[122] (Moshe Dayan, Israel's Defence Minister, 1967)

For Israelis, the Six-Day War meant that they had reclaimed the heartland of their ancient homeland, which galvanised Jewish nationalism.[123] Many Israeli Jews believed that Israel had the exclusive right to retain the newly captured territories based on their biblical, historical, and ancestral links to Judea and Samaria (i.e. West Bank), Jerusalem, and the Gaza Strip.[124] From this standpoint, 1967 catalysed the rise of 'neo-Zionist'[125] ideology and Jewish religious nationalism, making Israeli control and settlement of the territories a legitimate state mission.[126] Until today, this neo-Zionist ideology retains a powerful political grip[127] on Israeli state and foreign policy.[128] Similarly in public discourse, the territories have been defined as an essential element of the Jewish national project.[129] In short, they '...became identified with the essence of Jewish statehood and nationhood...'.[130]

Equally important, Israeli control over the territories is seen as a necessary defensive mechanism.[131] Indeed, the strategic depth Israel acquired territorially in 1967 proved to be a security asset in the Yom Kippur war 6 years later.[132] In 1969,

---

[122] Kimmerling, *Clash of Identities*, above n 112, 167.

[123] Ibid 284.

[124] Ibid 259. This idea became hegemonic among most segments of Israeli-Jewish society after the 1967 war. See Daniel Bar-et al., 'Psychological Legitimization - Views of the Israeli Occupation by Jews in Israel: Data and Implications' ('*Psychological Legitimization*'), in Daniel Bar-Tal and Izhak Schnell, *'The Impacts of Lasting Occupation' Lessons from Israeli Society* (Oxford University Press, 2012) 125 ('*The impacts of Lasting Occupation*').

[125] Neo-Zionism rests on a reinterpretation of Zionism with an emphasis on Judaism as a religion, in contrast to the secular Labour Zionist discourse stressing Judaism as a cultural tradition. See Asima Ghazi-Bouillon, *Understanding the Middle East Peace Process: Israeli Academia and the Struggle for Identity* (Routledge, 2009) 121. "Neo-Zionism barricades itself behind moral-historical and religious justifications of the exclusive right to the land while ignoring similar claims by the Palestinians." See Bar-Tal and Schnell, *'The Impacts of Lasting Occupation'*, above n 122, 513–15.

[126] Ram, *Israeli Nationalism,* above n 9, 36. See also Elizabeth G Matthews, *'The Israel-Palestine Conflict' Parallel Discourses* (Routledge, 2011), 6.

[127] See Matthews, above n 124, 6; The religious-ideological settlers have proved over recent decades to be the most astute political lobby in Israel. Even prime ministers intent on territorial compromise, such as Rabin and Barak, preferred to co-opt the settlers and enable settlement expansion. Yossi Alpher, *The Future of Israeli-Palestinian Conflict: Critical Trends Affecting Israel* (United States Institute of Peace September 2005) 8.

[128] Waxman, above n 6, 53.

[129] See Bar-Tal and Schnell, 'The Impacts of Lasting Occupation', above n 122, 173, 516.

[130] Waxman, above n 6, 57.

[131] Ghazi-Bouillon, above n 123, 122; Bar-Tal and Schnell, *'The Impacts of Lasting Occupation'*, above n 122, 519.

[132] After 1967, Israel's strategic depth grew to at least 300 km in the south, 60 km in the east, and 20 km of extremely rugged terrain in the north, a security asset that would prove useful in the Yom Kippur War 6 years later against Egypt and Syria.

Israel's foreign diplomat Abba Eban famously warned that withdrawal from the territories would be a return to 'Auschwitz borders',[133] a phrase echoed today. In this light, Arab hostility and anti-Semitism justify the Israeli occupation and expansion of the settlements.[134]

The presence of a sizeable Arab population in the territories, however, threatens Israel's national identity. Israelis remain torn between the nationalist urge to possess the historic land and the patriotic need to preserve a solid Jewish majority.[135] No government, right or left, has ever moved to formally annex all of the West Bank and Gaza, for to do so would tip the entire demographic balance.[136] From this standpoint, Israeli policy in the territories is borne out of an existential threat from the Palestinians,[137] as well as a desire to keep the 1967 dowry (the land) without marrying the bride (the Palestinians).[138] This demographic tension has encouraged a discourse that supports restricting Palestinian rights in order to secure the state's Jewish identity.[139]

Palestinian Narratives: Denial and Dispossession

> *It is this tenacious denial of Palestinians as a people that enables Israel to believe it can successfully impose a colonisation and ultimately succeed in overseeing docile inhabitants content to hew the wood and till the soil remaining them, while buying TV sets and washing machines.*[140]

What for Israelis constitutes redemption of the land is for Palestinians systematic dispossession and denial of national rights. The geo-political outcome of 1967 has no less transformed the Palestinian collective. Indeed, the re-unification of the three parts of historical Palestine (Israel, the West Bank, and Gaza), with all of its Arab inhabitants under Israeli rule, was a major trigger in the resurgence of Palestinian nationalism.[141] Paradoxically, Israel's military victory and seizure of the territories

---

[133] 'In the moral logic of the secular Israeli right then, Greater Israel is the answer to Auschwitz'. Atran, above n 92, 490–95.

[134] The settlers also justified settlements on Israel's security needs: '...conceding the rights of Jews to any part of the land would signal to Israel's enemies that it had gone soft...withdrawing from Judea and Samaria would leave Israel's narrow waist vulnerable to invasion; leaving the territories would turn them into a base for terrorism...'. Gadi Taub, *The Settlers And the Struggle over the Meaning of Zionism* (Yale University Press, 2010), 18.

[135] Kimmerling, above n 112, 259–60.

[136] Ibid 244.

[137] Nadim N. Rouhana 'Zionism's Encounter with the Palestinians: The Dynamics of Force, Fear, and Extremism' in Rotberg, above n 50, 130.

[138] Israeli PM Levy Eshkol after the Six-Day War as quoted in Taub, above n 132, 5.

[139] Bar-Tal et al., 'Psychological Legitimization', above n 122, 118.

[140] Raja Shehadeh 'Occupiers: Law and the Uprising' (1988) 67 (Spring) *Journal of Palestine Studies* 33, 42–43.

[141] Kimmerling, *Clash of Identities*, above n 112, 168.

helped crystallise Palestinian national identity.[142] In many ways, it forced Palestinians to assert their national aspirations and resist denial of their legitimacy as a distinct entity. Notably, a corollary of the Jewish nationalism from 1967 involved refuting the existence of Palestinian identity, and their collective rights to land and statehood.[143] Israeli PM Golda Meir expressed this attitude in 1969, when she famously said that: 'There was no such thing as the Palestinian people…They did not exist'.[144]

From this vantage, the results of 1967 made a lasting impact on the Palestinian national movement, namely the PLO and its political mobilisation. Following the war, its legitimacy derived from a Palestinian consensus on 'national liberation' as the goal and 'armed struggle' as the means to achieve it—core values expressed in the Palestinian national charter as amended in 1968.[145] In 1969, Yasser Arafat was elected chairperson of the Palestinian National Council and became a towering figure in the Palestinian cause for national independence. Indeed, the Palestinian violence that led to the First Intifada was about conscious engagement in the struggle for political expression.[146] Until today, the Palestinian narrative is coloured by an understanding of Israeli presence in the territories as dismissive of their identity and national claims.[147]

> *The settlements are to the Palestinians as bombs in Tel Aviv are to the Israelis.* (Palestinian Chief Negotiator, Saab Erekat)[148]

To Palestinians, the true assault on their nationhood began with a heavily subsidised Israeli settlement policy.[149] According to Khalidi:

> …[T]his is part of the gradual but so far inexorable century-old process whereby the Palestinians have been removed from more and more of their ancestral homeland…and their very identity and existence as a people placed into question.[150]

---

[142] 'Finally, with the occupation, the three Palestinian communities in the West Bank, the Gaza Strip and Israel were reconnected after nineteen years of separation'. Daniel Bar-Tal and Izhak Schnell, 'Occupied and Occupiers - The Israeli Case' (Introduction) in Bar-Tal and Schnell, *'The Impacts of Lasting Occupation'*, above n 122, 14 ('Occupied and Occupiers'); Kimmerling, *Clash of Identities*, above n 112, 168.

[143] Bar-Tal, et al. 'Psychological Legitimization', above n 122, 126.

[144] PM Golda Meir as quoted in Silberstein, above n 21, 216. See Nadim N Rouhana, 'Zionism's Encounter with the Palestinians: The Dynamics of Force, Fear, and Extremism' in Rotberg, above n 50, 123.

[145] Khalil Shikaki, 'The Peace Process, National Reconstruction and the Transition to Democracy in Palestine' (1996) 25(2) (Winter) *Journal of Palestine Studies* 5, 8 ('The Peace Process').

[146] The First Intifada (1987–1993) was a Palestinian uprising against the Israeli occupation of the West Bank and Gaza. It involved resistance and civil disobedience, consisting of general strikes and boycotts, as well as widespread throwing of stones and Molotov cocktails at the IDF and its infrastructure. Atran, above n 92, 493–95.

[147] Rashid Khalidi, *Palestinian Identity*, above n 95, xxiii.

[148] Matthews, above n 123, 5.

[149] In the late 1970s, the Israeli government initiated a heavily subsidised Jewish settlement policy. Bar-Tal and Schnell, 'Occupied and Occupiers', above n 140, 15.

[150] Rashid Khalidi, *Palestinian Identity, above n 95,* xxvi.

Indeed, the ongoing construction of Jewish settlements (often facilitated by destroying Palestinian homes)[151] is a perennial source of national humiliation revisiting the wound of 1948. Until today, Palestinians believe they are being stripped of their last land and water reservoirs.[152] To many, this creeping annexation dashes hopes for Palestinian statehood and the implementation of their right to self-determination.[153] In short, Israeli–Jewish settlements are plugged into the Palestinian collective threat perception and victimisation.[154]

Equally guiding the Palestinian mindset is the effect of occupation on the power dynamics. Since 1967, Israel's control over the territories has created an asymmetrical relationship between 'ruler' and 'ruled'.[155] In many respects, Palestinians remain completely economically dependent on Israel.[156] Until today, economic interest groups exist in Israeli society, which signify '… a sort of "settlement-occupation-industrial complex"' [157] that materially benefits from the occupation.

To this must be added the institutionalised inferiority of the Palestinians. While Jewish settlers are protected as Israeli citizens, Palestinians remain deprived of basic civil rights and are regulated under a military regime.[158] In this light, the occupation and 'hill-top fortress-like Israeli settlements'[159] solidify a sense of injustice for Palestinians. Not surprisingly, the 'occupation reality' with its daily humiliations for Palestinians, has become a central component of the national narrative. This legacy of harm and human rights abuse will be discussed in the next chapter. Ultimately, what for Israelis entail necessary defensive and religious measures are for Palestinian abuses and instruments of control.[160]

---

[151] Daniel Bar-On and Sami Adwan, 'The Psychology of Better Dialogue between Two separate but Interdependent Narratives' in Rotberg, above n 50, 209.

[152] Kimmerling, *Clash of Identities*, above n 112, 168.

[153] Rashid Khalidi, *Palestinian Identity,* above n 95, xxii.

[154] For example, Shikaki demonstrates a link between Israeli settlements and Palestinian threat perception. See Khalil Shikaki, *'Willing to Compromise' Palestinian Public Opinion and the Peace Process* (United States Institute of Peace, January 2006) 9 ('*Willing to Compromise*').

[155] "The geographical proximity… as well as the intimate and yet asymmetrical interactions between members of the two groups, have also shaped the identities of both peoples and internal structures of their societies." Kimmerling, *Clash of Identities*, above n 112, 301.

[156] Kimmerling, *Clash of Identities*, above n 112, 245. "The Palestinian economy has been totally dependent on Israel. Palestinian workers still seek employment in Israel by the tens of thousands" Shikaki, 'The Peace Process', above n 145, 8.

[157] Rashid Khalidi, *Palestinian Identity,* above n 95, Introduction to 2010 reissue, xxii.

[158] Bar-Tal and Schnell, *'The Impacts of Lasting Occupation'*, above n 122, 516. The double-standard of protecting the small Jewish settlements dispersed among the densely populated Palestinian population has been an open wound for Palestinians. See Kimmerling, *Clash of Identities*, above n 112, 249.

[159] Rashid Khalidi, *Palestinian Identity,* above n 95, Introduction to 2010 reissue, xxv.

[160] Ibid.

Conclusion

Thus, the political, ideological, and territorial consequences of 1967 touch raw national nerves and have a determinative effect on the Israeli–Jewish approach to the core issues of the Israeli–Palestinian conflict.[161] Any engagement with transitional justice will need to address the discursive implications of 1967. These narratives fuel the conflict and allow the violence, as each side '…justifies and legitimizes the most immoral acts and allows the attribution of one's own immoral behaviour to the rival's violence and external-situational factors'.[162] The historical experience of 1967 is thus entangled in debates over national identity and memory, and thus remains broader than its territorial dimension.

1.4 Part Three: Second Intifada (2000–2005)

Historical Outline

The al-Aqsa *Intifada*,[163] or the Oslo War[164] (Second Intifada), which erupted on 30 September 2000, is another significant turning point. Any engagement with transitional justice will need to contend with the legacy of bloodshed and discursive shifts heralded by the period between 2000 and 2005.[165] The large-scale violence that spread throughout the West Bank, Gaza, and Israel was ostensibly triggered by two events. The first was Israeli leader Ariel Sharon's provocative visit to the Temple Mount/Haram al-Sharif on 28 September intended to show Israel's attachment to the site.[166] The second was the killing of Palestinian protesters by Israeli police the

---

161 Bar-Tal et al., 'Psychological Legitimization', above n 122, 173–174.

162 Bar-Tal, 'Socio-psychological Foundations', above n 67, 1441; See also Daniel Bar-Tal and Gavriel Salomon, 'Israeli Jewish Narratives of the Israeli-Palestinian Conflict – Evolution, Contents, Functions and Consequences' in Rotberg, above n 50, 32.

163 The Second Intifada is also known as the *al-Aqsa* Intifada because it refers to the *al-Aqsa* mosque in Jerusalem, the place where the Intifada started following Israeli leader Ariel Sharon's controversial visit. It is the name of a mosque, constructed in the eighth century CE at *Al-Haram Al-Sharif*, also known as the Temple Mount in the old City of Jerusalem, a location considered the holiest site in Judaism and third holiest in Islam.

164 The Second Intifada has also been referred to as the 'Oslo War' by right-wing Israeli circles who consider it to be the result of concessions made by Israel under the Oslo Accords. See Itamar Rabinovich, *Waging Peace: Israel and the Arabs, 1948–2003* (Princeton University Press, 2004) 306. See also Devin Sper, *The Future of Israel* (Sy Publishing, 2004) 335.

165 Some consider the *Sharm el-Sheikh* Summit on 8 February 2005 as the end of the Second Intifada, when President Mahmoud Abbas and Prime Minister Ariel Sharon agreed to stop all acts of violence against Israelis and Palestinians and reaffirmed their commitment to the Roadmap for peace

166 According to Waxman, this visit aimed at displaying Israel's control over the site and its attachment to it generated angry Palestinian protesters. See Waxman, above n 6, 170.

next day, after angered demonstrators responded with violent rioting at the Mosque. Notwithstanding these proximate causes, the origins of the Second Intifada remain disputed and are largely associated with the failure of the Camp David II summit in July 2000 earlier that year.[167]

The decline of the Oslo peace process also contributed to the eruption of the Second Intifada. In 1993, the historic conclusion of the Israeli–Palestinian Declaration of Principles[168] reconfigured the conflict's political and ideological landscape. Thereafter, the Middle East peace process was initiated, heralding reciprocal acknowledgement of legitimacy between the two parties. The PLO and the State of Israel formally recognised each other, and agreed on a progressive handover of certain Palestinian-populated areas in the West Bank to the PA.[169] Whilst the Oslo Accords established a framework for limited Palestinian autonomy, they postponed the thornier questions such as borders, control over Jerusalem, and the refugees to 'final status negotiations', which were initially to have been concluded within 5 years.[170] The peace talks between the parties ground to a halt in 1995 and were by a number of rounds of negotiations including the Camp David Summit of 2000.

By 2000, Israelis and Palestinians had become increasingly disillusioned with the Oslo process. For Israelis, waves of suicide bombings eroded their faith in the negotiations. To a degree, Israel's national security concerns dominated the peace talks, and became the yardstick against which Israelis measured its progress.[171] By linking Oslo with demands to improve security, critics suggest the Israeli government could simply sit back and wait on the inevitable Hamas-led terrorism to de-rail the Accords.[172] The Palestinians had also grown frustrated with their deteriorating economic and political conditions.[173] For many during the period, it was believed that Israel did not genuinely seek to withdraw from the territories, much less enable

167 The Middle East Peace Summit at Camp David from 11 to 25 July 2000, took place between US President Bill Clinton, Israeli Prime Minister Ehud Barak, and PA Chairman Yasser Arafat. It failed with the latter two blaming each other for the failure of the talks.

168 Signed 13 September 1993, Israel-PLO, 32 ILM 1525 (entered into force 13 October 1993) ('*Oslo Accords*').

169 Under the 1995 Interim Agreement ('*Oslo II*'), the West Bank was divided into three administrative areas (Area A—full civil and security control by the PA; Area B—Palestinian civil control and joint Israeli–Palestinian security control; Area C—full civil and security control by Israel). See The Israeli–Palestinian Interim Agreement on the West Bank and Gaza Strip, 28 September 1995.

170 Eric Rosand "The Right to Return under International Law Mass Dislocation: The Bosnia Precedent?" (1998) 19 *Michigan Journal of International Law* 1091, 1124.

171 According to Michael, Israel's stringent security demands and desire to preserve the military status quo undermined its will to make concessions, and undercut the public's ability to identify with the potential benefits of Oslo. Kobi Michael, 'Chap. 9: The Geopolitical Environment as a Barrier to Resolution of the Israeli-Palestinian Conflict' in 'Barriers to Peace' above n 88, 345–6.

172 'Hence when a suicide car bomb, the Hamas response to Wye, exploded in a Jerusalem market (6 November 1998)…the Israeli government was quick to seize the opportunity by threatening to suspend the peace process'. Colin and Quirk Knox, Padraic, *Peacebuilding in Northern Ireland, Israel and South Africa: Transition, Transformation and Reconciliation* (Palgrave, 2000) 197–199.

173 'Living standards had actually declined, and unemployment increased during the years of the peace process'. See Waxman, above n 6, 170.

the creation of a viable Palestinian state.[174] Ultimately, deep grievances with the Oslo process were underlying triggers for the Second Intifada.

Overall, the Second Intifada signified a peak in violence between Israelis and Palestinians. Compared to the First Intifada (1987–1993), the number of casualties is far higher, and characterised by more armed attacks and acts of terrorism.[175] For Israelis, Palestinian suicide bombers claimed the lives of over 1000 Israelis, most of whom were civilians. On the Palestinian side, the number of fatalities was over 3500 with over 28,000 injured as a result of air attacks, targeted killings, and other violence (over half of whom were civilians).[176] Beyond the death toll, the Second Intifada and the demise of the peace process have had dire consequences on both the sides.[177]

National Narratives

Israeli Narratives: 'No Partner' and Radicalisation

> *Palestinians use...guided human bombs...they are supported by part of the civilian population, and by their families.* (Israeli Supreme Court, 2002)[178]

For Israelis, the Second Intifada was a vicious terrorist campaign deliberately waged by Palestinians against its citizens and the peace process. The severity and frequency of suicide attacks among a relatively small population caused severe

---

[174] Ibid; 'After 2000, the general view on each side was that the other side had failed the [Oslo] test and thereby revealed its true purpose. This fact was demonstrated, in Palestinian eyes, by the continued growth of Jewish settlements in the West Bank and Gaza...'. See Mark Tessler, *A History of the Israeli-Palestinian Conflict* (Indiana University Press; second edition, 2009) 183.

[175] Unlike the First Intifada (1987–1993) characterised as a popular uprising, symbolized by youths throwing stones at Israeli soldiers, the Second Intifada involved armed attacks and terrorism. See Tammy Sagiv-Schifter and Michael Shamir, 'Conflict, Identity and Tolerance: Israel and the Al-Aqsa Intifada' (2006) 27(4) *Political Psychology* 569, 570.

[176] See ibid.; See also Jacob Shamir, *Public Opinion in the Israeli-Palestinian Conflict: From Geneva to Disengagement to Kadima and Hamas* (United States Institute of Peace 2007) 7; B'Tselem – Statistics – Fatalities 29.9.2000 to 15.1.2005, *B'Tselem.*

[177] Social science research shows that Israelis and Palestinians are psychologically damaged by the conflict. A study conducted after the first 2 years of the Second Intifada of 1300 children by Tel Aviv University research shows that 70% of Palestinians in the West Bank and 30% of children in Jewish settlements are suffering from post-traumatic stress due to the bloodshed. See The Associated Press, 'Study: High Trauma Rate Among Palestinians, Settlers' Children' *Ha'aretz* (online), 2 July 2002 http://www.haaretz.com/news/study-high-trauma-rate-among-palestinian-settlers-children-1.40795; See also Alean Al-Krenawi et al., 'Analysis of trauma exposure, symptomatology and functioning in Jewish Israeli and Palestinian adolescents' (2009) 195 *The British Journal of Psychiatry* 427.

[178] H.C. 7015/02 *Ajuri v IDF Commander* 56 (6) P.D. 352 at 2 available at elyon1.court.gov.il/Files_ENG/02/150/070/A15/02070150.A15.pdf.

psychological damage,[179] exposing a high proportion of Israelis directly to the conflict. Indiscriminate attacks in crowded places within Israel from public transport to markets demoralised Israeli society. As the violence intensified, major government sources confirmed the belief that the attacks were pre-planned, directed, and orchestrated by the PA and by Arafat personally.[180] In this light, the PA and especially Arafat were entirely discredited, entrenching an official mantra of 'no partner for peace'.[181] This claim continues to shape Israel's view of the conflict.[182] Until today, Israelis widely regard Palestinian leaders as non-viable diplomatic counterparts.[183] Ultimately, the Second Intifada reawakened deep-seated fears about the Palestinians[184] and shattered Israeli optimism in the peace process.[185]

Moreover, the period radicalised Jewish–Israeli society and its view of Palestinians. Indeed, the violence strengthened the revival of Jewish nationalism,[186] increased political intolerance of Arabs and heightened collective threat perceptions.[187] According to Segev: 'The *Intifada* forced us to go back into the Zionist

---

[179] 'These experiences… clearly have caused severe psychological damage, expressed as posttraumatic stress disorder and other effects'. See Avraham Bleich et al., 'Exposure to terrorism, stress-related mental health symptoms, and coping behaviors among a nationally representative sample in Israel' (2003) 290 *Journal of the American Medical Association,* 612–20.

[180] The Israeli government claimed that the Second Intifada was a deliberate plan by the PA to initiate a campaign of violence in response to the breakdown of the Camp David summit. See generally 'Sharm el-sheikh Fact-Finding Commission Report' (2001) ('Mitchell Report (2001)'); Daniel Bar-Tal and Keren Sharvit, 'A Psychological Earthquake in The Israeli-Jewish Society: Changing Opinions Following the Camp David Summit and the Al-Aqsa Intifada' in Yaacov Bar-Siman-Tov (ed), *The Israeli-Palestinian Conflict: From Conflict Resolution to Conflict Management* (Palgrave Macmillan, 2007) 179 ('*The Israeli-Palestinian Conflict*'); See also Waxman, above n 6, 170.

[181] This is the phrase used by PM Ehud Barak that has since become a mantra for Israeli officials. See Waxman, above n 6, 171; See also David Makovsky, *A Defensible Fence: Fighting Terror and Enabling a Two state solution* (The Washington Institute for Near East Policy, 2004) xv.

[182] "The conception that Israel must not surrender to terror … [and] … we have no partner for talks on the other side, has hardly changed since October 2000" quoted in Bar-Tal and Sharvit, above n 178, 190.

[183] In January 2006, Israelis perceived the Hamas victory in the Palestinian elections as final proof of Palestinian renunciation of diplomatic means and negotiations with Israel. Further, the subsequent Hamas coup d'etat in Gaza in summer 2007 bolstered the Israeli view that the PA was no longer representative of the Palestinian people.

[184] 'It contended that Palestinians would never abandon their claims to historic Palestine and viewed Oslo merely as a first step towards achieving this aim rather than an end point to the conflict. This cocktail had a powerful effect on Israeli identity, influencing and shaping it….' Ghazi-Bouillon, above n 123, 121.

[185] Waxman, above n 6, 171. A public opinion poll by Tel Aviv University showed that it was the violence that broke out in September 2000 far more than the failure of Camp David that eroded Israeli faith in the peace process. Akiva Eldar, 'The revolutionary road to 194' *Haaretz* (online), 22 July 2002 https://www.haaretz.com/1.5200970.

[186] Ram, *Israeli Nationalism,* above n 9, 125–26.

[187] Kimmerling, *Clash of Identities*, above n 112, 283; Waxman, above n 6, 171; Sagiv-Schifter and Shamir, above n 173, 588.

womb…we feel as if we must fight for our lives again because of the Arabs'.[188] For Israelis, the brutal lynching of two military reservists in Ramallah was a manifestation of these fears.[189] Such violence bolstered support for harsh retaliatory aggression[190] and dehumanization of Palestinians.[191] It turned the discursive tide from conflict resolution and coexistence to one of conflict management and unilateralism.

Palestinian Narrative: Rage and Resistance

For Palestinians, the Second Intifada vented a collective rage over the continued occupation and disillusionment with Oslo.[192] In the eyes of many Palestinians, the peace process simply became another tool used by Israel to entrench its presence in the territories.[193] For example, between 1994 and 2000, Israel confiscated approximately 35,000 acres of land in the West Bank for bypass roads and settlements, and almost doubled its settlement population.[194] Continued restrictions on freedom of movement and daily humiliations during the Oslo period eroded Palestinian faith in the peace process.[195] There was also frustration with deteriorating economic circumstances.[196] Notably, the PLO denied that the Intifada was planned, and asserted 'Camp David represented nothing less than an attempt by Israel to extend the force it exercises on the ground to negotiations'.[197] Thus, deep grievances with Oslo and the occupation became central to the Palestinian narrative of the conflict.

---

188 Waxman, above n 6, 186.

189 On 12 October 2000, PA police arrested two Israeli reservists who accidentally entered Ramallah. A Palestinian mob stormed the Police station. Both soldiers were beaten, stabbed, and disemboweled, and one body was set on fire.

190 Ifat Maoz and Clark McCauley, 'Threat, Dehumanisation and Support for Retaliatory Agressive Policies in Asymmetric Conflict' (2008) 52 *Journal of Conflict Resolution* 93, 113; See also Yaacov Bar-Siman-Tov, 'Introduction' in Bar -Siman-Tov, *The Israeli-Palestinian Conflict*, above n 178, 6.

191 Dehumanization manifested in contempt and disgust towards Palestinians, who are seen by some Israeli Jews as inferior and/or even as subhuman. See Daniel Bar-Tal, 'From Intractable Conflict through Conflict Resolution to Reconciliation: Psychological Analysis' (June 2000) 21(2) *Political Psychology* 351; Ghazi-Bouillon, above n 123, 120.

192 Richard Falk, 'Azmi Bishara, the Right of Resistance, and the Palestinian Ordeal' (2002) 31(2) (Winter) *Journal of Palestine Studies* 19, 29 ('Azmi Bishara').

193 See Sarah Roy, 'Decline and Disfigurement: The Palestinian Economy After Oslo' in Roane Carey (ed) *The New Intifada: Resisting Israel's Intifada* (New York, 2001) 95 as cited in Waxman, above n 6, 170.

194 For example, between 1994 and 2000, Israel confiscated approximately 35,000 acres of land in the West Bank for bypass roads and settlements, and almost doubled its settlement population. Ibid.

195 Rashid Khalidi, *Palestinian Identity*, above n 95, xx.

196 'Living standards had actually declined, and unemployment increased during the years of the peace process'. Waxman, above n 6, 170.

197 See 'Mitchell Report (2001)', above n 178, 7.

Moreover, Palestinians viewed the Second Intifada as part of their ongoing struggle for national liberation. Indeed, the discourse of resistance became central to the Palestinian understanding of the violence.[198] According to Said: 'Their suicide missions, bomb throwing and provocative slogans are acts of defiance, …'.[199] As the violence escalated, it heightened the threat perception on the part of the Palestinians.[200] The widely seen images of Muhammad al-Durrah in Gaza on 30 September, shot as he huddled behind his father, reinforced that perception.[201] The Intifada's cycles of violence radicalized Palestinian society and bolstered support for retaliatory measures and popular support for suicide missions.[202] In sum, this period altered the Palestinian mindset. It transformed the discourse from diplomacy to armed struggle, from peace talks to the resumption of violent resistance against Israel.

In sum, the Second Intifada, coupled with the failure of Oslo, marked a significant narrative transition for both the nations. The period also inflamed the Palestinian memory of the 1948 *Naqba*.[203] Arguably, the *Naqba* and the fear of relinquishing the right of return was central to the Second Intifada.[204] Transitional justice will therefore need to address the implications of this event; not only in terms of human rights law, but also discursively, as its footprints are tracked across the national identity and memory of the parties even today.

Conclusion

The Israeli–Palestinian conflict is not only a conventional one for power and territory but also an existential one drawn from the collective memories of certain key historic events. Paradoxically, conflict identity and mutual rejectionism are what unite both the nations across time. It is contended that an ethos of victimhood cultivated on both sides contributes to the sustenance of the conditions and experiences of intractable conflict.[205] From this standpoint, all historical events since 1948, from 1967 to the Second Intifada, including the latest rounds of violence in Gaza, are

---

198 Shamir, above n 174, 23; 'Resistance is fundamental to the new Palestinian narrative. Indeed for Rouhana, preserving the memory of loss and discrimination is a central constituent of that narrative' quoted in Robert Rotberg 'Building legitimacy through Narrative' in Rotberg, above n 50, 11.

199 Edward Said, *Peace and its Discontents: Essays on Palestine in the Middle East Peace Process* (Vintage Books, 1996), 156.

200 Shikaki, *'Willing to Compromise'*, above n 152, 8.

201 See 'Mitchell Report (2001)', above n 178, 3.

202 Bar-Tal and Sharvit, above n 178, 190; See also Shikaki, *'Willing to Compromise'*, above n 152, 8.

203 The destruction of houses in the Rafah refugee camp, for example was described as a 'Second Nakba'. See writings in this vein in *al Hayat al-Jadida,* 11 January 2002 (with regard to Rafah); *al Quds,* 14 May 2002 (with regard to Jenin) cited in Milshtein, above n 95, 60.

204 Ibid.

205 See Bar-Tal, 'Socio-psychological Foundations', above n 66, 1443. See also Tint, above n 5, 242.

viewed through the same nationalistic prism, and each cycle of violence becomes yet another confirmation of each nation's collective memory.[206] In the final analysis, these conflicting narratives—and the existential and sociological purposes they serve—are fundamental to understanding the Israeli–Palestinian conflict and any meaningful efforts to resolve it.

[206] See Mathew A Weiner, 'Defeating Hatred With Truth: An Argument in Support of a Truth Commission as part of the solution to Israel/Palestine' (2005–2006) 38 *Connecticut Law Review* 123, 149.

Chapter 2
Legal Dimensions of the Conflict and Legacies of Human Rights Abuse

2.1 Introduction

Both Israelis and Palestinians buttress their respective histories and narratives by recourse to international law. Over the course of the conflict, leaders of both the nations have engaged in international law to mobilise their claims to 'justice', bolster political rights, and advance a partisan historical view of the conflict.[1] In recent years, international legal inquiries into Israeli–Palestinian hostilities have received wide attention.[2] It is therefore important to outline the legal dimensions of the conflict, in order to understand their points of friction and confluence and to gauge the relevant rights and duties of the parties. Equally important are the legacies of human rights abuse left by the three constituent events discussed in Chap. 1. For 1948, the debate over the Palestinian right of return in human rights law is pivotal. Regarding 1967, the applicability of international humanitarian law (IHL) and human rights law to the Palestinian territories[3] is axiomatic to the Israeli occupation. Finally, the Second Intifada unleashed a period of violence during which retaliatory attacks on civilians and impunity became routine. Notably, many international law aspects of

[1] See for example, George Bisharat et al., 'Mobilizing International Law in the Palestinian Struggle for Justice' 18 (3) (2018) *Global Justice*, [published online 31 July, 2018]. Israel has since its inception referred to international law to justify its legitimacy and conduct. Susan Akram, M. Dumper, M. Lynk and I. Scobbie (eds.) *International law and the Israeli-Palestinian conflict* (Routledge, 2011).

[2] For further discussion on the function and effect of international inquiries into Israel/Palestine, see Sharon Weill, "The follow up to the Goldstone report in Israel and beyond", in Chantal Meloni and Gianni Tognoni (eds.), *Is There A Court for Gaza?: A Test Bench for International Justice*, (Asser/Springer, 2012) 105–20; Sharon Weill and Valentina Azarova, "Israel's Unwillingness? The Follow-Up Investigations to the UN Gaza Conflict Report and International Criminal Justice", in (2012) *International Criminal Law Review* 12 (5) 905–35.

[3] For the purposes of this thesis, the term 'Palestinian territories' will be used to refer to the West Bank and Gaza Strip (also known as the 'Occupied Palestinian Territory').

J. Bracka, *Transitional Justice for Israel/Palestine*, Springer Series in Transitional Justice, https://doi.org/10.1007/978-3-030-89435-1_2

the Second Intifada are disputed including the duties of Palestinians as non-state actors and the legal character of the conflict itself.

Any serious reckoning with the past will need to address the key human rights violations committed during these periods and to settle the international legal framework capable of guiding the conduct of both nations. To be sure, an exhaustive analysis of every IHL and human rights violation throughout these historic events is beyond the scope of this chapter. For example, other significant abuses such as the cutting of water and electricity to Palestinian civilians in Gaza; torture and/or other cruel treatment in arbitrary detention are not directly examined. The foregoing analysis must home in on the most characteristic, symbolic, and severe violations of each period to reflect systemic patterns of abuse, and the commission of unlawful conduct on both the sides. It is unable to be comprehensive.

Similarly, this chapter is limited to cross-border Israeli–Palestinian abuses and, as such, does not address the human rights violations of Palestinians residing within Israel. This is because despite the conflict's inter-societal dimension, the IPTEC's primary focus is on transitional justice between two distinct national entities. To this end, the chapter is directed towards providing a solid foundation for the legal inquiry and mandate of a bilateral IPTEC. As will be proposed in Chap. 8, the IPTEC would squarely focus on IHL, human rights, and crimes against humanity allegedly committed by Israelis and Palestinians.

2.2 Part One (1948): The Palestinian Right of Return

The singular most important legal question triggered by 1948 is the Palestinian right of return. Indeed, the Palestinian side calls for human rights law to be the primary reference point in evaluations of this issue and has consistently argued that displaced Palestinians have a legally sanctioned right of return, which Israel is obliged to recognise.[4] Whilst the concept of return is reflected in IHL[5] and refugee law,[6] the major legal controversy surrounds the right's treatment in the UN General Assembly (UNGA) resolutions, international treaty obligations, and customary law. Notably, there is no authoritative Palestinian definition of what exactly constitutes the right of return. Given its symbolic resonance to the conflict and to national claims to 'justice', this legal discussion will be premised on the 1948 Palestinian refugees and their descendants' right of return to Israel proper. The issue of the 1967 displaced

[4] Kurt Renee Radley, 'The Palestinian Refugees: The Right to Return in International Law' (1978) 72 *American Journal of International Law* 587, 587.

[5] *Geneva Convention relative to the Protection of Civilian Persons in Time of War of August 12, 1949*, opened for signature 12 August 1949, 75 UNTS 287 (entered into force 21 October 1950) ('*Fourth Geneva Convention*') art 49 forbids the permanent evacuation of areas occupied during international conflicts.

[6] Refugee law, however, focuses on the voluntariness of repatriation, in other words on the right *not* to be returned, or forcibly repatriated, so long as the conditions that caused the original flight remain.

Palestinians has proven to be less contentious as it does not directly implicate the question of repatriation to 'Israel proper'.[7] Ultimately, as discussed in Chap. 1, the meanings and implications derived from 1948 and the Palestinian right of return strike at the very heart of both the parties' national legitimacy. Accordingly, it would be crucial for transitional justice, and any mechanism dealing with the past, to find ways to soberly engage with this event legally so as to assist in the reduction, de-escalation, and potential resolution of the conflict.

Relevant Palestinian Specific UN Texts (UNGA Resolutions)

The UN resolution most fervently cited as an affirmation of the Palestinian right of return is Resolution 194 adopted by the UNGA on 11 December 1948. Paragraph 11 of the resolution is recited and reaffirmed almost annually and refers to: '*... the [Palestinian] refugees wishing to return to their homes and live at peace with their neighbors should be permitted to do so at the earliest practicable date ...*'.[8] Although the Arab states originally rejected it,[9] this resolution has since been invoked as an authority for an immediate, unconditional, and wholesale repatriation of the Palestinian refugees to their original homes.[10] According to Boling[11] and Tomeh,[12] the Palestinian right of return is enshrined in paragraph 11. Proponents of Palestinian return insist that it entitles the refugees to choose whether they wish to return to Israel and to be compensated whether or not they choose to return.[13]

However, many refute the legal authority of paragraph 11. Firstly, scholars note that the resolution itself does not conceive of return as a matter of 'right', but rather

---

[7] Further Palestinian displacement occurred during the Six-Day War (1967) 'when approximately 500,000 Palestinians fled the West Bank and Gaza, of which over 200,000 were second-time refugees from the 1948 war' cited in Kathleen Lawand, 'The Right of Return of Palestinians in International Law' (1996) 8 *International Journal of Refugee Law* 532, 536–537.

[8] '*The General Assembly resolves that the [Palestinian] refugees wishing to return to their homes and live at peace with their neighbors should be permitted to do so at the earliest practicable date, and that compensation should be paid for the property of those choosing not to return and for loss or damage to property which, under principles of international law or in equity, should be made good by the Governments or authorities responsible*'. See GA Res 194, UN GAOR, 3rd Sess, UN Doc A/810 (1994), 24.

[9] The Arab states and Palestinian political groups originally rejected Resolution 194 as a legal nullity because it implicitly recognised Israel. Lex Takkenberg, *The Status of Palestinian Refugees in International Law* (Clarendon Press, 1998) 244.

[10] G J. Boling, *The 1948 Palestinian Refugees and the Individual Right of Return, An International Law Analysis* (Bethlehem: BADIL Resources Centre for Palestinian Residency and Refugee Rights, 2002) 10.

[11] Ibid, 12.

[12] George Tomeh quoted in Radley, above n 4, 601. Former Permanent Representative of Syria to the United Nations.

[13] Takkenberg, above n 9, 243.

is merely recommendatory.[14] Secondly, critics of paragraph 11 recall that UNGA resolutions do not normally constitute binding authority over sovereign states.[15] Indeed, Chapter IV of the Charter of the United Nations precludes the General Assembly from adopting binding resolutions except with regard to budgetary and internal UN affairs. Thus, it is argued, Israel is not obliged to comply with Resolution 194, and the fact of paragraph 11's reiteration in subsequent UNGA resolutions is of no legal consequence.[16] At the same time, although these resolutions have no obligatory character, they may constitute important evidence of customary international law on the matter.[17]

Nevertheless, beyond questions of legal force, the language and context of Resolution 194 also appears to circumscribe the nature of Palestinian repatriation. The wording of paragraph 11 must be considered in its entirety. For example, paragraph 11 of Resolution 194 carries within itself an ostensible condition that speaks of permission to individuals who wish to 'live at peace with their neighbors'. That no explanation of this phrase exists in debates leading to the adoption of Resolution 194 has rendered its textual certainty even more elusive.[18] Notably, paragraph 11 is but one element of a 15-paragraph resolution that foresaw a final settlement of all questions outstanding between the parties.[19] In this context, paragraph 11 also recommended the 'resettlement and economic and social rehabilitation of the refugees and the payment of compensation'.[20] Thus, reliance on Resolution 194 to claim unqualified return as the only legal remedy to the refugee problem would seem misplaced. Nowhere is Israel obliged to 'complete' or 'immediately and unconditionally effect' return.

In any event, notwithstanding what was envisaged in 1948, it seems clear more than six decades later that the issue of practicability has been significantly

[14] Ruth Lapidoth, 'Legal Aspects of the Palestinian Refugee Question' 485 *Jerusalem Viewpoints* (Jerusalem Centre for Public Affairs, 1 September 2002) 2 www.jcpa.org/jl/vp485.htm. ('Legal Aspects') 5; See also Tanya Kramer, 'The Controversy of a Palestinian "Right of Return" to Israel' (2001) 18 *Arizona Journal of International and Comparative Law* 979, 1004; Radley, above n 4, 601.

[15] Kramer, above n 14, 1004; see also Robbie Sabel, 'The Palestinian Refugees, International Law and the Peace Process' (2003) 21(2) *Refuge* 52, 55.

[16] In the words of Weil: '[n]either is there any warrant for considering that by dint of repetition, non-normative resolutions can be transmuted into positive law through a sort of incantatory effect'. Prosper Weil 'Towards Relative Normativity in International Law' (1983) 77 *American Journal of International Law* 413, 417, quoted in Sabel, above n 15, 55.

[17] Yoav Tadmor, 'The Palestinian Refugees of 1948: The Right to Compensation and Return.' (1994) 8 *Temple International and Comparative Law Journal* 403, 416; See also Luke Lee, 'The Right to Compensation: Refugees and Countries of Asylum.' (1986) 80 *American Journal of International Law* 532, 544.

[18] John Quigley, 'Displaced Palestinians and a Right of Return' (1998) 39 *Harvard International Law Journal* 171, 187 ('Displaced Palestinians').

[19] The wording of paragraph 11 must be considered in its entirety. See Kramer, above n 14, 1004.

[20] Resolution 194, above n 8, [11].

transformed. Both the Israeli resettlement of former Palestinian lands and the vast growth of the refugee population are cases in point. Indeed, the original 1948 refugees constitute perhaps 10% of today's Palestinian refugee population,[21] and there is no indication in Resolution 194 regarding the inclusion of their descendants. Accordingly, Dowty saliently reminds us that when the resolution was enacted, 'the war had not yet ended, demarcation lines were still fluid, ... so that simple return "to one's country" would have had little meaning apart from return to places of residence'.[22] Thus, the Conciliation Commission for Palestine (CCP) itself explained as early as 1951 that the physical conditions in this area had changed considerably since 1948 and 'that unrestricted repatriation of refugees was neither a feasible option nor the preferred one'.[23] In effect, the magnitude of the refugee crisis arguably diminishes both the legal application and scope of Resolution 194.

The uncertainty of the legal claim to Palestinian return based on Resolution 194 is reinforced by subsequent resolutions, which ostensibly depart from repatriation to Israel as the only durable solution. Thus, whilst it repeatedly reaffirmed Resolution 194 during the 1950s and 1960s, the UNGA also advocated programs insisting on resettlement of the refugees in Arab countries.[24] Moreover, UN Security Council (UNSC) Resolution 242 only affirms 'the necessity ... [f]or achieving a just settlement of the refugee problem'.[25] Thus, it is often argued that Resolution 242 has effectively superseded UNGA Resolution 194, particularly given that UNSC resolutions are legally binding.[26]

Indeed, since 1967, the international position on the Palestinian question has been reconfigured by the UNGA.[27] Resolutions adopted subsequently not only raised the issue of repatriation but also insisted on Palestinian

[21] Segal, for example, notes that approximately 30,000 of the 300,000 Palestinian refugees in Lebanon can be categorised as 1948 refugees. See Jerome Segal, 'Clearing up the Right-of-Return Confusion' (2001) 8(2) *Middle East Policy* 23, 29.

[22] Alan Dowty, 'Return or Compensation: The Legal and Political Context of the Palestinian Refugee Issue' (1994) *World Refugee Survey* 26, 30.

[23] Eyal Benvenisti and Eyal Zamir, 'Private Claims to Property Rights in the Future Israeli-Palestinian Settlement' (1995) 89 *American Journal of International Law* 295, 326.

[24] '[I]n the years 1952 through 1968, [the General Assembly] annually reaffirmed *Resolution 513*, emphasising public works projects by which the refugees might be resettled and reintegrated into the Arab communities where they were': See Radley, above n 4, 604.

[25] SC Res 242, UN SCOR, 22nd sess, 1382nd mtg, UN Doc S/RES/242 (22 November 1967) ('Resolution 242').

[26] Ruth Lapidoth, 'The Right of Return in International Law with Special Reference to the Palestinian Refugees' (1986) 16 *Israel Yearbook on Human Rights* 103, 118–19 ('The Right of Return'). cf Quigley, 'Displaced Palestinians', above n 18, 210; See also Boling, above n 10, 204.

[27] Radley, above n 4, 604.

self-determination.[28] UNGA resolution 3236 characteristically provides that the 'inalienable rights' of the Palestinian people include '[t]he right to self-determination without external interference' and 'the right to national independence and sovereignty'.[29] The General Assembly thereby changed its conception of the issue from a humanitarian question of refugees to a political question concerning the rights of a people.[30] UN recognition of Palestinian selfhood coincided, paradoxically enough, with a weakening in the PLO's position on the right of return. As these resolutions passed, the PLO 'was for the first time advocating a Palestinian state in only part of Palestine'.[31]

Overall, what seems clear is that since 1948 a range of options including compensation, resettlement, and self-determination (beyond solely repatriation) have been advocated by the UNGA as an adjunct to return in order to facilitate resolution of the conflict. This fact, coupled with the momentum of Palestinian self-determination, calls into question the legal and political currency of wholesale repatriation based on Resolution 194. In 2012, the UNGA passed a resolution conferring non-member observer-state status on Palestine 'to re-affirm the right of the Palestinian people to self-determination'.[32] Ultimately, the strength of legal arguments based on the UNGA resolutions are somewhat diminished by their non-binding nature, the textual uncertainty of the resolutions themselves, and with respect to actual return, the encouragement of equally authoritative remedies at international law (from resettlement to self-determination) to resolve the Palestinian refugee crisis.

[28] Takkenberg, above n 9, 258, notes that explicit recognition of a Palestinian right to self-determination is first contained in The Importance of the Universal Realization of the Right of Peoples to Self-Determination and of the Speedy Granting of Independence to Colonial Countries and Peoples for the Effective Guarantee and Observance of Human Rights; GA Res 2649 (XXV), UN GAOR, 25th sess, 1915th plen mtg, [5], UN Doc A/RES/2649 (XXV) (30 November 1970).

[29] See *Question of Palestine*, GA Res 3236 (XXIX), UN GAOR, 29th sess, 2296th plen mtg, art 2(1), UN Doc A/RES/3236 (XXIX) (22 November 1974) ('Resolution 3236') [1(a)]–[1(b)].

[30] Lapidoth, Radley and Justus R Weiner all protest that these resolutions call into question the very existence of Israel as a sovereign entity, as they grant Palestinians an absolute right of return to the Israeli State with the purpose of pursuing a separate nationalist identity: Lapidoth, 'The Right of Return', above n 26, 119; Radley, above n 4, 607; Justus R Weiner, 'The Palestinian Refugees Right to Return and the Peace Process' (1997) 20(1) *Boston College International and Comparative Law Review* 1, 42–3.

[31] Rashid Khalidi, 'Observations on the Right of Return' (1992) 21(2) *Journal of Palestine Studies* 29, 34.

[32] UNGA Res 67/19 (2012), A/RES/67/19, 4 December 2012. The Resolution upgraded Palestine's status at the UN and implicitly recognises Palestinian sovereignty. Notably, some states voting for the resolution 'underscored that statehood could only be achieved through dialogue between the parties implying that Palestine had not yet achieved statehood'. See Linda Keller, *The International Criminal Court and Palestine: Part 1* (JURIST-Forum, 29 January 2013) http://jurist.org/forum/2013/01/linda-keller-palestine-icc-part1.php.

International Human Rights Instruments

What then of the claim that Palestinian return can be grounded in the Universal Declaration of Human Rights[33] (UDHR), the International Covenant on Civil and Political Rights[34] (ICCPR), and the International Convention on the Elimination of All Forms of Racial Discrimination[35] (CERD)? Each of these human rights instruments unequivocally references such a right as a corollary of the right to freedom of movement. Article 12(4) of the ICCPR states that: '[n]o-one shall be arbitrarily deprived of the right to enter his own country'. Notably, human rights treaties tend to speak of a right to 'enter' one's country rather than 'return' to it, and considerable differences exist concerning the beneficiaries of the right as well as the limitations to which it may be subjected. Israel is a party to the CERD and the ICCPR and thereby legally bound by both the treaties.

However, the UDHR is only a Declaration adopted by the UNGA and accordingly has uncertain legal authority. Nevertheless, scholars widely regard the UDHR as reflective of customary international law,[36] and given that its provisions echo those contained in the treaties, it is worthy of consideration. In any event, some academics and UN organs assert the Palestinian right of return as an inalienable one, notwithstanding the absence of proper legal enforcement, and despite its interpretative and substantive ambiguity.[37] The difficulties with basing a Palestinian right of return on human rights law are manifold and warrant close scrutiny. Accordingly, this section addresses the unique challenges facing Palestinians under the human rights instruments as non-nationals, and as mass displaced persons seeking to invoke a right after a considerable passage of time. The potential for exigencies that may restrict the right's invocation under the treaties is also considered.

---

[33] Article 13(2) of the UDHR reads: '[e]veryone has the right to leave any country, including his own, and to return to his country'. GA Res 217A, UN GAOR, 3rd Sess, 183rd mtg, UN Doc A/810 (1948) 71.

[34] *International Covenant on Civil and Political Rights*, opened for signature 16 December 1966, 999 UNTS 171 (entered into force 23 March 1976) ('*ICCPR*'). Israel ratified the *ICCPR* on 3 October 1991, but is not a party to the Optional Protocol.

[35] *International Convention on the Elimination of Racial Discrimination*, opened for signature 7 March 1966, 660 UNTS 195 (entered into force 4 January 1969) ('*CERD*') art 5 provides in paragraph (d)(ii) for a right to 'leave any country, including one's own, and to return to one's country'. The phrase is taken verbatim from the UDHR and is therefore also considered in this section. Israel ratified *CERD* on 3 January 1979.

[36] Justus R Weiner, above n 30, 38.

[37] J D Ingles quoted in Lapidoth, 'The Right of Return', above n 26, 103; see also Eric Rosand 'The Right to Return under International Law Mass Dislocation: The Bosnia Precedent?' (1998) 19 *Michigan Journal of International Law* 1091, 1121.

Retrospectivity

Firstly, the retroactive application of human rights provisions to the events of 1947–1949 is uncertain. Commentators observe that it would be difficult to argue that Article 12 of the *ICCPR* is intended to apply to those who became refugees before the right took effect or that Israel assumed a duty to repatriate the 1948 refugees when it ratified the treaty in 1991.[38] From this standpoint, the *ratione temporis* rule applies so as to preclude the admissibility of Palestinian return.[39] Benvenisti contends: 'When the refugee problem was created, individuals enjoyed no rights under international law …'.[40] Indeed, non-retroactivity is a default rule in treaty interpretation,[41] and the ICCPR is firmly grounded in an explicit lack of retroactive application.[42] The CERD provision also contains no indication that it applies retrospectively to events occurring before a state's ratification of the treaty. Thus, Israel's conduct in 1947–1949 seems beyond the temporal reach of the human rights conventions.

Nevertheless, there exists an exception to the retroactive principle for 'continuing violations'. UN Human Rights Committee (HRC) jurisprudence indicates that when a violation predates the treaty's entry into force, but continues after that date, or where effects which of themselves constitute violations continue after a state ratifies, these breaches of the *ICCPR* will not be precluded from admissibility.[43] Arguably, Israel's refusal to allow Palestinian refugees and their descendants into

[38] According to Kent: 'It would be extraordinary if, by Israel's 1991 ratification, the words of Articles 12(4) or 13 reached back retroactively more than 40 years and implicitly overturned Israel's consistently maintained legal position that it had no obligation to allow the return of refugees from the 1947–49 conflict'. Andrew Kent, 'Evaluating the Palestinians' Claimed Right of Return' (2012) 34(1) *University of Pennsylvania Journal of International Law* 149, 198.

[39] Under Articles 1 and 3 of the First Optional Protocol, the Human Rights Committee of the ICCPR is precluded from adjudicating on a matter if it is inadmissible *ratione temporis* (by reason of time). See Melissa Castan and Sarah Joseph, *The International Covenant on Civil and Political Rights: Cases, Materials and Commentary* (Oxford University Press, 2013), 57.

[40] Benvenisti affirms: 'Then there is the question of retroactivity … At that time, individuals were objects of state's interests but had no standing to sue governments'. Eyal Benvenisti, 'The Right of Return in International Law: An Israeli Perspective', (2015) Tel Aviv University Faculty of Law ('The Right of Return'); See also Christian Tomuschat, 'Reparation for Victims of Grave Human Rights Violations' (2002) 10 *Tulane Journal of International and Comparative Law* 157.

[41] The basis of this rule flows from the generally recognized principle of international law, that treaties will not have a retroactive effect. See Castan and Joseph, above n 39, 57; See also JS Davidson, 'Admissibility under the Optional Protocol to the International Covenant on Civil and Political Rights' (1991) 4 *Canterbury Law Review* 337, citing arts 4 and 28 of the Vienna Convention on the Law of Treaties.

[42] Kent compares the *ICCPR* (which makes no reference to retroactive application) with the Refugee Convention art 1(A)(2) (stating explicitly that the term 'refugee' applies retroactively to individuals with certain characteristics). Kent, above n 38, 198.

[43] The HRC has found continuing violations in numerous cases, including *Kulomin v Hungary* (521/1991) (in the context of a period of pre-trial detention that began before the entry into force of the Optional Protocol for Hungary, but ended after that date) and *Gueye et al v France* (196/1985) (in the context of continuing discrimination) discussed in Castan and Joseph, above n 39, 60–65.

Israel since 1991 constitutes such a violation. Whilst the line between continuing and non-continuing violations is unclear,[44] denying entry to thousands of Palestinians, and their descendants, could amount to an ongoing act that continues to prevent the group from lawfully entering their country of origin.

Nationality Nexus

The meaning of the phrase 'own country' in the treaty-based instruments remains textually elusive. In particular, the determination of a Palestinian right of return is complicated by the severance of the State-national bond in 1948, brought about by a change of borders affecting the territory of origin.[45] Arguably, the Palestinians do not have the right to return to Israel, since they were displaced prior to the Israeli State's establishment, and thus as non-nationals fall outside the ambit of the provisions. Indeed, Kramer notes '... there was never a sovereign State of Palestine in which the Palestinian refugees were nationals'.[46] Not surprisingly, Israeli officials[47] and other scholarly reviews propagate this literal construction with some vehemence.[48]

Nevertheless, the insistence on a narrow test of citizenship to invoke the right of return seems unduly stringent. Rather, an expansive construction of 'own country' asserts that the existence of a 'close and enduring connection' to one's 'homeland' may be equally decisive.[49] Indeed, the International Court of Justice (ICJ) endorsed this approach in its landmark *Nottebohm* case, in which Liechtenstein petitioned for Guatemalan recognition of Friedrich Nottebohm as a Liechtenstein national.[50] The ICJ applied the criteria of 'tradition', 'establishment', 'interests', and 'family ties'

---

[44] This distinction is complex and might lie in the determination of when the impugned act or violation was 'completed'. See Castan and Joseph above n 39, 69.

[45] Thus, the question is begged as to whether the 'country' to which an individual is entitled to return is the State of which one holds formal nationality, or whether it connotes a link to a territory or land regardless of citizenship. Lawand, above n 7, 540.

[46] Kramer above n 14, 1008.

[47] Sabel argues that most international law instruments granting a right to re-entry are premised on nationality, evidenced by State practice, and the fact that the term 'national' is also used in the 1950 *European Human Rights Convention, Protocol No.4*, and in the 1969 *American Convention on Human Rights*. See Sabel, above n 15, 54.

[48] According to Radley "Article 13 (2) [of the UDHR] 'obliges' states to permit the return of their citizens or nationals only. The Palestinian refugees are, of course, not Israeli nationals, not by that state's definition, and significantly, also, not according to the refugees' own self-identity." Radley, above n 4, 613; see also Lapidoth, 'Legal Aspects', above n 12, 108.

[49] Takkenberg, above n 9, 237.

[50] *Nottebohm (Liechtenstein v Guatemala) (Second Phase)* [1955] ICJ Rep 4 ('*Nottebohm*'); See also Donna E Arzt and Karen Zughaib 'Return to the Negotiated Lands: The Likelihood and Legality of a Population Transfer Between Israel and a Future Palestinian State' (1991–2) 24 *New York University Journal of International Law and Politics* 1399, 1444. Proponents of the broader interpretation draw comfort from the subjective element of the *Nottebohm* principle in the Palestinian context. Lawand, above n 7, 559; Takkenberg, above n 9, 237; Amnesty International,

to hold that it was the 'substance' of Nottebohm's links with Liechtenstein, rather than a formal grant of citizenship, that was determinative in international law.[51]

Moreover, the comparative and contextual meaning of 'own country' lends support to a wider reading in the Palestinian context.[52] Such breadth seems all the more persuasive in view of the fact that a state-centred definition would defeat the object and purpose of protecting the right to return substantively.[53] In November 1999, the HRC issued *General Comment 27* on Article 12 of the ICCPR.[54] It asserted in paragraph 20 that the phrase 'his own country' is not limited to 'nationality in a formal sense' but rather was intended to include:

> individuals whose country of nationality has been incorporated in or transferred to another national entity … [and] stateless persons arbitrarily deprived of the right to acquire the nationality of [their long-term] residence.

Both enumerated categories of persons would appear to accommodate the factual complexity of the Palestinian refugees' plight.

The HRC has subsequently applied this broad view in the recent cases of *Nystrom v Australia*[55] and *Warsame v Canada*,[56] endorsing a 'factor-based' approach and an indicia of 'social bonding' to determine the strength of an individual's connection to 'his own country'.[57] In both the cases, the HRC prioritised the existence of clear,

---

'Israel and the Occupied Territories/Palestinian Authority. The Right to Return: The Case of the Palestinians' (Policy Statement, March 2001) 2.

[51] Mitchell Knisbacher, 'Aliyah of Soviet Jews: Protection of the Right of Emigration under International Law.' (1973) 14 *Harvard International Law Journal* 89, 97; The Court characterised this relationship as one of 'reciprocal rights and duties': *Nottebohm* [1955] ICJ Rep 4, 23.

[52] Contrary to Sabel, other commentators argue that the dichotomy between 'national' and 'country' in human rights documents clearly comports with the expansive approach, whereby "… the wider term 'his country' was chosen to include both place of nationality and place of origin." Susan Akram and Terry Rempel, 'Recommendations for Durable Solutions for Palestinian Refugees: A Challenge to the Oslo Framework.' (2000–01) XI The Palestine Yearbook of International Law 1, 51; see also Lawand, above n 7, 548.

[53] After all, in the words of Arzt and Zughaib "… these are broad-based human rights treaties, not a technical set of immigration regulations." Arzt and Zughaib, above n 50, 1445.

[54] Human Rights Committee, *General Comment No 27: Article 12 (Freedom of Movement)*, 67th sess, UN Doc CCPR/C/21/Rev.1/Add.9 (2 November 1999) UN ('*General Comment No 27*') [20].

[55] Human Rights Committee, *Views: Communication No 1557/2007*, UN Doc CCPR/C/102/D/1557/2007 (18 July 2011) ('*Nystrom v Australia*'). In this case, the HRC held that the deportation of Nystrom ("an absorbed member of the Australian community" whose mother, sister and nuclear family all live in Australia) to Sweden (a country where he does not speak the language and "to which he has no ties apart from nationality" in the formal sense) breached the *ICCPR*.

[56] Human Rights Committee, *Views: Communication No 1959/2010*, UN Doc CCPR/C/102/D/1959/2010 (21 July 2011) ('*Jama Warsame v Canada*').

[57] The HRC took into account: 'the strong ties' 'the presence of family' 'the language spoken', 'the duration of stay', and 'the lack of any other ties, than at best formal nationality with a country of origin.' Both cases concerned the prospective deportation of permanent residents to their formal countries of national origin (Sweden and Somalia respectively) due to extensive criminal records. In both instances, the authors emigrated at a very early age and spent most of their lives in their

ongoing, and longstanding ties to a country over the formal grant of citizenship.[58] Whilst the HRC does not necessarily resolve the interpretive ambiguity, it seems clear that the absence of formal nationality should not be granted substantive weight and that 'special ties to or claims' may be significant in the Palestinian context.[59] Nevertheless, it is worth recalling that even if Article 12(4) were to extend beyond citizens, it is difficult to imagine how it might also cover the descendants' of refugees who have never set foot in Israel.[60] The Palestinian right to return thus faces additional obstacles when claimed by individuals who have no physical links to the country nor have ever been its citizens.

Mass or Individual Rights?

The question of Palestinian return is further complicated by its collective or 'national dimension', and therefore, the extent to which an individually held human right applies to large-scale displacement. Several authors argue that mass movements of persons are beyond the freedom of movement provisions, and consequently, the right of return is inapplicable to displaced Palestinians.[61] Another view maintains that, rather than falling under international human rights law, the issue of mass repatriation is either a political problem or one of self-determination.[62] However, this line of argument appears tenuous in so far as it asserts that the right of self-determination and the right of return are mutually exclusive. In the words of Lawand: '[t]he implication is that the individual can only claim a right through the group …

resident countries (Australia and Canada respectively). The HRC overturned the previous strict interpretation of 'own country' in *Stewart v Canada* (583/93). For more details, see Castan and Joseph, above n 39, 417.

[58] Both cases seem to exceptionally demonstrate that even formal nationality per se, may be insufficient to determine the strength of an individual's connection to his or her 'own country'.

[59] Regarding the 1948 refugees right of return to Israel, the HRC (1998) has merely stated "the Committee urges Israel to respect the right to freedom of movement provided for under article 12, including the right to return to one's country." Notably, there are no references to a Palestinian 'right of return' in the subsequent Concluding Observations on Israel, issued in August 2003 or of September 2010. Concluding Observations on Israel, 18 August 1998, UN doc CCPR/C/79/Add.93, para 22. See Castan and Joseph, above n 39, 416.

[60] "Even if the article extends beyond citizens, it is hard to see how it covers non-citizens who have not been in a country for 40 years by the time that country joined the *ICCPR* and became bound by Article 12." Kent, above n 38, 199; See also Justus R Weiner, above n 30, 39–49, "ICCPR fails to support the Palestinian case for repatriation. This follows from the fact that the Palestinian refugees were never citizens of Israel. Nor do their offspring, most of whom have never visited Israel, meet the 'return to his country' test".

[61] Benvenesti and Zamir, above n 23, 325; See also R. Lapidoth, 'The Right to Return', above n 26, 114; Donna Arzt, "Palestinian Refugees: The Human Dimension of the Middle East Peace Process" (1995) *American Society of International Law: Proceedings of the 89th Annual Meeting* 369, 372.

[62] Stig Jagerskiold, '*The Freedom of Movement*', *The International Bill of Rights* (New York, 1981) 180, cited in Lawand, above n 7, 542; see also E. Rosand above n 37, 1128; Lapidoth, 'The Right of Return', above n 26, 123.

[which] is contrary to the objects and purposes of the human rights instruments generally'.[63] Moreover, in practice, it would unjustly endorse the suspension of the refugees' individual rights to freedom of movement pending the realisation of a Palestinian State. Similarly, the underlying political situation in a country to which return is sought should not necessarily bar an individual's entitlement to a right under international law.

At any rate, what seems clear is that neither the text nor the *travaux preparatiores* of the relevant UDHR, ICCPR, and CERD provisions actually support circumscribing return in this way.[64] Whilst the right to return is structured as an individual right, Quigley confirms that this is also true of most rights enumerated in international human rights instruments.[65] Further, legal scholars argue that a conservative reading of the provisions is belied by international practice.[66] It must be noted however that whilst freedom of movement should be interpreted in a way that is substantively meaningful, 'the article is [nonetheless] not a formula for determining state legitimacy or for resolving territorial disputes … its aims are in fact more modest'.[67]

Limitations

The additional difficulties with basing a Palestinian right of return on human rights law is that these instruments are conditioned by language that limits the right's invocation in certain circumstances. Article 29(2) of the UDHR speaks of the rights being qualified by the '*freedoms of others, the just requirements of morality, public*

[63] Lawand, above n 7, 543.

[64] Nowhere in the actual text of the instruments is the operation of the right of return qualified on the basis of group affiliation. Rather, in each instance, the relevant language refers to 'everyone'. In addition, the HRC in *General Comment 27*, paragraph 19 affirms this reading in so far as it states: '*[t]he right to return is of the utmost importance for refugees seeking voluntary repatriation. It also implies prohibition of enforced population transfers or mass expulsions to other countries*'. *General Comment No 27*, UN Doc CCPR/C/21/Rev.1/Add.9.

[65] Indeed, it is a historically self-evident fact that the movement of people takes on a collective dimension. Accordingly, to deny the availability of human rights simply because individuals form part of a mass group would render those rights illusory. See Quigley, 'Displaced Palestinians', above n 18, 211.

[66] Thus, Rosand points out that human rights treaties were the basis for guaranteeing return in recently signed peace agreements in order to resolve conflicts in Rwanda and Georgia, both of which produced hundreds of thousands of refugees and displaced persons. Rosand, above n 37, 1131. See also Quigley, 'Displaced Palestinians', above n 18, 236–37; Lawand, above n 7, 543; and Boling, above n 10, 40. Conversely, other commentators cite the lack of returns following mass displacement during conflict as evidence that the Right to Return applies only to individuals. See Benvenesti and Zamir, above n 23, 325; see also R Lapidoth, 'The Right of Return', above n 26, 114; Radley, above n 4, 613.

[67] Radley, above n 4, 614. Notably, the HRC in a recent consideration of Israel's obligations under the *ICCPR* (2014) makes no mention of the Palestinian right of return under Article 12(3). See Human Rights Committee, *Concluding Observations on the Fourth Periodic report of Israel*, CCPR/C/ISR/CP/4 (21 November 2014).

order and the general welfare in a democratic society'. This limitation allows governments a significant degree of freedom to curtail human rights in the face of real or perceived threats to national welfare and provides a potential defence to UDHR violations.[68] Indeed, scholars have marshalled the elasticity of this provision to argue that a mass return of Palestinian refugees would undermine the '*freedom of others*' and '*general welfare*' of Israel's citizens by calling into question ownership of homes, villages, and other properties long occupied by Israelis.[69] Accordingly, Israel's retreat from mass Palestinian return with respect to the UDHR's provisions might be justifiably mounted.

As for the ICCPR, the right to return enunciated in Article 12(4) is not subject to the more elaborate restrictions of Article 12(3) contained in the treaty based on national security, public order, and public health and morals.[70] Presumably then, it is arguable that the ICCPR does not allow a state to condition the right of return on such considerations. However, the incorporation of the modifier 'arbitrarily' in Article 12(4) might afford Israel significant leeway in its qualification of a Palestinian right of return. Indeed, the phrase implies the state has a right to interfere with the right to enter, so long as the interference is not 'in the absence of due process'.[71]

Unique to the ICCPR provision, 'arbitrarily' is a term steeped in contestation and interpretative ambiguity.[72] The HRC has stated, with regard to the meaning of 'arbitrary' in Article 12(4), 'even lawful interference provided for by law should be in accordance with the provisions, aims and objectives of the *Covenant* and should be, in any event, reasonable in the particular circumstances …'.[73] According to Boling, 'Israel … has flagrantly violated the ICCPR Article 2(1) non-discrimination provision protecting the Article 12(4) right of return'[74] and Israel's *Nationality Law* (1952) 'effectively "stripped" this entire group of their status as presumed nationals

[68] Samuel Bleicher, 'The Legal Significance of Re-Citation of General Assembly Resolutions.' (1969) 63 *American Journal of International Law* 444, 459–60.

[69] According to Lapidoth: 'the influx of more than one and half million mostly hostile refugees would without doubt violate "the rights and freedoms of others" in Israel and damage "public order and the general welfare in a democratic society".' See Lapidoth, 'The Right of Return', above n 26, 114–115; See also Joseph Alpher and Khalil Shikaki, *The Palestinian Refugee Problem and the Right of Return*, (Harvard University, 1998) 174. In this regard, a precise reversal of the initial dislocation could only be achieved at the cost of an even greater new dislocation.

[70] The qualifications listed in the *ICCPR* art 12(3) mirror those in Article 29 of the UDHR. They do not apply to art 12(4). This is because they precede art 12(4) and they refer only to the 'above-mentioned rights'.

[71] Lawand, above n 7, 547.

[72] According to one construction, 'arbitrarily' as a limitation must be 'strictly and narrowly construed'. See Louis Henkin, 'Introduction' in Louis Henkin (ed), *The International Bill of Rights: The Covenant on Civil and Political Rights* (Columbia University Press, 1981) 26.

[73] The HRC continues: '… The Committee considers that there are few, if any, circumstances in which deprivation of the right to enter one's own country could be reasonable. A State party must not, by stripping a person of nationality … arbitrarily prevent this person from returning to his or her own country'. See *General Comment No 27*, UN DOC CCPR/C/21/Rev.1/Add.9.

[74] Boling, above n 10, 40.

of Israel'.[75] Consequently, in her view, there is no reasonable basis for obstructing Palestinian repatriation.[76]

Nevertheless, whilst states may not arbitrarily de-nationalise their citizens in order to deprive them of return, or do so contrary to the principle of non-discrimination, Boling's argument seems somewhat misplaced. As the historical complexities of 1948 demonstrate, the Palestinian refugees were never Israeli citizens, and therefore could not have been said to be 'de-nationalised', arbitrarily, or otherwise.[77] As before, it is arguable that the demographic threat posed by the refugees as well as their descendants constitutes one of the few exceptional circumstances in which denial of a right to enter one's own country might be legitimately and, indeed, non-arbitrarily, circumscribed.[78] In sum, the interpretational questions with respect to the phrase 'arbitrary' illustrate that a Palestinian right of return to Israel under the ICCPR provisions is far from certain.

Derogations

There is also a question as to whether the public emergency clause of Article 4(1) of the ICCPR applies to Israel and allows it to derogate from its treaty obligations under Article 12(4). The ICCPR permits derogations 'in time of public emergency, which threatens the life of the nation'. Notably, the state of emergency, which the provisional government of Israel declared in 1948, has remained in force until today.[79] Although Israel has not made any explicit derogation to Article 12(4), it

[75] Ibid, 39.

[76] Ibid, 41–2.

[77] Moreover, rather than being racially driven, '[t]he right of a State to determine who are, and who are not, its nationals is an essential element of its sovereignty' of which Israel's *Nationality Law* is arguably an important expression. See Paul Weis, *Nationality and Statelessness in International Law* (Sijthoff and Noordhoff, 1979) 65.

[78] 'It is not a stretch to think that reasonable demographic or national security concerns could be a non-arbitrary basis to refuse entry to Palestinian refugees or their descendants'. Kent, above n 38, 199.

[79] In May 1948, Israel's Provisional Council declared a state of emergency under section 9 of the *Law and Administration Ordinance* (1948). In 1992, the Knesset passed the *Basic Law: The Government* (1992) requiring the state of emergency to be reviewed and approved annually. Under Article 38(b) of the amended Basic Law: The Government (2001), a state of emergency can only be declared for a period of 1 year, after which it must be reviewed. The Knesset routinely extends Israel's state of emergency.

informed the UN of its state of emergency at the time of its ratification of the ICCPR,[80] and thus could be said to have done so by implication.[81]

However, the validity of any Israeli derogation is subject to procedural and substantive compliance with the ICCPR.[82] Arguably, Israel's sweeping declaration of its emergency in 1991 falls short of its obligation to specify the 'provisions from which it has derogated'[83] and to include 'sufficient and precise information about its law and practice in the field of emergency powers'.[84] On this point, the HRC has reiterated its concerns from General Comment 29 (1998) in its Concluding Observations on Israel, that Israel '... should review the modalities governing the renewal of the state of emergency and specify the provisions of the Covenant it seeks to derogate from ...'.[85]

Moreover, Quigley argues that human rights law prohibits countries from declaring an emergency for an indefinite period of time.[86] Indeed, the HRC confirms in General Comment 29 that measures of derogation 'must be of an exceptional and temporary nature', 'designed to combat a serious public emergency'.[87] Nevertheless,

---

[80] '*International Covenant on Civil and Political Rights*' (8 September 2005) Status of Multilateral Treaties Deposited with the Secretary-General http://untreaty.un.org/ENGLISH/bible/englishinternetbible/partI/chapterIV/treaty6.asp at 1 October 2005 (declaration made by Israel 3 October 1991). According to its formal communication to the UN (1991), Israel maintains: '*Since its establishment, the Jewish State has been the victim of continuous threats and attacks on its very existence as well as on the life and property of its citizens. These have taken the form of threats of war, of actual armed attacks, and campaigns of terrorism resulting in the murder of and injury to human beings*'.

[81] Vic Ullom, 'Voluntary Repatriation of Refugees and Customary International Law' (2000–01) 29 *Denver Journal of International Law and Policy* 115, 142; '*International Covenant on Civil and Political Rights*' (8 September 2005) Status of Multilateral Treaties Deposited with the Secretary-General http://untreaty.un.org/ENGLISH/bible/englishinternetbible/partI/chapterIV/treaty6.asp.

[82] Under treaty law, derogations must satisfy a number of requirements, such as qualifications of severity, temporariness, proclamation and notification, legality, proportionality, consistency with other obligations under international law, and non-discrimination. Tahmina Karimova, *Rule of Law in Armed Conflicts Project: Derogation from human rights treaties in situations of emergency* (Geneva Academy of international humanitarian law and human rights) http://www.genevaacademy.ch/RULAC/derogation_from_human_rights_treaties_in_situations_of_emergency.php.

[83] *ICCPR* art 4(3).

[84] Human Rights Committee, *General Comment No 29: Article 4: Derogations during a State of Emergency*, 72nd sess, UN Doc CCPR/C/21/Rev.1/Add.11 (31 August 2001) ('*General Comment No 29*') [2], see also: HRC's Consolidated Guidelines for State Reports under the ICCPR, UN Doc CCPR/C/66/GUI/Rev.2, C3.

[85] See *Concluding Observations of the Human Rights Committee: Israel*, UN Doc CCPR/CO/78/ISR (5 August 2003); See also Concluding Observations on the Fourth Periodic Report of Israel, UN Doc CCPR/C/IS/R/CO/4 (21 November 2014) [10]; *Consideration of Reports Submitted by States Parties under Article 40 of the Covenant*, UN Doc CCPR/C/ISR/CO/3 (29 July 2010) [7]; *Consideration of Reports Submitted by States Parties under Article 40 of the Covenant*, UN Doc CCPR/CO/78/ISR (21 August 2003) [12]; *Consideration of Reports Submitted by States Parties under Article 40 of the Covenant*, UN Doc CCPR/C/79/Add.93 (18 August 1998) [11].

[86] Quigley, 'Displaced Palestinians', above n 18, 204.

[87] *General Comment No 29*, UN Doc CCPR/C/21/Rev.1/Add.11 [2].

whilst derogations must without doubt be strictly required by the exigencies of the situation,[88] it is arguable that both the duration and the intensity of the Israeli–Palestinian conflict have been as unprecedented as Israel's prolonged emergency. Indeed, that the fact Israel's emergency has lasted for over 50 years should not necessarily diminish its legitimacy.[89] Notably, General Comment 29 'does not deal with the … situation where a terrorist emergency lasts for such a long time as to achieve a state of de facto normalcy'.[90]

Whilst this argument, bolstered by the ongoing conflict, can be used to suspend mass Palestinian repatriation, it must not be broadly applied by Israel to justify blanket derogation from the ICCPR provisions.[91] Nevertheless, '[a] state declaring that it need not permit a refugee entry is materially different from a state declaring it would permit entry were it not for security concerns'.[92] Accordingly, by invoking the derogation clauses, Israel must implicitly acknowledge a theoretical obligation to repatriate in the absence of these presently extreme conditions, which seems unlikely. Notably, there is no language of derogation or limitation contained in CERD. At any rate, commentators defending the Israel's refusal to repatriate the Palestinians regularly invoke these clauses to undermine the binding effect of return.

Customary International Law

Finally, many argue that aside from the treaty provisions, the Palestinian right to return is binding under customary international law.[93] From this standpoint, Israel is legally obliged to repatriate the Palestinian refugees irrespective of its agreement, and even where the right of return is manifested in non-binding documents such as the General Assembly resolutions and perhaps the UDHR.[94] However, the right of return's customary law status requires both consistent State practice[95] and *Opinio*

[88] Derogation measures must be proportionate. See ICCPR at 4(1), and more generally Joan Hartman, 'Derogations from Human Rights Treaties in Public Emergencies' (1981) 22 *Harvard International Law Journal* 2.

[89] Kramer, above n 14, 1010–11.

[90] Sarah Joseph, 'Human Rights Committee General Comment 29' (2002) 2(1) *Human Rights Law Review* 81, 82.

[91] After all, '[i]t must be remembered that states of emergency have all too often acted as veils for gross abuses of human rights', ibid 98.

[92] Ullom, above n 81, 141–2.

[93] Lawand, above n 7, 546; see also Boling, above n 10, 43; cf. Lapidoth, 'The Right of Return', above n 26, 113.

[94] One study has posited that there may now exist in international law a specific right of return of the Palestinian people recognised by 'the juridical opinions and the international instruments…'. *UN Committee on the Exercise of the Inalienable Rights of the Palestinian People* (Publication Submitted by a Special Unit on Palestinian Rights) UN Doc ST/LEG/SER (1978), cited in Lapidoth, 'The Right of Return', above n 26, 113.

[95] JL Brierly, *The Law of Nations* (Oxford University Press, 6th ed, 1963) 59.

juris,[96] namely, that international practice was informed by an acknowledged sense of legal obligation.[97] Quigley notes that the pattern of UN resolutions referring to return as a right constitutes strong evidence of State practice that members of displaced groups are entitled to return to their home territory.[98] Despite the plethora of such resolutions, in the vast majority (as in *Resolution 194*), the UNGA simply 'encouraged' or 'urged' the international community to facilitate return and thus did not imply the existence of a legally binding obligation.[99] Moreover, States persistently objecting to the custom during its period of development are not bound once the custom crystallises.[100]

Consequently, the continued refusal of Israel to accept UN resolutions aimed at Palestinian return would modify its obligations in so far as they include repatriation in customary law. Whilst the customary basis of a right to repatriation arguably exists, its content remains far from certain.[101] The customs and practices of which it is comprised are not uniformly regarded as having established a principle that can be invoked by non-nationals or on a large-scale.[102] Further, similar sovereignty and policy considerations raised by Israel with respect to the human rights limitations and derogations apply.[103]

Conclusion

Ultimately, in the absence of international consensus, it seems difficult to fashion a persuasive case of Palestinian return based on customary law, UNGA resolutions, or human rights law instruments. There is a difference between acknowledging that an expansive right to return exists in international human rights law and recognising that in certain instances it may not be implemented. In the final analysis, international law alone seems ill equipped to cover the full claims of the Palestinian refugees, even if the right to return were to be recognised theoretically.

---

[96] Defined in J Fox, *Dictionary of International and Comparative Law* (Ocana Publications, 1992) as 'opinion that an act is necessary by rule of law'.

[97] See generally *Restatement of the Law, Third, Foreign Relations* (1987), cited in Ullom, above n 81, 125.

[98] Quigley, 'Displaced Palestinians', above n 18, 216; In particular, Boling cites the UNGA's annual reaffirmation of resolution 194 over five decades as indicative of the Palestinian right of return's incorporation into legal customary norms. Boling, above n 10, 48–9.

[99] Rosand, above n 37, 1136–1137.

[100] Rex Zedalis, 'Right to Return: A Closer Look.' (1992) 6 *Georgetown Immigration Law Journal* 499, 514–15.

[101] The general customary basis for a legal right of return is beyond the scope of this chapter. For a detailed discussion see Ibid 511; See also Ian Brownlie, *Principles of Public International Law* (Oxford University Press, 1998) 4–11.

[102] Zedalis, above n 100, 514.

[103] Ullom, above n 81, 142.

Moreover, Palestinian legal claims accompany an array of psychological and narrative demands about acknowledgment and legitimacy (Chap. 1) that require consideration beyond a technical legal framework. In this light, the wider paradigm of transitional justice and its capacity to reckon with the past (as will be discussed in Chaps. 3 and 4) offers a normatively appealing model for dealing with the 1948 claims. As recently as 2018, the 'Great March of Return' saw tens of thousands of Palestinian refugees demonstrating for their right to return based on the UNGA resolutions.[104] Although the protests were initially planned to last only 6 weeks, they ultimately continued during 2019.[105] In short, the unresolved status of the refugees from 1948 remains pivotal to the ongoing violence and the Israeli–Palestinian past. To this end, the legal mandate of the IPTEC (as discussed in Chap. 8) would meaningfully address the genesis of the conflict and the Palestinian right of return.

2.3 Part Two: 1967, Legal Regime in the Palestinian Territories

The international legal framework of Israeli control over the territories is essential to understanding the conflict and the outcome of 1967. Until today, the legal regime in this region remains contested. This section considers the binding nature of IHL, international occupation law and human rights law in the West Bank, Gaza and East Jerusalem and addresses the debate over the Israeli–Jewish settlements. Establishing the normative legal framework is central to identifying the rights and duties of the parties.

Applicability of IHL to the Territories

Traditionally, IHL applies to cases of occupation, and recent developments have also introduced human rights law into the mix, creating a complex interplay between the two bodies of law. Since 1967, Israel claims that neither of these systems pertains to the territories, preferring to regard them as 'disputed',[106] and thus beyond

---

[104] Between March and May 2018, thousands of Palestinians attended a non-violent march at the separation fence under the theme 'Return of a million', to draw attention to UNGA resolution 194 and to the dire humanitarian situation of Palestinian refugees in Gaza. See 'HRC Report of the independent international commission of inquiry on the protests in the OPT', A/HRC/40/74, [18]–[26].

[105] ICC, 'OTP Report on Preliminary Examination Activities 2019' (5 December 2010) [211] ('OTP Report 2019').

[106] This argument is grounded in the Israeli view that the territories had never been under either Jordanian (in the West Bank) or Egyptian (in Gaza) sovereignty. Thus, the IDF cannot be seen as an occupier that has usurped the territories from their legal owners. Daniel Bar-Tal and Izhak

the reach of IHL.[107] Indeed, the unique status of the West Bank and Gaza—with no sovereign governments[108]—led to Israel's consistent refusal to recognise the territories as 'occupied'.[109] By applying IHL solely to the rights and duties of sovereign states, Israel could contend that the Palestinians, '… as stateless peoples, are not the law's intended beneficiaries',[110] as well as preserve its own territorial claims. Despite this official position, Israel has undertaken to abide by what it refers to as 'the humanitarian provisions' of the Fourth Geneva Convention.[111] Either way, it is notable that Palestinian statelessness remains central to Israel's approach to the territories in both legal and political terms.[112]

The international legal community widely rejects Israel's formalistic position on the inapplicability of IHL. Resolutions of the UNSC[113] and the UNGA,[114] as well as

Schnell, *'The Impacts of Lasting Occupation' Lessons from Israeli Society* (Oxford University Press, 2012) 125.

[107] Under the *Fourth Geneva Convention* art 2(2), its provisions apply only to "occupation of the territory of a High Contracting Party".

[108] Egypt never asserted sovereignty over the Gaza Strip. In 1978, Egypt signalled an end to its control over Gaza in the Camp David Accords. On 31 July 1988, King Hussein surrendered all Jordanian claims to the West Bank to the PLO.

[109] See Meir Shamgar, 'Legal Concepts and Problems of the Israeli Military Government – The Initial Stage', in Meir Shamgar (ed), *Military Government in the Territories Administered by Israel, 1967–1980: The Legal Aspects* (Hebrew University Jerusalem, 1982); See also Justice Edmund levy, *Report on the legal Construction in Judea and Samaria* (2012), http://www.pmo.gov.il/Documents/doch090712/pdf.

[110] Lisa Hajjar, 'Human Rights in Israel-Palestine: The History and Politics of a Movement' (2001) 30(4) *Journal of Palestine Studies*, 21, 23.

[111] Israel's Attorney General Meir Shamgar expressed this approach in 1971. It has prevailed as the official Israeli position, despite the lack of enumeration of the provisions Israel considered 'humanitarian'. See Brigadier General Uri Shoham, 'The Principle of Legality and the Israeli Military Government in the Territories' (1996) 153 *Military Law Review* 245, 247; See also Meir Shamgar, 'The Observance of International Law in the Administered Territories' in Yoram Dinstein (ed), *Israel Yearbook on Human Rights: Volume 1* (BRILL, 1971) 262.

[112] Hajjar, above n 110, 23.

[113] As early as 1969, the UNSC has affirmed that Israel must scrupulously observe the provisions of the Geneva Conventions and international law governing military occupation. SC Res 271, 1512th mtg, UN Doc S/RES/271 (15 September, 1969). It has subsequently reaffirmed this position in numerous other resolutions. See: SC Res 446, 2134th mtg, UN Doc S/RES/446 (22 March 1979); SC Res 799, 3151st mtg, UN Doc S/RES/799 (18 December, 1992); SC Res 904, 3351st mtg, UN Doc S/RES/904 (18 March 1994).

[114] Over the years, the UNGA adopted several resolutions affirming that the *Fourth Geneva Convention* is applicable to the Palestinian territories and calling on Israel to accept de jure applicability of the Convention. GA Res 56/60, UN GAOR, 56th sess, 4th plen mtg, Agenda Item 88, UN Doc A/RES/56/60 (10 December 2001); GA Res 58/97, UN GAOR, 58th sess, 72nd plen mtg, Agenda Item 84, UN DOC A/RES/58/97 (9 December 2003); UNUN. See also: GA Res 67/119, UN GAOR, 67th sess, 59th plen mtg, Agenda Item 53, UN Doc A/RES/67/119 (14 January 2013). UN.

statements of states[115] and non-governmental international organisations (NGOs),[116] have consistently regarded the Fourth Convention and additional IHL norms as fully applicable to the areas occupied by Israel.[117] Significantly, the International Committee of the Red Cross (ICRC) also maintains that the Geneva Framework applies de jure to the West Bank, Gaza Strip and East Jerusalem.[118] In this light, Israel's argument that IHL only applies to occupation of a 'Contracting party' lacks substantial support and merit.

Indeed, the ICJ, in its 'Advisory Wall Opinion', rejected such a restrictive reading of Common Article 2 of the Conventions and noted the intent of the drafters to protect civilians under occupation regardless of how it came into existence.[119] Further, in its third paragraph, Common Article 2 requires a Contracting Party, such as Israel, to apply its rules even to a non-contracting 'power', as long as that power accepts and applies the Convention's provisions.[120] The PA formally acceded to the Geneva Conventions on 2 April 2014.[121] Finally, the Palestinian right to self-determination[122] also discredits Israel's claim of no prior sovereign, under which it is arguable that the Palestinians as people were de facto sovereigns of the territories in 1967. Imseis argues that sovereignty lies in the people, not in a government and thus it does not matter that the Palestinians did not have a government with official title to the territory in 1967.[123] There also exists the notion that the Palestinian peo-

---

[115] Even the US government, Israel's firmest ally, supports the applicability of IHL to the Israeli occupation.

[116] See for example, Amnesty International, 'Israel and the Occupied Territories: The Place of the Fence/Wall in International Law' (19 February 2004) 4.

[117] Benvenisti and Zamir, above n 23, 305.

[118] Annexe 1: Conference of High Contracting Parties to the Fourth Geneva Convention Declaration, ICRC (5 December 2001) http://www.icrc.org/eng/resources/documents/misc/5fldpj.htm.

[119] The ICJ flatly rejected Israeli claims on the inapplicability of the *Fourth Geneva Convention* to the West Bank. 'Legal Consequences of the Construction of a Wall in the Occupied Palestinian Territory' (ICJ Advisory Opinion 131, 9 July 2004) [94]-[95] ('Advisory Wall Opinion'). This claim has not gained serious support from the international community. See Eyal Benvenisti, *The International Law of Occupation* (Oxford University Press, 2012), xvii.

[120] '*Although one of the Powers in conflict may not be a party to the present Convention, the Powers who are parties thereto shall remain bound by it in their mutual relations. They shall furthermore be bound by the Convention in relation to the said Power, if the latter accepts and applies the provisions thereof*'.

[121] Following the UNGA resolution granting non-member observer state status to Palestine in November 2012, Palestine acceded to Geneva Conventions I-IV and *Protocol Additional to the Geneva Conventions of 12 August 1949, and Relating to the Protection of Victims of International Armed Conflicts June 8, 1977*, 1125 UNTS 3 ('Additional Protocol I') in April 2014.

[122] There exists broad legal consensus that recognises the Palestinians as people with an attendant right to self-determination within the territories. For more, see Catriona Drew, 'Self-determination, Population Transfer and the Middle East Peace Accords'. In: Bowen, Stephen, (ed.), *Human Rights, Self-determination and Political Change in the Palestinian Occupied Territories*. (Kluwer Law International: 1997) 119–168.

[123] Ardi Imseis, 'On the Fourth Geneva Convention and the Occupied Palestinian Territory' (2003) 44 *Harvard International Law Journal* 65, 97.

ple were the de facto sovereign of the land prior to occupation.[124] There is therefore an apparent consensus in the international community that at the very least, the Fourth Geneva Convention applies de jure to the territories. Thus, it will be assumed that Israel's presence in the territories is subject to the principles and norms of IHL.

Applicability of Occupation Law to Israel

Given its military presence in the Palestinian territories since 1967, Israel is also subject to the international law of occupation. Notwithstanding the nuanced and complicated relationship between this body of law and human rights law,[125] as well as its unclear application to Gaza, international occupation law is widely acknowledged as binding in the Palestinian territories. Indeed, the ICJ,[126] the UNGA,[127] and the UNSC, all regard Israel as an 'Occupying Power'.[128] The significance of classifying the Palestinian territories as occupied is that certain legal obligations are incumbent on Israel under the Hague Conventions of 1899 and 1907, and the Fourth Geneva Convention.[129] It is important to briefly review the evolution of the law of occupation as a basis for assessing Israeli conduct in the territories. As will be discussed, some difficulty exists concerning this body of law's operation in the Palestinian territories. Various challenges are rooted in the law of occupation itself,[130] as well as in changes on the ground within the territories in the context of the Oslo Accords, and Israel's withdrawal from Gaza, which complicate the delineation of Israel's international legal obligations.[131]

---

[124] Orna Ben-Naftali, Aeyal Gross and Keren Michaeli, 'Illegal Occupation: Framing the Occupied Palestinian Territory' (2005) 23 *Berkeley Journal of International Law* 551, 561.

[125] In certain cases, these two regimes conflict with one another. Though a primary goal of IHL is to limit suffering caused by war, the demands of human rights law go much further. 'Thus, complementarity sometimes gives away to an undeniable tension'. Grant Harris, 'Human Rights, Israel and the Political realities of Occupation' (2008) 41(1–2) *Israel Law Review* 87, 117.

[126] ICJ, 'Advisory Wall Opinion', above n 119.

[127] 'Israeli settlements in the Occupied Palestinian Territory, including East Jerusalem, and the occupied Syrian Golan'. http://unispal.un.org. 2012-12-01. Retrieved 2012-04-29.

[128] See SC Res 446, 2134th mtg, UN Doc S/RES/446 (22 March 1979); SC Res 452, 2159th mtg, UN Doc S/RES/452 (20 July 1979), SC Res 465, 2203rd mtg, UN Doc S/RES/465 (1 March 1980); SC Res 484, 2260th mtg, UN Doc S/RES/484 (19 December 1980). A conference of the parties to the *Fourth Geneva Convention* and the ICRC have also resolved that these territories are occupied and that the *Fourth Geneva Convention* provisions regarding occupied territories apply. See also Ruth Lapidoth, 'Legal Aspects', above n 14; Moshe Hirsch, *The Jerusalem question and its resolution* (Martinus Nijhoff Publishers, 1994) 351.

[129] *Occupation and International Humanitarian Law: Questions and Answers* (04 August 2004) International Committee of the Red Cross https://www.icrc.org/en/doc/resources/documents/misc/634kfc.htm.

[130] Arguably, the antiquated law of occupation has limited utility in the context of the prolonged nature of the Israeli occupation. See Harris, above n 125, 100.

[131] Ibid.

International Legal Regime of Occupation

The Hague Conventions reflect a detailed account of customary IHL on belligerent occupation[132] and have attained customary law status.[133] These instruments provide for the protection of occupied civilians, who at all times are entitled to respect for their persons, honour, family rights, religious conviction and practices, and protection of their private property.[134] Notably, after World War II, the Fourth Geneva Convention expanded both the nature and scope of protection afforded by occupation law[135] '... thus constituting a new and far broader bill of rights ...'[136] for occupied territories. Common Article 2 extended the application of occupation to include situations of conflict that lack an official declaration of war and armed resistance by the occupied population.[137] The substantive provisions of the Convention[138] also advanced protection of the individual rights of the occupied population over governmental military interests.[139] It imposes positive duties on the occupier with regard to protecting children, ensuring food and medical supplies, maintaining hospitals, providing certain due process rights, and providing certain rights of imprisoned persons.[140] In short, the Fourth Geneva Convention '... shifts the emphasis from political elites to peoples'.[141]

---

[132] The first international attempt to codify the law of occupation was the Brussels Declaration of 1874. The definition of occupation in the Brussels Declaration was 'a territory actually placed under the authority of a hostile army bounded by the territories around which it could establish and exercise authority'. *The Final Protocol and Project of an International Declaration Concerning the Laws and Customs of War, 27 August 1874* ('Brussels Declaration'); See Hague Regulations, art 42.

[133] Judgment of the Nuremburg International Military Tribunal (30 September 1946), 22; Trial of the Major War Criminals Before the International Military Tribunal: Nuremburg, 14 November 1945 to 1 October 1946, 411, 497 (1948). See also Knut Dormann, *Elements of War Crimes under the Rome Statute of the International Criminal Court: Sources and Commentary* (Cambridge University Press, 2003); Maurice H. Mendelson, 'The Formation of Customary International Law', (1998) 272 *Collected Courses of the Hague Academy of International Law*, 227–244.

[134] 'Brussels Declaration', above n 124, art 46.

[135] International Committee of the Red Cross, 'The Law of Armed Conflict: Belligerent Occupation' (2002) http://www.icrc.org/eng/assets/files/other/law9_final.pdf.

[136] Benvenisti, *The International Law of Occupation*, above n 113, 105.

[137] *Fourth Geneva Convention* art 2; art 4 also applies the Convention's provisions to 'protected persons' who, either during an armed conflict or during an occupation, find themselves in the hands of a party to the Convention of which they are not nationals.

[138] Article 75 of Additional Protocol I provided a minimum standard of fundamental rights to be enjoyed by 'persons who are in the power of a Party to the conflict and who do not benefit from more favorable treatment under the Conventions or under this Protocol'.

[139] 'Thus, it is the protection of the occupied civilian population, rather than the facilitation of governmental interests, which informs the *Fourth Geneva Convention*. This is a clear shift of concern from governments to people'. Ben-Naftali, Gross and Michaeli, above n 124, 564–5.

[140] *Fourth Geneva Convention* arts 32, 33, 34, 49, 65, 67, 51, 52, 50, 55, 59–62, 56, 57, 66, 69, 71–73, 76, 77, respectively.

[141] Benvenisti, *The International Law of Occupation*, above n 119, 105.

Nevertheless, significant elements of this legal framework are anachronistic.[142] As the Israeli case demonstrates, the need to apply occupation law beyond the traditional context of international armed conflict has now taken root in contemporary occupation law. Today, the widely accepted definition of occupation is 'the effective control of a power (be it one or more states or an international organization, such as the UN) over a territory to which that power has no sovereign title, without the volition of the sovereign of that territory'.[143] This modern, inclusive definition, though refuted by Israel, would apply to the Palestinian case[144] and allows for a substantive analysis of Israeli conduct to the extent that its military exercises 'effective control' in the territories. This definition is premised on the basic notion that occupation does not confer title, but is temporary,[145] and severs the link between sovereignty and effective control.[146]

Notably, Israel withdrew its settlements and military forces from the Gaza Strip in 2005. The question of whether this ended the Israeli occupation over this area remains open, and its determination depends on factual considerations related to 'effective control', which are beyond the scope of this inquiry.[147] However, even if one assumes that Gaza is no longer occupied, the legal regime of occupation applies to the rest of the Palestinian territory, which Israel continues to occupy, i.e., the West Bank including East Jerusalem, which constitutes a far more substantial area in terms of both territory and the extent of Jewish settlements.[148]

Israeli Position on Occupation

On occupation law and the territories, Israel has adopted a convoluted position, which in some ways rejects the very existence of an occupation. In the international political arena, Israeli governments and officials have preferred the term 'disputed

---

[142] For example, under the *Fourth Geneva Convention*, the qualifications of situations, which constitute occupation, require some nexus to an armed conflict. Ben-Naftali, Gross and Michaeli, above n 124, 565.

[143] Benvenisti, *The International Law of Occupation*, above n 113, 4; See also ibid 560.

[144] This modern definition includes the many different existing kinds of occupations including Israel's. See Adam Roberts, 'Prolonged Military Occupation: The Israeli Occupied Territories Since 1967' (1990) 84 *American Journal of International Law* 44, 51.

[145] Although not codified in an international instrument, this contemporary definition more closely corresponds with current interpretations of situations of occupation and the legal framework applicable to them. See, ICJ, 'Advisory Wall Opinion', above n 119; *Al-Skeini and Others v The United Kingdom*, App No 55721/07, Eur Ct HR (2011); *Issa v Turkey*, App No 31821/96, Eur Ct H.R (2005).

[146] Ben-Naftali, Gross and Michaeli, above n 124, 560.

[147] Plainly the notion of occupation implies the exercise of control. Yet it is unclear what degree of control amounts to occupation. Iris Canor, 'When Jus Ad Bellum Meets Jus in Bello: The Occupier's Right of Self-Defence against Terrorism Stemming from Occupied Territories' (2006) 19 *Leiden Journal of International Law* 129, 140.

[148] Ben-Naftali, Gross and Michaeli, above n 124, 551.

territories'.[149] As recently as July 2012, the Israeli Commission Levy Report concluded that the laws of belligerent occupation do not apply to '... the unique and *sui generis* historic and legal circumstances of Israel's presence in Judea and Samaria spanning over decades'.[150] According to Israel's Ministry of Foreign Affairs, the West Bank and Gaza should not be viewed as 'occupied' because their status can only be determined through negotiations, and there was no established and recognised sovereign prior to 1967.[151] As noted above, Israel uses this argument to dismiss the de jure application of the Fourth Geneva Convention to the territories. It is equally unpersuasive in the occupation context, particularly because as customary law, the applicability of the Hague Regulations is widely accepted.[152]

Although the government has never officially recognised the binding effect of occupation law in the territories,[153] Israeli authorities have generally administered the areas in accordance with this body of law.[154] Moreover, in recent decades, the State's attorneys have consistently argued before the Israeli Supreme Court[155] (HCJ) that Israel derives its authority in the territories from the international law of 'belligerent occupation', and in particular the Hague Conventions.[156] Since the late 1970s, the HCJ has formally applied the Hague Regulations to the territories and classified Israel's role in the territories as that of an occupying power.[157] Israel's HCJ

---

[149] FAQ: 'The Peace process with the Palestinians' (December, 2009) Mfa.gov.il; See also Justice Edmund Levy, 'Report on the Legal Status of Construction in Judea and Samaria' ('Levy Report'); Dore Gold, 'From Occupied Territories to Disputed Territories' Jerusalem Center for Public Affairs (2012), http://www.pmo.gov.il/Documents/doch090712.pdf.

[150] The Levy Report was commissioned by Israeli PM Netanyahu in 2012 to investigate the legality of Israeli presence in the territories and Jewish settlement activity. It was headed by former Israeli HCJ Justice Edmund Levy. Tovah Lazaroff, 'Legal report on outposts recommends authorization' *The Jerusalem Post* (online), 9 July 2012.

[151] Israeli MFA, 'Disputed Territories: Forgotten Facts About the West Bank and Gaza Strip' (1 February 2003) at http://www.mfa.gov.il/MFA/MFAArchive/2000_2009/2003/2/; see also UN Doc A/32/PV 27 (10 October 1977).

[152] See Roberts, above n 136, 64. For additional background on Israel's view of the Hague Regulations, see generally Nissim Bar-Yaacov, 'The Applicability of the Laws of War to Judea and Samaria (The West Bank and to the Gaza Strip)', (1990) 24 *Israeli Law Review* 485, 492–93, cited in Harris, above n 125, 92.

[153] For a brief, 4-month period, the Military Commander for the West Bank issued, and then repealed, an order that provided that military courts will observe the provisions of the *Fourth Geneva Convention* in matters concerning judicial proceedings, and that in case of contradiction between the order and the Convention, the Convention shall prevail in 'Levy Report'.

[154] Notably, Israel is one of the few occupying powers that formally applies the norms of belligerent occupation to the territory it occupies. David Kretzmer, 'The Law of Belligerent Occupation in the Supreme Court of Israel' (2012) 94 *International Review of the Red Cross* 207, 213.

[155] The Israeli Supreme Court in its capacity as the High Court of Justice adjudicates complaints against the Israeli public administration (HCJ).

[156] On the Israeli State's resort to the Geneva Conventions and the Hague regulations as the bases for exercising its powers, see generally David Krezmer, *The Occupation of Justice* (State University of New York Press, 2002) 197.

[157] HCJ 610/78 *Oiev and Others v Minister of Defense* 33(2) PD 113 [1979] (Isr.) 115; See also Yoram Dinstein, 'The Verdict in the Matter of Pithat Rafiah (HCJ 302/72 *Abu Hilou and Others v. The Government of Israel*)' (1974) 3 *Tel Aviv University Law* Review 934.

confirmed this interpretation on many occasions, most relevantly in its 2004 and 2005 rulings on the separation fence.[158] It is worth noting that the Israeli HCJ has not acknowledged however the de jure applicability of the Fourth Geneva Convention to the territories.[159] Nevertheless, the Court continues to draw on provisions of the Convention and consistently refers to the government's undertaking to comply with its 'humanitarian provisions'.[160]

Israeli Settlements

The debate over Israeli Jewish settlements in the West Bank (including East Jerusalem) is a hallmark of the conflict and inseparable from the occupation narrative. The legal dispute revolves around Article 49(6) of the Fourth Geneva Convention, which prohibits an occupier from transferring parts of its own civilian population into the territory it occupies.[161] As discussed earlier, the Geneva Conventions apply to cases of occupation. Indeed, an ICRC Study on Customary IHL (ICRC Study) affirms the customary status of this particular prohibition.[162] Nevertheless, successive Israeli governments maintain that the provision was solely intended to apply to the context of WWII 'forcible' migrations, and does not include 'voluntary' transfer into occupied territory.[163] More recently in 2012, the Levy Report concluded that Article 49(6) is not applicable to Israeli settlement activity in the West Bank and is therefore permissible under international law.[164] Israel's proponents also highlight the absence of a prior sovereign and claim that settlements

---

[158] The HCJ has ruled that Israel holds the West Bank under 'belligerent occupation'. See *Beit Sourik Village Council v Government of Israel and Commander of the IDF Forces in the West Bank* [2004] HCJ 2056/04 (Isr). ('Beit Sourik Case').

[159] Benvenisti, *The International Law of Occupation*, above n 119, 118–119.

[160] See the Beit Sourik Case, above n 150, 807; See also *Yassin et al., v Commander of Ketziot Detention Facility et al*, [2002] HCJ 5591/02, 403, 413 cited in Kretzmer, above n 154, 212.

[161] See also *Additional Protocol 1 to the Geneva Conventions of 12 August 1949, and Relating to the Protection of Victims of International Armed Conflicts, June 8, 1977*, 1125 UNTS 3 [Protocol I] art 85(4)(a). Israel is not a party to the Additional Protocol.

[162] The fact that Israel has not acceded to Additional Protocol therefore does not diminish its obligation of this fundamental IHL principle. ICRC, Study on Customary IHL, Rule 130: Transfer of Own Civilian Population into Occupied Territory, https://www.icrc.org/customary-ihl/eng/docs/v1_rul_rule130#Fn_2_7.

[163] For the Israeli position, see Israeli Settlements and International Law http://www.mfa.gov.il/mfa/go.asp?MFAHOjyzO; Ayelet Levy, 'Israel Rejects Its Own Offspring: The International Criminal Court' (1999) 22 *Loyola of Los Angeles International and Comparative Law Review*. 207, 230–31; Jean-Marie Henckaerts, 'Deportation and Transfer of Civilians in Time of War' (1993) 26 *Vanderbilt Journal of Transnational Law*. 469, 472.

[164] The Levy Report concluded: 'Israelis have the legal right to settle in Judea and Samaria and the establishment of settlements cannot, in and of itself, be considered illegal'. See 'Levy Report', above n 149.

are exclusively a political question, since under the Oslo Accords the Palestinians agreed to defer the issue to further negotiations.[165]

The Israeli position however is at odds with international legal consensus. Repeated resolutions of both the Security Council and the UNGA condemn Israeli settlements in the territories as a violation of the Fourth Geneva Convention.[166] In 2004, the ICJ's Advisory Opinion on the Wall concluded that by establishing settlements, Israel had breached its international obligations and could not rely on self-defence or necessity.[167] Numerous commentators maintain that even if Israel's use of force in 1967 was lawful, it does not confer legal title to territory nor validate its settlement policy.[168]

The Palestinian right to self-determination further bolsters this conclusion.[169] Israel's position on 'voluntary' transfer is also inconsistent with the ICRC commentary on the Fourth Convention, according to which Article 49(6) was intended to protect the interests of the occupied population, rather than the population of the occupier.[170] Parties to the Fourth Geneva Convention,[171] the ICRC,[172] as well as leading Israeli legal scholars[173] uniformly reject the Israeli interpretation. Of particular relevance, Article 8(2)(b)(viii) of the Rome Statute criminalises civilian transfers into occupied territory

---

[165] See Israeli Settlements and International Law (Israel Ministry of Foreign Affairs website) 20 May 2001; Jeffrey Helmreich, 'Diplomatic and Legal Aspects of the Settlement Issue' (Jerusalem Center for Public Affairs, Jerusalem Issue Brief 2(16) January 19, 2003).

[166] Numerous UN resolutions have stated that the building and existence of Israeli settlements are a violation of IHL, including UNSC resolutions in 1979 and 1980. See SC Res 446, 2134th mtg, UN Doc S/RES/446 (22 March 1979); SC Res 452, 2159th mtg, UN Doc S/RES/452 (20 July 1979), SC Res 465, 2203rd mtg, UN Doc S/RES/465 (1 March 1980); SC Res 484, 2260th mtg, UN Doc S/RES/484 (19 December 1980).

[167] ICJ, 'Advisory Wall Opinion', above n 119, [119]–[120]. The ICJ reached this conclusion based *inter alia* on SC Res 446, 2134th mtg, UN Doc S/RES/446 (22 March 1979).

[168] "The right to have recourse to self-defense does not include the right to permanently seize the territory of the attacked." Derek W Bowett, 'International Law Relating to Occupied Territory: A Rejoinder' (1971) 87 *Law Quarterly Review* 473, 475; Ben-Naftali, Gross and Michaeli, above n 124, 573; John Quigley, 'Living in Legal Limbo: Israel's Settlers in Occupied Palestinian Territory' (1998) 10 *Pace International Law Review* 1.

[169] This point was wholeheartedly approved by the ICJ, 'Advisory Wall Opinion', above n 119, [118]–[122].

[170] See Jean S Picet, 'Commentary – The Geneva Convention Relative to the Protection of Civilian Persons in the Time of War' (1958) 21, cited in Ben-Naftali, Gross and Michaeli, above n 124, 564.

[171] Declaration of the Conference of the Parties to the Fourth Geneva Convention, Dec 5, 2001, available at http://www.eda.admin.ch/eda/e/home/foreign/hupol/4gc/docum2.Par.0006.UpFile.pdf/mgOI12054gcdeclarne.pdf.

[172] 'Annexe 2—Conference of High Contracting Parties to the Fourth Geneva Convention: statement by the International Committee of the Red Cross' (ICRC website) https://www.icrc.org/en/doc/resources/documents/statement/57jrgw.htm.

[173] 'Their voluntary cooperation in the transfer does not diminish from its illicit character, pursuant to Article 49(6)'. Yoram Dinstein, *The International Law of Belligerent Occupation*, above n 350, 240; Benvenisti, *The International Law of Occupation*, above n 119, 140–41.

whether they are undertaken 'directly or indirectly'.[174] Given that Israel provides financial incentives to settlers, this provision could render Israeli officials criminally liable and may in part explain its decision not to ratify the Rome Statute.[175] In sum, Israel's settlement policy is unsupported by international law, and it will be assumed that the Fourth Geneva Convention applies to the Palestinian territories.

Applicability of Human Rights Law in the Territories

Treaties

Israel is a state party to seven of the nine core international human rights treaties.[176] Israel ratified CERD on 3 January 1979; and the ICCPR, the International Covenant on Economic, Social and Cultural Rights (ICESCR), the Convention against Torture and Other Cruel, Inhuman or Degrading Treatment or Punishment (CAT), the Convention on the Elimination of All Forms of Discrimination against Women (CEDAW), and the Convention on the Rights of the Child (CRC) on 3 October 1991. It also ratified the Convention on the Rights of Persons with Disabilities on 1 September 2012. Despite being a state party to these international treaties, Israel denies the applicability of these instruments to the territories.[177] Israeli officials maintain that international human rights norms do not formally apply to the Palestinians in the West Bank and Gaza, as they are not subject to Israel's sovereign territory and jurisdiction.[178] Since ratification, Israel has adamantly affirmed this claim in its periodic reports to the UN treaty monitoring bodies.[179] Thus, Israel argues it cannot be held accountable for ensuring the rights of the human rights treaties in the territories.

---

174 Rome Statute of the International Criminal Court, July 17, 1998, UN Doc A/CONF. 183/9; 37 I.L.M. 1002 (1998); 2187 UNTS 90, art 8(2)(b)(viii) ('Rome Statute'). The temporal limitation of the Rome statute vis a vis the Israeli-Jewish settlements will be discussed in Chap. 5.

175 Ben-Naftali, Gross and Michaeli, above n 124, 581.

176 UNHCR lists nine core international human rights instruments https://www.ohchr.org/EN/ProfessionalInterest/Pages/CoreInstruments.aspx. Israel is not a signatory to the International Convention on the Protection of the Rights of All Migrant Workers and Members of Their Families (18 December 1990) or the International Convention for the Protection of All Persons from Enforced Disappearance (20 December 2006).

177 UN Secretary-General, Rep of the Secretary-General Prepared Pursuant to General Assembly, Resolution ES-10/13, Annex I: Summary Legal Position of the Government of Israel, UN Doc A/ES-10/248 (24 November 2003) [4].

178 Committee on Economic, Social and Cultural Rights Forty-Seventh Session, Summary Record of meeting on Third periodic report of Israel on 28 March 2012, E/C/12/2011/SR.35, [35].

179 Most recently, in its fourth periodic report to the Human Rights Committee (12 December 2013), Israel reaffirmed the *ICCPR* does not apply to the Palestinian Territories, which, Israel contends, is not subject to its sovereign territory and jurisdiction, paragraph 48CPR/C/ISR/4; Israel mirrored this position in its third periodic report to the Committee on Economic, Social and Cultural Rights, 2 March 2012, E/C.12/ISR/Q/3/Add.1 [8].

Extra-Territorial Application: UN Bodies and Case Law

Israel's position remains contrary to the UN treaty monitoring bodies, which maintain that human rights law applies extraterritorially to the Palestinian territories.[180] In its recent Concluding Observations on Israel, the HRC,[181] the Committee on Economic, Social and Cultural Rights (CESCR),[182] as well as the Human Rights' Council's Universal Periodic Reviews (UPR) of Israel,[183] all affirm the applicability of international human rights treaties to Palestinians in the territories.

In particular, the ICCPR and CAT[184] contain jurisdictional clauses, which might specifically encompass the territories. Having ratified the ICCPR, Israel has undertaken 'to respect and to ensure to all individuals *within its territory and subject to its jurisdiction* the rights recognized in the present Covenant, without distinction …'.[185] For these clauses to include the territories, the Gaza Strip and the West Bank, including East Jerusalem, would need to be regarded as 'under [Israel's] jurisdiction'. The HRC has concluded that the ICCPR does apply to the territories, highlighting '… the long-standing presence of Israel's in these territories, Israel's ambiguous attitude towards their future status, as well as the exercise of effective jurisdiction by Israeli security forces therein'.[186] Finally, the HRC's General

180 See Concluding Observations of the HRC: Israel, 18 August 1998, CCPR/C/79/Add.93, [10]; Concluding Observations of the HRC: Israel, 21 August 2003, CCPR/CO/78/ISR [11]; Concluding Observations of the Committee on Economic, Social and Cultural Rights: Israel, 31 August 2001, E/C.12/1/Add.69, [11]; Concluding Observations of the Committee on Economic, Social and Cultural Rights: Israel, E/C.12/1/Add.27; Concluding Observations of the Committee against Torture (CAT/C/ISR/4), 23 June 2009 [11].

181 Concluding Observations of the HRC on the Fourth periodic report of Israel: Israel, 21 November 2014, CCPR/C/ISR/CO/4 at [5].

182 Concluding Observations of the Committee on Economic, Social and Cultural Rights: Israel, 16 December 2011, E/C.12/ISR/CO/3 [3].

183 Human Rights Council, *Report of the Working Group on Universal Periodic Review of Israel*, A/HRC/25/15, 19 December 2013 [136.30] (Maldives), Human Rights Council, *Report of the Working Group on Universal Periodic Review of Israel*, A/HRC/10/76, 8 January 2009 [100.1] [100.32] (Ireland), (Switzerland, Canada, Chile) Israel is recommended to '… *fully respect its human rights obligations, not only in its own territory, but also in places under its control, such as the OPT, as recalled by treaties and the ICJ*'.

184 The CAT includes the following provision which may include the Palestinian territories: 'Each State Party shall take effective legislative, administrative, judicial or other measures to prevent acts of torture in any territory under its jurisdiction'. *Convention against Torture and Other Cruel, Inhuman or Degrading Treatment or Punishment*, opened for signature 10 December 1984, 1465 UNTS 85 (entered into force 26 June 1987) ('*CAT*'), art 2(1).

185 *ICCPR* art 2(1).

186 HRC, *Consideration of Reports Submitted by States Parties Under Article 40 of the Covenant, Concluding Observations of the Human Rights Committee*, paragraph 10, UN Doc CCPR/C/79/Add.93 (18 August 1998). See also: HRC, *Concluding Observations: Israel*, paragraph 11, UN Doc CCPR/CO/78/ISR (21 August 2003); CCPR/C/ISR/CO/3 (2010) [5]; CCPR/C/ISR/CO/4 (2014).

Comment No. 31 supports the extraterritorial applicability of international human rights law to the territories.[187]

Moreover, international bodies and case law also assert the binding nature of Israel's human rights obligations in the territories.[188] The UNGA has reaffirmed in its resolutions that the ICCPR, ICESCR, and the CRC should be *respected* in the Palestinian territories.[189] The UNSC has adopted a more conservative approach and has not made explicit statements regarding the direct applicability of these human rights treaties.[190] Nevertheless, the UNSC implicitly resolved, with specific reference to the Arab–Israeli war of 1967 that 'essential and inalienable human rights should be respected even during the vicissitudes of war' in the areas affected by this conflict.[191]

Notably, the ICJ in its Advisory Opinion on the Wall[192] held that Israel's international obligations applied to the West Bank.[193] At paragraph 109, the ICJ reasons that, given the object and purpose of the ICCPR, 'it would seem natural that' State parties would be bound by its provisions even when they are exercising jurisdiction outside their national territory.[194] The Court affirmed that the ICCPR not only applies concurrently with IHL but also provides for extra-territorial applicability in situations of effective control, such as that exercised by Israel in the West Bank.[195] As for the ICESCR and the CRC, the ICJ concluded that in these cases too, Israel is bound by its treaty obligations in the areas where it exercises jurisdiction.[196] Based on ICJ jurisprudence,[197] it has also been widely accepted that an Occupying Power must abide by human rights obligations as the administrator of the territory and its

---

187 Human Rights Committee, *General Comment No 31 Nature of the General Legal Obligation Imposed on States Parties to the Covenant*, 26 May 2004, CCPR/C/21/Rev.1/Add.13 [10].

188 See UN Human Rights Council, 'Human Rights Situation in Palestine and Other Occupied Arab Territories' UN Doc A/HRC/8/17 (6 June 2008) [7].

189 See Special Commission to Investigate Israeli Practices Affecting the Human Rights of the Palestinian People and Other Arabs of the Occupied Territories, UN Doc A/66/427 (21 November 2011).

190 See SC Res 1544, 1972nd mtg, UN Doc S/RES/1544 (19 May 2004).

191 SC Res 237, 1361st mtg, UN Doc S/RES/237 (14 June 1967) (calling on Israel to respect human rights in areas affected by the 1967 conflict). The UNGA welcomed this resolution in UNGA Res 2253 (ES-V) of 4 July 1967.

192 ICJ, 'Advisory Wall Opinion', above n 119.

193 The ICJ relied heavily on its previous Advisory Opinion on the issue of nuclear weapons. ICJ, 'Advisory Wall Opinion', above n 119, [105]–[109].

194 From the *travaux preparatoires* of the *ICCPR*, the ICJ argues that the drafters did not intend to allow states to escape from their obligations if they were to exercise jurisdiction outside their national territory. Ibid [109].

195 Ibid [107]–[111].

196 Ibid [111]–[112].

197 The inseparability of human rights guarantees from the concept of trust was central to the ICJ Advisory Opinion concerning the Legal Consequences of the Continued Presence of South Africa in Namibia.

inhabitants.[198] Indeed, according to Ben-Naftali, Gross, and Michaeli, 'the longer the occupation, the heavier the weight to be accorded to the human rights of the occupied population'.[199]

It is worth adding that the Israeli HCJ has applied international human rights law to cases involving Palestinians in the territories.[200] Whilst treaties are not directly incorporated into Israeli legislation, given its dualist system of law, Israel's general approach, however, is to ensure that domestic legislation, policies, and practice comply with customary provisions and international human rights norms.[201] Jurisprudence of the HRC has also indicated the extra-territorial applicability of international human rights law.[202] Ultimately, it is arguable that Israel should be equally bound by its treaty commitments in Israel and the Palestinian territories alike.

Accountability Post-Oslo and 'Effective Control'

Israeli officials refer to the Interim Agreement (1995) (Oslo II 1995),[203] which contains a mutual commitment to human rights and the rule of law in the gradual transfer of responsibilities from Israel to the PA, stating that such issues are now under the jurisdiction of the Palestinians.[204] As recently as 2012, Israel asserted to the CESCR that: 'even if Israel exercised some physical control over the territories ...

---

[198] See Eyal Benvenisti, 'The Applicability of Human Rights Conventions to Israel and to the Occupied Territories' (1992) 26 (1) *Israel Law Review* 24–30; See also Noam Lubell, 'Human Rights Obligations in Military Occupation' (2012) 94 *International Review of the Red Cross* 317.

[199] Ben-Naftali, Gross and Michaeli, above n 124, 576.

[200] For example, the Israeli HCJ considered the competing claims of freedom of movement and freedom of religion in *Bethlehem Municipality & 21 others v. The State of Israel – Ministry of Defense*; HCJ 1890/03 (3 February 2005). It also considered human rights law for conditions of detention for security detainees in *Center for the Defense of the Individual founded by Dr. Lota Salzberger et al v Commander of the IDF Forces in the West Bank*; HCJ 3278/02, 25 April 2002; 28 July 2002, 15 October 2002.

[201] Human Rights Council Working Group on the UPR, *National Report Submitted in Accordance with Paragraph 15(A) of the Annex to Human Rights Council, Resolution 5/1, Israel*, A/HRC/WG.6/3/ISR/1, 25 September 2008 [30]. Notably, the Israeli HCJ deems human rights to be part of the natural law principles, and as such are an official source of law. See HCJ 5591/02 *Yassin v Commander of Ketziot Military Camp* 57(1) PD 403 [2002] (Isr.).

[202] In Human Rights Committee, *Views: Communication* No 52/1979, UN Doc CCPR/C/OP/1 (1984) ('*Burgos/Delia Saldias de Lopez v Uruguay*), the HRC reasoned that it would be unconscionable to interpret the responsibility under article 2 of the *ICCPR* as to permit a State party to perpetrate violations of the Covenant on the territory of another State, which violations it could not perpetrate on its own territory.

[203] The Israeli-Palestinian Interim Agreement on the West Bank and Gaza Strip, 28 September 1995, 36 I.L.M, 563. ('Oslo II 1995').

[204] See UN HRC Consideration of Rep. Submitted by States Parties under Article 40 of the Covenant, 2nd Periodic Rep, Add: Israel UN Doc CCPR/C/ISR/2001/2 (20 November 2001) [8]. Israel reiterated this position with identical wording in its reports to the CESCR.

the Covenant had been the responsibility of the PA'.[205] Indeed, Benvenisti concluded that '...Israel is not internationally responsible for ensuring human rights and humanitarian norms in the areas under the jurisdiction of the PA' because the PA is responsible in law and in fact for maintenance of public order and control of civil life in those areas.[206] This raises the question of whether joint Israeli–PA authority in certain spheres may diminish Israel's accountability in the territories.

As noted above, the legal and factual considerations related to the test of 'effective control' are complex, and beyond the scope of this inquiry. What is undisputed however is that until today, Israel maintains a degree of control and jurisdiction over many aspects of the Palestinian territories. Since Oslo II, Israel and its personnel have repeatedly entered and established control over the West Bank and Gaza and maintain control over the airspace, sea, exports, and imports into the territories.[207] Moreover, it is unlikely that the occupied Palestinians (at least in the West Bank)[208] exercise the necessary degree of authority so as to equal or supersede that of Israel and free Israel of its international responsibilities. Indeed, the ICJ has endorsed this position.[209] Whilst confirming that military and civil transfers took place under the Oslo Agreements, it stressed that 'as a result of subsequent events, they remained partial and limited'.[210] Ultimately, despite the PA's assumption of competence in the civil arena, it is strongly arguable that international human rights treaties and norms are applicable in the territories and bind Israel extraterritorially due to its ongoing control of the area.

Interplay with IHL

In denying the applicability of human rights to the occupation, Israel insists on the exclusive operation of the Hague Regulations to the territories[211] and has claimed that the treaty monitoring bodies have no mandate to address events occurring as

---

[205] Mr Karin (Israel) continued: '... since control, power and responsibilities had been transferred to the PA, Israel was unable to answer the Committee's questions'. CESCR, *Summary Record of the 35th Meeting:* E/C.12/2011/SR.35, 28 March 2012, [35].

[206] Eyal Benvenisti, 'Responsibility for the Protection of Human Rights Under the Interim Israeli-Palestinian Agreements' (1994) 28 *Israel Law Review* 297, 312.

[207] Omar M. Dajani, 'Stalled Between Seasons: The International Legal Status of Palestine During the Interim Period' (1997) 26 *Denver Journal of International Law and Policy* 29, 61.

[208] Regarding Gaza, Israel adamantly argues that following its withdrawal in 2005, '... Israel can clearly not be said to have effective control in the Gaza Strip, in the sense envisaged by the Hague Regulations'. See E/C.12/ISR/Q/3/Add.1 (2 March 2012) [6]. As discussed above, even if one assumes that Gaza is no longer occupied, the legal regime of occupation continues to apply to the West Bank including East Jerusalem.

[209] ICJ, 'Advisory Wall Opinion', above n 119, [77]–[78].

[210] Ibid.

[211] Notably, Israel simultaneously claims that the PA is bound to protect the human rights of Palestinians living in Area A and that it complies with its IHL obligations as an occupying power. The Israeli Military Court of Appeals has reiterated that the entire territory, including Area A,

part of the conflict.[212] According to Israel, the legal situation in the territories is *sui* generis, and therefore, only the IHL framework can appropriately '… administer the area whilst maintaining public order, safety and security'.[213] Yet again, the UN treaty monitoring bodies have rejected this argument and maintain that international human rights law applies concurrently with IHL in the West Bank and Gaza.[214] In its recent Concluding Observations on Israel, the HRC affirmed the applicability of the ICCPR during an armed conflict, as well as in a situation of occupation.[215] Similarly, the ICJ in its Advisory Opinion on the Wall[216] held that Israel's human rights obligations applied to its military occupation of the West Bank and do not cease in times of war.[217] Indeed, the ICJ applied both human rights law and IHL to the armed conflict between the Democratic Republic of the Congo and Uganda.[218]

It is therefore strongly arguable that both legal regimes exist in the territories and mutually reinforce one another.[219] With specific reference to situations of occupation, the UN Sub-Commission on Human Rights[220] persuasively demonstrates the

---

remains under belligerent occupation and Israel is bound by its IHL duties. See Military Prosecutor Appeal – Judea and Samaria 2016/07 *Issa (Ajouli) v. Military Prosecutor*, 16 May 2007; Appeals – Judea and Samaria 3924/06 *Sa'adi v. Military Prosecutor*, 17 October 2007.

[212] See Human Rights Commission, Consideration of Reports Submitted by State Parties under Article 40 of the Covenant, 2nd Periodic Report, Add., Israel, CCPR/C/ISR/2001/2 (20 November 2001) [8].

[213] Office of the Legal Advisor, Ministry of Foreign Affairs on the Applicability of the ICCPT to the Current Situation in the West Bank and the Gaza Strip, 15 July 1998. See also Israel's statements before the HRC, 63rd session, Summary Record of the 1675th Meeting, CCPR/C/SR. 1675 (15 July 1998) [21].

[214] For example, see paragraph 11 of CAT's concluding observations on Israel's fourth periodic report (CAT/C/ISR/CO/4 of 23 June 2009).

[215] See paragraph 5 of its concluding observations on Israel's fourth periodic report (CCPR/C/ISR/CO/4 of 21 November 2014) and paragraph 5 of its concluding observations on Israel's third periodic report (CCPR/C/ISR/CO/3 of 3 September 2010). The HRC reiterates its views from previous concluding observations. See CCPR/CO/78/ISR of 21 August 2003, paragraph 11 and CCPR/C/79/Add.93 of 18 August 1998 [10].

[216] ICJ, 'Advisory Wall Opinion', above n 119.

[217] The ICJ confirmed the applicability of the *ICCPR* and the *ICESCR* to the West Bank and that these protections do not cease in situations of armed conflict. See Ibid [105]–[106].

[218] Case concerning Armed Activities on the Territory of the Congo (Democratic Republic of the Congo v. Uganda), Judgment of 19 December 2005, I.C.J. Reports 2005, paras. 216–217. See also 'Fundamental standards of humanity' (E/CN.4/2006/87, chap. III), and UN Digest of jurisprudence of the UN and regional organizations on the protection of human rights while countering terrorism (New York and Geneva, 2003), ch I, sect (C); UNHCR, 'Human Rights, Terrorism and Counter-Terrorism' (Fact Sheet No 32, 2008) 12–13.

[219] The ICJ held that IHL is the applicable *lex specialis* to situations of armed conflict. However, the *lex specialis* rule does not oust the applications of human rights law. Rather, international human rights law can apply, but its scope is set by IHL norms. See ICJ, 'Advisory Wall Opinion', above n 119, [105]–[106]; See also ICJ, *Legality of the Threat or Use of Nuclear Weapons*, Advisory Opinion, Report 1996, (8 July 1995) ('Nuclear Weapons Opinion') [226].

[220] Sub-Commission on the Promotion and Protection of Human Rights, *Working Paper on the relationship between human rights law and international humanitarian law by Francoise Hampson and Ibrahim Salama*, E/CN.4/Sub. 2/2005/14, 21 September 2005.

overlap between IHL obligations and human rights norms.[221] Two leading Israeli international law academics have also shown how IHL and human rights law are 'on a continuum, rather than a dividing line' because of their shared purpose: the promotion of human dignity.[222] Of particular note, the Israeli HCJ has ruled that IHL and international human rights law may apply concurrently in the West Bank and Gaza, with IHL as the *lex specialis*, and human rights law available to fill gaps in IHL.[223] Accordingly, it appears there is solid footing for the applicability of both human rights law and IHL to the territories. As will be discussed in Chap. 8, the legal mandate of the IPTEC is grounded in this international legal framework. In particular, the Human Rights Committee of the IPTEC could help resolve the dispute around the applicable IHL and human rights law norms to the Israeli–Palestinian conflict and the respective duties of both parties.

2.4 Part Three: Second Intifada Legacies of Abuse

This section addresses the major human rights violations committed during the Second Intifada, and the parties' international obligations during the 2000–2005 period. Notably, many aspects of the Second Intifada are disputed, reflecting the unique complexity of these issues in international law. This consists of a long-term occupation: a PA, which is not a State but also not a non-governmental entity, asymmetrical warfare, and the blurring of lines between civilians and combatants.

The character of the conflict during the period is also relevant to an assessment of human rights violations. Both sides view the violence of the other as 'terrorism'. Israel regards all Palestinian attacks as terrorism, whether directed at military or civilian targets.[224] For Palestinians, IDF shootings at demonstrators, the use of tanks,

---

[221] One of the study's premises is that '[t]he notion of *lex specialis* does not place human rights law and IHL in an either/or situation for the totality of both sets of norms, which are two mutually supportive branches of the same discipline'. The study indicates a potential mutual reinforcement between the two sets of norms. Ibid [6].

[222] Ben-Naftali and Shany argue that an occupying power has responsibility for the human rights of the population in the territory over which it exerts potential or actual effective control. They investigate the potential coexistence of IHL and IHRL in the territories. Yuval Shany and Orna Ben-Naftali, 'Living in Denial: The Application of Human Rights in the Occupied Territories' (2003–2004) 37 *Israel Law Review* 17–118, 85.

[223] See *Public Committee against Torture in Israel et al. v. Government of Israel et al*, HCJ 769/02, 14 December 2006, ('Targeted Killing Case') [18]–[22].

[224] UN Commission on Human Rights, *Question of the Violation of Human Rights in the Occupied Arab Territories including Palestine: Report of the human rights inquiry commission S-5/1 of 19 October 2000*, Fifty-seventh session, Item 8 of the provisional agenda UN Doc E/CN4/2001/121 (16 March 2001) ('Commission on Human Rights Report (2001)') [23]; See also Human Rights Watch, 'Erased in a Moment: Suicide Bombing Attacks Against Israeli Civilians' (2002) 109, at https://www.hrw.org/report/2002/10/15/erased-moment/suicide-bombing-attacks-against-israeli-civilians; ('HRW Report (2002)').

helicopters, and targeted killings constitute state-sponsored terrorism.[225] Indeed, 'terrorism' is a highly contested term manipulated by both sides to condemn and to validate (counter-terrorist) use of force by the other.[226] In the legal arena, there exists no comprehensive definition of 'terrorism'. The international community has preferred to adopt a range of 'sectoral' anti-terrorism treaties addressing specific types of violence.[227] However, Cassese argues that terrorism is a customary crime,[228] and it has long been prohibited under IHL.[229] Overall, terrorism may be understood as violent acts that deliberately target civilians in pursuit of political or ideological aims.[230] Beyond rhetorical debate, it will be contended that the same legal prohibitions apply to both nations.

Applicability of IHL to the Second Intifada

Armed Conflict?

To determine whether IHL applies, the Second Intifada must first amount to an 'armed conflict'. A threshold question is therefore how to legally characterise the violence of the period. In particular, does the cycle of Palestinian terrorist attacks (in the name of national liberation), and Israeli retaliatory force (in the name of national security) rise to the level of 'armed conflict' within the meaning of IHL? Israel has argued that the Second Intifada constitutes an armed conflict due to the level of PA organisation and the intensity of attacks.[231]

The Israeli argument is based on thousands of incidents involving gunfire between the parties, as well as a belief that Palestinian violence was organised and

[225] Commission on Human Rights Report (2001), above n 224, [23].

[226] Richard Falk, 'Azmi Bishara, the Right of Resistance, and the Palestinian Ordeal' (2002) 31(2) (Winter) *Journal of Palestine Studies* 19, 20 ('Azmi Bishara'); Jacob Shamir and Khalil Shikaki, 'Self-serving Perceptions of Terrorism Among Israelis and Palestinians' 23(3) (2002) *Political Psychology* 537, 554.

[227] Ben Saul, 'Attempts to Define 'Terrorism' in International Law' (2005) 52 *Netherlands International Law Review* 57; UNHCR, 'Human Rights Terrorism and Counter-Terrorism', above n 218, 5.

[228] Antonio Cassese, *International Criminal Law* (Oxford University Press, 2003) 120–131; Antonio Cassese, 'Terrorism is Also Disrupting Some Crucial Legal Categories of International Law' (2001) 12 *European Journal of International Law* 993, 994.

[229] See *Fourth Geneva Convention* art 33(1) (prohibiting 'all measures … of terrorism'); 1977 Protocol I, art 51(2) and 1977 Protocol II, art 13(2) (prohibiting 'acts or threats of violence the primary purpose of which is to spread terror among the civilian population').

[230] UNHCR, 'Human Rights Terrorism and Counter-Terrorism', above n 218, 5.

[231] In the Targeted Killing Case, the State of Israel argued that since September 2000, Israel has been confronted with 'acts of combat and terrorism' and the applicable legal framework is therefore the laws of armed conflict. See Targeted Killing Case, above n 223 [10] (President Barak).

orchestrated by the PA.[232] In essence, Israel claims that it cannot be seen solely as an occupying power, but was also '... engaged in an armed conflict in which it is entitled to use military means, to suppress political demonstrations, ... to kill Palestinian leaders and to destroy homes and property in the interest of military necessity'.[233] Conversely, Palestinians regard the violence as a civilian uprising against an occupier's unlawful abuses that was instigated by loosely organised groups.[234] Ultimately, both Israeli and Palestinian positions seek to legitimate their own conduct during the period.

No doubt, the characterisation of a period of violence is legally challenging. IHL treaty provisions do not explicitly define the term 'armed conflict'.[235] The closest they come occurs in Article 1(2) of Additional Protocol II, where it is made clear that IHL does not apply to 'situations of internal disturbances and tensions, such as riots, isolated and sporadic acts of violence ...'.[236] In the seminal Tadić case, the ICTY defined an 'armed conflict' as including 'protracted armed violence between governmental authorities and organized armed groups. [Therefore,] IHL applies from the initiation of such armed conflict and extends beyond the cessation of hostilities until ... a peaceful settlement is achieved'.[237] This formulation leans heavily on ICRC Commentary[238] and has been repeated verbatim in all subsequent ICTY, ICTR, and ICC jurisprudence.[239]

Accordingly, an armed conflict can be found even though one side is not a contracting party, and even if the violence is temporarily halted.[240] It is generally

[232] 'Commission on Human Rights Report' (2001), above n 224, [38–39].

[233] Ibid.

[234] Overall, the Palestinians view the Second Intifada through the prism of an occupied people. They regard the violence as spontaneous eruptions of pent-up hostility. See Ibid [27]; See also UN Commission on Human Rights, *Question of the Violation of Human Rights in the Occupied Arab Territories, Including Palestine*, UN ESCOR, Supp No 3 at 38, UN Doc E/CN.4/1998/1 (1998), available at http://wwwl.umn.edu/humanrts/UN/1998/ResO01.htm.

[235] Common Article 2, for example, states that each respective Convention applies to all cases of declared war or of any other armed conflict which may arise. Common Article 3 provides no definitional clarification and simply applies to 'armed conflicts not of an international character occurring in the territory of one of the High Contracting Parties'. Caitlin Dwyer and Tim McCormack 'Chapter Three: Conflict Characterisation' in Raine Liivoja and Tim McCormack (eds.). *Routledge Handbook of the Law of Armed Conflict* (Routledge Handbooks. 2016) 49–50.

[236] Ibid.

[237] *Prosecutor v Tadic*, 1995 ICTY No IT-94-1-AR72, 70, 35 ILM 32, 54 (2 October) (decision on the defence motion for interlocutory appeal on jurisdiction). ('Tadic Case' Jurisdiction Decision).

[238] According to the ICRC Commentaries on the definition of armed conflict: 'It remains to ascertain what is meant by "armed conflict".... Any difference arising between two States and leading to the intervention of armed forces is an armed conflict within the meaning of Article 2, even if one of the Parties denies the existence of a state of war. It makes no difference how long the conflict lasts, or how much slaughter takes place'. GCI Commentary 32.

[239] Caitlin Dwyer and Tim McCormack 'Chapter Three: Conflict Characterisation' in Liivoja and McCormack, above n 235, 49–50.

[240] Donna Arzt, 'Can Law Halt the Violence? Palestinian Suicide Bombing and Israeli "Targeted Assassinations" under International Humanitarian Law' (2005) 11 *ILSA Journal of International and Comparative Law* 357, 359.

acknowledged that the level of intensity required for IHL is very low.[241] Additionally, as is the case in the Palestinian territories, Geneva IV governs 'all cases of partial or total occupation of the territory of a High Contracting Party, even if the said occupation meets with no armed resistance'.[242] From this standpoint, it seems apparent that the intense hostilities of the Second Intifada constitute an armed conflict under IHL.

It is worth noting that the HRC in 2001 disputed the existence of an armed conflict between Israelis and Palestinians in the period.[243] Nevertheless, it is strongly arguable that the IDF was indeed engaged in armed conflict with organised Palestinian terrorist organisations, including Hamas, as a result of the outbreak of violence in September 2000.[244] In fact, the Israeli HCJ has confirmed that IHL is the correct framework within which to determine the legality of Israeli and Palestinian conduct during the Second Intifada.[245] It is worth noting that even if the period is categorised as an armed conflict, entitling the IDF to greater latitude in the exercise of its powers, Israel remains bound by IHL and human rights law as will be discussed in the next section.

International Armed Conflict?

Assuming that the Second Intifada is an armed conflict, it must then be classified as either 'international' (traditionally fought between states) or 'non-international' (generally fought with a non-state actor), in order to determine the applicable norms. Increasingly, asymmetrical and transnational wars like the Israeli–Palestinian one are complicating this dichotomy.[246] On the one hand, an international armed conflict is harder to prove because of the legally unresolved status of Palestine as a state. On

---

[241] Jean S. Pictet (ed.), *The Geneva Conventions of 12 August 1949: Commentary, Fourth Geneva Convention Relative to the Protection of Civilian Persons in Time of War, Geneva* (ICRC, 1958) 34; Dietrich Schindler, 'The Different Types of Armed Conflicts According to the Geneva Conventions and Protocols', (1979), 63 (II) *The Hague Academy Collected Courses*, 131; Sylvain Vité, 'Typology of armed conflicts in International Humanitarian Law: Legal Concepts and Actual Situations' (2009) 91 (873) *International Review of the Red Cross* 76–77.

[242] *Fourth Geneva Convention* art 2.

[243] The HRC claimed '... that sporadic demonstrations/confrontations ... undisciplined lynchings ... acts of terrorism in Israel itself and the shooting of soldiers and settlers on roads leading to settlements by largely unorganized gunmen cannot amount to protracted armed violence on the part of an organized armed group'. Commission on Human Rights Report (2001), above n 224, [39–42].

[244] Targeted Killing Case, above n 223, [18] (President Barak).

[245] Ibid.

[246] For an in-depth discussion of the problems associated with the traditional classification of conflicts into either international or non-international see Roy S. Schöndorf, 'Extra-State Armed Conflicts: Is there a Need for a New Legal Regime?' (2005) 37 (1) *New York University Journal of International Law and Politics* 1, 3. Schondorf proposes to define any 'ongoing hostilities between a state and a non-state actor that take place, at least in part, outside the territory of the state', as 'extra-state hostilities'.

the other hand, the Israeli HCJ has characterised the conflict between Israel and Palestinian armed groups, including Hamas, as international in nature.[247] In 2005, the Court based its finding mainly on the idea that any armed conflict fought in the context of belligerent occupation qualifies as 'international'.[248] Until that year, all Palestinian terrorist organisations operated from areas occupied by Israel, including the West Bank and Gaza. The HCJ also posited that an armed conflict becomes 'international' once it 'crosses the borders of the state'.[249]

Nevertheless, many scholars consider that since the PA and Palestinian armed groups remain non-state actors, the conflict cannot be 'international', regardless of its cross-border dimension[250] and/or links to occupation. The effect of military occupation on the legal character of an armed conflict has been judicially disputed by the ICC.[251] Furthermore, many commentators have rejected the Israeli HCJ's position and prefer the U.S. Supreme Court's ruling in the Hamdan decision.[252] In that case, the Court regarded the war between the U.S. and al Qaeda in Afghanistan as a 'non-international armed conflict'.[253] Given the non-state character of Palestinian armed

[247] See Targeted Killing Case, above n 223; *A v. the State of Israel, Supreme Court of Israel*, Crim A 6659/06, 1757/07, 8228/07, 3261/08, 11 June 2008 ('Unlawful Combatants Judgement'). For a judgement in which the Israeli Supreme Court applies the laws of international armed conflict to Operation Cast Lead see *Physicians for Human Rights v. The Prime Minister of Israel*, Supreme Court of Israel, HCJ 201/2009, 19 January 2009 [14].

[248] The Israeli Supreme Court relied in part on Professor Cassese, who in his textbook on international law wrote that '[a]n armed conflict which takes place between an Occupying Power and rebel or insurgent groups – whether or not they are terrorist in character – in an occupied territory, amounts to an international armed conflict'. See Antonio Cassese, *International Law* (Oxford University Press, 2005), 420, as cited in the Targeted Killing Case, above n 223 [18].

[249] Targeted Killings Case, above n 223, [18]. For a reading of the Targeted Killings Judgement as characterising any cross-border armed conflict as international in nature, and a critique of this issue in the judgement, see Roy S. Schöndorf, 'The Targeted Killings Judgement – A Preliminary Assessment', (2007) 5 *Journal of International Criminal Justice* 301.

[250] See Anthony Dworkin, 'Are Israel and Hamas Committing War Crimes in Gaza?', 7 January 2009 available at http://www.crimesofwar.org/onnews/news-gaza3.html; Marko Milanovic, 'Lessons for human rights and humanitarian law in the war on terror: comparing Hamdan and the Israeli Targeted Killings case' (2007) 89 *International Review of the Red Cross* 384 ('the single defining characteristic of international armed conflicts has not been their cross-border, but their interstate, nature'). Compare Derek Jinks, 'The Applicability of the Geneva Conventions to the "Global War on terrorism"' (2005) 46 *Vanderbilt Journal International Law* 165 (arguing that the conflict between the U.S. and al-Qaeda should be regarded as a non-international armed conflict).

[251] In the Lubanga case, the ICC Trial Chamber found that 'the Ugandan military occupation of Bunia airport did not change the legal nature of the conflict' which remained a non-international one at all relevant times. *Prosecutor v Lubanga* Case no ICC-01/04-01/06, ICC Trial Chamber I, 14 March 2012 ('Lubanga Case') [565–567]; Liivoja and McCormack, above n 235.

[252] *Hamdan v. Rumsfeld*, United States Supreme Court, 548 U.S. (2006), 126 S. Ct. 2749. For a survey of the literature which interprets the Hamdan judgement as expressing the view that the conflict between the U.S. and al Qaeda is a non-international armed conflict see Eran Shamir-Borer, 'Revisiting Hamdan v. Rumsfeld's Analysis of the Laws of Armed Conflict' (2007) 21 *Emory International Law Review* 601; George P. Fletcher, 'The Hamdan Case and Conspiracy as a War Crime' (2006), 4 *Journal of International Criminal Justice* 444.

[253] Ibid.

groups, it is submitted that the violence of the Second Intifada is not easily characterised as an international armed conflict.

Non-international Armed Conflict?

The question then arises as to whether the Second Intifada constitutes a non-international armed conflict.[254] For conflicts between governmental authorities and non-state groups, the ICTY has indicated that non-state actors must be organised, and the violence sufficiently intense.[255] When one of these two conditions is not met, a situation of violence may well be defined as internal disturbances or internal tensions.[256] In such cases, the fighting could merely amount to 'banditry, unorganized and short-lived insurrections, or terrorist activities, which are not subject to IHL'.[257] These two elements are to be evaluated on a case-by-case basis after weighing up a series of relevant criteria.[258]

Organisation

Armed groups must have 'a sufficient degree of organization, in order to enable them to carry out protracted armed violence'.[259] Relevant factors include the group's internal hierarchy, the command structure and rules, the extent to which military equipment is available, the ability to plan and implement operations, and the extent

[254] Common Article 3 of the Geneva Conventions explicitly states that it applies to 'armed conflicts not of an international character'.

[255] *Prosecutor v. Tadić*, ICTY Case No. IT-94-1, Judgement (Trial Chamber), 7 May 1997, [561–8] citing GCII Commentary 33; GCIII Commentary 37 ('Tadic Case' Trial Chamber); See also ICTY, *Prosecutor v. Limaj*, Case No. IT-03-66-T, Judgment (Trial Chamber), 30 November 2005 [84]; ICTY, *Prosecutor v. Boskoski*, Case No. IT04-82, Judgment (Trial Chamber), 10 July 2008, [175]. These criteria have since been adopted by other international bodies. See, in particular ICTR, *Prosecutor v. Rutaganda*, Case No. ICTR-96-3, Judgment (Trial Chamber I), 6 December 1999, [93]; International Commission of Inquiry on Darfur, Report Pursuant to Security Council Resolution 1564 of 18 September 2004, 25 January 2005, [74–76].

[256] These two concepts, which designate types of social instability that do not pertain to armed conflict, have never been defined in law, despite the fact that they are referred to explicitly in Additional Protocol II. Article 1(2). See Vité, above n 241, 76–77.

[257] Tadic Case, Trial Chamber, above n 255 [562].

[258] ICTY, *Prosecutor v. Haradinaj*, Case No. IT-04-84-T, Judgment (Trial Chamber), 3 April 2008 [49]; ICTR, *Prosecutor v. Rutaganda*, above n 245 [93]; In his Commentary on the Geneva Conventions, Pictet suggests, by way of indication, a series of criteria that may be taken into account in this evaluation (see Pictet, above n 231, 49–50) cited in Vité, above n 241, 76–77.

[259] See Lubanga Case above n 241, [536]; *Prosecutor v Mbarushimana* (Decision on the Confirmation of Charges) (Case no ICC-01/04-01/10, ICC Pre-Trial Chamber I, 16 December 2011) [103].

of military involvement.[260] It is generally acknowledged that the threshold of organisation is a low one.[261] During the Second Intifada, a high level of organisation existed among Palestinian armed groups. The main actors who attacked Israeli military personnel and civilians involved Fatah, which is the dominant political force of the PA, and Hamas and Islamic Jihad. The Popular Front for the Liberation of Palestine (PFLP) also carried out attacks. Leaders of Hamas and Islamic Jihad openly espoused suicide attacks, and according to a 2002 report by Human Rights Watch (HRW Report), they were able to turn them on and off at will.[262] In particular, Hamas had a structured military force at the time, political and social power as well as de facto control over a defined territory in Gaza. Overall, Palestinian non-state groups appear to have been sufficiently organised.

Intensity

With regard to intensity, this relates to the requirement that the violence be 'more than sporadic or isolated'. The threshold of intensity for a 'non-international' armed conflict is higher than for an international one. However, caselaw reveals that in practice, the standard is met every time 'protracted armed violence' exists.[263] Relevant factors include the seriousness of attacks; the spread of violence over territory and period of time; the involvement of government forces; the number of victims and the mobilisation and distribution of weapons among both parties to the conflict.[264]

As discussed above, the violence of the Second Intifada spread throughout the West Bank, Gaza, and Israel and resulted in thousands of casualties. From September 2000 until 2005, the fighting was relatively continuous and grave, given frequent suicide-bombings inside Israel, thousands of Hamas rockets and large-scale IDF military operations. The extended timeframe seems to render the conflict 'protracted' and therefore sufficiently intense to qualify as a non-international armed conflict. It is also worth noting that the Second Intifada may be regarded as a non-international conflict, even though many of the acts of violence perpetrated were 'terrorist' in nature.[265]

---

[260] Lubanga Case, above n 241, [537]. See also ICTY, *Prosecutor v. Limaj*, above n 255 [89–90] and the sources cited therein.

[261] The fact that an armed group is able to engage in hostilities over a prolonged period of time is of itself significant evidence of 'organisation'. Liivoja and McCormack, above n 235, 53.

[262] 'HRW Report (2002)', above n 224.

[263] See Tadic Case, Jurisdiction Decision, above n 237, [70]; Vité above n 241.

[264] See Lubanga Case, above n 241 [538]; See also ICTY *Prosecutor v.* Limaj above n 245, [90] and [168]; For a review of the ICTY case law, see ICTY, *Prosecutor v. Boskoski*, above n 255, [177].

[265] In the Boškoski case, the ICTY considered crimes committed in connection with a conflict in Macedonia, between government forces and the Albanian National Liberation Army (NLA). Referring to the test established in the Tadić Case, the defendants argued that since the acts of NLA were of a terrorist nature, there was no armed conflict. The ICTY rejected their argument, finding

Customary IHL Norms

Ultimately, there exists no clear consensus as to whether the Second Intifada constitutes an international or non-international armed conflict. The law is unsettled in this area of IHL. Some commentators even advocate for the elimination of the distinction altogether.[266] Indeed, the overall legal character of the Israeli–Palestinian conflict remains unresolved. From this standpoint, it is worth applying the IHL norms that govern both the types of armed conflict.[267] Whilst Common Article 3 explicitly applies to 'armed conflicts not of an international character', its provisions are considered customary norms regulating every armed conflict. The ICJ explained that these IHL provisions amount to 'elementary considerations of humanity' which apply the moment an armed conflict begins.[268] The ICTY, in adopting this ruling, held that they reflect 'minimum mandatory rules' with respect to which 'the character of the conflict is irrelevant'.[269]

Overall, paragraph 1 (a) of Common Article 3 prohibits violence towards life and body of anyone who is not taking a direct part in the hostilities. Many additional customary IHL norms were identified by the ICRC as applicable to both the categories of armed conflict.[270] Regarding the Second Intifada, the following customary IHL norms are particularly relevant to the conduct of the parties:

---

that the intense and protracted nature of the violence, and the level of organization of the NLA, rendered the conflict a non-international armed conflict. *Prosecutor v. Boškoski* above n 255, [184–292].

[266] Emily Crawford, 'Unequal before the Law: The Case for the Elimination of the Distinction between International and Non-international Armed Conflicts' (2007) 20 *Leiden Journal of International Law* 441–465; James Stewart, 'Towards a Single Definition of Armed Conflict in International Humanitarian Law: A Critique of Internationalized Armed Conflict' (2003) 85 *International Review of the Red Cross* 313; Deidre Willmott, 'Removing the Distinction Between International and Non-International Armed Conflict in the Rome Statute of the International Criminal Court' (2004) 5 *Melbourne Journal of International Law* 196.

[267] A similar approach was adopted by the four UN Human Rights reporters who examined the violations of IHL and human rights law during the conflict between Israel and the Hezbollah in Lebanon in 2006. See UN Doc. A/HRC/2/7, 2 October 2006 [23] ('While the qualification of the conflict as international or non-international is complex, this report is mainly based on international customary law applicable in both forms of conflict').

[268] Military and Paramilitary Activities in and against Nicaragua (Nicaragua v. U.S.), Judgement, 1986 ICJ Rep. 14 ('Nicaragua Case') [114].

[269] Tadić, Case, Jurisdiction Decision, above n 237 [102].

[270] The study was published in two volumes in Jean-Marie Henckaerts and Louise Doswald-Beck (eds.) *Customary International Humanitarian Law* (ICRC and Cambridge University Press, 2005) ('ICRC Study on Customary IHL'). Conveniently, a list of the norms identified in the study is included in Jean-Marie Henckaerts, 'Study on Customary International Humanitarian Law-Annex: List of Customary Rules of International Humanitarian Law', (2005), 87 *International Review of the Red Cross* 198 (Annex to ICRC Study on Customary IHL). The ICRC, an organization based in Geneva, is considered the 'guardian' of IHL.

1. The parties to the conflict must at all times distinguish between civilians and combatants. Attacks may only be directed against combatants. Attacks must not be directed against civilians.[271]
2. Acts or threats of violence the primary purpose of which is to spread terror among the civilian population are prohibited.[272]
3. The parties to the conflict must at all times distinguish between civilian objects and military objectives. Attacks may only be directed against military objectives. Attacks must not be directed against civilian objects.[273]
4. Indiscriminate attacks are prohibited.[274]
5. The parties to the conflict must take all feasible precautions to protect the civilian population and civilian objects under their control against the effects of attacks.[275]

In sum, the direct targeting of the civilian population and the use of indiscriminate and disproportionate force are prohibited in every armed conflict as a matter of treaty and/or customary law. The customary status of all of the important rules mentioned above means they would bind both Israel and the Palestinians even where they are not a party to them.

Duties of Non-state Actors and Palestinian Obligations

IHL

Originally, IHL only applied to armed conflicts between States.[276] However, the law has broadened to include guerrillas fighting in wars of national liberation and against military occupation.[277] Today, there is a growing consensus that non-state actors can be held accountable under international law.[278] Regional institutions, such as the Inter-American Commission on Human Rights, often attribute responsibility to non-state armed groups (for example with respect to the Colombian guerrilla group FARC).[279] State practice, international case law, and scholarship have confirmed

---

[271] ICRC Study on Customary IHL, Rule 1.

[272] Ibid, Rule 2.

[273] Ibid, Rule 7.

[274] Ibid, Rule 11–12.

[275] Ibid, Rule 22.

[276] Cassese, *International Law*, above n 248, 327.

[277] Christopher Greenwood, 'Scope of Application of Humanitarian Law' in Dieter Fleck ed., *The Handbook of International Humanitarian Law* (Oxford University Press, 1995) 332.

[278] Annyssa Bellal, *The War Report 2017* (Geneva Academy, 2018); Katharine Fortin, *The Accountability of Armed Groups under Human Rights Law* (Oxford University Press, 2017) 27–68; Daragh Murray, *Human Rights Obligations of Non-State Armed Groups* (Hart, 2016) 120–154.

[279] See Christina M. Cerna, 'History of the Inter-American System's Jurisprudence as Regards Situations of Armed Conflict' (2011) 2 *International Humanitarian Legal Studies* 3–52; See also Inter-American Court of Human Rights, Second Report on the Situation of Human Rights in

that Common Article 3 can apply directly to non-state players.[280] In the words of the Special Court for Sierra Leone: '... it is well settled that all parties to an armed conflict, whether States or non-State actors, are bound by IHL, even though only States may become parties to international treaties'.[281]

At the same time, the precise legal means by which non-states become liable is debated.[282] For some scholars, they are simply bound by IHL due to customary law.[283] Thus, it is asserted that Common Article 3 reflects international custom and therefore governs each party to a conflict regardless of formal ratification.[284] Given the history and goals of IHL, this reasoning seems persuasive and could be applied to non-state actors during the Second Intifada.

Arguably, IHL obligations extend to the Palestinian armed groups of the period. This includes the PA, as well as other militant Palestinian factions, including Hamas, the al-Aqsa Martyrs Brigade and Islamic Jihad as armed parties to the conflict.[285] As well as custom, it is also worth noting that the PA assumed international legal obligations under the Oslo Accords in 1993. In particular, Oslo II specifically required PA security forces to ensure respect for IHL in the West Bank and Gaza.[286]

Moreover, given that the PA and potentially Hamas have governmental powers and assume state duties, the ILC Draft Articles on Responsibility of States for Internationally Wrongful Acts may be relevant.[287] Some provisions of the ILC Draft

---

Colombia (1993). UN resolutions have also referred to the responsibility under IHL of non-state actors such as the Sudan People's Liberation Army, Taliban, Hezbollah, and others.

280 In the Nicaragua Case, for example, the ICJ confirmed that Common Article 3 was applicable to the Contras, the non-state armed group fighting the Government of Nicaragua. See above n 258, [219] and [114]. See also Marco Sassoli, 'Taking Armed Groups Seriously: ways to improve their Compliance with International Humanitarian Law' 2010 (1) *Journal of International Humanitarian Legal Studies*, 12; Annyssa Bellal, Gilles Giacca, and Stuart Casey-Maslen, 'International law and Armed Non-State Actors in Afghanistan' (2011) 93 (881) *International Review of the Red Cross* 47, 53–55.

281 See for instance, *Prosecutor v. Sam Hinga Norman*, case SCSL-2004-14-AR72(E), Decision on preliminary motion based on lack of jurisdiction (child recruitment) (31 May 2004), [22].

282 Annyssa Bellal et al., above n 280, 53.

283 See for example, Daniel Bethlehem, 'The Methodological Framework of the Study' in Elizabeth Wilmshurst and Susan Breua (eds.), *Perspectives on the ICRC Study on Customary International Humanitarian Law* (Cambridge University Press, 2007–8); Jean-Marie Henckaerts, 'Binding Armed Opposition Groups through Humanitarian Treaty Law and Customary Law' (2003) 27 *Collegium* 123–38.

284 '... [a] convincing theory is that [insurgents] are bound as a matter of customary international law to observe the obligations declared by Common Article 3 which is aimed at the protection of humanity' quoted in *SCSL Prosecutor v. Morris Kallon and Brima Buzzy Kamara*, SCSL-2004-15-AR72(E) and SCSL-2004-16-AR72(E), Decision on Challenge to Jurisdiction: Lomé Accord Amnesty, Appeals Chamber, 13 March 2004 [45–47].

285 Cassese, *International Criminal Law*, above n 228, 76; 'HRW Report (2002)', above n 224, 47.

286 See 'Oslo II 1995' above n 203. art II. The PA formally acceded to the Geneva Conventions on 2 April 2014.

287 See 'Draft Articles on Responsibility of States for Internationally Wrongful Acts', prepared in 2001 by the International Law Commission ('ILC Draft Articles'); Demian Casey, 'Breaking the

Articles clarify that internationally wrongful acts may be attributed to non-state actors in certain circumstances.[288] Nevertheless, the ILC Draft Articles do not sufficiently address the responsibilities of non-state actors seeking statehood, like the Palestinians.[289] Furthermore, the Commentary observes that such questions fall outside the scope of the ILC Draft articles that primarily concern the responsibility of States.[290] Suffice to acknowledge that Palestinian non-state actors are bound by customary IHL provisions during the Second Intifada.

Human Rights Law

The applicability of human rights law to Palestinians is more controversial. This is because the human rights treaties were drafted to regulate the relationship between states and individuals and do not directly address non-states.[291] Arguably, '[e]fforts to establish explicit horizontal international human rights obligations for non-state actors have until now failed'.[292] At the same time, the relationship between IHL and human rights is evolving. Increasingly, academics have sought to expand human rights law protection in all circumstances and to ensure accountability for multiple actors.[293] There have also been attempts to modify the vertical conception of human rights law. This can be observed in the African human rights instruments, and in the Convention on the Rights of the Child and its Optional Protocol on children in

---

Chain of Violence in Israel and Palestine: Suicide Bombings and Targeted Killings under International Humanitarian Law' (2005) 32 *Syracuse Journal of International Law and Commerce* 311, 331.

[288] For example, Article 10 of the ILC Draft Articles addresses the responsibility of 'an insurrectional or other movement', providing that when such a movement becomes the 'new Government of a State', or 'succeeds in establishing a new State', the violations it committed whilst it was still a movement will be considered an act of that (new or existing) State.

[289] See Edith Brown Weiss, 'Invoking State Responsibility in the Twenty First Century' (2002) 96 *American Journal of International Law* 798, 799 (noting that the ILC Draft Articles 'do not deal sufficiently with the right of individuals and non-state entities to invoke the responsibility of states'); See also Arzt, 'Can Law Halt the Violence?' above n 240, 362.

[290] See Commentary 16 to Article 10. 'Commentaries to Draft Articles on Responsibility of States for Internationally Wrongful Acts, Report of the International Law Commission on the work of its 53rd session (A/56/10)' (2001) (II) *Year Book of the International Law Commission* Part II.

[291] Arguably, human rights treaties are 'neither intended, nor adequate, to govern armed conflict between the state and armed opposition groups'. Liesbeth Zegveld, *The Accountability of Armed Opposition Groups in International Law*, (Cambridge University Press, 2002) 54.

[292] Manfred Nowak and Karolina Miriam Januszewski, 'Non-State Actors and Human Rights' in Math Noortmann, August Reinisch and Cedric Ryngaert (eds), *Non-State Actors in International Law* (Hart 2015). 151.

[293] This type of approach has been advanced by leading authors in the field. See Philip Alston, 'The "Not-a-Cat" Syndrome: Can the International Human Rights Regime Accommodate Non-State Actors?' in Philip Alston (ed), *Non-State Actors and Human Rights* (Oxford University Press 2005) 3, 6; Andrew Clapham, *Human Rights Obligations of Non-State Actors* (Oxford University Press 2005) 271–312; Ibid, 129–132.

armed conflict.[294] Whether or not these developments impose direct duties on non-state groups is uncertain. However, they demonstrate a trend to hold actors accountable for human rights violations whatever their source.[295]

In that vein, there is some agreement that non-state armed groups are bound by human rights in certain circumstances, where they exercise de facto control over territory and adopt responsibilities analogous to a government.[296] There is no legal source indicating what level of 'authority' or 'control' is required to impose human rights duties on armed non-state actors.[297] However, this is more likely to be established when a non-state actor controls a portion of territory, like the PA in the West Bank or Hamas in Gaza. Arguably, the overarching need to regulate the relationship between those who govern, and those who are governed, justifies human rights law in these scenarios.[298] Armed non-state actors, like the Palestinians, may also be bound by international human rights based on customary law.[299] In 2010, the International Law Association concluded that even though non-state actors do not incur direct human rights obligations, they remain bound by basic *jus cogens* norms.[300] In 2001, the HRC identified arbitrary deprivations of life and liberty, freedom from torture, inhuman or degrading treatment, collective punishment, and fundamental principles of a fair trial as such norms.[301] Holding non-state armed groups accountable for core

[294] See Article 2 of the *African Union Convention for the Protection and Assistance of Internally Displaced Persons in Africa of 2009* ('The Kampala Convention'); Article 4 of the *Optional Protocol to the Convention on the Rights of the Child* on the involvement of children in armed conflict.

[295] Annyssa Bellal et al., above n 280, 64–74/Number.

[296] Andrew Clapham, 'Human Rights Obligations of Non-State Actors in Conflict Situations' (2006) 88(863) *International Review of the Red Cross* 491; See UN Human Rights Council, 'Human Rights Situation in Palestine and Other Occupied Arab Territories', UN Doc A/HRC/8/17, (6 June 2008) [8]–[9].

[297] Further reflection is demanded to determine when the requisite threshold of control has been met. Annyssa Bellal et al., above n 280, 71.

[298] Nigel Rodley, 'Can Armed Opposition Groups Violate Human Rights?' in Kathleen E. Mahoney and Paul Mahoney (eds), *Human Rights in the Twenty-first Century* (Martinus Nijhoff, 1993) 300; Liesbeth Zegveld, *The Accountability of Armed Opposition Groups in International Law* (Cambridge Studies in International and Comparative Law, Cambridge University Press, 2002) 149.

[299] See Clapham (2006), above n 296, 501–2.

[300] Norms of *jus cogens*—the peremptory norms of international law—are defined by Article 53 of the 1969 Vienna Convention on the Law of Treaties as norms 'accepted and recognized by the international community of States as a whole as a norm from which no derogation is permitted …'. See International Law Association, The Hague Conference 2010, *Non State Actors*, First Report of the Committee [3.2].

[301] There exists no definitive list of the human rights norms that form part of *jus cogens*. Human Rights Committee, 'General Comment No. 29: States of Emergency (Article 4)', UN Doc. CCPR/C/21/Rev.1/Add.11, 31 August 2001, 4–5.

human rights norms also reflects international criminal law which can assess the criminal responsibility of individual members of armed groups.[302]

From this standpoint, international human rights law could apply to Palestinian non-state actors during the Second Intifada. Many human rights groups have claimed that both the PA and Hamas were bound by human rights treaties throughout the violence.[303] Notably, since 1993, the PA, the PLO, and the Palestinian Legislative Council (PLC) have made numerous public statements and undertakings through which they declared themselves bound by international human rights obligations.[304] In particular, Article XIV of the 1994 agreement on the Gaza Strip and the Jericho Area provides for both Israel and Palestine to respect human rights norms. Moreover, the Palestinian Basic Law (2002) contains a number of articles protecting human rights as well as a commitment to abide by major international human rights instruments.[305] Hamas has also made public statements that it is committed to respect international human rights and humanitarian law.[306] Regardless of the extent to which Palestinians were technically bound by human rights law, it is worth noting their general willingness to subscribe to these norms, and their potential application during the period.

Palestinian International Legal Violations

Suicide Bombings and Rockets as War Crimes

> *We are going to go deep into Israel. We will turn their blood into rivers. We will follow the Israelis into their homes* ... [and] *on to their streets* .... (Palestinian militant shouting into a microphone[307])

Distinctive of the Second Intifada was the bloodshed of suicide missions. As noted above, members of Palestinian armed groups frequently attacked Israeli military

---

[302] This is the case regarding the crime of genocide and crimes against humanity, situations in which human rights violations are criminalized. See Rome Statute, Arts. 6 and 7; Jan Arno Hessbruegge, 'Human Rights Violations Arising from Conduct of Non-State Actors' (2005) (11) *Buffalo Human Rights Law Review* 21, 41–44; Philippe Currat, *Les Crimes Contre L'humanité dans le Statut de la Cour penale international* (Bruylant/L.G.D.J./Schulthess, 2006).

[303] 'HRW Report (2002)', above n 224; Amnesty International, 'Broken Lives – a year of Intifada' (2001) ('Amnesty Report (2001)').

[304] These undertakings have included assurances, decrees and declarations, and various agreements under the Oslo Accords signed with Israel, which stated that both parties would exercise their powers and responsibilities with 'due regard to internationally accepted norms and principles of human rights and the rule of law'.

[305] http://www.palestinianbasiclaw.org/2002-basic-law.

[306] See UN Human Rights Council, 'Human Rights Situation in Palestine and Other Occupied Arab Territories' UN Doc A/HRC/8/17 (6 June 2008) [8]–[9].

[307] Suzanne Goldenburg, '12 Dead in Attack on Hamas', *The Guardian* (online), July 23, 2003 https://www.theguardian.com/world/2002/jul/23/israel1.

personnel and civilians. In particular, Hamas and Islamic Jihad detonated bombs within Israel, in order to kill and maim large numbers of Israeli civilians.[308] Both the groups used suicide bombers in bars, buses, restaurants, and outside night-clubs in order to terrorise Israelis.[309] Leaders of Hamas and Islamic Jihad openly espoused suicide attacks.[310] Most disturbingly, a culture of martyrdom was fostered around this brutality.[311] In addition, Hamas fighters targeted Israeli civilians by daily launching Qassam and Grad rockets at population centres. Whilst Palestinians likely committed other violations in the period,[312] it was suicide bombings and rockets that became the key tactics and expressions of the Second Intifada.[313] Accordingly, this section will squarely focus on the legality of these acts.

The Prohibition Against Targeting Civilians

By deliberately targeting Israeli civilians, suicide bombings and rockets clearly violate fundamental norms of IHL. As noted above, it is forbidden to direct attacks against civilians in all circumstances. Common Article 3 expressly prohibits 'violence to life and person' when perpetrated against persons 'taking no active part in the hostilities'.[314] In addition to customary law, this principle is codified in numerous treaties. Thus, Article 51(2) of Additional Protocol I states: 'The civilian population as such, as well as individual civilians, shall not be the object of attack. Acts or threats of violence, the primary purpose of which is to spread terror among the

---

308 Hamas took responsibility for most of the suicide bombings in Israel and later for the Qasam rockets that targeted southern localities in Israel. See Baruch Kimmerling, *Clash of Identities: Explorations in Israeli and Palestinian Societies* (Columbia University Press, 2013) 169, 267.

309 For example, 21 people were killed and 84 injured when a Palestinian suicide bomber blew himself up among a group of young people waiting outside a disco near the Dolphinarium in Tel Aviv on 1 June 2001. The suicide bombing was claimed by *Hamas*. 'Amnesty Report' (2001), above n 303, 31.

310 'HRW Report (2002)', above n 224.

311 In Gaza, Hamas has been accused of training children as young as nine to become suicide bombers. Ibid; 'Amnesty Report' (2001), above n 303.

312 For example, the use in hostilities of children under the age of 15, the use of ambulances to transfer weapons and combatants in violation of the prohibition on perfidy may all be considered war crimes. Aeyal Gross and Orna Ben-Naftali, 'The Second Intifada' in Anthony Dworkin, Roy Gutman and David Rieff (eds), *Crimes of War (2.0): What the Public Should Know* (W Norton & Company, 2007).

313 Conducted as a single or double bombing, suicide bombings were generally conducted against 'soft' targets or 'lightly hardened' targets (such as checkpoints) to try to raise the cost of the war to Israelis and demoralize the Israeli society. The IDF cited a total of 22,406 Palestinian terrorist attacks since the beginning of the Second Intifada. See Robert A Caplan, 'Mending the Fence: How Treatment of the Israeli-Palestinian Conflict by the International Court of Justice at the Hague has Redefined the Doctrine of Self-Defense' (2005) 57(3) *Florida Law Review* 717, 724.

314 As noted above, this IHL prohibition is absolute and applies regardless of whether a party to the conflict is a state. See ICRC, *Commentary to the Fourth Geneva Convention* at http://www.icrc.org/ihl.

civilian population, are prohibited'.[315] The principle of distinction between civilian and military targets is enshrined in Article 48 of Protocol I.[316]

Notably, serious violations of Common Article 3[317] constitute war crimes under international criminal law and have been defined as such in the statutes of the ICTY and the ICTR.[318] Wilful killing, that is, intentionally causing the death of civilians and wilfully causing great suffering or serious injury are also war crimes under the ICC's Rome Statute.[319] Given that suicide attacks and rockets were launched with full knowledge of Israeli civilians as targets and that incidental deaths would occur, there seems to be little doubt about the intention to kill. This is evident by the choice of target in public places, and the timing of attacks, as well as claims of responsibility by Palestinian militant groups themselves. According to the HRW Report, '[t]he main thing [for Hamas leaders choosing their targets] is to guarantee that a large number of the [Israeli] enemy will be affected'.[320] Therefore, perpetrators and commanders who are part of organised Palestinian militant groups and who deliberately plan and carry out attacks against Israeli civilians commit war crimes.

Crimes Against Humanity

Palestinian violence during the Second Intifada may also constitute crimes against humanity under international criminal law. Generally, crimes against humanity refer to acts that, by their scale or nature, outrage the conscience of humankind.[321] Such crimes form part of *jus cogens* and constitute non-derogable rules of international law.[322] The term was first codified by the Nuremberg Tribunal[323] and has since been incorporated into international treaties, including the Rome Statute of the ICC.[324] Crimes against humanity are always prohibited, regardless of whether they occur

---

[315] First Additional Protocol 1. As of February 2019, 164 states had become parties to Additional Protocol I.

[316] Under IHL, attacks that are not aimed at military targets, are considered 'indiscriminate.' They are prohibited under Additional Protocol I and, under Article 48 constitute war crimes.

[317] 'Grave breaches' of the Fourth Geneva Convention are enumerated in Article 147 and include wilful killing, torture or inhuman treatment, and wilfully causing great suffering or serious injury to body or health.

[318] Steven Ratner, 'Categories of War Crimes' in Roy Gutman and David Rieff (eds), *Crimes of War* (WW Norton and Co, 1999).

[319] Article 8(2) of the Rome Statute defines war crimes among other things as wilful killing; attacking civilians, and causing excessive incidental death, injury or damage.

[320] 'HRW Report (2002)', above n 224.

[321] See Ian Brownlie, *Principles of Public International Law* (Clarendon Press, 1990) 512–13 (discussing the nature of *jus cogens* and crimes against humanity).

[322] Mahmoud Cherif Bassiouni, *Crimes Against Humanity: Historical Evolution and Contemporary Application* (Cambridge University Press, 2011).

[323] See Article 6(c) of the Nuremberg Charter 1945.

[324] Article 7 of the Rome Statute of the ICC defines crimes against humanity as the 'participation in and knowledge of a widespread or systematic attack against a civilian population', and 'the mul-

during armed conflict. So, even if the Second Intifada is not an 'armed conflict', this prohibition still applies.[325] Crimes against humanity essentially involve certain enumerated acts, such as killings or torture, that are committed intentionally as part of a widespread or systematic attack against a civilian population.[326] Arguably, the scale, frequency, target groups, and systematic nature of Palestinian suicide and rocket attacks set them apart from other abuses and may satisfy the basic elements of this crime.

Nevertheless, there may be some question around whether Palestinian non-state groups are capable of committing crimes against humanity. Originally, crimes against humanity connoted state crimes. Today, a broad consensus exists that private actors are capable of committing international crimes.[327] In the *Kunarac* case, the ICTY Appeals Chamber rejected the view that only a state actor could be the author or sponsor of a crime against humanity.[328] The ICTR reached a similar conclusion.[329] In Sierra Leone, members of the Armed Forces Revolutionary Council were found to have committed crimes against humanity with no effective territorial control or state-like infrastructure.[330] From this standpoint, members of Hamas and other Palestinian militant groups would be equally capable of committing crimes against humanity during the Second Intifada.

Arguably, some 'organisational policy element' or 'action' by a 'state or state like entity' is needed to establish non-state liability.[331] For the purposes of the Rome

tiple commission of [such] acts … against any civilian population, pursuant to or in furtherance of a State or organizational policy to commit such attack'.

325 The ICTY Tadic case ruled that crimes against humanity can take place during peacetime without a nexus to war or aggression. See Tadic Case Jurisdiction Decision, above n 237; William Schabas, *The Law of the Ad hoc Tribunals The UN International Criminal Tribunals: The Former Yugoslavia, Rwanda and Sierra Leone*. (Cambridge University Press, 2006), 23; Cassese, *International Criminal Law*, above n 228, 76.

326 Cassese, *International Criminal Law*, above n 228, 64.

327 Ibid; Joseph Rikhof, 'Crimes against Humanity, Customary International Law and the International Tribunals for Bosnia and Rwanda' (1996) 6 *National Journal of Constitutional Law* 232 at 254–261.

328 In that case, the Appeals Chamber concluded that the capacity of non-states expanded to the point where crimes against humanity can now be committed by members of non-state groups. See *Prosecutor v Kunarac* (Appeals Chamber Judgment), Case No IT-96-23-A and IT-96-23/1-A (12 June 2002) [98]; Mahmoud Cherif Bassiouni, *Crimes Against Humanity in International Criminal Law* (Martinus Nijhoff Publishers, 2nd rev. ed. 1999) 7–8.

329 Bassiouni, *Crimes Against Humanity in International Criminal Law*, above n 328, 14–19, 24, 197; See also *Prosecutor v. Kayishema et al.*, Judgment, Case No. ICTR-95-1-T, T.CH. II, 21 May 1999 [126].

330 *Prosecutor v. Brima* et al., Judgment, Case No. SCSL-04–16-T, T. Ch., 20 June 2007, at paras. 226, 238. See Prosecutor v. Brima, Kamara and Kanu, Case No. SCAL-04-16-T, Judgment (20 June 2007) Trial Chamber II at [253]. Robert Dubler, 'What's in a Name - A Theory of Crimes against Humanity' (2008) 15 *Australian International Law Journal* 85, 105.

331 Bassiouni, *Crimes Against Humanity in International Criminal Law*, above n 328, 71, 273–275; See also Cassese, *International Criminal Law*, above n 228 at 64; Joseph Rikhof, 'Crimes against

Statute, attacks must be in furtherance of a state or 'organisational policy'.[332] However, ICC jurisprudence to date has indicated that non-state actors do not have to demonstrate state-like qualities to be capable of satisfying this element of the offence.[333] The ad hoc Tribunal cases[334] have also ruled that a non-state group may commit crimes against humanity, as long as it is *capable* of committing a widespread or systematic attack, and there is no need for such an 'organisational policy'.[335] Notably, in practice, international tribunals have only tended to convict where an attack is linked in some loose way to a state or some de facto power.[336]

In this light, it is worth recalling that Hamas and other Palestinian militant groups officially claimed responsibility for suicide bombings and rockets throughout the Second Intifada period.[337] The attacks were not spontaneous or part of an uncontrolled group conflict,[338] but planned acts directed against civilians in response to Israeli conduct.[339] They represent organisational policy at the highest levels.[340] In the case of the al-Aqsa Martyrs' Brigades, control and responsibility appeared to have been centred at local levels.[341] In particular, suicide bombings were part of an intentional military strategy, which aimed to force an Israeli withdrawal from the territories.[342] In short, Palestinian attacks against Israeli civilians during the Second Intifada could equate with crimes against humanity.

Humanity, Customary International Law and the International Tribunals for Bosnia and Rwanda' (1996) 6 *National Journal of Constitutional Law* 232 at 254–261.

[332] Article 7(2) of the Rome Statute.

[333] See *The Kenyan Decision* (31 March 2010) where the majority affirm that it is not limited to state-like organisations. Decision Pursuant to Article 15 of the Rome Statute on the Authorization of an Investigation into the Situation in the Republic of Kenya, ICC Pre-Trial Chamber II, 31 March 2010, http://bit.ly/1VR9Qms [77–138] (majority judgment); and [33–67] (Dissenting Opinion of Judge Hans Peter-Kaul).

[334] According to the ICTY, in customary law, there is no requirement for an organisational 'policy' at all. See *Prosecutor v Kunarac* above n 318 [98].

[335] Gerhard Werle, *Principles of International Criminal Law* (TMC Asser Press, 2005) 228–229; Robert Dubler, above n 320, 105.

[336] For example, Dubler notes that '… militia groups such as the "Jokers" or Arkan's Tigers in Bosnia, the Interahamwe in Rwanda or around 23 different militia in East Timor in 1999 have been held to be authors of crimes against humanity because all gained support from state agencies and their acts were linked to a state or *de facto* power's policy, in a loose sense'. Robert Dubler, above n 330, 105.

[337] Hamas and Islamic Jihad have frequently claimed responsibility for suicide bombing attacks. Since January 2002, the al-Aqsa Martyrs' Brigades and the PFLP have also claimed responsibility for organising and carrying out such attacks. 'HRW Report (2002)', above n 224, 45–46.

[338] According to Bassiouni, the term 'widespread or systematic' both excludes spontaneous or uncontrolled group conflict and requires the element of 'policy' for non-State actors. Bassiouni, *Crimes Against Humanity in International Criminal Law*, above n 328, 245.

[339] Casey, above n 287, 335–6.

[340] See Middle East Policy Council, Conflict statistics at https://www.mepc.org/journal/middle-east-policy-archives; 'Amnesty Report (2001)', above n 303, 38.

[341] 'HRW Report (2002)', above n 224, 16.

[342] Ibid.

Justifications by Palestinian Armed Groups

Israelis Are Not Civilians

> *The Geneva Convention protects civilians in occupied territories, not civilians who are in fact occupiers. All of Israel, Tel Aviv included, is occupied Palestine. So we're not actually targeting civilians—that would go against Islam.* (Shaikh Ahmad Yassin, Hamas Leader[343])

Palestinian armed groups and their supporters often acknowledge that suicide bombings breach fundamental legal norms. However, they frequently invoke various claims to justify the violence. One such argument is that Palestinian attacks do not target civilians[344] or that those targeted in suicide bombings are not entitled to civilian immunity. For example, it has been frequently asserted that Israeli residents of settlements forfeit their civilian status because settlements are illegal, and/or since they carry military weapons for self-protection.[345] Leaders of Hamas and Islamic Jihad have further stated they consider all of Israel to be 'occupied territory', all Jewish Israelis to be reservists,[346] and thus all Israelis to be legitimate targets.[347]

None of these arguments have legal merit. As discussed earlier, the principle of distinction is a basic customary norm of IHL applicable in both international and non-international armed conflict. Accordingly, all Israeli civilians are protected against attack, unless and for such time as they take a direct part in hostilities.[348] Clearly, the lawfulness of any attack will depend on what exactly constitutes 'direct participation in hostilities', and therefore when direct participation begins and when it ends.[349] Arguably, reserve members of military forces are lawful targets only

---

[343] 'No Israeli targets off-limits, Hamas spiritual chief warns', Flore de Preneuf interview with Shaikh Ahmad Yassin, *St. Petersburg Times* (Florida), 11 August 2001. This statement was made in August 2001, following the Hamas suicide bombing attack on the Sbarro pizzeria cited in 'HRW Report (2002)', above n 224, 54.

[344] Despite overwhelming evidence to the contrary, members of armed Palestinian groups frequently deny that their operations target civilians, but seek to target only Israeli soldiers or police. See Ibid 50.

[345] Islamic Jihad spokesperson Ismail Abu Shanab told HRW: 'Every home and settler has a gun, and all these people are militants and targets. They can't hide in the uniform of a civilian …'. HRW interview, Gaza City, May 15, 2002, cited in ibid at 54.

[346] Shaikh Yassin said in an al-Hayat interview: 'They are all in the military, men and women … They wear civilian clothes inside Israel, and military clothes when they are with us …'. Fathi Sabbah, 'Hamas leader to al-Hayat: Resistance, not reform, is the Palestinian demand right now', *al-Hayat*, (May 22, 2002), translated in Mideast Mirror (London), May 22, 2002, cited in ibid.

[347] Ibid 54; Arzt, 'Can Law Halt the Violence?' above n 240, 360.

[348] ICRC Study on Customary IHL, above n 270, Rule 6.

[349] No precise legal definition of this term exists. The Inter-American Commission on Human Rights has stated it means: 'acts which, by their nature or purpose, are intended to cause actual harm to enemy personnel and matériel'. Inter-American Commission on Human Rights, Third report on human rights in Colombia; Inter-American Commission on Human Rights, *Case 11.137 (Argentina)* 811.

while on active duty, and otherwise benefit from protection as civilians.[350] Whilst it may be debated whether that would cover an attack on Israeli soldiers in uniform on weekend leave, it surely prohibits bombs which kill or maim innocent passengers on buses, or Israeli teenagers outside night clubs.[351]

Moreover, Israeli settlers equally remain entitled to civilian protections so long as they do not directly participate in hostilities. The mere unlawfulness of settlements does not render civilians living there legitimate military targets.[352] Ultimately, the argument for targeting Israeli settlers rests more on moral or political culpability,[353] rather than military threat.[354] From this standpoint, allowing Israeli settlers to be killed for political or moral wrongdoing risks being vigilante justice.[355]

Right to Armed Resistance

> *I am not a murderer .... Even if civilians are killed, it's not because we like it or are bloodthirsty. It is a fact of life in a people's struggle against a foreign occupier ....* (Hassan Salameh, Hamas member[356])

Palestinian armed groups have claimed that targeting civilians is beyond legal reproach, because of their struggle for 'national liberation'.[357] Many have sought to justify the violence as legitimate resistance to an oppressive occupation. As Al-Haq's director puts it, '... we understand violent action as another way to resist. Resistance is both a right and a duty ...'.[358] According to the former UN Special Rapporteur on Palestinian human rights, Richard Falk, the Palestinians enjoy a legally protected

---

350 IHL makes clear that reserve soldiers are considered civilians, until the time that they become subject to military command. Their incorporation into the regular armed forces is most frequently signified by wearing a uniform or other identifiable insignia. 'HRW Report (2002)', above n 224, 54.

351 Arzt, 'Can Law Halt the Violence?', above n 240, 360.

352 '... [V]iolence that intends to injure and kill that is directed at the settlements, which while illegal and armed, cannot be viewed persuasively as military targets' Falk, 'Azmi Bishara', above n 226, 27; Ibid.

353 According to Honerich, the culpability of settlers is most persuasive for those who voluntarily move into territories with the full knowledge of the international unlawfulness of their presence. Ted Honderich, *After the Terror* (Edinburgh University Press, 2003) 159.

354 David Rodin, *War and Self-Defense* (Oxford University Press, 2002) 84.

355 Ben Saul, 'Defending Terrorism: Justifications and Excuses for Terrorism in International Criminal Law' (2006) 25 *Australian Year Book of International Law* 177, 199 ('Defending Terrorism').

356 Jerrold M Post and Ehud Sprinzak, 'Terror's Aftermath: A convicted Hamas terrorist talks about his mission to destroy Israel', *Los Angeles Times*, (online) 7 July 2002, cited in 'HRW Report (2002)', above n 224, 51–2 https://www.latimes.com/archives/la-xpm-2002-jul-07-op-kaufman-story.html.

357 Ibid.

358 Al Haq's director quoted in Laure Fourest, 'Chapter 4: Human rights, civil society and conflict in Israel/Palestine' in Raffaele Marchetti and Nathalie Tocci (eds) *Civil society, Conflicts and the Politicization of Human Rights* (United Nations University Press, 2011), 90.

right to resist arising from their historic rights to self-determination.[359] He claims these rights are supported by de-colonisation and the legitimacy of an oppressed people engaging in armed struggle.[360] Indeed, liberation movements may enjoy a right to use force defensively against the forcible denial of their right to self-determination.[361] In this regard, Israel's denial of Palestinian national rights must be taken into account in evaluating recourse to force.

Whilst the Palestinian right of self-determination[362] may involve a right of resistance, it does not follow that all means are permissible.[363] Even Falk concedes that legitimate resistance is not without qualification, specifically the prohibition on wilfully targeting civilians.[364] Indeed, as noted above, Additional Protocol I extends IHL coverage to wars of national liberation and to armed conflicts against foreign occupation.[365] Although this particular provision has not yet attained customary status,[366] there exists wide support that fundamental rules of IHL apply even when exercising the right to self-determination.[367] Moreover, it is doubtful that armed groups express the will of the Palestinian people.[368] Many civilian attacks derive from extreme religious notions of martyrdom, rather than from the legitimate goal of self-determination.[369] Ultimately, any Palestinian right to resist does not negate criminal liability for deliberate and widespread killing of civilians, either by suicide bombing or by indiscriminate rockets.[370]

---

[359] Falk, 'International Law and the al-Aqsa Intifada' (2000) 217 *Middle East Report* 16 ('International Law'); See also Richard Falk and Burns H Weston, 'The Relevance of International Law to Palestinian Rights in the West Bank and Gaza: In Legal Defense of the Intifada' (1991) 32(1) *Harvard International Law Journal* 129.

[360] Falk refers to the historic 1960 UN General Assembly Declaration on the Granting of Independence to Colonial Countries and Peoples. Falk, 'Azmi Bishara', above n 226, 26–27.

[361] Recourse to force by self-determination movements is treated differently than recourse to force in 'ordinary' civil wars, in which international law is silent on rebel rights to use force against a government. Antonio Cassese, *Self-determination of Peoples: A Legal Reappraisal* (Cambridge University Press, 1996) 151–153.

[362] On the applicability of the right of self-determination to the Palestinian situation, see Catriona J. Drew, 'Self-Determination, Population Transfer and the Middle East Peace Process' in Stephen Bowen, *Human Rights, Self-Determination and Political Change* (Springer, 1997), 119–68.

[363] Gross and Ben-Naftali, above n 312.

[364] Falk, 'Azmi Bishara', above n 226, 22.

[365] Art 1(4) of Additional Protocol I. Notably, the PLO participated in the negotiation of Additional Protocol I from 1974 to 1977. Palestine formally acceded to the instrument in April 2014.

[366] ICRC Study on Customary IHL, above n 270, 387–389.

[367] HRW Report (2002), above n 224, at 51–2.

[368] Saul, 'Defending Terrorism', above n 355, 219.

[369] Ibid.

[370] Gross and Ben-Naftali, above n 312.

Retaliation and Reprisal

> *It's not targeting civilians. It is saying that if you attack mine I'll attack yours.* (Ismail Abu Shanab, Hamas leader[371])

Palestinian armed groups have also argued that suicide attacks are legitimate retaliation for excessive force applied by Israel. This justification has greatly resonated with the Palestinian public.[372] One Palestinian academic stated: 'None of us want to do these things. It is imposed on us. We know about the Geneva Conventions ... but what we see on the ground is something different'.[373] Nevertheless, an apparent failure by Israel to respect the laws of war does not relieve the Palestinians of their own legal obligations. Under IHL, those humanitarian duties are absolute, and not premised on reciprocity. The Geneva Conventions expressly prohibit reprisals against civilians.[374] Additional Protocol I is similarly unambiguous on such conduct.[375] This norm expresses a prevailing trend to prohibit reprisal attacks against civilians under all circumstances and to prevent vicious spirals of violence.[376] In this regard, real or perceived violations by Israel do not justify Palestinian reprisals that target or indiscriminately attack Israeli civilians.

Imbalance of Means

> *We don't have F-16s, Apache helicopters and missiles .... They are attacking us with weapons against which we can't defend ourselves. And now we have a weapon they can't defend themselves against ....* (Abdelaziz Rantisi, Hamas spokesman[377])

Finally, it is claimed that suicide attacks are legitimate because they compensate for the asymmetry of power between Palestinians and Israeli security forces.[378] Many Palestinians believe that attacks on civilians are their only weapon against ongoing

---

371 'HRW Report (2002)', above n 224, 51–2; Sheik Ahmed Yassin has also stated: 'The Jews attack and kill our civilians - we will kill theirs'. Paul McGeough, "Inside the mind of a suicide bomber" *Sydney Morning Herald* (13 April 2002). Islamic Jihad and Fatah leaders have made similar statements.

372 In a survey conducted by the Palestinian Center for Policy and Survey Research (PSR), 86% of Palestinians opposed the arrest of individuals who had carried out attacks inside Israel. PSR Public Opinion Poll no. 4, May 15–19, 2002 cited in 'HRW Report (2002)', above n 224, 51–2.

373 HRW interview, name withheld, Jenin, June 10, 2002, in Ibid.

374 *Fourth Geneva Convention*, art 33(3).

375 Additional Protocol I, art 51(6).

376 Theodore Meron, 'The Humanization of Humanitarian Law' (2000) 94 *American Journal of International Law* 239, 249–251.

377 Molly Moore and John Ward Anderson, 'Suicide Bombers Change Mideast's Military Balance', *Washington Post* (online), 18 August 2002 https://www.washingtonpost.com/archive/politics/2002/08/18/suicide-bombers-change-mideasts-military-balance/8e7e9f44-c71a-4dc9-861e-d0f5bea53150/?noredirect=on&utm_term=.bdfca3bcc070; 'HRW Report (2002)', above n 224, 56–7.

378 Ibid.

occupation and IDF use of military tanks, missiles, and warplanes.[379] Honderich defends Palestinian terrorism as a moral right and the only effective means for freeing Palestinians from Israeli domination.[380] In this regard, terrorism is considered as an essential 'weapon of the weak'[381] when facing modern, well-resourced, militarised states.[382] There is some appeal to this view, which assumes that the military inferiority of non-state actors is unjust and that law should redistribute power.[383]

Nevertheless, accepting this argument seems to defeat the very purpose of IHL since most wars are waged between forces of unequal means.[384] This is particularly true of national liberation struggles against incumbent states.[385] As noted above, Protocol I reaffirms that IHL still applies in those circumstances and that the prohibition on intentional attacks against civilians is absolute. There is no reason why unequal resources should trigger an entitlement to use irregular methods of warfare.[386] IHL must not be exploited to equalise power differences, as to do so risks widening the scope of violence.[387] Moreover, it is not obvious that there are no alternatives to suicide bombings. Attacking civilians to improve one's military or bargaining position may be strategic, but it is not of necessity.[388] Focusing on an imbalance of power seems to deny lawful tactics and diplomatic strategies that can be used to achieve political goals.[389]

---

[379] Neil MacFarquar, 'Hamas Henry Seeks Muslim Support for Suicide Raids', *International New York Times* (11 December 2001); See also Ibid.

[380] Honderich relies on anachronistic analogies with the deliberate killing of innocents by Western states in the naval blockade of Germany in the First World War, and by atomic bombing during the Second World War. See Honderich, above n 343, 170 quoted in Saul, 'Defending Terrorism', above n 355, 219.

[381] Yonah Alexander, 'Democracy and Terrorism: Threats and Responses' (1996) 26 *Israel Yearbook of Human* Rights 253, 257; Bradey Larschan, 'Legal Aspects to the Control of Transnational Terrorism: An Overview' (1986) 13 *Ohio Northern University Law Review* 117, 121.

[382] Michael Ignatieff, 'Human Rights, the Laws of War, and Terrorism' (2002) 69 *Social Research* 1137, 1150; Claudia Card, 'Making War on Terrorism in Response to 9/11' in James Sterba (ed), *Terrorism and International Justice* (Oxford University Press, 2003) 171, 174.

[383] Saul, 'Defending Terrorism', above n 355, 219.

[384] Nothing in IHL presupposes equality of power between adversaries. Meron, above n 366, 240; Ibid; 'HRW Report (2002)', above n 224, 56–7.

[385] 'HRW Report (2002)', above n 224, 56–7.

[386] Saul, 'Defending Terrorism', above n 355, 219.

[387] Ibid.

[388] Ibid.

[389] Ashrawi writes: 'Resistance comes in many different shapes and forms … building institutions is an act of resistance, staying on the land is an act of resistance, going to the UN is an act of resistance, joining institutions, international agencies and so on …'. Hanan Ashrawi, 'Reframing Resistance after the Second Intifada' (2015) 21(2) *The Brown Journal of World Affairs* 94, 98.

Arguably, killing civilians has been counter-productive to Palestinians, since it has often increased, not reduced, Israeli domination of Palestinian lives.[390] Ultimately, '... Palestinians must find ways to resist that do not rely on violence directed at Israeli civilians. Such a burden may be difficult ... but it can only be lifted by Palestinian ingenuity'.[391] In short, unequal military strength does not validate deliberate violence against Israeli civilians.

PA Accountability

One of the most contested questions of the Second Intifada concerns the responsibility and role of the PA. Israel has accused the PA of supporting civilian attacks by releasing incarcerated terrorists, by allowing PA security personnel to abet, and in some cases conduct terrorist operations, and by terminating security cooperation with Israel.[392] Israel maintains that the PA leadership has made no real effort to prevent anti-Israel terrorism, an allegation the PA vigorously refutes.[393] The PA officially denies having any role in Palestinian attacks against Israeli civilians.[394]

As noted above, the PA has security and legal obligations under the Oslo Accords. In particular, both the Interim Agreement (1995) and the Sharm el-Sheikh Memorandum (1999)[395] require the PA to take measures to prevent armed attacks against Israel.[396] Under these agreements, the PA is obliged to maintain security and public order in the territories under its control and to 'apprehend, investigate and prosecute perpetrators and all other persons directly or indirectly involved in acts of terrorism, violence and incitement'.[397] At the time of the Second Intifada, the PA assumed law enforcement responsibilities for the major cities and Palestinian population clusters, amounting to around 26% of the West Bank and 60% of the Gaza

---

[390] Arguably, Israel's construction of a security barrier, its continued expansion of settlements, and its retreat from Oslo indicate that terrorism has not practically advanced the Palestinian cause. Saul, 'Defending Terrorism', above n 355, 219.

[391] Falk, 'Azmi Bishara', above n 226, 22.

[392] See 'Sharm el-sheikh Fact-Finding Commission Report' (2001) ('Mitchell Report (2001)') 5; Mathew A Weiner, 'Defeating Hatred With Truth: An Argument in Support of a Truth Commission as part of the solution to Israel/Palestine' (2005–2006) 38 *Connecticut Law Review* 123, 148 citing Geoffrey R. Watson *The Oslo Accords* (Oxford University Press, 2000) at 225 (describing complaints by Israel that the PA prosecuted few suspects arrested for terrorist activity).

[393] Mitchell Report (2001), above n 392, 5.

[394] HRW Report (2002), above n 224, 109.

[395] In September 1999 Sharm el-Sheikh Memorandum, the parties pledged to take action against 'any threat or act of terrorism, violence or incitement' cited in 'Mitchell Report (2001)', above n 392, 5.

[396] See 'Oslo II 1995' above n 203.

[397] Ibid, Annex I, art 11(3)(c).

Strip.[398] Accordingly, the PA was bound to take all available measures, consistent with international law to prevent suicide or other attacks against civilians by the armed groups operating from these areas.[399]

Despite its legal obligations however, human rights reports conclude that the PA failed to take credible steps to prevent and deter suicide attacks or to bring those responsible to justice.[400] According to HRW: 'The greatest failure of President Arafat and the PA leadership is their unwillingness to deploy the criminal justice system to deter the suicide bombings, particularly in 2001, when the PA was most capable of doing so'.[401] The PA routinely failed to investigate, arrest, and prosecute persons believed to be responsible for these attacks and did not take available measures to reprimand, discipline, or bring to justice those members of its own security services who participated in such attacks.[402] On the rare occasions when Palestinians were arrested for killings of Israelis, they were released within a few hours or days by the PA.[403] In addition, President Arafat and other senior PA officials authorised payments, in several cases, to individuals who were known to have participated in attacks on Israeli civilians.[404]

Israeli Obligations During Second Intifada

IHL Norms

As discussed above, Israeli actions were subject to IHL norms during the Second Intifada. There is an apparent consensus that at the very least, the Fourth Geneva Convention applies de jure to the Palestinian territories.[405] Akin to the Palestinians, Israel is equally bound by customary IHL principles of distinction and proportionality. Given Israel's military and civilian presence in the territories, the IDF is also subject to the international law of occupation under international treaty and custom-

---

398 Of the 26% of the West Bank under PA security control, the PA shared joint security responsibility with Israel for 23%, and 3% was under its sole control. See Joel Beinin, 'The Demise of the Oslo Process', *Middle East Report Online*, March 26, 1999. https://merip.org/1999/03/the-demise-of-the-oslo-process/.

399 'The PA to the extent that it exercised authority, is legally bound to prevent the commission of such acts and to criminally prosecute the individuals who have ordered, organized, condoned, or carried them out'. 'HRW Report (2002)', above n 224, 57–58, 109.

400 Ibid; 'Amnesty Report (2001)', above n 303.

401 'HRW Report (2002)', above n 224, 109.

402 Ibid; According to Amnesty, the PA has signally failed to carry out proper investigations into the killings of Israelis by Palestinians. 'Amnesty Report (2001)', above n 303, 31.

403 Ibid.

404 Ibid.

405 As noted above, the ICRC and the UN have consistently maintained that the *Fourth Geneva Convention* fully applies to the Palestinian Territories and that the Palestinians are a protected population under the terms of the Convention.

ary law. As long as Israel maintains its effective control over the West Bank and Gaza, it is to bound to protect the civilian population as specified in Articles 47–78.[406] Of particular importance, Article 47 affirms 'the inviolability of rights' granted to an occupied civilian population, which cannot be suspended or evaded during the Second Intifada.[407]

Accordingly, Palestinians may not be wilfully killed, tortured, ill-treated, or suffer humiliating and degrading treatment by the IDF (Common Article 3). Their property may not be destroyed unless by military necessity (Article 53), and collective punishment and reprisals are prohibited (Article 33). Notably, Article 147 spells out a list of 'grave breaches' of the Geneva Convention which include: 'wilful killing, torture or inhuman treatment … wilfully causing great suffering or serious injury to body … or wilfully depriving a protected person of the rights of fair and regular trial …'. IDF conduct regarded as 'grave breaches' of the Geneva Conventions could constitute war crimes as well as potential crimes against humanity.

Human Rights Law

As discussed above, human rights law also binds Israel extraterritorially due to its ongoing control of the West Bank and Gaza. Accordingly, Israel must protect Palestinian human rights under the major UN human rights treaties it has ratified. These encompass the ICCPR, which contains non-derogable articles that include the right to life[408] (Article 6), and the right not to be subjected to torture or cruel, inhuman or degrading treatment (Article 7). Human rights law also includes rights with customary law status.[409] The Human Rights Committee has referred to the unlawfulness of arbitrary deprivation of life and liberty, and collective punishment as customary law.[410] All of these human rights apply to the Palestinians during the Second Intifada and bind the IDF accordingly. It is against this background that allegations of human rights violations and IHL breaches will be considered in the following section.

---

[406] Falk, 'International law', above n 359, 17.

[407] Ibid.

[408] The right to life, which is protected under human rights treaties (such as the *ICCPR*) has been described as 'the supreme right' because without its effective guarantee, all other human rights would be meaningless. See Human Rights Committee, General Comment No 6 (1982); Manfred Nowak, UN *Covenant on Civil and Political Rights: CCPR Commentary* (NP Engel, 2nd rev ed, 2005) 121; UNHCR, 'Human Rights Terrorism and Counter-Terrorism', above n 218, 8.

[409] Some human rights are recognised as having a special status as norms of *jus cogens* (peremptory norms of customary international law), which means that there are no circumstances in which derogation is permissible. UNHCR, 'Human Rights Terrorism and Counter-Terrorism', above n 218, 4.

[410] The HRC observed, in its General Comments No. 24 (1994) and No. 29 (2001), that some rights in the *ICCPR* reflect customary norms. *CERD*, in its Statement measures to combat terrorism also confirmed the principle of non-discrimination as a norm. UNHCR, 'Human Rights Terrorism and Counter-Terrorism', above n 218, 4.

Israeli Violations

Many Israeli measures taken to repress the Second Intifada constitute potential war crimes and/or crimes against humanity. The practices described below constitute some of the signature measures taken by Israel. As noted above, it is clearly not possible to analyse all the abuses suffered by Palestinians during the period. Rather, this section identifies a pattern of IDF violations. The first theme examines excessive and indiscriminate force from aerial bombardment, the destruction of property to the use of targeted killings. The second *modus operandi* involves Israeli measures with a collective punitive dimension; mass arrests, travel restrictions; and administrative detention of thousands of Palestinians.

Excessive and Indiscriminate Force

Demonstrations

> *It was clear from the start, that this Intifada, as distinct from the first one, was going to be fought with weapons, and not stones.* (Ben-Naftali and Gross[411])

The first Palestinian casualties of the Second Intifada occurred in violent clashes between the IDF and demonstrators.[412] It is strongly arguable that Israel used excessive force and violated basic IHL norms. 'The Israeli army's heavy handed tactics—including the use of tanks, helicopters and live ammunition against demonstrators blurred any distinction between combat and civilian zones'.[413] The UN Human Rights Commissioner described patterns of injury among Palestinians, which included a disproportionate number of injuries to the upper body, the head, and many from rubber-bullets fired at very close-range.[414] A Report by Physicians for Human Rights made similar observations.[415] According to an Amnesty International

[411] Gross and Ben-Naftali, above n 312.

[412] Most Palestinian deaths and injuries were caused by live ammunition (deaths: 93%; injuries: 20%). Palestinian demonstrations took place at 'symbolic areas'—where Palestinian land had been confiscated, near checkpoints, and on the way to Israeli settlements. Commission on Human Rights Report (2001), above n 224, 14.

[413] Gross, and Ben-Naftali, above n 312.

[414] Mary Robinson, Press conference, AFP (7 May 2002), cited in Lama Jamjoum, 'The Effects of Israeli Violations During the Second Uprising "Intifada" on Palestinian Health Conditions' (2002) 29(3) *Social Justice* 53, 66.

[415] Physicians for Human Rights documented numerous instances of 'shooting to kill' by Israeli soldiers as evidenced by wounds in the upper parts of the body and in the backs of demonstrators. See Physicians for Human Rights Report on the violence during the Second Intifada, cited in Falk, 'International law', above n 359, 17.

delegation, Israeli security forces moved swiftly from using non-lethal to lethal methods of crowd control.[416]

These findings are vigorously disputed by the IDF, which maintains that live ammunition was only used in life-threatening situations.[417] According to an official spokesperson, many demonstrators were armed, and Palestinian gunmen hid behind children.[418] This is at odds however with corroborated journalistic and NGO accounts from the period.[419] Indeed, Israeli group *B'Tselem* did not observe gunmen firing from among the demonstrators, and where gunmen were seen, they were located some distance away or removed by Palestinian security forces.[420] *B'Tselem* concluded that the IDF use of force did not take into account the size of the demonstrations.[421] NGO accounts also document other IHL violations including Israeli attacks on medical personnel and their marked vehicles and facilities.[422] On many occasions, Palestinian ambulances and first-aid workers were hindered from giving aid.[423]

At a minimum, it was incumbent upon Israel to respond with appropriate force to largely civilian demonstrations.[424] Notably, far greater efforts were undertaken by the IDF to avoid Palestinian fatalities during the First Intifada.[425] In demonstrations involving stone-throwing, or even slingshots or Molotov cocktails, a well-trained army should have been able to contain demonstrators without such heavy losses of life and widespread serious injury.[426] Conceivably, demonstrations could have been diffused with lesser methods of force, such as water cannons, tear gas, and soft rubber bullets (of the kind used in Northern Ireland).[427] There were also concerns

---

[416] The demonstrations and riots in the early days of the Second Intifada were studied by Amnesty International delegates, including a policing expert. They found that the Israeli security forces had tended to use military methods at first instance, rather than policing methods which prioritise the protection of human lives. 'Amnesty Report (2001)', above n 303, 15.

[417] 'Commission on Human Rights Report (2001)', above n 224, 14.

[418] There are up to 43,000 armed members of at least 11 separate security services created by the PA. 'Amnesty Report (2001)', above n 303, 15.

[419] Evidence of eyewitnesses who testified before the Human Rights Commission and international bodies place the IDF assessment in serious question. 'Commission on Human Rights Report (2001)', above n 224, 15.

[420] B'Tselem observed every demonstration that took place at Ayosh Junction in Ramallah for 10 days at the end of October 2000. See 'Illusions of Restraint, Human Rights Violations During the Events in the Occupied Territories, 29 September to 2 December 2000', (B'Tselem, December 2000) ('B'Tselem Report (2000)'). See also 'Amnesty Report (2001)', above n 303, 18.

[421] 'The response to a demonstration of hundreds of Palestinians was identical to one in which 50 Palestinians participate'. 'B'Tselem Report (2000)', above n 420.

[422] See Physicians for Human Rights Report on the violence during the Second Intifada, cited in Falk, 'International law', above n 359, 17.

[423] Amnesty International Report, *Israel and the Occupied Territories: Road to No-Where* (2006); 'Amnesty Report (2001)', above n 303, 15.

[424] Falk, 'International law', above n 359, 17.

[425] Ibid.

[426] 'Amnesty Report (2001)', above n 303, 15.

[427] 'Commission on Human Rights Report (2001)', above n 224, 15.

regarding the failure of IDF compliance with its own open-fire regulations relating to live ammunition in such circumstances.[428] In this regard, Israel failed to meet the IHL requirements of distinction and proportionality, and thereby showed a disregard for civilians in the proximity of demonstrations.

Operation Defensive Shield

As the violence of the Second Intifada intensified, the IDF responded with harsher force. In 2002, after a wave of suicide bombings, over 20,000 Israeli soldiers, accompanied by tanks, Apache helicopters, and F-16 warplanes attacked the most populous areas of the West Bank ('Operation Defensive Shield').[429] This included ground invasions of refugee camps and the military re-occupation of some territories.[430] An estimated 1500 Palestinians were killed and over 20,000 injured as a result of Israeli military assaults.[431] The fiercest fighting took place in the Jenin refugee camp. According to Israeli authorities, Jenin had become a central base for Palestinian terrorist groups and attacks.[432]

Reports from IHL groups indicate that severe violations of IHL were committed by Israel, resulting in a humanitarian crisis for civilians.[433] According to David Holley, an independent military expert: 'The military operations … appear to be carried out not for military purposes but instead to harass, humiliate, intimidate, and harm the Palestinian population'.[434] Both Amnesty International and Human Rights Watch reported that war crimes occurred in the Jenin refugee camp and in Nablus, including unlawful killings, a failure to ensure humanitarian relief and other violations.[435] A petition by Israeli Human Rights groups argued that the IDF attacked numerous civilian targets, including houses, schools, and hospitals, as confirmed by media reports, eyewitness testimonies, and the army itself.[436]

---

[428] Ibid.

[429] The Operation started early in March 2002 and lasted for several weeks. It was the largest military operation in the West Bank since the 1967 Six-Day War. The stated goal of the operation was to stop terrorist attacks.

[430] As the Second Intifada intensified, Israel began sealing off the Gaza Strip and re-occupying parts of the West Bank previously under Palestinian control.

[431] Jamjoum, above n 404, 65.

[432] The IDF spokesman attributed 23 of the 60 suicide bombers that attacked Israel in 2002 to Palestinians from Jenin. 'Suicide Bombers from Jenin' (Israel Ministry of Foreign Affairs, 2 July 2002), archived from the original on 5 July 2008.

[433] Jamjoum, above n 404, 54.

[434] See Amnesty International Report (4 November, 2002) *Israel and the Occupied Territories: The Heavy Price of Israeli Incursions* cited in ibid.

[435] Other alleged violations included the demolition of houses and property; the cutting of water and electricity to civilians; torture or other cruel treatment in arbitrary detention. ('Israel and the Occupied Territories Shielded from scrutiny: IDF violations in Jenin and Nablus') Ibid.

[436] HCJ 3022/02, *LAW*, ACRI, and *Adalah v. Commander of the Israeli Army in the West Bank, Yitzhak Eitan, and Chief of Staff of the Israeli Army, Shaul Mofaz*. https://www.adalah.org/en/content/view/7854.

Notably, the Israeli Supreme Court accepted the Israeli army's response that it was making every effort to prevent and minimise harm to civilians.[437] However, a UN Report confirmed that much of the fighting during the Operation occurred in heavily populated areas, and in many cases, heavy weaponry caused major harm to civilians.[438] Indeed, as noted above, customary IHL prohibits any attack that aims to terrorise civilians.[439] This would clearly include a military campaign of shelling Palestinian civilians in urban areas.

In this light, it seems the IDF breached fundamental IHL principles and failed to take all feasible measures to minimise harm to civilians.[440] An EU report stated: 'The massive destruction, especially at the center of the refugee camp … shows that the site had undergone an indiscriminate use of force, that goes well beyond that of a battlefield'.[441] It seems evident that Israeli patterns of force exceeded the scope of what is necessary to achieve its military goals.[442] Moreover, the IDF campaign displayed a pattern of serious human rights violations, especially the Palestinian right to life.[443] As noted above, the protection of the right to life obliges Israel to take all appropriate and necessary steps to safeguard the lives of those within its effective control.[444]

Destruction of Property

During Operation Protective Edge, the IDF demolished thousands of Palestinian houses and displaced numerous inhabitants. The shelling of residential areas and destruction of olive and citrus trees, nurtured by farmers over decades, caused enormous suffering.[445] Like others, Palestinians are deeply attached to their homes and agricultural land.[446] Destruction of private and public property is prohibited by

---

437 Ibid.

438 A UN fact-finding mission was established under UN Security Council Resolution 1405 (19 April 2002) into 'Operation Defensive Shield' following Palestinian charges of a massacre in Jenin. See UN Report of the Secretary-General prepared pursuant to General Assembly resolution ES-10/10 ('Report on Jenin'), United Nations, 30 July 2002.

439 Additional Protocol 1.

440 Gross, and Ben-Naftali, above n 312.

441 See Report on Jenin above n 428.

442 Falk, 'International law', above n 359, 17.

443 *ICCPR* art 6(1).

444 The ICJ affirmed the applicability of the *ICCPR* during armed conflicts, stating that 'the right not arbitrarily to be deprived of one's life applies also in hostilities'. Nuclear Weapons Advisory Opinion, above n 219, [25]; UNHCR, 'Human Rights Terrorism and Counter-Terrorism', above n 218, 12–13.

445 The IDF destroyed homes and a significant amount of agricultural land, especially in Gaza, which is already land starved. 'Commission on Human Rights Report (2001)', above n 214, 16.

446 Ibid.

Article 53 of the Fourth Geneva Convention, unless it is rendered absolutely necessary for military operations.[447] The scale of the physical devastation would make this difficult to establish for Israel.[448] For many, the use of force was excessive and intimidating, in the sense that the damage to civilian property outweighed military gain.[449]

Under Article 56 of the Fourth Geneva Convention, Israel is also bound to maintain public health infrastructure as an occupying power.[450] During the period, commercial and public health facilities were harmed,[451] including water reservoirs, electricity generators, pumping stations, telephone cables, and sewage/water treatment facilities.[452] According to the UNRWA, several Palestinian communities reported severe, continuous water shortages, and an accumulation of garbage that increased the risk of epidemics.[453] Such destruction of property by the IDF violates fundamental provisions of IHL.

Targeted Killings

> *If anyone has committed or is planning to carry out terrorist attacks, he has to be hit … It is effective, precise and just.* (Ephraim Sneh, Israeli Deputy Minister of Defense, 2001[454])

The Second Intifada heralded a policy of targeted killings. Attacking Palestinian leaders by missile or sniper became publicly defended by Israel at the highest levels.[455] Although the Israeli practice only caused a small number of deaths,[456] it

---

447 '*Any destruction by the Occupying Power of real or personal property belonging individually or collectively to private persons, or to the State, or to other public authorities, or to social or cooperative organizations, is prohibited, except where such destruction is rendered absolutely necessary by military operations*'.

448 Gross and Ben-Naftali, above n 312.

449 The UN Human Rights Commission concluded that the IDF has engaged in the excessive use of force at the expense of life and property in Palestine.'Commission on Human Rights Report (2001)', above n 224, 16; See also ibid.

450 '*To the fullest extent of the means available to it, the public Occupying Power has the duty of ensuring and maintaining … the medical and hospital establishments and services, public health and hygiene in the occupied territory …*'.

451 Gross, and Ben-Naftali, above n 312.

452 Jamjoum, above n 404, 64.

453 Ibid.

454 This comment was made in January 2001 cited in 'Commission on Human Rights Report (2001)', above n 214, 17 [53]–[55].

455 On 4 July 2001 a policy of 'active defence', involving 'intercepting terrorists' was announced by the Israeli security cabinet in ibid; see also 'Amnesty Report (2001)', above n 303, 25.

456 Targeted killings during the Second Intifada officially number at least 11, but the figure is probably somewhere between 25 and 35. 'Commission on Human Rights Report (2001)', above n 214, 18 [58]; 'Amnesty Report (2001)', above n 303, 26.

played an integral part in the cycle of violence.[457] Again and again, Israel responded to Palestinian terrorism, followed by yet another retaliatory attack.[458] Hamas leaders were common targets of such operations. One prominent example involved Salah Shehadeh, head of the Hamas' military wing in Gaza. On 23 July 2002, an Israeli missile razed his three-storey apartment building and adjacent structures to the ground.[459] Fourteen other persons were killed including a number of children.[460] Targeted killings often caused civilian casualties, with bystanders making up at least 30–35% of those killed in such attacks.[461]

The legality of targeted killings is hotly debated. In a 2001 Report, the U.N. HRC concluded that the measure breached customary human rights standards.[462] For Human Rights Watch: '... this is in essence a policy of killing without public accountability. The PM of Israel is effectively acting as prosecutor, judge, and jury ...'.[463] Indeed, several human rights instruments affirm the right to life and prohibit executing civilians without trial and/or judicial process.[464] Given the likely existence of an armed conflict during the period, IHL standards are also crucial.[465] Thus, many reports claim that targeted killings constitute 'wilful killings' of civilians which amount to grave breaches of the Fourth Geneva Convention (Article 147).[466]

On this view, Palestinian victims of Israeli strikes cannot be military targets because they do not take 'a direct part in hostilities' as required by Article 51(3) of Additional Protocol I.[467] However, Israel defends the practice as lawful warfare against legitimate targets.[468] According to the State, the victims of targeted killings

[457] Commission on Human Rights Report (2001) above n 214, 17 [53]–[55]; 'Amnesty Report (2001)', above n 303, 25.

[458] Casey, above n 287, 316.

[459] Peter Hermann, 'Mideast's Bitter Cycle of Attacks Renewed; Palestinians Vow Revenge for Hamas Leader's Death; 15 Die in Israeli 'Targeted Killing' *Baltimore Sun*, 14 July 2002, Al, cited in ibid 317.

[460] Ibid.

[461] Margot Dudkevitch, 'Halutz Says Targeted Killings Have 85% Success Rate', *Jerusalem Post*, 25 June 2003, 2; Palestinian Centre for Human Rights, *Statistics: Three Years of al-Aqsa Intifada* http://pchrgaza.org/special/statisics.htm.

[462] 'Commission on Human Rights Report (2001)', above n 224, 19 [61]–[63].

[463] Jamjoum, above n 404, 66.

[464] *ICCPR* arts 6, 14; UDHR arts 3, 10.

[465] Arguably, because the law of occupation and IHL also apply, these provisions are *lex specialis* and therefore take precedence over human rights and/or fill in the gaps of human rights law. 'Commission on Human Rights Report (2001)', above n 214, 19 [61]–[63].

[466] Ibid; See also Article 8 of the Rome Statute of the ICC defining war crimes as including grave breaches of the Geneva Conventions.

[467] Under Additional Protocol 1 art 51(3), civilians are protected 'unless and for such time as they take a direct part in the hostilities'.

[468] Targeted Killing Case, above n 223 [127]–[137].

have lost their civilian status by taking a direct part in hostilities.[469] For Israel, this includes those actively aiding and abetting Palestinian militants, or those planning, launching, and commanding attacks on Israeli citizens.[470] This reading was largely endorsed by the Israeli HCJ.[471] In this light, targeted killings comply with IHL norms.

The nature of the violence in this period makes interpreting 'taking a direct part in hostilities' difficult. After all, suicide attackers blur the principle of distinction, and defy conventional warfare. Though they dress and behave as civilians, most of the individuals targeted by Israel served as military commanders in the field and described themselves as such.[472] Given these complex realities, there is therefore some merit to a broader reading of Article 51(3).

On the other hand, targeting individuals in their cars, homes, or mosques when they are not engaged in armed conflict at the time of the attack is legally fraught.[473] There is scant support for such a practice,[474] which risks releasing Israel from its international duties.[475] Concern also exists around a lack of procedural safeguards to constrain the IDF.[476] Finally, by causing harm to civilian bystanders, the policy risks violating the principle of proportionality.[477] In many cases, the IDF had prior knowledge of the presence of civilians in its targeted operations.[478] Many attacks were

---

[469] Ibid [11], [138]; Israel argues that '[i]nternational law in general and the law of armed conflict in particular recognizes that individuals who directly take part in hostilities cannot then claim immunity from attack or protection as innocent civilians'. See Israeli MFA website, Palestinian Violence and Terrorism.

[470] Targeted Killing Case, above n 223 [12] (President Barak).

[471] Ibid.

[472] Israel's other targets are those who gather intelligence and who provide weapons, effectively supporting those targets who are for all intents and purposes military commanders. See Michelle Lesh, 'Case Notes: The Public Committee Against Torture in Israel v The Government of Israel - The Israeli HCJ Targeted Killing Decision' (2007) 8 *Melbourne Journal of International Law* 373, 397.

[473] It is worth recalling that taking part in hostilities only causes a temporary loss of protection. For example, killing militants when they are not posing an imminent threat to lives, when driving a car or exiting a mosque is prohibited. See Arzt, 'Can Law Halt the Violence?' above n 240, 361; Casey, above n 287, 337.

[474] There is no legal foundation in IHL for killing individuals on the basis of suspicion or even based on their prior menacing activities or possible future undertakings. 'Commission on Human Rights Report (2001)', above n 214, 19 [61]–[63].

[475] Ibid; Lesh, above n 472, 397.

[476] The legal guidelines are self-applied by the IDF, depending upon the accuracy of Israeli intelligence and upon good faith in limiting such tactics to circumstances of an exceptional character. 'Commission on Human Rights Report (2001)', above n 214, 18–19, [55], [61]–[63].

[477] *PCATI* (2006) HCJ 769/02, Reply Brief on Behalf of the Appellants (8 July 2003) [206], available from http://www.stoptorture.org.il at 18 October 2007 ('Appellants' Reply Brief').

[478] For example, the IDF noted that the attack on Hamas leader Shehadeh proceeded despite Israeli intelligence showing that his wife was present at the time and place of the attack. Dudkevitch, above n 451, 2.; Palestinian Centre for Human Rights, *Statistics: Three Years of al-Aqsa Intifada* http://pchrgaza.org/special/statisics.htm.

conducted in crowded urban spaces with a high likelihood of civilian casualties.[479] To the extent that targeted killing attacks were disproportionate, they constitute war crimes.

Collective Punishment

Throughout the Second Intifada, Israel used movement restrictions, house demolitions and mass arrests to combat Palestinian violence. Israel has justified these measures as reasonable and lawful security imperatives.[480] For Palestinians however, the closures and accompanying restrictions reflect a policy of collective punishment.[481] Ultimately, Israeli actions led to enormous hardship for Palestinian civilians. In economic terms, the Second Intifada devastated Palestinian society with high unemployment and poverty.[482] This section considers the legacy of human rights abuse with a collective and punitive dimension.

Movement Restrictions

The Second Intifada caused an unprecedent tightening of borders.[483] Palestinians were regularly subjected to daily curfews, road closures, and movement within the territories was curtailed. This intricate system included physical obstacles (checkpoints, roadblocks, the Wall[484]) and administrative restrictions (prohibited roads and

[479] Casey, above n 287, 341.

[480] Israel believes that its security measures, including border and road closures, represent reasonable, even restrained, measures of response to Palestinian violence. 'Commission on Human Rights Report (2001)', above n 224, 8; Ibid 9.

[481] Ibid 9.

[482] The Second Intifada devastated the Palestinian economy. For example, prior to the hostilities more than 150,000 Palestinians worked daily within Israel. By 2005, that number became less than 35,000. Under the stress of the Second Intifada the 'PA has fragmented, losing much of its ability to provide law and order and allowing more extreme groups to increase their autonomy and popular support'. Steven Erlanger, 'Intifada's Legacy at Year 4: A Morass of Faded Hopes' *New York Times* (New York) 3 October 2004, 16.

[483] The movement restrictions imposed on Palestinians during the Second Intifada were unprecedented in their nature and length. B'Tselem, *Civilians Under Siege: Restrictions on Freedom of Movement as Collective Punishment* (January 2001) https://www.btselem.org/publications/summaries/200101_civilians_under_siege; Jamjoum, above n 414, 58.

[484] Israel's security barrier (which Israel claims is to prevent suicide bombers) encircles the Israeli settlements and further restricts Palestinian freedom of movement. In some areas, it also separates Palestinian traders and farmers from their livelihoods. In 2004, the ICJ ruled that the barrier was illegal to the extent that it crosses the Green Line and violates human rights of the Palestinians. See ICJ, 'Advisory Wall Opinion', above n 119.

permit requirements).[485] *B'Tselem* described the impact of such restrictions on every aspect of Palestinian daily life.[486] They had a devastating effect on the economy, bringing two thirds of the population below the poverty line.[487] Israel also restricted Palestinian patients, health personnel, medical supplies, and humanitarian aid.[488] From 2002, preventing or hindering access to emergency medical facilities became a common occurrence.[489] Numerous reports document delayed medical care.[490] Denying Palestinians' freedom of movement constitutes a prima facie breach of the ICCPR (Article 12).[491] It also violates the ICSECR by causing severe socio-economic harm, potentially breaching the Palestinian right to a livelihood (Article 6), and acceptable standard of living (Article 11).[492]

Moreover, travel restrictions on those seeking acute medical care also contravene basic IHL norms. Articles 17 and 56 of the Fourth Geneva Convention require medical professionals and the sick open passage during conflict.[493] On several occasions, Israeli roadblocks hindered the delivery of medical supplies and humanitarian aid. Such actions violate Article 55 of the Fourth Geneva Convention.[494]

Israel has invoked security considerations to justify these restrictions. For example, the IDF's stated reason for curfews is that they are imposed not as punishment, but to stop attacks or in the search for a 'terrorist' cell.[495] The Israeli Supreme Court tends to accept this position and has confirmed that Israeli forces are lawfully entitled to prevent Palestinian free movement in the territories for security reasons.[496] On 8 April 2002, the Court rejected an appeal requesting an end to the siege and

---

[485] B'Tselem, *Restrictions on Movement* (11 November 2017) https://www.btselem.org/freedom_of_movement.

[486] B'Tselem, above n 637. See also Lama Jamjoum, above n 414, 58.

[487] 'Commission on Human Rights Report (2001)', above n 224, 24; See also Gross and Ben-Naftali, above n 312.

[488] Jamjoum, above n 414, 58.

[489] 'Commission on Human Rights Report (2001)', above n 224, 16.

[490] B'Tselem and the Israeli Physicians for Human Rights compiled a partial list of patients who died or developed complications due to movement restrictions. Available at https://www.btselem.org/sites/default/files/sites/default/files2/publication/200203_medical_treatment_eng.pdf; Jamjoum, above n 414, 60.

[491] '*Everyone has the right to freedom of movement and residence within the borders of each state*'.

[492] B'Tselem, *Restrictions on Movement: Effect of Restrictions on the Economy*; 'Commission on Human Rights Report (2001)', above n 224, 27.

[493] Medical personnel, including physicians and nurses, have been unable to reach their places of work regularly since the beginning of the intifada 'Infringement of the Right to Medical Treatment'. 'B'Tselem Report (2000)', above n 420.

[494] See Jamjoum, above n 414, 60.

[495] 'Amnesty Report (2001)', above n 303, 53.

[496] HCJ 2941/02, *Badia Ra'ik Suabta and LAW v. Commander of the Israeli Army in the West Bank*; and HCJ 2936/02, *Physicians for Human Rights-Israel v Commander of the Israeli Army in the West Bank*, decision delivered 8 April 2002.

attacks on emergency medical teams.[497] It stated that the Palestinian misuse of medical cover, hospitals, and ambulances obliges the IDF to act in order to prevent such unlawful activity.[498]

Whilst in some instances, security may justify temporary closures, the character and timing of the restrictions involved punitive elements.[499] During most of the period, Israel imposed a comprehensive closure and siege on millions of Palestinians, rather than on individuals posing an imminent threat.[500] According to *B'Tselem*, these measures practically imprisoned Palestinians within their own communities and were continuously enforced.[501] Numerous curfews lasted for many days after arrests had been made in respect of an incident.[502] Movement restrictions were also imposed exclusively on Palestinians. In many cases, their explicit aim was to ensure freedom of movement for the Israeli settler population at the expense of local Palestinians.[503] To claim a purely security rationale for such policies is unpersuasive.

House Demolitions

Israel imposed a policy of house demolitions during the Second Intifada.[504] This involved the destruction of a suspected terrorist's residence after lethal attacks against Israelis.[505] The rationale is that suicide bombers will be deterred if they know that their actions could harm their family's home.[506] Between October 2001

---

[497] Ibid.

[498] Ibid.

[499] 'Commission on Human Rights Report (2001)', above n 224, 24.

[500] Ibid.

[501] B'Tselem, *Civilians Under Siege*, above n 483; Jamjoum, above n 414, 58.

[502] For example, Palestinians in Hebron were under curfew almost continuously since October 2000. Theoretically, a curfew should cease as soon as suspected perpetrators have been arrested. Curfews should be imposed only in extreme circumstances and as a last resort. 'Commission on Human Rights Report (2001)', above n 214, 24; 'Amnesty Report (2001)', above n 303, 53.

[503] Ibid.

[504] House demolitions resumed after a 4-year stoppage by Israel. B'Tselem, *Through No Fault of Their Own: Punitive House Demolitions during the al-Aqsa Intifada* (November 2004) https://www.btselem.org/download/200411_punitive_house_demolitions_eng.pdf. ('B'Tselem, House Demolition Report').

[505] An internal Israeli review starting in October 2004 brought an end to the policy, but it was resumed in 2014. See Ed Farrian, *Human Rights Issues for the Palestinian population* (07 April 2005) Ministry of Foreign Affairs https://mfa.gov.il/mfa/aboutisrael/state/law/pages/human%20rights%20issues%20for%20the%20palestinian%20population%20-%20april%202005.aspx; Amichai, Cohen and Yuval Shany, 'House Demolition at Israeli Supreme Court: Recent Developments' *Lawfare* (online), 14 January 2019 https://www.lawfareblog.com/house-demolition-israeli-supreme-court-recent-developments.

[506] Ibid.

and January 2005, the IDF demolished around 668 Palestinian houses.[507] According to B'Tselem, they housed around 4000 persons and were demolished because of the acts of 333 Palestinians.[508] Human rights groups claim Palestinian occupants are rarely given prior warning of the demolition.[509]

Collective penalties and/or retaliatory measures are prohibited under Articles 33 of the Fourth Geneva Convention. Moreover, extensive destruction of property in occupied territories, without military necessity constitutes war crimes.[510] In addition, house demolitions contravene human rights standards. The Human Rights Committee deplored the measure for offending the ICCPR, particularly the right to freedom from arbitrary interference with one's home (Article 17) and the freedom to choose one's residence (Article 12).[511] The policy may also constitute a form of cruel, inhuman, and degrading punishment (Article 7).[512]

Nevertheless, Israel's HCJ accepts the claim that house demolitions are an effective deterrent.[513] According to the Court, the focus on deterrence and not retribution, proves that the measure is not aimed to punish; and cannot be regarded as collective punishment.[514] This characterisation seems unpersuasive. Deterrence is one of the declared goals of any criminal punishment, and the fact that a certain measure is primarily intended to deter does not negate its capacity to punish.[515] Indeed, the policy is directed at family members residing in their homes, and not at the terrorists themselves. In this regard, the measure clearly constitutes collective punishment.

---

[507] For statistics on homes demolished as an act of collective punishment, see 'B'Tselem, House Demolition Report', above n 494 and http://www.btselem.org/english/Punitive_Demolitions/Statistics.asp. These figures do not include the number of houses sealed or partially sealed, nor those demolished for other rationales, such as the alleged military reasons. See generally B'Tselem, *Demolition for Alleged Military Purposes* http://www.btselem.org/english/Razing/Statistics.asp.

[508] B'Tselem also claims that almost half of the homes demolished were never home to anyone suspected of involvement in attacks against Israelis. For statistics see B'Tselem, *House Demolition Report*, above n 494.

[509] Ibid; Israel claims that prior warning is given except in extraordinary. Cases. See HCJ 2977/02, *Adalah and LAW v Commander of the Israeli Army in the West Bank*, decision delivered 9 April 2002.

[510] Under Article 147, extensive destruction of property without military necessity is considered a 'grave breach' of the Geneva Conventions.

[511] The Human Rights Committee examined Israel's report on its implementation of the *ICCPR* in 1998, stated that it deplores the demolition of Palestinian homes as a means of punishment. CCPR/C/79/Add.93, [24]; 'Amnesty Report (2001)', above n 303, 54.

[512] Cohen and Shany, above n 505.

[513] The legality of house demolitions has been discussed by Israel's HCJ hundreds of times. See particularly HCJ 2977/02, *Adalah and LAW v Commander of the Israeli Army in the West Bank*, decision delivered 9 April 2002. Most recently in 2018, the HCJ issued three judgments on this issue: HCJ 6905/18 *Naji v IDF Commander of the West Bank*; HCJ 7961/18 *Na'alawa v IDF Commander of the West Bank*; HCJ 7961/18 *Jabbarin v IDF Commander of the West Bank*.

[514] Ibid.

[515] Cohen and Shany, above n 505.

Mass Arrests and Detention

Finally, several thousands of Palestinians were arrested and detained. During Operation Protective Edge alone Israeli forces arrest over 4000 Palestinians.[516] According to Amnesty International, a typical pattern of arrests in 2002 included Israeli forces calling, by loudspeaker, all male Palestinians between certain ages (usually 15 and 45) to report at an assembly point.[517] Some were immediately released, but most were blindfolded and handcuffed with plastic handcuffs.[518] Most of those arrested received no food for the first 24 h, were not allowed to go to toilets or afforded blankets.[519] Many Palestinians arrested were denied access to legal counsel.[520] Conducted in this manner, mass arrests constitute a form of cruel, inhuman, and degrading punishment (Article 7, ICCPR).[521]

Israel also administratively detained hundreds of Palestinians.[522] By the end of 2002, the number had reached more than 1000.[523] Administrative detention[524] is a potential breach of Article 10 of the UDHR and Article 14 of the ICCPR that confers Palestinians with the right to fair trial. The resort to such an expansive detention regime is justified by Israel as a 'state of emergency' necessity.[525] Israel defends its conduct by reference to the Fourth Geneva Convention, according to which a civilian may be interned or placed in assigned residence if 'the security of the detaining Power makes it absolutely necessary' or for 'imperative reasons of security'.[526]

No doubt, detention, and mass arrests arise from Israel's desire to protect the public's safety and national security concerns. Nevertheless, administrative detention is an 'extreme' measure that must be applied carefully, and in rare exceptions.

---

516 'Operation Defensive Shield (2002)' *Ynetnews* (online), 12 March 2009 https://www.ynetnews.com/articles/0,7340,L-3685678,00.html.

517 See Amnesty International, 'Israel and the Occupied Territories: The Heavy Price of Israeli Incursions' (2002) http://www.web.amnesty.org/.

518 Ibid.

519 Ibid.

520 Jamjoum, above n 414, 65.

521 Cohen and Shany, above n 505.

522 Israel's use of administrative detention is based on the British Mandate 1945 Defence (Emergency) Regulations which became the Israeli Law on Authority in States of Emergency. Administrative detention is for 6-month terms, although they can be extended barring appeal.

523 European Parliament, *Israel's Policy of Administrative Detention Policy Briefing*, (May 2012) 12; See also B'Tselem, *Statistics on Administrative Detention* (3 April 2019) https://www.btselem.org/administrative_detention/statistics.

524 'Administrative detention' is a term that covers the arrest and detention of individuals without charge or trial, usually for security reasons.

525 See *ICCPR*, UN treaty Collection, stating Israel's reservations to the Covenant, cited in Shiri Krebs, 'Lifting the Veil of Secrecy: Judicial Review of Administrative Detentions in the Israeli Supreme Court' (2012) 45(3) *Vanderbilt Journal of Transnational Law* 639, 655.

526 *Fourth Geneva Convention* arts 42, 78.

The Israeli HCJ has confirmed that it must only be used for prevention and never for punitive purposes, and only when the danger is posed by the individual person under detention.[527] However, Israel used this measure extensively and routinely during the period.[528] Thousands of Palestinians were arrested and even incarcerated without being convicted or even charged for lengthy periods of time.[529] Arguably, the alleged danger posed by hundreds of Palestinians could have been prevented through criminal proceedings, or an administrative measure less injurious to human rights.[530] In this regard, Israeli practices did not adequately respect the principle of proportionality.[531]

Conclusion

In the final analysis, it seems clear that the heavy-handedness and routine practice of closures, house demolitions and arrests were used punitively against an entire Palestinian population.[532] In this regard, they constitute human rights violations and violate Article 33 of the Fourth Geneva Convention, which prohibits collective punishment.

Israeli Self-Defence Claims

As discussed in Chap. 1, Israeli justifications for violence against Palestinians have deep existential and historical roots traceable to the conflict's genesis. In particular, the insecurity generated by suicide attacks translated into wide support for harsh Israeli responses during the Second Intifada.[533] For example, a study conducted during the period found that 72% of Israeli–Jews believed that greater military force

---

[527] See HCJ 3239/02 *Marab v IDF Commander* in the W Bank 57(2) PD 349, paras. 21–24 [2002] (Isr.); HCJ 7/48 *Al-Karbuteli v Minister of Def.* 2(1) PD 5, 97 [1949–50] (Isr.) (emphasizing the severity of this measure, which harms basic human rights, while accepting its necessity during states of emergency, [13]); see also HCJ 5784/03 *Salama v IDF Commander in Judea and Samaria* 57(6) PD 721, [7] [2003] (Isr.).

[528] B'Tselem, *Statistics on Administrative Detention*, above n 523.

[529] Ibid.

[530] HCJ 7015/02 *Ajuri v IDF Commander in Judea & Samaria* 56(6) PD 352, para. 25 [2002] (Isr.) (quoting HCJ 5667/91 *Jabarin v Commander of Military Forces in the W. Bank* 46(1) PD 858, 860 [1991] (Isr.)) ('There must be an objective relationship—a proper relativity or proportionality—between the forbidden act of the individual and the measures adopted by the Government').

[531] Ibid.

[532] 'Amnesty Report (2001)', above n 303, 61.

[533] For example, the Israeli public overwhelmingly supports the house-demolition policy. A survey conducted in 2018 by the Israeli Democracy Institute found that over 90% of Jews in Israel support the policy. Cohen and Shany, above n 505.

should be used against Palestinians.[534] On the international stage, Israel justified its use of force and 'counter-terrorist' measures as self-defence. It argued that the Israeli state can defend itself against 'armed attacks' under Article 51 of the UN Charter.[535] This legal claim is bolstered by a view that Palestinians are responsible for terrorist attacks and that unlawful aggression forced the IDF to respond.[536] It has also been argued that targeted killings are acts of anticipatory self-defence.[537] For Rivkin and Casey law-abiding states could use such force to protect themselves.[538]

No doubt, terrorist attacks present great challenges to states. Clearly, Israeli forces have a right to take measures that prevent and deter such violence, and are bound to protect individuals within their jurisdiction.[539] Israel is also entitled to consider its own security interests as an occupying power.[540] At the same time, the UN Charter is an uncertain basis for Israeli force.[541] Arguably, Article 51 only permits a state to respond to an attack by another state and cannot be invoked by an occupying power against militants.[542] The ICJ opined that Israel had effective

---

[534] *Peace Index* (March 2001) as quoted in Bar-Tal and Sharvit, above n 170, 185. Another study shows that during the 4 years of the Intifada between 60% and 70% of Israeli Jews supported every military operation initiated by Israel.

[535] Targeted Killing Case, above n 223 [10] (President Barak).

[536] See Israel's Response to the Report Submitted by the Special Rapporteur on the Right to Food, submitted to the Commission on Human Rights, 60th Sess, E/CN.4/2004/G/14, 5, 6 (26 November 2003) (indicating the Rapporteur's failure to take account of the Palestinians' responsibility for the encouragement of terror attacks against Israel, which form the basis of Israel's actions taken in self-defence).

[537] J Nicholas Kendall, 'Recent Development, Israeli Counter Terrorism: "Targeted Killings" Under International Law' (2002) 80 *North Carolina Law Review* 1069; Benjamin A Gorelick, 'Current Development, The Israeli Response to Palestinian Breach of the Oslo Agreement' (2003) 9 *New England Journal of International and Comparative Law* 651, 665.

[538] David B. Rivkin et al, 'Suicide Attacks are War Crimes, Targeted Killings Are Not' *Jerusalem Post*, 8 November 2002; Casey, above n 287, 341.

[539] Human rights law has recognized that, in specific circumstances, States have a positive obligation to take preventive operational measures to protect those at risk from the criminal acts of another, which certainly includes terrorists. See European Court of Human Rights, *Kiliç v Turkey*, No 22492/93, Judgement of 28 March 2000, [62]. See also Inter-American Court of Human Rights, *Velásquez Rodríguez v Honduras*, Judgement of 29 July 1988, [174]; UNHCR, 'Human Rights Terrorism and Counter-Terrorism', above n 218, 8.

[540] Ben-Naftali, Gross, and Michaeli, above n 124, 590.

[541] According to Benvenisti, there were areas in the Palestinian territories that were no longer 'effectively controlled' by Israel during the Second Intifada and would have enabled Israel used to force on the basis of self-defence. Eyal Benvenisti, 'Israel and the Palestinians: What Laws Were Broken?' in *Crimes of War*, 8 May 2002.

[542] In the Targeted Killings Case, the petitioners' argued that Israel could not use military force in the context of self-defence according to art 51 of the Charter of the United Nations in occupied territories. See Targeted Killing Case, above n 223 [14] (President Barak).

control over the territories in the Second Intifada and therefore could not use force in self-defence.[543]

Moreover, even if Israel had a right to self-defence, that right was not unlimited. Israel was obliged to follow IHL when engaging in armed conflict with militants.[544] Even force undertaken in self-defence, or against Palestinian aggression,[545] must respect international legal norms.[546] As noted in the ICJ Wall Opinion: '… those engaged in conflict … must, whatever the provocation, fight "with one hand [tied] behind their back" …'.[547] As discussed above, Israel however did not combat Palestinian violence with reasonable force. In both military campaigns and against demonstrations, Israel used severe measures and force that went beyond defensive action.[548] Acts in self-defence must only be motivated by self-preservation, and not political coercion or intimidation.[549] As discussed above, Israeli policies were also collective and punitive in character. In this regard, it is difficult to legally excuse Israeli conduct as mere acts of self-defence.

Israeli Impunity?

International criminal law requires perpetrators and their commanders to be held accountable for war crimes or crimes against humanity.[550] Indeed, there is no statute of limitations for such acts.[551] Nevertheless, it seems that Israel has failed to meaningfully investigate and prosecute commanders and soldiers for violations committed during the period. Except for a handful of cases, the IDF has not taken any serious steps to investigate its soldiers.[552] The fact that there was only one soldier

---

543 See ICJ, 'Advisory Wall Opinion', above n 113, [77]: According to Canor: 'Just as a state cannot argue self-defence against its own people, so, too, a state cannot argue self-defence against residents living under the occupation of its army'. Canor, above n 147, 140.

544 Casey, above n 287, 342; Saul, 'Defending Terrorism', above n 355, 188.

545 Defensive action against aggression is not a valid justification for breaches of IHL. Cassese, *International Criminal Law*, above n 218, 223; Casey, above n 287, 339.

546 As stated in the ICJ Nuclear Weapons Opinion, customary IHL is 'intransgressible'. Acts of self-defence must respect necessity and proportionality requirements. See Nuclear Weapons Advisory Opinion, above n 219, [79]; Casey, above n 287, 342; Saul, 'Defending Terrorism', above n 355, 214.

547 ICJ, 'Advisory Wall Opinion', above n 119 (separate opinion of Judge Higgins) [14].

548 An act remains defensive as long as it is a reasonable and proportionate response to imminent and unlawful force. Indiscriminate attacks on civilians can never be defensive. Saul, 'Defending Terrorism', above n 355, 203–204.

549 Ibid.

550 Leaders who order such crimes, who fail to take reasonable preventive action, or punish perpetrators are also responsible.'HRW Report (2002)', above n 224, 57–8.

551 Individuals who plan, organize, order, assist, commit, or attempt to commit them can be prosecuted at any time, as can those with command responsibility for such acts. Ibid.

552 'Commission on Human Rights Report (2001)', above n 224, 17, [52].

convicted for indiscriminate force during the Second Intifada, and then only sentenced to 28 days of imprisonment, attests to a culture of impunity.[553] Indeed, during the violence, the IDF designated many areas as 'closed military zones', barring access to journalists and denying access to NGOs, as well as to a UN fact-finding mission.[554] There were also claims that Israeli settlers killed and attacked Palestinians without legal recourse.[555] Overall, scarce accountability measures arising out of Operation Defensive Shield[556] and other Israeli practices cast doubt over the state's willingness to scrutinise its policies and leaders, as well as investigate and punish offenders for unlawful conduct.

Conclusion on Second Intifada

Any meaningful reckoning with the past will need to acknowledge, or at least address the thousands of Israeli casualties of Palestinian terrorism, and the thousands of Palestinian victims of Israeli counter-terrorist measures. Ultimately, the psychological earthquake of suicide bombing is crucial for Israelis, as are the conditions that lead to the hostilities for Palestinians. Suicide bombings, rockets, and excessive Israeli force constitute serious violations of IHL and may also constitute international crimes. Concluding this does not legitimise terror as a form of warfare, nor impair the ability of law-abiding states to protect themselves.[557] However, it does imply the need to make both sides accountable under international law. It also implies the need to investigate the claims and counterclaims surrounding systemic human rights violations.[558] The desirability of specific truth-telling and justice-seeking measures to Israelis and Palestinians will be considered in subsequent chapters.

---

553 See Gross and Ben-Naftali, above n 312.

554 Israel refused to allow a UN fact-finding mission into the West Bank. Jamjoum, above n 414, 54; Ibid.

555 On many occasions, settler violence during the Second *intifada* came as a response to Palestinian attacks. According to Amnesty, since the beginning of the period at least 10 Palestinians have been killed by settlers. In none of these cases has any settler been brought to justice.'Amnesty Report (2001)', above n 303, 29.

556 According to the Legal Department of the IDF, the army only carried out three internal investigations relating to Operation Defensive Shield. These appeared to relate to killings that were widely reported nationally and internationally.'Amnesty Report (2001)', above n 303, 19–20.

557 Casey, above n 287, 342.

558 'No killing in the territories is properly investigated so the claims and counter-claims continue to reverberate'. 'Amnesty Report (2001)', above n 303, 6.

2.5 Conclusion

The legacies of abuse arising from the Israeli–Palestinian conflict are substantial. They continue to haunt both nations and form part of ongoing violations and the conflict-narrative. The right of return from 1948 remains a flashpoint. As recently as 2018, the Gazan 'great march of Return' saw thousands of Palestinians demonstrating for the return of Palestinian refugees.[559] As a result of 1967, millions of Palestinians still live under a disputed international legal regime. For Israel, the occupation has created generations of soldiers at checkpoints, a complex legal and military order, and over half a million Israeli–Jews residing in settlements. For Palestinian society, the ongoing denial of collective and political rights remains an open wound.

Finally, the intensity of the Second Intifada set some enduring structural patterns of abuse. Many Israeli practices from this period, including house demolitions and administrative detention, have been reinstated.[560] Since Operation Defensive Shield, successive armed confrontations between the parties included two massive Israeli aerial and ground assaults on Gaza (Operations Cast Lead: 2008–2009 and Operation Protective Edge: 2014) while indiscriminate rocket attacks on Israel by Palestinian armed groups have continued.[561] Whilst Palestinians have abandoned suicide bombings, a new 'knife intifada' began in September 2015. Thus, indiscriminate attacks on civilians remain features of the violence. Accordingly, any engagement with transitional justice must deal with the human rights abuses entrenched by these periods. There is also the need to address a culture of impunity on both the sides. As noted above, Israelis and Palestinians insist on self-serving definitions of terrorism that legitimise the violence.

This chapter also demonstrated the international legal complexities raised by several aspects of the conflict. For example, regarding 1948, it is difficult to fashion a persuasive legal case of Palestinian return. No less complex would be attributing direct legal obligations on non-state Palestinian actors. Ultimately, international law alone is ill equipped to resolve the legacies of abuse created by the conflict. Moreover, the claims of both the nations are linked to broader demands about

[559] Between March and May 2018, thousands of Palestinians attended a non-violent march at the separation fence under the theme 'Return of a million', to draw attention to UNGA resolution 194 and to the dire humanitarian situation in Gaza. See 'HRC Report of the independent international commission of inquiry on the protests in the OPT', A/HRC/40/74, [18]–[26].

[560] The Israeli policy of house demolitions was fully reinstated in 2014, following a series of terror attacks. B'Tselem, maintains that 'over the years, Israel has held thousands of Palestinians in administrative detention for variable periods of time'. Cohen and Shany, above n 495; European Parliament, *Israel's Policy of Administrative Detention Policy Briefing*, (May 2012) 12; See also B'TSelem, *Administrative Detention Statistics*, above n 523.

[561] After 2001, Palestinians also fired Qassam missiles at targets within Israel, mostly from the Gaza Strip. Qassam attacks became more significant after 2003, causing a number of Israeli deaths and injuries as well as damage to property.

acknowledgement and legitimacy (Chap. 1) that require consideration beyond a strictly legal framework.

From this standpoint, the next two chapters consider the applicability of the transitional justice model to conflict resolution (Chap. 3), and to Israelis and Palestinians in particular (Chap. 4). They will examine the Oslo approach of conflict settlement, and the applicability of truth-telling, justice, and reconciliation to both the nations. Introducing transitional justice as a relevant dimension in peacebuilding may result in a paradigm shift and open new avenues for creative solutions to the historical and legal legacies of the conflict.

Chapter 3
Transitional Justice: 'Truth', 'Justice', and 'Reconciliation' in Conflict Resolution

3.1 Introduction

> *Successful contemporary peace building not only changes behavior but, more important, also transforms identities and institutional context. More than reforming play in the old game, it changes the game.*[1]

There is a growing interest in the desirability of truth-telling, justice-seeking discourse, and reconciliation processes to conflict resolution. Societies emerging from periods of violent conflict around the globe have considered diverse models of transitional justice and its mechanisms. This chapter highlights the significance of the transitional justice paradigm, and its capacity to apply a past-orientated retrospective as well as forward-looking restorative approach to conflict resolution. Given the centrality of history and the legacies of human rights abuse to Israelis and Palestinians, it is contended that engagement with transitional justice may play a determinative role in the resolution of the conflict, especially one that is so entangled in the politics of national identity.

As will be explored, transitional justice may serve as a relevant tool to foster truth-telling, historical justice, and reconciliation between warring nations. Introducing transitional justice as a relevant dimension in conflict resolution may result in a paradigm shift and open new avenues for imaginative and creative solutions to historical warfare.[2] In particular, this chapter will address the desirability of addressing the historical record to reckon with a nation's brutal past. It will be contended that justice-seeking discourse and human rights law are crucial to peace and conflict transformation and that reconciliation necessitates reshaping collective memory.

---

[1] Michael W Doyle, The John W. Holmes Lecture: Building Peace Global Governance 13 (2007), 1–15.

[2] Edward Kaufman, 'Human Rights Dimensions in Peace-making' in Elizabeth G Mathews, *'The Israel-Palestine Conflict' Parallel Discourses* (Routledge, 2011), 184.

J. Bracka, *Transitional Justice for Israel/Palestine*, Springer Series in Transitional Justice, https://doi.org/10.1007/978-3-030-89435-1_3

3.2 Part One: Theory and Meaning of Transitional Justice

Few concepts have gained as much momentum in recent decades as transitional justice. Whilst it remains contested, the term may be broadly described as 'a field of activity and inquiry focused on how societies address legacies of human rights abuses'.[3] Relatively quickly, it evolved into a normalised and globalised approach to countries emerging from conflict and political repression.[4] With few exceptions,[5] 'the no-action option' for such nations became either undesirable or no longer politically viable.[6] Transitional justice embodies a variety of judicial and non-judicial mechanisms from criminal prosecutions, truth commissions, and reparations programs to memorials.[7]

Tracing its origins to the Nuremberg tribunals, the field was reinvigorated in the mid-1990s as a response to democratisation in Latin America, the end of communism in Eastern Europe, and the negotiated transition in South Africa. Over the past 30 years, the practice and theory of transitional justice have consolidated the claim that meaningful 'transition' requires due regard for justice and a carefully conceived process to re-establish '... the rule of law, human rights ... address the plight of victims and provide accountability for perpetrators'.[8] In the international arena, transitional justice has crystallised into an international norm[9] and is today firmly grounded in international institutions, case law,[10] and international relations.

---

[3] Louis Bickford, 'Transitional Justice', in Dinah L. Shelton (ed.) *Encyclopedia of Genocide and Crimes Against Humanity* (Macmillan, 2004).

[4] Ruti G. Teitel, 'Transitional Justice Genealogy' (2003) 16 *Harvard Human Rights Journal* 69, 86 ('Transitional Justice Geneology').

[5] For example, both Mozambique and Northern Ireland decided against official measures confronting their pasts. The Mozambican 1992 Accord has no explicit provision on dealing with the past. The Northern Ireland Good Friday Accord is also lacking in specific transitional justice provisions with the exception of prisoner releases. Naomi Roht-Arriaza, 'Transitional Justice and Peace Agreements Working Paper' (2005) *Peace Agreements: The Role of Human Rights in Negotiations* 1–21, 5.

[6] ICTJ Fact Sheet, 'What is Transitional Justice' (2009) https://www.ictj.org/about/transitional-justice.

[7] The ICTJ stresses the importance of incorporating as many of the five approaches as possible because one alone may be insufficient. Ibid.

[8] Christian Tomuschat, 'Darfur, Compensation, for the Victims' (2005) 3 *Journal of International Criminal Justice* 579, 580–581. Tomuschat notes the value of transitional justice was acknowledged by the Security Council in UNSC Res. 1593, 31 March 2005, on Darfur in response to the Report of the International Commission of Inquiry on Darfur (the Commission) of 25 January 2005.

[9] See Jelena Subotić, *Hijacked Justice: Dealing with the Past in the Balkans* (Cornell University Press, 2016); Christine Bell, 'The "New Law" of Transitional Justice' in Kai Ambos, Judith Large and Marieke Wierda (eds.), *Building a Future on Peace and Justice: Studies on Transitional Justice, Conflict Resolution and Development: the Nuremberg Declaration on Peace and Justice* (Springer Verlag, 2009).

[10] Part of the legal basis for transitional justice is the 1988 *Velásquez Rodríguez* decision of the Inter-American Court of Human Rights, in which the court found that all states have four fundamental human rights obligations: to take reasonable steps to prevent human rights violations, to

Despite its proliferation and popularity, transitional justice remains an elusive and negotiable term. This is because the field is a relatively new, practice-driven, and inter-disciplinary one that defies a common theoretical language.[11] Notably, Teitel coined the term transitional justice '… as the conception of justice associated with periods of political change, characterized by legal responses to confront the wrong doing of repressive predecessor regimes'.[12] The International Center for Transitional Justice (ICTJ) defines transitional justice more broadly, as a 'process' that 'seeks recognition for victims and to promote possibilities for peace, reconciliation, and democracy'.[13] While some argue for a more narrowly defined concept limited to state-centred tools that operate during a specific transition period and focusing on legal aspects of violence,[14] others argue for a thicker understanding of transitional justice, in which 'dealing with the past' is not limited to fixed transitional periods or juridical mechanisms.[15]

In sum, the term 'transitional justice' will be used throughout this thesis in its widest conception,[16] to include all concerted efforts to redress gross human rights abuse as a result of large-scale political conflict. In the ensuing chapters, it will be submitted that the norms, lessons, and lexicon of transitional justice may apply to civil society contexts, as well as situations like the Israeli–Palestinian one, which fall short of a clear-cut post-conflict transition. It is this broader understanding of transitional justice that is relied upon in this dissertation. As will be discussed in Chaps. 4 and 5, the particular focus of transitional justice in the Israeli–Palestinian conflict is its role and normative value in ongoing conflict.

Although no consensus exists on meaning, the ideas of transitional justice used by international institutions and NGOs are largely based on common assumptions, goals, and normative underpinnings. Many of the basic elements of 'dealing with

---

conduct a serious investigation of violations when they occur, to impose suitable sanctions on those responsible for the violations, and to ensure reparation for the victims of the violations *Velásquez Rodríguez v. Honduras*, Inter-American Court Human Right (Ser. C) No. 4 (1988) ('*Velásquez Rodríguez case*'); See also ICTJ Fact Sheet, above n 6.

[11] For a detailed theoretical discussion, see Susanne Buckley-Zistel et al. (eds), *Transitional Justice Theories* (Routledge, 2014); Colleen Murphy The Conceptual Foundations of Transitional Justice (Cambridge University Press, 2017). See also Hakeem O. Yusuf *Transitional Justice, Judicial Accountability and the Rule of Law* (Routledge, 2010) Neil J. Kritz (ed) *Transitional Justice: How Emerging Democracies Reckon with Former Regimes (United States Institute of Peace Press, 1995).*

[12] Teitel, *Transitional Justice Genealogy*, above n 4, 69.

[13] ICTJ Fact Sheet, above n 6.

[14] See Colm Campbell, Fionnula Ni Aolain, and Harvey Colin 'The Frontiers Legal Analysis: Reframing the Transition in Northern Ireland' (2003) (66) *Modern Law Review* 317–45 ('*The Frontiers Legal Analysis*'); Christine Bell, 'Transitional Justice, Interdisciplinarity and the State of the "Field" or "Non-Field"' (2009) 3(1) *International Journal of Transitional Justice* 5–27.

[15] Kieran McEvoy, 'Beyond Legalism: Towards a Thicker Understanding of Transitional Justice' (2007) 34(4) *Journal of Law and Society* 411–440; See also Ron Dudai, 'A Model for Dealing with the Past in the Israeli-Palestinian Context' (2007) 1 *International Journal of Transitional Justice* 249; Rafi Nets-Zehngut, 'Transitional Justice and Addressing the History of Active Conflicts: The Case of the Israeli-Palestinian Conflict' (2011) (Unpublished) 1–27, 3.

[16] Roht-Arriaza, above n 5, 1.

the past', such as truth, justice, reconciliation, reparations, and institutional reforms share common threads and promote a very similar meaning of transitional justice. Most theorists and policy-makers resolutely defend the notion of 'dealing with the past' as the unique characteristic.[17] At its core, transitional justice embodies a liberal notion of progressive history,[18] a 'redemptive model in which the harms of the past may be repaired' in order to counter impunity and usher in the rule of law and a culture of human rights.[19] In short, the past is viewed through the prism of moving forward. Transitional justice discourse so defined is thus future-orientated as well as retrospective, and generally '... favors recognition, restitution, and reconciliation over retribution'.[20] This concept has been quickly adopted by the peace-building community and today constitutes an integral part of the liberal peace-building model.[21]

A 'Holistic' Menu of Measures

Transitional justice measures have become an almost automatic response to periods of human rights violations. Offering hope of recovery from conflict, they have been instituted in countries as diverse as Colombia, Canada, Morocco, and Australia. Indeed, the term 'transitional justice' has become synonymous with a wide category of legal and extra-legal mechanisms. Thus, in South Africa, truth-telling and reconciliation garnered enormous attention through the SATRC. In other cases, like the former Yugoslavia and Rwanda, international criminal prosecutions dominated transitional justice efforts. In this light, transitional justice is also 'a set of practices, mechanisms and concerns' that deal systematically with grave human rights abuses.[22]

Thus, a variety of tools are available for both victims and victimisers, which could theoretically apply to the Israeli–Palestinian conflict. The promotion of truth (through truth commissions or investigations on patterns of abuse); justice/criminal

[17] Bickford, above n 3.

[18] Teitel, *Transitional Justice Genealogy*, above n 4, 86.

[19] Rosalind Shaw and Lars Waldorf 'Introduction: Localizing Transitional Justice' in Rosalind and Waldorf Shaw, Lars with Pierre Hazan (eds), *Localizing Transitional Justice: Interventions and Priorities After Mass Violence* (Stanford University Press, 2010) 3.

[20] Mathew. A Weiner, 'Defeating Hatred With Truth: An Argument in Support of a Truth Commission as part of the solution to Israel/Palestine' (2005–2006) 38 *Connecticut Law Review* 123, 124.

[21] See Edward Newman, Roland Paris, and Oliver P. Richmond, 'Introduction' in Edward Newman, Roland Paris and Oliver P. Richmond (eds.), *New Perspectives on Liberal Peacebuilding* (United Nations University Press, 2009); Chandra Lekha Sriram, 'Justice as Peace? Liberal Peacebuilding and Strategies of Transitional Justice' (2007), 21(4) *Global Society* 579–591.

[22] Roht-Arriaza, above n 5, 1.

accountability (trials, amnesties, vetting[23]); reparations[24] (both financial and symbolic); and guarantees of non-recurrence (institutional reforms,[25] namely in the justice and security sector) are all examples of transitional justice measures.[26] Addressing a conflict's historical legacy also includes various mechanisms, such as museums, memorials, history textbooks reform, truth and reconciliation committees, and/or projects or committees that negotiate narratives.[27] Increasingly, transitional justice incorporates grass-root reconciliatory practices like reintegration and peace-building projects.

Ideally, transitional instruments should be combined and supplemented according to the post-conflict context. Above all, the duty to address past abuse '... does not mandate any particular mechanism or body—neither international tribunal nor truth commission'.[28] Rather, the idea is to somehow pursue the goals of transitional justice through many different forms and initiatives. Indeed, the ICTJ advocates a holistic and complementary approach to transitional justice.[29] Thus, in recent years, an important trend has been to apply any number of different mechanisms and practices at the same time.[30] Crafting transitional justice for conflict nations involves ethical debates on competing objectives and priorities. It raises practical concerns over political feasibility.[31] Ultimately, it is important to balance truth, justice, and reconciliatory goals, by engaging in complementary measures that best promote transitional justice overall.

---

[23] Vetting involves 'weeding out' (or lustration) mechanisms, whereby those involved in past violations (typically lower echelon functionaries) can be prevented by administrative or quasi-judicial means from public participation in the new institutions (such as in police forces).

[24] Reparations through which governments recognise and take steps to address the harms suffered. Such initiatives often have material elements (such as cash payments or health services) as well as symbolic aspects (such as public apologies or day of remembrance).

[25] Institutional reform of abusive state institutions such as armed forces, police, and courts, to dismantle—by appropriate means—the structural machinery of abuses and prevent recurrence of serious human rights abuses and impunity.

[26] Domenica Preysing, *Transitional Justice in Post-Revolutionary Tunisia (2011–2013)* (Springer Fachmedien Wiesbaden, 2016) 30.

[27] Andrew G. Reiter, Leigh A. Payne, and Tricia D. Olsen, *Transitional Justice in Balance: Comparing Processes, Weighting Efficacy* (United States Institute of Peace, 2010); Ruti Teitel, *Transitional Justice* (Oxford University Press, 2000) ('*Transitional Justice*').

[28] Roht-Arriaza, above n 5, 15.

[29] ICTJ Fact Sheet, above n 6.

[30] For example, far from being substitutes for trials, truth commissions are now often seen as complements to criminal processes, and a number of them have co-existed with ongoing criminal investigations. Roht-Arriaza, above n 5, 5.

[31] A country's political balance may be delicate, and a government may be unwilling to pursue wide-ranging initiatives. ICTJ Fact Sheet, above n 6.

3.3 Part Two: Debates on the Value of Truth, Justice, and Reconciliation

Three normative planks support the transitional justice paradigm: 'truth', 'justice', and 'reconciliation'.[32] They may be inter-linked, contradictory, or mutually enforcing, and their hierarchy is often contested, but ultimately transitional justice is based on an inherent combination of these three moral and ethical demands. The victim-centeredness and backward-looking aspects of transitional justice distinguish it from fields such as conflict resolution and peace building. This approach is considered both normatively required as well as pragmatically important for consolidating peace and democracy in the aftermath of conflict. The ensuing discussion examines the normative value of engaging the past, accountability and reconciliation by societies seeking to transcend conflict.

The Normative Value of 'Truth' and Engaging the Past

Peace if possible, but truth at any rate. (Martin Luther 1483–1546)

One of the fundamental premises of transitional justice is that truth-telling and setting the historical record straight are essential goals for conflict resolution. Thus, it is assumed that narrating a full account of a traumatic past is interlinked with the achievement of justice, reconciliation, social repair, healing, and institutional reform.[33] Whether by criminal process or truth commission, the idea of revisiting the past in order to move forward is deeply embedded in transitional justice discourse.[34] The right to the truth has also emerged as a legal concept at the national, regional,[35] and international levels[36] and relates to a state's obligation to provide information to victims, their families, and even society about the circumstances of serious human rights violations. The UNSC and international practice have repeatedly underlined the value of truth-telling for the consolidation of peace and

[32] Ibid; See also Marek M. Kaminski, Monika Nalepa and Barry O'Neill 'Normative and Strategic Aspects of Transitional Justice' (2006) 50 (3) *The Journal of Conflict Resolution*, 295–302.

[33] Donald Shriver, 'Truth Commissions and Judicial Trials: Complementary or Antagonistic Servants of Public Justice?' (2001) 16 *Journal of Law and Religion* 1, at 3.

[34] Teitel, *Transitional Justice Genealogy*, above n 4, 86.

[35] The Inter-American Court of Human Rights has recognised the right of relatives of the victims of forced disappearance to know their fate and whereabouts. See Velásquez Rodríguez Case, above n 10 [181]; Yasmin Naqvi, 'The Right to the Truth in International Law: Fact or Fiction?' (2006) 88(862) *International Review of the Red Cross* 245.

[36] The right to truth (sometimes referred to as 'the right to know') is fast emerging as a core standard for victims of human rights abuses, with the ICRC having already recognised it as a rule of customary international law. International Committee of the Red Cross, *Customary International Humanitarian Law: Volume I, Rules* (Cambridge University Press, Cambridge, 2005) 421.

reconciliation, and accountability.[37] In their assessment of ten transitional contexts, Long and Breke found that extensive truth-telling formed a core part of each successful reconciliation and was absent from all three unsuccessful ones.[38]

For truth commissions, a core modality of transitional justice practice, the past is closely associated with future possibilities of forgiveness, deterrence, and reconciliation. In South Africa, for example, the Truth and Reconciliation Commission (SATRC) was envisioned as a bridge between institutional racism and democracy in order to prevent a repetition of such acts 'in the future'.[39] Similarly, the past's pertinence to transition drives criminal prosecutions seeking to hold individuals accountable for previous crimes, through which it is assumed: 'The recall of past evil is [a] critical source of empowerment'.[40] Thus, the desirability of re-encountering the past is a foundational premise of both restorative and retributive models of justice.

Memory or Amnesia?

Nevertheless, dissenting voices undermine the very orthodoxy of a conflict-nation reckoning with history. After all, the value of engaging the past is 'under siege'[41] as a matter of 'intellectual historiography and human self-understanding'.[42] Overborne by the perils of the past, nations recovering from mass atrocity might arguably do better to forget.[43] Perhaps these fragile societies ought to invoke Nietzsche's aphorism that 'life in any true sense is impossible without forgetfulness'[44] by foregoing oral testimony and criminal investigations altogether. Capturing this poignant dilemma, Garton Ash writes: 'On the one side there is the old wisdom of the Jewish tradition: To remember is the secret of redemption ... on the other ... "Forgetting" ... is an essential factor in the history of a nation ...'.[45] Put simply, if what societies seek to recall is enormously selective, why choose to revisit mass trauma? Why should the progressive pull of the past pass as wisdom? Perhaps, there is indeed

[37] See e.g. UNSC Res 1606 (2005) on Burundi, preambular paras. 2 and 7; UNSC Res. 1593 (2005) on Darfur, Sudan, para. 5; SC Res. 1468 (2003) on the Democratic Republic of Congo, para. 5; SC Res. 1012 (1995). See Ibid.

[38] William J. Long and Peter Breke, *War and Reconciliation: Reason and Emotion in Conflict* (MIT Press, Boston, 2003) cited in Jonathan Doak, 'The Therapeutic Dimension of Transitional Justice: Emotional Repair and Victim Satisfaction in International Trials and Truth Commissions' (2011) 11 *International Criminal Law Review* 263, 274.

[39] *Promotion of National Unity and Reconciliation Act* 34 (1995).

[40] Ian Hacking, *Rewriting the Soul: Multiple Personality and the Sciences of Memory* (Princeton University Press, 1995) 213.

[41] Teitel, *Transitional Justice Genealogy*, above n 4, 86.

[42] Ibid.

[43] Mark Osiel, 'Ever Again: Legal Remembrance of Administrative Massacre' (1995–6) 144 *University of Pennsylvania Law Review* 463, 570 ('Ever Again').

[44] Friedrich Nietzsche, *On the Use and Abuse of History* 7–8 (1874) cited in Ibid 570.

[45] Timothy Garton Ash, *The File: A Personal History* 225–226 (Random House, 1997) cited in Shriver, above n 33, 26.

resonance to the maxim: '... let bygones be bygones. Sweep anything unpleasant under the rug [?]'[46]

However, such cries ring hollow, when neither the constructed nature of memory nor the inevitability of forgetting is capable of warding off selected aspects of the past. The problem continues to be the long shadow cast by trauma: '... the inability to forget, [even] when forgetting is entirely appropriate ...'.[47] Historical memories seem unavoidable in the context of intractable conflict.[48] In short, a society cannot simply toss a chapter of its history down the Orwellian memory hole. Thus, faced with the futility of erasing the past, collective repression[49] seems more perilous to a state's recovery in transition. Whilst: '... the motto "forget and move on" has its utilitarian attraction ... [it] is deceptive. Forgetting is a tricky business both psychically and politically'.[50] If governments are incapable of legislating amnesia, the crucial question is therefore not one between forgetting and memory but between what is remembered and how. The role of truth-telling in transitional justice is complex but operates safely on the assumption that a brutal past cannot simply be 'forgotten' even though 'memory is a process of both remembering and forgetting'.[51]

Dressing Wounds or Can of Worms?

There is an overwhelming consensus about the potential for truth-telling to bear sociologically meaningful fruit.[52] Arguably '[a] nation's unity depends on a shared identity, which in turn depends largely on a shared memory'.[53] Thus, the SATRC in disclosing its past '... became a mode of psychological repair, where denial could be superseded'.[54] For Courts and Commissions alike: 'speaking at public hearings ... can break an enforced silence and represent a point of closure and transition

[46] Christian Tomuschat, 'Clarification Commission in Guatemala' (May, 2001) 23 *Human Rights Quarterly* 233, 236.

[47] Osiel, *Ever Again*, above n 43, 570.

[48] Ifat Maoz, 'Multiple Conflicts and Competing Agendas: A Framework for Conceptualizing Structured Encounters Between Groups in Conflict-The Case of a Coexistence Project of Jews and Palestinians in Israel' 6 (2) *Peace and Conflict: Journal of Peace Psychology* 2000 (135–156).

[49] The Freudian notion of repression or denial of memory is predicated on the idea that what is repressed later returns through 'acting out' in Osiel, *Ever Again*, above n 43, 570.

[50] Shriver, above n 33, 27.

[51] Quoting Jack Kugelmas' famed comment in Brandon Hamber and Richard Wilson 'Symbolic Closure Through Memory, Reparation and Revenge in Post-Conflict Societies' (March 2002) 1 (1) *Journal of Human Rights* at 13.

[52] Aeyal Gross, 'The Constitution, Reconciliation and Transitional Justice: Lessons from South Africa and Israel' (2004) 40 *Stanford Journal of International Law* 47, 73.

[53] Jose Zalaquett, 'The Mathew 0. Tobriner Memorial Lecture: Balancing Ethical Imperatives and Political Constraints: The Dilemma of New Democracies Confronting Past Human Rights Violations' (1991) 43 *Hastings Law Journal* 1424, 1433.

[54] Hamber and Wilson, above n 51, 7.

in the grieving …'.[55] Concerning the victims' deep need for acknowledgement: 'The truth itself can also be understood as a form of reparation …'.[56] In this light, communal discursive processes around collective memory are central to the healing of individual victims, as has been demonstrated by Holocaust survivors, individuals in post-apartheid South Africa and post-genocide Rwanda.[57]

Nevertheless, objecting voices plausibly argue that in some cases truth-telling on a national scale may '… reanimate traumas, inflict new ones, and possibly work against reconciliation because it … reaffirms their victim ideologies …'.[58] In Rwanda for example, although the local village Gacaca courts claimed 'the truth heals', the hearings often caused renewed conflict, intimidation and even murder of witnesses.[59] Indeed, some studies have also shown that the construction of a collective narrative may lead neither to national healing nor to reconciliation in the wake of mass-atrocity.[60] Regimes in transition may also consciously choose not to engage the past in order to ease a political transition.[61]

However, for many, a past suppressed is a truth repressed, and this constitutes unfinished business for the task of reconciliation, on both the individual and the national levels.[62] Clearly, the extent to which truth-seeking can decisively reform society, or prevent the recurrence of mass-atrocity, is empirically uncertain. Indeed, there is no definitive study on the normative value of truth-telling to national social processes. As noted above, some studies reach conflicting conclusions and may be in tension in one another. However, on balance, it appears that that extensive truth-telling is instrumental to successful reconciliation efforts.[63] Although exposing the

---

[55] Ibid at 6.

[56] Miriam Aukerman, 'Extraordinary Evil, Ordinary Crime: A Framework for Understanding Transitional Justice' (2002) 15, *Harvard Human Rights Journal* 39, 79.

[57] Eric and Shain Langenbacher, Yossi (ed) *Power and the Past: Collective Memory and International Relations* (Georgetown University Press, 2010), 16.

[58] Ariel Meyerstein, 'Transitional Justice and Post-Conflict Israel/Palestine: Assessing the Applicability of the Truth Commission Paradigm' (2006–2007) 38 *Case Western Journal of International Law* 281, 360. See also generally Priscilla Hayner, *Unspeakable Truths* (Routledge, 2001).

[59] Susanne, Buckley-Zistel '"The Truth Heals"? Gacaca jurisdiction and the Consolidation of Peace in Rwanda' (2005): 80 (1–2) *Die Friedens Warte* 113–129.

[60] Olivia Lin, 'Demythologizing Restorative Justice: South Africa's Truth And Reconciliation Commission And Rwanda's Gacaca Courts In Context', (2005) (12) (1) *ILSA Journal of International & Comparative Law* 68; See also generally Priscilla Hayner 'Fifteen Truth Commissions--1974 to 1994: A Comparative Study' (1994) 16(4) *Human Rights Quarterly* 597–655.

[61] For example, after Franco's death, political elites in Spain elected to avoid dealing with the legacies of his dictatorship. Notably, today decades later, with democracy well established in Spain, calls for some sort of official reckoning with the past are increasing. Kevin Avruch, 'Truth and Reconciliation Commissions: Problems in Transitional Justice and the Reconstruction of Identity' (2010) 47 (1) *Transcultural Psychiatry* 37, 38.

[62] Ibid.

[63] William J. Long and Peter Breke, *War and Reconciliation: Reason and Emotion in Conflict* (MIT Press, Boston, 2003) cited in Jonathan Doak, 'The Therapeutic Dimension of Transitional Justice:

past cannot itself socially rehabilitate, its cathartic value ought not be invalidated at the expense of painful public recollection.

After all, the impact of collective truth-telling is not a zero-sum term analysis, and so persuasively remains, however complex, a policy preferable to silence and denial. As Zalaquette writes: '[t]he truth does not bring the dead back to life, but it brings them out from silence'.[64] Further, it is worth noting that individual processes of grief cannot be simplistically extrapolated on a national scale.[65] To this end, it might be argued that to forego any national response 'strikes at the very heart of human rights. Passivity then turns into permissiveness'.[66]

Relativising 'Truth'

Finally, critics challenge the very conceptual basis for 'truth-telling'; the notion that one version of the past can be singled out and established authoritatively. Truth-seeking with its focus on 'full truth',[67] 'unbiased examination',[68] and 'definitive historical record'[69] expresses a commitment to the prospect of 'truth',[70] which is, after all, an elusive goal. One, however, need not be a post-modernist to recognise the constructed nature of historical narrative.[71] Hence, not even the most well-meaning factual account of mass atrocity will ever be free from contestation, ideological taint or the fractured nature of lived memory. In this light, any mass production of memory is clearly '... more than a juiceless sequence of dates and facts or mere mnemonic cues'.[72] Notably, the SATRC Report itself discounted any singular forensic notion of 'truth' by distinguishing between four conceptions of truths: 'factual', 'personal', 'social', and 'healing'.[73]

At any rate, recognising the subjectivity and relativism of truth-telling should not diminish its value in transition. However intangible the task, or constructed the

---

Emotional Repair and Victim Satisfaction in International Trials and Truth Commissions' (2011) 11 *International Criminal Law Review* 263, 274.

[64] Zalaquett, above n 53, 1433.

[65] See Hamber and Wilson, above n 51, 12.

[66] Tomuschat, above n 46, 236.

[67] Ibid at 237.

[68] Gross, above n 52, 70.

[69] Antonio Cassese quoted in Laurel Fletcher, 'From Indifference to Engagement: Bystanders and International Criminal Justice' (2004–2005) 26 *Michigan Journal of International Law* 1013, 1019.

[70] Francois Du Bois, '"Nothing But the Truth": The South African Alternative to the Dilemma of Corrective Justice in Transitions to Democracy' in Emillios Christodoulidis and Scott Veitch (eds.) *Lethe's Law – Justice, Law and Ethics in Reconciliation* (Hart, 2001) 91.

[71] Jonathan Tepperman, 'Truth and Consequences' (March/April 2002) 81(2) *Foreign Affairs* 128, 134.

[72] Brian Havel, 'In Search of a Theory of Public Memory: The State, the Individual, and Marcel Proust' (Summer, 2005) 80 *Indiana Law Journal* 605 at 687.

[73] Du Bois, above n 70, 97.

content, '... the value of revealing the "truth" is not abstract',[74] either as a mode of acknowledgment or as a source of condemnation. In the words of Osiel:

> At a minimum, central truths, as relative as they may be, must be established in order to provide a historic record ... to dampen the spirits of revenge and renewed conflict, to educate people, and ultimately to prevent future victimization.[75]

Further, it might be equally contended: '... the division of truth into a large number of "truths" to some extent leads to its [further] distortion'.[76] In this light, it is arguable that beyond post-modern sensibilities, there is, after all: '... a bare bedrock of facts- about who did what to how many, when, and in what fashion—that must be authoritatively established ... for any legitimate public discussion ...'.[77] Above all else, stripped of its 'flatulent rhetoric' and 'glittering slogans'[78] truth-seeking in the wake of mass atrocity appears as much concerned with what happened, as with the lesson that what happened was wrong.[79] From this standpoint, transitional truth-telling, fractured, partial, and slippery, is also about moral context. In short, the paradoxical value of truth-telling, '... is to undo history'.[80]

The Normative Value of Justice and Human Rights Law

> *If peace is not intended to be a brief interlude between conflicts ... it must encompass what justice is intended to accomplish ...* (Mahmoud Cherif Bassiouni[81])

Transitional justice is also about creating a platform of justice to account for past abuses and injustice. It embodies the idea that justice can help move societies '... from overt, violent conflict to conflict resolution'.[82] Clearly, justice is a highly subjective term with different meanings to various constituents: for some it may be prosecuting political leaders, and for others it is being able to return to one's home and to live in peace.[83] Since the Second World War, retributive justice based on the

[74] Jonathan Tepperman, above n 71 at 134.

[75] Osiel, *Ever Again*, above n 43.

[76] Asher Maoz, 'Historical Adjudication: Courts of Law, Commissions of Inquiry, and "Historical Truth"' (2000) 18 (3) *Law and History Review* 559 at 568.

[77] Osiel, *Ever Again*, above n 43, 672.

[78] Ibid.

[79] 'Compelling Stories about the countries past ... aid our remembrance not only of the events themselves, but also of the moral judgements ...'. Ibid, 516.

[80] Teitel, *Transitional Justice Genealogy*, above n 4, 87.

[81] Mahmoud Cherif Bassiouni, 'Searching for Peace and Achieving Justice: The Need for Accountability' (1996) 59(4) *Law and Contemporary Problems* 9, 13.

[82] Kathleen. A Cavanaugh, 'Selective Justice: The Case of Israel and the Occupied Territories' (2002–2003) 26 *Fordham International Law Journal* 934, 934.

[83] Laurel Fletcher, 'Institutions from Above and Voices From Below: A Comment on Challenges to Group-Conflict Resolution and Reconciliation' (2009) 72 *Law and Contemporary Problems* 51, 54.

Nuremberg trials was the dominant paradigm.[84] In the post-Cold War era however, notions of restorative justice have become increasingly relevant as will be discussed in the subsequent chapters.[85] In all cases, justice-seeking discourse is premised on the belief that no durable peace is possible without due regard for the historical past.[86]

Whilst transitional justice measures might vary from prosecutions to non-criminal processes, the broad objectives of justice are essentially similar.[87] Firstly, as a matter of morality, perpetrators should be held accountable somehow to satisfy the demands of victims and the public.[88] Secondly, as a matter of law, accountability is intended to re-assert the rule of law and to prevent private vengeance.[89] Whether justice is retributive or restorative, absolute or relative, and whether a transitional form of justice based on human rights might be achieved, pursuing some kind of justice appears central to the process of reconciliation between parties to conflict.

Peace vs. Justice?

Nevertheless, many contest the relationship between retributive justice and peace. One of the tensions in transitional justice is how to reconcile the need to punish human rights violations ('retributive justice') with the pragmatics of reaching a political settlement and ending conflict ('peace'). Historically, the concern is that advocating for retributive justice can undermine peace.[90] Though it is widely accepted that both the goals are integral to reconciliation, some practitioners claim that conflict resolution may be obstructed by '... attempts to secure rights agendas, which are often rigid, idealistic, and unrealistic'.[91] This attitude is also premised on the belief that 'justice' is a subjective construct, and allowing it to become the subject of negotiations would only fuel the conflict.[92] According to Bar-Siman Tov, absolute values like justice may undermine the willingness of parties to make concessions, to compromise, or to take risks.[93]

[84] Ron Dudai and Hillel Cohen, 'Triangle of Betrayal: Collaborators and Transitional Justice in the Israeli-Palestinian Conflict' (2007) 6(1) *Journal of Human Rights* 37, 46.

[85] Aukerman, above n 56, 81.

[86] Cavanaugh, above n 82, 934.

[87] Mark Freeman, 'Transitional Justice: Fundamental Goals and Unavoidable Complications' (2000–2002) 28 *Manitoba Law Journal* 113, 114.

[88] Ibid.

[89] Ibid.

[90] Aukerman, above n 56, 81.

[91] Cavanaugh, above n 82, 934.

[92] Yoav Peled and Nadim Rouhana, 'Transitional Justice and the Right of Return of the Palestinian Refugees' (2004) 5 *Theoretical Inquiry Law* 317, 317.

[93] Yaacov Bar-Siman-Tov, 'Introduction: Barriers to Conflict Resolution' in Yaacov Bar-Siman-Tov (ed) *Barriers to Peace in the Israeli-Palestinian Conflict* (Jerusalem Institute for Israel Studies, 2011) 15, 15 ('*Barriers to Peace*').

Increasingly, however, recent post-conflict trends acknowledge that addressing past atrocity does not mean hampering stability and conflict resolution.[94] Upon this view, the advancement of peace and the rule of law may be harmonised with the pursuit of justice and accountability.[95] Thus, it may be concluded that the dichotomy between peace and justice is somewhat misleading. As Cherif-Bassiouni writes: 'Surely no-one can argue that peace is unnecessary and preferable to a state of violence. But the attainment of peace is not necessarily to the exclusion of justice, because justice is frequently necessary to attain peace'.[96]

Relativising 'Justice' with 'Human Rights Norms'

Moreover, there may be a conceptual bridge between justice and peace. Arguably the term 'justice' itself generates inflated expectations, when actually its goals may be more modest following mass atrocity. Thus, Teitel argues that at times of transition, what needs to be created is a relative notion of justice, as opposed to 'ordinary' justice during peacetime.[97] For instance, producing a joint understanding about past abuses or a meaningful public apology might be regarded as '... a preservative form of justice, which concededly sacrifices the aims of ideal justice for the more limited ones of assuring peace and stability'.[98] From a transitional justice perspective, negotiators and practitioners should therefore be encouraged to give due regard to both restorative and compensatory notions of justice, as well as to international human rights law.

Indeed, linking the framework of justice to human rights law may support political change and conflict transformation. Widening agreement on the universality of human rights law, and the proliferation of international instruments, has conferred human rights norms with a greater role in resolving conflict and peace agreements.[99] In the words of Kaufmann 'Introducing human rights as a relevant dimension may result in a paradigm shift and open new avenues for imaginative and creative solutions ...'.[100] From Latin America to South Africa, progress towards ceasing hostili-

[94] Ruti G. Teitel, 'Transitional Justice in a New Era' (2002) 26(4) *Fordham International Law Journal* 893, 896 ('*Transitional Justice in a New Era*'); See also Christine Bell, Colm Campbell and Fionnuala Ni Aolain 'Justice Discourses in Transition' (2004) 13(3) *Social and Legal Studies* 305 ('*Justice Discourses*').

[95] Teitel, *Transitional Justice in a New Era*, above n 94, 898.

[96] Bassiouni, above n 81, 12.

[97] Teitel, *Transitional Justice*, above n 27; Notably, Gross critiques this distinction. According to him 'Although grounded in the transition [justice] ... should not be limited to this period because justice is always in transition'. Gross, above n 52, 50.

[98] Teitel, *Transitional Justice*, above n 27, 51.

[99] See Colin Campbell, 'Peace and the Laws of War: the role of International Humanitarian Law in the Post-Conflict Environment' (2000) 82 (839) *Review of the International Committee of the Red Cross* 627–651, 628–631, and Christine Bell, *Human Rights and Peace Agreements* (Oxford University Press, 2000) 4.

[100] Edward Kaufman, above n 2, 184.

ties, ending gross violations, and reconciliation have been closely associated with attaching 'justice' to human rights law.[101] Whether it is the Dayton Accords[102] or Northern Ireland's piecemeal approach to past abuse,[103] it might be exceedingly hard to reach a political agreement without explicitly addressing demands for justice based on human rights law. In those countries and elsewhere, 'the legitimacy and sustainability of political processes are strengthened, not weakened, by including [IHL] and human rights standards'.[104]

From this standpoint, the interrelationship between peace, justice, and human rights is significant,[105] not only for principled normative reasons, but also for pragmatic ones. Many theorists posit that introducing human rights norms early into conflict resolution efforts '... is a formula that has both the potential for a smoother advance in the negotiation process, and contributes to the sustainability of peace accords'.[106] Fundamental civil and political rights, such as the right to life, freedom of movement, freedom from arbitrary detention, and the right to self-determination are highly relevant to peace efforts.[107] Proponents of this approach assert that drawing on objective legal criteria in conflict-related agreements makes an agreement both more possible and durable.[108]

---

101 Ibrahim Bisharat and Edward Kaufman, 'Introducing human rights into conflict resolution: the relevance for the Israeli-Palestinian peace process' (2002) 1(1) *Journal of Human Rights* 71, 72.

102 The General Framework Agreement for Peace in Bosnia and Herzegovina, also known as the Dayton Agreement was formally signed in Paris on 14 December 1995. It ended the three and half year-long Bosnian War. The Dayton Agreement contained numerous human rights provisions and annexes including implicit endorsement of the ICTY and the right of return. See Wolfgang Benedek et al. (eds.) *Human Rights in Bosnia and Herzegovina After Dayton: From Theory to Practice* (Nijhoff Publishers, 1999).

103 International human rights law played a crucial mediating role within the framework of the Good Friday Agreement itself, and indeed prior to it. Christine Bell, Campbell, Colm and Ni Aolain, Fionnuala 'Justice Discourses in Transition' (2004) 13(3) *Social and Legal Studies* 305, 315.

104 Mari Mustafa, 'The Negotiation Process: the Lack of Human Rights Component' (2003) 10(3) *Palestine Israel Journal* 5, 7 (2). See Anonymous, 'Human rights in Peace Negotiations' (1996) 18 (2), *Human Rights Quarterly* 249–258; Francis A. Boyle, 'Negotiating human rights in peace negotiations' (1996) 18 (3), *Human Rights Quarterly*, 515–516, and Felice D. Gaer, 'UN-Anonymous: Reflections on Human rights in Peace negotiations' 19 (1) (1997) *Human Rights Quarterly* 1–8.

105 Both at the normative level and as an empirical claim, the interrelationship between peace and justice has been underscored by prominent bodies such as the Carnegie Commission on Preventing Deadly Conflict. See Roger Fisher, William Ury, and Bruce Patton, *Getting to Yes: Negotiating Agreement Without Giving In* (Penguin, 1991).

106 Bisharat and Kaufman, above n 101, 72; Gross concurs that human rights discourse can play an important role in a conflict transformation processes. Gross, above n 52; See also Fisher et al., above n 105, 4.

107 Edward Kaufman, above n 2, 172.

108 See Fisher et al., above n 105; Mustafa, above n 104.

On the other hand, one must recall that human rights norms could also become 'unfulfilled promises'[109] and that they are mostly directed at the protection of individuals and not collective national groups.[110] Given the best practice elsewhere however, the discourse of human rights remains a valid lens to express the concept of 'justice' and provides a universal yardstick to assess the conduct of parties.[111] Indeed, in transitional societies, international legal standards are useful not only for future human rights protection but also in assessing past conduct.[112] In this light, notions of justice and human rights are integral elements of a sustainable peace process.[113]

The Normative Value of Reconciliation

Reconciliation is the third significant pillar of transitional justice. In recent years, theories of reconciliation have become increasingly present in political discourse,[114] borrowing from diverse disciplines such as history, philosophy, sociology, and political psychology. While reconciliation, both as a theoretical concept and as an empirical goal, remains under-defined,[115] it implies the long-term process of transforming relations between rivals from hostility to peaceful and harmonious ones.[116] Broadly speaking, reconciliation is about '... overcoming alienation, division and enmity ...

---

[109] Gross, above n 52, 98; Morton Horwitz, 'Rights' (1988) 23 *Harvard Civil Rights Civil Liberties Law Review* 393, discussing the tension inherent in the dual nature of rights. For the position that the rights discourse in the new South African political order hampered major reforms and left apartheid's economic hierarchies undisturbed see Makauwa Mutua, 'Hope and Despair for a New South Africa: The Limits of Rights Discourse' (1997) 10 *Harvard Human Right Journal* 63.

[110] Bisharat and Kaufman, above n 101, 73; Christine Bell, *On the Law of Peace: Peace Agreements and the Lex Pacificatoria* (Oxford University Press, 2008), 231.

[111] Arguably, the concept of 'justice' can be better conveyed in terms of respect for specific principles embodied in the articles of international covenants. Bisharat and Kaufman, above n 101, 76.

[112] Campbell et al., above n 14, *The Frontiers Legal Analysis*, 335.

[113] Aukerman, above n 56, 81; Bassiouni, above n 81, 13.

[114] Brandon Hamber and Grainne Kelly 'Beyond Coexistence: Towards a Working Definition of Reconciliation' in Joanna Quinn (ed), *Reconciliation (S) Transitional Justice in Postconflict Societies* (McGill-Queen's University Press, 2009) 287.

[115] 'The widespread use of the term reconciliation, its novelty in academic and political discourse, and its link to other concepts such as apology and forgiveness, overload the terms with multiple meanings ...' Nadim Rouhana, 'Identity and Power in Israeli-Palestinian Reconciliation' (2000/2001) 3(2) *Israeli Sociology* 277.

[116] Yaacov Bar-Siman-Tov, 'Dialectics between Stable Peace and Reconciliation,' in *From Conflict Resolution to Reconciliation*, ed. Yaacov Bar-Siman-Tov (Oxford University Press, 2004), 72 ('*From Conflict Resolution*'); Nevin Aiken, Learning to Live Together: Transitional Justice and Intergroup Reconciliation in Northern Ireland. (2010) 4 *International Journal of Transitional Justice*, 166, 168.

based on a shared commitment to communal solidarity'.[117] There exist therefore thicker and thinner notions of reconciliation that range from 'simple coexistence',[118] to what Osiel describes as 'liberal social solidarity'[119] in which former adversaries mutually respect and collaborate with one another.[120] Either way, reconciling past enemies is increasingly regarded as a pre-condition to surmounting conflict.

From Conflict Resolution to Conflict Transformation

After decades of focusing on conflict resolution,[121] social scientists are now devoting attention to prescriptive models of reconciliation based on social psychological theory.[122] Growing scholarship contends that after periods of mass violence, genuine and successful reconciliation must involve an element of 'identity negotiation' and 'conflict transformation'.[123] It is posited that conflict resolution alone, without such reconciliation, leaves historic grievances and injustices embedded in collective memories and narratives.[124] This is especially the case during intractable conflict,[125] which serves to close minds, and may prolong cycles of violence because of an

---

[117] Mark R Amstutz, *The Healing of Nations: The Promise and Limits of Political Forgiveness* (Boulder: Rowman and Littlefield, 2005) 97.

[118] Under this approach, reconciliation is nothing more than the cessation of hostilities. See Charles Villa-Vicencio, 'A Different Kind of Justice: The South African Truth and Reconciliation Commission' (1999) 1 *Contemporary Justice Review* 407–428.

[119] Mark Osiel, *Mass Atrocity, Collective Memory and the Law* (Transaction Publishers, 1999) quoted in David A Crocker, 'Reckoning with Past Wrongs: A Normative Framework' (March 1999) 13(1) *Ethics and International Affairs* 43, 60.

[120] Ibid.

[121] Broadly speaking, the conflict resolution model stresses an interest-based approach to international relations, which focuses mainly on problem-solving mediation. See for example Fen Osler Hampson, *Nurturing Peace: Why Peace Settlements Succeed or Fail* (US Institute of Peace Press 1996); Jacob Shamir and Khalil Shikaki, 'Determinants of Reconciliation and Compromise Among Israelis and Palestinians' (2002) 39 *Journal of Peace Research* 185, 186–187; See also Bar-Siman Tov, *From Conflict Resolution*, above n 116.

[122] Daniel Bar-Tal, 'From Intractable Conflict through Conflict Resolution to Reconciliation: Psychological Analysis (June 2000) 21(2) *Political Psychology* 351; See also John Paul Lederach, *Conflict Transformation* Conflict Information Consortium, University of Colorado http://www.beyondintractability.org/essay/transformation; Herbert Kelman, 'The Interdependence of Israeli and Palestinian National Identities: The Role of the other in Existential Conflicts' (1999) 55(3) *Journal of Social Issues* 581 ('*The Interdependence*'); Robert Rothstein, *How Not To Make Peace: 'Conflict Syndrome' and the Demise of the Oslo Accords*, United States Institute of Peace (March 2006).

[123] Ibid.

[124] Bar-Tal, above n. 122, 362–3; See also Yaacov Bar-Siman-Tov 'Dialectics between Stable Peace and Reconciliation' in Bar-Siman Tov, *From Conflict Resolution*, above n 116, 61, 245.

[125] Such conflicts are usually perceived as survival threatening, and of a zero-sum nature and protracted. See Bar-Tal, above n. 122; Kelman, *The Interdependence*, above n 122; Shamir and Shikaki, above n 121, 186–187.

entrenched conflict repertoire.[126] Accordingly, at the heart of the reconciliation process is changing the conflictive ethos.

In this light, a political formula or peace deal that merely terminates the conflict will fall short of overcoming the cognitive barriers that may foil the normalisation and stabilisation of peace relations.[127] While some conflicts reach the resolution phase, research suggests that a peace agreement alone does not guarantee sustainable peace.[128] Indeed, without conflict transformation and psychological change, violence is likely to be renewed, as has happened in the past, from Bosnia to Rwanda.[129] As Waxman concludes: 'Failure to take into account the importance of collective identities … will doom peace negotiations and the settlement of intractable conflicts'.[130]

Arguably, durable peacemaking and eventual reconciliation requires promoting social and cultural shifts that transform the collective narratives and identities of the parties.[131] This means engaging former enemies in redefining the antagonistic identities and belief systems that motivated past violence and re-creating a more positive system of relations.[132] Many practitioners in the field advance this view.[133] Bar-Tal refers to this process as the formation of an alternative 'peace ethos', an outcome that consists of mutual recognition, acceptance, trust, and positive attitudes, and sensitivity to the other party's needs and interests.[134]

---

[126] Bar-Siman-Tov, *From Conflict Resolution*, above n 116; See also Robert Rotberg (ed) *Israeli-Palestinian Narratives of Conflict: History's Double Helix* (Indiana University Press, 2006) 5; Bar-Tal, above n. 122; 'In many cases, the conflict itself becomes integral to the group identities in these societies and is therefore more difficult to unlock' quoted in Barbara Tint, 'History, Memory and Intractable Conflict' (Spring 2010) 27(3) *Conflict Resolution Quarterly* 239, 239.

[127] Yaacov Bar-Siman-Tov, 'Dialectics between Stable Peace and Reconciliation' in Bar-Siman Tov, *From Conflict Resolution*, above n 116, 61; Kelman, *The Interdependence*, above n 122.

[128] Rafi Nets-Zehngut, 'Passive Healing of the Aftermath of Intractable Conflicts' (Spring/Summer 2009) 14(1) *International Journal of Peace Studies* 39, 39 ('*Passive Healing*').

[129] Bar-Tal, above n. 122, 362–3; See also Yaacov Bar-Siman-Tov 'Dialectics between Stable Peace and Reconciliation' in Bar-Siman Tov, *From Conflict Resolution*, above n 116, 61.

[130] Dov Waxman, 'Introduction' in Dov Waxman, *The Pursuit of Peace and the Crisis of Israeli Identity* (Palgrave Macmillan, 2006), 6.

[131] Daniel Bar-Tal and Gemma H. Bennink, 'The Nature of Reconciliation as an Outcome and as a Process,' in Bar-Siman Tov, *From Conflict Resolution*, above n 122, 12.

[132] Herbert C. Kelman, 'The Role of National Identity in Conflict Resolution: Experiences from Israeli-Palestinian Problem-Solving Workshops', in *Social Identity, Intergroup Conflict, and Conflict Reduction*, Richard D. Ashmore, Lee J. Jussim and David Wilder eds. (Oxford University Press, 2001) 194.

[133] Ibid; Waxman, above n 130, 6; Shamir and Shikaki, above n 121, 186–187.

[134] Daniel Bar-Tal, 'From Intractable Conflict through Conflict Resolution to Reconciliation: Psychological Analysis' (June 2000) 21(2) *Political Psychology* 351, 352.

Bridging Narrative and Collective Memory

The social psychological field also stresses the value of historic truth to reconciliation.[135] In diverse contexts, truth-and-reconciliation projects, historical enquiries, and various commemorative efforts have become instrumental to advancing reconciliation and democratisation.[136] As Teitel recalls: 'In the post-Cold war phase historical production was fundamental to building a state's political identity, and control over construction of an alternative history could lie with multiple actors …'.[137] Indeed, the word 'truth' now appears in the official names of most reconciliation commissions. It has become routine to consider how truth-recovery mechanisms can contribute to reconciliation.[138]

More specifically, reconciliation involves specific actions that acknowledge the past, like revisiting the history of the conflict, expressing an apology and offering reparations.[139] Bush and Folger stress the value of acknowledgement and recognition as the basis for transformative processes.[140] There is thus broad consensus that reconciliation demands the creation of a new common outlook of the past—a change of collective memories.[141] It is posited that once there is a shared and acknowledged perception of the past, both parties take a significant step towards achieving reconciliation.[142] Osiel refers to this as 'liberal social solidarity', whereby transitional societies pluralise the past in order to overcome their brutal legacies.[143] For Gross, it is about seeking a 'bridging narrative' to foster legitimacy and a sense of

---

[135] Rouhana, above n 112; Crocker, above n 116; Kelman, above n 122, *The Interdependence*, 581.

[136] 'In contexts as diverse as Guatemala, South Africa, Rwanda, Turkey, Chile, Bosnia, and Kosovo, collective memory of traumatic episodes has become a constitutive part of efforts to come to terms with the past, rebuild social trust, and re-establish the rule of law'. Eric Langenbacher and Yossi Shain, (ed) *Power and the Past: Collective Memory and International Relations* (Georgetown University Press, 2010), 16.

[137] Teitel, *Transitional Justice Genealogy*, above n 4, 87.

[138] Hamber and Kelly, above n 114, 289–290.

[139] Tint, above n 126, 251; Nets-Zehngut, *Passive Healing*, above n 128, 40.

[140] Robert Bush and Joseph Folger, *The Promise of Mediation* (Jossey-Vass 1994).

[141] Acknowledgement of the past implies at least recognising that there are two (legitimate) narratives of the conflict. See Bar-Siman-Tov, *From Conflict Resolution*, above n 116; Daniel Bar-Tal and Gavriel Salomon, G. 'Israeli-Jewish Narratives of the Israeli-Palestinian Conflict: Evolvement, Contents, Functions and Consequences' in Rotberg above n 126, 37–38; Bar-Tal, above n. 122; See also Priscilla Hayner, 'In pursuit of Justice and Reconciliation: Contributions of Truth-telling' in Cynthia Arnson (ed.), *Comparative peace processes in Latin America* (Stanford University Press. 1999) 363–383; Aletta Norval, 'Truth and Reconciliation: The Birth of the Present and the reworking of history' (1999) 25 *Journal of African Studies* 499–519.

[142] Through the process of negotiation, in which the one's own past is critically revised and synchronised with that of the other group, a new narrative can emerge. With time, this new historical account should substitute each side's dominant narrative of collective memory. Ibid.

[143] Osiel, *Ever Again*, above n 43, 471.

inclusion.[144] At times of transition, a common historical narrative must therefore be developed and publicly disseminated to advance reconciliation.[145]

Critiquing and Defending Reconciliation

While nobody disputes the value of reconciliation, some suggest that transformative processes are too psychologically taxing and may inhibit termination of long-term conflict.[146] 'They compel one to give up deeply entrenched self-serving beliefs about one's in-group goals, to admit to dark chapters … to forgive unforgivable atrocities and to show mercy for those seen as brutal enemies not long ago'.[147] Indeed, conditions for ensuring reconciliation are usually perceived as an advanced stage of the process of establishing peace and not necessarily part of conflict resolution.[148]

In this light, it is worth querying whether reconciliation is even possible in the wake of mass abuse. Bandes suggests that transitional justice unreflectively applies concepts from a personal therapeutic context for legal and policy prescription.[149] Fletcher asks: 'One individual may forgive another for a transgression, but what does it mean for communities to reconcile?'[150] There is thus the concern that politicians exploit the rhetoric of reconciliation to 'indulge in the illusion that they had put the past behind them'.[151] For example, some victims who testified at the SATRC complained of 'false reconciliation', whereby they felt compelled to forgive their

[144] Gross, above n 52, 82.

[145] 'Successful mediation involves finding an alternative narrative, which promotes a new story for the relationship and one that is incongruent with the continuation of the conflict'. Tint, above n 126, 249–250; 'The ability to develop a new and shared view of the past is seen as a key element to reconciliation processes'. Daniel Bar Tal and Gemma Bennink, 'The Nature of Reconciliation as an Outcome and as a Process' in Bar-Siman Tov, *From Conflict Resolution*, above n 116, 12.

[146] Tint, above n 126, 245; John Paul Lederach, *Conflict Transformation* Conflict Information Consortium, University of Colorado http://www.beyondintractability.org/essay/transformation; Shamir and Shikaki, above n 121, 188.

[147] Shamir and Shikaki, above n 121, 188.

[148] Yaacov Bar-Siman-Tov, 'Chapter 5: Justice and Fairness as Barriers to the Resolution of the Israeli-Palestinian Conflict' in Bar-Siman-Tov, *Barriers to Peace*, above n 93, 182.

[149] Susan Bandes, 'Victims, Closure and the Sociology of Emotion' (2009) 72 *Law and Contemporary Problems* 1; Laurel E. Fletcher and Harvey M. Weinstein, 'Violence and Social Repair: Rethinking the Contribution of Justice to Reconciliation' 24 *Human Rights Quarterly* 573, 592–95 (2002) (critiquing the argument that criminal trials for mass violence promote therapeutic healing for individual victims).

[150] Fletcher, above n 83. 53.

[151] See Michael Ignatieff, 'Articles of Faith' (1996) 5 *Index on Censorship* 96, 110–22.

perpetrators for political gain.[152] Finally, there are those who object to coercing mutuality or contrition based on religious notions of forgiveness.[153]

Nevertheless, critics of reconciliation ignore the grassroot support and long-term processes required for lasting conflict resolution. Minimalist theories of conflict resolution often entail top-down interest-driven measures imposed by political elites with an emphasis on short-term tasks, such as signing a ceasefire and demilitarisation. This leaves peace deals fragile and far less amenable to success by alienating rather than commanding the support of large segments of society.[154] Thus, Daly suggests that while transition happens at the top institutional level, a broader transformational dimension of justice, requiring metamorphosis at all levels of society, is important for reconciliation.[155] Similarly, Lederach describes the need for a framework that transcends a narrow view of peace building to include a web of activities that envision the entire body politic.[156]

Advocates of reconciliation thus confirm the need to move beyond short-term crisis orientation and consider conflict resolution as a broader endeavour, which involves various societal institutions and channels.[157] In this light, reconciliation need not be dismissed as an ambitious set of transformative outcomes and unrealistic interactions, but rather it may be regarded as a crucial nation-wide building process that fosters sustainable peace over time.[158]

Regarding the viability of reconciliation, it is worth distinguishing personal reconciliation between victims and perpetrators, which may be too demanding, from national reconciliation, which Dwyer argues is more achievable.[159] What is required if former rivals are to share an interdependent future is not demanding individuals to overcome their traumas or to expect healing or forgiveness, but rather the development of some form of bridging narrative. It is about transforming relationships

---

[152] Brandon Hamber, Dineo Nageng and Gabriel O'Malley, *'Telling it like it is: Survivors' perceptions of the Truth and Reconciliation Commission' and Suggestions for the Final Report* (The Centre for the Study of Violence and Reconciliation Johannesburg, South Africa 1998).

[153] Hamber and Kelly, above n 114, 287–289; Susan Dwyer, 'Reconciliation for Realists' 13 (1999) *Ethics and International Affairs*, 81–98.

[154] Formal conflict resolution often involves only the leaders, and the majority of society members may not accept the political compromises they made, or even if they do, they may maintain conflict narratives that fuel the conflict. Formal resolutions of conflicts may be unstable: they may collapse as in the case of Angola. Daniel Bar Tal and Gemma Bennink, 'The Nature of Reconciliation as an Outcome and as a Process' in Bar-Siman Tov, *From Conflict Resolution*, above n 116, 12.

[155] Erin Daly, 'Transformative Justice: Charting a Path to Reconciliation' (2001–2) 12(1 & 2) *International Legal Perspectives* 73.

[156] Lederach discusses four distinct and necessary dimensions in post-conflict peace building: the socio-political, the socio-economic, the social-psychological, and the spiritual. John Paul Lederach, 'Beyond Violence: Building Sustainable Peace' in Eugene Weiner (ed.) *The Handbook of Interethnic Co-existence* (Continuum, 1998). 236, 245.

[157] Daniel Bar-Tal, 'Societal Beliefs of Intractable Conflicts' (1998) 9 *International Journal of Conflict Management* 22, 35.

[158] Hamber and Kelly, above n 114, 302.

[159] Dwyer, above n 153, 89–95, 246.

damaged through warfare—a complex, difficult, and slow process[160]—that contains paradoxes and contradictions,[161] but which is ultimately profound and worthwhile.

3.4 Conclusion

In the final analysis, transitional justice discourse is exceedingly valuable for societies seeking to transcend conflict. As discussed, truth-telling, accountability through human rights norms, and reconciliation processes are both normatively as well as pragmatically desirable after large-scale violence. These goals have contributed to the signing of peace agreements in various contexts from the Good Friday Agreement to the Dayton Accords and have promoted co-existence and national catharsis. The next chapter will therefore consider the relevance of the transitional justice paradigm in the Israeli–Palestinian setting.

---

[160] Valery Peel, 'A Survey of Reconciliation Processes in Bosnia and Herzegovina: the Gap between People and Politics' in Joanna R (ed) Quinn, *Reconciliation (S) Transitional Justice in Postconflict Societies* (McGill-Queen's University Press, 2009), 208.

[161] David Bloomfield, 'The Concept of Reconciliation' in David Bloomfield, Teresa Barnes, and Luc Huyse (eds.) *Reconciliation after Violent Conflict: A Handbook* (International Institute for Democracy and Electoral Assistance, 2003) 10–18 cited in Hamber and Kelly, above n 114, 288.

Chapter 4
The Applicability of Transitional Justice to the Israeli–Palestinian Conflict

4.1 Introduction

> *Neither Israelis nor Palestinians can afford to ignore the mistakes of Oslo or to give up on the possibility of peace. The proposal to reconcile the two populations is not utopian; it is necessary.* [1]

This chapter explores the normative value of engaging with the fundamental goals of transitional justice to promote the resolution of the Israeli–Palestinian conflict. Indeed, as will be discussed, the Oslo process was a based on a fraught paradigm, which undermined historical memory and unhelpfully de-coupled discourses of justice, human rights, and reconciliation from peacemaking. Thus, the ensuing discussion will consider the potential relevance of truth-telling, justice-seeking, and reconciliation to Israelis and Palestinians.

Ultimately, it will be contended that these normative objectives are essential to any viable, meaningful, and sustainable conflict resolution process between the two nations grounded in the political framework of the two states envisaged by Oslo. Whilst the boundaries and viability of the two-state solution remain contested, the idea retains the support of significant proportion of Israelis and Palestinians, the EU, and the US. Of relevance to transitional justice, the two-state separation envisioned for Israel and Palestine would require extensive cooperation and joint agencies that could draw on the goals of the field. No doubt, the Israeli–Palestinian peace scenario is different from reconciliation within a single nation, but as will be discussed, transitional justice need not exclusively concern single societies transitioning into a liberal democracy after conflict.

[1] Zinaida Miller, 'Settling with History: A Hybrid Commission of Inquiry for Israel/Palestine' (2007) 20 *Harvard Human Rights Journal* 293, 323 (*'Settling with History'*).

J. Bracka, *Transitional Justice for Israel/Palestine*, Springer Series in Transitional Justice, https://doi.org/10.1007/978-3-030-89435-1_4

4.2 Part One: The Existing Israeli–Palestinian Paradigm of Conflict Resolution

Excluding Transitional Justice

Although the Oslo Accords marked a significant milestone towards peace, transitional justice has been all but absent in diplomatic efforts between the two nations. With the initiation of Oslo, both the sides crossed a critical threshold of mutual acknowledgement. The Israeli government officially recognised the PLO as a legitimate entity, and the Palestinians meanwhile, recognised the right of the State of Israel to exist in peace and security.[2] To a degree, this ended the rhetorical warfare of mutual denial, under which '...both sides withheld recognition as if it were the ultimate weapon in a peculiar version of mutual deterrence'.[3]

Nevertheless, the terms transitional justice and dealing with the past have not yet been seriously considered in the Israeli–Palestinian setting.[4] Goals of truth-telling, justice, and reconciliation were conspicuously removed from the diplomatic process, and 'proposals for such mechanisms have not been engaged with even in the margins of the political arena'.[5] Attempted settlements, including those at Oslo (1993), the Camp David Summit (2000), and the Taba Summit (2001), primarily addressed the territorial dimensions of the conflict, and the institutional arrangements, such as the nature of the Palestinian administration, borders, and security arrangements.[6] Several proposals since Oslo, including the Arab-Peace Initiative (2002), the Road Map (2002), the Nusseibeh-Ayalon Initiative (2002), the Geneva Initiative (2003), the Bush Initiative (2007), and the Annapolis Peace Conference (2008) continue to mirror this pragmatic approach. In sum, a major feature of the political landscape is that it continues to frame conflict resolution in practical and material terms, deliberately

---

[2] Mathew. A Weiner, 'Defeating Hatred With Truth: An Argument in Support of a Truth Commission as part of the solution to Israel/Palestine' (2005–2006) 38 *Connecticut Law Review* 123,141.

[3] 'For just as the Israelis...persisted in denying the Palestinians the legitimacy attached to an independent national identity, so did the Palestinians and the Arab world consistently deny that the Israelis were a people, or that Zionism could be considered a legitimate national movement'. Rashid Khalidi, *Palestinian Identity: The Construction of Modern National Consciousness* (Columbia University Press, 1997) 205.

[4] Rosalind Shaw and Lars Waldorf with Pierre Hazan (eds), *Localizing Transitional Justice: Interventions and Priorities After Mass Violence* (Stanford University Press, 2010) 237.

[5] Ron Dudai, 'Does Any of this Matter?' Transitional Justice and the Israeli-Palestinian conflict' in David Downes, Rock, Paul, Chinkin, Christine and Gearty, Conor (eds), *Crime, Social Control and Human Rights: From moral panics to states of denial - Essays in honour of Stanley Cohen* (Willan Publishing, 2007) 340. (*'Does Any of this Matter?'*).

[6] For example, Oslo II (1995) established important organs of Palestinian self-government and called for Israeli military redeployment from parts of the territories. See Geoffrey Watson, *The Oslo Accords: International Law and the Israeli-Palestinian Peace Agreements* (Oxford University Press, 2000) at 44. See also Jill Alisson Weiner, 'Israel, Palestine and the Oslo Accords' (1999–2000) 23 *Fordham International Law Journal* 230, 245.

avoiding thorny issues of the past, like questions of legitimacy, narratives, justice, collective memory, and remedies for human rights abuse.

Sidelining '1948' and 'Justice'

> *What happened in 1948 is the subject of controversy, and the peace process shouldn't be the arena in which historical truth is pronounced.* (Israeli Attorney-General Elyakim Rubinstein)[7]

Most significantly, Oslo sidestepped 1948 and the festering dispute over the genesis of the conflict. Notwithstanding the centrality of the Palestinian displacement, or perhaps precisely because of it, there have been few attempts to address the historical dimensions of the dispute at the political level. Indeed, both Oslo (1993) and Oslo II (1995) expressly deferred the question of the Palestinian refugees, the status of Jerusalem and existing Jewish settlements until final negotiations '...postponing any "policing of the past" to a future unspecified stage.'[8] Thus, the deepest desires of the parties for mutual validation of their collective memories from 1948, namely Palestinian acceptance of a Jewish state, and Israeli recognition of the Nakba, were sidelined.[9] Ultimately, Oslo was an attempt to solve the problem of the occupation without fundamentally questioning the existing political, social and historical discursive structures supporting the conflict.[10] 'History now began in 1967...Fundamental questions of justice, such as the 1948 refugees were placed on the political back burner'.[11]

Moreover, the Oslo paradigm exposed the cleavage between the two parties on 1948 and the relevance of justice to the political process. As Bell argues: '[i]n both their text and their implementation, the Israeli-Palestinian peace agreements demonstrate a complete divorce between the concept of peace and the concept of justice'.[12] To a degree, the security doctrine dominated the Oslo peace process and became the yardstick against which Israelis measured its progress. Arguably, Israel's desire to preserve the military status quo undermined its will to make concessions,

---

[7] Shaw and Waldorf, above n 4, 237.

[8] Lauri King-Irani, 'To Reconcile or be Reconciled?: Agency, Accountability and Law in Middle-Eastern Conflicts' (2004–2005)328 *Hastings and International and Comparative Law Review* 369, 375; See also Kathleen Cavanaugh, 'Selective Justice: The Case of Israel and the Occupied Territories' (2002–2003)26 *Fordham International Law Journal*, 934, 940–941.

[9] Jacob Shamir and Khalil Shikaki, 'Public Opinion in the Israeli-Palestinian Two-Level Game' (2005) 42 *Journal of Peace Research* 311, 315.

[10] Asima Ghazi-Bouillon, *Understanding the Middle East Peace Process: Israeli Academia and the Struggle for Identity* (Routledge, 2009) 92.

[11] Ibid 78.

[12] Christine Bell, *Peace Agreements and Human Rights* (Oxford: Oxford University Press, 2000) 205 ('*Peace Agreements*').

denied Palestinian symbolism and honour,[13] and undercut the public's ability to identify with the potential benefits of Oslo.

For Israelis, the negotiations were centred on the fate of 1967, assuming that a territorial agreement based on separation would in time lead to peace (building on the relatively successful examples of peace treaties between Israel and Egypt and Israel and Jordan).[14] Conversely, for Palestinians, the 1948 war, the refugee question, and notions of justice were critical to the negotiations. According to Pappe: 'The Palestinian view deals with the more distant past, and less visible layers of the conflict focusing on responsibility, guilt and justice'.[15] Whilst some plans[16] involved attempts to deal with 1948, none of them sought to fully grapple with the psychological and historical barriers of this past nor envisaged a transitional justice mechanism.

Sidelining Human Rights

The Oslo paradigm also sidelined moral, human rights, and international legal elements from the peace process. No explicit human rights or international law provisions were contained in either the DOP (1993) or the subsequent Israeli–Palestinian agreements. Oslo II (1995) required both Israelis and Palestinians to pay 'due regard' to 'internationally-accepted norms...of human rights'.[17] Nevertheless, the Wye Agreement (1998) makes no reference to human rights obligations and only vaguely refers to the responsibilities of the Palestinian police.[18] The Road Map (2002) does not address human rights at all.

---

[13] Kobi Michael, 'Chapter 9: The Geopolitical Environment as a Barrier to Resolution of the Israeli-Palestinian Conflict' in Bar-Siman-Tov, above n 13,345–6.

[14] Yaacov Bar -Siman-Tov, 'Introduction: Barriers to Conflict Resolution' in Ibid, 15, 26.

[15] Ilan Pappe, 'The Visible and Invisible in the Israeli-Palestinian Conflict' in Lustick Ann M. Lesch and Ian S (ed) *Exile and Return: predicaments of Palestinians and Jews* (University of Pennsylvania Press, 2005) 279–296, 279; See also Ibid.

[16] As will be discussed below, Barak's Peace proposal at Camp David (2000) made some attempt to include 1948 into the peace process. On the issue of return, he made a symbolic offer to allow an amount of Palestinian refugees into Israel proper on the basis of family reunification.

[17] Oslo II (1995) also required both sides to take measures designed to fight and prevent terrorism and obligated the Palestinians 'to remove anti-Semitic and anti-Israel clauses [from the Palestinian National Charter]'. Watson, above n 6, 46.

[18] The Wye River Memorandum has a reference only to the obligation of Palestinian police to behave according to 'internationally accepted norms of human rights and the rule of law'. The Israeli delegation led by PM Netanyahu was allegedly adamant in refusing to accept any commitment to human rights standards. See Mari Mustafa, 'The Negotiation Process: the lack of human rights component' (2003) 10(3) *Palestine Israel Journal* 5, 9. See also Ibrahim Bisharat and Edward Kaufman, 'Introducing human rights into conflict resolution: the relevance for the Israeli-Palestinian peace process '(2002) 1(1) *Journal of Human Rights* 71, 78.

Indeed, the brokered agreements failed to outline any legal measures, human rights standards or mechanisms to examine and/or resolve past abuses, nor to '...consider the impact of post-agreement practices on the human rights of ordinary civilians'.[19] Oslo's language of 'future arrangements' also ignored an evaluation of present legal realities.[20] Accountability and institutional mechanisms that are 'an essential component of any transitional process [were] conspicuously absent'.[21] The leaderships of both the Israeli Labour Party and the PLO may have avoided human rights language out of pragmatic considerations.[22] Oslo was also shaped by Israel's hegemonic security discourse,[23] which regarded justice and human rights issues as barriers to peace.[24]

By contrast, it is worth noting that human rights clauses were tightly threaded through Northern Ireland's peace accords, and the European Convention on Human Rights set the standards for domestic law.[25] So too for South Africa, human rights institutions were instrumental to establishing and legitimating the new democratic order.[26] In Cyprus, political negotiations generally acknowledge the historical experience of displacement, along with the need for legal compensation for the refugees.[27] This is an alternative to the broad rejectionism in Israeli discourse regarding the Palestinian refugee issue.[28] Arguably, the Oslo Accords' exclusive focus on practical clauses and the sidelining of human rights is a source of their weakness.[29] Overall, the Israeli–Palestinian peace process has a paucity of vocabulary for contesting human rights abuse, unlawful practices (from settlements to suicide bombing) and contemplating accountability and/or restorative justice mechanisms.

---

[19] Mustafa, above n 18, 9.

[20] Zinaida Miller, 'Perils of Parity: Palestine's Permanent Transition' (2014) 47 *Cornell International Law Journal* 331, 415 (*'Perils of Parity'*).

[21] Cavanaugh, above n 8, 955; Bisharat and Kaufman, above n 18, 78.

[22] Bisharat and Kaufman, above n 18, 81.

[23] Yaacov Bar -Siman-Tov, 'Introduction: Barriers to Conflict Resolution' in Bar-Siman-Tov, above n 13, 27.

[24] Asaf Lebovitz 'Why the Left cannot bring Peace' Haaretz article; See also Nadim Rouhana, 'Identity and Power in Israeli-Palestinian Reconciliation' (2000/2001) 3(2) *Israeli Sociology* 277, 300 (*'Identity and Power'* (2000)).

[25] Bisharat and Kaufman, above n 18, 79.

[26] While many criticisms are made of different aspects of the South African approach, it is the case that Bell puts first among her case studies in a summary ranking of the human rights measures included in various peace deals, 'according to detail and capacity to deliver change'. The Israel/ Palestine deal comes last. See Bell, *Peace Agreements*, above n 12, 231.

[27] Akin to the Israeli–Palestinian conflict, the problem of refugees, property, and compensation is laden with historic significance in Cyprus. Dahlia Scheindlin, 'Lessons from Cyprus for Israel-Palestine: Can Negotiations Still Work?' (Mitvism, September 2016) 8.

[28] Ibid.

[29] Bisharat and Kaufman, above n 18, 81.

Sidelining Reconciliation

The discourse of reconciliation was also excluded from the Israeli–Palestinian peace process. There have been very few significant reconciliation actions taken by major leaders on either side. In fact, some important leaders in both the camps have denounced attempts at reconciliation actions.[30] Arguably, the Oslo process fell short of fundamentally affecting Israeli or Palestinian policy, society, and identity. Thus, despite military withdrawals and the creation of the PA, Israel's approach to settlement building did not really change, nor for example did Palestinian demands to return to their original homes.[31] Rather, the Oslo framework embodied a top-down pragmatic approach of 'conflict settlement' in which territorial compromise was of cardinal importance, and reconciliation was at best, a marginal concern.[32] In this way, '…the lack of truth and reconciliation initiatives ensured the negotiations remained an elite process between political and diplomatic leaderships without wider circles of society being engaged...'.[33] Oslo was essentially a political process that did not seek to resolve the conflict at a grassroot level.

The dissociation of the Israeli–Palestinian peace process from an overarching concept of 'reconciliation' is of major significance.[34] Indeed, contrary to the peace processes in either Northern Ireland or South Africa, 'the Oslo process was about *separation*, rather than *accommodation*…while the end game (partition) was accepted by both sides, the Agreements were [merely] left to provide the interim measures to achieve the divorce'.[35] For example, Knox and Quirk demonstrate how leaders in Northern Ireland and South Africa were more actively engaged in 'building peace', contrasting the situation in Israel, where the process is described as still about 'making peace' devoid of considerations of justice and reconciliation.[36] For example, the Good Friday Agreement (1998) explicitly recognised the 'tragedies of the past', 'the achievement of reconciliation', and 'the protection and vindication of the human rights of all'.[37]

Notably, Barak's Peace proposal at Camp David (2000) made some attempt to introduce reconciliation into the peace process. On the issue of return, he made a symbolic offer to allow an amount of Palestinian refugees into Israel proper on the

---

[30] Louis Kriesberg, 'The Relevance of Reconciliation Actions in the Breakdown of Israeli-Palestinian Negotiations, 2000' (2002) 27(4) *Peace and Change* 546. 564–5.

[31] Ghazi-Bouillon, above n 10, 92.

[32] Jacob Shamir and Khalil Shikaki, 'Determinants of Reconciliation and Compromise Among Israelis and Palestinians' (2002) 39 *Journal of Peace Research* 185, 189, 198.

[33] Ron Dudai, 'A Model for Dealing with the Past in the Israeli-Palestinian Context' (2007) 1 *International Journal of Transitional Justice* 249, 253 (*'A Model'*).

[34] Aeyal Gross, 'The Constitution, Reconciliation and Transitional Justice: Lessons from South Africa and Israel' (2004) 40 *Stanford Journal of International Law* 47, 55.

[35] Cavanaugh, above n 8, 959.

[36] Colin and Quirk Knox, Padraic, *Peacebuilding in Northern Ireland, Israel and South Africa: Transition, Transformation and Reconciliation* (Palgrave, 2000) 197–198.

[37] The Belfast Agreement 10 April 1998, Declaration of Support: 2.

basis of family reunification.[38] Nevertheless, the Israeli negotiating team rejected recognition of responsibility for 1948, and refused to address the principle of return to Israel proper. Although Barak officially raised issues and possible solutions avoided in previous negotiations, Israeli conduct and Barak's own statements seemed to belie any offers of reconciliation.[39] Reconciliation actions at the unofficial and sub-elite level have also been sparse.[40] Accordingly, the prevailing rhetoric of 'peace talks' between Israelis and Palestinians is of 'separation and disengagement', rather than dialogue and truth-telling, and this above all else, echoes the prevailing political wisdom that historical justice and reconciliation have no meaningful role to play in the conflict's resolution.

4.3 Part Two: Normative Value of Transitional Justice to Israelis and Palestinians

Value of Engaging the Past and Truth-Telling

> *Recognizing that narratives matter acknowledges that the societies themselves have a deep stake in both the continuation and the ending of the conflict. It implies that the two societies have to recognize—not ignore—each other, and must squarely face each other's deepest beliefs....*[41]

A greater appreciation of the separate narratives that inform Israelis and Palestinians could plausibly contribute to peacebuilding and conflict resolution. Indeed, it is contended that, rather than obstructing negotiations, an honest and full accounting of the past for both Israelis and Palestinians is in fact the discursive and cognitive bridge required to reconcile both the nations. More specifically, a minimal requirement of any resolution will require a thorough reckoning with Israeli–Palestinian history by squarely addressing issues of collective memory, an ethos of victimhood, and the historical taboo of 1948.

Critiquing Oslo: Is the Past Too Potent to Ignore?

It is worth critiquing the prevailing notion that facing the past obstructs resolution of the Israeli–Palestinian conflict. In addition to Oslo's architects, many commentators and scholars maintain that the discussion of historic truths as futile and

---

[38] Tamar Hermann, 'Reconciliation: Reflections' in Bar-Siman-Tov, above n 13, 56.

[39] Ibid; During Barak's time as PM, Israelis expanded Jewish settlements, built more bypass roads, and demolished Palestinian homes. Kriesberg, above n 30, 565.

[40] Ibid, 564–5.

[41] Walid Salem, Benjamin Pogrund and Paul Scham (ed) *Shared Histories: A Palestinian-Israeli Dialogue* (Left Coast Press, 2005), 2.

counter-productive. Zakay and Fleisig regard Israelis and Palestinians debating history as an irrational distraction from 'realistic' solutions.[42] This approach is premised on the belief that '...each party has its own version of history, and usually a strong sense of victimization...Discussions of these facts will only lead to irresolvable clashes of narratives...and leave the parties frustrated'.[43] Based on her experience with Israeli–Palestinian workshops, politician, and academic Tamir claims: 'I have found that an attempt to expose the facts is not particularly useful...if the peace process is to move forward it cannot proceed based on an investigation of the past...Peace cannot be grounded in competition over past suffering'.[44]

Nevertheless, it is arguable that the perceived undesirability of dealing with the past contributed to the demise of Oslo and continues to significantly obstruct the conflict's resolution. According to several commentators, the avoidance of historical narratives, whether by negotiators or between the two publics, was a key element in the diplomatic breakdown. Dajani,[45] Dudai,[46] Miller,[47] and Golan-Agnon[48] all cite Oslo's failure to discuss history as a central cause of the impasse between Israelis and Palestinians. Indeed, given the socio-psychological underpinnings of the conflict (as discussed in Chap. 1), both sides' national narratives are arguably too steeped in collective memory to be dismissed.

A study by the US Institute for Peace on Oslo concluded that: 'history cannot be ignored in negotiations of communal conflict'.[49] Thus, despite formally de-coupling the peace talks from the past, each side remained caught up in its own psychological repertoire without realising it.[50] According to Dudai, this seriously hampered the parties' ability to deal with any of the substantive issues in solely 'material' terms.[51] Rothstein notes how the sidelining of the past at Camp David exacerbated tensions

---

[42] Dan Zakay and Dida Fleisig, 'The Time Factor As a Barrier to Resolution of the Israeli-Palestinian Conflict' in Bar-Siman-Tov, above n 13,17.

[43] Nadim Rouhana and Daniel Bar-Tal, 'Psychological dynamics of ethno-national conflict: The Israeli-Palestinian case'.(1998). 53 *American Psychologist'*, 761–770.

[44] Yael Tamir quoted in *The Feasibility of a Tribunal on Palestine* (Euro-Med Human Rights Network, January 2003) 30.

[45] Salem et al., above n 41, 2.

[46] Dudai *'Does any of this matter?'*, above n 5, 341.

[47] Miller, *Settling with History*, above n 1, 313.

[48] Daphna Golan-Agnon, 'Between Human Rights and Hope - What Israelis Might Learn from the Truth and Reconciliation Process in South Africa' (2010) 17 *International Review of Victimology* 31, 45.

[49] See Omar Dajani, 'Surviving Opportunities: Palestinian Negotiating Patterns in Peace Talks with Israel' in Tamar Cofman Wittes (ed.) *How Israelis and Palestinians Negotiate: A Cross-Cultural Analysis of the Oslo Peace Process* (U.S. Institute of Peace Press, 2005) 39, 69.

[50] Salem et al., above n 41, 4; Robert Rothstein, *How Not To Make Peace: 'Conflict Syndrome' and the Demise of the Oslo Accords*, United States Institute of Peace (March 2006).

[51] Ron Dudai and Hillel Cohen 'Dealing with the Past when the Conflict is still Present' Civil Society Truth-seeking Initiatives in the Israeli-Palestinian Conflict' in Shaw and Waldorf, above n 4, 235. (*'Dealing with the Past'*).

over the negotiations on land, refugees, and settlements.[52] For example, when Palestinians discuss refugees and the right of return, Israelis interpret a frontal attack on their national legitimacy. Regarding settlements and borders, what for Israelis are legitimate security measures is for Palestinians a perpetuation of dispossession and occupation. In sum, the peace process underestimated the historical shadow cast over all the major issues.

Moreover, the refusal to engage the past has arguably fuelled the 'meta-conflict' and made it harder to resolve.[53] Far from 'letting go of the past', the omission of history has in fact sustained perceptions of victimhood and an ethos of conflict. 'Thus, each violent attack by extremists from either side easily derails the process, "confirming" for each side that the other only wishes to destroy them'.[54] Israeli–Palestinian negotiations have proved insufficient in making these deep fears go away; in fact, in light of actions on the ground (mainly settlements and violence), they have only heightened them. In failing to address both peoples' basic yearnings, the Oslo paradigm was bound to fall short. For Palestinians, peace without some recognition of their suffering in 1948 seems inconceivable. Likewise for Israelis, the failure to recognise the Jewish people's historical links repudiates their deepest desires for acceptance into the region. Ultimately, the peace process became an arena in which: '…rumors and hearsay have triumphed over historical truth in the absence of any kind of authoritative approach to uncovering the pains of the past'.[55]

In this light, the architects of Oslo may have underestimated the importance of historical memory to conflict resolution. The assumption that 'borders can be discussed, lines moved, territories exchanged…'[56] without addressing the conflict at the deepest levels seems fraught. As Dudai concludes: 'These issues cannot be resolved on purely technical and forward-looking terms without engaging with each side's narratives and historical sensitivities'.[57] Ultimately, Oslo did not grasp the extent of the discursive barriers impeding the peace process.

Understanding this also sheds light on the importance of history to resolving the conflict at present. Indeed, the legacies of the Israeli–Palestinian past are no less formidable today. As discussed in Chap. 2, the recent 'Great March of Return' (2018) saw tens of thousands of Palestinian refugees demonstrating for their 1948 'right to return' at the Gaza border. Thus, it is submitted that recognising the past, and its conflicting versions is desirable to bridging the rhetorical divide. Squarely facing collective memory and mythology is no less important to peacemaking than devising technical formulas for border control and land swaps. This was true during the Oslo period and arguably remains the case three decades on.

---

[52] Rothstein, above n 50, 12–13.

[53] Dudai *'Does any of this matter?'*, above n 5, 341.

[54] Ibid 343.

[55] Andrew Rigby, *Justice and Reconciliation: After the Violence* (Lynne Rienner Publishers), 148.

[56] Golan-Agnon, above n 48, 45.

[57] Dudai and Cohen 'Dealing with the Past', above n 51, 235.

Value of Countering Denial and Impunity

Truth-telling is also relevant to counter the collective denial of human rights abuses on both sides across all major events of the conflict. Until today, some Palestinians sanctify as legitimate resistance suicide-bombing and terrorist attacks on civilians, while some Israelis dismiss military excesses and occupation abuses as unavoidable 'counter-terrorist' security measures.[58] For example, more than 4 years after the end of the 2014 Gaza–Israel conflict, in which some 1460 Palestinian civilians were killed, many in allegedly unlawful attacks, the Israeli authorities had indicted only three soldiers for looting and obstructing an investigation.[59] In August 2016, the Military Advocate General announced the closure of investigations into 12 incidents, despite evidence that some should be investigated as war crimes.[60]

Thus, until such cultures of impunity and historic responsibilities are faced, '…the current power imbalance between the parties will not allow for reconciliation, simply because the unchallenged narratives that guide each party's behaviour do not allow for compatible political moves'.[61] In this light, Israelis and Palestinians will need to consider peacebuilding, not only in terms of separation and co-existence, but also in terms of conflict transformation and mutual acknowledgement of past abuses. Truth-telling appears paramount to meaningful resolution of the conflict.[62]

Desirability of 'Justice' and Human Rights to Israelis and Palestinians

No less important to Israelis and Palestinians are issues of justice, acknowledgment, and accountability for human rights abuse. The ethos of injustice is deeply embedded into the struggle. Like the historical narratives, it is one of the 'organising principles' of each nation's beliefs and positions in the conflict.[63] As Rouhana observes: 'From a Palestinian viewpoint, injustice is at the core of the conflict and, therefore,

---

[58] A study conducted during the Second Intifada noted that 27% of Israeli Jews thought it justifiable to violate human rights in the territories because of terrorism. Ifat Maoz and Clark McCauley, 'Threat, Dehumanisation and Support for Retaliatory Agressive Policies in Asymmetric Conflict '(2008) 52 *Journal of Conflict Resolution* 93, 94.

[59] *Network of Concerned Historians*, Annual Report 2017 (July 2017) 62.

[60] Ibid.

[61] Nadim Rouhana, 'Group Identity and Power Asymmetry in Reconciliation Processes: The Israeli Palestinian Case '(2004) 10(1) *Journal of Peace Psychology* 33, 43 (*'Group Identity'*).

[62] 'Responding to these denials and myths is no less important than any attempt to reach yet another sophisticated technical formula for security arrangements or control of Jerusalem…'. Dudai *'Does any of this matter?'*, above n 5, 343.

[63] Elazar Barkan, 'Considerations Toward Accepting Historical Responsibility' in Lustick Ann M. Lesch and Ian S (ed) *Exile and Return: predicaments of Palestinians and Jews* (University of Pennsylvania Press, 2005) 85–105; Robert Rotberg (ed) *Israeli-Palestinian Narratives of Conflict: History's Double Helix* (Indiana University Press, 2006), 2; Salem et al., above n 41.

achieving some sort of justice is central for conflict resolution'.[64] Given the asymmetric power relations, Palestinians also demand procedural justice, whereby Israelis recognise them as equal partners in any peace process.[65]

Similarly for Israelis, the mass trauma wrought by terrorist acts, solider abductions, urban bombardment, Jewish persecution,[66] Arab warfare, and rejectionism may not be easily dismissed. For Israelis, historic justice is also framed in terms of national recognition. Until today, Israel demands acknowledgement of their perceived moral right to exist as a Jewish state.[67] Moreover, many Israelis regard the Palestinian armed struggle, which has included attacks on civilians and Jews outside Israel, as morally reprehensible. For many Israelis, the need for justice include Palestinian assurances that they are not out to destroy them and an acknowledgement of past wrongs. Thus, a vital requirement for conflict resolution between the parties is to facilitate recognition of their historic rights, acceptance of responsibility, and some form of atonement for the past.[68]

Arguably, Oslo's failure to compensate or to acknowledge Israeli victims of Palestinian terrorism, or the thousands of Palestinian casualties caused by Israel, was a source of the accords' weakness.[69] By excluding human rights and (more generally) international law principles and standards from the political process, the conflict narrative and historic grievances remained intact, and the accords could implicitly endorse continuing violations.[70] Thus, Cavanaugh warns: 'As the current situation reveals, transitional mechanisms that fail to address the underpinnings of

[64] Rouhana, *'Identity and Power'* (2000), above n 24, 23.

[65] 'But I think real principle and real justice have to be implemented before there can be true dialogue. Real dialogue is between equals, not between subordinate and dominant partners'. Edward W. Said, *Peace and its Discontents: Essays on Palestine in the Middle East Peace Process* (Vintage Books, 1996) 38.

[66] 'It is obvious that there was no responsibility, whatsoever, direct or indirect by the Palestinians for the holocaust. But this innocence did not exempt them from the effects of the holocaust that culminated in the establishment of the State of Israel…Palestinians have to be able to work on their reaction to holocaust in the direction of being able to recognize and acknowledge the other's agony and suffering on a human basis…'. See Salem et al., above n 41,152.

[67] In May 2014, PM Netanyahu ruled out any deal with the Palestinians unless they recognise Israel as the Jewish state and give up their refugees' right of return. Although Palestinians now recognise Israel they deny the essence of Zionism—the Jewish people's right to establish a Jewish state in Palestine.

[68] Peled and Rouhana suggest along these lines that meaningful symbolic gestures, particularly official recognition of past injustices, are as important as more tangible redress. See Yoav Peled and Nadim Rouhana, 'Transitional Justice and the Right to Return of the Palestinian Refugees' (2004) 5 *Theoretical Inquiries in Law* 317. See also Rashid Khalidi, 'Attainable Justice: Elements of a Solution to the Palestinian Refugee Issue' (1998) 33(2) (Spring) *International Journal* 233, 239.

[69] Mathew Weiner, above n 2, 148; Bisharat and Kaufman, above n 18, 79.

[70] Arguably, Oslo's ambiguity regarding the application of the Geneva Conventions allowed for continued settlement construction and land expropriation in contravention of Articles 49 and 49. See Cavanaugh, above n 8, 955.

conflict and so detach the concepts of peace and justice, will most certainly fail'.[71] Many authors echo the claim that without a minimum consensus on the moral basis for negotiations and some recognition of past abuse, it is doubtful that the conflict can be resolved or that peaceful relations can be established.[72]

Justice as a Barrier or Bridge?

Justice will destroy all of us, so let so let's think of less than justice.[73]

Nevertheless, the exclusion of justice from Israeli–Palestinian conflict resolution is principally defended. Many theorists claim that justice is a subjective, biased, and protected value,[74] and allowing it to become the subject of negotiations would only fuel further conflict. Arguably, principled demands are impervious to rational argument or compromise.[75] At present, both the nations tend to frame their historical narratives and ethos of justice as protected values that are not subject to negotiation, bargaining, or compromise.[76] The desire for recapturing the past, and loss of pride, especially among the weaker side '…leads to embedding of distrust into the warp and woof of the conflict itself'.[77] This tendency to anchor justice in conflict narrative and faith may indeed pose an obstacle to peace. Moreover, demands of historical justice arguably heighten paranoia among Israelis, rather than increase their sympathy to Palestinian claims. Arguably, a Palestinian attachment to absolute justice and victimhood is a formidable barrier to conflict resolution.[78] In the words of Israeli negotiator Ben-Ami: 'the Palestinian leadership was not searching for a solution but for justice'.[79]

---

[71] Ibid 960.

[72] Miller, *Settling with History*, above n 1, 307; Yaacov Bar-Siman-Tov, 'Chapter 5: Justice and Fairness as Barriers to the Resolution of the Israeli-Palestinian Conflict' in Bar-Siman-Tov, above n 13,196; Dudai *'Does any of this matter?'*, above n 5, 343.

[73] Hadas Baram 'Roundtable 1948: Independence and the *Nakba*'. (2008) 15 (1 &2*) Palestine-Israel Journal* 114.

[74] 'Both sides frame their historical narratives and ethos of injustice as protected values that are not subject to negotiation, bargaining or compromise'. Yaacov Bar-Siman-Tov, 'Chapter 5: Justice and Fairness as Barriers to the Resolution of the Israeli-Palestinian Conflict' in Bar-Siman-Tov, above n 13,196.

[75] 'The historical debate [on justice] only constitutes a barrier…because it almost certainly leads each side to solidify its thinking and permanently fix its version, preventing the finding of a creative solution...'. Yechiel Klar, Keren Sharvit and Dan Zakay and '"If I Don't Get Blown Up…": Realism in Face of Terrorism in an Israeli Nationwide Sample'. (2002) 7 *Risk Decision and Policy*, 203–219.

[76] Yaacov Bar-Siman-Tov, 'Chapter 5: Justice and Fairness as Barriers to the Resolution of the Israeli-Palestinian Conflict' in Bar-Siman-Tov, above n 13,196.

[77] Rothstein, above n 50,13.

[78] Yaacov Bar-Siman-Tov, 'Chapter 5: Justice and Fairness as Barriers to the Resolution of the Israeli-Palestinian Conflict' in Bar-Siman-Tov, above n 13,207.

[79] Shlomo Ben-Ami 'A Front without a Rearguard: A Voyage to the Boundaries of the Peace Process' (2004) *Yediot Ahronoth* Tel Aviv (Hebrew) quoted in Ibid 207.

However, one could also persuasively refute the need to exclude justice from Israeli–Palestinian peace efforts. Firstly, there exists the potential for broad agreements on basic principles of justice.[80] 'Even if the parties accept a conception of justice independent of realistic external moral guidelines, there is still space within this contextual subjectivity for agreement on some components of justice'.[81] As discussed above, human rights law can be linked to the framing of justice. For example, Israelis and Palestinians could agree on some basic human rights law standards that targeting civilians, unlawful detention, and expulsions are unjust or that mutual respect for both the nations' self-determination and IHL is a virtue.[82] In this way, shared notions of justice might strengthen political negotiations and legitimate peace efforts rather than weaken them. Ultimately, '[t]he issue is not whether parties should use a framework of justice, but rather which framework of justice the parties should use'.[83]

From this standpoint, it is contended that international human rights norms should inform the discourse of justice in the Israeli–Palestinian context. As with other countries, international legal principles have supported the negotiating process, as well as guided the texts of peace agreements with universal moral standards. As discussed above, there are ample instances in which specific human rights issues were addressed in the resolution of ethno-national conflicts, including those involving refugees, systemic human rights abuses, and war crimes.[84]

Introducing a human rights dimension into conflict resolution may generate innovative measures of acknowledgment and compensation to help resolve the Palestinian right of return. For the conflict over 1967, applying a human rights discourse to the occupation could help reorient the Israeli public towards its democratic rather than nationalist tendencies. For Israelis, Jewish nationalism continues to legitimate the occupation and the placing of settlements 'above moral-human considerations'.[85] Approaching the occupation from a human rights perspective, the Israeli public might be encouraged to accept that the territories are in fact 'occupied' and that some of its policies have violated international law and moral standards to which Israel itself subscribes.[86] A language of justice as human rights

---

[80] Rouhana, *Group Identity*, above n 61, 47.

[81] Ibid.

[82] Ibid.

[83] Ibid, 48.

[84] Mustafa, above n 18, 7.

[85] Until today, Israeli leaders stir religious nationalist sentiment to justify the state's conduct and presence in the territories. See Gadi Taub, *The Settlers And the Struggle over the Meaning of Zionism* (Yale University Press, 2010), 45; Dan Zakay and Dida Fleisig, 'The Time Factor As a Barrier to Resolution of the Israeli-Palestinian Conflict' in Bar-Siman-Tov, above n 13, 264–299.

[86] 'But by far, the occupation of the West Bank and Gaza since 1967 is Israel's most glaring violation of democratic rights and liberal values'. Taub, above n 85, 32; Daniel Bar-Tal (et al), 'Psychological Legitimization -Views of the Israeli Occupation by Jews in Israel: Data and Implications' in Daniel Bar-Tal and Izhak Schnell, *'The Impacts of Lasting Occupation' Lessons from Israeli Society* (Oxford University Press, 2012), 175.

norms could bolster attempts to settle the Israeli–Palestinian conflict. By creatively addressing a range of victims' rights with truth recovery and acknowledgement mechanisms, concerns about justice need not be pushed aside for political expediency.

Justice to Reduce Asymmetry of Power

Deference to justice and human rights might also ameliorate the power imbalance between Israelis and Palestinians, which has hampered negotiations. Arguably, Israel's power-orientated military culture regarding Palestinians informs the political process.[87] Many Palestinians feel that conflict resolution efforts have been sorely lacking in procedural justice and moral legitimacy.[88] Critics of Oslo argue that the process merely entrenched injustice,[89] by imposing a 'hegemonic peace', in which the consistent element is Israeli domination and Palestinian supplication.[90] Given Israel's geo-political superiority, Palestinians have a well-founded fear of Israel dictating the terms of any peace deal. The Oslo paradigm tended to promote aspects of transition that preserved the relative power imbalance on the ground and the status quo, based on Israeli military concerns.[91]

No one argues that Israel should ignore valid security concerns. However, by showing more willingness to recognise the Palestinian experience of injustice and 1948, it is likely negotiations would yield more positive results. Framing concessions in the language of justice might be equally decisive. For example: 'Rather than conceding they will 'give up' territories…the Israeli authorities should stress that the Palestinians have an inherent right to a state in part of historic Israel of Palestine'.[92] By bridging the gap through symbolic gestures, 'the dominant actor's measures can persuade the weak to feel empowered to negotiate acceptance of other claims'.[93]

[87] Baruch Kimmerling, *Clash of Identities: Explorations in Israeli and Palestinian Societies* (Columbia University Press, 2013) 255.

[88] Yaacov Bar-Siman-Tov, 'Chapter 5: Justice and Fairness as Barriers to the Resolution of the Israeli-Palestinian Conflict' in Bar-Siman-Tov, above n 13, 200–201.

[89] 'This is not a reconciliation between two equals: it is a situation where dominance of one over the other prevails, and where after a century of conflict there is an unequivocal winner and a clear loser'. Khalidi, above n 3, 204; Pappe insists that Oslo is but a reflection of the Israeli–Palestinian power imbalance and likely to perpetuate injustice. Pappe, above n 15, 38.

[90] See Glenn E. Robinson, 'The Peace of the Powerful' in *The New Intifada: Resisting Israel's Apartheid* Roane Carey, ed. (Verso, 2001); Said, above n 65, 37.

[91] Miller, *Perils of Parity,* above n 20, 411.

[92] Edward Kaufman 'Human rights dimensions in peace-making' in Elizabeth G Mathews, *'The Israel-Palestine Conflict' Parallel Discourses* (Routledge, 2011) 181.

[93] Ibid, 180.

Moreover, there is a qualitative value of justice to counter an asymmetry of power with a discourse of mutual respect.[94] Indeed, some of Israel's negotiators admitted that the Oslo process could have been conducted with more direct and egalitarian dialogue, one that respected Palestinian notions of honour and justice.[95] Whilst Israelis are indeed the stronger party, human rights standards are equally relevant to them as victims of ongoing terrorism.[96] In this light, human rights and 'justice' may be reciprocal demands based on shared interests and national concerns. In sum, justice is simply too important to be declared irrelevant and traded for a minimalist conflict-settlement approach, which merely perpetuates the unequal balance of power.

Desirability of Reconciliation to Israelis and Palestinians

Value of Reconciliation as Conflict Transformation

In addition to truth-telling and justice-seeking measures, Israelis and Palestinians will need to engage in reconciliation efforts to achieve sustainable peace. As noted in Chap. 3, identity-based conflicts are the most susceptible to intractability.[97] Given the nature of the Israeli–Palestinian struggle as one characterised by antagonistic belief systems and national identities, it is arguable that thicker models of reconciliation based on conflict transformation are most desirable. Precisely because the gap and contradictions between national claims appear so vast and unbridgeable, reconciliation efforts are particularly relevant. As discussed, the goals of reconciliation would seek to form new relationships between Israelis and Palestinians by addressing historical grievances while working toward future cooperation.[98] As Oslo's demise demonstrates, reaching a purely political formula for resolving the Israeli–Palestinian conflict is insufficient.[99]

---

[94] 'The asymmetry of having an overwhelming advantage may appear to be extremely helpful…[but] when negotiating with those who have known nothing but powerlessness for nearly forty years, empowerment is the name of the game'. Ibid.

[95] See Uri Savir, *The Process: 1100 Days that Changed the Middle East.*(Vintage, 1999); Yaacov Bar-Siman-Tov, 'Chapter 5: Justice and Fairness as Barriers to the Resolution of the Israeli-Palestinian Conflict' in Bar-Siman-Tov, above n 13, 200–201.

[96] 'It is crucial to remind ourselves that universal rights apply to any individual, be they a terrorist, a refugee or a settler'. Kaufman, above n 92, 189.

[97] Barbara Tint, 'History, Memory and Intractable Conflict' (Spring 2010) 27(3) *Conflict Resolution Quarterly* 239, 244; Daniel Bar-Tal, 'Societal Beliefs of Intractable Conflicts' (1998) 9 *International Journal of Conflict Management* 22, 35.

[98] Hania Bekdash, 'Information Brief - Reconciliation: Lessons for Peace and Justice in Palestine' (2009) (Part One) *The Palestine Centre* 1–6.

[99] Kriesberg, above n 30, 565.

Value of Grass Roots Reconciliation and Empathy

> *Israelis and Palestinians continue to recoil from one another…through glasses that attribute satanic characteristics to the other... A process of reconciliation will not cause the two peoples to become friends, but it will, perhaps, enable them to turn over a new leaf.*[100]

Grassroot approaches to reconciliation are especially valuable to Israelis and Palestinians, given the pernicious effects of conflict on clouding mutual perceptions. As discussed, a crucial reason for the collapse of Oslo was the failure of public education on both the sides to humanise the 'enemy' and create an awareness of the historical issues. A fundamental transformation of the conflict must rest on more substantial discursive changes relating to justice, truth-telling, mutual regard, and mutual security. 'Those changes must occur at the elite level but also to a significant degree at all other levels of each society'.[101] In this light, reconciliatory projects that foster a genuine sense of honesty and human compassion, and which directly involve civil society, may assist the parties to address the core elements of the conflict.[102] In short, 'peace is not the absence of war, it is the negation of the conflict culture'.[103] Halphern and Weinstein argue that empathy is critical to reconciliation, noting that: 'co-existence without empathy is superficial and fragile'.[104] 'The starting point is overcoming nationalism and ethnocentrism. Without this, no Palestinian-Israeli dialogue on historiographical, moral, and philosophical levels is possible'.[105] Ultimately, creating a platform for grassroot reconciliation would greatly enhance the prospects of peace in the Middle East.

Value of Bridging Narrative and Critical History

Most significantly, reconciliation will need to afford proper weight to historic truth, critical history, and forging an authoritative narrative around the conflict's major events. As detailed in Chap. 1, the existing Israeli–Palestinian relationship is often treated as zero-sum in terms of the differing historical narratives. Cultivating a nuanced historic truth, independent of polarised collective memory, is therefore central to reconciliation. Critical history should impel the deconstruction and

---

[100] Uzi Bensimon, 'Needed Reconciliation', *Haaretz,* 12 October 2005.

[101] Kriesberg, above n 30, 565.

[102] Bar-Tal, above n 97, 35.

[103] Ariel Meyerstein, 'Transitional Justice and Post-Conflict Israel/Palestine: Assessing the Applicability of the Truth Commission Paradigm' (2006–2007) 38 *Case Western Journal of International Law* 281, 304.

[104] '…Just below the surface is mistrust, resentment and even hatred'. Brandon Hamber and Grainne Kelly 'Beyond Coexistence: Towards a Working Definition of Reconciliation' in Joanna R (ed) Quinn, *Reconciliation (S) Transitional Justice in Postconflict Societies* (McGill-Queen's University Press, 2009), 288–289.

[105] Pappe, above n 15, 293.

reformulation of the hegemonic Palestinian and Israeli narratives.[106] Arguably, a precondition to conflict resolution is reconciliation with Israeli–Palestinian history.[107]

Indeed, formulating a common historical narrative is not impossible. For example, a joint German, Czech, and Slovak historical commission succeeded in drafting a common interpretation of the events of 1938–1947. A similar joint historical reconciliation project could be conceived for Israelis and Palestinians. 'It may present a unified story that not everyone will agree on but it would be a powerful starting point to a necessary conversation'.[108] In a bow to this concept, the Geneva Accords (2003) (which will be discussed in Chap. 7) emphasise the need for reconciliatory mechanisms in addition to compensation and resettlement. The Accords specifically mention historical narrative and mutual understanding regarding the past.[109] Ultimately, in the Israeli–Palestinian context, conflict transformation requires an examination and reformulation of the narrative itself.

Value of Reconciliatory Gestures

More specifically, reconciliation could usefully involve specific actions that acknowledge the past, like revisiting the history of the conflict, expressing an apology and offering reparations to Israelis and Palestinians.[110] In this light, the reconciliatory goal of transitional justice is uniquely placed to have historical rights and injustices acknowledged. For example regarding 1948, Israelis continue to officially deny any responsibility for the creation of the refugees (Chap. 1), and Palestinians still refuse, by and large, to recognise the consequences of their long-term rejection of Israel's right to exist as a Jewish state.[111] Reconciliatory gestures around these issues could therefore 'help to move the conflict from the realm of exchanging pieces of territory under near-compulsion to a relationship that encompasses the human history of each side, as understood and experienced by the protagonists'.[112] Arguably, even small actions towards reconciliation may generate increased trust and understanding and reciprocated actions between Israelis and Palestinians. [113]

---

[106] Ibid.

[107] Meyerstein above n 103, 302.

[108] Bekdash, above n 98.

[109] Geneva Initiative, The Geneva Accord: A Model Israeli-Palestinian Peace Agreement, art. 7.14(i), Dec. 12, 2003, available at http://www.geneva-accord.org (follow 'The Accord' hyperlink). See also Miller, *Settling with History*, above n 1, 307.

[110] Rafi Nets-Zehngut, 'Passive Healing of the Aftermath of Intractable Conflicts' (Spring/Summer 2009) 14(1) *International Journal of Peace Studies* 39, 40; Tint, above n 97, 251.

[111] Many Palestinians distinguish between at least two levels of legitimacy: the legitimacy of Israel to exist and the legitimacy of Israel to exist as a Jewish state. See Nadim N. Rouhana 'Zionism's Encounter with the Palestinians: The Dynamics of Force, Fear, and Extremism' in Rotberg, above n 63, 138.

[112] Salem et al., above n 41, 2.

[113] Kriesberg, above n 30, 564.

Conclusion

Ultimately, the three central pillars of transitional justice (truth, justice, and reconciliation) are highly relevant to the Israeli–Palestinian conflict. Transitional justice may therefore be theoretically and practically conceived so as to give Israeli and Palestinian civil society and victims a central role in repairing the relationship between them. In this way, the field could strive for at least enough truth-telling, justice, and reconciliation to make a significant contribution to resolution of the struggle.

4.4 Part Three: Transitional Justice Mechanisms: Obstacles and Opportunities for the Israeli–Palestinian Conflict

Introduction

As noted in Chap. 3, there is no 'one size fits all' approach to dealing with the past. Transitional justice literature often highlights the problem of cultural differences between practitioners and participants in transitional justice activities.[114] Thus, any truth, justice, or reconciliation institution conceived for Israelis and Palestinians will need to be particularised. It must accommodate the unique historical context and political culture of the conflict discussed in Chap. 1. Notwithstanding the relevance of transitional justice to the Middle-East, there exist several objections to implementing such measures in this particular context, both at present, and even in a post-conflict future. Traditionally, transitional justice envisages one high-profile state-sanctioned mechanism created at the end of a conflict. However, the inter-state nature of the Israeli–Palestinian struggle, the continuity of leadership, and the ongoing violence each present unique challenges. At both a theoretical and practical level, it is therefore worth addressing the obstacles to and opportunities of transitional justice for Israelis and Palestinians.

Expanding the Theoretical Framework for Israeli–Palestinian Mechanisms

Beyond 'Overnight Transition'

One of the principal objections to transitional justice in the Middle East is that such measures are typically envisaged in the post-conflict stage. Thus truth, justice, and reconciliation efforts are described as premature, unrealistic, and inapplicable

[114] Rafi Nets-Zehngut, 'Transitional Justice and Addressing the History of Active Conflicts: The Case of the Israeli-Palestinian Conflict' (2011) 1–27, 3 ('Transitional Justice').

whilst war rages.[115] Indeed, transitional justice is dominated by theory and practice regarding non-active conflicts, focusing on the time periods *after* conflicts have ended.[116] Its mechanisms are commonly conceived for a political transition, involving a clear turning point and regime change from an authoritarian state to a democratic one.[117] In this light, transitional justice mechanisms appear more appropriate and effective in post-conflict societies, and/or where transitions are relatively linear.[118] In short, the 'paradigmatic transition'[119] involves a new liberal order and/or a political settlement between two political entities at the conclusion of hostilities.

What, then, of transitional justice for conflicts at varying stages of political and social transition like the Israeli–Palestinian one? How does one contend with theory narrowly drawn around the cessation of hostilities and linear regime change? Arguably, the orthodox discourse is 'somewhat problematic, in that it implies a defined period of flux after which a post-transitional state sets in'.[120] Rather, as the etymology of 'transition' makes clear, the term itself intimates a journey.[121] Teitel herself acknowledges that 'not all transformations exhibit the same degree of "normative shift".'[122] Indeed, many post-conflict nations remain in '...varying degrees of legal, political, emotional, physical, and social dysfunction in the wake of gross violations of human rights'.[123] For example, decades after its political transition to democracy, transitional justice remains as relevant as ever to South African society.[124] 'In reality, there are few examples of "ideal liberal transitions" where a clearly repressive and non-democratic regime is

[115] Adrien Wing, 'A Truth and Reconciliation Commission for Palestine/Israel: Healing Spirit Injuries?' (2008) 17(1) *Transnational Law and Contemporary Problems* 139, 141. See also Dudai, '*A Model*', above n 33, 250.

[116] Mahmoud Cherif Bassiouni (ed.) *Post-Conflict Justice* (New York: Transnational Publishers, 2002); Lavinia Stan, *Transitional Justice in Eastern Europe and the Former Soviet Union: Reckoning with the Communist Past*. (Routledge, 2010).

[117] Fionnuala Ni Aolain and Colm Campbell, 'The Paradox of Transition in Conflicted Democracies,' (2005) 27(1) *Human Rights* Quarterly 172,173; The term 'transition' is also referred to as the interval between one political regime and another. Guillermo O'Donnell and Philippe C. Schmitter, *Transition from Authoritarian Rule: Tentative Conclusions about Uncertain Democracies* (Johns Hopkins University Press, 1986).

[118] See Ni Aolain and Campbell, above n 117, 172.

[119] Ibid.

[120] Naomi Roht-Arriaza, 'Transitional Justice and Peace Agreements Working Paper' (2005) *Peace Agreements: The Role of Human Rights in Negotiations* 1–21, 1.

[121] Christine Bell, Colm Campbell, and Fionnuala Ni Aolain 'Justice Discourses in Transition' (2004) 13(3) *Social and Legal Studies* 305, 314.

[122] 'Indeed, one might conceptualise transitions along a transformative continuum in their relation to the predecessor regime and value system varying in degrees from "radical" to "conservative" change'. Ruti Teitel, *Transitional Justice* (Oxford University Press, 2000), 6.

[123] Miller, *Settling with History*, above n 1, 294.

[124] Elias O. Opongo, Jim Stormes, Kifle Wansamo, Peter Knox (eds.) *Transitional Justice in Post-Conflict Societies in Africa*, (Hekima Institute of Peace Studies and International Relations, 2015).

replaced by a clearly democratic rule-of-law...Usually, it is a matter of degree, and such changes seldom take place overnight'.[125]

In this light, any strict dichotomisation of 'transition' is questionable.[126] As will be discussed in subsequent chapters, the role of transitional justice in consolidated democracies such as the US, Australia, and Canada demonstrates that transitional justice is not unique to heightened periods of political transition. Indeed, states facing ongoing political violence, from Turkey, Northern Cyprus to Kenya and Colombia have all implemented a suite of transitional justice measures.[127] It may therefore be concluded that '...transition should be an invariable element of the justice equation, not only in times of heightened change, but at all times'.[128]

Indeed, this theoretical development is increasingly recognised by the field itself. In recent years, the ICTJ has acknowledged that transitional justice must be '...adapted to societies transforming themselves after pervasive human rights abuse. In some cases, these transformations happen suddenly; in others, they may take place over many decades'.[129] Accordingly, transition need not involve an identifiable starting and end point, but may involve longer and more fragmented processes as reflected by Northern Ireland's engagement with transitional justice.[130] In sum, the traditional concepts and mechanisms of transitional justice still apply to situations, which fall short of a clear-cut transition, like the Israeli–Palestinian one.

Beyond 'One Rainbow Nation'

From South Africa to Sierra Leone, transitional justice mechanisms are typically triggered within a single society. Gross observes that, whereas for South Africa, reconciliation and integration guided the transition from apartheid, the existence of two distinct and nationalistic societies in Israel/Palestine invites a different discourse.[131] Accordingly, many challenge the applicability of transitional justice to Israelis and Palestinians as the endgame is one of separation rather than

---

[125] Thomas Obel Hansen, 'Transitional Justice: Toward a Differentiated Theory' (2011) 13 *Oregon Review of International Law* 1, 5.

[126] 'A strict distinction ignores that justice should always be both backward- and forward-looking...'. See Gross, above n 34, 51.

[127] Hansen, above n 125; Yeliz Budak, 'Dealing with the Past: Transitional Justice, Ongoing Conflict and the Kurdish Issue in Turkey' (2015) 9 *International Journal of Transitional Justice* 219, 224.

[128] Gross affirms that issues of transitional justice are not unique to such periods and that the law should consistently engage these questions and play a dis-entrenching role. Ibid 52.

[129] ICTJ Fact Sheet, *'What is Transitional Justice'* (2009) https://www.ictj.org/about/transitional-justice

[130] Ni Aolain and Campbell, above n 117, 172.

[131] Gross, above n 34, 101–102.

unification.[132] Campbell and Aoláin confirm: 'a two-state solution would bring little immediate need for a common understanding of overlapping historical legacies'.[133] From this standpoint, the value of a transitional justice mechanism is questionable, especially when Israelis and Palestinians are seeking 'amicable divorce' and not 'harmonious marriage'.

It is worth recalling however that the inter-state nature of Israeli–Palestinian conflict is not clear-cut.[134] Today, there is more than one million Palestinian/Arab–Israelis residing within Israel proper, and there is about half a million Israeli settlers residing within the Palestinian territories under Israeli military occupation. There is therefore a high degree of inter-connectivity between the two entities based on security, economy, trade, and holy sites, not to mention geographical proximity.[135] 'These two nations share territory, resources and a vast history, regardless of whether they eventually share a state'.[136] Moreover, the reality of this inter-dependence means it is likely to continue even after any formal creation of a Palestinian state.[137] According to Scheindlin, 'Even the two-state separation envisioned for Israel and Palestine will require extensive cooperation and joint agencies that can draw on Cypriot models'.[138]

No doubt, the Israeli–Palestinian peace scenario is different from reconciliation within a single nation, but it is still far from a de-colonisation process or a political truce between two independent states. Arguably, this conflict bears the hallmarks of both an intra-societal and inter-societal dispute,[139] to which transitional justice mechanisms are no less relevant and meaningful.[140] Finally, transitional justice approaches can be initiated regarding transitions involving two or more political

---

[132] Stanley Cohen, 'Justice in Transition? Prospects for a Palestinian-Israeli Truth Commission' (1995) 194/195 *Middle East Report* 2; Ni Aolain and Campbell, above n 117, 211.

[133] Ni Aolain and Campbell, above n 117, 211.

[134] Dudai, *'A Model'*, above n 33, 253.

[135] Mathew Weiner, above n 2, 151; '[T]he geography of the region is so intimate that the two states will have to share resources such as electricity grids and water for the foreseeable future, not to mention the shared infrastructure, security cooperation and economic links'. David Makovsky, 'Middle East Peace through Partition' (2001) 80 (2) *Foreign Affairs* 42 cited in Dudai, *'A Model'*, above n 33, 253.

[136] Miller, *Settling with History*, above n 1, 323.

[137] In the words of Benvenisti, Israel proper, and the West Bank and Gaza, even after the establishment of an independent Palestinian state, would still be 'a single eco-system'. See 'An Interview with Meron Benvenisti', (*Bitterlemons*, January 19, 2004) cited in Dudai, *'A Model'*, above n 33, 253.

[138] According to Scheindlin, the Cypriot context is relevant to Israel/Palestine as both conflicts involve two entities on a bounded geographic region. Dahlia Scheindlin, 'Lessons from Cyprus for Israel-Palestine: Can Negotiations still work?' (MITVIM, The Israeli Institute for Foreign Policies, September 2016).

[139] Michael J. Mattler, 'The Distinction Between Civil Wars and International Wars and Its Legal Implications' (1994) 26 *New York University Journal of International Law and Politics* 655–700; Mary Kaldor, *New and Old Wars: Organized Violence in a Global Era* (Polity Press, 2006), 2.

[140] Mathew Weiner above n 2, 151.

systems. Notably, the inter-state nature of the Former Yugoslavia and East Timor/Indonesia[141] disputes did not prevent the use of transitional justice mechanisms. Thus, a range of political contexts can give rise to truth and justice measures. Ultimately, transitional justice need not exclusively concern single societies transitioning into a liberal democracy.

Beyond 'Major Regime Change'

The continuity of political leadership in both Israeli–Palestinian societies also raises doubts about the feasibility of mechanisms.[142] There exists a conceptual objection to applying tools traditionally used during regime change to situations where there is no real political transition.[143] The fact that Israelis remain in power defies the dominant characteristic of new transitional regimes, which commonly seek to distance themselves from the prior order.[144] Similarly in the Palestinian territories, the PA and Hamas continue to govern, notwithstanding a potential status change to statehood. Accordingly, one might query the institutional capacity to genuinely examine legacies of abuse in which the same actors are implicated. This is no trivial objection, in so far as it relates to official transitional justice initiatives like state-sanctioned truth commissions.

Nevertheless, it is strongly arguable that a profound regime change, or new political order, is not a precondition for truth and justice seeking endeavours. As will be discussed in subsequent chapters, transitional justice tools have been applied in diverse cases without any political transition at all. Thus, consolidated democracies, such as Australia, Canada, and the US have all drawn on transitional justice to deal with legacies of injustice.[145] Countries facing ongoing political violence, such as Kenya, Colombia, and Uganda, have also implemented transitional justice measures.[146] They have also been used in 'conflicted democracies' experiencing prolonged periods of political violence.[147] Regarding Northern Ireland, Ni Aolàin and

---

[141] A similar post-conflict scenario is East-Timor/Indonesia, where in addition to internal transitional justice mechanisms initiated by both states, a bilateral truth commission, the Commission for Truth and Friendship was also established.

[142] Dudai, '*A Model*', above n 33, 252.

[143] Jens Iverson, 'Transitional Justice, *Jus Post Bellum,* and International Criminal Law: Differentiating the Usages, History and Dynamics '(2013) 7 *International Journal of Transitional Justice* 413, 419.

[144] Meyerstein, above n 103, 322.

[145] Canada's Truth Commission (2008) focused on the legacies of Indian residential schools and indigenous-settler relations. Australia held a National Inquiry (1995) into the Separation of Aboriginal and Torres Strait Islander Children from Their Families. A US truth commission (2004) was established in Greensboro to examine events of November 1979 when members of the Klu Klux Klan fired into a racially mixed gathering of political activists, killing five and wounding ten.

[146] Hansen, above n 125; Budak, above n 127.

[147] Countries dealing with legacies of abuse and political violence without major regime change are often described as 'conflicted democracies'. This is broadly defined as states experiencing pro-

Campbell observe: 'authoritarian entities may not be the only kind of states to leave in their wake a legacy of...systematic rights violations'.[148]

Accordingly, after decades of warfare, it is arguable that Israel is no less wanting of transitional justice measures, and may even be more capable of implementation than 'paradigmatic transitions'.[149] After all, unlike new regimes coming to power with 'high moral capital [and] low bureaucratic capacity',[150] Israel has the benefit of mature civil apparatuses and liberal institutions as an established democracy.[151] Arguably, '...the continuation of the same order...in Israel...may even be an advantage, by removing the temptation for revenge or a witch hunt of former adversaries'.[152] In this light, political continuity need not obstruct Israeli and Palestinian transitional justice efforts.

Beyond Middle-East Exceptionalism

Finally, some resist transitional justice based on religious cultural and/or historical grounds. Arguably, Middle-eastern societies are wrapped in 'a sturdy coating of cultural Teflon'[153] that frustrates restorative justice efforts. Such objections presume that '...tribal vengeance trumps reconciliation'.[154] According to Cohen, comparisons with other post-conflict countries are '...either sadly irrelevant or premature'.[155] For example, for most Israelis, '...the comparison of Israel with apartheid South Africa is unacceptable...because it challenges the basic belief that the...conflict was imposed upon Israel, and is so unique that it cannot be compared with any other conflict in the world'.[156]

Nevertheless, it is worth resisting over-stated Israeli–Palestinian exceptionalism regarding transitional justice measures.[157] Firstly, despite the rise of religious

longed communal or political violence even where the political structures could be considered 'democratic'. Ni Aolain and Campbell, above n 117, 174.

[148] Ibid.

[149] 'In 'paradigmatic transitions' there is a clear shift from an authoritarian regime to a democratic one, or from a state of civil war to a state of peace. In this case, there is little capacity for reform prior to the transition'. Ibid.

[150] Bruce Ackerman, *The Future of Liberal Revolution* (Yale University Press, 1992) 72.

[151] While some refer to Israel as the 'only democracy in the Middle East', others describe it as an 'ethnocracy', essentially a democracy only for Jewish people. As'ad Ghanem,. 'State and Minority in Israel: The case of Ethnic State and the Predicament of its Minority' (2010) 3(21) *Ethnic and Racial Studies* 428–448. Either way, its political structures can be broadly characterised as democratic.

[152] Adam Heribert and Kogila Moodley, *Seeking Mandela: Peacemaking Between Israelis and Palestinians* (Temple University Press, 2005), 156.

[153] Ibid.

[154] King-Irani, above n 8, 379.

[155] Stanley Cohen, above n 132, 4.

[156] Golan-Agnon, above n 48, 33.

[157] Miller, *Settling with History*, above n 1, 323.

extremism and the currency of religious motifs in the conflict, the Israeli–Palestinian dispute is primarily a secularist-nationalistic one.[158] Secondly, transitional justice has played a role in numerous conflict regions from Africa to the Balkans, notwithstanding festering ethnic, nationalist, and cultural divisions. In the words of Allen: '...there is no reason to believe that Africans are more inclined towards reconciliation than other people'.[159] Indeed, '[t]he Augustinian and Hobbesian tendencies displayed by Israel and the Palestinians respectively are not reflections of essentialised cultural traits or socio-psychological collective tendencies'.[160] Whilst transitional justice tools ought to be tailored to the Israeli–Palestinian context, there is no plausible reason to disqualify, out of hand, the lessons and experiences learnt by other conflict nations.

Theoretical Conclusions

In sum, devising mechanisms during conflict between two distinct political entities without a major regime change probes the limits of the normative discourse of transitional justice.[161] By the same token, transitional justice is not a fixed paradigm, but an ever-expanding concept that must evolve to remain relevant. In the words of the ICTJ: 'New practical challenges have forced the field to innovate as settings have shifted from Argentina and Chile where authoritarianism ended, to societies such as Bosnia... Liberia...where the key issue is shoring up peace'.[162] No longer is post authoritarian political change needed for transitional justice to apply.

Accordingly, based on a more holistic and inclusive view of the field, creative truth, justice, and reconciliation efforts may be initiated regardless of the conflict's degree of activity or the linearity of the transition. Ultimately, the goals of transitional justice are fundamentally tied to 'the aspiration of transition',[163] both towards justice for past crimes and the creation of a new political reality. Notwithstanding its complexity and uniqueness, the fact remains that the Israeli–Palestinian conflict is

---

[158] Khaled Diab, '*The Israeli-Palestinian Conflict Is Not About Religion*' (*Ha'aretz,* August 17, 2015) http://www.haaretz.com/opinion/.premium-1.671543. According to Diab, 'Extremists call it a "holy war," but this conflict has always been about the very secular issues of territory, injustice and identity'.

[159] Tim Allen, *War and Justice in Northern Uganda: An Assessment of the International Criminal Court's intervention.* (LSE Crisis States Research Centre, 2005), 5.

[160] Dan Rabinowitz, 'Israel and the Palestinian Refugees: Postpragmatic Reflections on Historical Narratives, Closure, Transitional Justice, and Palestinian Refugees' Right to Refuse' in Barbara Rose Johnston and Susan Slyomovics (eds) *Waging War, Making Peace: Reparations and Human Rights* (Left Coast Press, 2009) 225–239, 232

[161] 'Transitional justice has begun to lose its original focus and is increasingly used to refer to all manner of "transitions", to the point where it is unclear if any substantial transition is required for the term to be applied'. See Iverson, above n 143, 413.

[162] ICTJ Fact Sheet, above n 129.

[163] Iverson, above n 143, 419.

the source of widespread human rights violations. Transitional justice mechanisms offer a way to deal with this violence and address the legacies of past abuse.

Expanding Practice: Transitional Justice in Active Conflict

Over the past decade, transitional justice during ongoing conflict has become a new and rapidly evolving field. According to Par Engstrom, this is a fundamental development that distinguishes contemporary transitional justice.[164] Teitel argues that as a result of globalisation and intensified political violence, transitional justice has become the rule rather than the exception.[165] What was once viewed as an exceptional legal response to post-conflict conditions is now more routinely applied in the course of hostilities.[166] Accordingly, truth commissions, criminal trials, and other measures are being conceived for periods of profound violence or extreme political instability. Indeed, the reality that societies exhibit various stages of 'transition',[167] coupled with the rise of tribunal justice, have seen transitional justice '...become an overarching legal and political mantle'[168] to help resolve active conflict. In this light, '...transitional justice has moved forward in the sequencing of events'.[169]

Accountability and Reparations in Colombia

For example, States are using transitional justice practices during hostilities as a way to end conflict. Of particular note, Colombia has adopted accountability and reparation mechanisms to foster conditions for a viable peace agreement.[170] Since

---

[164] Par Engstrom, 'Transitional Justice and Ongoing Conflict', in Chandra Lekha Sriram, Jemima Garcı'a-Godos, Johanna Herman and Olga Martin-Ortega (eds.) *Transitional Justice and Peacebuilding on the Ground: Victims and Ex-Combatants*, (Routledge, 2013), 42.

[165] Ruti G. Teitel, 'Transitional Justice Genealogy' (2003) 16 *Harvard Human Rights Journal* 69, 71.

[166] Rachel Kerr, 'Tyrannies of Peace and Justice? Liberal Peacebuilding and the Politics and Pragmatics of Transitional Justice' (11) 1 (2017) *International Journal of Transitional Justice*, 176–185.

[167] According to the World Bank's 2011 published report on conflict, security, and development, while more than one and a half billion people are living today in conflict-affected countries, many of these conflicts do not fit neatly into categories of either 'war' or 'peace'. Arguably, the Israeli–Palestinian conflict corresponds with this trend, oscillating between violent periods and relative calm.

See https://siteresources.worldbank.org/INTWDRS/Resources/WDR2011_Full_Text.pdf

[168] Christine Bell, Colm Campbell and Fionnuala Ni Aolain, 'Transitional Justice: Re(Conceptualising the Field' '(2007) 3(2) *International Journal of Law in Context* 81, 86.

[169] Hansen, above n 125, 26.

[170] Colombia developed a comprehensive transitional justice scheme of transitional justice from 2005 initially through the Law of *Justice and Peace*, with the aim of achieving peace with the paramilitary groups. The clear link between the de-mobilisation of illegal armed groups and the

2005, the Colombian National Reconciliation and Reparation Commission has investigated gross human rights violations, and more than 30,000 paramilitaries have been demobilised.[171] In June 2011, Colombia passed the Victims' Law ('*Ley de Victimas*') to establish a rights-based scheme for victims to reparations, truth, and justice—and to make perpetrators accountable. The Victims' Law also declares a right of restitution for those dispossessed of land or forced to abandon it.[172] Summers describes Colombia's mechanism as an innovative process of transitional justice within a framework where no significant political or social change has occurred.[173] She concludes it '…marks a significant re-thinking of transitional justice'.[174] Others agree Colombia offers hope for achieving truth, redress, and responsibility in circumstances typically guided by a security perspective, rather than a justice and reconciliation one.[175]

Shadow Effect of ICC

The rise of international criminal jurisdiction over the past decade has also led to the pursuit of justice during armed conflict. Judicial interventions in situations of ongoing violence has brought transitional justice much closer to the fields of conflict resolution and peacemaking.[176] The first tribunal established in this context was the ICTY.[177] Subsequent examples have included the Special Court for Sierra Leone (SCSL) and, most significantly, the ICC.[178] The ICC has issued arrest warrants in various ongoing conflicts, including in Uganda, the Democratic Republic of the

rights of the victims is the main feature of the Colombian process. See Jemima Garcia-Godos and Knut Andreas O 'Transitional Justice and Victims' Rights before the End of a Conflict: The Unusual Case of Colombia' (2010) 42 *Journal of Latin American Studies* 487.

171 'Human Rights Watch, *Breaking the Grip? Obstacle to Justice For Paramilitary Mafias in Colombia'* (2008) http://www.hrw.org/sites/default/files/reports/colombia1008webwcover.pdf

172 Nicole Summers, 'Colombia's Victims' Law' (2012) 25 *Harvard Human Rights Journal*, 219, 220.

173 Ibid.

174 Ibid.

175 Lisa J. Lamplante and Kimberly Theidon, 'Transitional Justice in Times of Conflict: Colombia's Ley de Justicia y Paz' (2006) 28 *Michigan Journal of International Law* 49; See also Hansen, above n 125, 34.

176 Par Engstrom, above n 164, 41.

177 The ad hoc Court was established by Resolution 827 of the U.N Security Council, passed on 25 May 1993. Its mandate was to prosecute serious crimes committed during the Yugoslav Wars since 1991, and to try their perpetrators. The Dayton Agreement was reached in November 1995 ending the conflict.

178 Established in 2002 via the Rome Statute, the ICC is a treaty-based body with jurisdiction over genocide, crimes against humanity, war crimes, and aggression committed on the territory of state parties, or by its nationals. See the Rome Statute of the International Criminal Court (entered into force 1 July 2002) 2187 UNTS 90 (ICC Statute), arts 5, 6, 7, 8.

Congo (DRC), the Sudan, and Libya.[179] According to the former ICC Prosecutor: 'My Office is part of a new system dealing with a complex new reality: transitional justice during ongoing conflicts...The ICC's mandate...requires that we engage in judicial proceedings in relation to conflicts even before they have ended...'.[180]

Indeed, the 'shadow effect' of the ICC may motivate warring governments to adopt measures to end hostilities and/or address ongoing violations. Notably, the ICC adjudicates atrocities states are unwilling or unable to investigate.[181] Thus, governments may thwart ICC intervention by addressing wartime abuses domestically, including through transitional justice mechanisms. For example, the Prosecutor's warnings 'that he is "keeping an eye on Colombia"—appears to have had significant influence on the shaping of domestic responses to accountability'.[182] In 2007, the Ugandan government commenced transitional justice processes[183] after referring its ongoing armed conflict to the ICC.[184]

Arguably, the threat of prosecution is a weapon in the diplomatic arsenal against belligerents during wartime.[185] When the severity of ICC threats are escalated through official actions, such as a formal criminal investigation or arrest warrants, they can serve as a form of public rebuke to challenge a regime or a rebel group.[186] The result may be an even greater incentive to encourage negotiation of a peace settlement, or arrange a peaceful exit from power.[187] According to Teitel, ICJ

---

[179] The situation in Libya was the ICC's sixth investigation. In 2011, three arrests warrants were issued in this investigation: against Muammar Gaddafi, Saif Al-Islam Gaddafi and Abdullah Al-Senus.

[180] Luis Moreno Ocampo, 'Transitional justice in Ongoing Conflicts' (2007) 1 *International Journal of Transitional Justice* 8–9, 8.

[181] The principle of complementarity is built into the ICC's institutional design pursuant to Article 17 of the ICC Statute. Investigations of alleged war crimes do not begin automatically, because the ICC must next find that a State is either unwilling or unable to address those charges.

[182] The American Non-Governmental Organizations Coalition for the ICC, An ICC Investigation of Colombia? (August 11, 2005) in Hansen, above n 125, 33.

[183] In 2007, the Ugandan government and the LRA entered into the Juba Agreement which sets up 'Special Tribunals' to hear the gravest crimes committed during the conflict, while referring the rest to 'alternative justice' mechanisms that rely on local transitional justice practices. The Juba Agreement also stipulates that a reparation fund to victims must be set up. See Ibid, 36.

[184] In 2003 President Musevini of Uganda referred crimes committed by the Lord's Resistance Army (LRA) in Northern Uganda to the ICC.

[185] Uganda's referral to the ICC 'should be viewed as one weapon in the arsenal in fighting the still active rebels'. Hansen, above n 125, 35.

[186] 'While the ICC issuing arrest warrants against LRA leaders in 2005 was celebrated by many commentators, the Court's failure to investigate Ugandan army atrocities has been criticised as an example of selective justice. See HRW: ICC takes decisive steps for justice in Uganda' https://www.hrw.org/news/2005/10/14/icc-takes-decisive-step-justice-uganda; See also David Mendeloff, 'War Crimes and Hollow Threats: Assessing the Coercive Logic of ICC Intervention in Ongoing Conflicts'. Minerva Conference Paper 2011, p.3.

[187] 'The potential for arrest creates fear...it could motivate the accused to move directly to the bargaining table in the hope of negotiating an amnesty as happened with the LRA's Joseph Kony after his indictment'. Mendeloff, above n 186; '...When peace talks with the LRA appeared to

'...offers the potential for regime de-legitimisation that can support or even instigate transition'.[188] In sum, transitional justice efforts and the ICC may play an important role in still conflicted and largely non-transitional societies.

Challenges and Opportunities for Active Conflict

Despite the foray into active conflict, the application of various transitional justice mechanisms during wartime remains under-researched. 'There is still doubt as to whether transitional justice in active conflicts is effective at all'.[189] Indeed, the theoretical success of mechanisms during hostilities may be difficult to assess empirically.[190] For example, it may take years, or even decades, for social scientists to be able to fully assess whether transitional justice has been successful in achieving its ambitious goals.[191] Of particular relevance to Israelis and Palestinians, even studies that address the conflict as an active one typically do so '...from a prescriptive point of view rather than analysing how transitional justice has been used...'.[192] Arguably, the focus of practitioners tends to be on the pre-resolution phase of the Israeli–Palestinian conflict, such as '...incorporating truth-telling mechanisms into peace negotiations...',[193] or on constitutional reform.[194] It is therefore important to recall that major efforts to evaluate transitional justice within the Israeli–Palestinian setting are sorely lacking.

There are other political and practical challenges for truth and justice processes during wartime. For example, the pursuit of justice is by no means assured by the shadow effect of the ICC. Judicial intervention as a coercive tool may be limited by the lack of enforcement and a belief that perpetrators act according to threats of prosecution.[195] Academics also caution that conceptual expansion of transitional justice into ongoing conflict invites political exploitation and could lead to a host of 'dubious nation-building projects'.[196] Regarding Colombia, it is arguable that 'much

---

stand a real chance of success, and the rebels unsurprisingly made clear that they perceived the arrest warrants as the key obstacle to reaching an agreement, new developments took place'. Hansen, above n 125, 35.

[188] Teitel, above n 165, 90.

[189] Nets-Zehngut, *'Transitional Justice'* above n 114, 4.

[190] Judy Barsalou, 'Trauma and Transitional Justice in Divided Societies' April 13, 2005 United States Institute of Peace.

[191] Andrew Reiter, 'Chapter 13: Measuring the Success (or Failure) of Transitional Justice', in Olivera Simic (ed), *An Introduction to Transitional Justice* (Routledge 2017), 271.

[192] Nets-Zehngut, *'Transitional Justice'* above n 114, 4.

[193] Dudai, *'A Model'*, above n 33, 249–267.

[194] Gross, above n 34.

[195] David Mendeloff, 'War Crimes and Hollow Threats: Assessing the Coercive Logic of ICC Intervention in Ongoing Conflicts'. Minerva Conference Paper 2011, p.4.

[196] Jelena Subotić, 'The Transformation of International Transitional Justice Advocacy' (2012) 6 (1) *International Journal of Transitional Justice* 106–125, 116. See also Christine Bell, *On the Law*

more than…attempting to achieve liberalization and governance reform, transitional justice…provides central actors with a tool for controlling an ongoing conflict and maintaining the status quo...'.[197] From this standpoint, 'transitional justice has a malleable quality, and is sufficiently indeterminate to make it particularly susceptible to strategic instrumentalism'.[198] Thus, wartime initiatives may be viewed cynically as Western intervention[199] or mere lip-service.[200]

Nevertheless, transitional justice efforts also present opportunities for active conflicts like the Israeli–Palestinian one. As discussed in Chap. 3, there is a normative value to truth, justice, and reconciliation efforts as part of conflict resolution. From Latin America to South Africa, progress toward political resolution has been closely connected to early transitional justice measures.[201] Of the various processes, many may be implemented before a formal political transition occurs.[202] Thus, projects like memorials, textbook reform and unofficial commissions, could be presently contemplated to sow the seeds of reconciling the past even before an Israel–Palestinian accord is formally concluded.[203] They may result in a paradigm shift and open new avenues for imaginative and creative solutions.[204] In this light, far from being premature, transitional justice measures may in fact play an invaluable role in the region.[205] Arguably, such measures have the potential to herald earlier support, healing, and trust between the parties and to promote termination of the conflict by extending the boundaries of debate.[206]

Moreover, truth and justice-seeking efforts could promote negotiations and bolster peace accords during ongoing conflict. For example, the inclusion of accountability mechanisms might restore a broader societal involvement in the development

of Peace: Peace Agreements and the Lex Pacificatoria (Oxford University Press, 2008), 256. ('On the Law of Peace').

[197] Hansen, above n 125, 34: See also Catalina Diaz, Challenging Impunity from Below, Grassroots Activism and the Struggle for Change 189 (Kieran McEvoy and Lorna McGregor eds., 2008).

[198] Bell, *'On the Law of Peace'*, above n 196, 257; Bell et al., above n 168, 86; See also Hansen, above n 125, 16.

[199] For example, imposing western concepts on non-western societies. Rachel Kerr 'Review of books on Transitional Justice' (2011) 5 *International Journal of Transitional Justice,* 319–330; Patricia Lundy, 'Exploring home-grown transitional justice and its dilemmas: A case study of the historical enquiries team, Northern Ireland' (2009) 3 *International Journal of Transitional Justice*, 321–340.

[200] Bell, *'On the Law of Peace'*, above n 196, 256.

[201] Bisharat and Kaufman, above n 18, 72.

[202] Dudai and Cohen,'Dealing with the Past' above n 51, 230.

[203] Nets-Zehngut, *'Transitional Justice'* above n 114, 2–3.

[204] Kaufman, above n 92, 184.

[205] Peter T. Coleman, *The Five Percent: Finding Solutions to (Seemingly) Impossible Conflicts* (Public Affairs, Perseus Books, 2011); Mihaela Mihai, 'Transitional Justice and the Quest for Democracy: A Contribution to a Political Theory of Democratic Transformations' (2010) 23(2) *Ratio Juris* 183, 194.

[206] Dudai, *'A Model'* above n 33, 253; Nets-Zehngut (n 58) 20.

and implementation a peace agreement.[207] 'It may begin independently of the conflict resolution process, before the opposing sides even begin to negotiate…'.[208] Many negotiation theorists claim that introducing justice and human rights law early into conflict resolution efforts '…is a formula that has…the potential for a smoother advance in the negotiation process...'.[209]

According to recent research by Loyle and Binningsbø, measures such as prosecuting wrongdoers, compensating victims and pardoning rebels positively influence both the intensity and the termination of armed conflict.[210] Their findings indicate that governments (as well as rebels) successfully use such processes in order to end armed conflict and reach a negotiated settlement.[211] This is consistent with previous transitional justice research, which suggests that measures initiated during conflict have a pacifying effect and can serve as a tool for conflict resolution or de-escalation.[212]

Beyond Quick-Fixing Ongoing Conflict

At the same time, it is worth conceding that expectations of transitional justice in active conflict must be recalibrated. Instead of critiquing such measures as a set of under-researched quick-fix outcomes, they should be regarded as long-term nation-building processes that foster peace over time.[213] This suggests that beyond offering a measure of truth, justice, and healing during wartime, it may be too much to expect a conclusive end to the violence or a short-term regime change. As Hansen notes, '…as long as the very stakeholders subjected to accountability maintain influence and power',[214] transitional justice cannot transform governance overnight. Rather more modestly, the Colombian case demonstrates: '…how in fact it is possible to achieve some kind of justice while attempting to limit the violent conflict.

---

[207] 'The requirement for the past asserts the pragmatic importance of the rule of law to future peace-building efforts. For many, therefore, the move towards transitional justice marks a creative and progressive attempt to insert requirements of justice into peace agreement brokering, even if partially or imperfectly'. Bell, *'On the Law of Peace'*, above n 196, 255–6.

[208] Daniel Bar-Tal, 'From Intractable Conflict through Conflict Resolution to Reconciliation: Psychological Analysis '(June 2000) 21(2) *Political Psychology* 351, 356.

[209] Bisharat and Kaufamn, above n 18, 72; Gross concurs that human rights discourse can indeed play an important role in a conflict transformation process. Roger Fisher, William Ury, and Bruce Patton, Getting to yes, Penguin, 1991, (1997), p 4.

[210] Cyanne E. Loyle and Helga Malmin Binningsbø, 'Justice during Armed Conflict: A New Dataset on Government and Rebel Strategies' (2018) 62(2) *Journal of Conflict Resolution* 442–466.

[211] Ibid 460.

[212] See Tricia, Olsen, Leigh A. Payne and Andrew G. Reiter. *Transitional Justice in Balance: Comparing Processes, Weighing Efficacy'*. (United States Institute of Peace Press, 2010); Lie, Tove Grete, Helga Malmin Binningsbø, and Scott Gates 'Post-conflict Justice and Sustainable Peace'. (2007) Paper Presented at DC Area Workshop on Contentious Politics, College Park, MD.

[213] Hamber and Kelly, above n 104, 302.

[214] Hansen, above n 125, 35.

This also suggests that this case cannot easily be evaluated according to the same standards as used in contexts of ended conflict or ended regime oppression'.[215]

Indeed, the US Institute of Peace Report confirms the need to move away from current thinking of mechanisms, as 'single shot approaches or quick one-time fixes [which] usually fall short of expected goals'.[216] From this standpoint, transitional justice measures may be viewed more leniently on a long-term trajectory.[217] 'Transitional justice on this view is an optimistic 'hooray word' that means some justice in place of none…'.[218] As noted by Coleman: 'there are no simple solutions to intractability…we must find ways to intervene earlier when disputants can still see the humanity and validity of the other's needs'.[219] From Latin America to South Africa, progress towards political resolution has been closely connected to early transitional justice measures.[220]

4.5 Conclusion

In the Israeli–Palestinian context, transitional justice mechanisms could play an important role at present. As concluded earlier, many authors claim that without a minimum consensus on the moral basis for negotiations, and some recognition of past abuse, it is doubtful peaceful relations can be established. According to studies on current reconciliation activities between Israeli and Palestinian youth: 'transformative practices can still be effective, and possibly even more relevant in the harsh context of a violent conflictual socio-political reality'.[221] Realistically any transitional justice mechanism is distant from resolving the Israeli–Palestinian conflict. However, given the gravity of the situation, the potential for a small positive impact remains significant. Choosing the means to address the past is one of transitional justice's threshold dilemmas. Accordingly, the next two chapters will therefore consider the potential role of the ICC and truth commissions in the Israeli–Palestinian conflict.

---

[215] Ibid, 34–35.

[216] Judy Barsalou, 'Trauma and Transitional Justice in Divided Societies' April 13, 2005 United States Institute of Peace.

[217] 'Thus, while a lenient approach to transitional justice will understandably anger and frustrate most victims, surely there might be some consolation in the prospect of justice at some point in the future, whether it be in a national, foreign or international forum. In the meantime, the victims can at least enjoy a measure of peace and democracy'. Mark Freeman, 'Transitional Justice: Fundamental Goals and Unavoidable Complications'(2000–2002) 28 *Manitoba Law Journal* 113, 120.

[218] Bell, *'On the Law of Peace'*, above n 196, 255–6.

[219] Coleman, above n 205; 'By filtering negative affects through the strainer of equal respect for both victims and victimizers, transitional justice can provide an important mechanism for steering the polity towards democracy'. Mihai, above n 205, 194.

[220] Bisharat and Kaufman, above n 18, 72.

[221] Ifat Maoz, 'An Experiment in Peace: Reconciliation-Aimed Workshops of Jewish-Israeli and Palestinian Youth'(2000) 37(6) *Journal of Peace* 721, 733.

Chapter 5
International Criminal Justice, the ICC, and the Israeli–Palestinian Conflict

5.1 Introduction

This chapter assesses the contours, challenges, and aspirations of ICJ in the Israeli–Palestinian context. As foreshadowed in Chap. 3, a range of mechanisms exist to pursue transitional justice and accountability from reparations, institutional reform to the creation of war memorials.[1] However, criminal trials and investigations remain a flagship tool of the field. Given their primacy in transitional justice and the ICC's examination into Palestine, it is worth evaluating the desirability and feasibility of ICJ to the Israeli–Palestinian conflict with a special focus on the ICC.

Notably, over the past decade, the UN and other international legal inquiries into Israeli–Palestinian hostilities have received wide attention, particularly in relation to Gaza.[2] However, their current practical and normative value seems to have been eclipsed by progress at the ICC. As will be discussed, 'universal jurisdiction' has also led to failed attempts to prosecute prominent Israeli officials for alleged war crimes under European criminal law. Accordingly, the relevance of ICJ to the region is primarily explored through the debate over the wisdom and implications of an ICC intervention. This is because Israelis and Palestinians appear unlikely to agree to an ad hoc or hybrid tribunal anytime soon. It is also because the very raison d'être of the ICC was to become a permanent home to adjudicate serious international crimes. Unsurprisingly, the PA's decision to join the Court in 2015 has instigated a

---

[1] ICTJ Fact Sheet, "What is Transitional Justice" (2009) https://www.ictj.org/about/transitional-justice

[2] For further discussion on the function and effect of international inquiries into Israel/Palestine, see Sharon Weill, 'The follow up to the Goldstone report in Israel and beyond', in Chantal Meloni and Gianni Tognoni (eds.), *Is There A Court for Gaza?: A Test Bench for International Justice,* (Asser/Springer, 2012) 105–20; Sharon Weill and Valentina Azarova, 'Israel's Unwillingness? The Follow-Up Investigations to the UN Gaza Conflict Report and International Criminal Justice' (2012) 12 (5) *International Criminal Law Review*, 905–35.

J. Bracka, *Transitional Justice for Israel/Palestine*, Springer Series in Transitional Justice, https://doi.org/10.1007/978-3-030-89435-1_5

fiery debate over the ICC, exposing tensions between ICJ and the Middle East peace process, as well as the suitability of retributive justice for the region.

This chapter critiques the potential role of the ICC in the Israeli–Palestinian conflict, whether its intervention is politically and legally plausible, and whether it is desirable for the court to intervene. It will identify some of the obstacles to jurisdiction over Israel's alleged crimes in Gaza, and the Israeli settlements, concluding that they are formidable. The opening of an investigation into the complex situation of Palestine is far from assured. Notwithstanding, the 2019 OTP determination that a 'reasonable basis' exists to proceed with an ICC investigation,[3] a number of jurisdictional issues will not disappear. There is likely to be no shortage of challenges and appeals during the investigation and prosecution phases based on other questions of complementarity, gravity, and the interests of justice. In this regard, prosecuting Israelis and Palestinians is no legal slam-dunk. Proceedings are likely to stall for several years and even ultimately fail to deliver on international calls for justice and accountability. Moreover, it will be contended that beyond polarised rhetoric or technical legal debate, any meaningful resolution of the conflict will need to include questions of historical responsibility and account for the existential aspects of both nations' pasts.

5.2 Part One: The Field of International Criminal Justice

Until the 1990s, legal immunity and social amnesia were transitional default settings. New post-authoritarian states could rely on amnesties for past crimes to reach peace agreements.[4] However, after the Cold War, public outrage over the Balkans and the Rwandan genocide spurred the UN to turn the tide against impunity. This trend has been aptly described as a 'justice cascade',[5] indelibly altering the post-conflict landscape.[6] Today, ICJ involves determining the legal responsibility of individuals for egregious acts.[7] Owing its genesis to World War II's Nuremberg and

[3] ICC Prosecution Request Pursuant to Article 19(3) for a Ruling on the Court's territorial jurisdiction in Palestine ICC-01/18 (20 December 2019), https://www.icc-cpi.int/CourtRecords/CR2020_00161.PDF ¶93 [hereinafter OTP 2019 Request].

[4] In Latin America, many of these amnesties were steadily whittled away by the Inter-American Court or national courts. See Neil Kritz (ed.) *Transitional Justice: How Emerging Democracies Reckon with Former Regimes* (US Institute of Peace Press, 1995) xxi–xxii.

[5] Ellen Lutz and Kathryn Sikkink, 'The Justice Cascade: The Evolution and Impact of Foreign Human Rights Trials in Latin America,' (2001) 2(1) *Chicago Journal of International Law* 1–34; Kathryn Sikkink, *The Justice Cascade: How Human Rights Prosecutions Are Changing World Politics* (W.W. Norton, 2011).

[6] Laurel Fletcher, 'Institutions from Above and Voices From Below: A Comment on Challenges to Group-Conflict Resolution and Reconciliation' (2009) 72 *Law and Contemporary Problems* 51.

[7] Jens Iverson, 'Transitional Justice, *Jus Post Bellum,* and International Criminal Law: Differentiating the Usages, History and Dynamics '(2013) 7 *International Journal of Transitional Justice* 413, 421.

Tokyo Trials, the investigation and prosecution of gross human rights abuses have become central components of transitional justice. Recent examples include the UN-established ICTY and ICTR. There have also been the voluntary creation of 'hybrid' courts or tribunals[8] such as the Special Court for Sierra Leone, Special Panels of the Dili District Court in Timor Leste, and the Extraordinary Chambers in the Courts of Cambodia.

Most significantly, the ICC was established in 2002 as the first permanent international criminal court. It aims to bring individuals (not states) that have been involved in international crimes to justice where countries are unable or unwilling to do so. More broadly, there is now a solid bedrock of international criminal law.[9] There are binding international standards established through treaties, customary international law, and judicial practice from the international criminal tribunals. Today an international legal duty exists to investigate, prosecute, and punish perpetrators of international crime including 'grave breaches' of human rights law, genocide, torture, and cruel and inhuman treatment.[10] In sum, human rights trials and international prosecutions are key elements in the response to mass atrocity.

The Prosecution Preference

In recent decades, the cardinal value of criminal trials and IHL have profoundly shaped transitional justice.[11] As the field of ICJ expanded, it came to dominate post-conflict engagement.[12] Despite extensive criticism of the post-war and ad hoc

[8] Hybrid courts and tribunals have emerged as 'third generation' courts established to investigate and prosecute human rights offenses. These courts consist of both international and domestic justice actors. Caitlin Reiger, *'Where to From Here for International Tribunals?' Considering Legacy and Residual Issues* (International Center for Transitional Justice Briefing, September 2009).

[9] Antonio Cassese, *International Criminal Law* (Oxford University Press, 2003) 120–131.

[10] The responsibility to investigate is codified in several treaties including the Geneva Conventions and recognized as binding obligation under customary law. See for example Rule 158 of customary IHL in Jean-Marie Henckaerts and Louise Doswald-Beck (eds.) *Customary International Humanitarian Law* (ICRC and Cambridge University Press, 2005), 87 *International Review of the Red Cross* 198; See also Diane E Orentlicher, '*Setting Accounts: The Duty to Prosecute Human Rights Violations of Prior Regime'*, 100 *Yale Law Journal* 2537, 2548 (1991) (arguing that international law requires prosecution of human rights violations).

[11] See Mahmoud Cherif Bassiouni, 'Accountability for Violations of International Humanitarian Law and Other Serious Violations of Human Rights' in Mahmoud Cherif Bassiouni (ed.) *Post-Conflict Justice* (Transnational Publishers, 2002) 6–7; Ruti G. Teitel, 'Transitional Justice Genealogy' (2003) 16 *Harvard Human Rights Journal* 69, at 72–74 (describing war crimes trials as being part of the 'first phase of transitional justice' that took place after World War II).

[12] Gideon Boas, 'What Is International Criminal Justice?' in Gideon Boas, William A. Schabas and Michael P. Scharf (eds.) *International Criminal Justice: Legitimacy and* Coherence (Edward Elgar Publishing, 2012), 1–24.

tribunals,[13] solid support remains for ICJ.[14] While legal practitioners often debate the feasibility of trials, many share the view that prosecution is the means of choice to counter impunity.[15] Roht-Arriaza writes that trials became the '…essential element of transitional justice—without trials everything else was incomplete at best, and a sham at worst'.[16] This has fuelled the assumption that alternative approaches, such as truth commissions or other non-judicial measures, are somewhat inferior.[17] Even those championing non-prosecution options often concede the normative preference for retributive justice and trials.[18] Advocates of ICJ thus conclude that '…whatever salutary effects it can produce, an official truth-telling process is no substitute for enforcement of criminal law through prosecutions'.[19]

[13] Nancy Armoury Combs, *Guilty Pleas in International Criminal Law: Constructing a Restorative Justice Approach.* (Stanford University Press, 2007); Mark Drumbl, *Atrocity, Punishment and International Law* (Cambridge University Press, 2007); Mark Findlay and Ralph Henham, *Beyond Justice: Achieving International Criminal Justice* (Palgrave McMIllan, 2010); Hans Kochler, *Global Justice of Global Revenge? International Criminal Justice at the Crossroads* (Springer, 2003); Danilo Zolo, *Victors' Justice: From Nuremberg to Baghdad* (Verso Books, 2009).

[14] See for example Jose Alvarez, 'Crimes of States/Crimes of Hate: Lessons from Rwanda', 24 *Yale Journal of International Law* 365, 365–366 (1999); Chris Tenove and Peter Dixon, 'International Criminal Justice as a Transnational Field: Rules, Authority and Victims' (2013) 7 *International Journal of Transitional Justice* 393, 407.

[15] Erin Daly, 'Transformative Justice: Charting a Path to Reconciliation' (2001–2002) 12(1 & 2) *International Legal Perspectives* 73, 100; See also Mary Margaret Penrose, 'Lest We Fail: The Importance of Enforcement in International Criminal Law', (1999) 15 *Amsterdam University of International Law Review.* 321, 373 ('Punishment, via criminal prosecutions, is perceived as the most favored method of combating impunity').

[16] Naomi Roht-Arriaza, 'Transitional Justice and International criminal justice: a fraught relationship' (November 25 2013) *Oxford University Press's Blog* http://blog.oup.com/2013/11/transitional-justice-international-criminal-justice-relationship-pil/ ('Transitional Justice and ICJ').

[17] Tenove and Dixon, above n 14, 407.

[18] See Stephan Landsman, 'Alternative Responses to Serious Human Rights Abuses: Of Prosecution and Truth Commissions' (1996) 59 *Law and Contemporary Problems* 81 at 83 (arguing that the best response is usually the 'vigorous prosecution of perpetrators'); Martha Minow, *Between Vengeance and Forgiveness: Facing History after Genocide and Mass Violence* (Beacon Press, 1998), (noting that most commentators believe prosecution is the best option and truth commissions should be used only when prosecution is impossible).

[19] Orentlicher, above n 10, 2546; see also Juan E. Mendez, 'In Defense of Transitional Justice' in James McAdams (ed.) *Transitional Justice and the Rule of Law in New Democracies* (University of Notre Dame Press, 1997 1997) 1, 15.

Conceptual Tension: Is ICJ a Tool or a Field?

In this light, conceptual tension exists between transitional justice and ICJ.[20] Some theorists claim that '[m]ore than just a mechanism in transitional justice's toolkit, ICJ is a "field" in itself'.[21] Arguably, because ICJ draws on three other well-established fields (interstate diplomacy, criminal justice, and human rights advocacy), it can '…mobilize authority in ways that make it more powerful at a global level than "place-based" approaches to transitional justice'.[22] On this view, ICJ is not a single instrument among others, but wields particular authority to provide the most legitimate and potent response to mass violence.[23]

Nevertheless, as the value of other measures like truth commissions become clearer, ICJ is also understood as a subset of transitional justice. Notably, the new transitional landscape promotes a wider array of processes.[24] Indeed, 'transitional justice has itself undergone a shift towards the local'.[25] As discussed, transitional justice strategies are mindful to avoid a 'one size fits all' model, especially one externally imposed by the international community. Whilst prosecutions continue to play a distinctive role,[26] they are, after all, only one method of redressing human rights abuse.[27] In this light, the debate over whether ICJ 'counts' as a field is less relevant.[28] Indeed, ICJ practitioners typically locate their work within the broader aims and practices of transitional justice and often suggest trials contribute to

[20] Roht-Arriaza, '*Transitional Justice and ICJ*', above n 16.

[21] Tenove and Dixon, above n 14, 393; Iverson, above n 6, 420.

[22] Tenove and Dixon, above n 14, 393.

[23] 'A field-based approach to ICJ helps explain why and how ICJ actors accrue and wield authority. We believe it also helps explain why ICJ is a key component – perhaps the most powerful component – in the broader universe of transitional justice'. Ibid, 406.

[24] Naomi Roht-Arriaza, 'The New Landscape of Transitional Justice,' in Naomi Roht-Arriaza and Javier Mariezcurrena (eds.) *Transitional Justice in the Twenty-First Century*, (Cambridge University Press, 2006).

[25] Rosalind Shaw and Lars Waldorf, with Pierre Hazan (eds), *Localizing Transitional Justice: Interventions and Priorities After Mass Violence* (Stanford University Press, 2010) 4.

[26] For example, international criminal law is generally seen as providing the legal framework for transitional justice Ruti G. Teitel, *Transitional Justice* (Oxford University Press, 2000). Departing from Teitel, Campbell suggests the special role of ICJ derives from the specific form of social association in criminal law, rather than any transitional qualities of law as such. See Kirsten Campbell, 'Reassembling International Justice: The Making of 'the Social' in International Criminal Law and Transitional Justice' (2013) 8 *International Journal of Transitional Justice* 53, 61.

[27] Roht-Arriaza, '*Transitional Justice and ICJ*', above n 16.

[28] Tenove and Dixon, above n 14, 406; Christine Bell, 'Transitional Justice, Interdisciplinarity and the State of the "Field" or "Non-Field"' (2009) 3(1) *International Journal of Transitional Justice* 5–27. For other approaches to defining the field, see Pablo de Greiff, 'Theorizing Transitional Justice,' in *Transitional Justice*: Nomos Li, Melissa S. Williams, Rosemary Nagy and Jon Elster (eds.) (New York University Press, 2012).

truth-telling and reconciliation.[29] Despite a fraught relationship,[30] ICJ remains wedded to transitional justice.

5.3 Part Two: ICC Procedural History in Israel/Palestine

No doubt, an international prosecutor could build a solid case against both Israelis and Palestinians regarding any number of breaches of international criminal and humanitarian law over the course of the conflict. There is no shortage of scholarship and human rights reports discussing alleged breaches of international criminal law and international humanitarian law (IHL) on both sides. On the Israeli front, civilian settlements into the Palestinian territories are commonly cited as IHL violations[31] and war crimes.[32] Human Rights Watch even recently concluded that deprivations of Palestinians by Israeli authorities are so severe that they amount to crimes against humanity of apartheid and persecution.[33] It is equally not difficult to find reports that Palestinians, particularly Hamas, have committed serious crimes against Israelis, such as suicide bombings during the Second Intifada.[34] Some commentators have even noted that Hamas rocket attacks on Israeli civilians might in fact be easier to establish than alleged Israeli war crimes.[35] In sum, there are credible accounts of unlawful practices that could expose both sides to international criminal prosecutions.

---

[29] Boas, above n 12; For a reflection on ICJ's contribution to historical truth telling, see, Gerry J. Simpson, 'Law's Promise: Punishment, Memory and Dissent,' in *Law, War and Crime: War Crimes Trials and the Reinvention of International Law* (Polity Press, 2007).

[30] Roht-Arriaza, '*Transitional Justice and ICJ*', above n 16.

[31] Numerous UN resolutions have stated that the building and existence of Israeli settlements are a violation of IHL. See e.g. UNSC resolutions 446 (Mar. 22, 1979); S.C. Res. 799 (Dec. 18, 1992); S.C. Res. 904 (Mar. 18, 1994); S.C. Res. 2334 (Dec. 23, 2016).

[32] The Rome Statute criminalises civilian transfers into occupied territory whether they are undertaken 'directly or indirectly'. Rome Statute of the International Criminal Court art 8(2)(b)(viii), July 17, 1998, 2187, U.N.T.S 90, [hereinafter Rome Statute]. See e.g. Orna Ben-Naftali, Aeyal Gross and Keren Michaeli, *Illegal Occupation: Framing the Occupied Palestinian Territory* 23 BERKELEY J. INT. LAW 551, 581 (2005).

[33] On 27 April 2021, Human Rights Watch (HRW) launched its report 'A Threshold Crossed: Israeli Authorities and the Crimes of Apartheid and Persecution'. See https://www.hrw.org/report/2021/04/27/threshold-crossed/israeli-authorities-and-crimes-apartheid-and-persecution

[34] See e.g. UN Commission on Human Rights, *Question of the Violation of Human Rights in the Occupied Arab Territories including Palestine: Report of the human rights inquiry commission* S-5/1, E/CN4/2001/121 (March 16, 2001) [hereinafter Commission on Human Rights Report 2001] ¶¶ 23; Human Rights Watch, 'ERASED IN A MOMENT: SUICIDE BOMBING ATTACKS AGAINST ISRAELI CIVILIANS' (2002) 109 https://www.hrw.org/report/2002/10/15/erased-moment/suicide-bombing-attacks-against-israeli-civilians [hereinafter HRW Report 2002].

[35] See e.g. Linda M. Keller, 'The International Criminal Court and Palestine: Part 11,' JURIST-FORUM (February 5, 2013) www.jurist.org/forum/2013/02/linda-keller-palestine-icc-part2.php; Kevin Jon Heller, *The ICC in Palestine: Be Careful What You Wish For'* JUSTICE IN CONFLICT, (April 2, 2015) https://justiceinconflict.org/2015/04/02/the-icc-inpalestine-be-careful-what-you-wish-for/

ICC Route

Over the past decade, a bid for Palestinian statehood and direct engagement with international law paved the way for an ICC intervention. During the Israel–Gaza armed conflict (2008–2009) ('Operation Cast Lead'), the PA lodged a declaration with the ICC Registrar, seeking to recognise the jurisdiction of the Court based on Article 12(3) of the Rome Statute.[36] Whilst on 3 April 2012, the OTP declined to continue its preliminary examination because Palestine was not a state, the decision deferred the statehood issue to the 'relevant bodies' at the UN or the ICC Assembly of States.[37] On 4 December 2012, the UNGA passed a resolution conferring non-member observer-state status on Palestine,[38] which arguably amounts to a de facto or implicit recognition of statehood.[39]

Having gained this recognition, Palestine joined a number of international treaties[40] including the Rome Statute. On 1 January 2015, the PA lodged a declaration under Article 12(3) accepting the jurisdiction of the ICC over alleged crimes committed 'in the occupied Palestinian territory, including East Jerusalem, since June 13, 2014'.[41] This timeframe indicates the PA's desire for the ICC to investigate

---

[36] Under Article 12(3) of the Rome Statute, 'a state which is not a Party to this Statute' may lodge a declaration that accepts the jurisdiction of the Int'l Criminal Court [ICC] 'with respect to the crime in question'. Rome Statute, art. 12(3), above n 33. The government of Palestine lodged such a declaration on January 22, 2009, accepting jurisdiction for 'acts committed on the territory of Palestine since 1 July 2002'.

[37] See Valentina Azarov, *ICC Jurisdiction in Palestine: Blurring Law and Politics*, JURIST-FORUM (April 9, 2012), https://jurist.org/forum/2012/04/valentina-azarov-icc-palestine.php

[38] GA Res 67/19, UN Doc A/RES/67/19 (Dec. 4, 2012). Notably, some states voting for the resolution 'underscored that statehood could only be achieved through dialogue between the parties implying that Palestine had not yet achieved statehood'. See Keller, above n 35.

[39] To some legal scholars, this upgrade is capable of clearing the path for the OTP. The UNGA decided 138 votes in favour to 9 against to accord to Palestine a 'State' status in the UN. See e.g. George Bisharat, *Why Palestine Should Take Israel to Court in The Hague*, THE NEW YORK TIMES, (January 29 2013). Notably, other legal scholars like Quigley assert that Palestine had already qualified as a state for the purposes of the Rome Statute. John Quigley, *The Palestine Declaration to the International Criminal Court* 35 RUTGERS L.J. 1(2009).

[40] On 3 and 7 April 2014, the Palestinian Authority (PA) acceded to 14 international treaties including the International Covenant on Civil and Political Rights, 16 December 1966, 999 U.N.T.S. 171; Convention on the Rights of the Child, 20 November 1989, 1577 U.N.T.S. 3, International Covenant on Economic, Social and Cultural Rights, 16 December 1966, 993 U.N.T.S. 3; Convention on the Prevention and Punishment of the Crime of Genocide, 9 December 1948, 78 U.N.T.S. 277 and the Convention against Torture and Other Cruel, Inhuman or Degrading Treatment or Punishment, 10 December 1984, 1465 U.N.T.S. 85.

[41] On 2 January 2015, the government of Palestine acceded to the Rome Statute, which entered into force on 1 April 2015. See ICC Press Release, *The State of Palestine Accedes to the Rome Statute'* (January 7, 2015), https://www.icccpi.int//Pages/item.aspx?name=pr1082_2; *State of Palestine, Declaration Accepting the Jurisdiction of the International Criminal Court* (31 December 2014), https://unispal.un.org/DPA/DPR/unispal.nsf/0/93EEF1935D2E78E285257DC4006B7C2F

alleged crimes committed during the 2014 war in Gaza (Operation Protective Edge). Thus, on 1 April 2015, Palestine became the 123rd state party to the Rome Statute.

ICC Preliminary Examination

On 16 January 2015, the ICC Prosecutor opened a preliminary examination into the situation in Palestine.[42] Specifically, under Article 53(1) of the Rome Statute, the Prosecutor must consider issues of jurisdiction, admissibility, and the interests of justice in making her determination to open a formal investigation. On 22 May 2018, the OTP received a referral from the Government of the State of Palestine regarding the situation in Palestine since 13 June 2014 with no end date (2018 State Referral).[43] The scope of the preliminary examination covers alleged Israeli war crimes in the West Bank and East Jerusalem, settlements activities, forced removal as well as demolition of property, and eviction of Palestinians from homes.[44] The OTP also considered alleged Israeli crimes against humanity, the crimes of persecution, transfer and deportation of civilians, and apartheid.[45] With respect to the Gaza hostilities of 2014 and to the 2018 violence, the OTP examined alleged crimes both by members of Palestinian armed groups and by members of the IDF.[46]

OTP Referral on 'Statehood'

On 20 December 2019, the ICC Prosecutor announced her intention to close the preliminary examination in an Article 19(3) request for the ICC PTC to rule on territorial jurisdiction (2019 OTP Request).[47] It is the first time the OTP has formally confirmed its belief that a 'reasonable basis' exists to open a formal investigation

---

[42] See ICC Press Release, *The Prosecutor of the International Criminal Court, Fatou Bensouda, Opens a Preliminary Examination of the Situation in Palestine* (16 January 2015), https://www.icc-cpi.int/Pages/item.aspx?name=pr1083

[43] The State of Palestine, Referral by the State of Palestine Pursuant to Articles 13(A) and 14 of the Rome Statute ¶ 9 (15 May 2018) [hereinafter Referral by the State of Palestine]. See also Statement by ICC Prosecutor, Mrs. Fatou Bensouda, on the Referral Submitted by Palestine, Int'l Crim. Ct. of the Prosecutor (22 May 2018), https://www.icc-cpi.int//Pages/item.aspx?name=180522-otp-stat

[44] ICC, Office of the Prosecutor Report on Preliminary Examination Activities 2018 ¶ 269–271 (5 December 2018) [hereinafter OTP Report on Preliminary Examination Activities 2018].

[45] Ibid. at ¶ 271.

[46] Ibid. at ¶ 261–267, 274, 275.

[47] ICC, Office of the Prosecutor Request pursuant to Article 19(3) for a Ruling on the Court's Territorial Jurisdiction in Palestine, ICC-01/18, ¶ 93 (20 December 2019) [hereinafter OTP Jurisdiction Request 2019].

into the situation of Palestine under Article 53(1).[48] As a result of a 2018 State Referral,[49] the Prosecutor is no longer required to seek authorisation of the PTC to do this.[50] Nevertheless, the OTP requested a ruling on the validity and scope of the ICC's territorial jurisdiction, noting that this 'foundational question' requires 'expeditious' resolution by the PTC.[51] Specifically, the OTP seeks confirmation that the 'territory' over which the ICC may exercise jurisdiction comprises the West Bank, including East Jerusalem, and Gaza.[52] At present, the PTC has 120 days from 30 April 2020 to determine whether Palestine is a 'state' under the Rome Statute, and in turn, whether the situation falls within the Court's jurisdiction.

Notably, the 2019 OTP Request elaborates on her finding that both parties committed war crimes during the 2014 hostilities in Gaza (Operation Protective Edge). Regarding IDF members, she refers to the crimes of 'intentionally launching disproportionate attacks in at least three incidents; wilfully killing and/or causing serious injury to body or health and intentionally directing an attack against Red Cross personnel or institutions'.[53] Regarding members of Hamas and Palestinian armed groups, the Prosecutor specifies 'the crimes of intentionally directing attacks against civilians and civilian objects; using protected persons as shields; wilfully depriving protected persons of the rights of fair and regular trial and wilful killing and torture or inhuman treatment and/or outrages upon personal dignity'.[54]

Significantly, the Prosecutor concludes that members of the Israeli authorities have committed war crimes in the West Bank that include 'inter-alia' the transfer of Israeli civilians' into Israeli settlements since 13 June 2014.[55] This paragraph leaves open the possibility that other settlement-related activities such as forcible transfer of Palestinians and demolition of property would be part of any investigation into the West Bank.[56] Finally in relation to the 2018 violence, the Prosecutor considers that any investigation may also probe alleged crimes committed by IDF members using 'non-lethal and lethal means' against those who participated in the Great March of Return demonstrations, which began in March 2018 on the Gazan

[48] Ibid. at ¶ 2, 93.

[49] Referral by the State of Palestine, above n. 43.

[50] OTP Jurisdiction Request 2019, above n. 47 at ¶ 4.

[51] The Prosecutor justifies the referral for the practical conduct of the investigations, the efficiency of the proceedings and in order to provide an opportunity for victims, the referring State and others to participate in the case and 'thereby endow its decision with greater legitimacy'. Ibid. at ¶ 6.

[52] Ibid.

[53] Ibid. at ¶ 94 (citing Rome Statute, arts. 8(2)(b)(iv)); 8(2)(a)(i), 8(2)(a)(iii), or arts 8(2)(c)(i)) (article 8(2)(b)(xxiv), or 8(2)(e)(ii)).

[54] Ibid. (citing Rome Statute, arts.8(2)(b)(i)-(ii), or 8(2)(e)(i)); 8(2)(b)(xxiii) 8(2)(a)(vi)or 8(2)(c)(iv); 8(2)(a)(i), or 8(2)(c)(i);(article 8(2)(a)(ii), or 8(2)(c)(i); 8(2)(b)(xxi), or 8(2)(c)(ii)).

[55] Ibid. at ¶ 95.

[56] Ibid.

border.[57] This event 'reportedly resulted in the killing of over 200 individuals, including over 40 children, and the wounding of thousands of others'.[58]

Recent Developments

On 28 January 2020, the PTC responded to the OTP 2019 Request by requesting Israel, Palestine, and the victims in the situation to submit written observations on the question of jurisdiction.[59] In addition, States, organisations, and/or persons were allowed to submit *amicus curiae* filings. The PTC stated that this step was necessary due to the 'complexity and novelty' of the Prosecutor's request.[60] Arguably, this legitimacy seeking trend, set by the OTP, seeks to share the burden of decision-making in Palestine.

During February and March 2020, an unprecedented number of *amicus curiae* briefs were filed with the court. Some distinguished scholars[61] and specialised NGOs supported the Israeli[62] and Palestinian[63] positions on jurisdiction, respectively. Seven states (namely Australia, Austria, Brazil, the Czech Republic, Germany, Hungary, and Uganda) submitted that Palestine does not meet the definition of 'State' under the statute and cannot establish ICC jurisdiction. Conversely, Palestine, the League of Arab States (representing 22 countries) and the Organization of Islamic Cooperation (representing 57 countries) echoed the OTP's decision that Palestine qualifies as a 'state' and endorsed the jurisdictional basis to investigate. On 29 April 2020, over 180 Palestinian and international organizations and individuals filed an open letter in support of the ICC's intervention in Palestine.[64] The

---

[57] Ibid. at ¶ 96.

[58] Ibid.

[59] Int'l Criminal Court, Situation in the State of Palestine, ICC-01/18–14, Order setting the procedure and the schedule for the submission of observations (28 January 2020).

[60] Ibid. at ¶ 15.

[61] For example, Professors Richard Falk, William Schabas, and John Quigley filed submissions in support of Palestinian statehood and ICC jurisdiction. Conversely, Professors Eyal Benvenisti and Malcolm N Shaw rejected Palestine's capacity to constitute a state under Article 12 of the Rome Statute.

[62] Pro-Israel groups included the Lawfare Project, the Institute for NGO Research, Palestinian Media Watch, and the Jerusalem Center for Public Affairs, The Israel Forever Foundation, UK Lawyers for Israel, B'nai B'rith UK, the International Legal Forum, the Jerusalem Initiative and the Simon Wiesenthal Centre.

[63] Pro-Palestinian groups included the Palestinian Bar Association, MyAQSA Foundation, the Palestinian Center for Human Rights, Al-Haq Law in the Service of Mankind, Al-Mezan Center for Human Rights, and Aldameer Association for Human Rights.

[64] These Palestinian human rights organisations included Al-Haq, Al Dammeer Association for Human Rights, the Palestinian Centre for Human Rights (PCHR), and Al Mezan Center for Human Rights. For details of the letter see http://www.alhaq.org/advocacy/16795.html

Prosecutor responded to the submissions by confirming her initial findings.[65] The OTP concluded that it '…has carefully considered the observations of the participants and remains of the view that the Court has jurisdiction over the Occupied Palestinian Territory'.[66]

Subsequently, the PTC requested the PA to clarify whether Palestine still regards the Oslo Accords as binding in light of a statement made by President Abbas.[67] On 19 May 2020, President Abbas declared that the PA was absolved from all its agreements with Israel because of threats to imminently annex parts of the West Bank.[68] The PTC requested additional information to help determine the Court's jurisdiction.[69] On 5 June 2020, the PA responded by insisting the President's remarks have no legal bearing on the questions before the Court and are not part of the formal record.[70] A statement made by the OTP 3 days later echoed this view and reiterated its position that 'the Oslo Accords do not bar the exercise of the Court's jurisdiction in Palestine'. Ultimately, this exchange seems to be merely a rhetorical one. It leaves the complex jurisdictional questions to be resolved by the PTC unchanged.

On 5 February 2021, the ICC Pre-Trial Chamber I rendered its much-anticipated decision on the Prosecutor's request for a ruling on territorial jurisdiction in the Situation in Palestine (2019 OTP Request),[71] the Chamber decided by a majority,[72] that the Court may exercise criminal jurisdiction in Palestine, namely Gaza, the West Bank, and East Jerusalem. The ruling stressed that it was not determining the question of Palestinian statehood in international law, neither adjudicating nor prejudging a border dispute, but solely determining jurisdiction for the Rome Statute.[73] The PTC noted 'that disputed borders have never prevented a State from becoming a State Party to the Statute and, as such, cannot prevent the Court from exercising its jurisdiction'.[74] According to the majority, the Prosecutor is now obliged to open

[65] ICC, Prosecution Response to the Observations of Amici Curiae, Legal Representatives of Victims, and States, ICC-01/18-131, (30 April 2020), https://www.icc-cpi.int/CourtRecords/CR2020_01746.PDF

[66] Ibid. at ¶ 100.

[67] Int'l Criminal Court, Situation in the State of Palestine, Order requesting additional information, ICC-01/18–134 (26 May 2020) at ¶ 6 https://www.icc-cpi.int/CourtRecords/CR2020_02105.PDF [hereinafter PTC Request on Oslo 2020].

[68] ICC, The State of Palestine's response to the Pre-Trial Chamber's Order requesting additional information, ICC-01/18–13 (5 June 2020) at ¶ 7 [hereinafter Palestine's Response on Oslo 2020].

[69] PTC Request on Oslo 2020, above n 67 at ¶ 6.

[70] Palestine's Response on Oslo 2020 at ¶ 6.

[71] OTP Jurisdiction Request 2019.

[72] Int'l Criminal Court, Situation in the State of Palestine, ICC-01/18, Decision on the 'Prosecution request pursuant to article 19(3) for a ruling on the Court's territorial jurisdiction in Palestine' (5 February 2021) [hereinafter PTC Jurisdiction Ruling 2021]. The PTC affirmed the Court's jurisdiction in a 2:1 vote (in favour of French Judge Perrin de Brichambaut and Beninese Judge Alapini-Gansou, against Hungarian Judge Kovács).

[73] Ibid. at ¶ 130.

[74] Ibid. at ¶ 115.

an investigation, having determined that a reasonable basis exists to do so.[75] Indeed, on 3 March 2021, the OTP confirmed its opening of an investigation into the Situation in Palestine.[76]

Unsurprisingly, Palestinian leaders welcomed the move as a vindication of their strategy at the ICC.[77] PA official Hussein al-Sheikh even described the judgement as 'a victory for rights, justice, freedom and moral values in the world'.[78] Conversely, Israeli PM Netanyahu was quick to deride the Court and the investigation as 'pure anti-Semitism'.[79] The US State Department opposed the ruling and restated its established position that 'the court's jurisdiction should be reserved for countries that consent to it'.[80] Regardless of the backlash, it seems clear that a legal rubicon has been crossed. At least in theory, both Israeli soldiers and Palestinian militants are accountable to the Hague for their past conduct. At the same time, no legal action is expected anytime soon. The ICC decision itself warns of a 'protracted' and 'resource-intensive' period for identifying potential cases for investigation.[81] It concludes with an apparent disclaimer that 'further questions of jurisdiction' may still arise when arrest warrants and summons are issued.[82] The lengthy dissent of Judge Peter Kovacs could also provide a sound basis for future judicial review.[83]

---

[75] Ibid. at ¶ 65.

[76] Statement by ICC Prosecutor, Mrs. Fatou Bensouda, respecting an investigation of the Situation in Palestine, INT'L CRIM. CT. OF THE PROSECUTOR (3 March 2021) https://www.icc-cpi.int/Pages/item.aspx?name=210303-prosecutor-statement-investigation-palestine

[77] Nabil Shaath, a senior aide to Palestinian leader Mahmoud Abbas, welcomed the decision and said it proved the Palestinians were right to go to the ICC. FRANCE 24, 5 February 2021 https://www.france24.com/en/middle-east/20210205-icc-rules-it-has-jurisdiction-over-palestinian-territories-clears-way-for-probe-of-israeli-actions

[78] Ibid.

[79] PM Netanyahu 'The decision of the International Court to open an investigation against Israel today for war crimes is absurd. It's undiluted antisemitism and the height of hypocrisy'. https://govextra.gov.il/foreign-affairs/icc/home/?gclid=CjwKCAiA65iBBhB-EiwAW253W3ZnUBkKR4qe0hK-C2htcR7PpHwYm7V7hUXdsc9oh7_LTGeoGML-hBoCN

[80] See Ned Price, Opposing International Criminal Court Attempts to Affirm Territorial Jurisdiction Over the Palestinian Situation US State Dept, Press Statement (5 February 2021) https://www.state.gov/opposing-international-criminal-court-attempts-to-affirm-territorial-jurisdiction-over-the-palestinian-situation/

[81] PTC Jurisdiction Ruling 2021 at ¶ 86.

[82] Ibid. at ¶ 130.

[83] Although Judge Kovacs supported opening an investigation, he disagreed with the majority's reasoning on geographical scope and jurisdiction over Israeli nationals. See Partly Dissenting Opinion Judge Kovacs Int'l Criminal Court, Situation in the State of Palestine, ICC-01/18, Decision on the 'Prosecution request pursuant to article 19(3) for a ruling on the Court's territorial jurisdiction in Palestine' (5 February 2021) ¶ 367–379.

5.4 Part Three: Jurisdictional Hurdles at the ICC

In light of the 2019 OTP Request, it seems that so far as the Prosecutor is concerned, the Rome statute requirements relating to subject-matter jurisdiction and admissibility, and thus complementarity have all been met at the preliminary examination stage. At the same time, the Prosecutor has herself acknowledged that 'it is no understatement to say that determination of the Court's jurisdiction…touch[es] on complex legal and factual issues'.[84] The unusually large involvement of States, civil society groups and the far-reaching implications of the case make this clear. In this regard, the game is not over and there is still much to play for.

This section outlines the four major hurdles obstructing the OTP in Palestine, namely the question of Palestinian statehood and territory complementarity, gravity, and the interests of justice. It is contended that each jurisdictional barrier raises complex legal and factual questions, and they ultimately cast doubt over the OTP's jurisdictional capacity to proceed with a formal and viable investigation in the near future. Notwithstanding the Prosecutor's conclusion to the contrary, it remains unclear whether the procedural preconditions have in fact been met for exercising ICC jurisdiction under the Rome Statute in the situation in Palestine.

Palestinian Statehood and Territory

Arguably, the Palestinian statehood question is an easy one for judicial determination at the ICC. After all, the UN Secretary-General (UNSG) has accepted Palestine's accession to the Rome Statute, and the Prosecutor has concluded that Palestine is a 'state' for the purpose of the Court's territorial jurisdiction.[85] The OTP seems assured that it could prosecute war crimes committed all over the Palestinian territories, including the West Bank, East Jerusalem, and the Gaza Strip.[86] At the same time, the Prosecutor openly acknowledges the 'unresolved' and contentious nature of Palestine's statehood, indicating that many questions remain open.[87] Whilst the Court has ruled that Palestine does qualify as a state for jurisdictional purposes, the Rome Statute does not exist in a legal or political vacuum. Accordingly, various plausible legal and factual arguments can still be raised against the Court's ruling on the statehood question.

---

[84] OTP Jurisdiction Request 2019, above n 47 at ¶ 5.

[85] Since 2015, the OTP has confirmed that it treats the GA vote as conclusive, but the ICC has never formally ruled on this issue. Ibid. at ¶ 5; See David Luban, 'Some Legal Questions', JUST SECURITY (2 January 2015) https://www.justsecurity.org/18817/palestine-icc-legal-questions

[86] OTP Jurisdiction Request 2019, above n 47 at ¶ 3.

[87] Ibid. at ¶ ¶ 5, 181.

Accession as Jurisdiction?

The Prosecutor's primary claim is that Palestine's accession to the ICC is sufficient to indicate statehood for establishing the court's jurisdiction.[88] She even suggests that the PTC could simply rely on Palestine's ratification in 2015 without considering statehood at all under general international law.[89] Unsurprisingly, Israel's Attorney-General insists that '…a substantive legal inquiry into the precondition of the Court's jurisdiction cannot be averted'.[90] According to Israel, the context and language of Palestine's accession were highly qualified by disclaimers and deferrals concerning the legal status of 'Palestine' and are therefore wholly inadequate for settling the Court's jurisdiction.[91] For example, the 2012 UNGA Resolution, on which the Palestinian accession relied, was passed 'without prejudice' to the legal question of 'Palestinian Statehood'.[92] Indeed, the OTP itself has previously affirmed that Palestine should be viewed as a 'State' solely for the purposes of acceding to the Rome Statute and lodging an Article 12(3) declaration.[93] Similarly, Palestinian participation in the ICC Assembly of States Parties was facilitated 'without prejudice' to the legal question of statehood.[94]

At the same time, whilst accession may not equate to statehood,[95] the PTC remains capable of ruling on jurisdiction without having to address the broader

---

[88] OTP Jurisdiction Request 2019, above n 47 at ¶ 7–8

[89] '…the Court is not required to make a pronouncement with respect to or resolve Palestine's Statehood under public international law more generally'. Ibid. at ¶ 42.

[90] Israel's Attorney General (AG) released a memo challenging ICC jurisdiction the same day the OTP's 2019 Request was issued. State of Israel, Office of the Attorney General, The International Criminal Court's lack of jurisdiction over the so called 'situation in Palestine' Exec. Sum ¶ 5, 18. (2019) [hereinafter state of Israel A-G Memo 2019].

[91] Ibid.

[92] G.A. Resolution 67/19 (2012), above n 28, ¶ 2. Arguably, the resolution concerned a 'procedural matter of Palestinian representation within the UN alone.' state of Israel A-G Memo 2019, above n 90, Exec. Sum ¶ 5.

[93] In its 2018 Prelim Report, the OTP stated that its summary was 'without prejudice to any future determinations by the Office regarding the exercise of territorial or personal jurisdiction by the Court'. See OTP Report on Preliminary Examination Activities 2018, above n 44; state of Israel A-G Memo 2019, above n 90, ¶ 3.

[94] The President of the Assembly of State Parties explicitly clarified that 'the Assembly takes such [procedural] decisions in accordance with the Rules of Procedure of the Assembly, independently of and without prejudice to decisions taken for any other purpose, including decisions of any other organization or organs of the Court regarding any legal issues that may come before them'. Assembly of States Parties to the Rome Statute of the International Criminal Court, ICC-ASP/13/20, ¶ 3 (8–17 December 2014).

[95] ICC membership supports claims for Palestinian statehood, even if ratification of treaties is not a formal criterion for assessing statehood under the Montevideo Convention. See generally David Bosco, *Palestine in The Hague: Justice, Geopolitics, and the International Criminal Court*, 22 Global Governance 155, 168 (2016); See also Thomas Obel Hansen, *What Are the Consequences of Palestine Joining the International Criminal Court?*, e-int'l rel. (6 April 2015), http://www.eir.info/2015/04/06/what-are-the-consequences-of-palestine-joining-the-international-criminal-court/

debates on Palestinian statehood.[96] The Rome Statute does not define 'State', and so the Judges could technically adopt the OTP's interpretation under the 'all States' formula in Article 125(3).[97] On this view, the Court exercises jurisdiction based solely on the 2015 procedural determination of the UNSG and UNGA practice that Palestine constitutes a 'State'.[98] Indeed, it might contradict the principle of effectiveness to permit an entity to join the ICC and later deny the natural consequence of its membership, namely the exercise of jurisdiction.[99]

It is strongly arguable however that any 'thin' application of international law on this question would comprise the court's legitimacy. It seems unwise for the Judges to simply invoke a non-binding UN resolution on an administrative matter to resolve jurisdiction in Palestine.[100] By its own terms, the 2012 UNGA Resolution was limited to a procedural upgrade of the Palestinian representation within the UN alone. Rather, the term 'State' in Article 12(2) should be interpreted based on general international law principles governing sovereign statehood.[101] This seems most consistent with the drafters' intentions of the Rome Statute,[102] and the clear need for the ICC to authoritatively exercise its mandate, especially in relation to a non-state party. In short, the PTC should not have dodged the substantive bullet on statehood where clear legal parameters have not been met.

OTP's Substantive Case

The Prosecutor makes an alternative case for ICC jurisdiction based on a relatively modern approach to statehood. Traditionally, an entity must meet four criteria set out in the Montevideo Convention of 1933 to be considered a state: a permanent

---

[96] OTP Jurisdiction Request 2019, above n 47 at ¶ 42 ('…the Court is not required to make a pronouncement with respect to or resolve Palestine's Statehood under public international law more generally').

[97] See Rome Statute, above n 32, art 125(3): 'This Statute shall be open to accession by all States. Instruments of accession shall be deposited with the Secretary-General of the United Nations'. Ibid. at ¶ 7.

[98] Ibid. (Simply put, a State under article 12(1) and article 125(3) should also be considered a State under article 12(2). There is no reason why this logic should not apply to Palestine.)

[99] Ibid. at ¶ 105.

[100] See Yan Ling, *Non-States Parties and the Preliminary Examination of Article 12(3) Declarations* in QUALITY CONTROL IN PRELIMINARY EXAMINATIONS: VOLUME II, 462 (Morten Bergsmo & Carsten Stahn eds., 2018); Yaël Ronen, *Recognition of the State of Palestine: Still Too Much Too Soon?*, in SOVEREIGNTY, STATEHOOD AND STATE RESPONSIBILITY – ESSAYS IN HONOUR OF JAMES CRAWFORD 229, 231 (Christine Chinkin and Freya Baetens eds., 2015).

[101] STATE OF ISRAEL A-G MEMO 2019, above n 90, ¶ 9; See also Steven Kay and Joshua Kern, ARTICLE 15 COMMUNICATION: PRECONDITIONS TO THE EXERCISE JURISDICTION UNDER ARTICLE 12 OF THE ROME STATUTE (2019) (referring to article 31(4) of the VCLT (if 'any "special meaning" is to be given to a treaty provision, it must be shown to have been so intended by the parties').

[102] Bassiouni (2010) (the Chairman of the Diplomatic Conference's Drafting Committee) has 'attest[ed] to the fact that referrals under Article 12(3) were intended to be by [sovereign] States only'. OTP Jurisdiction Request 2019, above n 47 at ¶113; see also STATE OF ISRAEL A-G MEMO 2019, above n 90, ¶ 11.

population, a defined territory, effective government over the population, and the capacity to enter into relations with other states.[103] The OTP claims that 'the exceptional circumstances of Palestine call for a case-specific application of traditional statehood criteria to it'.[104] Given the PA's limited powers and authority over large parts of the territories,[105] the Prosecutor duly notes the difficulties with Palestine satisfying the effective government requirement of statehood.[106] However, she regards Israel's expansion of settlements and the security barrier as unlawful measures capable of relaxing the normative criteria of statehood.[107] Moreover, the OTP draws on the Palestinian right to self-determination and 'statehood in the territories'[108] as legally remedial of the governance deficit and sufficient to establish ICC jurisdiction.[109] The Prosecutor also cites bilateral recognition of Palestine by 138 States as significant to her determination.[110]

Relaxing Governance: Too Novel and Partisan?

Whilst the OTP's approach has normative appeal, it is perhaps too ambitious for an international court to use as a basis for criminal jurisdiction. The Prosecutor's remedial application of international law to statehood is novel and judicially untested and does not command unequivocal support.[111] Notably, both the ICTY in assessing the

[103] See Convention on the Rights and Duties of States (Montevideo Convention), December 26, 1933 165 L.N.T.S. 19. [hereinafter *Montevideo Convention*]; OTP Jurisdiction Request 2019, above n 47 at ¶ ¶ 43, 136.

[104] OTP Jurisdiction Request 2019, above n 47 at ¶ 138.

[105] '...Palestine's authority appears largely limited to Areas A and B of the West Bank and subject to important restrictions.' Ibid. at ¶ 145.

[106] Under the Montevideo Convention, the creation of a State requires, inter alia, a government with full governmental powers over the territory that it claims. See the rules of international law enshrined in the Montevideo Convention, art. 1, above n 79.

[107] 'In sum, the negative impact of the above illegal measures and practices on Palestine's effective authority....and more fundamentally on the realisation of the Palestinian people's right to self-determination, warrant a case-specific application of the traditional statehood criteria...'. OTP Jurisdiction Request 2019, above n 47 at ¶ ¶ 9137, 178.

[108] 'Further, the OPT [Occupied Palestinian Territories] has long been recognised as the territory where the Palestinian people are entitled to exercise their right to self-determination and to an independent and sovereign State'. Ibid. at ¶ 138.

[109] '...the Prosecution does not consider that Palestine's governance shortcomings are fatal to its status for the purpose of the Court's jurisdiction'. Ibid. at ¶ 146.

[110] Ibid. at ¶ ¶ 124–132.

[111] For example, the OTP cites Crawford for the idea that Israel's unlawful conduct in 'restricting Palestinian self-determination supports Palestine's claim to statehood'. However, Crawford himself did not consider this proposition applicable to Palestine because of Israeli-Palestinian permanent status negotiations (as noted by the OTP itself). See Ibid. at ¶ ¶ 142–43; See also James R. Crawford, The Creation of States in International Law 448 (2016) [hereinafter *Creation of States*].

Milosevic case[112] and the Badinter Arbitration Commission on issues arising from the dissolution of Yugoslavia[113] adhered to the well-established Montevideo formula. At the same time, the statehood test is 'neither exhaustive nor immutable',[114] and the governmental criterion has indeed been relaxed in certain contexts. For example, Bosnia and Croatia were overwhelmingly recognised as States even though they did not have effective government control over the entirety of the territory at issue.[115]

Nevertheless, the idea that Israel's unlawful conduct and impact on Palestinian self-determination should bolster claims to statehood is problematic. It implicitly presumes that, but for the Israeli settlements and the security barrier, the PA would effectively exercise control over all of the territories and enjoy independent statehood. This idea is controversial given, for example, that the PA does not control over 40% of the Palestinian population in the Gaza Strip where Hamas governs, nor has it ever exercised powers over East Jerusalem which until 1967 was under Jordanian control.[116] By glossing over factors that contribute to the current governance situation in Palestine, the Prosecutor strays into political terrain.[117] The OTP seems to be holding one party responsible for all the realities on the ground.[118] A partisan narrative of the conflict should not be used to salvage legal deficiencies in Palestine's case for statehood.

---

[112] Prosecutor v. Slobodan Milošević, Case No. IT-02-54-T, Decision on Motion for Judgement of Acquittal, ¶¶ 85–115 (Int'l Crim. Trib. for the Former Yugoslavia, Jun.16, 2004).

[113] Opinion No. 8 of Conference on Yugoslavia Arbitration Commission: Opinions on Questions Arising From the Dissolution of Yugoslavia, 31(6) I.L.M. 1488, 1522–1523 (November 1992) ('a state's existence or non-existence had to be established on the basis of universally acknowledged principles of international law concerning the constituent elements of a state').

[114] See e.g. MALCOLM N. SHAW, QC, INTERNATIONAL LAW 158 (2017) [hereinafter *International Law*]; JAMES R. CRAWFORD, BROWNLIE'S PRINCIPLES OF PUBLIC INTERNATIONAL LAW 118 (2019) ('Not all the conditions are necessary, and in any case further criteria must be employed to produce a working definition').

[115] *See* Shaw, *International Law,* above n 90, at 159–160; Matthew Craven and Rose Parfitt, *Statehood, elf-determination and Recognition,* in MALCOLM EVANS, INTERNATIONAL LAW 224 (2018) ('[B]oth Bosnia-Herzegovina and Croatia were recognized by the EC as independent States in 1992 at a time at which the governments concerned had effective control over only a portion of the territory in question"); See also *Creation of States* above n 87 at 57 (further noting that "the requirement of 'government' is less stringent than has been thought, at least in particular contexts').

[116] STATE OF ISRAEL A-G MEMO 2019, above n 90, ¶37.

[117] The Palestinian Authority and Hamas also lack control over other aspects of governance in the territories, such as airspace and tax collection under the Oslo Accords. Arguably, there are many contributing factors (beyond Israeli conduct) that impinge on the realisation of the Palestinian people's right to self-determination from failed peace agreements, systemic corruption to terrorist activities.

[118] OTP Jurisdiction Request 2019, above n 47 at ¶157 (The OTP make a throwaway line that 'one party is not solely responsible' for the impasse in Palestine but insists that the Court cannot and should not attempt to identify all the contributing factors).

Self-determination and Borders

The OTP too easily conflates self-determination with the achievement of statehood.[119] Whilst the Palestinian right to self-determination has long been connected with a state, that right may also be exercised by free pursuit of economic, social, and cultural development based on political equality.[120] In particular, the Prosecutor seems to confuse the unlawfulness of Israeli settlements with the existence of Palestinian sovereignty in all of the West Bank and East Jerusalem, including for example, highly disputed areas like the Jewish quarter in Jerusalem's old city. For example, the OTP cites UNSC Resolution 2334 (2016) and other UN resolutions condemning the Israeli settlements as proof that Israel does not have sovereign title over the territories.[121] However, non-recognition of Israeli sovereignty over the territories is not the same as international recognition of Palestinian sovereignty in all of the territories. Indeed, the Palestinians themselves have claimed that Jerusalem and certain parts of the West Bank are *corpus separatum* over which neither Israel nor the PA has sovereignty.[122] In sum, the ICC should avoid demarcating a highly disputed border for jurisdictional purposes.[123]

Delegation and Oslo

Finally, the ICC must address whether a Palestinian state could validly delegate criminal jurisdiction over its territory and nationals. Arguably, the Court's treaty-based system is limited to the scope of authority conferred by Member-States.[124]

---

[119] See Ibid. at ¶[150] ('there is a general accord among the international community that the Palestinian people have a right to self-determination and are entitled to an independent and sovereign State in the Occupied Palestinian Territory'). However, a distinction between self-determination and statehood is maintained by scholarship and practice. See *Creation of States,* above n 87 at 446; Legal Consequences of the Separation of the Chagos Archipelago from Mauritius in 1965, Advisory Opinion, 2019 I.C.J 169, ¶¶ 156–157 (25 February 2019) [hereinafter ICJ Chagos Advisory Opinion]; DAVID RAIC, STATEHOOD AND THE LAW OF SELF-DETERMINATION 444–445 (2002); Christian Tomuschat, *Secession and Self-Determination, in* SECESSION: INTERNATIONAL LAW PERSPECTIVES 23, 24 (Marcelo G. Kohen ed., 2006).

[120] *Creation of States,* above n 87 at 127–128; ICJ Chagos Advisory Opinion, above n 95 at ¶156.

[121] OTP Jurisdiction Request 2019, above n 47 at ¶¶ 157–178.

[122] Relocation of the United Stated Embassy to Jerusalem (Palestine v. United States of America), Application Instituting Proceedings (28 September 2018), available at https://www.icj-cij.org/files/case-related/176/176-20180928-APP-01-00-EN.pdf (last accessed: 19 December 2019); STATE OF ISRAEL A-G MEMO 2019, above n 90, ¶ 46.

[123] 'Politically, this will place the Prosecutor into the midst of one of the world's most flammable disputes'. Kay and Kerne, above n 77 at 24; See also Luban, above n 85.

[124] Fundamentally, the ICC draws its authority from states' consent to delegate their powers under Article 12 of the Rome State. Michael A Newton, *How the International Criminal Court Threatens Treaty Norms* 49 VANDERBILT J. TRANSANT'L L. 371, 408–14 (2016).

This conforms with a functional view of the Rome Statute[125] and the drafter's intent to reject universal jurisdiction.[126] Nevertheless, the OTP claims that recognising Palestine's jurisdiction is most consistent with the treaty's objectives.[127] Indeed, the ICC is geared towards ending impunity and enforcing the law on behalf of vulnerable groups where the court's role is most significant.[128] The creation of 'legal black holes' over which no state exercises sovereignty seems contrary to the statute.[129] On the other hand, it is no less arguable that the Court must stay faithful to the treaty's jurisdictional foundations and should not assume authority outside its institutional limits.[130] After all, the ICC was also intended to pay due deference to state sovereignty.

To this end, some academics invoke the Oslo Accords as a limitation on Palestine's capacity to delegate jurisdiction.[131] The recent dissent of Judge Peter Kovacs would clearly support this approach.[132] Israel has argued that the Oslo Accords exclude Israelis and the settlements from Palestinian jurisdiction and as a consequence from the ICC's authority.[133] Indeed, Palestinian courts are legally incapable of prosecuting Israelis for settlement-related crimes, or any other offence in the territories.[134] Nevertheless, the OTP has dismissed this obstacle by distinguish-

---

[125] A functional approach is one that interprets the Rome Statute in light of the objectives of the Court. See Malcolm Shaw, *The Article 12(3) Declaration of the Palestinian Authority, the International Criminal Court and International Law* 9 J. INT. CRIM. JUSTICE 301(2011); Yuval Shany, *In Defence of Functional Interpretation of Article 12(3) of the Rome Statute: A Response to Yaël Ronen'* 8 J. INT. CRIM. JUSTICE 329, 339 (2010).

[126] Conversely, according to a universalist theory, ICC jurisdiction is grounded in a broader entitlement of states and the international legal community as a whole. On this view, ICC jurisdiction is not solely derived from the territorial or national jurisdiction of a specific state. See Ibid, 331–33; Carsten Stahn, *The ICC, Pre-Existing Jurisdictional Treaty Regimes, and the limits of the Nemo Dat Quod Non Habet Doctrine - A Reply to Michael Newton*, 49 VAND. J. TRANSNAT'L L. 443 (2016) 447–8.

[127] OTP Jurisdiction Request 2019, above n 47 at ¶ 180.

[128] Ibid. (citing Rome Statute, Preamble at ¶ 11).

[129] Shany, above n 125 at 337.

[130] Arguably, the adoption of the delegation concept by its nature limits the ICC's jurisdiction and therefore cannot be disregarded on the basis of purposive interpretation.

[131] Newton, above n 124 at 408–14; Eugene Kontorovich, Israel/Palestine–The ICC's Uncharted Territory, 11 J. INT'L CRIM. JUST. 979, 988–89 (2013). at 990; Shaw, above n 104 at 301; Shany, above n 125 at 339.

[132] In this regard, Judge Kovács recognises that the Oslo Accords considerably curtail Palestinian criminal jurisdiction Ibid. at ¶ 130,372 ff.), which is why only this restricted jurisdiction should be delegated to the ICC.

[133] Oslo established a twofold limitation on the PA' s jurisdiction: *ratione personae* by excluding Israeli nationals and *ratione loci* by excluding Israeli settlements as territory. In the 1995 Interim Agreement (Oslo II), and more specifically in its Legal Annex, the Palestine Liberation Organization (PLO) and Israel agreed that the criminal jurisdiction of the newly created PA only covers offences committed by Palestinians and/or non-Israelis in the territory, whereas the term 'territory' excludes settlements and military locations. See Israel–Palestinian Interim Agreement on the West Bank and the Gaza Strip (28 September 1995), 36 ILM 557 (1997) (Oslo II), art XVII and Annex IV, art 1.

[134] Hannes Jöbstl, *An Unlikely Day in Court? Legal Challenges for the Prosecution of Israeli Settlements Under the Rome Statute* Israel Law Review' 51(3) ISR. LAW REV. 339, 350–1 (2018).

ing between Palestine's *enforcement* jurisdiction and its *prescriptive* jurisdiction.[135] On this view, Palestine retains its authority to vest the ICC with jurisdiction, even though it cannot enforce criminal law over Israelis and most of the territories. At a theoretical level, this is a relevant distinction.[136] In practice, however, the PA does not have any recognised authority (prescriptive or otherwise) over Israeli nationals, the settlements, or East Jerusalem. In this regard, even a broader view of delegation[137] is at odds with legal and factual realities on the ground. Ultimately, the ICC would need to meaningfully resolve this precondition to jurisdiction.

Complementarity

Complementarity is another admissibility hurdle at the ICC.[138] Indeed, the Court may only exercise jurisdiction where Israeli/Palestinian national legal systems fail to do so, including where they purport to act, but are unwilling and/or unable to genuinely carry out credible investigations (and, where warranted, prosecutions).[139] The ICC recognises that States have the primary duty to prosecute international crimes and that its jurisdiction should be complementary to national criminal jurisdictions.[140] In her 2019 OTP Request, the Prosecutor indicated that she will continue to review the 'scope and genuineness' of relevant and ongoing Israeli proceedings for crimes allegedly committed by members of the IDF.[141] However, she noted, there is no question that the alleged crimes committed by Palestinian armed groups in Gaza are not being investigated and are thus fair game for the ICC.[142]

---

[135] According to the OTP, Oslo only limits the Palestine's jurisdiction to enforce the law, but not the jurisdiction to prescribe it. OTP Jurisdiction Request 2019, above n 47 at ¶ ¶ 183–184; See also Stahn (2016) above n 126 at 450 (distinguishing between jurisdiction to prescribe and jurisdiction to enforce) and Shaw, *International Law,* above n 90, at 483.

[136] This distinction is in line with general jurisdictional theories under international law. See e.g. Shany, above n 125 at 339 and Stahn, above n 126 at 450.

[137] See Office of the Prosecutor, Situation in the Islamic Republic of Afghanistan—Public redacted version of 'Request for authorisation of an investigation pursuant to article 15', ICC-02/17, p. 27, fn. 47 (20 November 2017).

[138] The legal framework resulting from the complementarity principle is laid down in Article 17 of the Rome Statute, which regulates admissibility. See e.g. Marcus Benzing, *The Complementarity Regime of the International Criminal Court: International Criminal Justice between State Sovereignty and the Fight against Impunity'* 7 MAX PLANCK. UNYB. 595(2003); Okechukwu Oko, *The Challenges of International Criminal Prosecutions in Africa* 31 FORDHAM INT'L L. J. 362 (2008).

[139] See Rome Statute, above n 32, at art 17.

[140] Ibid. (Both the preamble and Article 1 of the Rome Statute define the ICC as 'complementary to national criminal jurisdictions'.)

[141] OTP Jurisdiction Request 2019, above n 47 at ¶ 94.

[142] Ibid; See also OTP Report on Preliminary Examination Activities 2019 at ¶ 224.

The 'first limb' of complementarity requires the OTP to check the existence or absence of legal 'activity' at the national level.[143] Originally, national proceedings needed to encompass both the same person and the same conduct under investigation at the ICC.[144] In recent years, case law has held that a 'large overlap' between incidents being investigated by the OTP and the national authorities might be enough to render a case inadmissible.[145] In Afghanistan, however, the PTC observed that 'the information about investigation efforts at the domestic level in the US... [did] not show that criminal investigations or prosecutions have been conducted *on the incidents referred to and relied upon* by the Prosecution…'.[146] Similarly in Georgia, the Prosecutor proceeded with an investigation because Russia had not opened the 'relevant' domestic proceedings identified in the OTP requests.[147] Accordingly, the OTP is likely to scrutinise not just the existence of legal activity but the scope of Israeli investigations into alleged crimes.

Gaza and March of Return

Arguably, Israel has a track record of conducting investigations into alleged international crimes. In the aftermath of Operation Cast Lead, the Israeli military ordered five cumulative legal inquiries into Israeli warfare in Gaza (2009).[148] Regarding Operation Protective Edge (2014), the OTP noted that '…the information available indicates that all of the relevant incidents are or have been the subject of some form of investigative activities at the national level within the IDF military justice system'.[149] The IDF has further conducted its own legal examination and investiga-

143 This includes the following two scenarios: a. The state having jurisdiction is investigating or prosecuting the case (Article 17(1)(a)); or b. The state has investigated and decided not to prosecute (Article 17(1)(b)). See Rome Statute, above n 32, at art 17.

144 Prosecutor v. Thomas Lubanga Dyilo, ICC – 01/04–01/06, ¶31 (9 March 2006).

145 See Prosecutor v. Saif Al-Islam Gaddaffi, ICC – 01/11 – 01/11 – 344- Red, ¶89 (31 May 2013); Prosecutor v Gaddaffi and Al – Senussi, ICC – 01/11 – 01/11, 21, Judgement on the appeal of Libya against the decision of the Pre –Trial Chamber of 31 May 2013, ¶¶ 71 – 77 (May 2014).

146 ICC, Decision Pursuant to Article 15 of the Rome Statute on the Authorisation of an Investigation into the Situation in the Islamic Republic of Afghanistan ICC-02/17–33 12 April 2019 | Pre-Trial Chamber II | Decision at ¶79.

147 The Prosecutor determined that '…no concrete and progressive steps have been taken in Russia to ascertain the criminal responsibility of those involved in the alleged crimes related to the potential case(s) identified in the Request'. ICC, OTP, Report on Preliminary Examination Activities in Georgia (2015), ¶256 (12 November 2015).

148 Operation Cast Lead was subject to an independent Israeli Commission of Inquiry headed by a former Supreme Court justice THE PUBLIC COMMISSION TO EXAMINE THE MARITIME INCIDENT OF 31 MAY 2010 (THE TURKEL COMMISSION) PART ONE (Jan. 2010) [hereinafter TURKEL REPORT PART I]. See Philip Willams, 'Israeli Military Orders Inquiry Into the Recent Gaza Conflict', THE WORLD TODAY, (12 March, 2009), http://www.abc.net.au/worldtoday/content/2008/s2521408.htm

149 OTP Report on Preliminary Examination Activities 2018, above n 44 at ¶279; This was also again confirmed in the OTP's 2019 Preliminary Report. OTP Report on Preliminary Examination Activities 2019, *INT'L CRIM. CT., OFFICE OF THE PROSECUTOR, REPORT ON PRELIMINARY EXAMINATION ACTIVITIES 2019 ¶ 211 (2019) [hereinafter OTP REPORT ON PRELIMINARY EXAMINATION ACTIVITIES 2019]*, at ¶ 224.

tions into alleged incidents involving the shooting of demonstrators during the Great March of Return (2018–2019).[150] The IDF legal division, namely Israel's Military Advocate General (MAG) opened criminal investigations into the deaths of 11 demonstrators.[151] As recently as 2019, the OTP determined that the Israeli MAG is a 'competent authority for investigation' under the Rome Statute.[152]

It is not enough, however, that relevant proceedings in these cases exist; they must also be established as genuine and credible. In particular, the OTP must evaluate the un/willingness[153] and/or in/ability[154] of the parties to carry out such proceedings. Israel could cite the Second Turkel Commission Report (2013) to show that its examination mechanisms into alleged war crimes generally comply with international standards.[155] The Ministry of Foreign Affairs insists that 'Israel maintains a multi-layered investigations system, with numerous checks and balances to ensure impartiality...'.[156] Conversely, the UN Gaza Commission of Inquiry Report (2014) raised serious concerns about the country's investigative mechanisms for IHL.[157]

---

[150] According to media reports, one internal IDF probe into the deaths of 153 demonstrators was led by IDF Brigadier General Moti Baruch. Ibid. at ¶ 226.

[151] On 28 October 2019, one such investigation led to the conviction of one IDF soldier in relation to the killing of a teenager who took part in the demonstrations on 13 July 2018. OTP Report on Preliminary Examination Activities 2019, above n 149, at ¶ 216.

[152] See 'Situation on Registered Vessels of Comoros, Greece and Cambodia, Final decision of the Prosecutor concerning the "Article 53(1) Report"' (ICC-01/13–6-AnxA), dated 6 November 2014, as revised and refiled in accordance with the Pre-Trial Chamber's request of 15 November 2018 and the Appeals Chamber's judgment of 2 September 2019 (2 December 2019) [hereinafter *Mavi Marnara Appeal 2019*] ¶ 26; 'Bensouda said that one reason that she would not open a criminal probe was that the case had been probed by the IDF legal division'. Yonah J. Bob, *Did Palestinians push ICC Prosecutor into complimenting IDF?*, JERUSALEM POST, December 4, 2019 https://www.jpost.com/Arab-Israeli-Conflict/Did-Palestinians-accidentally-push-ICC-Prosecutor-into-complimenting-IDF-609766

[153] See Rome Statute, above n 32, at art 17(2) (requires determinations as to whether national proceedings are aimed at 'shielding' persons from criminal responsibility, whether there has been unjustified delay, or whether investigations or prosecutions are being conducted independently and impartially).

[154] See Rome Statute, above n 32, at art 17(3) (requires determinations as to whether, the State is unable to obtain the accused or the necessary evidence and testimony or otherwise unable to carry out its proceedings).

[155] THE PUBLIC COMMISSION TO EXAMINE THE MARITIME INCIDENT OF 31 MAY 2010, SECOND REPORT: ISRAEL'S MECHANISMS FOR EXAMINING AND INVESTIGATING COMPLAINTS AND CLAIMS OF VIOLATIONS OF THE LAWS OF ARMED CONFLICT ACCORDING TO INTERNATIONAL LAW (February 2013), 49 (though making a series of recommendations for further improvement [hereinafter TURKEL REPORT PART II]. See *generally* Amichai Cohen and Tal Mimran, *The Palestinian Authority and the International Criminal Court*, ISRAEL DEMOCRACY INSTITUTE, 10 February 2015, https://en.idi.org.il/articles/5216

[156] Israel Ministry of Foreign Affairs, Israel's Investigation of Alleged Violations of the Law of Armed Conflict (14 June 2015), http://mfa.gov.il/MFA/ForeignPolicy/IsraelGaza2014/Pages/IsraelInvestigation-of-Alleged-Violations-of-Law-of-Armed-Conflict.aspx

[157] See UN Human Rights Council, Report of the Independent Commission of Inquiry on the 2014 Gaza Conflict Established Pursuant to Human Rights Council Resolution S-21/1, A/HRC/29/52 (24 June 2015), 25 June 2015) ¶ 633 [hereinafter *UNHRC Gaza Report 2014*].

The Report identified '...a number of procedural, structural and substantive shortcomings...which compromise Israel's ability to adequately fulfil its duty to investigate'.[158] In March 2018, the Israeli State Comptroller also criticised aspects of the investigative legal framework.[159]

Theoretically, the OTP might regard the Israeli investigations as deficient[160] or too focused on low-level perpetrators.[161] For example, regarding Gaza (2014), Israel's MAG opened criminal investigations into 19 soldiers and not a single one was prosecuted.[162] The IDF recently closed its largest investigation of the period into the 'Black Friday Incident'[163] without any criminal charges.[164] Regarding the Great March of Return (2018), Israel's internal IDF probe only led to the conviction of one IDF soldier.[165] This might impact any assessment on the adequacy of Israeli investigations. On the other hand, it is worth recalling that the ICC must give precedence to domestic courts operating in good faith and genuine effort.[166] Ultimately, despite the criticisms, Israeli themselves have implemented extensive accountability efforts to investigate alleged war crimes.[167] Moreover, Israel's military justice

[158] Ibid. at ¶ 618 (The Report also concluded that 'significant further changes are required').

[159] An investigation launched by the state comptroller in January 2015 and published in March 2018 noted that Israel's legislation concerning war crimes is not fully in line with international law; that the IDF's reporting procedure only covers deliberate attacks on civilians (and hence not all war crimes); and that the IDF has no effective investigation policy of allegations of war crimes. See State Comptroller, Operation 'Protective Edge': IDF Activity from the Perspective of International Law particularly with regard to Mechanisms of Examination and Oversight of Civilian and Military Echelons (March 2018).

[160] In a June 2016 report, Human Rights Watch noted that there had been no 'meaningful progress in providing justice for serious laws-of-war violations during the 2014 conflict', See Human Rights Watch, *Palestine: ICC Should Open Formal* Probe (June 5, 2016), https://www.hrw.org/news/2016/06/05/palestine-icc-should-open-formal-probe

[161] The OTP might consider whether there is a 'deliberate focus of proceedings on low-level or marginal perpetrators despite evidence on those more responsible'. Office of the Prosecutor, Policy Paper on Preliminary Examinations (November 2013) ¶ 48.

[162] See Bar Levy & Shir Rozenzweig, *Israel and the International Criminal Court: A Legal Battlefield,* 19 Strategic assessment 29, 135 (2016).

[163] OTP Jurisdiction Request 2019, above n 47 at ¶ (mentioning 'three incidents' of war crimes allegedly committed in Gaza during 2014). It is likely that one of these incidents refers to the Black Friday battle that took place in Rafah after the abduction of the body of Lt. Hadar Goldin.

[164] See Yonah J. Bob, *IDF Closes Largest War Crime Probe of 2014 Gaza War*, Jerusalem Post (15August2018),https://www.jpost.com/Israel-News/IDF-closes-largest-war-crimes-probe-of-2014-Gaza-war-564946

[165] OTP Report on Preliminary Examination Activities 2019, above n 149, at ¶ 216.

[166] According to the ICJ, good faith is central to international law, '[o]ne of the basic principles governing the creation and performance of legal obligations, whatever their source'. Nuclear Tests (Australia v. France),1974 I.C.J. 253, 268 (December 20); Nuclear Tests (New Zealand v. France), 1974 I.C.J. 457, 473 (December 20). See Cohen and Mimran, above n 133.

[167] Adam Oler, *The Looming Demise of the ICC's Complementarity Principle: Israel, U.S. Interests, and the Court's Future*, 31 Emory Int'l. rev. 001, 1008 (2017); See also State of Isr., The 2014 Gaza Conflict (7 July-26 August 2014): Factual and Legal Aspects (May 2015), 218 [hereinafter State of Isr., The 2014 Gaza Conflict].

system compares favourably with the investigative mechanisms of other democratic countries.[168] It would be difficult for the ICC to justify intervention based on a claim that Israeli investigations are inadequate.[169]

Settlements

In her 2019 OTP Request, the Prosecution concluded that the potential case(s) that would arise from investigating the Israeli settlements 'would be admissible pursuant to article 17(1)(a)-(d) of the Statute'.[170] Accordingly, Israel, more than ever, remains exposed to prosecutions for settlement-related activities in the West Bank and East Jerusalem.[171] This is because the Israeli government has maintained that the establishment of Jewish settlements is not unlawful[172] and domestic law does not prohibit it.[173] Given state policy, Israel has not investigated or prosecuted its own senior leadership, the IDF, and/or relevant ministries for their involvement in the settlement enterprise.[174] This reality could constitute a case of 'total inactivity' to investigate the relevant allegations before the ICC.[175] In such cases, the OTP might simply

---

[168] The Second Turkel Commission (2013) found that 'Israel's system compares favourably [sic] with the investigative mechanisms of other democratic countries, including Australia, Canada, Germany, the Netherlands, the United Kingdom and the United States'. TURKEL REPORT PART II, above n 133; See also David Bosco, *How to Avoid Getting Hauled Before The Hague*, FOREIGN POL'Y(1April2015),https://foreignpolicy.com/2015/04/01/how-to-avoid-getting-hauled-before-the-hague-palestine-internationalcriminal-court/

[169] Based on Article 17(2), the OTP would face an uphill battle to try to prove bad faith ('unwillingness' in the language of the Statute) on the part of Israel. According to Dershowitz: 'If it were to be ruled that the Israeli legal system does not provide the required complementarity to deny the ICC institution jurisdiction as "a court of last resort", then no nation would pass that test'. Alan M Dershowitz, *Response to My Friend Luis Moreno Ocampo on the ICC and the Palestinian Situation*, JUST SECURITY 20 January 2015) www.justsecurity.org/19248/response-friend-luis-moreno-ocampo-international-criminal-court-palestinian-situation

[170] OTP Jurisdiction Request 2019, above n 47 at ¶ 94.

[171] Legal Consequences of the Construction of a Wall in the Occupied Palestinian Territory, Advisory Opinion, 2004 I.C.J. 136 (9 July 2004) [hereinafter *ICJ Advisory Wall Opinion*] (concluding that by establishing settlements, Israel had breached its international obligations and could not rely on self-defence or necessity) at ¶ ¶ 119–120.

[172] Political discourse around Israel's settlement policy rarely acknowledges its unlawful or 'criminal' nature. Michael G Kearney, *On the Situation in Palestine and the War Crime of Transfer of Civilians into Occupied Territory* 28 CRIM. L. FORUM 1, 4 (2017).

[173] OTP Report on Preliminary Examination Activities 2018, above n 44 at ¶277.

[174] Rome Statute, above n 32, art. 8(2)(b)(viii) (individuals are only liable if they are public authorities or if their conduct is otherwise attributable to the state). In this regard, those most indictable are the Israeli PM, the military commander in the West Bank, or the heads of the Division of Settlement in the Jewish Agency. See Yaël Ronen, *Taking the Settlements to the ICC? Substantive Issues'* 111 AM J. INT. L.57, 60 (2017); Kearney, above n 172 at 25.

[175] See ICC PreTrial Chamber II, 'Decision pursuant to Article 15 of the Rome Statute on the authorization of an investigation into the situation in the Republic of Kenya', Situation in the Republic of Kenya, No.ICC-01/09–19 (31 March 2010), ¶¶ 53,70. [hereinafter *ICC Kenya Decision*].

bypass consideration of the adequacy of Israel's justice system (the second limb of the complementarity analysis).

Nevertheless, it bears noting that Israeli jurisprudence[176] has investigated certain aspects of settlement activity that falls within the scope of the ICC examination. Specifically, the HCJ has addressed the legality of appropriation of land and construction of settlements,[177] the demolition of Palestinian property and eviction of Palestinian residents from homes,[178] the regularisation of construction,[179] and the planning and authorisation of settlement expansion.[180] Most recently, on 9 June 2020, the HCJ nullified a law that would legalize the status of Israeli–Jewish settlements partially built on privately owned Palestinian land in the West Bank.[181] The OTP has reportedly considered a number of HCJ decisions relating to the legality of specific governmental actions connected to the settlements.[182] For so long as the Israeli court has made genuine factual and legal determinations with respect to such conduct, the number of potential settlements cases admissible before the ICC could be reduced.[183]

On the other hand, the value of Israeli case law might be diminished by the HCJ's refusal to rule on the overall legality of the settlement policy.[184] Arguably, the issue's non-justiciability and lack of prosecutions amount to 'shielding' suspects from

---

[176] Steven Kaye and Joshua Kern, 'Complementarity and a Potential Settlements Case: A Response to the OTP's Report on its Preliminary Examination of the Situation in Palestine' OPINIO JURIS 14 March 2019 http://opiniojuris.org/2019/03/14/complementarity-and-a-potential-settlements-case-a-response-to-the-otps-report-on-its-preliminary-examination-of-the-situation-in-palestine/ (noting that where there is a dispute which engages individual petitioners' rights under IHL, human rights, and national administrative law, affected communities have a right of civil and public law redress in Israel concerning settlements).

[177] HCJ 606/78 and HCJ 610/78, Saliman Tawfiq Ayyub v Minister of Defence & ors [1979].

[178] HCJ 5667/11 *Deirat Rafaya Village Council v The Minister of Defense.*

[179] See also HCJ 7957/04, *Zaharan Yunis Muhammad Mara'abe & ors v The Prime Minister of Israel & ors.* ¶31; HCJ 2056/04, *Beit Sourik Village Council v The Government of Israel & or.* ('Beit Sourik'), ¶23.

[180] HCJ 390/79, *Izzat Muhammed Mustafa Dweikat* et al. *v The State of Israel & ors.* In this case, the petition addressed the legality of establishing a civilian settlement on the outskirts of Nablus on land privately owned by Arab residents.

[181] The Law for the Regularization of Settlement in Judea and Samaria was approved in February 2017 but has now been rendered unconstitutional. HCJ 1308/17, *Silwad Municipality, et al. v. The Knesset, et. al* [2020].

[182] OTP Report on Preliminary Examination Activities 2018, above n 44 at ¶277; OTP Report on Preliminary Examination Activities 2019, above n 149, at ¶ 220.

[183] Kaye and Kern, above n 176 at ¶ 6.

[184] For example see HCJ 4481/91 Bargil v. GoI; See e.g. DAVID KRETZMER, THE OCCUPATION OF JUSTICE: THE SUPREME COURT OF ISRAEL AND THE OCCUPIED TERRITORIES 83 (2002) (arguing that the HCJ has done its utmost to avoid ruling on the general legality of establishing settlements and that the HCJ's approach is overly formalistic. Sharon Weill, *Arguing International Humanitarian Law Standards in National Courts – A Spectrum of Expectations* in THE GREY ZONE – CIVILIAN PROTECTION BETWEEN HUMAN RIGHTS AND THE LAWS OF WAR (Mark Lattimer and Phillipe Sands QC (eds.), (2018), 232 (argues that the HCJ serves as an apologist for the executive which acts to grant legitimacy to the government and its policies).

criminal responsibility.[185] Nevertheless, the HCJ has acted in good faith in determining that individual claimants have suffered violations of their rights under Israeli law, which encompass rights under customary IHL and international human rights law in various cases.[186] Given this judicial activity, the OTP might need to further evaluate the lack of will and/or capacity of Israeli authorities to genuinely investigate the question of settlements.[187]

'Gravity'

ICC jurisdiction and admissibility also entail an evaluation of the criterion of 'gravity'. The Rome Statute limits the Court's jurisdiction to 'the most serious crimes of concern to the international community as a whole'.[188] The OTP must consider whether the alleged crimes are sufficiently grave 'considering their scale, nature, manner of commission, and their impact on victims and affected communities'.[189] According to the PTC, the basic inquiry involves both quantitative and qualitative factors, as well as whether those accused bear the greatest responsibility for the commission of the alleged crimes.[190]

Gaza and March of Return

On the one hand, indiscriminate targeting of civilians arising out of the hostilities in Gaza could satisfy the gravity definition. This seems to be supported by the findings of the UNHCR Commission's Report on Operation Protective Edge in Gaza

---

[185] See Sharon Weill, *The Situation in Palestine in Wonderland: An Investigation into the ICC's Impact in Israel* in QUALITY CONTROL IN PRELIMINARY EXAMINATION: VOLUME 1. (M Bergsmo and C. Stahn. eds.), (2018) 498–499; See also Yael Stein, *Fake Justice: The Responsibility Israel's High Court Justices Bear for the Demolition of Palestinian Homes and the Dispossession of Palestinians*, (B'tselem Publication,(February 2019) 47.

[186] Kaye and Kern, above n 176

[187] According to Kaye and Kern, the OTP should pay a qualified deference to Israeli HCJ decisions when conducting complementarity analysis with respect to a potential settlements case. They argue that this position is consistent with a textual interpretation of the Rome Statute, the Court's jurisprudence to date, and sound policy reasons too. See Ibid.

[188] Rome Statute, above n 32 arts 5, 53, 17(1) (d). Article 53 makes gravity of the crime a requirement before the OTP initiates an investigation/prosecution. Article 17(1)(d) clarifies that the ICC shall rule a case inadmissible if it is not 'of sufficient gravity to justify further action by the Court'.

[189] OTP Report on Preliminary Examination Activities 2018, above n 44 at ¶278.

[190] ICC Kenya Decision, above n, 153, at ¶¶ 59–60; Pre-Trial Chamber III, 'Situation in the Republic of Côte d'Ivoire, Corrigendum to 'Decision Pursuant to Article 15 of the Rome Statute on the Authorisation of an Investigation into the Situation in the Republic of Côte d'Ivoire' ICC-02/11–14-Corr (3 October 2011) ¶ 204.

(2014)[191] and the civilian fatality rate.[192] On the other hand, demonstrating high-level systematic planning is no easy task for the OTP at an evidentiary level.[193] Moreover, the scale of atrocities must be quite extensive before the ICC Prosecutor can proceed.[194] Given that many ICC cases involve large-scale systematic killings as well as mass displacement, it is unclear whether rocket attacks on Israel and/or aerial bombardment of Palestinians are sufficiently grave to warrant prosecutions.[195] For example, in granting the OTP requests to open investigations into Kenya and the Congo, the PTC noted the gravity and scale of the violence was in the several thousands.[196] The Prosecutor has indicated that the primary criterion is the 'number of victims', particularly the number of deaths,[197] which seem to be comparatively low in Gaza. This is also the case in respect of the Great March of Return which resulted in the killing of around 200 individuals.[198]

At the same time, the ICC has accepted sufficient gravity in situations of much smaller scale and numbers of victims[199] which could assist the OTP in Palestine. Indeed, the Mavi Marmara Incident (2010), which resulted in only 10 deaths, sustained two successful appeals against the OTP's decision to close the case because it lacked the requisite gravity.[200] Ultimately, the gravity criterion remains elusive

---

[191] See UNHRC Gaza Report 2014, above n 147, ¶ 668.

[192] Gazan civilian casualty rates estimates range between 70% by the Gaza Health Ministry, 65% by United Nations Protection Cluster by OCHA (based in part Gaza Health Ministry reports), and 36% by Israeli officials. See STATE OF ISR., THE 2014 GAZA CONFLICT, above n 145; *Statistics: Victims of the Israeli Offensive on Gaza since 08 July 2014*, PALESTINIAN CENTRE FOR HUMAN RIGHTS, (16 September 2014) Statistics: Victims of the Israeli Offensive on Gaza since 8 July 2014

[193] INT'L CRIMINAL CRT, OTP, POLICY PAPER ON CASE SELECTION AND PRIORITISATION ¶ 40 (15 September 2016).

[194] See GIDEON BOAS ET AL., INTERNATIONAL CRIMINAL PROCEDURE 85 (2011)

[195] Daniel Benoliel and Ronen Perry, *Israel, Palestine and the ICC* (32(1) MICH. J. INT. 73, 120 (2010) ('Gravity assessment, as it seems, begs a proper comparative assessment of events during any conflict, and the Israel-Gaza conflict in particular, both internationally and among the parties involved in the particular cycle of violence').

[196] In Kenya, the Prosecutor contended that over 1000 people were killed, there were over 900 acts of documented rape and sexual violence, approximately 350,000 people were displaced, and over 3500 were seriously injured. In Congo, the OTP noted reports of thousands of deaths by mass murder and summary execution in the DRC since 2002.

[197] Luis Moreno-Ocampo, *Integrating the Work of the ICC into Local Justice Initiatives* 21 AM. U. INT'L L. REV. 497, 498 (2006).

[198] OTP Jurisdiction Request 2019, above n 47 at ¶ 96.

[199] In the situation of Georgia, ten killings, 50–55 physical injuries, and potentially hundreds of outrages upon personal dignity were seen as a 'compelling indicator of sufficient, and not of insufficient gravity'. Pre-trial Chamber I, ICC-01/15, Decision on the Prosecutor's request for authorization of an investigation, ¶ 26 (27 January 2016).

[200] On 2 December 2019, after examining the case for a third time, the Prosecutor reaffirmed her previous conclusions that there was no basis for prosecution because it lacked the requisite 'gravity'. Mavi Marmara Appeal 2019, above n 130 ¶ 4.

law until the Rome Statute came into force in 2015.[207] Theoretically, if the crime had crystallised into custom,[208] the PA could submit another Article 12(3) declaration in order to extend the Court's temporal jurisdiction to 1 July 2002, the date of entry into force of the Rome Statute.[209] This would nonetheless still exclude ICC jurisdiction over the vast majority of Israeli settlement activities, which commenced shortly after the Six-Day War in 1967.[210]

Notably, scholars query whether population transfers constitute a 'continuous crime' and might thereby help to widen the ICC's temporal scope over the settlements.[211] A continuous crime involves ongoing conduct committed and maintained over time.[212] Arguably, the regular and repeated transfer of Israeli civilians into Palestinian territories meets this definition.[213] In a decision on Côte d'Ivoire, the PTC noted that the Court could generally investigate and exercise jurisdiction over conduct outside its authorised mandate for ongoing and continuous crimes.[214] On the other hand, ICC case law is scarce on such questions.[215] Continuous crimes were discussed during negotiations, but the Rome Statute is ultimately silent on this issue.[216]

---

[207] Since the domestic criminal law of either Israel or Palestine has never contained a criminal provision against population transfer, settlement activities on Palestinian territory would not have been a criminal offence until accession to the Rome Statute. Ronen, above n 174 at 59; Jöbstl, above n 134 at 349.

[208] The customary status of Article 8(2)(b)(viii), the date it crystallised into a norm and whether it could even bind Israel on that basis, all remain legally uncertain and disputed. See Andreas Zimmermann, *Israel and the International Criminal Court – An Outsider's Perspective* 34 ISR. YB. HUM. RTS 231, 241–42 (2006); Jöbstl, above n 134 at 349; Ronen, above n 174 at 58–9.

[209] In the case of crimes allegedly committed by nationals of a non-state party the Court must consider whether the crime in question was customary at the relevant time. Bruce Broomhall, *Article 22* in THE ROME STATUTE OF THE INTERNATIONAL CRIMINAL COURT (Otto Triffterer and Kai Ambos, eds) 956 (2016).

[210] Jöbstl, above n 134 at 349.

[211] This might allow the ICC to consider pre-2015, or even pre-2002 related conduct. See e.g. Kearney, above n 172 at 1.

[212] Article 14(2) of the ILC Articles on the Responsibility of States for Internationally Wrongful Acts. See Alan Nissel, *Continuing Crimes in the Rome Statute* 25 MICH. J. INT. L. 653, 661(2004).

[213] The OTP's preliminary examination reports seems to support the OTP focusing on direct transfers as they refer extensively to the construction of new housing units and mention subsidies and other incentives only in passing. ICC OTP, Preliminary Examinations Report 2017 ¶¶ 59–61. Jöbstl, above n 134 at 350–1; Kearney, above n 172 at 31.

[214] ICC, Decision pursuant to Article 15 of the Rome Statute on the Authorisation of an Investigation into the Situation in the Republic of Côte d'Ivoire, ICC-02/11–14, Pre-Trial Chamber, 15 November 2011, ¶¶ 179–180. Jöbstl, above n 134 at 361–2.

[215] Jöbstl, above n 134 at 361–2.

[216] The only exception is a footnote to the crime of enforced disappearance, which is generally perceived as a continuous crime. 'Elements of Crimes', Official Records of the Assembly of States Parties to the Rome Statute of the International Criminal Court ICC-ASP/1/3/Add.1 (Vol II) 135 (3–10 September 2002). See Carsten Stahn, Mohammed M El Zeidy and Héctor Olásolo, *The International Criminal Court's* Ad Hoc *Jurisdiction Revisited* 99 AM. J. INT. L. 421, 429 (2005); Jöbstl, above n 134 at 360. Commentary to the Rome Statute explains that '[t]he Rome Statute is

Moreover, the basis for concluding that settlement activity is a continuous crime is uncertain.[217] It remains unclear which aspects of the activity would be regarded as the consequence of earlier conduct or as new conduct.[218] For example, the construction of Israeli settlements may have long-term consequences, but its continuing effects do not necessarily render the act a continuous one.[219] Thus, in *Nahimana*, the ICTR Appeals Chamber concluded that it had no jurisdiction over incitement to genocide that occurred in 1993, even though such acts had continued until the time period that fell within the tribunal's temporal jurisdiction.[220]

Ultimately, it is no simple task for the OTP to demonstrate that Israeli settlement activity since 2014 is sufficiently grave to warrant prosecution.[221] According to OTP guidelines, the 'scale' component of gravity has a temporal component: '[L]ow intensity' crimes over a long period apparently are less grave than brief, intense eruptions'.[222] In this regard, it is questionable as to whether a political campaign of

---

silent in regard to violations which are committed prior to the entry into force of the Statute and continued afterwards…references in future cases to acts pre-dating the entry into force of the Statute may be useful in establishing the historical context but they may not be (sic) form the basis of a charge'. See Case Matrix Network, *ICC Commentary* art. 11, http://www.casematrixnetwork.org/cmn-knowledge-hub/icccommentary-clicc/commentary-rome-statute/commentary-rome-statute-part-2-articles-11-21/#c1976

[217] Kamari Maxine Clarke, *Refiguring the Perpetrator: Culpability, History and International Criminal Law's Impunity Gap'* 19 INT. J. HUM. RTS. 5 (2015) 592–614, 596–597 (noting that continuing violations such as colonialism or apartheid challenge strict notions of legal time and thereby present unstable questions of perpetratorhood and create multivalent legal dilemmas such as questions of jurisdiction, admissibility, and evidence).

[218] Zimmermann argues that the term 'transfer' describes a physical displacement, which is completed once a settler has migrated to occupied territory, irrespective of whether he or she remains there. Andreas Zimmermann, *Palestine and the International Criminal Court Quo Vadis? Reach and Limits of Declarations under Article 12(3)* 11 J. INT. CRIM. L. 324 (2013); See also WILLIAM SCHABAS, THE INTERNATIONAL CRIMINAL COURT: A COMMENTARY ON THE ROME STATUTE 342 (2016); Kearney, above n 172 at 31; Ronen, above n 174 at 59–60; Jöbstl, above n 134 at 360.

[219] 'As a matter of fact, once settlers have already been settled in an occupied territory, their transfer has been completed even if they then continue to be induced [by state incentives] to stay in such territory.' Zimmermann, above n 218, 324.

[220] The ICTR held that the relevant radio broadcasts could not constitute one continuing incitement to commit genocide because the crime is completed once the material in question is published. ICTR, *Prosecutor v Nahimana and Others,* Judgment, ICTR-99-52-A, Appeals Chamber, 28 November 2007, ¶¶ 723–725 cited in Ibid. c.f. Kearney, above n 172 at 28 ('International criminal law on the scope and nature of continuing crimes does not support such a restrictive opinion' citing dissenting Judgements from the ICTR Appeal Chamber in *Nahimana* et al. *v The Prosecutor,* ICTR-99-52-A, 28 November 2007. Partly Dissenting Opinion of Judge Shahabuddeen ¶ 23 and Partly Dissenting Opinion Of Judge Fausto Pocar ¶ 2).

[221] In recent years, somewhere between 3000 and 5000 Israeli Jews have migrated into the West Bank annually, the vast majority of population growth is from births, which are much harder to fit into the 'deport or transfer' category of crime.

[222] See ICC, Office of the Prosecutor, 'Policy Paper on Preliminary Examinations', (November 2013) ¶ 62.

facilitating civilian migration[223] albeit in breach of IHL should meet the admissibility threshold at the ICC.

'Interests of Justice'

The final criterion allows the Prosecutor to decline a case when it would not be in 'the interests of justice' to proceed. This element is understood by reference to gravity and the interests of victims.[224] According to OTP policy, a presumption in favour of investigation or prosecution applies.[225] No clear guidance exists however, concerning the content of the term 'interests of justice', nor in what exceptional circumstances the OTP could close a case on this basis.[226] For good reason, OTP policy is reluctant to take into account countervailing security concerns, or the possibility that an ICC investigation and/or prosecution could escalate conflict.[227] However, it is worth noting that the Rome Statute does not dictate this rather narrow interpretation of the 'interests of justice'.[228] Since Article 53(1)(c) foresees the possibility that pursuing a case may not be 'in the interests of justice', it follows that the concept of justice must be broader than criminal justice.[229] Yet ICC practice reveals wide discretionary usage of criteria, specifically regarding the role and definition of the 'interests of justice'.[230]

[223] Notably, an OTP Report used the term 'migration' to describe the conduct criminalised in Article 8(2)(b)(viii) rather than apply the Statute's terminology of 'transfer' See ICC, Office of the Prosecutor, Report on Preliminary Examination Activities (2015) ¶ 68.

[224] Rome Statute, above n 32, at art. 53(1)(c).

[225] International Criminal Court, Office of the Prosecutor, Policy Paper on the Interests of Justice (September 2007), 1–3. [hereinafter *OTP Policy Paper on the Interests of Justice*).

[226] Ibid.

[227] See *OTP Policy Paper on the Interests of Justice,* above n 225 at 9 (The Paper seems to acknowledge the relevance of countervailing security concerns within the context of peace processes, but reaffirms that the 'broader matter of international peace and security is not the responsibility of the Prosecutor; it falls within the mandate of other institutions').

[228] Robert P. Barnidge Jr. *Palestinian Engagement with the International Criminal Court: From Preliminary Examination to Investigation?,* 7(2) J. MID. E. & AFR. 109–123 (2016); See also Drazan Đukic, *Transitional Justice and the International Criminal Court—in 'The Interests of Justice'?,* 89 (867) INT. REV. RED CROSS 695–700 (2007).

[229] Notably, OTP policy '...fully endorses the complementary role that can be played by domestic prosecutions, truth seeking, reparations programs, institutional reform and traditional justice mechanisms in the pursuit of a broader justice'. See *OTP Policy Paper on the Interests of Justice'*, above n 225 at 8.

[230] Roy S. Lee, *The Rome Conference and Its Contributions to International Law*, in THE ICC: THE MAKING OF THE ROME STATUTE: ISSUES, NEGOTIATIONS AND RESULTS (Roy S. Lee, ed.) 35 (1999) (noting that the ICC drafters' contemplation of the peace-justice tension refers to a 'delicate balance between the search for international justice...and the need for the maintenance of international peace and security'). See also Benoliel and Perry, above n 195, at 120.

Recent ICC case law has only added to this ambiguity. On 12 April 2019, the PTC rejected the Prosecutor's request to open an investigation into Afghanistan based on Article 53(1)(c).[231] The Chamber decided that an official investigation would not be 'in the interests of justice' due to the amount of time that had passed since the preliminary examination,[232] the scarce cooperation obtained by the Prosecutor,[233] political changes in Afghanistan and important states,[234] the interests of victims,[235] and the Court's limited resources.[236] The PTC's primary concern was that any official investigation into Afghanistan would be ultimately unsuccessful and inconclusive.[237] Despite drawing much criticism,[238] Israeli officials embraced this decision and connected the dots to Israel/Palestine.[239]Akin to Afghanistan, several years have lapsed since the ICC preliminary examination commenced in Palestine. Arguably, the political situation in the Middle-East has also deteriorated, and the Court's limited resources would similarly frustrate investigative and prosecutorial efforts. Difficulties in securing even minimal cooperation from the relevant authorities in Israel and Gaza are not trivial. In this light, the PTC application of Article 53(1)(c) could hinder the OTP in Palestine.

Nevertheless, on 5 March 2020, the Appeals Chamber reversed the PTC ruling and authorised the Afghanistan investigation. Specifically, the Appeals Chamber decided that the PTC erred in considering the 'interests of justice' at all.[240] It seems the PTC erroneously reached its decision given the reasonable basis to conclude that the 'most serious crimes' had occurred and that any case concerning those crimes

---

[231] ICC, Decision Pursuant to Article 15 of the Rome Statute on the Authorisation of an Investigation into the Situation in the Islamic Republic of Afghanistan ICC-02/17–33 12 April 2019 | Pre-Trial Chamber II | Decision.

[232] Ibid. at ¶¶ 91–92.

[233] Ibid.

[234] Ibid. at ¶94.

[235] Ibid. ('…[I]t is unlikely that pursuing an investigation would result in meeting the objectives listed by the victims favoring the investigation, or otherwise positively contributing to it').

[236] Ibid. at ¶95.

[237] Ibid. at ¶¶ 91–96.

[238] See Gabor Rona, 'More on What's Wrong with the ICC's Decision on Afghanistan' (*Opiniojuris* online, 15 April 2019 http://opiniojuris.org/2019/04/15/more-on-whats-wrong-with-the-iccs-decision-on-afghanistan/; Alex Whiting, 'The ICC's Afghanistan Decision: Bending to U.S. or Focusing Court on Successful Investigations?' (*Just Security* online, April 12, 2019) https://www.justsecurity.org/63613/the-iccs-afghanistan-decision-bending-to-u-s-or-focusing-court-on-successful-investigations/

[239] '[W]hat we have here is a correction of injustice, and it is an act that has far-reaching influence with regard to the conduct of the international system in relation to the State of Israel…' Netanyahu Congratulates Trump on ICC Decision Not to Investigate U.S. Forces (*HAARETZ* online, 14 April 2019),https://www.haaretz.com/israel-news/.premium-netanyahu-congratulates-trump-on-iccdecision-not-to-investigate-u-s-forces-1.7119243

[240] 'The PTC erred in giving any consideration to the factors identified under Article 53(1)(a)-(c), including the interests of justice'. ICC, Judgment on the Appeal against the decision on the authorisation of an investigation into the situation in the Islamic Republic of Afghanistan, ICC-02/17 OA4 (5 March 2020) at ¶ 99 [hereinafter Appeals Decision in Afghanistan 2020].

would have been admissible.[241] Whilst the Judges did not address Article 53(1)(c) substantively, they concluded that 'the PTC did not properly assess the interests of justice', noting that it did not consider 'the gravity of the crimes and the interests of victims as articulated by the victims themselves'.[242] In sum, the Judges described the PTC decision as 'cursory, speculative and…not refer[ing] to information capable of supporting it'.[243]

The implications for Palestine are uncertain. On the one hand, this decision lends support to the Prosecutor commencing an investigation based on her own assessment of Article 53(1)(c). Indeed, given the 2018 State Referral in Palestine, the OTP has already asserted the ability to open a case without needing the Court's consent.[244] On this view, the Prosecutor's 'interests of justice' analysis is not open to judicial review like it was in the *proprio motu*[245] situation of Afghanistan.[246] In her 2019 OTP Request, the Prosecutor concluded that 'there are no substantial reasons to believe that an investigation would not serve the interests of justice' in Palestine.[247] The Prosecutor has not provided her substantive assessment and has yet to be requested to do so.[248] The Appeals Chamber in Afghanistan highlighted that Article 53(1)(c) is formulated in the negative.[249] Accordingly, the OTP is not required to affirmatively determine that an investigation would serve the 'interests of justice' in Palestine. At any rate, opening a case might help to address the gravity of allegations against Israelis and Palestinians, to reject violence and to offer human rights protection to victims.[250]

[241] Ibid.

[242] Ibid. at ¶ 49.

[243] Ibid.

[244] OTP Jurisdiction Request 2019, above n 47 at ¶ 4.

[245] Under Article 15(3) of the Rome Statute, a *proprio motu* situation mandates judicial review of an OTP decision to begin an investigation. This would include the OTP's assessment of the interests of justice.

[246] Some pro-Israel advocates reject the validity of Palestine's 2018 State referral for the period pre-dating Palestine's accession to the Rome Statute on 1 April 2015. On this view, the OTP would require an Article 15(4) authorisation for this period making its 'interests of justice' assessment reviewable. ICC, Corrigendum to 'International Jewish Lawyers observations on the "Prosecution request pursuant to article 19(3) for a ruling on the Court's territorial jurisdiction in Palestine" (ICC-01/18–12)', ICC-01/18–98-Corr, (17 March 2020) ¶¶ 71–74; ICC, Corrigendum to 'Submissions Pursuant to Rule 103 (The Israel Forever Foundation)' ICC-01/18–108-Corr (20 March 2020) ¶¶ 71–74.

[247] OTP Jurisdiction Request 2019, above n 47, at ¶¶ 2, 97.

[248] In December 2019, the OTP wrote that 'Although she does not consider it necessary for the Chamber's determination, the Prosecutor is ready to provide her assessment of the criteria under article 53(1) to the Chamber'. Ibid. ¶ 97 *(*footnote 341).

[249] Appeals Decision in Afghanistan, above n 240, ¶49.

[250] See Chantal Meloni, *On Palestinian, International law and the ICC,* Justice in Conflict (31 March 2015) https://justiceinconflict.org/2015/03/31/on-palestine-international-law-and-the-international-criminal-court/

On the other hand, the ICC Judges are yet to conclusively resolve the law. The Appeals Chamber in Afghanistan failed to address the PTC's substantive findings nor its application in such complex cases.[251] Arguably, for the 'interests of justice' to be effectively achieved, this criterion needs to be positively defined or risk becoming arbitrary.[252] What exactly constitutes 'substantial reasons' that would be contrary to the 'interests of justice'? The legal parameters are unclear, and so the viability of any prosecution in Palestine as well as state cooperation remain relevant to an assessment of whether or not to continue with an investigation.[253] Every sign indicates that neither Israel nor Hamas would agree to provide witnesses, evidence or transfer defendants to the Hague. The OTP cannot ignore the possibility that a fruitless investigation would not materially advance the interests of justice either locally or internationally.

It seems clear that Article 53(1)(c) involves assessing both the situation at hand and the Court's broader mandate.[254] The Prosecutor has herself acknowledged that the interests of justice must be interpreted in accordance with the object and the purposes of the Rome Statute.[255] No doubt, ploughing ahead with Palestine would divert precious resources from other important OTP activities and exigent situations. It might seem defeatist to yield to political variables or reward obstruction. Yet, a Prosecutor who ignores such realities in Palestine does so at her peril. An over-zealous OTP would exacerbate tensions on the ground, interfere with non-legal considerations, and ultimately undermine the 'interests of justice' overall.[256]

---

[251] 'Although it rebuked the PTC for abusing its discretion in its interests-of-justice analysis, this was a critique of the PTC's process, not its arguments'. David Luban, *The Interests of Justice at the ICC, A Continuing Mystery,* JUST SECURITY (17 March 2020) https://www.justsecurity.org/69188/the-interests-of-justice-at-the-icc-a-continuing-mystery/

[252] Solon Solomon, *Broadening International Criminal Jurisdiction?: The Rome Statute 'Interests of Justice' Clause as a Prosecutorial Platform,* 4(1) INT'L HUM. RTS. L. REV. 68–70 (2015).

[253] Article 53 (1) of the Rome Statute give the Prosecutor the right to decline to initiate an investigation or suspend a prosecution. In these cases, the interests of justice act as a basis for the Prosecutor to refrain from any action.

[254] According to Luban, what we see here is a clash between two competing and credible views of 'the interests of justice', one focused on individual situations and one on the overall mission of the Court, above n 251.

[255] See *OTP Policy Paper on the Interests of Justice,* above n 225 at 9.

[256] According to Israel's MFA, the Palestinian decision to initiate proceedings at the ICC, is 'a political, hypocritical and cynical maneuver. [It] contradicts the core purposes for which the Court was founded and will bring about the destructive politicization of the Court as well as undermine its standing'. ISR. MIN. FOREIGN AFFAIRS, http://mfa.gov.il/MFA/PressRoom/2015/Pages/Palestinian-Authority-joins-the-ICC-Israel-response-1-Apr-2015.aspx

Conclusion

Ultimately, the obstacles to ICC jurisdiction over Israel's alleged crimes in Gaza, the Great March of Return, and the Israeli–Jewish settlements are significant. So too are the cooperation and other non-substantive barriers an ICC intervention would face. How the incoming ICC Prosecutor, British lawyer Karim Khan proceeds with this investigation remains to be seen. In certain cases, grave criminal allegations are simply not enough to ensure prosecutorial success given the legal, technical, and practical constraints.[257] Suffice it to say, a fruitful investigation into the complex situation of Palestine is far from assured. It might therefore be worth conceding that the ICC has a less 'messianic' role to play than commonly assumed in the Israeli–Palestinian conflict.

5.5 Part Four: Normative Objections to ICJ and Prosecution Preference

Many welcome the potential contribution of international prosecutions to the Israeli–Palestinian conflict based on its normative goals. Conceivably, invoking ICC jurisdiction could end '...Israeli impunity...promote peace in the Middle East, and help uphold the integrity of international law'.[258] Others claim the ICC '...would allow for an expert determination of the merits of the claims of atrocities...'.[259] Nevertheless, the potential benefits of the ICC addressing aspects of the Israeli–Palestinian conflict are not clear-cut and should be re-evaluated within a broader framework of transitional justice as a 'holistic' strategy and against the fundamental goals of ICJ. This section casts doubt over the normative priority given to the ICC in the Middle East. Notably, ICC debates in Palestine dominate international legal scholarship around the conflict, with little scholarly attention devoted to transitional justice or other non-retributive justice measures for the region.

---

[257] As the Court's Prosecutor has acknowledged in a qualified statement, this is the case with ISIS. See Statement of the Prosecutor of the International Criminal Court, Fatou Bensouda, on the alleged crimes committed by ISIS, April 8, 2015 available at: https://www.icc-cpi.int/Pages/item.aspx?name=otp-stat-08-04-2015-1

[258] Bisharat, above n 39.

[259] Julian Ensbey, *Israel, Palestine and the ICC,* THE COMMENT FACTORY (January 192,009); Lauri King-Irani, *To Reconcile or be Reconciled?: Agency, Accountability and Law in Middle-Eastern Conflicts* 28 HASTINGS. INTL. & COMP.L. REV. 369, 386 (2004–2005).

Retribution and Victims' Rights

At its core, criminal prosecutions centre on retribution or 'just deserts' theory. The idea is that crimes of mass atrocity '...deserve punishment as a matter of morality and fundamental considerations of justice'.[260] Indeed, victims of serious war crimes may tend to favour prosecutions.[261] When reflecting on their needs, trials can play a vital role in restoring dignity and paving the way for personal healing.[262] In recent years, the rights and interests of victims have broadened the discourse and authority of ICJ.[263] Indeed, inclusion of victim participation and reparation rights at the ICC has advanced the role of victims in international trials.[264] To this end, the ICC issued a decision in July 2018 to establish 'a system of public information and outreach activities among the affected communities and particularly the victims of the situation in Palestine'.[265] Retributive justice thus holds great intuitive appeal for victims in the Middle-East.

Nevertheless, it is arguable that prosecutions predicated on retributive justice are too focused on punishing perpetrators.[266] In the wake of mass atrocity, some reject

---

[260] This is the 'just-deserts theory' cited in Miriam Aukerman, *Extraordinary Evil, Ordinary Crime: A Framework for Understanding Transitional Justice*, 15 HARV. HUM. RTS. J. 39, 56 (2002). By contrast, Cassese argues that the purpose of international trials '...is not so much retribution as stigmatisation of the deviant behavior'. Antonio Cassese, *On the Current Trends towards Criminal Prosecution and Punishment of Breaches of International Humanitarian Law*, 9 EUROPEAN JOURNAL OF INTERNATIONAL LAW 4 (1998).

[261] See Stephan Parmentier, Marta Valias, and Elmar Weitekamp, *How to Repair the Harm after Violent Conflict in Bosnia? Results of a Population-Based Survey,* 27 NETH. Q. HUM. RTS. 27–44 (2009). Almost all of the Bosnian respondents (94%) to their survey agreed or strongly agreed that perpetrators should be prosecuted.

[262] Nigel Biggar, *Making Peace and Doing Justice. Must We Choose?* in BURYING THE PAST, MAKING PEACE AND DOING JUSTICE AFTER CIVIL CONFLICT 10 (Nigel Biggar ed., 2001). There is also evidence that victims experience a sense of relief following the arrest, conviction and punishment of the perpetrator(s). By contrast, in cases where the guilty are not brought to justice, victims may experience 'pronounced feelings of indignation...with mistrust in the legal system...'. See Daniel Shuman and Alexander McCall Smith, JUSTICE AND THE PROSECUTION OF OLD CRIMES: BALANCING LEGAL, PSYCHOLOGICAL AND MORAL CONCERNS (2000); Brandon Hamber, TRANSFORMING SOCIETIES AFTER POLITICAL VIOLENCE: TRUTH, RECONCILIATION, AND MENTAL HEALTH (2009) 123–124.

[263] The expanding power and reach of human rights advocacy have played a pivotal role. See Luke Moffett, *The Role of Victims in the International Criminal Tribunals of the Second World War*, 12 INTERNATIONAL CRIMINAL LAW REVIEW 245–270 (2012); Godfrey M. Musila, RETHINKING INTERNATIONAL CRIMINAL LAW: RESTORATIVE JUSTICE AND THE RIGHTS OF VICTIMS IN THE INTERNATIONAL CRIMINAL COURT (2010); Tenove and Dixon, above n 14 at 409.

[264] Article 68(3) of the Rome Statute establishes a general right of victims to present their 'views and concerns' at different stages of Court proceedings.

[265] OTP Report on Preliminary Examination Activities 2018, above n 44 at ¶¶ 269–271.

[266] Jens Iverson, *Transitional Justice, Jus Post Bellum, and International Criminal Law: Differentiating the Usages, History and Dynamics* 7 INT.L J. TRANSIT. JUSTICE 413, 431(2013).

retributivism in favour of broader transitional goals.[267] For example, it has been argued that prosecutions may undermine a nation's peacebuilding or reconciliation efforts.[268] Arguably, '[i]f punishment is a prerequisite, reconciliation between the perpetrators and their victims is impossible'.[269] Regarding South Africa, Mbeki writes: '....Had there been a threat of Nuremberg-style trials over members of the apartheid security establishment, we would never have undergone the peaceful change'.[270] Thus, the principal case against retribution is rooted in consequentialism and a deep discomfort with the notion of vengeance.

Moreover, prosecutions apply an exceedingly narrow notion of justice. A nation's experience of 'justice' may be highly divisive and subjective,[271] as highlighted by the mixed reactions to indictments at the ICTY in the Former Yugoslavia. Whilst members of one ethnic group protested, members of the other celebrated.[272] The nature of prosecutions does not necessarily allow those proceedings to establish a broad consensus that 'justice' has been done.[273] In the Israeli–Palestinian context, where military occupation, collective memory, and structural violence form part of the conflict, social, economic, and political justice may be just as important as legal justice in the criminal sense.[274]

---

[267] Retributivism, as Nino contends: 'presupposes that it is sometimes appropriate to redress one evil with another evil...however, [in] my moral arithmetic...we have "two evils" rather than one good'. Carlos Santiago Nino, *Radical Evil on Trial and a Consensual Theory of Punishment* in PUNISHMENT: A PHILOSOPHY PUBLIC AFFAIRS READER 95 (John Simmons et al. eds, 1995); Malamud Goti, *Transitional Governments in the Breach: Why Punish State Criminals?* 12(1) HUM. RTS. Q. 1–16 (1990).

[268] On a theoretical level, retributive measures might not only not be conducive to nation-building, but it may in fact the nation's healing process. See Mathew. A Weiner, *Defeating Hatred With Truth: An Argument in Support of a Truth Commission as part of the solution to Israel/Palestine*, 38 CONN. L. REV. 123, 127 (2005–2006).

[269] Aukerman, above n 260 at 82.

[270] Thabo Mbecki, AFRICA: THE TIME HAS COME: SELECTED SPEECHES 29 (1998).

[271] Delivering justice usually means different things to different people. See Hugo Van der Merwe, *Delivering Justice During Transition: Research Challenges* in ASSESSING THE IMPACT OF TRANSITIONAL JUSTICE: CHALLENGES FOR EMPIRICAL RESEARCH 138 (Hugo van der Merwe, Victoria Baxter and Audrey Chapman eds, 2009).

[272] There were mixed reactions by Bosnian Serbs and Bosnian Muslims to the news of the arrest, in July 2008, of the indicted war criminal Radovan Karadzic. See Janine Natalya Clark, *The State Court of Bosnia and Hercegovina: A Path to Reconciliation?* 13 CONTEMP. JUSTICE. REV. 371, 375 (2010).

[273] Weiner, above n 268 at 127.

[274] In their review of representative surveys from Bosnia and Herzegovina, Croatia, Rwanda, Uganda, and Iraq, Weinstein et al. conclude that 'we cannot assume that legal justice is desired or the highest priority in all countries after periods of repression or violence'. Harvey M. Weinstein, Laurel E. Fletcher, Patrick Vinck, and Phuong Pham, *Stay the Hand of Justice: Whose Priorities Take Priority?* in LOCALIZING TRANSITIONAL JUSTICE: INTERVENTIONS AND PRIORITIES AFTER MASS VIOLENCE (Rosalind Shaw & Lars Waldorf, with Pierre Hazan eds.) (2010) 47.

International trials also risk favouring the culpability of the accused, over the dignity of victims.[275] Indeed, criminal proceedings, with their punitive focus and narrow evidentiary paradigm, are notorious for excluding victims from telling their 'whole story'.[276] Even once a perpetrator is brought to justice, trials are not geared to generate closure or satisfaction with sentencing.[277] In this light, the ICC may not sufficiently address the needs of victims and may even risk re-traumatising them.[278] In a conflict, like the Israeli–Palestinian one, with mutual legacies of human rights abuse, no intervention should threaten to re-victimise either population. Indeed, the legal representatives of Palestinian Victims in Gaza recently expressed their concern over 'the ostensibly narrow scope of the investigation into the crimes suffered by the Palestinian victims of this situation'.[279] Even if the PA succeeds in securing an ICC investigation, there will remain major legal and moral lapses that frustrate those advocating justice on behalf of Palestinians.

Most importantly, questions of history, memory, and recognition of the past are essential to Israelis and Palestinians and yet are largely outside the legal purview of the ICC. Beyond punishment and sentencing of individual offenders, a vital requirement of each nation is acknowledgement of historic rights, acceptance of responsibility, and some form of atonement for the past.[280] In essence, the parties' demands of justice are more than just retributive, but rather involve national and historic claims, which are far better captured by a restorative view of justice.[281] For example, since 1948, Palestinians have remained wedded to the justness of their claim to return to their homes. For Israelis, accountability for terrorist acts, soldier abductions, and urban bombardment are paramount. It is difficult to imagine how putting

---

[275] Aukerman, above n 260 at 54; See also Stephan Landsman, *Those Who Remember the Past May Not Be Condemned to Repeat it,* 100 MICH. L. REV. 1564, 1571 (May 2002).

[276] Donald Shriver, *Truth Commissions and Judicial Trials: Complementary or Antagonistic Servants of Public Justice?* 16 J. L. & RELIGION 1, 8 (2001).

[277] Research of the ICTY suggests much dissatisfaction amongst victims in terms of sentencing. In a comprehensive study of the experiences of 1400 survivors of the Yugoslav conflict, Basoglu et al. found that the perceived lack of punishment for perpetrators gave rise to a sense of injustice. See Metin Basoglu et al., *Psychiatric and Cognitive Effects of War in Former Yugoslavia: Association of Lack of Redress for Trauma and Post-traumatic Stress Reactions*, 294 J. AM. MED. ASS. 580–590 (2005). See also Sanja Ivkovic, *Justice by the International Criminal Tribunal for the Former Yugoslavia,* 37 STAN. J. INT. L. 255–346 (2001).

[278] For a review of challenges the ICC has faced vis-à-vis victim participation, see Carla Ferstman, REPORT: THE PARTICIPATION OF VICTIMS IN INTERNATIONAL CRIMINAL COURT PROCEEDINGS: A REVIEW OF THE PRACTICE AND CONSIDERATION OF OPTIONS FOR THE FUTURE (2012); Christine Van den Wyngaert, *Victims before International Criminal Courts: Some Views and Concerns of an ICC Trial Judge,* 44 CASE W. RES. J. INT. L. 475–496 (2011).

[279] ICC, Submission on Behalf of Palestinian Victims Residents of the Gaza Strip with confidential Annex ICC-01/18–135 at ¶ 4 (4 June 2020).

[280] Yoav Peled and Nadim Rouhana, *Transitional Justice and the Right to Return of the Palestinian Refugees,* 5 THEORETICAL. INQ. L. 317 (2004); See Rashid Khalidi, *Attainable Justice: Elements of a Solution to the Palestinian Refugee Issue,* 33(2) INT. J. 233, 239 (1998).

[281] Ron Dudai, A Model for Dealing with the Past in the Israeli-Palestinian Context, 1 INT'L J. TRANSITIONAL JUST. 249, 249–50 (2007).

a handful of Palestinians or Israelis in the dock would be able to resolve these historic claims. No verdict at the Hague would assuage the Jewish state's desire for acknowledgment, nor the Palestinian grievances from 1948 and afterwards. In this regard, the ICC alone remains an inadequate tool for transitional justice in the region.

Deterrence

International trials are also intended to deter.[282] The goal is to prevent both potential violators[283] and victims from taking vengeance themselves.[284] Arguably formal investigation by the ICC into the situation of Palestine might create a credible deterrent against future atrocities. Indeed, since April 2015, both the Palestinians and Israelis alike have been potentially within the Court's reach. In this way, '…Palestine's ICC membership could actually enhance Israeli security, by giving the Palestinian leadership incentives to curb attacks on Israel. If this came to pass, it would be an example of the ICC working as it is supposed to, as a deterrent to international crime'.[285] There exists the hope that threats of ICC prosecutions could limit and/or even prevent ongoing abuses.

Thus, for the past 5 years, the OTP has kept a watchful eye on Israeli and Palestinian conduct, issuing annual preliminary examination reports and periodic statements. The OTP recently stressed that it 'continues to closely monitor relevant developments in the region, and to assess new allegations and information available concerning the alleged commission of Rome Statute crimes...'.[286] There is evidence that the ICC examination commands the attention of senior Israeli leadership and is taken seriously by the military authorities.[287] In short, the ICC is far from being an irrelevant actor.

Nevertheless, the effectiveness of deterrent theory is also questionable in theory and practice. For example, a review of deterrence literature conducted by legal theorists concluded that there was no basis for inferring that increased severity of

---

[282] Mahmoud. Cherif. Bassiouni, *Searching for Peace and Achieving Justice: The Need for Accountability*, 59(4) LAW & CONTEMP. PROBLEMS 18 ('The relevance of prosecution…is that through their effective application, they serve as deterrence, and thus prevent future victimization. Their relevance to justice is self-evident').

[283] Kieran McEvoy, Beyond Legalism: Towards a Thicker Understanding of Transitional Justice, 34 J.L. & SOC'Y 411 (2007) at 438.

[284] Minow, above n 18 at 49 (discussing trials in Israel, Argentina, Germany, Poland, Yugoslavia and Rwanda); See also Weiner, above n 268, at 126.

[285] Luban, *Some Legal Questions*, above n 85.

[286] OTP Report on Preliminary Examination Activities 2019, above n 149, at ¶ 229.

[287] For example, in January 2018, Israel's National Security Council warned members of the Knesset's Foreign Affairs and Defense Committee that the ICC was likely to move from the examination to the investigation phase soon with respect to alleged Israeli crimes. Alan Baker, *Palestinian Manipulation of the International Criminal Court*, JERUSALEM CTR. FOR PUB. AFF. (21 January 2018), http://jcpa.org/will-the-international-criminal-court-disregardinternational-law/

sentence had any deterrent effect and was inconclusive.[288] There is also scant evidence that international trials actually prevent genocides or gross human rights abuses.[289] In truth, no one really knows how to deter those individuals who commit acts of mass destruction in ethno-national conflicts.[290] Indeed, many of the worst atrocities in the former Yugoslavia occurred after the ICTY was established.[291]

Whilst ending impunity is crucial, it is unclear how ICC indictments of senior Israeli or Palestinian officials would serve either the broader goal of deterrence or conflict-specific deterrence. In particular, political and ideologically motivated offenses like the Israeli settlements, or Hamas rockets, have proven stubbornly resistant to the threat of international punishment in The Hague. Indeed, for the past 5 years, there has been a marked increase in hostilities between the parties and new outbreaks of violence. To be sure, the ICC's examination has put Israelis and Palestinians on notice. However, prosecutions are perhaps not the most effective means to prevent abuses in such conflicts. In this regard, long-term peacebuilding and the transformation of society might be most beneficial to deterrence.[292]

Positive Complementarity

ICC enthusiasts advocate the value of 'positive complementarity'. The OTP has stated that one of the main goals of preliminary examinations is to encourage genuine domestic accountability.[293] The claim is that the threat of ICC action will galvanise states to investigate and prosecute international crimes themselves.[294] In the situation of Palestine, one could certainly make the case that the preliminary

---

[288] Andrew Von Hirsch et al., Criminal Deterrence and Sentence Severity (1999); Kader Asmal, *The Second Annual Grotius Lecture: International Law and Practice: Dealing With the Past in the South African Experience*, 15 American University International Law Review 1211, 1221 (2000); see also Cronin-Furman Kate, *Managing Expectations: International Criminal Trials and the Prospects for Deterrence of Mass Atrocity,* 7 International Journal of Transitional Justice 434 (2013).

[289] Minow, above n 18 at 49; Aukerman, above n 260 at 66.

[290] Minow, above n 18 at 46 (discussing trials in Israel, Argentina, Germany, Poland, Yugoslavia and Rwanda).

[291] Neier notes that the genocide in Rwanda also occurred after the establishment of the ICTY, Neier argues that the tribunal's creation '[certainly... did not make the authors of grave crimes in other parts of the world worry about being called to account'. Aryeh Neier, *The Quest for Justice,* New York Review Books, 31, 32 (2001).

[292] Daly, above n 15 at 106.

[293] The Policy Paper on Preliminary Examinations uses the term 'positive complementarity' to refer to a situation where national judicial authorities and the ICC 'function together' to create an 'interdependent, mutually reinforcing international system of justice'. OTP Report on Preliminary Examination Activities 2013, above n 139, at ¶¶ 93–94, 100–01 (2013); Yahli Shereshevsky, *International Decisions*, 113(2) Am. J. Int. L. 366–67 (2019).

[294] See William W. Burke-White, *Implementing a Policy of Positive Complementarity in the Rome System of Justice,* 19 CRIM. L. F. 59, 70 (2008).

examination involves 'soft power' as a result of the Prosecutor's wide discretion and her place on the international stage.[295]

Since 2015, Israel has shown a greater willingness to cooperate with the ICC's examination in Palestine, particularly in relation to the 2014 Gaza conflict.[296] In 2016, the Israeli government opened a 'dialogue' with the OTP and helped to facilitate its visit to the region, involving outreach and education activities.[297] Notably, hours after the Prosecutor issued her statement on alleged crimes committed during the March of Return (2018–2019), the IDF leadership announced that it would launch an inquiry into the conduct of its troops in those incidents in Gaza.[298]

Nevertheless, little empirical evidence exists to show that the ICC actually triggers genuine accountability measures.[299] In fact, a recent Human Rights Watch report noted that such expectations of preliminary examinations should be

[295] See Carsten Stahn, *Damned If You Do, Damned If You Don't: Challenges and Critiques of Preliminary Examinations at the ICC,* 15 J. INT'L CRIM. JUST. 413 (2017). Accordingly, as David Bosco notes, 'the [office's] discretion is broad during this phase of the [C]ourt's work [and n]either the Rome Statute nor the Rules of Procedure and Evidence offer any significant guidance on how to conduct preliminary examinations, although they do make clear that the prosecutor may seek additional information and may take oral or written testimony during this phase'. David Bosco, *The International Criminal Court and Crime Prevention: Byproduct or Conscious Goal,* 19 MICH. ST. U. COLL. L. J. INT'L L. 163 (2011).

[296] In recent years, Israel has offered international lawyers and experts unprecedented in-person access to its own military lawyers including an in-depth discussion of its views on IHL. Sharon Weill and Valentina Azarova, *The 2014 Gaza War: reflections on jus ad bellum, jus in bello, and accountability* in THE WAR REPORT: ARMED CONFLICT IN 2014, 360, 386–387 (Annyissa Bellal ed., 2015); Yahli Shereshevsky, *Back in the Game: International Humanitarian Lawmaking by States* 37(1) BERK. J. INT'L LAW. 35–36 (2019).

[297] See Tom Miles, *Israel 'Engaging' with ICC over Gaza War Crimes Inquiry: Prosecutor,* REUTERS (3 June 2016), https://www.reuters.com/article/us-israel-palestinians-icc-idUSKCN0YP1CT; see also 2016 OTP Report on Preliminary Examination Activities, at ¶143; Statement of the Prosecutor of the International Criminal Court, Fatou Bensouda, Ahead of the Office's Visit to Israel and Palestine from 5 to 10 October 2016 (5 October 2016) (emphasizing that the purpose of the visit was to 'undertake outreach and education activities', but not to 'engage in evidence collection in relation to any alleged crimes', 'undertake site visits' or 'assess the adequacy of the respective legal systems to deal with crimes that fall within ICC jurisdiction').

[298] See *Israel to Probe Gaza Border Deaths Avoiding International Investigation,* ASHARQ ALA-WSAT (10 April 2018), https://aawsat.com/english/home/article/1232846/israel-probe-gaza-borderdeaths-avoiding-international-investigation

[299] See Paul Seils, *Making Complementarity Work: Maximizing the Limited Role of the Prosecutor* in THE INTERNATIONAL CRIMINAL COURT AND COMPLEMENTARITY: FROM THEORY TO PRACTICE 989, 1012 (Carsten Stahn and Mohamed M. El Zeidy eds, 2011) (noting that whereas publicizing a situation under preliminary examination may well have a catalytic influence, there is no proof of it having made a difference.); Geoff Dancy and Florencia Montal, *Unintended Positive Complementarity: Why International Criminal Court Investigations Increase Domestic Human Rights Prosecutions,* 111 AM J. INT'L. L. 689 (2017).

'modest'.[300] Many scholars recognise the limits of positive complementarity.[301] In practice, the OTP has not closed a single preliminary examination on the basis that domestic processes have rendered ICC action unnecessary.[302] For example, there is no indication '…that ICC activity with respect to the U.S. activities in Afghanistan has prompted U.S. authorities to take more seriously their obligations to prosecute torture and other international crimes'.[303] A disconnect exists between normative goals and reality.

This is particularly true in Israel/Palestine. In line with positive complementarity, Israel has investigated specific incidents in the aftermath of the 2014 Gaza conflict. Similar investigations were instigated following the March of Return (2018). Nevertheless, the ICC examination seems to have had no positive impact on the Israeli settlements. On the contrary, the OTP's shadow may have produced the reverse effect on Israeli policy.[304] As recently as 2017, Israel adopted the Settlement Regulation Law.[305] 'Rather than being dissuaded by the ICC, the Israeli parliament affirmed its sovereignty and authority in opposition to that pressure…'.[306]

---

[300] Human Rights Watch, 'Pressure Point: The ICC's Impact on National Justice – Lessons from Colombia, Georgia, Guinea, and the United Kingdom' (2018), https://www.hrw.org/sites/default/files/report_pdf/ij0418_web_0.pdf; Elizabeth Evenson, Balkees Jarrah, Elise Keppler, Juan Pappier, & Param-Preet Singh, *The ICC's Impact on National Justice: Can the ICC Prosecutor Catalyze Domestic Cases?,* EJIL TALK! (6 December 2018) https://www.ejiltalk.org/the-iccs-impact-on-national-justice-can-the-icc-prosecutor-catalyze-domestic-cases

[301] See, Ibid. Thomas Obel Hansen, *Complementarity (In)action in the UK?,* EJIL TALK! (7 December 2018) https://www.ejiltalk.org/complementarity-inaction-in-the-uk;Weill, *Palestine in Wonderland*, above n 185 at 493, 507–19.

[302] Thomas Obel Hansen, '*The Policy Paper on Preliminary Examinations: Ending Impunity through 'Positive Complementarity?'* https://papers.ssrn.com/sol3/papers.cfm?abstract_id=2939139; Thomas Obel Hansen, *Opportunities and Challenges Seeking Accountability for War Crimes in Palestine Under the International Criminal Court's Complementarity Regime,* 9 (2) NOTRE DAME J. INT. & COMP. L. 1, 27 (2019).

[303] Following a 10-year preliminary examination of the situation in Afghanistan, in November 2017, the Prosecutor noted that 'no national investigations or prosecutions have been conducted or are ongoing against those who appear most responsible for the crimes allegedly committed by members of the US armed forces' and the CIA. Int'l Criminal Court, Office of the Prosecutor, Public Redacted Version of 'Request for Authorisation of an Investigation Pursuant to Article 15', ICC-02/17–7-Red.20, ¶¶ 299, 312 (20 November 2017) (noting that the complementarity assessment was complicated by the fact that US authorities did not engage her Office).

[304] The OTP itself recognised that 'Despite the clear and enduring calls that Israel cease activities in the Occupied Palestinian Territory deemed contrary to international law, there is no indication that they will end. To the contrary, there are indications that they may not only continue, but that Israel may seek to annex these territories'. OTP Report on Preliminary Examination Activities 2019, above n 149, at ¶177.

[305] Law for the Regulation of Settlement in Judea and Samaria adopted in February 2017.

[306] 'The external threat of the ICC ended up strengthening the walls of separation between local law and international'. Weill, '*Palestine in Wonderland*', above n 185, at 518.

Israel's judicial response to alleged abuses committed during the March of Return protests reflects a similar trend.[307] Presumably, the ICC would have pushed the Israeli HCJ to be more interventionist in Israeli military policy.[308] However, the Israeli HCJ has been reluctant to intervene in such cases since the ICC involvement began in 2009.[309] For example, in the 2018 Yesh Din case,[310] the Israeli Court dismissed two petitions by six human rights NGOs who challenged the IDF's violent engagement with the demonstrators at the Gazan border. It is therefore questionable whether the ICC has led to more domestic accountability measures in Israel.

Individual Responsibility

ICJ is also a means of holding senior perpetrators, planners, or instigators accountable for past atrocities.[311] Arguably, by assigning blame to specific individuals, the remainder of society is freed from implicit guilt, which can aid national reconciliation.[312] Indeed, not all Palestinians are suicide bombers, and not every Israeli citizen is a Jewish settler. Thus, individualised guilt '...counteracts the misleading notion of collective guilt and does not smear the name of an entire group'.[313] Ultimately, the aim of prosecuting powerful leaders at the ICC (whether political or military) is to help strengthen the rule of law.

Nevertheless, the multi-dimensional aspect of responsibility for every event in the conflict, from 1948 to Gaza and military occupation to terrorism somewhat defies any singular allocation of culpability. To be clear, an ICC warrant is issued in

---

[307] Over the past decade, the HCJ's increased deference to the IDF also seems to result from the Court's growing self-identification as a domestic actor as opposed to an international one. Yahli Shereshevsky, *Targeting the Targeted Killings Case – International Lawmaking in Domestic Contexts*, 39 MICH J. INT'L.L. 241, 261–66 (2018).

[308] Yahli Sharshevsky, *'Back in the Game'*, above n 296.

[309] This reticence can be explained by the fact that the logic of positive complementarity does not work in the context of general policies where those responsible are the highest-ranking officers and government officials. Ibid.

[310] HCJ 3003/18 *Yesh Din – Volunteers for Human Rights v. Chief of General Staff, IDF* (24 May 2018) (Isr.) https://supreme.court.gov.il

[311] The phrase used in Article 1 of the Statute for the Special Court in Sierra Leone is that that the court has 'the power to prosecute persons who bear the greatest responsibility for serious violations of international humanitarian law and Sierra Leonean law', http://www.sc-sl.org/scsl-statute.html

[312] '[T]rials establish individual responsibility over collective assignation of guilt, i.e., they establish that not all Germans were responsible for the Holocaust, nor all Turks for the Armenian genocide... - although, of course, there may be a great number of perpetrators; justice dissipates the call for revenge'. Alvarez, above n 14 at 373–374 (1999) paraphrasing Antonio Cassese, *Reflections on International Criminal Justice,* 61 MODERN LAW REVIEW 1 (1998); See also Andrew Rigby, JUSTICE AND RECONCILIATION: AFTER THE VIOLENCE, 5 (2001).

[313] Heribert Adam and Kogila Moodley, SEEKING MANDELA: PEACEMAKING BETWEEN ISRAELIS AND PALESTINIANS 122 (2005).

the name of a particular person and does not account for the complex political factors or historical narratives that contributed to the violence.[314] In conflicts like the Israeli–Palestinian one, guilt is also embedded into the national and ideological context that gives rise to the alleged crimes (be it religious Zionism or Palestinian resistance). For example, it is worth noting that the systemic nature of the Israeli–Jewish settlement project, namely its organization and its embedment in state apparatus, renders it to some extent beyond the reach of individual criminal liability.

Moreover, human rights abuses: '...usually involve massive complicity by large numbers of perpetrators, at all levels...'.[315] Individual criminal liability does not neatly fit situations where mass segments of society are implicated in the violations.[316] Indeed, for Israelis and Palestinians, the 'webs of collaboration'[317] tend to transcend a simple victim/perpetrator binary. In pursuing a small number of elites, the ICC risks fostering a false sense of collective moral blamelessness.[318] Ultimately, it might be conceded that ICJ is simply ill-equipped to deal with the complex 'grey-zone of complicity', which is spread so diffusively throughout Israeli and Palestinian societies.[319]

Feasibility and Selectivity

There is also the question of feasibility in placing the current Israeli military and political officials on trial or prosecuting the military wing of Hamas.[320] Often 'criminal trials are impractical because, much like in the Chilean or El Salvadorian contexts, those most likely to be accused of crimes are the people most likely to hold

[314] Notably, jurisprudence regarding mass atrocity in recent years has seen trials go beyond the lens of individual fact patterns to make broader findings that uncover how an abusive system functioned. The development of ICTY jurisprudence around the notion of command responsibility is an excellent case in point. Vasuki Nesiah, *Truth* vs. *Justice? Commissions and Courts* in HUMAN RIGHTS AND CONFLICT, 384 (Jeff Helsing and Julie Mertus eds, 2006).

[315] Alvarez, above n 14 at 467.

[316] Daly, above n 15 at 105.

[317] Ron Dudai and Hillel Cohen, *Triangle of Betrayal: Collaborators and Transitional Justice in the Israeli-Palestinian Conflict,* 6(1) JOURNAL OF HUMAN RIGHTS 37 (2007).

[318] 'Under such conditions, the most that could be expected of ICJ is to relate to the perpetrator as an exception, a "bad apple" in an otherwise well-cultivated orchard'. Karen Engle, Anti-Impunity and the Turn to Criminal Law in Human Rights, 100 CORNELL L. REV. 1069, 1120 (2015); See also H. Steinert, Fin De Siecle Criminology, 1 THEORETICAL CRIMINOLOGY 111–29 (1997); See also McEvoy, above n 283 at 438.

[319] Ariel Meyerstein, *Transitional Justice and Post-conflict Israel/Palestine: Assessing the Applicability of the Truth Commission Paradigm,* 38 CASE WESTERN RESERVE JOURNAL OF INTERNATIONAL LAW 281, 313–314 (2006–2007).

[320] For example, it is likely that most of the Hamas leaders responsible for rocket attacks against Israel during the 2009 Operation Cast Lead are probably dead (e.g., Ahmed Jabari). See Kevin Jon Heller, 'The ICC in Palestine: Be Careful What You Wish For', above n 35.

power'.[321] One must therefore recognise that only a small number of even the worst perpetrators will ever be brought to justice. Moreover, those who end up on trial are ironically not the most responsible, but the most 'available'.[322] The prosecution strategy for large-scale crimes often focuses on organisers of crime, rather than those of lower rank who also bear criminal responsibility. The ICC has very limited resources and only tries defendants it can get its hands on. An Israeli or Palestinian official who does not want to be put in the dock could simply stay at home or limit his or her travel. ICJ is thus radically selective and may risk granting 'de facto amnesty' to those who dodge the prosecutorial bullet.[323] This may create an impression that justice is not being done.[324]

Arbitrary limitations on jurisdiction may also prove problematic. As discussed, the reference to 'gravity' is essential to case selection at the ICC and thus accounts for only the gravest violations of the conflict. Arguably, any likely ICC charges would be overly narrow and would not represent the range and nature of the crimes committed during the conflict.[325] The ICC would thus be unable to address the broader humanitarian dimensions of Israeli and Palestinian suffering, such as historical displacement, poverty in Gaza, or breaches of collective political rights in the territories. Moreover, the ICC could only ever exercise jurisdiction from 13 June 2014. At best, the ICC would ignore the vast majority of alleged crimes committed over the course of the conflict.[326] Even if an international court could prosecute all perpetrators successfully, this would not adequately address the legacies associated with past abuses.[327]

---

[321] Weiner, above n 268, at 153.

[322] Alex Boraine, *Truth and Reconciliation in South Africa: The Third Way* in TRUTH V JUSTICE: THE MORALITY OF TRUTH COMMISSIONS (Robert Rotberg and Dennis Thompson eds, 2000).

[323] Notably, using political 'big-wigs' as the main candidates for justice comes with a historical price tag. It often means turning a blind-eye to the vast number of agents and low-level collaborators implicated in past crimes. Thus, what is lauded as individual justice may in fact be a de facto way of exculpating many with blood on their hands. See Shriver, above n 255, at 7 and Gary Jonathan, STAY THE HAND OF VENGEANCE: THE POLITICS OF WAR CRIMES TRIBUNALS 300 (2000).

[324] By restricting ICC charges to high-level accused, the possibility of dealing with perpetrators who have a direct link with victims is eliminated. See Human Rights Watch, 'The Selection of Situations and Cases for Trial before the International Criminal Court', at ¶ 13 (October 2006).

[325] The ICC has faced criticism in its investigations in the Democratic Republic of the Congo (DRC), particularly in the case against Thomas Lubanga, a leader of one of the major militias in Ituri. See Joint letter to the Chief Prosecutor of the ICC, by Avocats Sans Frontières, Center for Justice and Reconciliation, Coalition Nationale pour la Cour Pénale Internationale—RCD, Fédération Internationale des Ligues des Droits de l'Homme, Human Rights Watch, ICTJ, Redress, Women's Initiatives for Gender Justice, at hrw.org/english/docs/2006/08/01/congo13891_txt.htm

[326] Meyerstein, above n 319 at 310.

[327] Priscilla Hayner, UNSPEAKABLE TRUTHS: CONFRONTING STATE TERROR AND ATROCITY 14 (2001).

Legal Norms and Moral Standards

Many scholars extol the didactic virtues of ICJ to dispense justice and '…enable the community ritually to affirm its guiding principles'.[328] ICJ offers the hope of 'moral transformation' and 'norm projection'.[329] Some even claim that ICJ wields particular authority to provide the most legitimate and potent response to mass violence.[330] Indeed, international tribunals have established new legal and moral standards.[331] Arguably, the ICC, as the key enforcement mechanism for ICJ norms could promote established principles and accountability in the Middle-East.[332] Any potential intervention might be used as a way to challenge and level the Israeli–Palestinian conflict narrative.[333]

Nevertheless, the ICC does not command universal support. The Rome Statute is regarded as deeply flawed by Israel[334] and is opposed by the US.[335] Israelis are particularly cynical about the use of international law for political ends, a strategy

---

[328] Martii Koskenniemi, *Between Impunity and Show Trials*, 1 Max Planck Yearbook of United Nations Law 10 (2002). See also Mark Osiel, *Ever Again: Legal Remembrance of Administrative Massacre*, 144 University of Pennsylvania Law Review 463 (1995–6); Lawrence Douglas, *The Memory of Judgement: Making Law and History in the Trials of the Holocaust* 6 (2001).

[329] David Luban, *After the Honeymoon: Reflections on the Current State of International Criminal Justice* 11 Journal of International Criminal Justice 510 (2013) ('After the Honeymoon').

[330] 'A field-based approach to ICJ helps explain why and how ICJ actors accrue and wield authority. We believe it also helps explain why ICJ is a key component – perhaps the most powerful component – in the broader universe of transitional justice'. Tenove and Dixon, above n 14, at 406.

[331] Following the *Akayesu* conviction at the ICTR, rape is now recognised as a crime against humanity. See *Prosecutor v Akayesu* (Jean Paul), Case no ICTR-96-4-T (1998). The ICTY case of *Kunarac* brought wartime acts of sexual violence within international legal scrutiny. See *Prosecutor v. Kunarac* et al., Case No. IT-96-23-T & IT-96-23/1-T, Judgement (Int'l Crim. Trib. for the Former Yugoslavia, 22 February 2001); Christopher Scott Maravilla, *Rape as a War Crime: The Implications of the International Criminal Tribunal for the Former Yugoslavia's Decision in Prosecutor v. Kunarac, Kovac, & (and) Vukovic on International Humanitarian Law,* 13 Florida Journal of International Law 321–343 (2000–2001).

[332] Michael Kearney and John Reynolds, *Palestine and the Politics of International Criminal Justice* in The Ashgate Research Companion to Int. Criminal Law: Critical Perspectives 429 (William Schabas et al. eds., 2013).

[333] Mark Kersten, *The ICC in Palestine: Changing the Narrative, Rattling the Status Quo,* Justice in Conflict (7 April 2015) https://justiceinconflict.org/2015/04/07/the-icc-in-palestine-changing-the-narrative-rattling-the-status-quo/

[334] On 28 August 2002, Israel informed the UN Secretary General that it no longer intends to become a state party to the Rome Statute of the ICC. Israel's usual argument against the ICC is that the crime of population transfer in occupied territories should not have been included in the Rome Statute. See http://mfa.gov.il/MFA/ForeignPolicy/Issues/Pages/PA-appeal-to-the-ICC--Jan-2015.aspx

[335] The US government has consistently opposed an international court that could hold US military and political leaders to a uniform global standard of justice. The policies of the Trump administration do not bode well for the ICC. US dissatisfaction with the Palestinians engaging the ICC can be seen, for example, in the minutes of a meeting between George Mitchell and Saab Erekat on 21 October 2009.

known as 'law-fare'.[336] For Israel and its supporters, Palestinian recourse to the ICC is 'diplomatic blackmail'.[337] Arguably, Palestinian engagement at the ICC is far more motivated by politics than the ideals of international justice.[338] Indeed, previous international investigations into the conflict have been dismissed as biased, lacking credibility and inherently political.[339] Israel is accustomed to being accosted in international bodies, and prosecutions would simply confirm that hostile perception.[340]

Ultimately, the ICC is dependent on cooperation and assistance from both the sides if it is to speak law to power and claim a measure of moral legitimacy. Presently, the ICC may be too fragile to play a leading role in transitional justice for the Middle East. In recent years, the ICC has encountered harsh political and legal setbacks, which undermine its global authority.[341] The presence of the ICC in Israeli public debate has even declined, along with its reputation.[342] In an era of populism and suspicion of international institutions, that is not something to easily dismiss. The ICC thus remains at risk of being charged with politicisation, which risks producing neither justice nor peace.[343] Indeed, why ought we to assume that a verdict from The Hague is the only method of norm-projection for Israelis and Palestinians? Sending signals which condemn war crimes might be more effectively conveyed by other transitional justice initiatives and *normative* institutions such as truth commissions or civil society initiatives.

Indeed, broader conceptions of justice, particularly restorative justice models, have not yet received adequate academic recognition, attention, and realization in the Israeli–Palestinian context. Notably, even former ICC Prosecutor Ocampo

---

[336] Keller, above n 35, at 2.

[337] See Dershowitz, above n 169 'Palestinians called joining the international bodies a "paradigm shift"... In turn, Israel called Palestinian accession to the international treaties "blackmail"'. Meloni, above n 204. C.f. William Schabas, *Foreword* in IS THERE A COURT FOR GAZA? vi (Chantal Meloni and Gianni Tognoni eds, 2012) ('The "lawfare" libel is nothing more than frustrated resistance to the availability of new mechanisms and institutions whereby international law can be applied to present conflicts, including those involving Israel and Palestine').

[338] Nimrod Karin, *The Establishment of the International Criminal Tribunal for Palestine (Part II)*, JUST SECURITY (22 January 2015) https://www.justsecurity.org/19301/establishment-international-criminal-tribunal-palestine-part-ii/

[339] On the use of ICJ as a weapon in political struggles, and the importance of acknowledging the ICC's political dimensions, see Sarah Nouwen and Wouter Werner, *Doing Justice to the Political: The ICC in Uganda and Sudan,* 21 EUR. J. INT'L LAW 941 (2012).

[340] See Dershowitz, above n 169.

[341] In 2016, several African countries indicated their intention to withdraw from the ICC. This tide was reversed, however, after South Africa and the Gambia withdrew their notifications to the UN, leaving Burundi as the only country formally seeking withdrawal. The OTP has also endured legal setbacks. Faced by Kenyan government intransigence and witness intimidation, Madame Bensouda had to close the Kenya case against President Uhuru Kenyatta for lack of evidence.

[342] Weill, '*Palestine in Wonderland*', above n 185 at 519.

[343] The prospect of the ICC becoming mired in a nation's internal politics has been an ongoing concern. See Safia Swimelar, *Guilty Without a Verdict: Bosniaks' Perception of the Milošević Trial* in THE MILOŠEVIĆ TRIAL: AN AUTOPSY 189 (Timothy William Waters ed., 2013).

conceded that 'Israel could achieve an even bigger impact while avoiding the intervention of the Court by inviting Palestine to create a "bilateral fact-finding committee" with experts representing all the parties to investigate alleged crimes committed by any party'.[344] 'The point is that the drama of trials and punishments is not the only method of norm projection'.[345]

Truth-Telling and Reconciliation

ICJ is also lauded for its truth-telling function.[346] Arguably, the ICC would allow for an expert determination of particular war crime allegations. Indeed, the OTP has already reviewed information from reliable sources on alleged crimes committed by both the parties to the 2014 Gaza Conflict, as well as in the West Bank and East Jerusalem since 13 June 2014.[347] An investigation might also provide a moral basis upon which to acknowledge that both sides are responsible for abuses. Nevertheless, judicial proceedings are blunt truth-telling instruments which risk distorting the complexity, and sensitive historical dimension of conflict. After all, trials are adversarial contests where truth-seeking and consensus building are often discarded in favour of 'winning'. In so doing, it is arguable that the ICC might constrain the truth-seeking exercise by pitching victims against perpetrators as mere adversaries.[348]

Arguably, the existential connotations of Israeli and Palestinian narratives are far too important and axiomatic to collective identity to be ignored. Given that the ICC is also limited by its temporal jurisdiction, it would be unable to establish a complete historical record of the conflict. To that end, legal discourse might compromise meaningful truth-telling for Israelis and Palestinians. Indeed, evidentiary inquiry and technical debate are unlikely to address the experience of Palestinian

---

[344] Ocampo continues: 'This committee, which could also include international experts, could provide the evidence collected to Palestinian or Israeli Courts with jurisdiction over the case. I am not sure if the current state of the relations between the parties makes it feasible to develop such a common mechanism, but I am presenting it because I see its enormous advantages It would create a buffer between both parties and the ICC and it would foster a strong complementarity system for all the parties'. Luis Moreno Ocampo, Palestine's Two Cards: A Commitment to Legality and an Invitation to Stop Crimes, JUST SECURITY (Jan. 12, 2015), www.justsecurity.org/19046/palestines-cards-commitment-legality-invitation-stop-crimes/ [https://perma.cc/N6EP-EYG6] (archived Jan. 21, 2021).

[345] Luban, *'After the Honeymoon'*, above n 329 at 511.

[346] Aukerman, above n 260 at 73.

[347] To date the OTP has reviewed over 320 reports as well as related documentation and supporting material. This includes information from individuals, groups, States, and NGOs. See ICC, Office of the Prosecutor, 'Report on Preliminary Examination Activities on the Situation in Palestine' (14 November 2016).

[348] See Stephan Landsman, *Those Who Remember the Past May Not Be Condemned to Repeat it*, 100 MICH. L. REV. 1564, 1571 (2002).

dispossession or Israeli national security.[349] In this light, international prosecutions remain an imperfect means to address the past and reshape collective memory.

Finally, judicial intervention might interfere with reconciliatory efforts. Indeed, many argue that ICJ is not only irrelevant, but harmful to overall processes of social reconstruction.[350] Some have even challenged the use of trials for dealing with past violence in Latin America, the Balkans, and Rwanda.[351] Arguably, criminal prosecutions do not promote reconciliation because they are both adversarial and divisive.[352] 'Trials separate victims and perpetrators...They do nothing to bring people together'.[353] 'Legal justice' fails to address structural injustices and conflict narratives, and may therefore impede the improvement of relations. Embitterment of the Croats and Serbs over the ICTY is a case in point.[354] Rwanda's fractured relationship with the ICTR is also worth noting.[355] Thus, far from achieving reconciliation, the ICC might fuel hostility and mistrust between Israelis and Palestinians, especially if one sides believes it is being unjustly or exclusively held accountable.

5.6 Conclusion

There is no doubt that the situation in Palestine presents the ICC with formidable challenges. Given the jurisdictional and admissibility hurdles discussed above, the Court's ability to intervene is far from assured. Notwithstanding the Prosecutor's decision to proceed with an investigation, Israeli and Palestinian leaders sitting on the docks at the Hague remains a distant scenario. Moreover, ICJ alone is inadequately equipped to capture the complex legacies of trauma inherited by both the

---

[349] Scholars note the limitations of legal paradigms, and the disjuncture between law and history when it comes to reckoning with large-scale political events through trials. See Brian Havel, *In Search of a Theory of Public Memory: The State, the Individual, and Marcel Proust* 80 INDIANA L. J. 605 (2005); Mark Osiel, *Ever Again: Legal Remembrance of Administrative Massacre* 144 UNIV. PEN. L. REV. 463, 661 (1995–6).

[350] Naomi Roht-Arriaza, *Editorial: Transitional Justice and International Criminal Justice*, 7(3) INT'L. J. TRANSITIONAL JUSTICE 383–392 (2013).

[351] Carlos Nino, RADICAL EVIL ON TRIAL (1996); Mark Osiel, MASS ATROCITY, COLLECTIVE MEMORY, AND THE LAW (1997); Jose Alvarez, *Rush to Closure: Lessons of the Tadic Judgment,* 96 MICHIGAN LAW JOURNAL 20, 31 (1998); Robert Howse and Jennifer Llewellyn, Institutions for Restorative Justice: The South African Truth and Reconciliation Commission, 49 UN. TORONTO L.J, 355, 358 (1999).

[352] Daly, above n 15 at 105; see also Minow, above n 18 at 26 (noting that 'Reconciliation is not the goal of criminal trials except in the most abstract sense').

[353] Daly, above n 15 at 105.

[354] See Anthony Borden, *Milosevic at the Bar*, THE NATION (1 April 2002). Though Milosevic was brought to trial along with other officials from his former regime, the adverse effects (and lack of positive effects) of his trial back in Yugoslavia were disturbing. Borden writes, 'If the tribunal hoped to break through Serbia's deep rejection of any responsibility for the wars and atrocities, the proceedings appeared to be having the opposite effect'.

[355] Alvarez, above n 14, at 366–67.

nations. This is because the conflict involves a diverse and broad set of actors and events, far beyond the ICC's jurisdictional reach and focus. It is also because the normative goals of ICJ might compromise other steps necessary for justice and conflict resolution, like historical truth-telling and national reconciliation.

Ultimately, beyond polarised rhetoric or procedural debate at the ICC, any meaningful reckoning with the past would need to include questions of collective responsibility and institutional policy. To understand international human rights law in the Middle East as solely or exclusively involving trials is not only short-sighted but places an unrealistic burden on judicial bodies like the ICC.[356] At the same time, the ICJ route must not be entirely discounted. After all, a comprehensive transitional justice strategy involves judicial and non-judicial mechanisms, retributive and restorative elements. Ultimately, retributive justice alone is ill-equipped to capture the complex legacies of trauma inherited by both the nations. From this standpoint, it is submitted that other more flexible tools of transitional justice, with broader goals and modes of inquiry, must also be seriously considered. The desirability of thicker notions of justice for Israelis and Palestinians and particularly a truth commission model is therefore addressed in the next chapter.

[356] Janine Natalya Clark, *Peace, Justice and the ICC: Limitations and Possibilities*, 9 J. INT. CRIM. JUSTICE 521, 543 (2011).

Chapter 6
The Applicability of Truth Commissions to the Israeli–Palestinian Conflict

6.1 Introduction

The previous chapter examined the limits of international criminal trials as a tool for transitional justice. It was concluded that ICJ, as represented by an ICC intervention, is a relatively impractical and ineffective means of addressing the nature and complexity of the Middle East conflict. Given the need for complementary approaches, this chapter explores the applicability of truth commissions and restorative justice theory to Israelis and Palestinians. Notably, as discussed in Chap. 3, a range of other transitional justice mechanisms and processes exist to pursue truth-telling, justice, and reconciliation.[1] However, truth commissions remain a key 'staple of the transitional justice menu'.[2] Yet scant attention has been devoted to this mechanism in the Israeli–Palestinian setting. This chapter therefore evaluates the possibilities of the truth commission model for the region based on the three normative pillars of transitional justice. It also seeks to evaluate the applicability of an IPTEC as developed and explored in Chap. 8.

As will be discussed, broader conceptions of justice, truth-telling, and reconciliation arguably better serve the goals of transitional justice in the Israeli–Palestinian context. This wider paradigm is more geared towards acknowledging the pervasive suffering experienced by both nations. A truth commission could also circumvent some the obstacles posed by an exclusively individualised and retributive approach

---

[1] For example, Gross has written about constitutional making and reconciliation. Aeyal Gross, 'The Constitution, Reconciliation and Transitional Justice: Lessons from South Africa and Israel' (2004) 40 *Stanford Journal of International Law* 47. Benvenisti has considered compensation for property rights in Israeli–Palestinian negotiations around 1948. Eyal Benvenesti and Eyal Zamir 'Private Claims to Property Rights in the Future Israeli-Palestinian Settlement' (1995) 89 *American Journal of International Law* 297.

[2] Naomi Roht-Arriaza, 'Transitional Justice and Peace Agreements Working Paper' (2005) *Peace Agreements: The Role of Human Rights in Negotiations* 1–21, 2.

J. Bracka, *Transitional Justice for Israel/Palestine*, Springer Series in Transitional Justice, https://doi.org/10.1007/978-3-030-89435-1_6

to transitional justice. Whilst the chances of such a truth-telling enterprise are slim at present, it is worth recalling that '…truth commissions have often emerged in conflict situations where shortly before the chances for their establishment were slim, as well'.[3] In sum, it will be argued that the success of a truth commission rests upon its ability to sidestep vengeance in order to promote restorative justice, empathy, and shared moral discourse—the very steps required to resolve the Israeli–Palestinian struggle.

6.2 Part One: Defining Truth Commissions

In less than three decades, the truth commission has evolved into a widely regarded mechanism commanding solid support.[4] It offers a restorative lens through which to view post-conflict justice. Hayner classically defines truth commissions as temporary state-sanctioned bodies that focus on the past and investigate patterns of abuse, rather than one event.[5] They normally engage in an examination of historical violence (resulting in a published report), provide a platform for victims to tell their stories (sometimes through public hearings), recommend reforms, and contribute to reconciliation.[6] Ultimately, truth commissions address conduct that raises the most politically and morally sensitive issues facing a community.[7]

Indeed, commissions of varying types have been established in close to 40 different countries. They first appeared in Latin America, as the region transitioned from dictatorships to democracies, and then increasingly surfaced in Asia and Africa.[8] The first modern official transitional commission was Argentina's inquiry into the Disappearance of Persons (1983).[9] In Argentina, and later in Chile, incoming civilian governments used the mechanism to investigate and document abuses of prior military regimes. Truth commissions gained force as a 'second-best' option where

---

[3] Ron Dudai and Hillel Cohen, 'Triangle of Betrayal: Collaborators and Transitional Justice in the Israeli-Palestinian Conflict' (2007) 6(1) *Journal of Human Rights* 37, 52.

[4] 'The historical analogies to today's truth commissions range from international commissions of inquiry to many forms of national investigative bodies…' Harvard Law School, 'Truth Commissions: A Comparative Assessment' (Paper presented at the Inter-disciplinary Discussion Held at Harvard Law School, (1997) 10 ('Harvard Law School Paper').

[5] Priscilla Hayner, *Unspeakable Truths: Facing the Challenge of Truth Commissions* (Routledge, 2002), 14 ('Unspeakable Truths').

[6] Rosalind Shaw and Lars Waldorf with Pierre Hazan (eds.), *Localizing Transitional Justice: Interventions and Priorities After Mass Violence* (Stanford University Press, 2010), 231.

[7] *Harvard Law School Paper*, above n 4, 10.

[8] Additional information about individual truth commissions can be found on the United States Institute of Peace website (http://www.usip.org/library/truth.html1#tc).

[9] It was created by President Raúl Alfonsín of Argentina on 15 December 1983. The Commission issued the *Nunca Más* (Never Again) Report, which documented human rights violations under the military dictatorship known as the National Reorganisation Process.

trials were deemed too confronting or impractical.[10] Truth commissions were also incorporated into UN sponsored peace accords in El Salvador, Guatemala, Sierra Leone, Democratic Republic of Congo, Burundi, and elsewhere.[11] Within two decades, truth commissions became a 'staple of the transitional justice menu'.[12]

More Than Second-Best

No commission has been both celebrated and criticised as much as the SATRC.[13] It marked an audacious attempt to address the crimes of apartheid in a non-vengeful way and has often been considered 'the most far-reaching and the most effective of its genre'.[14] The SATRC was created in 1995 after national calls for truth-telling and the White National Party's demands for amnesties.[15] Its innovative framework, which conditioned amnesty on full disclosure by perpetrators, ushered in a valid alternative to criminal trials.[16] Unlike in Latin America, the SATRC was established by Parliament rather than presidential decree and held open hearings instead of in-camera investigations.[17] The commission's powers, budget, and size were all unprecedented, far exceeding those of previous commissions in Argentina, Chile, and El Salvador (the models on which the SATRC was based).[18] Given its scale and significance, the SATRC will be the truth commission most considered over the course of this chapter.

Ultimately, supporters of the SATRC did not just argue that a truth commission was a second-best alternative, they insisted that a well-run commission could

[10] Roht-Arriaza, above n 2, 2.

[11] For a listing and discussion, see Hayner, *Unspeakable Truths,* above n 5.

[12] Roht-Arriaza, above n 2, 2.

[13] Ruti G. Teitel, 'Transitional Justice Genealogy' (2003) 16 *Harvard Human Rights Journal* 69, 78 ('Transitional Justice Genealogy'); See Truth and Reconciliation Commission of South Africa Report (Truth and Reconciliation Commission eds., 1999); Promotion of National Unity and Reconciliation Act, No. 34 (1995) (establishing the Truth and Reconciliation Commission). For an in-depth account of its history, see Alex Boraine, *A Country Unmasked: Inside South Africa's Truth and Reconciliation Commission* (Oxford University Press, 2000).

[14] Heribert Adam and Kogila Moodley, *Seeking Mandela: Peacemaking Between Israelis and Palestinians* (Temple University Press, 2005), 134.

[15] The SATRC was the product of a political deal between the former white-minority regime and the African National Congress (ANC) to usher in democracy. The fear of violence in the 1990–1995 period was central to the design. See Rita Kesselring, *Bodies of Truth: Law, Memory and Emancipation in Post-apartheid South Africa* (Stanford University Press, 2017).

[16] Laurel E. Fletcher and Harvey M. Weinstein et al., "Stay the Hand of Justice: Whose Priorities Take Priority?" in Shaw and Waldorf, above n 6.

[17] Adam and Moodley, above n 14, 128.

[18] These unparalleled resources included search-and-seizure powers and the right to issue court-backed subpoenas.

accomplish things no trial could provide.[19] From this standpoint, one could now view the commission as a 'first best solution', not just 'an ineffective bromide where criminal prosecutions are inadequate, politically risky, or undesirable'.[20] In the two decades following the SATRC, more than 20 truth commissions were established as a primary response to patterns of widespread human rights abuse. These include repeat commissions in countries where the first commission was unduly constrained.[21] Truth commissions have also surfaced in stable democracies such as Canada and Australia, and in East Germany after communism.[22] Whilst it does not constitute a nation's complete response to the past, the truth commission is gaining force as an instrumental transitional justice tool.[23]

Normative Goals

Advocates of commissions typically laud their ability to create an authoritative record of the past, provide a platform for victims, recommend changes to deter future violations, and establish responsibility for human rights violations.[24] Supporters of truth commissions also invoke peace and nation-building as destinations to which these institutions lead.[25] In essence, the goals of truth-commissions rest on the three pillars of transitional justice outlined in Chap. 3, namely truth-telling, justice, and reconciliation. With respect to Israelis and Palestinians, many academics welcome the potential contribution of a truth commission. Both Weiner and Meyerstein claim, it is the best method for addressing human rights abuses in this context, because it could provide an officially acknowledged history, foster reconciliation, and provide legitimacy to the existing Israeli and emerging Palestinian

[19] Roht-Arriaza, above n 2, 2.

[20] Robert Howse and Jennifer Llewellyn, 'Institutions for Restorative Justice: The South African Truth and Reconcilation Commission' (1999) 49 *University of Toronto Law Journal* 355, 356; See also Martha Minow, *Between Vengeance and Forgiveness: Facing History after Genocide and Mass Violence* (Beacon Press, 1998).

[21] Chile's National Commission for Truth and Reconciliation was followed by a National Commission on Political Imprisonment and Torture; the Nepalese Truth Commission (1990–1991) was followed by a new commission in 2014; and there have been calls for a new truth commission to supplement the Panama Truth Commission established in 2000.

[22] Canada's truth commission focused on the legacies of Indian residential schools and indigenous-settler relations. Australia held a National Inquiry into the 'Separation of Aboriginal and Torres Strait Islander Children from their Families'. Germany has held two truth commissions on human rights violations in former East Germany.

[23] Howse and Llewellyn, above n 20, 356; See Minow, above n 20.

[24] Margaret L. Popkin and Naomi Roht-Arriaza, 'Truth as Justice: Investigatory Commissions in Latin America', (1995) 20 *Law and Society Inquiry* 79, 80; Hayner, *Unspeakable Truths,* above n 5, 24.

[25] Ibid.

democracies.[26] Indeed, there exists a small chorus of practitioners who seriously advocate consideration of this model.[27] The next section therefore explores the capacity and limits of a truth commission in the Israeli–Palestinian setting based on the three normative goals of transitional justice (Chap. 3). It bears noting that the normative goals and legitimacy of any such truth-telling endeavour would depend on its official or unofficial character which will be explored in Chaps. 7 and 8.

6.3 Part Two: Truth Commissions and 'Justice'

> *Contrary to popular perception, restorative justice is not just a program, but a new 'paradigm' or pattern of thinking....* [28]

Truth commissions pursue justice through official acknowledgement of past injustice, identifying institutional responsibility, and setting a new moral framework.[29] Unlike trials, which focus on past crimes, truth commissions are more forward-looking and lean on broader notions of restorative justice. Generally speaking, restorative justice is about restoring victims, offenders, and communities.[30] In this way, restorative justice does not aim to achieve individual criminal justice but to establish equality, humanity, and respect among a traumatised community. Thus, the SATRC saw itself as 'foregoing punishment in favour of reconciliation'.[31] Arguably, '[r]estorative justice is not so much concerned with punishment as with

---

[26] Mathew. A Weiner, 'Defeating Hatred With Truth: An Argument in Support of a Truth Commission as part of the solution to Israel/Palestine' (2005–2006) 38 *Connecticut Law Review* 123, 125; Ariel Meyerstein, 'On the Advantage and Disadvantage of Truth Commission for Life: Dreaming an Israeli-Palestinian Truth Commission' (2003) 45 *Journal of Church and State* 457, 460 ('Dreaming an Israeli-Palestinian Truth Commission'); See also Ariel Meyerstein, 'Transitional Justice and Post-conflict Israel/Palestine: Assessing the Applicability of the Truth Commission Paradigm' (2006–2007) 38 *Case Western Reserve Journal of International Law* 281 ('Transitional Justice and Post-conflict Israel/Palestine').

[27] Cohen and Dudai, above n 3, 54; Miller also proposes a hybrid commission of inquiry for Israel/Palestine to address 1948 and the creation of the Palestinian refugees. Zinaida Miller, 'Settling with History: A Hybrid Commission of Inquiry for Israel/Palestine' (2007) 20 *Harvard Human Rights Journal* 293; See also Adrien Wing, 'A Truth and Reconciliation Commission for Palestine/Israel: Healing Spirit Injuries?' (2008) 17(1) *Transnational Law & Contemporary Problems* 139

[28] Many regard restorative justice as a 'new pattern of thinking' about crime and justice. See Daniel, Van Ness, and Karen Heetderks Strong, *Restoring Justice* (Anderson Publishing Company, 2002) 15; Howard Zehr, *Changing Lenses: A New Focus For Crime and Justice* (Herald Press, 1990) 175; Robert K Ame and Seidu M Alidu, 'Truth and Reconciliation Commissions, Restorative Justice, Peacemaking Criminology and Development' (2010) 23(3) *Criminal Justice Studies* 253, 256.

[29] *Harvard Law School Paper,* above n 4, 11.

[30] Gross, above n 1, 74; Ame and Alidu, above n 28, 256; David Crocker, 'Truth Commissions, Transitional Justice and Civil Society', in Robert I. Rotberg and Dennis Thompson (eds.), *Truth v Justice: The Morality of Truth Commissions* (Princeton University Press, 2000), 99–112, 105.

[31] Adam and Moodley, above n 14, 128.

correcting moral imbalances and restoring broken relationships...'.[32] In short, truth commissions innovate the concept of justice itself and may offer a new reparative ingredient for the Israeli–Palestinian conflict.

Beyond 'An Eye for an Eye'

As discussed in the previous chapter, retributive justice may be ill-suited to large-scale political conflict. Retributive justice rests on a very narrow concept of individual blame. Arguably, '[criminal] Justice falls limp before monster-sized evil'.[33] For example, the ICTY and the ICTR indicted and imprisoned war criminals, and yet widespread accountability remained elusive.[34] For some sociologists, the solution therefore lies outside the criminal legal paradigm.[35] Whilst trials promote punishment, restorative theory identifies practices 'that include victims and perpetrators and involve concrete consideration of the needs of each for restoration'.[36] For truth commissions, 'justice' is more about meeting demands of multiple players in post-conflict society. Thus, 'justice' can encompass truth-telling, reform of state institutions, reparations for victims and creative initiatives to forge reconciliation.[37] It may also include investigations of individuals or institutions implicated in human rights violations and thus lead to recommendations regarding war crimes trials, but it is not limited to this. In essence, truth commissions offer a thicker version of justice than that pursued through international criminal justice, one that is likely better placed to address Israeli and Palestinian national demands and claims.

As discussed in earlier chapters, questions of history, memory, and recognition of the past are essential to Israelis and Palestinians and yet are largely outside the legal and normative purview of the ICC. Beyond punishment and sentencing of individual offenders, a vital requirement of each nation is acknowledgement of historic rights, acceptance of responsibility and some form of atonement for the past.[38]

---

[32] Gross, above n 1, 74.

[33] Donald Shriver, *An Ethic for Enemies: Forgiveness in Politics* (Oxford University Press, 1998) 8.

[34] For example, in Rwanda, after a genocide that killed some 800,000 people, the ICTR had issued indictments against only 96 people by the end of its tenure in 2015. The ICTR convicted 61 individuals: 32 of whom are currently serving sentences, 22 of whom have completed their sentences, and seven of whom died while serving their sentences. The Tribunal acquitted 14 individuals and transferred the cases against 10 individuals to national jurisdictions.

[35] Richard, Quinney, 'The Way of Peace: On Crime, Suffering, and Service' in Hal Pepinsky and Richard Quinney (eds.), *Criminology as peacemaking* (Indiana University Press, 1991).

[36] Howse and Llewellyn, above n 20, 375.

[37] Paul Van Zyl, 'Dilemmas of Transitional Justice: The Case of the South African Truth and Reconciliation Commission' (1999) 52 (2) *Journal of International Affairs* 647.

[38] See Yoav Peled and Nadim Rouhana, 'Transitional Justice and the Right to Return of the Palestinian Refugees' (2004) 5 *Theoretical Inquiries in Law* 317; See Rashid Khalidi, 'Attainable Justice: Elements of a Solution to the Palestinian Refugee Issue' (1998) 33(2) (Spring) *International Journal* 233, 239.

In essence, the parties' demands of justice are more than just retributive, but rather involve national and historic claims, which are far better captured by a restorative view of justice.[39] For example, since 1948, Palestinians have remained wedded to the justness of their claim to return to their homes. For Israelis, accountability for terrorist acts, soldier abductions, and urban bombardment are paramount. It is difficult to imagine how putting a handful of Palestinians or Israelis in the dock would be able to resolve these historic claims. In short, no verdict at the Hague will assuage the Jewish state's desire for acknowledgement nor the Palestinian grievances from 1948 and afterwards.

Widening the Net of Accountability: Complicity and Collaboration

> *Truth commissions have the capacity to address accountability and justice on multiple registers: at the individual level and the structural level....*[40]

Moreover, truth commissions allow for a broader assessment of accountability beyond individual criminal guilt. Academics caution against a false sense of collective moral blamelessness fostered by ICJ.[41] For example, Nuremberg arguably failed to provide a wider structural responsibility for German citizens as 'willing executioners' of the holocaust.[42] Many scholars thus advocate restorative justice for Israelis and Palestinians, because the conflict involves a diverse and broad set of actors, beyond the simple formula of high-level perpetrators on whom the ICC focuses.[43] As discussed in Chap. 5, the multi-dimensional aspect of responsibility for every event of the conflict defies any unilateral allocation of culpability. Arguably, truth commissions set in motion accountability processes that address transitional society collectively and offer a more complex account of those responsible.

---

[39] Ron Dudai, 'A Model for Dealing with the Past in the Israeli-Palestinian Context' (2007) 1 *International Journal of Transitional Justice* 249.

[40] Vasuki Nesiah, 'Truth vs. Justice? Commissions and Courts', in Jeff Helsing and Julie Mertus eds., *Human Rights and Conflict*, (USIP, 2006) 384.

[41] Engle writes: 'Under such conditions, the most that could be expected of International criminal justice is to relate to the perpetrator as an exception, a "bad apple" in an otherwise well-cultivated orchard'. Karen Engle, 'Anti-Impunity and the Turn to Criminal Law in Human Rights' (2015) 5(100) *Cornell Law Review* 1120; See also Kieran McEvoy, 'Beyond Legalism: Towards a Thicker Understanding of Transitional Justice' (2007) 34(4) *Journal of Law and Society* 411, 438.

[42] Many have condemned the 'justice' advanced at Nuremberg as 'victor's justice' doing more to consolidate the Allies' victory off the battlefield than to provide accountability for the Holocaust. See for example, Daniel J. Goldhagen, *Hitler's Willing Executioners: Ordinary Germans and the Holocaust* (Knopf, 1996) 2.

[43] Meyerstein, *'Transitional Justice and Post-conflict Israel/Palestine'*, above n 26.

For example, much of the abuse in South Africa was perpetrated, supported, and maintained in a systematic manner. Through its event hearings and Final Report, the SATRC could attribute responsibility to diverse segments of society from the judiciary, media to the Church. In the Israeli–Palestinian context, the 'webs of collaboration'[44] and categories of guilt are no less ambiguous. Most of the Jewish population is conscripted into the Israeli army, and many continue to serve reserve duty. Beyond this, there is an argument that the entire Israeli–Jewish population is in some way complicit in the administration of the occupation.[45] On the Palestinian side, collaborators include those indirectly engaged in hostilities who aid and abet Palestinian militants in killing Israelis, or plan and prepare attacks.[46] From this standpoint, truth commissions can generate a process of collective accountability, requiring everyone from Israeli soldiers and bystanders to Palestinian civilians and abettors, to examine their role in past abuses. As discussed in Chap. 5, this is something trials are not designed to generate, with their focus on holding key perpetrators accountable for past atrocities.

Institutional Accountability

To pursue a path of justice, truth commissions may also focus on the role of institutions in human rights abuse. As discussed in Chap. 5, retributive justice tends to address crime as an individual-based phenomenon. Nevertheless, the involvement of political, educational, and social institutions are significant factors in large-scale violence. Regarding South Africa: '…the real wrong was the apartheid system itself, a focus on individual offences, or crimes, abstracts from this overwhelming reality and risks moral arbitrariness'.[47] The SATRC also addressed accountability by examining the roles played by various professions and institutions in resisting or facilitating human rights abuse.[48] Likewise, establishing the responsibility of Israeli and Palestinian institutions is as important as determining individual criminal

[44] Cohen and Dudai, above n 3, 38.

[45] 'Ordinary Israelis are somewhat implicated if only through paying the taxes that support the country's massive defense budget, electing officials that continue to pursue problematic policies such as settlement-building, or merely by remaining silent in the face of the abuses of its government against the Palestinian civilian population'. See Meyerstein, *'Transitional Justice and Post-conflict Israel/Palestine'*, above n 26, 315.

[46] On collaborators in Palestinian society, see Human Rights Watch, 'Justice Undermined Balancing Security and Human Rights in the Palestinian Justice System' 23, (2001). http://www.hrw.org/reports/2001/pa/isrpal101.pdf

[47] In most transitional contexts, the abuses of the past that demand attention are political in nature. By definition, political crimes are not the result of purely individual action. Howse and Llewellyn, above n 20, 375.

[48] For example, by holding hearings on the role of the medical and legal professions under apartheid, the SATRC focused national attention on issues such as professional codes of conduct. See Van Zyl, above n 37, 657.

liability. Unlike the post-conflict context of the SATRC, it would be more challenging to address institutional accountability during ongoing conflict. However, by focusing on the administration of the occupation, and the infrastructure of terrorism, an Israeli–Palestinian commission could delve more widely into past injustice and moreover, could recommend institutional reforms directed at improving the prospects of future peace. In this way, accountability and justice are best accomplished by scrutinising the institutions responsible for past crimes and producing recommendations for their reform.

Selling Out 'Justice'?

Nevertheless, truth commissions have also encountered critics who challenge the model as an unnecessary compromise or obstruction of justice.[49] Invariably, tensions exist between the moral demands of criminal justice, and non-punitive approaches to gross human rights abuse.[50] Arguably, 'real' justice is '...often thought to necessitate punishment, not acknowledgement and dialogue'.[51] From Chile to Ghana, truth commissions have been said 'to cobble together a constituency of compromise and appeasement'.[52] Others critique the perceived deficient and quasi-judicial standards of truth commissions, and lack of enforcement powers,[53] claiming they are ultimately poor and toothless substitutes to criminal trials. Truth commissions risk being seen by Israel and/or the PA as a soft option at best, or at worst, another political smoke screen for dodging prosecutions.[54]

There is also the claim that truth commission are incompatible with justice for victims. Many query whether victims are truly better served by restorative justice; and some researchers have interviewed survivors in South Africa, Rwanda, and Cambodia where the desire for retributive justice was strongly expressed following events there.[55] Regarding South Africa, the SATRC was arguably a denial of justice

[49] Mainstream activists such as Ken Roth of Human Rights Watch and Aryeh Neier accuse truth commissions of obstructing justice because their emphasis on reconciliation and restorative justice lets perpetrators off too easily. See Jonathan Tepperman, 'Truth and Consequences' (2002) 81(2) *Foreign Affairs* 128–145.

[50] See Howse and Llewellyn, above n 20, 369.

[51] Ibid 356.

[52] Nesiah, above n 40, 378.

[53] Frederik Van Zyl Slabbert, 'Truth Without Reconciliation, Reconciliation Without Truth' in James Wilmot and Linda. Van de Vijver (eds.), *After the TRC: Reflections on Truth and Reconciliation in South Africa* (Ohio University Press, 2001) 62 (finding insufficiencies in the South African TRC procedures, evidentiary standards and legality).

[54] Reed Brody, 'Justice: The First Casualty of Truth?', *The Nation* 2001 in Eric Brahm, 'Uncovering the Truth: Examining Truth Commission Success and Impact' (2007) 8 *International Studies Perspectives* 16, 22.

[55] Wendy Lambourne, 'Justice and Reconciliation: Post-conflict Peacebuilding in Cambodia and Rwanda' in Mohamed Abu-Nimer (Ed.), *Reconciliation, Justice, and Coexistence, Theory and*

because the amnesty provision robbed victims of their right to criminal and civil recourse.[56] This 'injustice' was exacerbated by a flawed reparations process.[57] This is a serious concern for Israelis and Palestinians for whom as discussed, justice narratives are existentially paramount.

Nevertheless, the claim that transitional justice is only possible after exacting retribution is questionable. As discussed above, this view subscribes to an unnecessarily myopic conception of justice that is itself narrower than what Israelis and Palestinians are demanding. It is also inconsistent with the need to apply a holistic approach to transitional justice mechanisms. For example, through its process, the SATRC did in fact provide the opportunity for victims and not just violators to tell their stories, and eventually (to some extent), to be compensated.[58] In the Chilean case, few victims expressed a desire for vengeance, but rather '…stressed that in the end, what really mattered to them was that the truth be revealed, that the memory of their loved ones not be denigrated or forgotten...'.[59] Ultimately, this issue is closely tied to the desires of victims which can only be ascertained through empirical work and which are in any event unlikely to be uniform.

Finally, sentencing and punishment are not the only registers of accountability. Even those perpetrators granted amnesty through a truth commission could receive retribution in the form of social and moral censure. For example, although the SATRC did not gather information to pursue prosecutions, the hearings contributed to accountability through public shaming.[60] Truth commissions can also elicit

Practice (Lexington Books, 2001) 311–337; See also Richard Wilson, 'Reconciliation and Revenge in Post-apartheid South Africa: Rethinking legal pluralism and human rights' (2000) 41 (1) *Current Anthropology,* 75–98 cited in Kevin Avruch, 'Truth and Reconciliation Commissions: Problems in Transitional Justice and the Reconstruction of Identity' (2010) 47 (1) *Transcultural Psychiatry* 37.

[56] This very argument was the subject of a constitutional challenge to the South African amnesty provisions. See *Azanian People's Organization (AZAPO) and Others v. President of the Republic of South Africa and* Others (1996) 8 B.C.L.R. 1015 (CC). The challenge failed on the grounds that the constitution allowed for the limitation of rights in the interests of national unity and reconciliation. Hugo Van der Merwe, 'Reconciliation and justice in South Africa: Lessons from the TRC's community Interventions' in Mohamed Abu-Nimer (ed.), *Reconciliation, Justice, and Coexistence* (Lexington Books, 2001) 187–207.

[57] Although the Reparation and Rehabilitation Committee of the SATRC could award reparations, it had to contend with a large discrepancy between victims' expectations and its capacity and willingness to deliver. The SATRC had no money of its own to disburse to survivors and could only make recommendations. See Catherine Jenkins, 'After the Dry White Season: The Dilemmas of Reparation and Reconstruction in South Africa' (2000) 16 *South African Journal of Human Rights* 415, 415–17.

[58] Ibid, 356.

[59] Jose Zalaquett, 'Balancing Ethical Imperatives and Political Constraints: The Dilemma of New Democracies Confronting Past Human Rights Violations: The Mathew O. Tobriner Memorial Lecture (1991)' (1992) 43 *Hastings Law Journal* 1425, 1437.

[60] See Dumisa Ntsebeza, 'The Uses of Truth Commissions: Lessons for the World' in Rotberg and Thompson, above n 30, 158, 164 (explaining that in the South African context '[flor amnesty applicants to be prepared to run the gauntlet of public dismay, censure, and even ostracism was a heavy price to pay') quoted in Weiner, above n 26,130.

accountability and justice through naming[61] and using a range of non-judicial sanctions such as community service.[62]

'Some Better Than None': Relative Justice for Transition

> *Justice would not be foregone, but pursued to the extent possible given the existing political restraints.* [63]

Even if one concedes the superiority of trials as a matter of principle and admits to defects in restorative justice, truth commissions may still be the preferred avenue of accountability. Indeed, it is strongly arguable that restorative rather than retributive justice is paramount at times of transition. Conceivably, at times of transition, what needs to be created is a relative notion of justice, as opposed to 'ordinary' justice, as understood during peacetime.[64] For instance, producing a joint understanding about past abuses or a meaningful public apology might be regarded as '...a preservative form of justice, which concededly sacrifices the aims of ideal justice for the more limited ones of assuring peace and stability'.[65] 'Justice, one might argue, does not encompass the whole of the moral universe. Other values may exist against which justice may be weighed...'.[66] From this perspective, Israeli and Palestinian negotiators and practitioners should give due regard to broader notions of justice grounded in instrumental concerns.

It should also be recalled that truth commissions play an invaluable role in justice where prosecutions are simply impracticable. In various transitional contexts, truth commissions end up becoming a forum of last resort. For example, in Sierra Leone, the sheer scale of violations made prosecution of all perpetrators impossible. In East Timor, prosecutorial capacity was limited because of human and financial resource constraints and in South Africa, the imperatives of a negotiated peace rendered

---

[61] Some truth commissions are empowered to name names in making findings. When prosecutions are unlikely, this may be an important way of providing individualised accountability. See Nesiah, above n 40, 383.

[62] The community reconciliation process in East Timor is an interesting model in this regard. All defendants charged with 'lesser' crimes were channelled through a community reconciliation process where, if found guilty, they faced a community service requirement rather than a criminal sanction. See ibid.

[63] Zalaquett, above n 59, 1437.

[64] Teitel refers to an understanding of a non-ideal 'compromised justice that is constitutive of the conditions under which it is chosen'. Ruti G. Teitel, *Transitional Justice* (Oxford University Press, 2000) 227 ('Transitional Justice'). According to Gross 'Although grounded in the transition, [justice]...should not be limited to this period because justice is always in transition'. Gross, above n 1, 50.

[65] Teitel, *Transitional Justice*, above n 64, 51.

[66] Howse and Llewellyn, above n 20, 370; Miriam J Aukerman, 'Extraordinary Evil, Ordinary Crime: A Framework for Understanding Transitional Justice' (2002) 15 *Harvard Human Rights Journal* 39, 45.

prosecutions too politically volatile.[67] In any event, given the scale of mass atrocity, transitional societies are only ever capable of prosecuting a tiny fraction of perpetrators, which often results in a de facto amnesty.[68]

Truth commission may therefore be the only avenue to ensure that victims have access to some measure of accountability.[69] This is because often '...political power dictates judicial response'.[70] This is pertinent in the Israeli–Palestinian setting, where those accused of war crimes are the individuals most likely to negotiate an agreement and retain power. It is an inescapable fact that power relations between Israelis and Palestinians will constrain judicial responses to the conflict. From this more pragmatic standpoint, Israelis and Palestinians may need to embrace 'justice to the extent possible', based on a model of restorative justice.[71]

Complementarity: ICC and Truth Commissions?

> *International criminal justice and truth commissions are thus inevitable co-workers in transitional contexts.*[72]

It must also be emphasised that truth commissions and criminal justice are not mutually exclusive endeavours. Many truth commissions, like Chile's,[73] may turn over findings to prosecuting authorities.[74] Moreover, truth commissions may be unable to deliver sentences, but their determinations may be used during trials, either as evidence or as contextual information.[75] For example, the Peruvian Truth and Reconciliation Commission contained a special unit to collect evidence for

[67] See Nesiah, above n 40.

[68] Van Zyl, above n 37, 661; 'Therefore, each war crimes trial is an exercise in partial justice to the extent that it reminds us that the majority of war crimes remain unpunished. If Yugoslavia, why not Somalia; if Rwanda, why not Guatemala?' Gerry Simpson, 'Didactic and Dissident Histories in War Crime Trials'. (1996–1997) 60 *Albany Law Review* 801, 810.

[69] See Nesiah, above n 40.

[70] Meyerstein, '*Dreaming an Israeli-Palestinian Truth Commission*', above n 26, 468; For example, at the time of South Africa's transition, Van Zyl writes 'The political and historical circumstances that prevailed...made it virtually impossible for the leadership...to refuse to agree to some form of amnesty'. Van Zyl, above n 37, 661.

[71] See Neil Kritz, (ed.), *Transitional Justice, Country Studies* (United States Institute of Peace Press, 1995) 487; Howse and Llewellyn, above n 20, 370.

[72] Phillippe Flory, 'From Strangers to Partners: International Criminal Justice and Truth Commissions' (2015) 13 *Journal of International Criminal Justice* 19, 21.

[73] Chile may offer the paradigmatic example of a transformed political environment making it possible to revisit prosecution options. In this context, the work of an earlier truth commission provided an invaluable archive of evidentiary resources gathered at a time closer to that of the original crime. Nesiah, above n 40, 383–384.

[74] Hayner, *Unspeakable Truths,* above n 5, 16.

[75] Jason S. Abrams and Priscilla Hayner, 'Documenting, Acknowledging and Publicizing the Truth', in Mahmoud Cherif Bassiouni (ed) *Post-Conflict Justice* (Transnational Publishers, 2002).

criminal investigation.[76] Indeed, truth commissions laid the foundations for subsequent prosecutions in both Argentina and Chile.[77] They can therefore be particularly valuable in advancing criminal accountability long-term.

The UN has also supported the parallel operation of judicial and non-judicial mechanisms in Cambodia,[78] Sierra Leone,[79] and East Timor.[80] Not only can these tools complement each other, but each one may benefit from the other. The simultaneous experience of the Special Court and the TRC in Sierra Leone led William Schabas (a member of the Commission) to observe that truth commissions and courts can work productively together.[81] He concludes: 'This complementary relationship may have synergistic effect on the search for post-conflict justice as part of the struggle against impunity'.[82] In practical terms, cooperation between these two institutions is complex, as they contend with delicate issues from evidence to witness-sharing.[83] Nevertheless, truth commissions may continue to be regarded as complementary to the criminal justices process.

---

[76] Roht-Arriaza, above n 2, 21.

[77] '[T]he National Commission on the Disappeared in Argentina played a critical role in the trials against members of the former military junta leadership, serving as a model for the positive relationship that can exist between truth commissions and later prosecutions'. See Hayner, *Unspeakable Truths,* above n 5, 93–94.

[78] In Cambodia, Prime Minister Hun Sen proposed a truth commission to operate alongside trials. This was supported by the UN International Commission of Inquiry and seen as a way to address the numerous cases that would not be investigated by the ECCC. Hayner, *Unspeakable Truths,* above n 5, 206.

[79] In Sierra Leone, the UN Secretary-General and Security Council took into account the future creation of the Sierra Leonean Truth and Reconciliation Commission (TRC), noting that this institution would be better suited to deal with secondary offenders.

[80] In Timor-Leste, the Commission for Reception, Truth and Reconciliation (CAVR) was established by the UN Transitional Administration in East Timor (UNTAET) to work alongside the Special Panels for Serious Crimes (the Special Panels). See Flory, above n 72, 27.

[81] The author was also a member of the Sierra Leone Truth and Reconciliation Commission. See William Schabas, 'A Synergistic Relationship: The Sierra Leone Truth and Reconciliation Commission and the Special Court for Sierra Leone' (2004) 15 *Criminal Law Forum,* 3–54 ('A Synergistic Relationship'); William Schabas, 'The Relationship Between Truth Commissions and International Courts: The Case of Sierra Leone', (2003) 25(4) *Human Rights Quarterly* 1035–1066.

[82] Schabas, *A Synergistic Relationship,* above n 81.

[83] The Sierra Leone experience also reflects poor institutional collaboration between a court and a truth commission. For example, the potential use of information gathered by the Special Court and the Sierra Leonean TRC may have caused reluctance from some witnesses and perpetrators to testify in front of these commissions. Flory argues that 'in the end, the relationship between the TRC and SCSL functioned at its best when these two institutions did not have to cooperate'. See Flory, above n 72, 39; See also Rosalind Shaw, *Rethinking Truth and Reconciliation Commissions: Lessons from Sierra Leone* (United States Institute of Peace Special Report, 2005) 4.

Conclusion

In sum, given the hostile political terrain, it might be plainly more important that Israelis and Palestinians experience a relative notion of justice, rather than the ICC flexing its retributive muscles. This does not foreclose the possibility of future criminal prosecutions, but it does mean, that for now, and until a formal peace treaty is concluded, a truth commission is the most feasible and beneficial option overall. As discussed above, violence in the region is institutional and endemic, requiring a more nuanced assessment of accountability than the one offered by ICJ. Moreover, in cultures of impunity such as the Israeli–Palestinian one, the choice is not between 'strong' retributive justice and 'weak' restorative justice. Rather, it is between a truth commission and silence.[84] In this light, it might be concluded that a truth commission, '…rather than being devoid of justice, is, in fact, a model of justice'.[85]

6.4 Part Three: Truth Commissions and 'Truth-Telling'

Broader 'Truths'

> *Patterns, trends, tendencies, and the big picture are often the pieces most missing from the history of transitional societies.* [86]

Supporters of truth commissions also claim they are better placed to achieve truth-recovery and are, in this respect, superior to any court or tribunal. 'The appeal of the model is its ability to offer a broader historical perspective, rather than mere judgments in isolated cases'.[87] Commissions target a wider range of human rights violations than the narrow set that may constitute international crimes.[88] For instance, they may expose acts of institutional violence, violations of social and economic rights, systemic discrimination, and other misdeeds perpetrated by the state or by groups.[89] Further, unlike a verdict, the final report of a commission does not

---

[84] Charles S. Maier, 'Doing History, Doing Justice: The Narrative of the Historian and of the Truth Commission' in Rotberg and Thompson, above n 30, 269.

[85] Howse and Llewellyn, above n 20, 371.

[86] Audrey Chapman and Patrick Ball, 'The Truth of Truth Commissions: Comparative Lessons from Haiti, South Africa, and Guatemala' (2001) 23 *Human Rights Quarterly* 1, 41.

[87] Teitel, 'Transitional Justice Genealogy', above n 13, 78; According to Ball and Chapman, truth commissions are far better suited to pursue 'macro-truth', the assessment of contexts, causes, and patterns of human rights violations, than 'micro-truth' dealing with the specifics of particular events, cases, and people. Ibid 41.

[88] Jens Iverson, 'Transitional Justice, *Jus Post Bellum,* and International Criminal Law: Differentiating the Usages, History and Dynamics' (2013) 7 *International Journal of Transitional Justice* 413, 414.

[89] As discussed above, the responsibility of the state and 'social truths' of past crimes are disregarded by criminal courts. See Chapman and Ball, above n 86.

represent a 'final point' that can be reduced to the sort of 'forensic' truths established by ICJ. Most significantly, as investigative bodies, truth commissions can delve more fully into the past and establish the broader context of conflict. For example, one of the SATRC's goals was to establish 'as complete a picture as possible of the causes, nature and extent of the gross violations of human rights…'.[90]

Akin to South Africa's apartheid, the political struggle between Zionism and the Palestinian national movement is ideologically driven and spans decades. Ultimately, 'truth' is a complex and nuanced concept, which requires social context. Understanding the socio-psychological dimensions of the conflict is paramount to meaningful truth-telling. As discussed in Chap. 1, a more complete historical record of 1948, 1967, and the Second Intifada is vital to frame the violations of human rights in the region. No less important are discursive mechanisms that can forge an authoritative bridging narrative around these events. Thus, the idea that the Israeli–Palestinian conflict could be limited to the temporal and personal scope of any criminal inquiry, or the singular actions of a few individuals 'seems to deny the basic reality and character of the conflict'.[91] As Mamdani concludes, writing about the South African context to focus on individualised criminal prosecutions threatens to decontextualise the conflict beyond comprehension.[92] In short, history benefits when viewed through a wider lens.

Quality of 'Truths'?

Nevertheless, some critics impeach the quality and authority of commission findings, claiming they are inferior to prosecutions.[93] Nino suggests that 'truth' 'is much more precise and much more dramatic when done through trial'.[94] Similarly, Roht-Arriaza writes: 'Only trials could provide for the confrontation of evidence and witnesses that would create an unimpeachable factual record'.[95] Arguably, truth commissions might fail to explore key features of historical 'truth', which involve

---

[90] This was set out in the Promotion of National Unity and Reconciliation Act 34 of 1995.

[91] Meyerstein, *'Transitional Justice and Post-conflict Israel/Palestine'*, above n 26, 317.

[92] Mahmood Mamdani, 'A Diminished Truth' in James Wilmot and Linda van de Vijver (eds.) *After the TRC: Reflections on Truth and Reconciliation in South Africa* (Ohio University Press, 2001) 58.

[93] Juan E. Mendez, 'In Defense of Transitional Justice' in, James McAdams, ed. *Transitional Justice and the Rule of law in New Democracies* 1, 16 (arguing that society has more faith in truth produced at trial since courts are stricter than truth commissions in examining evidence).

[94] Carlos Santiago Nino, *Radical Evil on Trial* (Yale University Press, 1996). Mark Osiel also argues that trials are preferable to truth commissions in shaping public memory because they are more dramatic. Mark J. Osiel, 'Why Prosecute? Critics of Punishment for Mass Atrocity' (2000) 22(1) *Human Rights Quarterly* 118, 136.

[95] Roht-Arriaza, above n 2, 3; According to Dixon and Tenove, truth commissions lack the moral authority and technical capability that gives ICJ purchase. Chris Tenove and Peter Dixon, 'International Criminal Justice as a Transnational Field: Rules, Authority and Victims' (2013) 7 *International Journal of Transitional Justice* 393, 407.

the full disclosure of violations and the names of perpetrators.[96] In this view, without judicial powers, and adversarial cross-examination procedures, truth commissions do not '…establish what perpetrators had in mind and [so cannot] refute their "official story"'.[97] Prosecutors may also be unwilling to use a commission's findings because they fail to meet stricter evidentiary standards.[98] Even in cases where commissions compel testimony, they have been criticised for producing narrative, which does not delve deeply enough into 'truth'.[99]

Admittedly, legal proceedings are superior to truth commissions in determining the guilt or innocence of particular individuals.[100] Nevertheless, as discussed in the previous chapter, it is doubtful they reflect a complete account of mass-atrocity or are uniquely placed to establish an authoritative record. Indeed, truth commission reports have implicated high reaches of state authority in systematic violations in numerous political contexts. The SATRC produced a five-volume report that established an official record of the experiences of white and black South Africans from 1960 until 1990.[101] In Chile and El Salvador, the TRC reports were published and widely disseminated.[102] Thus, truth commissions are no less a legitimate forum of accountability than trials regarding contested events.[103] Truth commissions may also be just as effective at theatricalising history.[104] The SATRC's victims'hearings, for example, were broadcast throughout the media and watched by millions of viewers.[105]

Finally, there is no guarantee that stricter procedural standards improve truth-finding. Rather, fuller documentation and abundant witnesses could make truth commissions sharper tools of historical investigation.[106] Arguably, '…in the wake of

---

[96] Osiel, above 94, 136.

[97] Ibid.

[98] Onur Bakiner, 'Truth Commission Impact: An Assessment of How Commissions Influence Politics and Society'. (2014) 8 *International Journal of Transitional Justice* 6, 25.

[99] Regarding the SATRC, Hayner writes: 'Unfortunately, the commission did not often use the strong powers that it had at its disposal, and was sometimes criticized for holding the mission of reconciliation above that of finding the truth' Hayner, *Unspeakable Truths*, above n 5, 42.

[100] David A Crocker, 'Reckoning with Past Wrongs: A Normative Framework' (March 1999) 13(1) *Ethics and International Affairs* 43, 51 ('Reckoning with Past Wrong').

[101] Truth and Reconciliation Commission of South Africa Report (1999) ('SATRC Report').

[102] In El Salvador, a survey showed widespread acceptance of that truth commission's findings. Priscilla Hayner, 'Fifteen Truth Commissions—1974 to 1994: A Comparative Study' (1994) 16(4), *Human Rights Quarterly* 597, 628 ('Fifteen Truth Commissions').

[103] Truth commissions share with transitional trials the establishment of a 'contested national history'. Miller, above n 27, 297; See also Teitel, *Transitional Justice*, above n 64, 84.

[104] Richard Wilson 'The Sizwe will not go away: The Truth and Reconciliation Commission, Human rights and Nation-Building in South Africa' (1996) 55 (2) *African Studies* 1, 20.

[105] The victims' hearings occupied the center stage of the SATRC, leading some critics to disparage it as the 'Kleenex Commission'. Meyerstein, '*Dreaming an Israeli-Palestinian Truth Commission'*, above n 26, 478; 'The televised confrontations between victims and perpetrators before the SATRC, may be as good or better at capturing the public imagination'. Aukerman, above n 66, 74.

[106] Crocker, '*Reckoning with Past Wrongs'*, above n 100, 51.

gross human rights violations, gruesome photographs, flagrant hearsay and perpetrator confessions are essential to developing an accurate picture of the past'.[107] In the Chilean context, 'Official documentation was made available to the commission, including autopsy reports...which, although by and large inconclusive, nevertheless provided useful pieces of information'.[108] Moreover, if they trade amnesty for confession, truth commissions can elicit information from perpetrators that is unlikely to emerge from a criminal trial.[109] Finally, many concerns about the quality of a commission's truth-telling can be addressed in the institutional design phase. Tailoring a truth commission accordingly will be fully explored in the final chapter.

Narrative 'Truths': Revealing as Healing

> *The truth itself can also be understood as a form of reparation. When the silence is broken, and families learn where the bodies are buried...the injury caused by past abuse may begin to be repaired.*[110]

The truth-telling of a commission is also claimed to serve a reparative function. Giving victims an official platform to tell their stories is '...thought to have a powerful healing effect on those who have suffered'.[111] Legal proceedings may allow victims to testify, but they do not constitute a comprehensive mechanism in which a large number of survivors can expose the atrocities they suffered. With trials, 'The strict regulation of testimony and establishing facts...constricts the cathartic potential of such discourse'.[112] It is worth recalling that, despite the increasing role of victims at the ICC, many remain critical of the participation provisions. Pena and Carayon write: 'Trials in a distant town thousands of miles away will have little relevance for victims and affected communities if they are not adequately recognised as a constituency

[107] Aukerman, above n 66, 74.

[108] 'The available documentation was usually abundant and reliable...The commission also heard the testimony of retired military, police, and former secret police personnel' Zalaquett, above n 59, 1434.

[109] 'The primary sources of information concerning those infamies, the perpetrators themselves', notes the late South African Constitutional Court Justice John Didcott, 'would hardly be willing to divulge it voluntarily, honestly, and candidly without the protection of exemptions from liability' cited in Aukerman, above n 66, 74.

[110] Ibid, 79.

[111] Tepperman, above n 49, 130; According to Herman: 'Victims make meaning and sense out of their experiences through narration, and under certain circumstances, storytelling contributes to psychological healing after trauma'. Judith Herman, *Trauma and Recovery: The Aftermath of Violence--From Domestic Abuse to Political Terror* (Basic Books, 1997).

[112] Flory, above n 72, 26.

whose interests are at the heart of the justice process'.[113] As discussed in Chap. 5, the ICC may not sufficiently address the needs of victims.[114]

In this light, many academics champion the idea that 'narrative or personal' truths are vital to the 'memory-work' undertaken by truth commissions.[115] Indeed, by validating testimony, truth commissions can support the credibility of trauma by helping to restore dignity to survivors.[116] For example, Ghana's National Reconciliation Commission provided many victims with '…the first formal occasion and a safe forum to narrate their experiences without any fear of reprisals or worry about high legal fees'.[117] In South Africa, 'narrative truths' were central to the SATRC, as evidenced by the final report[118] and the public hearings (particularly of the Human Rights Violations Committee).[119] The Chilean TRC also invoked the therapeutic value of testimony.[120] In sum, truth commissions prioritise victim-centred 'truths' and offer greater potential for personal catharsis than trials.

Truth Vs. Reconciliation: Catharsis or Can of Worms?

> *While the TRC may have helped to create some base level of trust within the country as a whole, our findings suggest this was not the case on the individual level….*[121]

---

[113] Pena and Carayon find that while there is great potential, the ICC's victim participation provisions to date have not adequately provided for the needs of victims. See Mariana Pena and Gaelle Carayon 'Is the ICC Making the Most of Victim Participation?' (2013) 7 (3) *International Journal of Transitional Justice* 518–535.

[114] For example, the solutions proposed by the ICC to address victim participation, collective applications, common legal representatives, and registration—all risk minimising any potential recognition that participation might afford. For a review of the challenges faced by the ICC vis-á-victim participation, see Carla Ferstman, *Report: The Participation of Victims in International Criminal Court Proceedings: A Review of the Practice and Consideration of Options for the Future* (Redress Trust, 2012); Christine Van den Wyngaert, 'Victims before International Criminal Courts: Some Views and Concerns of an ICC Trial Judge,' *Case Western Reserve Journal of International Law* 44 (2011): 475–496.

[115] Chapman and Ball, above n 86, 12; Peled and Rouhana, above n 38, 328; See also Brahm, above n 54, 20.

[116] Chapman and Ball, above n 86, 3; See also Crocker, *'Reckoning with Past Wrongs',* above n 100, 52.

[117] Ame and Alidu claim that Ghana's NRC offered victims the opportunity to be acknowledged and their stories validated. Ame and Alidu, above n 28, 258–9.

[118] In its final report, the SATRC acknowledged the 'healing potential of storytelling, of revealing the truth before a respectful audience and to an official body' *SATRC Report*, above n 101, 351.

[119] 'Approximately two thousand witnesses and victims appeared before the SATRC in public hearings. Another nineteen thousand witnesses and victims provided the commission with testimony'. See Hayner, *Unspeakable Truths,* above n 5, 42; See also Chapman and Ball, above n 86, 12.

[120] See Report of the Chilean National Commission on Truth and Reconciliation (Volume 1), 16–17 cited in Chapman and Ball, above n 86, 12.

[121] Brandon Hamber, Dineo Nageng and Gabriel O'Malley 'Telling It Like It Is... Understanding the Truth and Reconciliation Commission from the Perspective of Survivors' (2000) 26 *Psychology in Society* 18–42.

Many refute the cathartic value of truth commissions.[122] Minow claims that truth commissions are ultimately utilitarian in nature.[123] That is, commissions 'treat survivors and their recovery as a means toward a better society rather than as persons with dignity and entitlements to justice'.[124] In the South African context, many victims felt that the 'truths' elicited from the SATRC were only partial and did not satisfy their expectations.[125] Indeed, the Trauma Centre for Victims of Violence and Torture in Cape Town estimated that more than half of the victims it worked with experienced serious psychological problems after testifying or regretted their participation in the hearings.[126] Typically, truth commissions provide victims with only a few minutes to tell their stories with no follow-up support.[127] Under such conditions, there is contradictory anecdotal evidence about 'truth' re-igniting anger and causing post-traumatic stress.[128] In this light, '[t]here is room for skepticism about the relationship between the acknowledgment of the past and victim empowerment'.[129]

Nevertheless, a commission's psychological benefits cannot be discounted. For example, the ability to speak out in front of a respectful institutional body was viewed overall in South Africa as an effective way to begin the process of personal healing and reconciliation.[130] No less true is the fact that repressing memory can have more adverse psychological consequences, as evidenced by the Latin American experience with political disappearances.[131] It is also worth recalling that healing is not a simple or objective process that may be engineered overnight by any single intervention.[132] Above all else, the 'truth' elicited from commissions provides survi-

---

[122] For a critique of the cathartic argument used to promote the creation of truth commissions see Shaw, above n 83; See also Hayner, *Unspeakable Truths,* above n 5, 133–153.

[123] Minow, above n 20, 80.

[124] Ibid.

[125] Hamber's South African research found that although many victims appreciated the need to pursue reconciliation for the greater good, they felt the impunity afforded to perpetrators was unfair to them at a personal level. Brandon Hamber, *Transforming Societies After Political Violence: Truth, Reconciliation, and Mental Health* (Springer, 2009) ('Transforming Societies').

[126] See Jonathan Doak, 'The Therapeutic Dimension of Transitional Justice: Emotional Repair and Victim Satisfaction in International Trials and Truth Commissions' (2011) 11 *International Criminal Law Review* 263. 278.

[127] Brandon Hamber, *The Burdens of Truth: An Evaluation of the Psychological Support Services and Initiatives Undertaken by the South African Truth and Reconciliation Commission* (Centre for the Study of Violence and Reconciliation, 1999) ('The Burdens of Truth'); Avruch, above n 55, 37.

[128] As the SATRC process demonstrated, while some victims felt profoundly empowered by telling their stories, others felt angrier and faced post-traumatic stress. Brahm, above n 54, 22.

[129] Yael Tamir quoted in *Harvard Law School Paper*, above n 4.

[130] According to interviews conducted by South Africa's Centre for the Study of Violence and Reconciliation, the process of unleashing the stories, revealing the hidden traumas, and covering latent tensions is largely considered a positive contribution by some 25 organisations. Hamber, *The Burdens of Truth*, above n 127.

[131] Herman, above n 111.

[132] Hamber, 'Transforming Societies', above n 125.

vors with some official acknowledgement of the past. Arguably, the value of truth commissions might be described more accurately as *acknowledging the truth* rather than seeking the truth.[133] This is particularly important in the Israeli–Palestinian context, where victims on both the sides seek institutional acknowledgement of their national suffering.

Conclusion

By investigating systemic abuse, identifying victims, establishing historical records, and educating the public on its work, a truth commission can meaningfully pursue the truth around past violations. Ultimately, the broader inquisitorial mode of truth commissions seems well placed to recover truth in the Israeli–Palestinian setting. This is because the drama of international trials and punishment is not the only authoritative method of setting the record straight. It is also because Israeli and Palestinian victims require a measure of personal catharsis and collective acknowledgement beyond what the ICC or trials can realistically provide at this stage.

6.5 Part Four: Truth Commissions and 'Reconciliation'

Truth commissions can play a crucial role in forging reconciliation, fostering mutual understanding and providing assistance to victims.[134]

National Reconciliation

Unlike criminal trials, which are adversarial, past-orientated and can be divisive,[135] truth commissions prioritise nation-building and social catharsis.[136] Truth commissions created since the SATRC have typically included the term 'reconciliation' in their titles and mandates to reflect this. Examples include Yugoslavia's Truth and Reconciliation Commission, the Truth and Reconciliation Commission in Sierra Leone, and the Ghanaian National Reconciliation Commission (NRC). Guided by

133 Hayner, '*Fifteen Truth Commissions*' above n 102.

134 Van Zyl, above n 37, 663.

135 Erin Daly, 'Transformative Justice: Charting a Path to Reconciliation' (2001–2) 12(1 & 2) *International Legal Perspectives* 73, 105; See Minow, above n 20, 26 (noting that '[r]econciliation is not the goal of criminal trials except in the most abstract sense').

136 'They are victim-centred approaches to resolving conflict…This offers the potential of re-uniting and strengthening the nation and offer a better alternative…than criminal prosecution could ever offer any of the parties involved'. Ame and Alidu, above n 28, 263.

principles of restorative justice, truth commissions aim to contribute to national reconciliation through truth-telling, broad local involvement in their processes and by fostering empathy between former rivals. Victims have an opportunity to confront and potentially reconcile with perpetrators.[137] Drawing on the experience of Ghana, '...the opportunity created by the establishment of the NRC opened the vent to healing the trauma and pains inflicted upon the Ghanaian people and offered the prospect for national reconciliation'.[138] In many national contexts, victim testimony has been crucial to national reconciliation efforts.[139]

From this standpoint, a truth commission has something meaningful to offer Israelis and Palestinian 'as a mechanism through which the two populaces can begin to explore their troubled past, helping them to understand the grievances that divide them and the sufferings that unite them'.[140] As concluded in Chap. 3, durable peacemaking requires promoting social and cultural shifts to transform conflict narrative. This means redefining the antagonistic belief systems that guided violence and recreating a more positive system of relations between the two nations (Chap. 4).[141] Ultimately, if changing an ethos of conflict is central to peacebuilding, then a victim-centred truth commission could be vital for Israelis and Palestinians. For wider society in the region, the details uncovered may provide a broader education for the public that aids reconciliation efforts.[142]

Notably, various commissions have interpreted reconciliation differently. In South Africa, it was vested with Christian notions of forgiveness. In Chile, it meant simply non-violent coexistence between former enemies.[143] The goals of reconciliation might be realised in terms of minimum acknowledgement,[144] deterrence by discrediting perpetrators,[145] advancing democracy,[146] or through a commitment to

---

[137] Flory, above n 72, 26.

[138] Ame and Alidu, above n 28, 263.

[139] Doak, above n 126, 290.

[140] Meyerstein, '*Dreaming an Israeli-Palestinian Truth Commission*', above n 26, 460; See also '*Transitional Justice and Post-conflict Israel/Palestine*', above n 26; Weiner, above n 26, 125.

[141] Herbert C. Kelman, 'The Role of National Identity in Conflict Resolution: Experiences from Israeli-Palestinian Problem-Solving Workshops', in Richard D. Ashmore, Lee J. Jussim and David Wilder (eds) *Social Identity, Intergroup Conflict, and Conflict Reduction* (Oxford University Press, 2001); Jacob Shamir and Khalil Shikaki, 'Determinants of Reconciliation and Compromise Among Israelis and Palestinians' (2002) 39 *Journal of Peace Research* 185, 186–187.

[142] Abrams and Hayner, above n 75.

[143] Cohen and Dudai, above n 3, 46.

[144] Timothy Ash, *True Confessions* (The New York Review of Books, 1997) 44, 33–38; Abrams and Hayner, above n 75.

[145] Mike Kaye, 'The Role of Truth Commissions in the Search for Justice, Reconciliation and Democratisation: The Salvadorean and Honduran Cases'. (1997) 29 *Journal of Latin American Studies* 693–716.

[146] Political reconciliation in Philpott's view manifests as democratic state building in societies that are not established democracies. Daniel Philpott. *Just and Unjust Peace: An Ethic of Political Reconciliation* (Oxford University Press, 2012).

human rights.[147] In this light, identifying the nature of the reconciliation sought in the Israeli–Palestinian context is fundamental.

Beyond Forgiveness and Repentance

Although truth commissions can contribute to reconciliation at the collective level, many critics challenge their fitness for interpersonal healing.[148] For example, based on empirical data, Chapman questions the efficacy of the SATRC's approach to forgiveness and healing, and its capacity to promote thicker notions of reconciliation.[149] In the Chilean case, one study stresses 'that neither victims…nor the general population believe that forgiveness can [even] be achieved'.[150] Critics of the SATRC suggest that its strong language of forgiveness put pressure on some victims and forced reconciliation that was not genuine and even psychologically hurtful.[151] Seeking to turn perpetrators into 'repentant sinners' is no less fraught. In practice, genuine acceptance of guilt or responsibility was not widespread in the SATRC hearings.[152]

Accordingly, as concluded in Chap. 3, interpersonal healing should be distinguished from reconciliation in a larger political and social context.[153] Fundamentally, the SATRC reflects the danger of conflating the individual with the collective, the personal with the political, and therapeutic change with more pragmatic reconcili-

[147] Abrams and Hayner, above n 75.

[148] Critics, including members of the religious community, also questioned the appropriateness of a truth commission attempting to promote forgiveness between victims and perpetrators. Audrey Chapman and Bernard Spong, *Religion and reconciliation in South Africa: Voices of religious leaders* (Templeton Foundation Press, 2003).

[149] Chapman analyses transcripts of the SATRC human rights violation hearings and amnesty hearings with participants conducted as part of the project. This data show the limitations of the SATRC in promoting forgiveness and reconciliation in a meaningful way. Audrey Chapman, 'Truth Commissions and Intergroup Forgiveness: The Case for the South African Truth and Reconciliation Commission' (2007) 13(1) *Peace and Conflict: Journal of Peace Psychology* 51, 69.

[150] Manual Cárdenas et al., 'How Transitional Justice Processes and Official Apologies Influence Reconciliation: The Case of the Chilean "Truth and Reconciliation" and "Political Imprisonment and Torture"'. (2015) 26 *Journal of Community and Applied Social Psychology* 515, 530.

[151] According to Baker: 'Victims faced with moral pressure [to forgive] by the TRC were further victimized'. Judith Baker, 'Truth Commissions' (2001) 51 (3) *University of Toronto Law Journal* 309, 314.

[152] This claim is based on participant observation and recorded confessions. Adam and Moodley, above n 14, 128–129; 'At the amnesty hearings perpetrators were reluctant to acknowledge their wrongdoing or to offer meaningful apologies, expressions of regret, or some form of compensation to those who had suffered'. Chapman, above n 149, 69.

[153] As Derrida argues, 'a distinction is necessary between forgiveness and repentance and the TRC process functioning as a political strategy or a psychotherapeutic economy'. Jacques Derrida, 'On Forgiveness' in Mark Dooley and Michael Hughes (English translation) *On Cosmopolitanism and Forgiveness* (Routledge, 2001) 25, 41–43.

ation.[154] The reality is that, in the Israeli–Palestinian context, even though some individuals may wish to forgive the perpetrator, the need to secure communal political claims might render forgiveness impossible. More importantly, since it is usually agents of the Israeli state or PA/Hamas who perpetrate crimes in their name, forgiveness at an individual level may leave macro national wounds unhealed. In sum: 'Fuzzy notions of reconciliation, healing and forgiveness resonate more with normative sermons than with social reality'.[155] From this standpoint, as will be discussed in the final chapter, any Israeli–Palestinian truth commission could avoid framing reconciliation within religious notions of interpersonal healing.

Empathy as Reconciliation

> *Empathy for the enemy, before, during, or after the violence of war is an essential ingredient to the healing of enmity. To empathise with enemies is to weaken one's readiness to kill them.* (Donald Shriver[156])

As examined in Chap. 4, it is important to draw on a model of grassroots reconciliation that focuses more modestly on fostering empathy between Israelis and Palestinians. 'Empathy' may be defined as an 'other' oriented emotional response elicited by and congruent with the perceived welfare of someone else.[157] 'Empathy is the ability to understand another's needs and fears. Empathic emotions include sympathy, compassion, soft heartedness…and tenderness'.[158] In short, empathy leads to the development of an understanding of the 'other'. Such a process enables the bridging of psychological obstacles that divide parties and nations.[159] As discussed in Chaps. 1 and 3, this is critical to resolving the Israeli–Palestinian conflict. One important method of encouraging such 'bridging and cognitive development'

[154] See Andre Du Toit, 'The moral foundations of the South African TRC: Truth as acknowledgment and justice as recognition' in Rotberg and Thompson, above n 30, 122–140.

[155] 'The Politics of Reconciliation and Justice' in Adam and Moodley, above n 14, 136.

[156] Shriver, above n 33, 125.

[157] C. Daniel Batson, Nadia Ahmad, David A. Lishner, and Jo-Ann Tsang, 'Empathy and Altruism' in Charles R. Snyder and Shane J. Lopez, *Handbook of Positive Psychology* (Oxford University Press, 2002) 487.

[158] Ibid.

[159] Daniel Bar-Tal, 'From Intractable Conflict through Conflict Resolution to Reconciliation: Psychological Analysis' (June 2000) 21(2) *Political Psychology* 351; See also John Paul Lederach, *Conflict Transformation* Conflict Information Consortium, University of Colorado. http://www.beyondintractability.org/essay/transformation; Herbert Kelman, 'The Interdependence of Israeli and Palestinian National Identities: The Role of the other in Existential Conflicts' (1999) 55(3) *Journal of Social Issues* 581.

is the use of 'story-telling' as it may create a fresh perspective on conflict and the 'other'.[160]

Arguably, truth commissions are an important vehicle for this type of reconciliation through empathy-building. Murphy demonstrates how truth commissions contribute to political reconciliation through respect for moral agency and humanisation.[161] She identifies three capacities exercised by 'moral agents in their interactions with others': recognising the demands made by others and their normative authority to make such demands, empathising with others, and being motivated by the demands of others and responding to the emotional address of others.[162] By providing victims with a platform to tell their stories of suffering, testimony can 'take people out of their comfort zone…'.[163] It requires both the sides to view their actions '..from the outside, from the other side's perspective'.[164] The African word 'Ubuntu' implying both 'compassion' and 'humanity' was the concept invoked by the SATRC to capture this kind of phenomenon.[165]

Thus, a truth commission could be significant in fostering empathy between Israelis and Palestinians, which is a central component of reconciliation. As discussed in Chap. 4, a crucial reason for the collapse of Oslo was the failure of public education, on both the sides, to 'humanise the enemy' and to create an awareness of the historical issues. This does not suggest national hugs, tears, or even national catharsis. It simply means that reconciliation involves some measure of perception change or social transformation, whether in the victim, the perpetrator, or both. This is something a truth commission model could offer Israelis and Palestinians.

---

[160] Daniel Bar On and Fatima Kassem, 'Storytelling as a way to work through Intractable Conflict' (2004) 60 *Journal of Social Issues* 289; Jeff Corntassel, Chaw-win-is, and T'lakwadzi 'Indigenous storytelling, truth-telling and community approaches to reconciliation', (2009) 35(1) *English Studies in Canada* 137–159.

[161] Colleen Murphy, *A Moral Theory of Political Reconciliation* (Cambridge University Press, 2012) 48.

[162] Ibid; See also David Shoemaker, 'Moral Address, Moral Responsibility, and the Boundaries of the Moral Community', (2007) 118 *Ethics* 70–108.

[163] Mark Drumbl provides an alternative metaphor: 'Individuals must peel off the layers of their own prejudice and involvement'. Mark Drumbl, 'Sclerosis: Retributive Justice and the Rwandan Genocide' (2000) 2 *Punishment and Society* 288, 295.

[164] Daly, above n 135, 86.

[165] In his judgement against the death penalty, Justice Langa assigned special weight to 'Ubuntu' as representing a culture that emphasises communality and interdependence, and recognises the person's status as a human being entitled to unconditional respect, dignity, value, and acceptance. CCT 3/94 S. v. Makwanyane and Another, 1995 (3) SALR 391, 480–81 (CC) quoted in Gross, above n 1.

Local Involvement and Institutional Reform

Truth commissions may also facilitate reconciliation through a structure that maximises communal involvement and through other practical measures, such as its recommendations. Unlike a criminal trial, which is largely limited to a verdict of individual guilt or innocence, commissions boast a broader palette of reconciliatory gestures that include recommendations, reparations, and political reform.[166] For example, the final report of the SATRC was a five-volume document that made far-ranging recommendations for the future, including reparations for all the victims identified.[167] As concluded in Chap. 4, reconciliation between Israelis and Palestinians could usefully involve concrete actions and restorative practices, like revisiting the history of the conflict, expressing an apology and symbolic gestures.[168]

By creating the conditions for institutional reform, truth commissions can also bridge the gap between 'citizenry and state', and ultimately provide ways in which the population could reconcile with official institutions.[169] For example, in the wake of the SATRC, the South African Defense Force and the South African police, both of which had a long history of abuse against black South Africans, underwent major reform.[170] In El Salvador and Chile, truth commission investigations were able to bolster reforms related to the judiciary, military training, and governmental institutions.[171] As discussed above, because Israeli–Palestinian violence is more institutional than interpersonal, truth commissions would be better equipped to effect reconciliation in this context.

What is more, truth commissions reach a broader group of citizens than trials.[172] Much of the abuse in the Israeli–Palestinian conflict is perpetrated, supported, and maintained by most of the population in some way. Thus, for any social transformation to occur, reconciliation must involve not just the formal perpetrators and victims but also the silent majority.[173] This could be extremely beneficial in the Israeli–Palestinian context, which involves a diverse and broad set of actors beyond a few high-level perpetrators.

---

[166] The practices may vary widely, including therapy for victims, apology or acceptance of responsibility, community service, what Braithwaite calls 're-integrative shaming' quoted in Howse and Llewellyn, above n 20, 375.

[167] Tepperman, above n 49, 134.

[168] Howse and Llewellyn, above n 20, 375.

[169] Miller, above n 27, 297.

[170] See Vanessa Johnstone, 'UET apologises for role in Bika's death: Department begins reconciliation process', *Cape Argus* 11 (June 6, 2001) quoted in Daly, above n 135, 86.

[171] Brahm, above n 54, 28.

[172] Richard Goldstone, 'Justice as a Tool for Peace-Making: Truth Commissions and International Criminal Tribunals' (1996) 28 *New York University Journal of International Law and Politics* 485–503.

[173] The involvement of the community is also important in the transitional process, as the transformation by definition involves the rebuilding of community. Howse and Llewellyn, above n 20, 380.

Reconciling the Past: 'Narrowing the Lies'

> *...Social truth signifies the dialogic process of sharing experiences with the aim of transcending the divisions of the past...It is here where truth borders reconciliation.*[174]

Truth commissions have the potential to begin a common moral conversation about the past. 'Reconciliation', according to Kelman, 'does not require writing a joint consensual history, but it does require admitting the other's truth into one's own narrative'.[175] In this light, truth commissions are said to inform social debate,[176] and in so doing improve social relations between former rivals. For instance, the 'very presence' of the SATRC 'provided a tangible set of reference points to which people were forced to respond'.[177] The SATRC was extremely effective in publicising the plight of victims and past atrocities.[178] Ignatieff has famously written that commissions can only 'reduce the number of lies that can be circulated unchallenged in public discourse'.[179] Individual testimonies '...serve as a basis for collective memory for events which were previously erased from the official national memory'.[180] Their records establish mainstream acceptance of legal violations, even if the origins and causes of the abuse remain disputed.

In the Israeli–Palestinian context, it seems clear that reconciliation is not possible so long as the past remains so polarised and disputed (Chap. 1). Whilst human rights abuses are ignored, justified, or denied, there is no way to build interpersonal trust between the nations. At the very least, the truth commission model could offer Israelis and Palestinians the ability to create a massive authoritative written, audio, and video record of abuses that helps to reconcile the past. The existence of this record does not necessarily mean that one joint consensual history could be achieved,

---

[174] Susanne Buckey-Zistel, 'Transitional Justice in Divided societies—Potentials and Limits' (September 2009) Paper presented at the 5th European Consortium for Political Research General Conference, Potsdam Universität 14.

[175] Herbert Kelman, 'Reconciliation as Identity change: A social-psychological perspective' in Yaacov (ed) Bar-Siman-Tov, *From Conflict Resolution to Reconciliation* (Oxford University Press, 2004).

[176] Mahmood Mamdami, 'Truth and Reconciliation Commission Public Discussion: Transforming Society Through Reconciliation: Myth or Reality?' cited in Daly, above n 135, 91.

[177] Jennifer Balint, 'Law's Constitutive Possibilities: Reconstruction and Reconciliation in the Wake of Genocide and State Crime' in Emilios Christodoloudidis and Scott Veitch, (eds.) *Lethe's Law: Justice, Law and Ethics in Reconciliation* (Hart Publishing, 2001) 143.

[178] The media event of the TRC captured the attention of all South Africans and stimulated public debate about past human rights violations for more than 2 years. Only a few societies have been able to achieve such an intensive public reckoning with their own recent past during the immediate post-authoritarian era. Gunnar Theissen, 'Common Past, Divided Truth: The Truth and Reconciliation Commission in South African Public Opinion', Paper presented at the Workshop on Legal Institutions and Collective Memories International Institute for the Sociology of Law (IISL) Oñati, Spain, 22–24 September 1999, 51.

[179] Michael Ignatieff, 'Articles of Faith' 5 (1996), *Index on Censorship* 113.

[180] Michael Humphrey, 'From Terror to Trauma. Commissioning Truth for National Reconciliation' (2000) 6 (1) *Social Identities* 7–27.

but it does mean starting a moral conversation. 'As long as one side's freedom fighter or revolutionary is regarded as the other side's terrorist, it is unlikely that the stories could ever be reconciled. However, the record could be allowed to speak for itself'.[181] Indeed, the challenge in the Middle-East is to find ways in which truth recovery could tackle not just the forensic details of the violations but also the broad societal justifications afforded to them.[182] In sum, if the SATRC 'narrowed the range of permissible lies' about apartheid, an Israeli–Palestinian truth commission might help the two nations narrow the range of mythology and rhetoric framing their legacies of abuse (Chap. 2).[183]

Reconciliation as a 'Process'

Finally, as discussed in Chap. 3, reconciliation need not be an ambitious set of transformative outcomes, but rather could constitute nation-building processes that foster change over time.[184] For South Africa, Ndebele notes: '[t]he TRC hearings were not an event, but a process that will continue in the future…'.[185] Viewed in this way, a truth commission does no more than lay the ground-work and/or creates the conditions for reconciliation to occur.[186] For example, various reconciliation programs were devised and implemented by South African civil society as a direct result of the SATRC.[187] Ultimately, it is too much to expect major collective shifts following

[181] Wing, above n 27,154.

[182] Ron Dudai, 'Does Any of this Matter?' in David Downes, Rock, Paul, Chinkin, Christine and Gearty, Conor (eds), *Crime, Social Control and Human Rights: From moral panics to states of denial - Essays in honour of Stanley Cohen* (Willan Publishing, 2007) 344.

[183] Ibid.

[184] 'Our research suggests that national reconciliation does not automatically transform communities, but that does not mean the value of national processes (which also include reparation strategies for victims or even trials) should be underestimated. They can help to create conditions conducive to better relationships to create a common vision for the future, and to build social, intergroup, and individual reconciliation over the long-term'. Brandon Hamber and Grainne Kelly 'Beyond Coexistence: Towards a Working Definition of Reconciliation' in Joanna R (ed) Quinn, *Reconciliation (S) Transitional Justice in Postconflict Societies* (McGill-Queen's University Press, 2009), 302.

[185] Professor Ndebele of University of Cape Town quoted in Daly, above n 135, 91.

[186] Ibid.

[187] For example, in June 2001, the health sciences faculty of the University of Cape Town launched a 6-month 'reconciliation programme' that 'will involve introspection, examination of acts of discrimination or oppression against black students, during the university's long history'. This programme was launched as a direct response to the SATRC. Vanessa Johnstone, 'UCT apologises for role in Bika's death: Department begins reconciliation process', *Cape Argus* 11 (June 6, 2001) in Ibid.

intractable conflict, but '…[t]ruth commissions can set the stage and initiate changing discourses about a divisive past, if perhaps only in the next generation'.[188]

Conclusion

Overall, truth commissions involve local communities in a reconciliation process, which can help build the bridge to a post-conflict future. Despite their shortcomings, they do allow victims to recreate trauma in an inclusive public forum. Most importantly, a truth commission could foster empathy between Israelis and Palestinians and enable the idea of shared suffering to become part of each nation's collective memory. As concluded in Chap. 5, individual retributive justice is less suited to such processes of social reconstruction. In this light, a truth commission may provide the parties with a platform for reconciliation, which could mark the beginning of a shared moral conversation about the past.

6.6 Part Five: Truth Commission Limitations

Truth commissions are no magic bullets. In fact, some scholars persuasively challenge their capacity to deliver.[189] For all their hype and normative claims, many commissions are hampered by political inaction, underfunding, and low bureaucratic capacity. In Guatemala, for example, despite the president's initial support, the commission's report was not implemented, and its recommendations were largely ignored after a regime change.[190] Similarly, the government of East Timor did not publicise its commission's final report for fear of post-conflict tensions.[191] Only a comparatively small number of commissions established between 1974 and 2009 actually supported victims' demands for acknowledgement and

[188] Adam and Moodley, 'Chapter Seven: The Politics of Reconciliation and Justice' in Adam and Moodley, above n 14,136.

[189] See Amy Gutmann and Dennis Thompson, 'The Moral Foundations of Truth Commissions' in Rotberg and Thompson, above n 30, 22; Richard Wilson, 'Challenging Restorative Justice' (2004) 2(7) *Human Rights Dialogue*, 15, 15; Miller, above n 27, 297.

[190] Henry J Steiner, 'Introduction' in *Harvard Law School Paper*, above n 4, 7.

[191] Ultimately, the Final report was barely disseminated amongst the public. The 'truth', it was feared, would poor oil into open wounds. Monika, Schlicher 'Geschichte eines Scheiterns. Strafverfolgung und Versöhnung in Osttimor' (2007) (43) (1–2) *Der Überblick*, 39–41 quoted in Susanne, Buckley-Zistel 'Transitional Justice in Divided Societies—Potentials and Limits (September 2009).

compensation.[192] Such failures also beset the 'successful' SATRC. There were almost no follow-up prosecutions,[193] and paltry reparations were awarded to victims.[194]

Further, whilst commissions hold great intuitive appeal for their supporters, 'truth', 'justice', and 'reconciliation', for all their allure, are fundamentally ethereal and relative concepts difficult to assess empirically, with few attempting to do so.[195] 'Defining success, even in a single geographical context, is a complicated process. It is extremely difficult to evaluate the overall effectiveness...given the differing perspectives of victims and perpetrators'.[196] Arguably, no overwhelming evidence exists to demonstrate that commissions actually work, and '...much is driven by normative conviction'.[197] Accordingly, one must acknowledge the practical difficulty of crafting collective narrative.[198] There is valid concern that truth commissions are unable to resolve deeply contested pasts.[199]

To be fair however, such criticisms are also true of other modalities of transitional justice such as ICJ. As discussed in Chap. 5, prosecutions also face bureaucratic and procedural impediments, and they are no less contingent on political will and normative claims. Might one proclaim the deterrent value of an ICC indictment with any greater scientific certainty? Are claims about the beneficial effects of ICJ any less philosophical and theoretical in nature? Overall, it might be conceded that: 'the tension between justice and reconciliation and revenge, prosecution and amnesty, is grounded as much in principled debate, as in a tug of war between deep emotions, unresolved memories and uncertain futures'.[200]

---

[192] Buckey-Zistel, above n 174, 15.

[193] There was a de facto policy of non-prosecution after the life of the SATRC. The government sent a directive not to pursue those involved in the pre-apartheid era. The Prosecutor's Office was only staffed by two policemen. Van Zyl, above n 37, 662.

[194] Implicit in the deal of the SATRC was the promise that victims were to be given reparations. They ended up with one sixth of what the SATRC recommended. The victims received approximately R43 000 (a symbolic once-off payment, far less than the over R120 000 that the SATRC recommended).

[195] 'Specifically, most studies focus on a small biased subsample of cases, rely on anecdotal evidence and normative conviction, and fail to follow the truth commission's legacy beyond its immediate reception'. Brahm, above n 54, 16.

[196] Judy Barsalou, 'Trauma and Transitional Justice in Divided Societies' (United States Institute of Peace Press, 2005).

[197] Brahm, above n 54, 21.

[198] Avruch, above n 55, 38.

[199] 'While truth commissions play an important fact-finding role in national reconciliation processes, current evidence suggests that the ability of truth commissions to put the past to rest by making it a matter of public record is illusory'. See Sharon Lean 'Is Truth Enough? Reparations and Reconciliation in Latin America' in John C. Torpey (ed) *Politics and the Past: On Repairing Historical Injustices* (Littlefield Publishers,2003) 170.

[200] Charles Villa-Vicencio, 'Reconciliation as Political Necessity: Reflections in the wake of Civil and Political Strife' 3 in Joseph Yav Katshung, *The Relationship between the International Criminal Court and Truth Commissions: Some Thoughts on how to build a bridge across retributive and restorative justices*, (Position Paper Centre for Human Rights and Democracy, 2008);

Ultimately, for Israelis and Palestinians, a comprehensive and holistic approach to transitional justice is arguably most relevant to engaging their past. This is not only because there will always be an 'impunity gap' (after seven decades of conflict no mechanism could address all accounts of abuse), but perhaps more importantly, there is moral weight to warring nations leaning on broader notions of justice, truth, and reconciliation in their efforts towards peace.[201] From this standpoint, the success of truth commissions should be measured not by whether truth, justice, and reconciliation have in fact occurred, but by the extent to which they lay the ground-work for these goals to be achieved long-term.

6.7 Conclusion

Israelis and Palestinians could glean valuable theoretical and practical lessons in conflict resolution and transitional justice from prior national experiences of truth commissions. Accordingly, this chapter provides a solid theoretical basis for the institutional design of an IPTEC. The desirability of thicker notions of justice, broader truth-telling, and normative collective change make the model worthy of contemplation. It is precisely because of the wide extension of the conflict throughout each society that relative notions of justice, victim acknowledgement, and national reconciliation are significant.

For Israelis and Palestinians however, whist bilateral negotiations are stalled and the conflict rages, it would seem implausible to implement any such official mechanism at present. This is because Israeli and Palestinian politicians are unlikely to agree to a state sanctioned TRC without first reaching a peace agreement. It is also because neither society seems willing and/or able to embark upon such a formal process in the face of ongoing hostilities. However, this does not mean that any truth-telling mechanism would be unfeasible: the challenge is to find ways to engage with the commission model within the current political realities. In this light, the next two chapters will contemplate the conception and architecture of an unofficial Israeli–Palestinian truth commission spearheaded by civil society.

Meyerstein writes: '…most international lawyers and policymakers have until now settled for well-meaning, but thoroughly unsupported declarations about the power of prosecutions and truth-commissions'. Meyerstein, *'Transitional Justice and Post-conflict Israel/Palestine'*, above n 26, 311.

[201] Justin M Swartz, 'South Africa's Truth and Reconciliation Commission: A Functional Equivalent to Prosecution' (1997) 3 *De Paul Dig International Law* 13, 19.

Chapter 7
Transitional Justice and Civil Society

7.1 Introduction

Civil society has played an important role in every country that has experienced a successful transitional justice endeavour. (Priscilla Hayner[1])

This chapter explores the normative value of civil society to transitional justice and its potential role in the Israeli–Palestinian conflict. There is a growing body of scholarship and practice that gives recognition and a prominent role to grassroot approaches to transitional justice. As will be discussed, a nation's non-state actors are often well placed to devise, guide, and prioritise the goals of truth, justice, and reconciliation. The involvement of civil society in peacemaking through civic representation and consultation is becoming an essential transitional justice strategy. Thus, Sect. 7.2 begins by describing why civil society is enormously valuable and even indispensable to the work of transitional justice, especially during ongoing conflict. Beyond state-centric theory and legalism, it will be submitted that the norms, lessons, and lexicon of transitional justice mechanisms apply equally to civic actors and unofficial projects.

Section 7.3 focuses on precisely how civil society has developed creative and engaging measures to expose the past in several diverse settings, without, and often against, the state. Focusing in particular on unofficial truth initiatives, this part demonstrates how they have been successfully orchestrated in various contexts comparable to the highly politicised Israeli–Palestinian one. As will be illustrated, non-state truth-recovery is an important response to the past and has the potential to mobilise a national response. In cases like the Israeli–Palestinian one, civil society occupies

[1] Priscilla Hayner, 'Responding to a Painful Past: The Role of Civil Society and the International Community' in Mo Bleeker and Jonathon Sisson (eds), 'Dealing with the Past: Critical Issues, Lessons Learned, and Challenges for Future Swiss Policy' (KOFF Series Working Paper, Swisspeace, 2004).

J. Bracka, *Transitional Justice for Israel/Palestine*, Springer Series in Transitional Justice, https://doi.org/10.1007/978-3-030-89435-1_7

a particularly important role given the absence of official transitional justice mechanisms, and the presence of state actors who are unwilling and/or unable to pursue transitional justice agendas.

Ultimately, it is in the hands of local Israeli and Palestinian civic actors to cultivate transitional justice initiatives at present. Thus, Sect. 7.4 outlines the specific landscape of Israeli–Palestinian peacebuilding and the human rights field. Moreover, Sect. 7.5 explores the various factors that obstruct Israeli and Palestinian non-state actors from fully embracing transitional justice. In recent years however, several unilateral and collaborative initiatives have emerged. Section 7.6 outlines their major activities and contends that, despite the challenges, they promote recognition of wrongdoing, reconciliation, and recasting of the historical debate in the region. Ultimately, this chapter argues for sustained support of civic peacebuilding within a framework of long-term conflict transformation and transitional justice. It provides the theoretical and practical foundations for the conception of an IPTEC to be fully explored in the next chapter.

7.2 Part One: Value of Civil Society to Transitional Justice

State-Centric Theory

Traditionally, transitional justice theory is narrowly confined to official truth and justice mechanisms.[2] The field remains heavily influenced by the liberal peace and top-down, state-centric view of conflict resolution,[3] and a narrow focus on 'legalism'.[4] Transitional justice has increasingly been 'institutionalised' into costly official supra-state and 'state-like' structures.[5] Most empirical research on transitional justice thus addresses the formal and legal steps taken by national

[2] See Paul Gready and Simon Robins, 'Rethinking Civil Society and Transitional Justice: Lessons from Social Movements and "New" Civil Society' (2017) 21(7) *The International Journal of Human Rights* 956, 957.

[3] The liberal peace theory, which privileges the notion of pacification through state political and economic liberalisation is embedded in transitional justice. See Roland Paris, 'Peacebuilding and the Limits of Liberal Internationalism' (1997) 22(2) *International Security* 54. See also Paul Gready and Simon Robins, 'From Transitional to Transformative Justice: A New Agenda for Practice' (2014) 8(3) *International Journal of Transitional Justice* 339.

[4] Kieran McEvoy, 'Beyond Legalism: Towards a Thicker Understanding of Transitional Justice' (2007) 34(4) *Journal of Law and Society* 411, 414.

[5] For example, at the level above the state, McEvoy notes the ICTY, ICTR, and ICC. At the national level, we have seen the growth of hybrid tribunals and truth commissions. Ibid 421. See Rachel Kerr, *The International Criminal Tribunal for the Former Yugoslavia: An Exercise in Law, Politics and Diplomacy* (Oxford University Press, 2004); LJ van den Herik, *The Contribution of the Rwanda Tribunal to the Development of International Law* (Brill, 2005) 50.

governments and/or international political institutions.[6] By contrast, little theoretical attention has been paid to non-state mechanisms. Grassroot actors involved in truth, justice, and reconciliation efforts remain 'below the gaze' of the transitional justice mainstream.[7]

Rise of Civil Society

Over recent decades, interest in human rights and democratic norms has spurred the rapid growth of civil society.[8] International judicial interventions (from the ICTY to the ICC) have also signalled that states are no longer the sole transitional justice actors.[9] While civil society is a contested concept,[10] it is generally constituted from: 'All public spheres, separate from the apparatus of the state…which serve as locations of political participation and discursive interaction'.[11] Characterised by a diverse range of actors and groups,[12] civil society can reach down into the local village level and make use of various techniques that combine elements of truth-telling, justice, and reconciliation.[13] In short, 'Two dimensions—national/international, or truth commission/trial—are no longer enough to map the universe of transitional justice efforts'.[14]

Overall, transitional justice practitioners value civil society in formal transitional justice processes. According to the ICTJ, civil society plays a vital role in mobilising public opinion and lobbying decisionmakers, in calling for legislative reform, providing information and support to formal institutions, and working with truth

---

[6] David Backer, 'Civil Society and Transitional Justice: Possibilities, Patterns and Prospects' (2003) 2(3) *Journal of Human Rights* 297, 297.

[7] Kieran McEvoy and Lorna McGregor (eds), *Transitional Justice from Below: Grassroots Activism and the Struggle for Change* (Hart, 2008).

[8] Margaret E Keck and Kathryn Sikkink, *Activists Beyond Borders: Advocacy Networks in International Politics* (Cornell University Press, 1998); Thomas Risse-Kappen, Stephen C Ropp and Kathryn Sikkink (eds), *The Power of Human Rights: International Norms and Domestic Change* (Cambridge University Press, 1999).

[9] Yeliz Budak, 'Dealing with the Past: Transitional Justice, Ongoing Conflict and the Kurdish Issue in Turkey.' (2015) 9(2) *International Journal of Transitional Justice* 219, 222–223.

[10] David Crocker, 'Transitional Justice and International Civil Society: Toward a Normative Framework' (1998) 5(4) *Constellations* 492, 500.

[11] The literature on definitions of civil society is enormous. Seminal recent texts include the Global Civil Society Yearbooks published by the Global Civil Society Programme at the LSE. Quoted in Gready and Robins, 'Rethinking Civil Society', above n 2, 958.

[12] Throughout this chapter, 'civil society' will be used as a conceptual term to refer to a broad spectrum of political and non-political actors, such as grassroots organisations, religious groups, and universities.

[13] Naomi Roht-Arriaza, 'Transitional Justice and Peace Agreements Working Paper' (2005) *Peace Agreements: The Role of Human Rights in Negotiations* 1–21, 5.

[14] Ibid 5.

commissions to disseminate their findings and recommendations.[15] NGOs are often lauded for their ICJ efforts in assisting courts and prosecutions through evidence collection and advocacy. For example, during the Pinochet regime in Chile, there was 'a concerted strategy by activists and victims to document incidents of abuse, to force authorities to recognize arrests…'.[16] In general, civil society has been an effective catalyst of formal transitional justice instruments.[17]

Civil Society and Official Truth Commissions

Civil society has also been described as the 'essential ingredient' in a truth commission.[18] Non-state actors have been able to participate in and improve the process at all stages, from initial debates to the implementation of recommendations.[19] For example in Chile, two local religious organisations[20] collected thousands of judicial transcripts concerning disappearances during the 17-year Pinochet dictatorship. Such records were vital for the investigations of the National Commission for Truth and Reconciliation, which had to complete its work in only 18 months.[21] In Guatemala, the Project for the Recovery of Historical Memory (REHMI)[22] was

[15] International Center for Transitional Justice, *Truth Commissions and NGOs: The Essential Relationship* (2004) 9. For example, South African civil society was fundamental to the creation and work of the SATRC. See also Brandon Hamber, Tlhoki Mofokeng and Graeme Simpson, 'Evaluating the Role and the Function of Civil Society in a Changing South Africa: The Truth and Reconciliation Commission as a Case Study' (Paper presented at The Role of Southern Civil Society Organisations in the Promotion of Peace Seminar, Catholic Institute of International Relations, London, 10 November 1997).

[16] This campaign, particularly the efforts of the *Vicaria de La Solidaridad*, had no discernible judicial effect, but did contribute to shifting public sentiment in favour of political liberalisation and generated a wealth of evidence that was a natural lead-in to Chile's National Commission on Truth and Reconciliation. Jorge Correa Sutil, '"No Victorious Army Has Ever Been Prosecuted …": The Unsettled Story of Transitional Justice in Chile' in A James McAdams (ed), *Transitional Justice and the Rule of Law in New Democracies* (University of Notre Dame Press, 1997).

[17] Gready and Robins, 'Rethinking Civil Society', above n 2, 961; See also Susanne Buckley-Zistel, 'Transitional Justice in Divided Societies – Potentials and Limits' (Paper presented at the fifth European Consortium for Political Research General Conference, Potsdam Universität, 10–12 September 2009), 5.

[18] Priscilla Hayner, *Unspeakable Truths: Transitional Justice and the Challenge of Truth Commissions* (Routledge, 2001) 34.

[19] For example in Argentina: 'We must emphasize the invaluable assistance the commission received from human rights organizations'. Argentine Commission on the Disappeared, *Nunca Más: The Report of the Argentine National Commission on the Disappeared* (Farrar Straus Giroux, 1986) 429; See generally, International Center for Transitional Justice, above n 15.

[20] The ecumenical Comité de Cooperación Para la Paz en Chile (1974–75) and the Roman Catholic Church's Vicaría de la Solidaridad (1976–92).

[21] Crocker, 'Transitional Justice and International Civil Society', above n 10, 505.

[22] The Oficina de Derechos Humanos del Arzobispado (Human Rights Office of the Archbishop of Guatemala) conducted the project called the 'Proyecto de Recuperación de la Memoria Histórica'

exceedingly beneficial to the national Commission for Historical Clarification, (CEH).[23] REMHI made a massive contribution by gaining thousands of testimonies from sectors of the indigenous population to which the CEH might not otherwise have gained access.[24] Generally, civil society has been enormously valuable and even indispensable to the work of truth commissions.

Truth commissions also enjoy a symbiotic relationship with civil society.[25] Many commissions have influenced the ways in which human rights groups and others seek to deal with legacies of the past. Thus, NGOs and victim associations have been at the forefront of the creation of official truth commissions, with NGO involvement often determining their success.[26] In Brazil, during the debate over, and creation of, the National Truth Commission, many universities and social groups set up local and regional committees, with different powers and investigative purposes.[27] In various Brazilian states across the country, they created local 'Memory and Truth Committees' that provided instrumental logistical and grassroot support for Brazil's National Truth Commission.[28] Similarly, in South Africa, bottom-up initiatives that transpired about a decade prior to the end of apartheid were essential for building the legitimacy of the SATRC.[29]

Through advocacy and lobbying efforts, civil society can also influence truth commissions to be more responsive to victims' concerns. For example, in countries where states initially chose not to publish the final report[30] or adopt a reparations program,[31] civic activism led to policy change.[32] In South Africa, NGOs effectively

(Recovery of Historical Memory Project, REMHI). It had the support of more than 70 churches, human rights organisations, and NGOs worldwide.

[23] UN assistance in the mid-1990s contributed to the creation of a *Comisión Nacional de Esclarecimiento Histórica* (Commission for Historical Clarification, CEH).

[24] International Center for Transitional Justice, above n 15, 30.

[25] See ibid. See also Hugo van der Merwe, Polly Dewhirst and Brandon Hamber, 'Non-Governmental Associations and the Truth and Reconciliation Commission: An Impact Assessment' (1999) 26 *Politikon: South African Journal of Political Studies* 55; Louis Bickford, 'Unofficial Truth Projects' (2007) 29 *Human Rights Quarterly* 994, 1002.

[26] International Centre for Transitional Justice, above n 15, 30.

[27] Eduardo González and Howard Varney (eds), *Truth Seeking: Elements of Creating an Effective Truth Commission* (Amnesty Commission of the Ministry of Justice of Brazil, 2013) 10.

[28] Ibid.

[29] Crocker, 'Transitional Justice and International Civil Society', above n 10, 505.

[30] In Nepal, Sri Lanka, and Haiti, it took human rights organisations several years of lobbying to make the government publish their truth commissions' final report. Onur Bakiner, 'Truth Commission Impact: An Assessment of How Commissions Influence Politics and Society' (2014) 8(1) *International Journal of Transitional Justice* 6, 23.

[31] In South Africa, Guatemala, Peru, and Sierra Leone, reluctant governments found themselves pressured into legislating reparations programs. In East Timor, domestic and international groups successfully lobbied for the 2012 National Reparations Programme Bill. Ibid.

[32] Human rights groups were crucial in publishing abridged versions of the final report in Peru, East Timor, and Sierra Leone. Ibid.

pressured parliament to hold the SATRC amnesty hearings in public.[33] To varying degrees, there is evidence that a truth commission's long-term impact is greatly enhanced by civil society mobilisation and participation.[34]

'Transitional Justice from Below': Independent Actors

Civil society has been traditionally relegated to a secondary role in transitional justice, serving only to complement, support, or criticise the work of state institutions.[35] Thus, '[c]ommentators use official mechanisms as the main point of reference, with civil society essentially mimicking or gap-filling…'.[36] For example, valuable evidence collected by civil society is typically consigned to a subsidiary role in most official investigations: it is used to supplement direct testimony, but not actively solicited or made a focal point.[37]

Nevertheless, scholars and practitioners are challenging the assumption that civil society must necessarily play a secondary role. Thicker concepts of transitional justice treat civil society as actors in their own right, who can act as independent providers of transitional justice, not just as conduits or critics of state-led institutions.[38] Backer identifies seven primary roles for civil society in respect of transitional justice efforts: data collection and monitoring; representation and advocacy[39]; collaboration, facilitation, and consultation; service delivery and intervention; acknowledgement and compensation; parallel or substitute authority; and research and education.[40] Gready and Robins use the term 'new civil society' to describe a range of 'counter-publics' which actively contest mainstream social, political, and transitional paradigms.[41] Civil society can constitute an independent site to monitor,

---

[33] Priscilla B Hayner, *Unspeakable Truths: Confronting State Terror and Atrocity* (Routledge, 2002); David K Androff, 'Can Civil Society Reclaim Truth? Results from a Community-Based Truth and Reconciliation Commission' (2012) 6 *The International Journal of Transitional Justice* 296, 299.

[34] Onur Bakiner, *Truth Commissions: Memory, Power, and Legitimacy* (University of Pennsylvania Press, 2016), ch 6.

[35] Ron Dudai, 'Deviant Commemorations: Civil Society and Dealing with the Past in Active Conflicts' (Paper presented at The Potential Role of Transitional Justice in Active Conflicts, Hebrew University Jerusalem, 13–15 November 2011).

[36] Gready and Robins, 'Rethinking Civil Society and Transitional Justice', above n 2, 957.

[37] Priscilla Hayner, 'Same species, Different Animal: How South Africa Compares to Truth Commissions Worldwide' in Charles Villa-Vicencio and Wilhelm Verwoerd (eds), *Looking Back, Reaching Forward: Reflections on the Truth and Reconciliation Commission of South Africa* (University of Cape Town Press, 2000) 38.

[38] Dudai, 'Deviant Commemorations', above n 35.

[39] Backer, above n 6, 313.

[40] Ibid 313.

[41] Gready and Robins, 'Rethinking Civil Society', above n 2, 958.

evaluate, and guide national conduct towards achieving transitional justice.[42] Many NGOs are working to replace a 'culture of impunity' with a 'culture of rights'.[43] Indeed, there is a growing awareness that: 'Civil society actors can take action where no formal mechanisms exist, lead efforts to set up such mechanisms, as well as provide a space where citizens can engage with the ideas and possibilities of transitional justice'.[44]

This wider view of the value of civil society in transitional justice measures lends more credibility than ever before to grassroot transitional justice measures and non-state actors.[45] Indeed, civil society has initiated and developed some of the most creative and robust transitional justice measures around the globe.[46] In Ghana, Sierra Leone, East Timor, and Peru, local organisations played primary roles in shaping the justice mechanisms used to confront past crimes.[47] Unofficial truth projects further occupy terrain traditionally held by the state. From Brazil to Guatemala, NGOs have conducted fact-finding missions on par with truth commissions.[48]

Comparative Advantage in Ongoing Conflict

Arguably, civil society is particularly well-placed to perform transitional justice tasks during active conflict. In 'situations where national governments remain ineffective, aloof or otherwise incapable of responding properly to the needs of transition'.[49] Victims and survivor groups, NGOs, and ex-combatant associations can play pivotal roles in confronting past abuse.[50] For several years around the

---

[42] Such monitoring and assessment are part of what Jean Drèze and Amartya Sen call 'public action'. Jean Drèze and Amartya Sen, *Hunger and Public Action* (Oxford University Press, 1989) 275–279 in Crocker, 'Transitional Justice and International Civil Society', above n 10, 507.

[43] Crocker 'Transitional Justice and International Civil Society', above n 10, 507.

[44] Gready and Robins, 'Rethinking Civil Society', above n 2, 959.

[45] Alison Brysk, 'Introduction: Transnational Threats and Opportunities' in Alison Brysk (ed), *Globalisation and Human Rights* (University of California Press, 2002) 1–19, cited in Patricia Lundy, 'Paradoxes and Challenges of Transitional Justice at the 'Local' Level: Historical Enquiries in Northern Ireland' (2011) 6(1) *Journal of the Academy of Social Sciences* 89, 92.

[46] Priscilla Hayner, 'Responding to a Painful Past', above n 1, quoted in Gready and Robins, 'Rethinking Civil Society', above n 2, 961.

[47] Ibid.

[48] The *Nunca Más* Commission in Brazil was a 5-year underground project, under the direction of the Archdiocese of Sao Paulo, that compiled evidence about abuses suffered by 17,000 victims of repression. See Stanley Cohen, 'State Crimes of Previous Regimes: Knowledge, Accountability, and the Policing of the Past. Law and Social Inquiry' (1995) 20(1) *Law & Social Inquiry* 7, 16; The Project to Recover the Historical Memory (REMHI) in Guatemala was also a comparably massive civil undertaking: 6000 testimonies collected by local citizens recruited by the Archdiocese of Guatemala City, providing the basis for a detailed report.

[49] Dudai, 'Deviant Commemorations' above n 35.

[50] McEvoy and McGregor, above n 7; See also Backer, above n 6, 301.

globe, local groups, trade unions, and social religious organisations have acted against the state to bring resolve to violent conflicts.[51] They can, for example, fill gaps resulting from political incapacity, respond more flexibly and efficiently than bureaucratic structures to opportunities, and facilitate legitimacy, participation, and sustainability in local contexts.[52] Even in seemingly intractable settings, civil society may actively intervene through unofficial measures, which will be extensively discussed in the next section of this chapter.[53]

The role of civil society is especially significant in the Middle East, where ongoing conflict has rendered both the PA and the Netanyahu government relatively incapable and/or unwilling to officiate transitional justice practices. Without a political accord, and against heightened tensions, it seems inconceivable that an official institution such as the SATRC could be implemented in the region or that formal measures like reparations, reforms, or prosecutions would be seriously contemplated at present. Furthermore, as concluded in Chap. 5, international prosecutions alone are an inadequate tool for transitional justice. From this standpoint, local unofficial actors may be the only agents for pursuing truth, justice, and reconciliation, absent political will and institutional capacity.

Peacemaking (Civic Representation and Mobilisation)

The involvement of civil society in peacemaking is becoming an essential transitional justice strategy. As discussed in Chap. 3, peace agreements tend to involve interest-based negotiations[54] or 'elite pact-making'.[55] Whilst this model has some merit,[56] its capacity to adequately address long-term communal conflict is questionable. Top-down peacemaking can leave political deals fragile.[57] There is therefore

[51] Jessica Nevo, Tammy Pustilnick and Ami Asher (eds), 'Report of the Truth Commission on the Responsibility of Israeli Society for the Events of 1948–1960 in the South' (Final Report: English Digest, March 2016) 5. ('Zochrot Commission Report').

[52] Roger Duthie, *Building Trust and Capacity: Civil Society and Transitional Justice from a Development Perspective* (International Centre for Transitional Justice, 2009), cited in Gready and Robins, 'Rethinking Civil Society', above n 2, 961.

[53] *Zochrot Commission Report*, above n 51, 5.

[54] See Roger Fisher, William L Ury and Bruce Patton, *Getting to Yes* (Penguin Books, 1991).

[55] Celia McKeon, 'Public Participation in Peace Processes: Comparative Experience and Relevant Principles' in Terry Rempler, *Rights in Principle, Rights in Practice* (BADIL, 2009) 339.

[56] 'This model of peacemaking has successfully contributed to the ending of civil wars in a number of countries: Sierra Leone, Tajikistan and El Salvador. This success should certainly not be underestimated, and neither should the enormous challenges of simply getting the armed parties to the table'. In ibid.

[57] Yaacov Bar-Siman-Tov (ed), *From Conflict Resolution to Reconciliation* (Oxford University Press, 2004) 12.

growing appreciation of the need for local authorship and participation in the lead up to peace processes.[58]

To this end, civil society offers a web of peacebuilding activities that envision the entire body politic.[59] Civil society actors have the potential to engage in public deliberation, achieve consensus on basic policies, stimulate public discussion, and lend democratic legitimation to a peace process. Regarding Cyprus, Kanol claims: 'Time and energy should be spent more on peace-building efforts that penetrate into ideas and identities of the Cypriots, than on negotiations between the leaders…'.[60] He persuasively demonstrates how civil society can be a crucial actor in reversing the negative political rhetoric between the North and South.[61] In Northern Ireland community-based reconciliation projects helped transform the hostile mindsets and antagonistic attitudes leading up to the Good Friday Agreement.[62] According to Aiken, these are factors that may, in no small part, help account for the resumption of power-sharing governance and the signing of the historic accord in that country.[63] Arguably, the involvement of civil society in peacebuilding and negotiations is both normatively and politically desirable.

Given the psychological foundations of the Israeli–Palestinian conflict, civic participation in the peace process is particularly pertinent. Arguably Israeli–Palestinian society was not sufficiently transformed or sensitised to peace in order to reach a more stable political accommodation with the Oslo Accords.[64] From this standpoint, each nation's collective identity is too steeped in conflict to be ignored by peacemakers, and resolved by diplomatic agreements alone.[65] There is therefore a need to involve Israeli and Palestinian civil society in the diplomatic process throughout all of its stages.[66] Ultimately, Israeli and Palestinian non-state actors must mobilise

[58] Report of the Secretary-General on The Rule of Law and Transitional Justice in Conflict and Post-Conflict Societies, UN Doc S/2004/616 (2004) para 17, cited in Patricia Lundy, 'Exploring Home-Grown Transitional Justice and its Dilemmas: A Case Study of the Historical Enquiries Team, Northern Ireland' (2009) 3(3) *International Journal of Transitional Justice* 1, 325.

[59] John Paul Lederach, 'Beyond Violence: Building Sustainable Peace' in Eugene Weiner (ed), *The Handbook of Inter-ethnic Co-existence* (Continuum, 1998) 236, 245.

[60] Although the success of civic peacebuilding in Cyprus is questionable, Kanol argues that the opportunity for a successful outcome exists if civil society can 'increase work-related activities, apply a more participative strategy, and act in a coordinated way'. Direnq Kanol, 'Civil Society's Role in Peace-Building: Relevance of the Cypriot Case' (2010) 9(1) *Journal on Ethnopolitics and Minority Issues in Europe* 26.

[61] Ibid.

[62] Nevin T Aiken, 'Learning to Live Together: Transitional Justice and Intergroup Reconciliation in Northern Ireland' (2010) 4 *International Journal of Transitional Justice* 166, 172–3.

[63] Ibid.

[64] Louis Kriesberg, 'The Relevance of Reconciliation Actions in the Breakdown of Israeli-Palestinian Negotiations, 2000' (2002) 27(4) *Peace and Change* 546, 565.

[65] Herbert C Kelman, 'The Interdependence of Israeli and Palestinian National Identities: The Role of the other in Existential Conflicts' (1999) 55(3) *Journal of Social Issues* 581, 596.

[66] Ibid 596.

transitional justice in order to instigate, inform, and endorse a political accord, so that it may become more achievable, representative, and sustainable.[67]

Peacemaking: Civic Consultation and Drafting

Moreover, many countries have benefitted from civic involvement in advancing and devising transitional justice goals during peace negotiations. As discussed in Chap. 3, an essential element of conflict resolution is the inclusion of transitional justice considerations into any potential peace accord. Arguably, civil society can facilitate the kind of inclusive dialogue this requires,[68] and through consultation contest decisions driven by political self-interest, for example, amnesty provisions, as part of a watchdog or monitoring function.[69]

For example, during the Northern Ireland negotiations leading up to the Good Friday Agreement, the political parties involved consulted extensively with civil society and local communities on truth and justice issues. Thus, in 1997, the Northern Ireland Office established a Victims' Commission that released a report recommending, among other provisions, increased access to compensation for victims, trauma counselling, and support services in the accord.[70] The Northern Ireland Women's Coalition was another significant civic player. Created as a cross-community political women's party,[71] the group played a significant role in the drafting of the Good Friday Agreement and effectively contributed to the promotion of a Northern Ireland women's agenda and giving women a voice in the peace talks.[72] According to McKeon: 'it is widely acknowledged that the Women's Coalition played a crucial role in ensuring the inclusion of sensitive issues, demystifying the political process and showing civil society's capacity to engage in political decision-making'.[73]

---

[67] Edy Kaufman, Walid Salem and Juliette Verhoeven (eds), *Bridging the Divide: Peacebuilding in the Israeli-Palestinian Conflict* (Lynne Rienner, 2006) 81.

[68] Kora Andrieu, 'Civilizing Peacebuilding: Transitional Justice, Civil Society and the Liberal Paradigm' (2010) *Security Dialogue* 41(5) 537–58.

[69] Gready and Robins, 'Rethinking Civil Society', above n 2, 961.

[70] Sir Kenneth Bloomfield, 'We Will Remember Them: Report of the Northern Ireland Victims Commissioner, Sir Kenneth Bloomfield KCB' (Belfast: Stationery Office, 1998) in Aiken, above n 62,lxii 176.

[71] The Women's Coalition in Northern Ireland was successful at the negotiation table because it was able to create space for the inclusion of local concerns in the broader negotiation process. 'Toward a framework of Transitional Justice in Israel/Palestine' (Workshop with Zochrot and Transitional Justice Institute of Ulster University, Summary Lessons Paper, 9–12 November 2015).

[72] Véronique Molinari, 'Putting Women in the Picture: The Impact of the Northern Ireland Women's Coalition on Northern Irish Politics' (2007) 32(1) *Études Irlandaises* 109.

[73] The Good Friday Agreement was signed in April 1998 and subsequently endorsed by a public referendum. The representative political process was a key factor in determining its acceptability to the wider public in Northern Ireland. McKeon, above n 55, 342.

In Guatemala too, civil society made an invaluable contribution to complex peace negotiations.[74] For example, the Center for Human Rights Legal Action helped implement human rights in the Guatemalan peace process and promote 'the involvement of a broad cross section of civil society representatives in the process'.[75] The UN-brokered Framework Agreement (1994) 'recognized the role played [in earlier negotiations]...by the various sectors of organized civil society and gave them a legitimate place within the negotiating process in an Assembly of Civil Society (ACS)'.[76] The Guatemalan ACS[77] devised consensus papers on substantive topics of negotiation, including the creation of a truth commission, agreements on indigenous rights, and on socioeconomic goals.[78] Although the process had its shortcomings,[79] 'Many of the Assembly's proposals were adopted into the drafting of the relevant peace accord on the topic'.[80] Whitefield observes that consultation with civil society both 'fuelled public discussion and enhanced the validity of the peace process within Guatemalan society at large'.[81] Arguably the ACS was 'uniquely responsible for getting the peace negotiators to tackle the root causes of the conflict...and of some remedies'.[82]

In this light, the involvement of Israeli and Palestinian civil society in peacemaking and political negotiations may assist both nations to address and resolve the core elements of the conflict.[83] The experiences of both Northern Ireland and Guatemala lend support to the capacity of civil society to shape transitional justice at the political and diplomatic level and to inform the peace agenda during active conflict. Ultimately, non-state actors can herald a more inclusive and participatory approach to transitional justice that may positively impact the Israeli–Palestinian peace process.

---

[74] Crocker, 'Transitional Justice and International Civil Society', above n 10, 503.

[75] Announcement of Briefing, 'Guatemala After the Peace Accords', Washington Office on Latin America and Center for Human Rights Legal Action, Washington DC, 6 March 1997 in ibid. 507.

[76] The Agreement was reached between the Guatemalan government and the Guatemalan National Revolutionary Union. Ibid 503.

[77] Chaired by a Catholic Bishop, the ACS comprised representatives not only of grassroots NGOs but also of political parties, universities, and small and medium business associations.

[78] Crocker, 'Transitional Justice and International Civil Society', above n 10, 503.

[79] For example, the ACS failed to involve the agro-business elite, which led to the undermining of several ACS suggestions on socio-economic reform and land distribution. Crocker, 'Transitional Justice and International Civil Society', above n 10, 503; McKeon, above n 55, 344.

[80] McKeon, above n 55, 344.

[81] Teresa Whitefield, 'The Role of the UN in El Salvador and Guatemala: A Preliminary Comparison' (Paper presented at Comparative Peace Processes in Latin America, Woodrow Wilson International Centre for Scholars 13–14 March 1997) 16–17, cited in Crocker, 'Transitional Justice and International Civil Society', above n 10, 503.

[82] According to Whitefield, the ACS helped broaden the peace negotiations to address the original sources of a conflict. Ibid.

[83] Daniel Bar-Tal, 'Societal Beliefs of Intractable Conflicts' (1998) 9 *International Journal of Conflict Management* 22, 35.

Challenges

It is worth noting that civil society is not always successful or sufficiently influential to have an impact in the pursuit of transitional justice. In transitional settings, civil society groups often encounter many challenges and limitations,[84] as observed in diverse political contexts. For example, in Guatemala, civil society groups lobbied unsuccessfully for the national truth commission to be more victim-centred, and in South Africa non-state actors were powerless to rectify the inadequate reparations paid to victims.[85] These, and other factors (e.g., local unity, institutional capacity, access, and competence) have a bearing on whether or not they effectively impact the state and/or wider society.[86] The specific challenges facing Israeli and Palestinian civil society will be thoroughly investigated in Sect. 7.4 of this Chapter. However, broadly speaking, there is clearly an inequality of arms between civil society and the state, with the latter being far better equipped to implement transitional justice mechanisms, and to influence the agenda and structure of peace negotiations. For example, governments play an indispensable role when it comes to prosecutions, compensation, and commemoration.[87] In short, '...civil society must not be absolutized as the new source of salvation...'.[88]

Conclusion

Nevertheless, it is also clear that non-state actors effectively engage transitional justice through broad-based representation, advocacy, public debate and consultation particularly where the state is weakened by conflict, and/or reluctant to embrace a human rights agenda. As discussed, transitional justice has grown from a narrow class of official institutions to wider social and political processes. It has also evolved from civil society in the service of the state, to becoming a more independent agent of truth, justice, and reconciliation. As will be discussed in the next section, civil society commands a relative advantage in terms of local knowledge and moral authority at the grassroot level. In order to engage with the full spectrum of

---

[84] Civil society is often under-developed, under-equipped, and divided, not to mention politicised and financially dependent. See Swedish NGO, Foundation for Human Rights, *The Status of Human Rights Organizations in Sub-Saharan Africa* (1994).

[85] Androff, above n 33, 299–300.

[86] John W Harbeson, Donald Rothchild and Naomi Chazan (eds), *Civil Society and the State in Africa* (Lynne Rienner, 1994); Backer, above n 6, 301.

[87] Peter B Evans, Dietrich Reuschemeyer, and Theda Skocpol, *Bringing the State Back In* (Cambridge University Press, 1985); Michael Schudson, 'The Public Sphere and Its Problems: Bringing the State (Back) In' (1994) 8(2) *Notre Dame Journal of Law, Ethics and Public Policy* 8, 529–46.

[88] Crocker, 'Transitional Justice and International Civil Society', above n 10, 508–9.

possibilities for dealing with the past in the Israeli–Palestinian context, non-state actors must be afforded greater relevance and attention.

7.3 Part Two: Unofficial Transitional Justice Mechanisms and Truth-Seeking

As discussed in Chap. 3, transitional justice is a broad field that includes *all* concerted efforts to redress gross human rights abuse as a result of intractable conflict. Nevertheless, the popularity of transitional justice and its extensive use in human rights activism[89] means that it risks becoming a 'catch-all' term for every kind of conflict intervention or a synonym for peacebuilding per se.[90] It is therefore worth distinguishing transitional justice measures from purely political projects, legal advocacy, and/or a wide range of socio-economic peacebuilding activity. The definitional key is to move from simple documentation of abuses or isolated confidence-building measures to more complex mechanisms that counter official denial of the past and that seek to promote accountability and redress for mass violations of human rights. Dudai calls such truth-telling initiatives 'deviant commemorations', because of the way they act against the dominant values in their own communities.[91] This section therefore focuses on examples of unofficial truth-telling that challenge state policy and national narrative in order to transform conflict. It also seeks to demonstrate the value of civil society in those processes, which has been discussed at a more theoretical level above.

Value of Unofficial Truth-Seeking Measures

Civil society actors are making a particularly important contribution to transitional justice mechanisms through unofficial truth-telling activities. As noted in Sect. 7.2 of this chapter, NGOs and community groups have established many such projects in various political contexts. Increasingly, transitional justice scholars are advocating for local truth-seeking processes particularly where official mechanisms are unavailable.[92] Bickford has labelled such initiatives as 'unofficial truth projects'.[93]

---

[89] Domenica Preysing, *Transitional Justice in Post-Revolutionary Tunisia How the Past Shapes the Future* (Springer, 2011–2013) 29.

[90] Buckley-Zistel, above n 17.

[91] An important element in deviant commemoration is addressing abuses committed by one's own in-group against members of an ethnic, national, or religious out-group. Dudai, 'Deviant Commemorations', above n 35, 2.

[92] Laura Arriaza and Naomi Roht-Arriaza, 'Social Reconstruction as a Local Process' (2008) 2(2) *International Journal of Transitional Justice* 152.

[93] Bickford, above n 25.

In his leading study on the subject, he recognises that unofficial truth initiatives may serve as replacements for official measures, for example, when a formal truth commission is not possible (e.g. Brazil and Northern Ireland); as precursors to state-backed measures (Iraq); and/or as complimentary to state initiatives (Guatemala).[94] This fluidity demonstrates the potential benefit of civic truth-seeking over formal or international interventions, because: '…they are usually rooted in local communities, creative, adapted to local culture and circumstance and responsive to local needs'.[95]

Drawing on unofficial truth commissions that have operated in hostile political settings from Brazil to Northern Ireland, this section will advocate for the value of an unofficial truth project in the Israeli-Palestinian context based on two fundamental arguments. Firstly, civil society efforts are the only feasible avenue for meaningful truth-recovery in the current political climate in the Middle East. Secondly, unofficial truth projects may be more desirable based on their local legitimacy, and capacity to lay the foundations for more formal and complementary transitional justice institutions.

Unofficial Vs. Official Truth Commissions

In some cases, unofficial truth projects are comparable to formal truth commissions.[96] They can sometimes replicate the goals, and often the form and content, of formal truth commissions.[97] For example, some of the projects discussed below have mimicked truth commissions in certain aspects, especially in their production of a final report. In others, like the Greensboro Truth and Reconciliation Commission, there were public hearings, while the Brazilian NGO Nunca Mais Project states that 'it merits comparison with other truth commissions'.[98] Overall, unofficial truth initiatives address and expose the truth about past abuses, at times consciously emulating the work of formal truth commissions.[99]

Notwithstanding their proliferation, the truth commission paradigm remains classically confined to 'officially sanctioned, authorized or state-empowered

---

[94] Ibid.

[95] Androff, above n 33, 300–301.

[96] Bickford, above n 25.

[97] Priscilla Hayner explores what she calls 'semi-official and unofficial inquiries' in the 1990s, referring to examples in Honduras, Northern Ireland, and in Rwanda. Hayner, *Unspeakable Truths: Confronting State Terror and Atrocity,* above n 33.

[98] Catholic Church, Archdiocese of Sao Paulo (Brazil), 1986, *Torture in Brazil: A Shocking Report on the Pervasive Use of Torture by Brazilian Military Governments, 1964–1979* (Joan Dassin ed., Jaime Wright, trans); Stanley Cohen, 'State Crimes of Previous Regimes', above n 48, 16.

[99] Bickford, above n 25, 1002.

bodies'.[100] It often excludes non-state inquiries.[101] There exists a normative preference for state-led truth mechanisms, given their relative advantage over civil society endeavours. For example, in the South African context, it is arguable that the creation of the SATRC, as an official state enterprise, was vital to its success.[102] Du Toit writes: '...while a civil society initiative would have been able to speak truth *to* power, the TRC was able to speak truth *on behalf of* (the new) power, achieving more influence than civil society could'.[103] Ultimately, civil society-led truth commissions encounter difficulties in obtaining the status, visibility, and recognition more easily afforded to state-sanctioned projects.[104]

Nevertheless, official sanction does not necessarily confer greater judicial power and legitimacy. Firstly, the ability to subpoena witnesses by even official truth commissions is the exception not the rule.[105] Teitel explains how all truth-seeking investigations, state-mandated or otherwise, are circumscribed and ultimately reliant on social consensus.[106] After all, there are also examples of poorly received official truth commissions.[107] Secondly, 'the construction of a plausible public truth depends on other ratifying processes outside of the government and emanating from the people'.[108] In this regard, the greater inclusion of victims' voices may lend more weight to truth-recovery. From this standpoint, the professionalism and perceived objectivity of truth-telling is arguably what matters most. Thus, in the Brazilian context, '...reliance on official documents, reputable lawyers, and the respected role of the Church is arguably considered much more legitimate than a hypothetical alternative, such as a truth commission, that is seen as politicized or weak'.[109] In other words, the moral authority of truth-telling appears more contingent upon the context from which it emerges, rather than state involvement per se.

---

[100] Priscilla B Hayner, *Unspeakable Truths: Facing the Challenge of Truth Commissions* (Routledge, 2011) 14.

[101] Freeman goes as far as to suggest that the definition of 'truth commissions' excludes any 'non-state' inquiry. Mark Freeman, *Truth Commissions and Procedural Fairness* (Cambridge University Press, 2006) 18.

[102] Andre Du Toit, 'Experiments with Truth and Justice in South Africa: Stokenstrom, Ghandi and the TRC' (2005) 31(2) *Journal of Southern African Studies* 419.

[103] Ibid.

[104] Bickford, above n 25, 1027.

[105] The SATRC was unique in this regard. Most official truth commissions lack judicial power as in El Salvador, Guatemala and Peru. Ruti G Teitel, *Transitional Justice* (Oxford University Press, 2000) 81.

[106] Ibid.

[107] In El Salvador, the truth commission's findings were flatly rejected by top government and military leaders. In Nigeria, the general population regarded the overall effort as an unserious 'soap opera'. Bickford, above n 25, 1027.

[108] Ibid.

[109] Ibid.

Viable Alternatives to Official Truth-Telling

Moreover, state-centric conceptions of truth commissions too easily dismiss the value of civic forms of truth-seeking, particularly when formal institutions are unfeasible or simply unavailable.[110] In cases like the Israeli–Palestinian one, where there is insufficient political will to establish a truth commissions, civic projects '…may represent viable alternative strategies, and can be seen as more legitimate interlocutors for the task of confronting the past'.[111] As mentioned above, in certain settings they become de facto replacements for official measures.[112] For instance, in countries like Brazil and Uruguay in 1984 and 1985, or Northern Ireland in 1998, the creation of an official truth commission was politically unfeasible, and civil society was forced to pick up the slack.[113] Thus, unofficial truth-recovery is an essential vehicle to addressing the past and may play an invaluable role in catalysing formal transitional justice mechanisms.

Brazil

In Brazil, for example, an unofficial truth-telling project called 'Nunca Mais' ('Never Again') coordinated by the World Council of Churches exposed irrefutable evidence of systematic torture by the Brazilian state.[114] Working from 1979 to 1982, while the military was still in power, lawyers and other researchers investigated the use of torture against the regime's political opponents, secretly copying documents from military trial transcripts of 1964–1979 and gathering testimony from political prisoners. The project resulted in the publication of a final report that '…became a best seller and had lasting effects on Brazilian society, receiving as much attention, if not more than an official report would have'.[115] According to Bickford, Nuncas Mais is best understood as 'a replacement for a truth commission, since an official truth commission was unlikely at that time'.[116]

---

[110] Ron Dudai and Hillel Cohen, 'Dealing with the Past when the Conflict is Still Present: Civil society Truth-Seeking Initiatives in the Israeli-Palestinian Conflict' in Rosalind Shaw, Lars Waldorf and Pierre Hazan (eds), *Localizing Transitional Justice: Interventions and Priorities After Mass Violence* (Stanford University Press, 2010).

[111] Bickford, above n 25, 995.

[112] Ibid 1004.

[113] Ibid.

[114] Brasil's *Nunca Mais* proved conclusively that torture was an essential part of the military justice system and that judicial authorities were clearly aware of the use of torture to extract confessions. See Lawrence Weschler, *A Miracle, a Universe: Settling Accounts with Torturers* (University of Chicago Press, 1998).

[115] In 1985, the Archdiocese of São Paulo published a report called Brasil: Nunca Mais (Brazil: Never Again, or Torture in Brazil) about the widespread use of torture during Brazil's military regime. Weschler, above n 114.

[116] Bickford, above n 25, 1007.

Ultimately, the Brazilian civil society effort laid the foundations for national engagement with the past. One decade later, the democratic government established a Special Commission on Political Deaths and Disappearances (the CEMDP)[117] that disbursed nearly 40 million reais of reparations.[118] In 2007, the book *Right to Memory and to Truth* outlined the results of the 11 years of work by the CEMDP, thus serving as the first official report by the Brazilian State to directly accuse members of the military for crimes such as torture. The authors of Brazil's unofficial Nunca Mais were instrumental in this process.[119] More recently, the Brazilian National Truth Commission (2012–2014) and its report also resulted from a complex and dynamic process of negotiation that involved diverse local commissions around the country and civil society actors.[120]

Northern Ireland

Several truth-seeking efforts in Northern Ireland were also led by civil society in the absence of official transitional justice institutions. Like Brazil, they emerged at a time when the political climate effectively ruled out the creation of an official tribunal or truth commission.[121] One prominent example is the Ardoyne Commemoration Project (ACP), a local effort, that focused on personal testimonies from the small nationalist community of Ardoyne in Northern Belfast.[122] Through the collection of over 300 oral interviews, the ACP sought to record the stories of around 100 people killed during the 'Troubles'. The ACP emerged in 1996 as a result of the community's desire to acknowledge and commemorate the victims as 'a counter to state-sanctioned forgetting and to 'tell their story' from the perspective of the community'.[123] Their report, 'Ardoyne: The Untold Truth', was published in 2002.

The work of the cross-community NGO, Healing Through Remembering (HTR), is another example of civic truth-telling in Northern Ireland. Since 2001, the group has been tasked with independently '...seeking views on the development of truth

[117] In 1995 Law No. 9.410, known as the Law of the Disappeared, allowed for the creation of a Special Commission on Political Deaths and Disappearances (the CEMDP), established and installed in the Ministry of Justice of Brazil and sanctioned by the president.

[118] The estimated liability of the government is 4 billion reais ($1.5 billion). 'Brazil's armed forces: Resurrecting the Right to History', *The Economist* (São Paolo), 25 November 2004.

[119] For example, Paulo Vannuchi, one of the authors of Brazil's *Nunca Mais*, helped to complete this book.

[120] Nina Schneider and Gisele Iecker de Almeida, 'The Brazilian National Truth Commission (2012–2014) as a State-Commissioned History Project' in Berber Bevernage and Nico Wouters (eds), *The Palgrave Handbook of State-Sponsored History After 1945*. (Palgrave Macmillan, 2018).

[121] In the interest of stability, the issue of responsibility was left unresolved in the 'fault-neutral' framework of the Belfast Agreement. Christine Bell, 'Dealing with the Past in Northern Ireland' (2003) 26 *Fordham International Law Journal* 1095, cited in Aiken, above n 62, 175.

[122] Ardoyne Commemoration Project, *Ardoyne: The Untold Truth* (Beyond the Pale Publications, 2002).

[123] Ibid 2.

and justice processes for Northern Ireland'.[124] After a lengthy consultation process, HTR submitted a final report to the government recommending several truth-recovery projects,[125] which included collective storytelling and the creation of a permanent memorial or museum to the victims of the Troubles.[126] The HTR also launched a 'national day of private reflection' in June 2007, an event usually initiated by governments.[127] According to Dudai and Cohen: 'the HTR initiative is an example of how, when leaderships are reluctant to initiate such activities, civil society can partly fill the vacuum by taking the lead'.[128] Aiken also lauds the HTR's aiding of transitional justice efforts. He concludes that although much of the work is conceptual, it is invaluable for 'promoting greater dialogue around addressing the past in Northern Ireland'.[129]

Russia

The Russian NGO 'Memorial'[130] is a final example of unofficial truth-telling within a hostile political setting. Established in 1988, Memorial has been pushing for justice and recognition for the victims of the Soviet regime, when it became clear that no official mechanism would do so.[131] Despite evidence of mass human rights violations during the Communist period, virtually nothing has been done to contend with this violent past, '…no-one has been prosecuted, no-one has officially apologized… '.[132] Thus, Memorial has been engaging in the systematic collection of historical evidence from the Stalinist era. Among other things, it produced statistical records,

---

[124] Office of the First Minister and Deputy First Minister, Victims Unit, *Reshape, Rebuild, Achieve* (April 2002). See Aiken, above n 62, 180.

[125] Healing Through Remembering, *The Report of the Healing Through Remembering Project* (June 2002).

[126] Healing Through Remembering, *Making Peace with the Past: Options for Truth Recovery Regarding the Conflict in and about Northern Ireland* (October 2006).

[127] HTR invited individuals to reflect individually and privately upon the conflict in and organised several activities around this reflection day.

[128] Dudai and Cohen, above n 110, 234.

[129] Aiken, above n 62, 180.

[130] Memorial's full name is 'Memorial: An International Historical, Educational, Human Rights and Charitable Society'. It is an association of organisations created in 1981 by famous dissident and Nobel Peace Prize winner Andrei Sakharov.

[131] According to its Charter, Memorial aims: 'to promote the revelation of the truth about the historical past and perpetuate the memory of the victims of political repression exercised by totalitarian regimes'. See Memorial, 'The Historical-Enlightenment Work of Memorial' http://www.memo.ru/eng/history/intro.htm (in Russian).

[132] Kora Andrieu, 'An Unfinished Business: Transitional Justice and Democratization in Post-Soviet Russia' (2011) 5 *International Journal of Transitional Justice* 198.

conducted interviews, and investigated mass graves and former detention camps.[133] By 1998, the association's archives contained more than 50,000 files on victims.[134] It also erected a monument to the victims of Stalinist repression.

Nevertheless, the struggle between civil society and the Russian state is not an easy one, with officials significantly impeding Memorial's activities.[135] For example, the offices of 'Memorial' were targeted and their leaders persecuted.[136] The association has also faced many administrative hurdles with official registration, recruitment, and even just opening a bank account.[137] On the other hand, since the Russian state has refused to take any official transitional justice action, it therefore fell on civil society to deal with the legacies of the past.[138] In such contexts, civil society may become a viable alternative to the state, compensating for its inaction.[139]

According to Andrieu, Memorial's impact has been huge because of the revelations made, its engagement with victims, and defiance of state-sanctioned history.[140] The group is still active today, and continues to expose the past and document current human rights abuses, most notably in Chechnya, Dagestan, and Ossetia.[141] Memorial's work seems to confirm that unofficial truth-telling can lay the groundwork for transitional justice even within challenging political frameworks and semi-authoritarian regimes. This example is particularly relevant to the PA whose culture is far less democratic than Israel's (as will be discussed below in Sect. 7.4) and therefore demonstrates that transitional justice practices can take place, and those goals pursued, even in the context of a repressive governmental environment. The absence of official truth and justice mechanisms does not necessarily mean that the past cannot be addressed.[142]

---

[133] This is done through an electronic database of the victims of political terror in the USSR. For more details, see Marcia A Weigle, *Russia's Liberal Project: State–Society Relations in the Transition from Communism* (Pennsylvania University Press, 2000) 106–113.

[134] This included camp memoirs, letters, rehabilitation documents and names of Gulag prisoners. Andrieu, 'An Unfinished Business', above n 132, 215.

[135] Ibid 216.

[136] Ibid.

[137] In November 2008, masked and armed men from the Russian general prosecutor's office entered Memorial's St Petersburg office and confiscated its entire archives. In July 2009, Memorial's representative in Chechnya, Natalia Estemirova, was killed. See Ibid.

[138] 'These constraints, as well as the crying absence of any committed elite effort to deal with the past, means that social action has become the only way to keep memory alive in Russia'. Ibid 220.

[139] Ibid.

[140] Ibid.

[141] Ibid.

[142] Ibid.

Unofficial Civic Advantage

It is also arguable that civil society projects may be relatively more advantageous than state-led enterprises. According to Bickford, they are superior in terms of community-level truth-telling.[143] This is because an unofficial project potentially '...allows "voices from below" to be heard and heeded'.[144] Given the prominent role of victims within both Israeli and Palestinian societies, civic initiatives would have a distinct advantage in the Middle East. By mobilising victims and survivors, documenting abuse, and issuing formal findings, unofficial truth inquiries '...have often generated public support and catalysed official action, leading to stronger official inquiries and other measures'.[145]

For example, the investigation by the Peace and Justice Service in Uruguay[146] 'was more comprehensive, accurate and widely distributed than the little-known and anaemic government report that was released later'.[147] In Guatemala, REHMI recorded close to 6500 testimonies and documented more than 55,000 human rights violations.[148] Despite not being officially sanctioned, the project's final report was well publicised and highly influential.[149] Local citizens conducted interviews in 18 languages across the country, which gave REMHI the capacity to reach into the most rural areas of Guatemala 'linguistically, geographically, and culturally...surpassing the capacity of the CEH'.[150] The interviews also went far beyond the standard truth commission statement-taking format, asking reflective and personal questions that allowed the project to gain a broader understanding of both victims and the events. The REHMI process also lead to more local empowerment by including the community and religious leaders.[151]

---

[143] Bickford, above n 25, 995.

[144] See Patricia Lundy, 'Community, Truth-telling and Conflict Transformation: A Case Study from the North of Ireland' (Paper presented at The Second International Conference on Interdisciplinary Social Sciences, Ulster University, July 2007).

[145] González and Varney, above n 27, 10.

[146] The Report 'Uruguay: Nunca Más' was produced by the organisation SERPAJ (Fundación Servicio Paz y Justicia).

[147] David Crocker, 'Truth commissions, Transitional Justice and Civil Society' in Robert Rotberg and Dennis Thompson (eds), *Truth v. Justice: The Formal Efficacy of Truth Commissions - South Africa and Beyond* (Princeton University Press, 2000) 13.

[148] The Oficina de Derechos Humanos del Arzobispado (Human Rights Office of the Archbishop of Guatemala) conducted the project called the 'Proyecto de Recuperación de la Memoria Histórica' (REMHI). It had the support of more than 70 churches, human rights organisations, and NGOs worldwide.

[149] The Report 'Guatemala: Nunca Más' was released on April 1998. See Backer, above n 6, 304–5; Roberto Cabrera, 'Should We Remember? Recovering Historical Memory in Guatemala', in Brandon Hamber (ed), *Past Imperfect: Dealing with the Past in Northern Ireland and Societies in Transition* (International Conflict Research Institute and University of Ulster, 1998).

[150] International Centre for Transitional Justice, above n 15, 30.

[151] Ibid.

Civil society processes may also enjoy a greater moral or local authority precisely because they operate outside the state. As the experience of Guatemala demonstrates, unofficial truth efforts tend to emphasise popular participation, and can more positively impact locals and victims. Many of the non-state projects described above have subsequently won impressive wider recognition.[152] From this standpoint, it is arguable that they are preferable to 'top-down' truth commissions.[153]

Most importantly, civil truth projects are best understood on their own terms, and not just as second-best alternatives to official truth commissions.[154] Arguably, both official and unofficial commissions have strengths and weaknesses: 'Neither approach is inherently superior in terms of truth recovery'.[155] Moreover, it is not particularly useful to compare civil society projects against ideal-type truth commissions, '...especially where the political climate makes the establishment of an official commission unlikely. The potential of such initiatives should be weighed in relation to existing reality, not in comparison to unattainable hypothetical official commissions'..[156] As noted, this is particularly relevant in the Israeli–Palestinian context, where the creation of an official commission remains a distant scenario.

It is also worth recalling that unofficial truth projects and state-sanctioned commissions are not mutually exclusive endeavours. Whilst political and practical demands may inhibit the creation of official institutions at a particular stage, a holistic approach to transitional justice can ensure all relevant measures are integrated and complementary (Chap. 4). To this end, unofficial projects may serve as precursors and/or become complementary to state-backed measures.[157] Arguably, a rigid dichotomy of oppositional NGOs on the one hand, and official governmental sponsorship on the other, should be rejected.[158] For example, the mandate of the Iraq History Project was specifically designed to pave the way for a formal truth commission.[159] As discussed above, Guatemala's REMHI invaluably supported the work of the national truth commission.[160] Thus, civil society-led initiatives can play a catalytic role in transitional society and may instigate as well as complement official commissions.

---

[152] Bickford, above n 25, 1027.

[153] See Lundy, above n 144.

[154] Laura Arriaza and Naomi Roht-Arriaza, 'Waiving a Braid of Histories' in Rosalind Shaw, Lars Waldorf and Pierre Hazan (eds), *Localizing Transitional Justice: Interventions and Priorities After Mass Violence* (Stanford University Press, 2010).

[155] Bickford, above n 25, 995.

[156] Dudai and Cohen, above n 110, 231.

[157] Bickford, above n 25, 995.

[158] See Ron Dudai, 'Does any of this matter? Transitional Justice and the Israeli-Palestinian conflict' in David Downes et al. (eds), *Crime, Social Control and Human Rights: From Moral Panics to States of Denial - Essays in Honour of Stanley Cohen* (Willan Publishing, 2007) 345.

[159] Iraq History Project, *Iraq History Project Testimonies* (International Human Rights Law Institute, 2007); Bickford, above n 25, 1004–5.

[160] González and Varney, above n 27, 10.

Challenges

Although civic truth efforts are clearly significant, they may be undermined by operating beyond and/or against the state. The Russian example of 'Memorial' demonstrates how vulnerable unofficial truth projects become when pitted against a powerful national entity. Whilst in many respects, the Israeli and Palestinian context is distinctly more liberal, the risk of political and/or legal attacks against a non-state inquiry would be formidable. For example, by way of fact-finding, Israeli government archives routinely deny access to documentation concerning state-sanctioned human rights violations.[161] The PA is no less hostile to such efforts as will be discussed in Sect. 7.4 below. Ultimately, as demonstrated in Chap. 1, both Israeli and Palestinian officials exploit the past. Neither entity would welcome a narrative that is contrary to the one the government deploys for its own legitimacy.

In addition, an unofficial truth-initiative might lack credibility for Israelis, because their country is formally a democratic one with high internal moral legitimacy. This is distinguishable from the Brazilian and Russian authoritarian contexts. In established liberal nations, there is often an illusion of normalcy and legitimacy surrounding the state and its institutions.[162] As will be discussed, this emboldens the Israeli government to undermine civil society and deny the existence of human rights abuses, and its own role in the conflict. Indeed, the current political establishment is clearly against this kind of truth-telling initiative, which would make the work of any unofficial truth commission significantly harder.

On the other hand, it is precisely in such cases that Israeli/Palestinian civil society may be best positioned to devise and implement truth and justice-seeking efforts. In nations mired in conflict, and in which many of the original perpetrators remain in power, any state-led initiative would invariably raise questions about its even-handedness and neutrality. As long as the current Israeli and Palestinian governments remain in power, the likelihood that they could undertake a dispassionate review of the events of the conflict seems unlikely. For example, there exists a perception amongst Palestinians that Israeli military investigations are not genuinely independent or impartial and fail to deliver justice.[163]

To some extent, unofficial and locally driven truth projects may have an inherent advantage when they undermine the official narrative of an incumbent state. For example, the Brazilian Nunca Mais project was particularly powerful because it could establish official responsibility for politically motivated abuses based on the

[161] In April 2016, a report by the Akevot Institute for Israeli–Palestinian Conflict Research, Point of Access, found that public access to 99% of 14 million archival records kept in Israel's State Archive and IDF archives was blocked due to unauthorised decisions. Network of Concerned Historians, *Annual Report 2017* (July 2017) 62.

[162] 'Towards a framework of Transitional Justice in Israel/Palestine' Workshop with Zochrot and Transitional Justice Institute of Ulster University Summary Paper (9–12 November 2015).

[163] See Network of Concerned Historians, above n 161, 62.

military records themselves, making denial impossible.[164] Perhaps an inclusive Israeli–Palestinian project that analyses, verifies, records, and seeks to understand the competing narratives could facilitate the shift from duelling monologues to engaging dialogues, and move the conflict beyond the diplomatic impasse it is challenged to address.

Conclusion

As the above analysis demonstrates, civil society has developed creative and engaging efforts to expose the past in diverse settings–without, and often against, the state. They have operated in hostile political contexts (Brazil), semi-authoritarian regimes (Russia), and in nations without any centralised approach to transitional justice (Northern Ireland). Their activities mostly replicate those undertaken by official commissions, such as producing reports, conducting public hearings, or meticulously documenting past abuses.[165] The Brazilian and Northern Ireland experiences also demonstrate the value of 'sequencing' truth-recovery efforts in highly politicised contexts 'with intra-communal truth recovery being the first necessary "building block" for people to develop the sense of self-confidence, security and receptiveness necessary to grapple with the much more contentious issues surrounding intercommunal truth recovery'.[166] In sum, non-state truth-recovery is an important response to the past, and has the potential to challenge official narrative, and mobilise a national response.

Akin to the countries discussed, the Middle East is a highly politicised context, in which little prospect exists for a national truth commission. As concluded in Chap. 5, an imminent ICC intervention is also far from assured and seems undesirable in terms of broader peace, truth-telling, and justice goals. Whilst conflict in the region is raging, there is no political incentive on either side to formally investigate past abuses. In this light, civic engagement may be the only way to credibly investigate, document and expose human rights violations, as well as to apply transitional justice considerations to the conflict. Finally, civic projects may be desirable as tools of conflict transformation for Israelis and Palestinians, particularly during active conflict.

---

164 See Catholic Church, Archdiocese of Sao Paulo (Brazil), 1986. *Torture in Brazil: A Shocking Report on the Pervasive use of torture by Brazilian Military Governments*, 1964–1979 (Joan Dassin ed., Jaime Wright, trans.) xvii.

165 Dudai and Cohen, above n 110, 234.

166 Ardoyne Commemoration Project, above n 122, 2.

7.4 Part Three: Israeli–Palestinian Civil Society: Capacity and Challenges

Introduction

What then of the current landscape of civil society in the region? How capable and equipped are local non-state actors to create an unofficial transitional justice mechanism at present? At the outset, it must be made clear that neither Israeli nor Palestinian civil societies are homogeneous. Their diversity and fragmentation along ethnic, religious, and ideological lines are significant.[167] Both the Israeli and Palestinian communities are also subject to their own 'internal tensions and conflicts, as well as antagonisms or cooperation with one another'.[168] Moreover, the conflict's asymmetry means that Israeli civic groups develop activities in an environment structured by the state, whereas the Palestinian ones do not.[169] Five decades of military occupation have hindered the growth and power of Palestinian civic institutions.[170]

Nevertheless, both the nations share a similar spectrum of civic qualities from political engagement, religious extremism to violent resistance. This section addresses the contribution made by peacebuilding and human rights groups to mitigating the Israeli–Palestinian conflict, and its limitations. It provides a snapshot of existing human rights and peacebuilding actors and contends that, despite the challenges, there is ample evidence that Israeli–Palestinian civil society could play a vital role in creating the conditions for a transitional justice process.

Defining Israeli/Palestinian Civil Society Actors

> *[H]ow does one determine that a given action undertaken by civil society actors is a step towards peace? Which definition of peace?*[171]

Civil society is a contested concept. Given that it involves diverse players, the term could apply to a wide range of Israeli and Palestinian groups that either promote or

[167] Laure Fourest, 'Chap. 4: Human Rights, Civil Society and Conflict in Israel/Palestine' in Raffaele Marchetti and Nathalie Tocci (eds), *Civil society, Conflicts and the Politicization of Human Rights* (United Nations University Press, 2011) 80.

[168] Ibid 76; Manuel Hassassian, 'Civil Society and NGOs Building Peace in Palestine' in Edy Kaufman, Walid Salem and Juliette Verhoeven (eds), *Bridging the Divide: Peacebuilding in the Israeli-Palestinian Conflict* (Lynne Rienner, 2006) 59.

[169] Ibid; Fourest, above n 167, 76.

[170] Hassassian, above n 168, 64.

[171] Fourest, above n 167, 79.

hinder peacebuilding, human rights, and transitional justice.[172] Naturally, truth, justice, and reconciliation actors are not free from political taint.[173] 'On both sides, civil society groups are instrumentalised to advance not an agenda of peace or justice in some abstract sense but a parochial claim that, seen from the other side, is, in fact, an obstacle to resolution'.[174] In short, one man's peacebuilder is another man's warmonger.

It is difficult to theoretically frame Israeli–Palestinian civil society. On the one hand, a wider view could include illiberal, extremist, or violent elements from Hamas[175] to the Israeli settler's Price Tag Movement.[176] On the other hand, reducing Israeli–Palestinian civil society to a small progressive subset is conceptually fraught.[177] Unhelpfully, civil society researchers tend '…to have a blind spot for grassroots activities that contravene their own political preferences…'.[178] Thus, a directory of some 80 Israeli, Palestinian, or joint peacebuilding organisations excludes reference to any rightist groups opposed to the Oslo process.[179] Naturally, there are also rightist and religious NGOs invoking the language of 'peace and justice'.[180] It is worth resisting a simplistic all-encompassing and overly optimistic approach to examining NGOs. Accordingly, any analysis of Israeli–Palestinian civil society must be multi-dimensional and not presuppose that human rights groups are politically neutral.[181]

Nevertheless, whilst civil society is fragmented, and although extremist groups are part of a continuum of unofficial activity, this chapter will focus on civic efforts most conducive to the normative goals of transitional justice (as defined in Chap. 3). Broadly speaking, 'Israeli/Palestinian civil society' for the purposes of this thesis will refer to organised engagement in non-violent peacebuilding and human rights activity aimed at transforming mutual perceptions, policies, and/or relations in order to resolve the conflict. This section also confines its inquiry to cross-border

172 Timothy Waters, 'Clearing the Path: The Perils of Positing Civil Society in Conflict and Transition' (2015) 48 *Israel Law Review* 165, 165.

173 Ibid.

174 Ibid.

175 Although now in government, Hamas has and retains many features of a popularly based civil society organisation. Ibid 181.

176 Tag Mechir, a movement within the West Bank settler community, seeks to extract a price for acts of Palestinians or Israelis that the group's members see as harmful to the Israeli–Jewish settler movement. 'Israeli Mosque Entrance Torched in Suspected Price Tag Attack', *Jewish Telegraphic Agency* (online), 18 April 2014, https://www.jta.org/2014/04/18/israel/israeli-mosque-entrance-torched-in-suspected-price-tag-attack.

177 Waters, above n 172, 165.

178 Ibid 175.

179 Kaufman, Salem and Verhoeven (eds), above n 67, 223. (noting that only groups that provided information were included in the directory).

180 The human rights rhetoric has also been taken up by religious civil society actors, both Jewish and Muslim, as one of the bases of their involvement in the community. They tend to include human rights within the framework of religious references.

181 Fourest, above n 167, 79.

Israeli–Palestinian activity in order to identify the **civic** potential for a binational transitional justice mechanism to be conceived in Chap. 8. As noted in Chap. 2, despite the conflict's inter-societal aspect, the primary focus of the thesis is on the potential for transitional justice between two distinct national Israeli and Palestinian entities.

Israeli–Palestinian Civic Peacebuilding and Human Rights

From First Intifada to Oslo

In order to grasp how transitional justice might gain a stronger footing in the region, it is necessary to appreciate the local peacebuilding and human rights field. For nearly as long as there has been an Arab–Jewish conflict in the Holy Land, Arabs, and Jews have established civic initiatives aimed at resolving it.[182] Until the early 1990s, Israeli–Palestinian peacebuilding organisations were scant. Since the early 1980s, Israeli society has produced hundreds of NGOs focusing on peaceful Arab–Jewish relations inside Israel and the human rights of the Arab–Israeli minority.[183] However, the First Palestinian Intifada[184] galvanised the region's civil society. Palestinians in the territories organised underground educational, economic, and social institutions to support civil disobedience against Israel.[185] Israelis also began embarking on direct dialogue with Palestinian leaders and launching peace programs.[186]

The advent of the Oslo process and formal mutual Israeli–Palestinian recognition inspired a surge of joint civic activity. International donor communities supported a whole new genre of groups that popularised coexistence and mutual acceptance.[187] The Seeds of Peace programme came to symbolise a popular new model of Israeli–Palestinian encounters.[188] Equally, the Palestinian Center for Rapprochement

---

[182] A 2016 study lists 500 joint Arab–Jewish non-violent activities dating back to the twilight of the Ottoman era. Sheila H Katz, *Connecting with the Enemy: A Century of Palestinian-Israeli Joint Nonviolence*, (University of Texas Press, 2016).

[183] On Israeli Palestinian NGOs generally, see Shany Payes, *Palestinian NGOs in Israel: The Politics of Civil Socie*ty (Tauris Academic Studies, 2005).

[184] The First Intifada was a Palestinian uprising against Israeli military rule in the West Bank, Gaza Strip, and East Jerusalem, which began in December 1987. See Chapter One for more detailed information.

[185] The popular uprising was the 'crucible of a Palestinian civil society operating independently of Israel and leading, rather than following, the exiled leadership of the PLO'. Mary Elizabeth King, *A Quiet Revolution: The First Intifada and Nonviolent Resistance* (Nation Books, 2007).

[186] Ned Lazarus, *A future for Israeli-Palestinian peacebuilding* (Britain Israel Communications and Research Centre, 2017) 33–34.

[187] Hassassian, above n 168, 80.

[188] Founded in 1993, Seeds of Peace is a peacebuilding and leadership development organisation headquartered in NYC. Its main program is to bring youth and educators from areas of conflict to its camp in Maine. See the organisation's website at www.seedsofpeace.org.

Between People (PCR) lead Palestinian civil society in dialogue with Israelis.[189] The 1995 'Oslo II' agreements established an official 'people to people' programme aimed at generating grassroots support. There were also official bilateral initiatives paralleling the work of civil society at multiple levels.[190] Basically, the Oslo era transformed a handful of activists and projects into an Israeli/Palestinian peacebuilding civil society.

Second Intifada to Today

The violence of the Second Intifada, and the collapse of Oslo, dealt a severe blow to the fledgling field. Approximately half of the cross-border peacebuilding projects active in 2000 ceased in the first year of the hostilities.[191] Two decades of failed negotiations, the rise of extremism, and two wars in Gaza have further damaged the 'peace camp' and cross-border dialogue.[192] The freedom of movement of activists has also become more limited. Until the second Intifada, Israeli and Palestinian human rights activists met frequently and collaborated extensively. Today, with the walls, checkpoints, and regulations, it is very difficult for Israeli human rights activists to get into the territories, and it is almost impossible for Palestinians to leave the territories and enter Israel.[193] According to Fourest, '...Palestinian and Israeli civil societies have grown increasingly and dramatically oblivious to one another since the Second Intifada'.[194]

Nevertheless, the peacebuilding community has not entirely disappeared. According to a recent 2017 study by the Britain Israel Communications and Research Centre (BICOM),[195] a core group of peacebuilding NGOs have persevered despite the Second Intifada, adapting projects, and revising strategies for the harsh

---

[189] PCR was responsible for underground schools and dialogue groups with Israeli supporters of nonviolent struggle. See the organisation's website at www.pcr.ps.

[190] This included 'twinning' and partnerships between schools and other institutions outside the peacebuilding field. LC Endresen, *Contact and Cooperation: The Israeli-Palestinian People-to-People Program*. (FAFO Institute for Applied Social Science, 2001).

[191] This was particularly the case for governmental or municipal-based partnerships and others dependent on any degree of official goodwill. Avivit Hai and Shira Herzog, *The Power of Possibility: The Role of People-to-People Programs in the Current Israeli-Palestinian Reality* (Economic Cooperation Foundation, 2005).

[192] Operations Cast Lead and Protective Shield, as well as the Qassam rocket launches from Gaza into southern Israel have further segregated Palestinians and Israelis.

[193] Daphna Golan and Zvika Orr, 'Translating Human Rights of the Enemy: The Case of Israeli NGOs Defending Palestinian Rights' (2012) 46 *Law and Society Review* 781, 806.

[194] Fourest, above n 167, 75.

[195] BICOM is a UK-based organisation which acts to promote awareness of Israel and the Middle East in the UK. BICOM publishes significant research materials such as briefings, reports, and a journal on the region. Lazarus, above n 186, 31.

and recent practice demonstrates only partial consistency in application.[201] In short, there are no assurances that the Gazan hostilities or the Great March of Return will meet the gravity threshold for prosecutions.

Settlements

Regarding settlements, there are also no guarantees that the voluntary transfer of Israeli civilians would qualify as sufficiently egregious. Firstly, an occupied power's settlement activity is not a 'grave breach' of the Geneva Conventions[202] under Article 8(2)(b)(viii) of the Rome Statute.[203] The OTP has never investigated a situation defined primarily by non-grave breaches, nor that do not involve mass killing, wounding, or physical coercion.[204] Whilst it is arguable that settlements are nonetheless war crimes[205] that contribute to other serious human rights and IHL violations,[206] limited precedent exists that this activity warrants prosecutions.

Secondly, the OTP would at best have jurisdiction over settlement activity from 13 June 2014. The Court's temporal jurisdiction, which Palestine accepted retroactively from 13 June 2014, does not easily extend to the Israeli settlements. This is because population transfers were never criminalised in either Israeli or Palestinian

---

[201] Eugene Kontorovich, *When Gravity Fails: Israeli Settlements and the Admissibility at the ICC* 47(3) Isr. L. Rev. 379, 381–2 (2014) [hereinafter *When Gravity Fails*] (noting that the ICC Rome Statute and its drafting history offer no definition of 'gravity'. 'The Court has never defined it, and in almost all the situations before the Court the gravity of the crimes has been manifest, involving situations of mass atrocity as contemplated by the Preamble').

[202] Article 85(4)(a) of Additional Protocol I expanded the category of 'Grave Breaches' to include wilful breaches of Article 49 of Geneva Convention IV. Israel has not ratified the Additional Protocol while Palestine ratified it in 2014. Kearney, above n 172 at 13.

[203] Israeli settlements appear to violate Article 8(2)(b)(viii) of the Rome Statute, above n 32, which prohibits '[t]he transfer, directly or indirectly, by the Occupying Power of parts of its own civilian population into the territory it occupies'. The language is lifted almost verbatim from Article 49(6) of the Geneva Convention (IV).

[204] Kontorovitch, *When Gravity Fails,* above n 201 379 ('No modern international criminal tribunal has ever prosecuted crimes that do not involve systematic violence and physical coercion'). See also Robert Cryer et al., An Introduction to International Criminal Law and Procedure (2010) ('So far, all situations in which investigations have been initiated involved hundreds or thousands of the gravest forms of crimes (such as murder or sexual violence)').

[205] Kearney, above n 172 at 4.

[206] A UN Human Rights Council Fact-Finding Mission concluded Israeli settlements materially contribute to systematic and widespread human rights violations against Palestinians and that Israel is committing serious breaches of its obligations under the right to self-determination and IHL. See UN Human Rights Council, Report of the Independent International Fact-Finding Mission to Investigate the Implications of the Israeli settlements on the Civil, Political, Economic, Social and Cultural Rights of the Palestinian People throughout the Occupied Palestinian Territory, including East Jerusalem, A/HRC/RES/22/63 (7 February 2013) ¶¶104–11; OTP Jurisdiction Request 2019, above n 47 at ¶ 9.

post-Oslo political landscape.[196] The Alliance for Middle East Peace (ALLMEP)[197] NGO network recently added its 100th member. There are at least 164 organisations currently engaged in peace, conflict resolution, or cross-conflict civil and human rights work in the Israeli and the Palestinian territories.[198]

Moreover, a new wave of joint Israeli–Palestinian peacebuilding groups developed in response to the changing context. Grassroots initiatives such as Ta'ayush and Machsom Watch combined aspects of nonviolent direct action, human rights monitoring, and humanitarian relief to oppose the checkpoints and the Separation Barrier.[199] In particular, Bethlehem became the focus of nonviolent activity as three new organisations formed despite the violent nature of the Second Intifada, including the Palestinian Center for Conflict Resolution and Reconciliation (CCRR), Wi'am, and Holy Land Trust.[200] Other Palestinian NGOs based in Ramallah and Jerusalem have kept the momentum of nonviolent resistance alive, such as Middle East Nonviolence and Democracy (MEND) and the Center of Community Development and Democracy.[201] The contemporary peacebuilding community continues to include a resilient and professionalised[202] sector of civil society activists and NGOs. Despite the political impasse, militant opposition, and public inertia, Israeli–Palestinian peacebuilding remains a vital and diverse field.

Israeli and Palestinian Human Rights Groups

The work of human rights groups is also essential to mapping the civic landscape. Human rights discourse continues to command a prominent space in international relations, as well as in Israel.[203] Using a variety of strategies, many human rights groups were established in the late 1980s to expose Israel's military abuses and to defend the rights of Palestinians.[204] NGO's such as B'Tselem,[205] the Israeli

---

[196] At least 66 pre-Second Intifada organisations remain active today. Ibid 36.

[197] See the organisation's website at http://www.allmep.org.

[198] There are at least nine degree-granting academic programmes in conflict resolution, multiple research centres, and a host of less formal, local initiatives. Lazarus, above n 186, 17.

[199] See Maia Hallward, 'Building Space for Peace? Israeli and Palestinian Activism in the Second Intifada' (2009) 21(3) *Global Change, Peace and Security* 309.

[200] Omri Arens and Edward Kaufman, 'The Potential Impact of Palestinian Nonviolent struggle on Israel: preliminary lessons and projections for the future' (2012) 66(2) *Middle East Journal* 231, 239.

[201] Ibid.

[202] Today's leading organisations are often skilled in articulating theories of change, establishing indicators, and speaking the language of impact assessment. Lazarus, above n 185, 36.

[203] Golan and Orr, 'Translating Human Rights of the Enemy', above n 193, 782.

[204] Lazarus, above n 186, 33.

[205] B'Tselem, the Israeli Information Center for Human Rights in the Occupied Territories, is the largest organisation documenting human rights violations in the territories. B'Tselem www.btselem.org.

Information Center for Human Rights in the Occupied Territories, and the Public Committee Against Torture focus mainly on monitoring and reporting violations in the territories. Others, such as Physicians for Human Rights, Machsom Watch, and Hamoked for Defense of Individuals provide individual Palestinians with legal and advocacy assistance.[206] The Association for Civil Rights in Israel (ACRI)[207] focuses on petitioning the High Court in precedent-setting cases regarding the violation of Palestinian rights. These groups have been collecting testimonies and documenting violations for decades, all of which might 1 day lay the foundations for a transitional justice mechanism.

Although the operational space of Israeli groups is far broader, there are also examples of Palestinian human rights organisations. In 1979, Law in the Service of Man (LSM) was the first Palestinian human rights group to pursue legal strategies (monitoring, reporting, and advocacy) to challenge the Israeli narrative by documenting routine military abuses.[208] Today, the Palestinian Center for Human Rights,[209] al-Haq,[210] the Alternative Information Center,[211] and the Ramallah Center for Human Rights Studies in the West Bank[212] all play strong roles in producing high-quality and widely distributed information. Indeed, a wide spectrum of recognised Palestinian civil society actors supported efforts for the PA to join the ICC.[213] Without doubt, the achievements of these human rights organisations have been impressive.[214]

[206] HaMoked—www.hamoked.org.il; The Association of Civil Rights—www.acri.org.il; The Public Committee against Torture—www.stoptorture.org.il.

[207] ACRI is Israel's largest and oldest human rights organisation. www.acri.org.il/en/.

[208] Lisa Hajjar, 'Human Rights in Israel-Palestine: The History and Politics of a Movement' (2001) 30(4) *Journal of Palestine Studies* 21, 25.

[209] http://pchrgaza.org/en/

[210] Al Haq is a notable West Bank human rights organisation. It is often considered as a tireless and effective voice in its cause. http://www.alhaq.org/

[211] The Alternative Information Center (AIC) is a joint Palestinian–Israeli NGO which 'engages in dissemination of information, political advocacy, grassroots activism and critical analysis of the Palestinian and Israeli societies as well as the Israeli–Palestinian conflict'.

[212] The Ramallah Center for Human Rights Studies (RCHRS) is an independent Palestinian NGO that advocates human rights, democracy and tolerance from a secular perspective.

[213] Bill van Esveld, 'Why Palestine Should Seek Justice at the International Criminal Court', *Ma'an News Agency*, republished by Human Rights Watch, 6 December 2013 http://www.hrw.org/news/2013/12/06/why-palestine-shouldseek-justice-international-criminal-court.

[214] For example, 48 employees work for the Association for Civil Rights in Israel. Some 60,000–80,000 people access their website each month. See Daphna Golan-Agnon, 'Between Human Rights and Hope—What Israelis Might Learn from the Truth and Reconciliation Process in South Africa' (2010) 17 *International Review of Victimology* 31 39.

Challenges for Israeli–Palestinian Civic Peacebuilding and Human Rights

Embattled Field

At the same time, Israeli/Palestinian peacebuilding and human rights activity remain a relatively small and embattled field. Out of more than 20,000 active registered NGOs in Israel, fewer than 5% are advocacy groups, and even less are dealing directly with the conflict.[215] The fact that such a small proportion of Israeli civil society engages the conflict reflects a willingness among many Israelis to ignore it, and to unilaterally separate from the Palestinians.[216] 'Israeli public opinion seems to favour a strategy of conflict management by hiding the conflict behind the Wall'.[217]

On the Palestinian side, the proportion of such civic initiatives is even smaller. In recent years, many Palestinians have grown suspicious of human rights discourse,[218] as a result of Oslo's failure and the multiplication of NGOs[219] with no visible impact.[220] The seeming impotence of the international community to end the conflict has not helped. Lack of consensus and a stalled peace process have also caused the political demobilisation of large sectors of Palestinian society, 'as the people are genuinely uninterested, fatigued or imbued with a sense of futility regarding their efforts'.[221]

Among both the societies, peace NGOs are accused of disloyalty, betrayal, and even of 'airing dirty laundry' in public. For Palestinians, cooperation with Israelis is often branded as 'normalisation of the occupation'.[222] Many Palestinian NGOs have taken up this position, rejecting out of hand projects that artificially unite Israelis with Palestinians. For example, the Palestinian Universities (with the exception of

[215] 164 active peacebuilding/human rights organisations are but a fraction of the NGOs in Israel. See Lazarus, above n 186, 17.

[216] Invoking a need for 'separating' from the Palestinians has become the default position across left and right of Israeli politics. Abe Silberstein and Nathan Hersh, 'Israel's Left Goes Right', *New York Times*, 21 December 2017.

[217] Fourest, above n 167, 80.

[218] 'Decades of Israeli occupation, in which law was used to dispossess and disempower rather than protect Palestinians, fostered a skepticism about law's positive possibilities'. Hajjar, 'Human Rights in Israel-Palestine', above n 208, 25.

[219] Secular NGOs, whether local or international, enjoy a poor reputation among Palestinians, in so far as they are suspected or accused of being profit oriented and focusing on useless abstract concepts. Fourest, above n 167, 80.

[220] Persons involved in such NGOs are ironically referred to as 'Power-point people'. According to Golan and Orr, the influence of human rights litigation on the reality of four million occupied Palestinians is questionable. Golan and Orr, 'Translating Human Rights of the Enemy', above n 193, 782.

[221] Hassassian, above n 168, 80–81.

[222] The policy of anti-normalisation is a grassroots Palestinian movement that urges Palestinians (and others) to refrain from collaborating with Israelis as a form of non-violent resistance to the occupation.

Al-Quds) and the Palestinian NGO network have officially boycotted any joint activity with their Israeli counterparts.[223] Some Palestinian peacebuilding advocates experience harassment from anti-normalisation activists, whose bullying tactics include blacklisting and threats.[224] In Israel, vandalism and verbal attacks against peace activists as 'Leftists' and 'Jewish traitors' are also common. Activities and statements from the extreme right are buoyed by supportive rhetoric from the government. The lack of political engagement between Israelis and Palestinians also hinders cooperation and/or normalisation between the two sides.[225]

Official Hostility

Marginalisation and stigmatisation have also taken their toll. There are few government statements supporting joint activities, and almost no thought by officials on how to make this an integral part of the peace process and of peacemaking.[226] In fact, in recent years, the 'right-wing' bloc Netanyahu government has made strident attempts to undermine the work of NGOs. In 2016, the Knesset passed the 'NGO Transparency Law', requiring civil society organisations to disclose their degree of funding from foreign entities, in an attempt to impugn the loyalty of peace and human rights NGOs that are primarily supported by international donors.[227] This move reflects the current political climate of seeking to silence critical engagement with the conflict and revive traditional Zionist narratives. The 'Nakba law'[228] (2011) also provides an excellent example of this official trend. Arguably, the Israeli state discursively constitutes human rights groups as a security threat.[229]

---

[223] The Palestinian NGO network even expelled one of its member organisations for continuing to engage in such activities. Mohammed Dajani and Gershon Baskin, 'Israeli-Palestinian Joint Activities: Problematic Endeavour, but Necessary Challenge' in Edy Kaufman, Walid Salem and Juliette Verhoeven (eds), *Bridging the Divide: Peacebuilding in the Israeli-Palestinian Conflict* (Lynne Rienner, 2006) 99.

[224] In 2014, for example, a 2-day 'Minds of Peace' conference in Ramallah in the West Bank was broken up by anti-normalisation activists, who hung a poster over the hotel entrance stating: 'Normalisation [with Israel] is an act of treason'. Lazarus, above n 186, 17.

[225] Hassassian, above n 168, 80–81.

[226] Dajani and Baskin, above n 223, 96–7.

[227] The law requires Israeli NGOs to report more than 50% of funding received from foreign public sources and to indicate on all publications that they are funded by 'foreign agents'. Failing to abide by these rules will be considered a criminal offence.

[228] The Nakba Law is an amendment empowering the Minister of Finance to reduce monetary support for bodies or institutions (e.g. schools, universities or local authorities) that fund events or actions marking the date of Israel's establishment as a day of mourning (or undermining the existence of Israel as a Jewish and democratic state). *Budget Principles Law* (Amendment #40), 5771–2011, SH No. 2286, 686–7.

[229] Neve Gordon, 'Human Rights as a Security Threat: Lawfare and the Campaign against Human Rights NGOs' (2014) 48(2) *Law & Society Review* 311, 312.

Similarly, the PA has sought to de-legitimise critical human rights and peace organisations as disrupting or undermining 'national unity'.[230] For instance, most joint peace activities within the Palestinian education system have had to rely on private schools because the Palestinian Ministry of Education has prevented such programmes from gaining access to public schools under its jurisdiction.[231] The Palestinian Ministry of Higher Education advocates a policy of non-cooperation with the Israeli Higher Learning institution.[232] The PA also discredits local human rights groups as 'foreign', a critique that resonates with many Palestinians because of an enduring perception that human rights are 'Western'.[233] Given the absence of state support, this field is therefore prone to donor fatigue, volatility, and 'turnover'. Many veteran groups have closed doors, downscaled, or have had to reset strategy.[234] Overall, despite the international visibility enjoyed by Israeli and Palestinian NGOs, their size, means of action, and local impact are relatively limited.[235]

'Small But Significant'

> *Dozens of viable organisations have been established in each of the last three decades, while the strategies employed for cross-conflict engagement have grown.*[236]

Despite the diplomatic impasse, ideological opposition, and the 'silent majority', Israeli–Palestinian peacebuilding remains a vital, diverse, and resilient field. The civic repertoire has endured and evolved. Individual organisations have closed doors, re-branded or rebooted, but peacebuilding approaches have steadily grown in volume and sophistication. New NGOs like Women Wage Peace (WWP) have risen to prominence.[237] In October 2016, tens of thousands of women, Arab and Jewish, Israeli and Palestinian rallied throughout the country urging the government to renew peace negotiations. Approximately 4000 Israeli and Palestinian women marched from Jericho to Jerusalem, where they joined 20,000 protestors outside the Israeli PM's residence. 'In the process, they illustrated the enduring potential of grassroots organising, and the resonance – even today – of a well-crafted campaign of peace advocacy'.[238] The rise of the extreme right in Israel has also generated a

---

230 Hajjar, 'Human Rights in Israel-Palestine', above n 208, 29.

231 Dajani and Baskin, above n 223, 97.

232 Hassassian, above n 168, 80–81.

233 Hajjar, 'Human Rights in Israel-Palestine', above n 208, 31.

234 Alongside at least 164 active organisations, the BICOM research finds at least 77 initiatives that have either ceased to exist (41) or whose status is unclear at present (36), some closing after a decade or more of activity. Lazarus, above n 186, 17.

235 Mohammed Abu-Nimer, 'Nonviolent Action in Israeli and Palestine: A Growing Force' in Edy Kaufman, Walid Salem and Juliette Verhoeven (eds), *Bridging the Divide: Peacebuilding in the Israeli-Palestinian Conflict* (Lynne Rienner, 2006) 147.

236 Lazarus, above n 186, 17.

237 Ibid.

238 Ibid 13.

degree of counter-mobilisation among some mainstream elements in Israeli society.[239] Overall, Israeli–Palestinian peacebuilding is a larger, and more diverse field than commonly assumed.

Since the Second Intifada, a host of sceptics have questioned whether peacebuilding projects have had any impact at all.[240] Nevertheless, 'Evaluation and scholarship have validated the effectiveness of numerous civic peacebuilding strategies'.[241] Indeed, the breadth and depth of existing research is substantial for a field that has only existed for a few decades.[242] 'It is doubtful that similar scrutiny has been applied to civil society peacebuilding in any comparable conflict context, including the Northern Ireland precedent'.[243]

Even within the current climate, sustained advocacy campaigns have achieved meaningful policy change. For instance, NGOs like EcoPeace have played a major role in convincing the Israeli government to reform its allocation of natural resources independent of final status negotiations.[244] Since 2016, Israel has more than doubled its water supply to Palestinians in the territories. In another example, the Near East Foundation (NEF) Olive Oil Without Borders project has facilitated cross-border trade and cooperation between thousands of Palestinian and Israeli olive producers. Many such projects have documented positive attitudinal shifts.[245] It is therefore premature to eulogise Israeli and Palestinian civil actors, and discount their instrumental value.

> *The human rights organizations are the only ones that create some kind of bridge-albeit a problematic and imperfect one-in a reality in which Israelis and Palestinians meet almost always as enemies.*[246]

Human rights NGOs have also left their imprint on state policy. Notwithstanding many courtroom losses,[247] legal advocacy has engendered some historic wins and

---

[239] For example, Israel's President Reuven Rivlin is the most prominent of a number of long-time right-wing politicians now advocating inclusive politics toward Arab citizens, respect for human rights and expressing consistent opposition to incitement and violence. Ibid 17.

[240] According to Fourest, today, civil society in Israel/Palestine has nothing but a symbolic impact. Fourest, above n 167, 80; Mathew Kalman, 'Will Seeds of Peace Ever Bloom?', *Haaretz*, 15 September 2014.

[241] Lazarus, above n 186, 17.

[242] The local field has a steadily growing 'paper trail' of evaluation reports, meta-evaluations, scholarly studies, and qualitative research. Ibid 39.

[243] Ibid.

[244] EcoPeace is a trilateral Israeli/Palestinian/Jordanian environmental NGO. In 2013, EcoPeace convinced the Israeli government to release fresh water from the Sea of Galilee into the Jordan for the first time in 50 years. More controversially, EcoPeace has campaigned for water to be resolved independently from political negotiations. Lazarus, above n 186, 29.

[245] After the Olive Oil Without Borders project, 90% of participants reported increased trust in 'the other' and 77% indicated the intention to continue cross-border cooperation. Interview conducted by BICOM with Near East Foundation (NEF) Director Charles Benjamin, cited in ibid.

[246] Golan and Orr, 'Translating Human Rights of the Enemy', above n 193, 808.

[247] Analysis of human rights litigation in Israel often equates courtroom losses to 'no impact'. See ibid.; Shlomo Mizrahi and Assaf Meydani, 'Political Participation via the Judicial System: Exit,

prompted institutional shifts. For example, in September 1999, after rejecting numerous appeals, the Israeli Supreme Court ruled that the use of physical force by Israeli security services was illegal.[248] This decision changed interrogation protocols, and whilst it did not decisively end torture, some of the more brutal practices routinely employed against Palestinians in detention were abandoned.[249] Other victories include the rulings on Alfei Menashe,[250] Beit Sourik,[251] and Bil'in,[252] which ordered the Israeli government to change the route of the separation fence. Ultimately, the HCJ voided the route of the fence along more than 30 of the 40 km that were in dispute in these petitions.[253] Many human rights achievements also occur 'in the shadow of the High Court'. For example, Hamoked observes that over 70% of its petitions against restrictions of Palestinian movement are cancelled even before court, because once the appeal is submitted, the 'security-motivated' restrictions are lifted.[254] Finally, human rights petitions create a valuable legal record of the violations.[255] In the words of Israeli–Palestinian attorney Fatma El Ajou of Adalah: 'the High Court is the best record of the occupation'.[256]

In this light, human rights activists bear witness to the suffering and bring the voices of the tortured and the detained to the lounge rooms of the public.[257] Their tremendous value became particularly clear during the last two Gaza wars, 'when they helped civilian victims of the offensive receive medical care, warned against the Israeli army's disproportionate use of weapons, called on Israel to avoid targeting civilians, and reported to international bodies'.[258] Overall, despite the challenges

---

Voice and Quasi-Exit in Israeli Society' (2003) 8 *Israel Studies* 118; Maayan Geva, 'Human rights litigation and the transition from policing to warfare: the case of Israel and its governance of the West Bank and Gaza in the Al-Aqsa Intifada' (2017) 49(3) *The Journal of Legal Pluralism and Unofficial Law* 294, 295.

[248] HCJ 5100/94 The Public Committee Against Torture in Israel v. The State of Israel (1999). The petition was submitted by Israeli NGOs HaMoked, Center for the Defence of the Individual, the Association for Civil Rights in Israel and the Public Committee against Torture in Israel. B'Tselem also published a significant report on torture in 1991 which galvanised legal action.

[249] Golan and Orr, 'Translating Human Rights of the Enemy', above n 193, 793.

[250] HCJ 7957/04 Zaharan Yunis Muhammad Mara'abe v. The Prime Minister (2005).

[251] HCJ 2056/04 The Beit Sourik Village Council v. The Government of Israel (2004).

[252] HCJ 8414/05 Ahmed Issa Abdallah Yassin v. The Government of Israel et al. (2007).

[253] These petitions were submitted by Israeli NGOs, HaMoked and Center for the Defence of the Individual.

[254] David Kretzmer, *The Occupation of Justice: The Supreme Court of Israel and the Occupied Territories* (State University of New York Press, 2002) 189.

[255] Lisa Hajjar argues for NGO litigation as a means of documentation because court proceedings provide knowledge of alleged abuses. Lisa Hajjar, *Virtual Roundtable* (February 2008) Adalah: The Legal Center for Arab Minority Rights in Israel, Accessed 18 July 2017. http://adalah.org/newsletter/eng/feb08/roundtable/Hajjar.html

[256] Golan and Orr, 'Translating Human Rights of the Enemy', above n 193, 793.

[257] Ibid 808.

[258] Ibid.

and limitations, human rights NGOs do important work, with the impact of litigation extending far beyond the Israeli courtroom.[259]

Civic Capacity

Whilst at present, Israeli–Palestinian civil society is too small to achieve macro-political change, local actors remain capable of reforming policy and shaping the conflict narrative. It is worth recalling that the operational space occupied by the human rights groups in Israel is far broader than it was in South Africa during apartheid.[260] They are working in a political context with more freedom of expression, less censorship, and less personal risk associated with human rights activism. As noted above, the active involvement of South African civil society about a decade prior to the end of apartheid was instrumental to building the legitimacy of the SATRC.[261]

Many factors have developed over the past two decades which also make Palestinian society more conducive to human rights norms and civil society. For example, a tolerance for divergent opinions has evolved into an intrinsic value and tradition among Palestinians.[262] According to Hajjar, Palestinian human rights organisations today form part of '…a larger constellation of NGOs that enjoy legitimacy as home-grown, and historically active, on behalf of the needs and interests of [their] society'.[263] 'Another major factor is the development of a participatory political culture in which elections and popular consent are considered legitimate'.[264]

Despite the cynicism for human rights, this discourse remains a reference point for most activists in the region, who continue to frame their struggle within IHL and human rights law.[265] It is also worth recalling that 'anti-normalisation' does not necessarily mean anti-Israeli. Opinion ranges within Palestinian society regarding this strategy,[266] and many Palestinian NGOs, which officially reject contact with Israel, collaborate with their Israeli counterparts under the radar or aspire to such

[259] 'The processes of change unfolding in court demonstrate that a case lost does not necessarily indicate zero influence on state policy'. Geva, above n 247, 295; Kretzmer, above n 254, 189. Michael Sfard, 'The human rights lawyer's existential dilemma' (2005) 38(3) *Israel Law Review* 154.

[260] Golan-Agnon, above n 214.

[261] Crocker, 'Transitional Justice and International Civil Society', above n 10, 505.

[262] Hassassian, above n 168, 65.

[263] Hajjar, 'Human Rights in Israel-Palestine', above n 208, 29.

[264] A good example is the active political participation of women, which is an essential part of Palestinian civil society today, and has a crucial impact on the establishment and consolidation of pluralist thinking and democratic rule. Hassassian, above n 168, 65.

[265] Fourest, above n 167, 93.

[266] For some Palestinian peacebuilding activists, engagement with Israelis is a crucial avenue for advocating Palestinian rights. Palestinian peacebuilding advocate Aziz Abu Sarah argues that 'normalisation' has become an outmoded term, a catch-all argument against Israeli–Arab cooperative efforts and a cover for character assassination in Palestinian politics. Lazarus, above n 186, 17.

co-operation in the future.[267] Accordingly, civic capacity exists for peacebuilding and human rights groups to bear fruit for transitional justice.

7.5 Part Four: Israeli/Palestinian Civic Resistance to Transitional Justice

Notwithstanding inroads made by peacebuilding and human rights groups, Israelis and Palestinians have struggled to mobilise transitional justice. As discussed in Chap. 4, the terms 'truth-telling', 'historical justice', and 'reconciliation' have not been popularised in the region and do not serve as established markers of this line of activity.[268] Whilst a small number of such projects do exist (as discussed below), the desirability of dealing with the historical past has not entered the lexicon of mainstream NGOs, peacebuilders or the public. Many groups are involved in or support peace advocacy and human rights, yet few of them consciously and explicitly frame their activities within the context of transitional justice. Naturally, 'civil society is both an independent agent for change and a dependent product of existing structures'.[269] Thus, Israeli and Palestinian civil societies reproduce the fault-lines of prevailing political assumptions and rhetoric. This section briefly outlines the various factors that explain why Israeli and Palestinian civil societies have been unable to fully embrace transitional justice.

Hegemonic Security Discourse

> *...it was difficult to find human rights organizations which are openly against the occupation.*[270] (Aeyal Gross)

Most Israeli NGOs conform to a Zionist discourse on security and do not directly challenge official narratives on the legitimacy of the ongoing occupation. As discussed in Chap. 1, military control over the territories is widely regarded by Israelis as a necessary defensive mechanism.[271] Moreover, the IDF is glorified as a moral

---

[267] According to Fourest, 'Driving the Jews into the sea' has no reality whatsoever in dominant Palestinian discourse and hopes. Fourest, above n 167, 79.

[268] Rosalind Shaw, Lars Waldorf, and Pierre Hazan (eds), *Localizing Transitional Justice: Interventions and Priorities After Mass Violence* (Stanford University Press, 2010).

[269] Raffaele Marchetti and Nathalie Tocci, above n 167. 'Conflict Society: Understanding the Role of Civil Society in Conflict' (2009) 21(2) *Global Change Peace & Security* 201, 202.

[270] Comments by Aeyal Gross at a faculty seminar of the Minerva Center for Human Rights, Neve Shalom, 12 January 2007; Golan-Agnon, above n 214, 39.

[271] Ghazi-Bouillon, above n 122, 122; Bar-Tal and Schnell, *'The Impacts of Lasting Occupation'*, above n 112, 519.

institution in Israel and maintains a powerful grip on Israelis.[272] Thus, Israeli NGOs may produce important reports defending Palestinian rights in the territories, or develop worthy peace projects, but they avoid taking a clear political stand against the military occupation, the primary source of human rights violations.[273] Since the Israeli public largely perceives IDF conduct as justified against Palestinian violence, there is a tendency to avoid recognising the occupation per se as a major cause of Palestinian suffering. Arguably, civil society in South Africa was far more 'political' in nature and did not hesitate to challenge the legitimacy of apartheid[274] or repudiate the structural violence against Black South Africans.[275]

By contrast, Israeli human rights groups seek to mediate Palestinian suffering through 'neutral', 'apolitical', and 'legal' language that conforms to the national discourse on security.[276] 'Even Peace Now, the backbone of the Israeli peace movement is remarkably guarded, carefully avoiding official participation in public demonstrations'.[277] Despite their opposition to Israeli settlement policy, Peace Now leaders remain loyal to the national consensus on supporting the army.[278] Thus, B'Tselem once explained that the organisation is political 'with a small p not a capital P' and sends the Israeli public a message that has to be 'softened, tried and tested with great caution'.[279] B'Tselem has shifted its position in recent years.[280] Indeed,

---

[272] Israel has been in a state of war since its creation. Its security specialists have continually shaped the dominant views within public opinion and civil society on questions of war and peace. At present, there is only a very limited amount of Israelis who refuse to serve in the IDF. Fourest, above n 167, 81; See also Abu-Nimer, above n 235, 147.

[273] Fourest, above n 167, 79.

[274] As Cohen has commented, '[i]n South Africa the struggle for legality and basic civil rights was inseparable from the overall political struggle'. Stanley Cohen, 'The Human Rights Movement in Israel and South Africa: Some Paradoxical Comparisons' (1991) *The Harry S Truman Institute* (Hebrew University, Jerusalem, Occasional Papers No 1).

[275] Johan Galtung and Tord Hoivik, 'Structural and Direct Violence—A Note on Operationalization' (1971) 8(1) *Journal of Peace Research* 73.

[276] In Israel, numerous NGOs use the human rights discourse to assert their non-political identity. Fourest, above n 167, 79; Golan and Orr, 'Translating Human Rights of the Enemy', above n 193, 801.

[277] Giles Fraser, 'Against the war: the movement that dare not speak its name in Israel', *The Guardian* (London), 6 August 2014.

[278] Peace Now avoids any direct confrontation with Israeli military forces on the ground, with many serving in the army or reserves. See David Hall-Cathalah, *The Peace Movement in Israel 1967–1987* (St Martins Press, 1990); Mordechai Ben Or, *In Pursuit of Peace: A History of the Israeli Peace Movement* (United States Institute of Peace Press, 1996).

[279] Orr and Golan conducted interviews with Jessica Montell (former Executive director) and Najib Abu Rokaya (formerly director of field coordinators in B'Tselem), 7 July 2009. Daphna Golan Zivka Orr, 'Human Rights NGOs in Israel: Collective Memory and Denial' (2014) 18(1) *The International Journal of Human Rights* 68, 75.

[280] Since 2017, B'Tselem has taken a more public stand against the Israeli occupation. For example, B'Tselem Executive Director Hagai El-Ad made a speech in 2018 to the UN Human Rights Committee that was highly critical of the occupation, comparing Israeli policies to apartheid-era South Africa and urging the international community to act on their behalf. See for example: https://www.btselem.org/duty_to_end_occupation

whilst there are notable exceptions,[281] most groups remain reluctant to explicitly call for an end to the occupation. By and large, Israeli civil society refrains from challenging the military, or other core foundations of the occupation.

Sidelining 1948 and Collective Rights

From their perspective, the rights of the Palestinians begin in 1967....(Fayrouz Sharqawi[282])

Mirroring the Oslo paradigm, the issue of Palestinian refugees, and their right of return, is consciously ignored by Israeli NGOs.[283] The 'Nakba' (as discussed in Chap. 1) does not feature prominently in the human rights discourse.[284] Virtually all human rights organisations are consumed by 1967 and focus on ongoing human rights abuses. For example, ACRI, the leading group on civil and political rights in Israel does not work on questions specifically related to 1948.[285] A similar approach is adopted by B'Tselem, which '...has never written a report on this issue and is reluctant to openly and publicly discuss the *Nakba* and the future rights of 1948 Palestinian refugees'.[286] Arguably, the pressing need to respond to the current human rights situation in the territories explains the lack of engagement with the past.[287] Nevertheless, it is also clear that the sensitivity and political taboos around this event inhibit civil society.[288]

> *Israeli human rights organizations deal mostly with individual Palestinians and leave issues pertaining to collective rights to the politicians.*[289]

[281] For example, Machsom Watch, Yesh Din, established in 2005, and Women in Black were the first human rights NGOs to question the wisdom of 'not doing politics' and 'not calling to end the occupation.' Golan and Orr, 'Translating Human Rights of the Enemy', above n 193, 806.

[282] Fayrouz Sharqawi served as a media coordinator at the Association for Civil Rights in Israel (ACRI). He comments on the non-committal approach of ACRI regarding the Nakba: '...The discourse about the 1948 Palestinians [citizens of Israel] focuses on their civil rights. The discourse has nothing to do with history and their ties to the Palestinian people' quoted in Golan and Orr, 'Human Rights NGOs in Israel', above n 279, 69–72.

[283] Ibid 69–72.

[284] This is the case for a wide range of organisations, from those that focus on Palestinian human rights in the territories to those that focus on economic and social rights within Israel. Ibid.

[285] Ehud Uziel, ACRI's campaign and new media manager and IHL Program manager, stated: 'This is an issue for which ACRI has not yet formulated a position and has not gotten into.' Ibid 72–73.

[286] Ibid.

[287] For example, Jessica Montell, former executive director of B'Tselem, explained that the organisation's limited resources are directed at the urgent cases taking place right now. Interviews conducted by Orr with Jessica Montell. Ibid.

[288] 'The organisations fear that their current ability to make change and assist people whose rights have been violated (limited and partial as this ability is) would be lost or severely damaged if they engaged in 'political' taboo issues such as the Nakba...'. Ibid 75.

[289] Exceptions to this rule are the Palestinian–Israeli organisations, Adallah and Mossawa, both of which advocate for collective rights. They are, however, concerned primarily with the collective

Moreover, unlike some other transitional contexts, human rights discourse in Israel stresses individual rights.[290] Despite the collective rights of Palestinians[291] (e.g. self-determination) and the violations against Palestinian as a group (e.g. collective punishment), human rights practice revolves around petitioning the courts for individual Palestinians.[292] Legal advocacy is disassociated from the national context, particularly the Palestinian experience of 1948.[293] For example, most human rights groups like ACRI[294] act according to the existing framework on Palestinian land rights without even mentioning the Nakba which informed the current reality.[295] In the words of an intern: 'B'Tselem supports the human rights of the Palestinians in the Occupied Territories, but not the struggle of the Palestinians as a people for rights to identity and freedom'.[296] In sum, neither the 'structural violence' of the conflict nor the historical experiences that gave rise to them are the focus of Israeli civil society. Overall, NGO activities concern individuals and current abuses, without vigorously challenging the fundamental reasons why Israel perpetuates the occupation or denies the Nakba.

Legalism

Furthermore, human rights groups adopt legal discourse as the primary language of activism rather than the richer vocabulary of transitional justice.[297] The Israeli human rights movement pursues litigation as a key strategy in its efforts to intervene in the conflict.[298] Many NGOs inform Palestinians of their rights, assist in

rights of Palestinians inside Israel and less with those in the territories. Golan-Agnon, above n 214, 40–41.

[290] In Israel, as was the case in South Africa and Northern Ireland, the conflict centres on collective political rights, yet the organisations in Israel are focused on individual violations. Ibid 39.

[291] According to Allen: 'the right to self-determination, which has some potential of challenging the settler colonial structures, has not, by and large, entered into these NGOs' discourse and court petitions'. Lori Allen, 'The Rise and Fall of Human Rights: Cynicism and Politics in Occupied Palestine' (Stanford University Press, 2013).

[292] Notably, the Israeli HCJ will not hear any discussion pertaining to collective rights of Palestinians.

[293] Golan and Orr, 'Human Rights NGOs in Israel', above n 279, 74.

[294] ACRI's mandate pertains to the civil, political, and legal rights of individuals. Thus while ACRI was critical of some of the Israeli state's practices in the territories, the organisation has never pursued a role of challenging the occupation, promoting the cause of Palestinian national/collective rights, or asserting a position independent of the state's on the applicability of the Fourth Geneva Convention. Hajjar, above n, 25.

[295] Golan and Orr, 'Human Rights NGOs in Israel', above n 279, 74.

[296] Interview conducted by Orr with Amany Khalefa, 29 February 2012. Golan and Orr, 'Translating Human Rights of the Enemy', above n 193, 801.

[297] Ibid 791.

[298] Geva, above n 247, 296.

challenging legislation and petition Israeli courts. Notably, 'these organizations are not active at the grass roots level, but stress legal strategy'.[299] Instead of collective truth-telling or reconciliation, their focus is on the legal system and technical debate,[300] which reflects the 'legalisation' of Israeli society.[301] Arguably, human rights litigation is an attempt to solve the problem of the occupation without fundamentally questioning the existing political and historical structures that support the conflict. Indeed, despite the courtroom successes, 'all the victories belong to individual Palestinians and hence do not constitute a challenge to the system'.[302] From this standpoint, some query the impact of litigation on the daily lives of Palestinians,[303] and view the court as a legitimising institution of the occupation.[304] NGO practitioners have also doubted the benefits of their legal work. One NGO director described these groups as 'a fly on the emperor's nose'.[305] Human rights litigation is therefore limited, and legal discourse has a paucity of vocabulary for addressing history, justice, memory, and conflict transformation.

299 Golan-Agnon, above n 214, 39.

300 'Dozens of Israeli jurists working for the government and the army argue over legal interpretations with jurists from international and Israeli human rights organizations'. Golan and Orr, 'Translating Human Rights of the Enemy', above n 193, 792.

301 There are more lawyers per capita in Israel than in any other country in the world. Golan-Agnon, above n 214, 40–41.

302 Thus, for example, the human rights organisations did not challenge the overall logic and justice of building a wall on Palestinian land, but merely opposed the exact location of certain stretches of that wall. Ibid.

303 According to Golan and Orr, the influence of human rights NGOs on the reality of four million Palestinians living under oppressive military occupation is negligible. Golan and Orr, 'Translating Human Rights of the Enemy', above n 193, 782; See also Orna Ben-Naftali, *PathoLAWgical Occupation: Normalizing the Exceptional Case of the Occupied Palestinian Territory and Other Legal Pathologies in International Humanitarian Law and International Human Rights Law: Pas de Deux* (Oxford University Press, 2011) 129–200.

304 David Kretzmer argues that by exercising a limited measure of liberal justice, the court has legitimised the Israeli occupation and contributed to its continuance. Kretzmer, above n 254; See also Gad Barzilai, 'Between the Rule of Law and the Laws of the Ruler: The Supreme Court in Israeli Legal Culture' (1997) 49(2) *International Social Science Journal* 193, 202.

305 Golan and Orr quote NGO directors who at a conference entitled 'Forty Years of Occupation: What Have We Done, What Have We Achieved and What Next?' critically discussed the impact of their work. One director suggested their work amounts to carefully rearranging chairs on the deck of the Titanic, and another said that legal practice is comparable to sticking notes on the Wailing Wall. Golan and Orr, 'Translating Human Rights of the Enemy', above n 193, 781–2.

Palestinian Law-Fare and Absolute Justice

Palestinian civil society also tends to reject the term 'transitional justice', as it is seen to erode something essential in their quest for historical justice. Thus, many Palestinian groups remain wedded to utopian conceptions of return to their homes[306] and absolute justice.[307] Among Palestinians, NGOs are seen as '...effective in producing creative avenues of the national struggle, raising the sophistication of the fight from the streets and the rocks to the pen and opinions of men and women'.[308] Generally the goal of Palestinian civil society is to end the occupation and its 'evils' and not to promote conflict resolution.[309] Whilst Israeli peace activists tend to be motivated by social and cultural concerns, for Palestinians, such activities are more pragmatic and political platforms.[310] In this regard, when Palestinians do refer to transitional justice, it seems to be part of a human rights discourse that is strategically deployed as a political tool or weaponised against Israel.[311]

For example, unlike Israeli human rights NGOs that strive to be 'apolitical', the work of Palestinian groups seem to serve more overt nationalist political purposes. Thus, on the one hand, an ICC bid by Palestinian civil society is an effort to advance transitional justice, but on the other, it is part of a broader strategy to assert Palestinian statehood and label Israelis as war criminals.[312] Likewise, invocations of apartheid to describe the occupation, and related calls for boycott divestment and sanctions against Israel (BDS),[313] are intensely polemical even though they are part

---

[306] As noted in Chapter One, Palestinian discourse on return remains utopian, abstract, and nostalgic. For example, the BADIL Resource Center for Palestinian Residency and Refugee Rights is a human rights group committed to protect and promote the rights of Palestinian refugees and internally displaced persons to their *homes of origin*.

[307] As discussed in Chapter One, Palestinians narratives are often framed in zero-sum absolute terms. For example, in March 2017, Fathi Nemer, Program Officer at Ramallah Center for Human Rights Studies wrote an op-ed stating, 'The ethnic cleansing, massacres and colonialism needed to establish Israel can never be justified, regardless of who was there first...'. On its website, Al Haq writes: 'As Israel celebrates 61 years of independence, it must not be forgotten that its creation was based on settlement and colonisation of Palestinian land'.

[308] Hassassian, above n 168, 80.

[309] Benjamin Gidron, Stanley N Katz, and Yeheskel Hasenfeld (eds) *Mobilizing for Peace: Conflict Resolution in Northern Ireland, Israel/Palestine, and South Africa.* (Oxford University Press, 2002).

[310] Fourest, above n 167, 86.

[311] Ibid, 79.

[312] For example, the Palestinian Center for Human Rights (PCHR) is a leader in the ICC campaign. Arguably, this group commonly ignores the existence of terrorism against Israeli civilians and presents a one-sided version of the conflict based on a Palestinian narrative of suffering. The PCHR also used its legal advocacy "as a platform to lobby international forums and disseminate statements demonizing Israel." https://www.ngo-monitor.org/ngos/palestinian_center_for_human_rights_pchr_/

[313] In 2005, Palestinian civil society called for a global campaign to use the tactics of BDS against Israel and its institutions. Overwhelmingly popular, over 170 organisations, Palestinian women's organisations, trade unions and student groups support BDS.

of a conscious legal strategy for Palestinians.[314] The politicisation of human rights[315] therefore affects the credibility of the transitional justice paradigm. In the eyes of many Israelis, discussions on the ICC and truth commissions are yet another weapon in the diplomatic battlefield and instrument of law-fare (as discussed in Chap. 5). Broadly speaking, Palestinian civil society, as the political underdog, remains more committed to the national struggle than to the complex goals of truth-telling and reconciliation or what is left of the peace process.[316]

Public Hostility

Finally, civic resistance to transitional justice is also because NGOs must struggle against a tide of largely hostile public opinion regarding peacebuilding and human rights discussed above. This could be attributed, in part, to the mutual internalisation of victimhood explored in the Chap. 1. In Israel, there has been a harsh rejection of dissident civil society initiatives. As noted, the left-orientated peace camp is often depicted within Israel as Jewish traitors.[317] Similarly for Palestinians, those engaged in joint civic activity are viewed as collaborators with the enemy and/or abettors of the occupation. The anti-normalisation movement has taken its toll on joint activities between the two sides. Thus, many challenges persist in preparing the ground for a truth and reconciliation forum in the Israeli–Palestinian setting.

Conclusion

This section outlined some of the civic and discursive challenges facing transitional justice in the region. On the Israeli side, peacebuilding and human rights are commonly confined to 'apolitical' legal campaigns divorced from the historical context. For Palestinians, such activities tend to be driven by highly politicised notions of absolute justice and national resistance. In general, both the parties are constrained by fatigue and frozen political prejudices, reflecting a wholesale lack of enthusiasm for transitional justice.

---

[314] Waters, above n 172, 180.

[315] Many have examined the various uses of the term 'human rights' and explored how human rights claims have been deployed in specific political, historic, and cultural settings. Kenneth Cmiel, 'The Recent History of Human Rights' (2004) 109(1) *The American Historical Review* 117; see also Mark Goodale and Sally Engle Merry (eds), *The Practice of Human Rights: Tracking Law between the Global and the Local* (Cambridge University Press, 2007).

[316] Hassassian, above n 168, 72.

[317] Heribert Adam and Kogila Moodley, *Seeking Mandela: Peacemaking Between Israelis and Palestinians* (Temple University Press, 2005), 157.

Notably, opposition to transitional justice is not unique to the Middle East. For example, in Northern Ireland, Unionist opposition to engagement with the past also obstructed local truth-recovery efforts.[318] Based on qualitative fieldwork, Lawther argues that 'denial' and 'silence' were instrumental to political elites and security forces resisting transitional justice efforts in Northern Ireland.[319] Such dynamic is visible in other transitional contexts dealing with uncomfortable aspects of the past.[320] As discussed in Chap. 1, groups in conflict tend to form selective 'collective memories' that 'focus mainly on the other side's responsibility for the conflict and its misdeeds' while at the same time 'concentrating on their own self-justification, self-righteousness, glorification and victimization'.[321]

In this regard, denial and silence around legacies of violence are endemic to ethno-national conflict. These particular challenges, as well as those facing human rights and peace groups more generally, must be taken into account when conceiving any transitional justice project in the region. As will be discussed in Chap. 8, participatory and bilateral steps exist to perhaps mitigate some of the obstacles facing Israeli and Palestinian civil initiatives and resistance to transitional justice.

7.6 Part Five: Unofficial Israeli–Palestinian Transitional Justice Activity

In recent decades, small cracks have appeared in the hegemonic discourses discussed above. Notwithstanding the obstacles, pockets of Israeli/Palestinian civil society are seeking to weaken national resistance to exploring the past. Today, some notable civic transitional justice efforts deal with historic abuses, and more recognition exists about the limits of human rights litigation and peacebuilding advocacy. Civil society is extremely frustrated with the failed peace process and the ongoing violations of human rights. There is a growing feeling that new practices must be trialled to bring the conflict closer to an end. Aware that the current regime will not lead a 'peace with justice and reconciliation' process, a handful of groups are re-telling the story of the Israeli occupation and 1948.

In general, Israeli–Palestinian transitional justice projects inform national discourse through two goals: denunciation and reconciliation.[322] The first aim is

---

[318] Cheryl Lawther, 'Denial, Silence and the Politics of the Past: Unpicking the Opposition to Truth Recovery in Northern Ireland' (2013) 7 *The International Journal of Transitional Justice*, 157–177.

[319] Ibid.

[320] For example, see Matt James, 'A Carnival of Truth? Knowledge, Ignorance and the Canadian Truth and Reconciliation Commission', 6(2) (2012) *International Journal of Transitional Justice* 182–204, on efforts to deal with the past in a settled democracy.

[321] Daniel Bar-Tal, 'Collective Memory of Physical Violence: Its Contribution to the Culture of Violence', in Ed Cairns and Michael D. Roe (eds), *The Role of Memory in Ethnic Conflict*, (Palgrave Macmillan, 2003), 78.

[322] Dudai, 'Deviant Commemorations', above n 35, 2.

distinctly introspective, involving unilateral measures that encourage members of (mainly) Israeli–Jewish society to acknowledge their own abuses. The second goal is collaborative, reaching out across the Israeli–Palestinian divide, recognising the suffering of the 'other', and fostering mutual understanding as a tool of conflict transformation.[323] The organisations cited below reflect a transitional justice discourse that is more explicit, and one that consciously and provocatively challenges official narratives. This section outlines their major activities and contends that despite the challenges, they promote recognition of wrongdoing, reconciliation, and recasting of the historical issues.

Unilateral Transitional Justice Measures

Since the late 1990s, unofficial truth-telling and accountability efforts have started negotiating the complex past and collective denial. Notably, an essential feature of such measures is that they involve exposing abuses committed by one's own in-group against members of an ethnic, national, or religious out-group.[324] Almost all of the unilateral projects discussed below are about influencing members of Israeli–Jewish society to acknowledge its wrongdoing against Palestinians. Notably, the Palestinian polity, as the weaker party, is less empowered to unilaterally transform its conflict narratives.[325] Nevertheless, national memory and history has been a platform for mobilising transitional justice and identity construction across both the societies.

Academia and History

> *As Palestinians we demand consideration and reparations from them without in any way minimizing their own history of suffering and genocide...we must think of our histories together...free of any exclusionary, denial-based schemes....*(Edward Said[326])

As discussed in Chap. 1, the story of 1948 is being re-told by Israeli academics who challenged the hegemonic Zionist narrative of the conflict. Dubbed the 'New Historians', they transformed traditional repertoires of the past. Thus, in Israel,

---

[323] Ibid.

[324] 'Truth-telling which exclusively addresses victims of an in-group—for example Israeli projects which only address attacks against Israelis, would be a completely different affair, as in most societies commemorating the victims of one's own side is a legitimate and encouraged activity'. Dudai, 'Deviant Commemorations', above n 35, 2.

[325] Rafi Nets-Zehngut, 'Transitional Justice and Addressing the History of Active Conflicts: The Case of the Israeli Palestinian Conflict' (Working Paper No 2, The Leonard Davis Institute for International Relations, The Hebrew University of Jerusalem, 7 April 2014) 20.

[326] Edward Said, *The End of the Peace Process, Oslo and After* (Granta Books, 2000) 209.

critical scholarship of 1948 led to marked shifts in popular memory,[327] with official history textbooks being re-written,[328] and increased diplomatic willingness to acknowledge responsibility for the Palestinian displacement.[329] For example, during Israeli–Palestinian peace talks in Taba (2001), '...Israeli negotiators went where no Israeli officials went before: they considered the right of return, and a quasi-statement that acknowledges the Palestinian tragedy and Israel's share of the responsibility'.[330] Revised historical narratives influenced the political elites and seemed to open up new possibilities for negotiable trade-offs.[331] More broadly, as discussed in Chap. 1, the central critiques of the New Historians withstood a torrent of Zionist outrage, disclaimers, and apologetics. Ultimately, they raised a wide-ranging debate that spilled over from scholarly journals and academic conferences into the public domain.[332]

At the same time, Palestinian writers have challenged Arab world histories of 1948 '...marked by apologetics, self-justification, onus-shifting and conspiracy theories'.[333] Thus, Khalidi, a leading Palestinian historian, exposes the tendency in Palestinian historiography to produce a narrative that denies any agency or responsibility for its own fate.[334] Indeed, in recent years, '...there has been less reluctance on the part of the Palestinians to broach the theme of Palestinian failure, bespeaking the growing maturity of Palestinian historiography'.[335] Nevertheless, as discussed in Chap. 1, Palestinian historiography lacks the robust self-criticism of its Israeli

---

[327] A 2008 public opinion reflected a major shift in Israeli–Jewish popular memory of the conflict, which used to be more Zionist-orientated, especially in the first decade after 1948. Nets-Zehngut, above n 325, 15.

[328] '...While until 1999 the Ministry of Education's approved history and civic text books presented by and large the Zionist narrative, since 2000 they have presented the Critical one (at least until 2004)'. See Ibid 9.

[329] Michal Ben-Josef Hirsch, 'From Taboo to the Negotiable: The Israeli New Historians and the Changing Representation of the Palestinian Refugee Problem' (2007) 5 *Perspectives on Politics* 241; Nets-Zehngut, above n 325.

[330] Hirsch, above n 329, 247.

[331] According to Daniel Levy, a member of the Israeli Delegation to Taba, 'the historical work or the New Historians was part of the material they read in preparation for the negotiation', cited in ibid. 251; '...[T]he 2000 Camp David and the 2001 Taba Israeli-Palestinian peace summits witnessed a significant change. At that time, the Critical narrative regarding the exodus was so prevalent in Israel that it was hard for Israeli negotiators to ignore it'. See Nets-Zehngut, above n 325, 14.

[332] Uri Ram, *Israeli Nationalism: Social Conflicts and the Politics of Knowledge* (Routledge, 2010) 30; Dr. Daphna Shraga also noted that in recent years the Nakba has emerged as a legitimate subject of discussion. '1948 Refugees: Proceedings of an International Law Workshop, Hebrew University of Jerusalem Faculty of Law, 14–15 December 2016' (2018) 51(1) *Israel Law Review* 47, 106.

[333] Eugene L Rogan and Avi Shlaim (eds), *The War for Palestine, Rewriting The History of 1948* (Cambridge University Press, 2001) 2.

[334] See Rashid Khalidi, *Palestinian Identity: The Construction of Modern National Consciousness* (Columbia University Press, 1997). Khalidi devotes the concluding section of his final chapter to the Palestinian proclivity for the 'portrayal of failure as triumph'.

[335] Ibid.

counterparts. Notwithstanding this asymmetry, historical developments have paved the ground for re-conceiving 1948.

After decades of collective denial,[336] a new Palestinian attitude has also surfaced towards Holocaust memory. In recent years, leading Palestinian academics have openly criticised the propensity to diminish the Jewish tragedy.[337] Both Said and Bishara argue that Palestinian recognition of the Holocaust is vital to the national cause, both morally and instrumentally.[338] They herald a new approach to Palestinian collective memory, particularly in the way they challenge the role of the 'other'.[339] In March 2014, Dajani, a Palestinian professor, led a group of Palestinian students from Al-Quds University to visit Auschwitz.[340] It was part of a joint educational project, seeking to teach students about the suffering that shaped the historical consciousness of the 'enemy'.[341] Despite success with participants, Dajani was personally vilified and physically threatened upon his return from Poland.[342] Nevertheless, this backlash also demonstrates how forcefully the project challenged the collective narrative of Palestinians. In the words of one participant: 'We have made Palestinians talk publicly about a topic that was once taboo'.[343] Notably, Dajani himself remains undeterred and told Haa'retz that he is planning to return to Jerusalem and plan more such Holocaust trips.[344] This educational project remains one of the few examples of unilateral reconciliation within Palestinian society. It is particularly significant as an unofficial Palestinian truth-telling project that contends with the history of the 'rival'. As discussed in Chap. 1, the holocaust and the 'Jewish victim' narrative arising from this historical event remains central to the 1948 debate.

---

[336] Gilbert Achar's work can be considered the best book on the subject to have illustrated the culture of denying the Holocaust in the Middle East. Gilbert Achar, *Arabs and the Holocaust: The Arab-Israeli War of Narratives* (Metropolitan Books, 2009).

[337] Said, above n 326, 209; Azmi Bishara, 'The Arabs and the Holocaust' (Summer, 1996) 53 *Zemanim* 56–74 (Hebrew); Azmi Bishara (1996). 'On Chauvinism and Universalism' (Winter, 1996) 55 *Zemanim* 102–107, (Hebrew).

[338] Ibid.

[339] Ibid.

[340] It was the first organised visit of Palestinian students to visit the Auschwitz-Birkenau State Museum. Matthew Kalman, 'Palestinian Teaches Tolerance via Holocaust', *The New York Times* (New York), 20 April 2014; Matthew Kalman, 'Palestinian Students Visit Auschwitz in First Organized Visit', *Haaretz* (Tel Aviv), 28 March 2014.

[341] The project involved the Friedrich Schiller University Jena and Ben-Gurion University of the Negev for their part, the Israeli students visited the Dheisheh refugee camp near Bethlehem.

[342] In January 2015, Dajani's car was set on fire and destroyed in front of his home. 'Arsonists Torch Car Belonging to Palestinian Prof. who Led Auschwitz Trip', *Haaretz*, 18 January 2015.

[343] Zeina M Barakat, 'A Palestinian Student Defends Her Visit to Auschwitz', *The Atlantic* (online), 28 April 2014 https://www.theatlantic.com/international/archive/2014/04/a-palestinian-student-defends-her-visit-to-auschwitz/361311/

[344] Nadine Epstein, 'Mohammed Dajani Daoudi: Evolution of a Moderate', *Moment* (online), 17 July 2014.
https://momentmag.com/mohammed-daoudi-evolution-moderate/

Zochrot

The hiking tour and testimony…can be seen as an ephemeral truth commission that appears and disappears around the country in every tour. Zochrot's booklet can be thought of as a 'report'….[345]

Perhaps the most prominent transitional justice group in Israel is Zochrot[346] ('remembering' in Hebrew), which conducts truth-telling activities on 1948. This small activist NGO, based in Tel Aviv, seeks to promote awareness and accountability for the Palestinian Nakba among Israeli–Jewish society. It was founded on the belief that Israeli denial of the Palestinian national disaster obstructs reconciliation between the two nations.[347] In practical terms, Zochrot distributes informational resources and oral history[348] and organises memorial events[349] and historical tours in Hebrew. Zochrot also prepares educational kits describing Palestinian history and 1948, which since 2009 has been distributed among Israeli–Jewish history and civic teachers.[350] One of its signature activities is signposting around Israel to mark destroyed Palestinian villages from 1948.[351] 'Physically marking these villages and holding public discussions…may encourage a more ethical discourse…[it] is intended to set in motion a process of catharsis...'.[352] In 2013, Zochrot launched the iNakba, an application for mobile phones which garnered some international media attention.[353]

---

[345] Yifat Gutman, 'Transcultural Memory in Conflict: Israeli-Palestinian Truth and Reconciliation' (2011) 17(4) *Parallax* 61, 71.

[346] See the Organisation's website: http://zochrot.org/en

[347] One of the self-defined purposes of Zochrot is for Israeli Jews to acknowledge the practical and moral responsibility for the Palestinian Nakba.

[348] Zochrot has produced numerous booklets, each describing the events that occurred in the 1948 War in a specific Palestinian locality. The booklets are based on the work of the 'new historians' and the oral histories of former Palestinians residents. Eitan Bronstein, 'The Nakba in Hebrew: Israeli-Jewish Awareness of the Palestinian Catastrophe and Internal Refugees' in M Nur (ed), *Catastrophe Remembered – Palestine, Israel and the Internal Refugees* (Zed Books, 2005) 215–241.

[349] Each year Zochrot organises on Independence Day a public commemoration of the Nakba in order to educate Israelis about the Palestinian catastrophe.

[350] Or Kashty, 'Mitachat leapo shel misrad hachinuch irgun smol mefits lamorim chomer limud al hanakba hafalestinit' ['Under the nose of the Ministry of Education, a leftish organization disseminates to the teachers educational material about the Palestinian Nakba'], *Haaretz*. 6 April 2009. (In Hebrew).

[351] Posting signs at destroyed Palestinian villages is part of a larger campaign to bring Nakba awareness to the country. In this context, Zochrot has invited Jewish people to join guided visits in order to learn about the Nakba.

[352] Eitan Bronstein, 'The Nakba—Something that did not occur (although it has to occur)' in Terry Rempel (ed), *Rights in Priciple- Rights in Practice: Revisiting the Role of International Law in Crafting Durable Solutions for Palestinian Refugees* (BADIL Resource Centre, 2011) 321.

[353] This application allows you to locate on the map of Israel villages destroyed by militias in 1948 and provide information concerning deportation of their Palestinian inhabitants. Jodie Rudoren, 'Navigating Lost Villages in Israel', *New York Times* (New York), 13 May 2014.

Zochrot is also engaged in legal advocacy. In March 2006, after Zochrot petitioned the HCJ, Israeli authorities conceded to post new signs at Canada Park that commemorate the prior existence of Palestinian villages on this site.[354] Zochrot claimed the signs originally posted by the Jewish National Fund (JNF) were 'selective exclusions of segments of local history'.[355] Zochrot further requested the JNF take similar action at all sites it is responsible for across the country. Ultimately, the JNF rejected this proposal.[356] Further, shortly after the case, one of the new signs posted in Canada Park disappeared, and the other was vandalised.[357] Despite these practical setbacks, one must not underestimate Zochrot's discursive contribution to the present political landscape, as a 'movement of alternative memory'.[358] Indeed, the group has raised mainstream awareness of the 1948 legacy. According to Gordon, a politics professor at Ben Gurion University: 'A decade ago, if I mentioned the Nakba in a class…,hardly any of them would have known...Now 80 or 90 per cent would know'.[359] Gordon attributes this directly to Zochrot's activities.[360] In this sense, Zochrot produces counter-memory as a knowledge-based strategy for political change.[361]

Most recently, Zochrot established an unofficial public truth commission in October 2014 to address Israeli responsibility for the displacement of Negev Bedouins during 1948–1960.[362] Seven commissioners, Israeli Jews and Palestinians,

---

[354] See HCJ 5580/05 *Zochrot v. The Military Commander for Judea and Samara* [June 5, 2006] (unpublished) on the Zochrot website for case background and legal arguments. In sum, the petition sought to include a historic account of the prior existence of Palestinian villages *Yalu* and *Imwas* that were destroyed following the Six-Day War in 1967.

[355] See, the High Court of Justice Petition No. 5580/05 Id. See also, Amiram Barakat, 'The JNF Will Post Signs Commemorating the Palestinian Villages that Were Destroyed', *Haaretz,* 26 July 2005.

[356] According to the former director of Zochrot Eitan Bronstein, the JNF first refused the request to update all of its signs, then suggested a partial revision of its signage system, but eventually withdrew all its suggestions, thereby maintaining the existing situation. Irus Braverman, 'Planting the Promised Landscape: Zionism, Nature, and Resistance in Israel/Palestine' (2009) 49(2) *Natural Resources Journal* 317, 353.

[357] The new signs were posted in May 2006, but 1 month later one of the signs disappeared. In July the remaining sign was vandalised rendering the text referring to the Palestinian villages illegible.

[358] Ram observes: 'What is remarkable about Zochrot is not its size or impact, but rather the fact that it openly offers an explicit and direct antithesis to the Israeli regime of forgetting…'. Uri Ram, 'Ways of Forgetting: Israel and the obliterated Memory of the Palestinian Nakba' (2009) 22(3) *Journal of Historical Sociology* 366, 389; Yifat Gutman, 'Looking Back to the Future: Counter-Memory as Oppositional Knowledge-Production in the Israeli-Palestinian Conflict' (2005) 65(1) *Current Sociology* 1, 2.

[359] http://www.middleeasteye.net/news/israelis-rattled-search-truth-about-nakba-96376998

[360] Ibid.

[361] Gutman, above n 358, 12–13.

[362] *'The Truth Commission for Exposing Israeli Society's Responsibility for the period of 1948–1960 in the South'.* Its mandate was '…to expose the injustices committed against the Palestinian population in the Negev, especially from 1948–1960, and publish a conclusive report...'. See *Zochrot Commission Report*, above n 51.

all active in civil society and academia, were appointed.[363] They heard testimonies by displaced Palestinians, as well as Israeli–Jews who lived in the south, and Jewish fighters who participated in the 1948 operations.[364] On International Human Rights Day, 10 December 2014, the Zochrot Commission held an open public hearing in Be′er-Sheva, featuring seven Bedouin and Jewish witnesses.[365] The Final Report was published in December 2015 and sought 'to facilitate public discussion of Israeli society's moral, political and legal responsibility and provide recommendations for redress'.[366] Overall, the Zochrot Commission recommended that Israel and Jewish–Israeli society acknowledge their responsibility for the injustices and crimes of the 1948 war and its aftermath towards the civilian Bedouin population. The Report also recommended raising awareness of the Nakba in Israeli society and that innovative forms of protest on the ground such as the planning of three Bedouin settlements for internally displaced persons be considered.[367]

The commission's impact was limited. Neither the report nor the public hearings have managed to significantly challenge denial of the Nakba within Israeli–Jewish society. They triggered little media reaction and, in practice, were disregarded, lacking the reach to persuade mainstream Israelis of any wrongdoing.[368] Whilst the commission received some media attention, it did not come close to reaching high level policymaking.[369] Being on the far left of the Israeli political spectrum, Zochrot did not command, and probably did not seek, legitimacy in the public eye.[370] To be sure, Zochrot remains a fringe group in Israel, relegated to the outer orbit of the Israeli Left at a time when the right wing enjoys unprecedented political and cultural dominance. Its ability to make change is limited by the bounds of public and official discourse.

The impact of the Commission was not empirically evaluated. However, according to researcher Kadman, its value lies in standing against 'erasure' and 'forgetting'.[371] By challenging mainstream denial of 1948, the commission serves as a counterweight to official state memory. 'Doing so places the group squarely at the nerve centre of Israeli society'.[372] Through its Commission, Zochrot could establish a new historical and testimonial archive of the Nakba. By focusing exclusively on

---

[363] Huda Abu-Obaid, Prof. Avner Ben-Amos, Wasim Biroumi, Adv. Shahda Ibn Bari, Dr. Munir Nuseibah, Dr. Nura Resh, and Dr. Erella Shadmi.

[364] The Commissioners also heard expert testimony and perused relevant archive materials. *Zochrot Commission Report*, above n 51, 5.

[365] Ibid.

[366] Ibid 6.

[367] Ibid 26–29.

[368] Dr. Shraga quoted in 'Proceedings of an International Law Workshop', above n 332, 108.

[369] Dudai and Cohen, above n 110, 251.

[370] 'Proceedings of an International Law Workshop', above n 332, 108.

[371] Noga Kadman, *Erased from Space and Consciousness: Israel and the Depopulated Palestinian Villages of 1948* (Indiana University Press, 2015).

[372] Daniel Yadin, '*Truth on Trial, Unearthing the Legacy of the Nakba*' (14 February 2018) https://thepolitic.org/truth-on-trial-unearthing-the-legacy-of-the-nakba/

Israel's south, the enquiry helped to bring the Bedouin experience of 1948 into the Nakba story. The displacement of the Bedouin Arabs of the Negev Desert, which stretches over most of the south of Israel, is a less-recognised part of 1948, and commonly overlooked by historians.[373]

Thus, the Zochrot Commission may have had limited impact in Israel, but it does contribute to the testimonial and historical record. The English version of the Final Report is 30 pages long, and contains excerpts of testimony and several pages of background and analysis that are available online.[374] Indeed, in March 2016, the Zochrot Truth Commission submitted its Final Report to the UN Rapporteur on the Right to Truth, Reparation, and Guarantee of Non-Recurrence for the public record.

Moreover, such truth-telling activities could impact collective memory and dialogue in the future. In the long term, Zochrot's work might be used as a tool of conflict transformation like the unofficial truth-telling measures discussed above in Sect. 7.3. The potential pre-figurative value of such a project, and lessons learned for a potential IPTEC are further discussed in Chap. 8. Ultimately, the Zochrot commission serves as a partial and imperfect attempt to apply the truth commission model to the Israeli–Palestinian conflict.[375] In the words of the Zochrot Final Report:

The Truth Commission was a preliminary attempt to imagine transitional justice in the difficult reality of an intractable conflict...We believe that this bold step would offer an example and inspiration for future truth-seeking and other civil society efforts, along the lines of our recommendations and also in ways that cannot yet be imagined.[376]

Breaking the Silence

> *Cases of abuse towards Palestinians,...have been the norm for years, but are still explained as extreme... Our testimonies portray a much grimmer picture...While this reality is known to Israeli soldiers and commanders, Israeli society continues to turn a blind eye.*
>
> Breaking the Silence Website[377]

A significant group documenting Israeli abuses against Palestinians for Israelis is 'Breaking the Silence' (BtS) ('Shovrim Shtika' in Hebrew). This local NGO consists of mainly young Israeli soldiers and veteran combatants, who seek to expose

---

[373] Thus, for example, Walid Khalidi did not include Bedouin communities in the list of 418 depopulated Palestinian villages in his book. Walid Khalidi (ed.), *All That Remains: The Palestinian Villages Occupied and Depopulated by Israel in 1948* (Institute for Palestine Studies, 1992). Similarly, Kadman excludes Bedouin sites from her study. See Kadman, above n 371.

[374] Jessica Nevo, Tammy Pustilnick, and Ami Asher, *Truth Commission on the Responsibility of Israeli Society for the Events of 1948–1960 in the South* (March 2016) Zochrot https://zochrot.org/uploads/uploads/653355e3e054eac11b738f649a4d9a4e.pdf

[375] 'This Truth Commission is the first of its kind in Israel. It is the first application of the transitional justice paradigm in the context of the Israeli-Palestinian conflict'. Ibid 7.

[376] Ibid 29.

[377] See the organisation's website: http://www.breakingthesilence.org.il/

the Israeli public to daily life in the territories, and to stimulate debate about the legacy of the occupation.[378] Founded in March 2004 by a handful of soldiers, this group has interviewed hundreds of combatants who have served in the territories since September 2000, and disseminated their testimony using the website, booklets, exhibitions, lectures, and house meetings.[379] This group also conducts tours around Hebron to thousands of Israelis, 'with the aim of giving the Israeli public access to the reality which exists minutes from their own homes...'.[380] To date, BtS has collected testimonies from over 1000 soldiers who represent all strata of Israeli society and cover nearly all units that operate in the territories.[381] It has also published accounts related to Israel's major military operations in Gaza.[382] As with Zochrot, BtS produces online publications which materially add to the testimonial and historical record of the conflict and its abuses.[383]

Nevertheless, the group remains on the social fringes. It is under constant attack from senior political figures who claim it is unreliable[384] and unpatriotic.[385] PM Netanyahu has condemned BtS in the Knesset,[386] and in 2015, the Education Minister proposed a Bill threatening to block its speakers from state schools.[387] PM Netanyahu attempts to dissuade other states from funding the group.[388] In 2017, the

[378] Breaking the silence explicitly calls for an end to the occupation. See the organisation's website: http://www.breakingthesilence.org.il/

[379] According to Breaking the Silence: 'All the testimonies publish are meticulously researched, and all facts are cross-checked with additional eye-witnesses and/or the archives of other human rights organizations also active in the field'. See the organisation's website: http://www.breakingthesilence.org.il/

[380] Ibid.

[381] Ibid.

[382] For example, the Breaking the Silence testimonies from Operation Cast Lead revealed a sharp disparity between the official IDF narrative of the Gaza campaign and the events on the ground as seen through the eyes of combat soldiers. Gila Orkin, 'Why Is Israel Trying to Break Breaking the Silence?' *Forward* (New York), 14 August 2009, 11.

[383] https://www.breakingthesilence.org.il/testimonies/publications

[384] The NGO has been criticised for publishing anonymous accounts. A 2016 investigation by a television program confirmed the integrity of the organisation, but also said that a few of the testimonies painted a distorted picture. Itai Rom, 'What Have We Learned from Six Months with Breaking the Silence?', *HaMakor,* Channel 10 (in Hebrew) 12 July 2016.

[385] The Israeli political establishment has been hostile to the activities of the group since it was founded in 2004. It believes that BtS emphasises negative aspects of Israeli military operations and threatens its state security, 'part of an advocacy campaign intended to harm Israel's image overseas'. Harriet Sherwood, 'Former Israeli Soldiers Break the Silence on Military Violations', *The Guardian* (London), 16 May 2011.

[386] Barak Ravid, 'Netanyahu: Breaking the Silence's Attempt to Gather Intel on IDF Soldiers Is Intolerable', *Haaretz* (Jerusalem), 20 March 2016.

[387] Toi Staff, 'Stormy debate erupts over bill to ban Breaking the Silence from schools', *The Times of Israel* (online), 27 December 2016 https://www.timesofisrael.com/stormy-debate-erupts-over-bill-to-ban-breaking-the-silence-from-schools/

[388] In April 2017, PM Netanyahu cancelled a meeting with Germany's foreign minister, Sigmar Gabriel, after the statesman had met with the Breaking the Silence group during his visit to Israel.

Israeli State Attorney's office opened a criminal investigation against the BtS spokesperson.[389] Right-wing NGOs have also mobilised against the group. Im Tirtzu[390] boycotts BtS lectures and events and distributes leaflets labelling the organisers as 'liars who try to delegitimise Israel'.[391] NGO Monitor attacks the external funders of the group as 'foreign enablers' who are seeking '...the demonization and smearing of Israeli society'.[392]

At the same time, BtS has acquired a special standing in the eyes of the Israeli public, and in the media, because its activists identify as soldiers. This endows the group with a high level of credibility.[393] 'It has been the use of this soldier's voice which has consistently propelled Breaking the Silence into the national consciousness'.[394] Respected members of the Israeli security establishment have defended the NGO.[395] In 2015, retired military General Amiram Levin said that 'Breaking the Silence strengthens the IDF and its morality'.[396] Notably, unlike the human rights groups discussed above, this group deliberately eschews legalistic language in favour of a discourse of morality.[397]

In this regard, unofficial interventions are endowed with a social authority to vindicate victims and to generate social awareness of unacknowledged violations.[398] Arguably, soldier testimony during conflict could constitute a form of 'social

389 Jacob Magid, 'Police probe Breaking the Silence official who claimed to beat Palestinian', *The Times of Israel* (online), 23 June 2017 https://www.timesofisrael.com/police-open-probe-into-breaking-the-silence-official-after-confession/

390 Im Tirtzu is a right-wing organisation which calls for a 'second Zionist revolution', aimed mainly at defending and promoting Israel and its Jewish character. It has more recently been associated with increasingly public attacks on Breaking the Silence.

391 James Eastwood, 'Chap. 6: Creating a Moral Conversation: The Public Activism of Breaking the Silence' in James Eastwood (ed), *Ethics as a Weapon of War Militarism and Morality in Israel* (Cambridge University Press, 2017) 213.

392 Daniel Laufer, 'Why does Europe support Breaking the Silence's radical anti-Israel agenda?' *Jewish Advocate*, 8 December 2017, 7.

393 Factually, soldiers appear more credible because they were eyewitnesses and participants in the events they describe. Socially, serving the nation through military participation still holds high symbolic rewards in Israel. Eastwood, above n 391, 213.

394 Ibid.

395 In 2016, a number of retired senior Israeli security and military figures expressed support and admiration for BtS. Former General Ami Ayalon wrote that 'Breaking the Silence protects IDF soldiers in the impossible situation in which politicians have abandoned them'. 'Two New Israeli Defense Brass Join in Support for Breaking the Silence', *Haaretz* (Tel Aviv) 22 December 2015.

396 Isabel Kershner, 'Israeli Veterans' Criticism of West Bank Occupation Incites Furor', *New York Times* (New York) 23 December 2015.

397 Eastwood, above n 391, 197.

398 Janine Clark, 'Transitional Justice as Recognition: An Analysis of the Women's Court in Sarajevo' (2016) 10(1) *International Journal of Transitional Justice* 67–87; Christine Chinkin, 'Women's International Tribunal on Japanese Military Sexual Slavery', (2001) 95(2) *American Journal of International Law* 335–41.

control' and political action 'from below'.[399] In a post-dictatorial context, informal public 'outings' and 'shaming' in Latin America contributed to accountability for human rights abuses. Known as 'Escraches' in Argentina,[400] and 'Funa' in Chile,[401] the civic practice involved local actors confronting perpetrators to expose their identity and past crimes. The Funa and Escraches generated a measure of social disapproval and community condemnation absent state-led sanction.[402] In a similar vein, BtS has marked and signified events, policies, and military practice as 'deviant', where the Israeli state and military continue to deny any wrongdoing. Recent attempts to ban BtS from state schools reflect the level of social threat and impact the group has in being able to challenge the IDF's moral authority.

In sum, BtS, like the human rights groups discussed above, aims to reclassify legacies of the past in Israel. It is also worth recalling that dissent within Israeli civil society, and resistance to BtS activities 'is itself an intervention in debates about memory, remembrance and memorialisation—which is to say, it is itself transitional justice'.[403] Indeed, despite the local controversies, both BtS and B'Tselem have actually expanded their international work in recent years. Ultimately, BtS demonstrates the value of local testimony and moral activism, even against social militarism and ongoing conflict.

Collaborative Initiatives

Beyond unilateral measures directed at one society, collaborative efforts between Israelis and Palestinians are also negotiating the past. Since the early 2000s, Israeli–Jews and Palestinians have collaborated in various projects in which they jointly address the historical narratives of the conflict. Among other things, this involves finding common narratives, reducing the gaps between narratives, or agreeing on two parallel but legitimate narratives.[404] Beyond joint truth-telling, these initiatives are also informed by reconciliation, and particularly the contact hypothesis,[405]

---

[399] Ron Dudai, 'Transitional justice as social control: Political transitions, Human rights Norms and the Reclassification of the Past: Transitional justice as social control' (2017) 69(2); *British Journal of Sociology* 13; Mary Pat Baumgartner 'Social Control From Below' in Donald Black (ed.) *Toward a General Theory of Social Control* (FL: Academic, 1984).

[400] Francesca Lessa, *Memory and Transitional Justice in Argentina and Uruguay: Against Impunity*, (Palgrave Macmillan, 2013). 64–5.

[401] Cath Collins, *Post-transitional Justice: Human Rights Trials in Chile and El Salvador*, (Penn State University Press, 2010). 114.

[402] Ron Dudai, 'Transitional justice as social control: Political transitions, Human rights Norms and the Reclassification of the Past: Transitional justice as social control' (2017) 69(2)).

[403] Waters, above n 172, 178.

[404] Rafi Nets-Zehngut, 'Palestinian and Israelis Collaborate in Addressing the Historical Narratives of their Conflict' (2013) 5 *Quest* 232, 238.

[405] According to conflict resolution theory, the contact hypothesis is the idea that under certain conditions such as equality, sustained interaction, and cooperation on common goals, intergroup

which regards inter-group contact as crucial to conflict resolution.[406] This rationale[407] has spawned various unofficial projects between Israeli and Palestinian academics, teachers, soldiers, bereaved families, and policy figures, despite the conflict's persistence or perhaps precisely because of it.

Shared Histories: Historians

In 2002, a project called 'Shared Histories' brought Israeli–Jewish and Palestinian academics together to discuss their historical narratives.[408] Three Jerusalem-based institutions conducted workshops in Israel and Cyprus for historians, journalists, and activists to explore key events of the conflict.[409] The primary aim was to increase mutual understanding of each party's narrative and to respect discursive differences. The process was grounded in cultural context and inter-subjective interaction, with the concept of narrative implying the existence of multiple 'truths'.[410] In 2005, the outcome of these workshops was published in a book, which attracted some media attention.[411] Ultimately, Shared Histories is a rare example of collaborative scholarship between Israelis and Palestinians. As discussed in Chap. 1, the field tends to be entrapped in parallel historical realities.[412] The authors here initiated what is essentially a joint truth-telling project, which values understanding the unfamiliar and the 'other'.[413] Readers can witness first-hand a respectful confrontation between two

---

contact can lead to a reduction in prejudice. Herbert C Kelman, 'Creating the Conditions for Israeli-Palestinian Negotiations' (1982) 26(1) *Journal of Conflict Resolution* 39; Ronald Fisher, *Interactive Conflict Resolution* (Syracuse University Press, 1997).

[406] 'These ideas of dialogue as changing constructions of self and other, and as enabling, through mainly experiential, affective processes to include the other within the self, resonate with recent reformulations of the contact hypothesis'. Ifat Maoz, 'An Experiment in Peace: Reconciliation-Aimed Workshops of Jewish-Israeli and Palestinian Youth' (2000) 37(6) *Journal of Peace Research* 722.

[407] Ellis and Maoz maintain that even emotional argument and deaf dialogue (i.e. articulations of mutual rejection) may increase tolerance by broadening horizons and exposing inconsistencies in conventional reasoning. Donald G Ellis and Ifat Maoz, 'Online Argument between Israeli Jews and Palestinians' (2007) 33 *Human Communication Research* 291–307.

[408] This project involved three Jerusalem-based institutions: The Truman Institute for the Advancement of Peace, Panorama (The Palestinian Center for the Dissemination of Democracy and Community Development), and Yakar's Center for Social Concern. P Scham, W Salem and B Pogrund, *Shared Histories – A Palestinian-Israeli Dialogue* (Left Coast Press, 2005).

[409] The topics discussed included: the Zionist settlement in Palestine/Eretz Israel (1982–1914), the Palestinian national movement (1919–1939), the UN resolution of 1947 to establish independent Jewish and Arab states, the 1948 War, and religious aspects of the conflict.

[410] Scham, Salem and Pogrund, above n 408.

[411] Ibid.

[412] This is what Kelman refers to as the laws of negative interdependence. Kelman, 'The Interdependence of Israeli and Palestinian National Identities', above n 65.

[413] Adrienne Desse, Noor Ali, and Alice Mishkin, 'Learning about Palestinian Narratives: What are the Barriers for Jewish College Students?' (2014) 20(4) *Peace and Conflict: Journal of Peace Psychology*, 365.

competing versions of the past. The project is particularly notable, given that it occurred at the height of the Second Intifada.[414] In this regard, academic collaboration is an example of integrating transitional justice into national memory.

Peace Research Institute in the Middle East (PRIME): Teachers

> *Teach as best you can, and perhaps*
> *a generation will come that will do great wonders,*
> *And do not burden the youth in your community....* (Esh-Shawqiyyat, Ahmed Shawqi)

PRIME is an NGO established by Palestinian and Israeli researchers whose purpose is to pursue mutual coexistence and peacebuilding through joint research and outreach activities. In 2002–2003 PRIME conducted a project with high school curricula.[415] In workshops conducted over several years, Israeli–Jewish and Palestinian teachers developed a joint school textbook juxtaposing each party's narratives of the conflict.[416] The booklets were published gradually over the years,[417] each one covering a different historical period: an inclusive textbook comprised of all three previous booklets was published in 2009.[418] They were written in Hebrew and Arabic, and taught in both Israeli and Palestinian schools. The parallel history project was not intended to enter mainstream pedagogy or gain state approval.[419] Rather, the project focused on the role of teachers as agents of change.[420] This is significant given that both sides have used official textbooks which perpetuate negative stereotyping and polarised history.[421] Although the Israeli Ministry of Education opposed

[414] If Israeli and Palestinian intellectuals can engage in dialogue of this level, at that time, it should be possible to debate these issues substantially and productively in academic forums further removed from the violence.

[415] Sami Adwan and Dan Bar-On, 'Shared Histories Project: A PRIME Example of Peace-Building Under Fire' (2004) 17 *International Journal of Politics, Culture and Society* 513.

[416] Nets-Zehngut, above n 404, 239.

[417] 2003, 2005, and 2007.

[418] Sammy Adwan, Daniel Bar-on, Andres Musalem, and Eyal Nave, *Lilmod et Hanerative Hahistory shel Ha'aher – Falistinim Veisraelim* [*Studying the Narrative of the Other – Palestinians and Israelis*] (Beit Jallah: PRIME, 2003) (In Hebrew).

[419] 'We did not try to advertise the textbook or bring it to the attention of the ministries of education, because the public and the ministries were paralysed and haunted by the conflict, not the peace process'. Adwan and Bar-On, above n 415, 514.

[420] Shoshana Steinberg and Dan Bar-On, 'The Other Side of the Story: Israeli and Palestinian Teachers Write a History Text Book Together' (2009) 79(1) *Harvard Educational Review* 104, 111.

[421] Sammy Adwan and Ruth Firer, *The Narrative of Palestinian Refugees During the War of 1948 in Israeli and Palestinian History and Civic Education Textbooks* (UNESCO, 1997); Sammy Adwan and Ruth Firer, *The Narrative of the 1967 War in the Israeli and Palestinian History and Civics Textbooks and Curricula Statement* (Eckert Institute, 1999).

the initiative,[422] many welcomed the two-narrative approach. In some universities and teacher training colleges, the material is being used in conflict resolution courses and for history teachers.[423] It should also be noted that some of the projects received widespread local and international attention.[424]

Further, the very process of developing alternative textbooks is significant. Through the joint workshops, Israeli and Palestinian teachers had positive transformative experiences.[425] Most of the encounters transpired under severe conditions of asymmetry of power relations of Israeli occupation and Palestinian suicide bombing.[426] According to the co-founders: 'The textbook helped us to maintain our 'island of sanity' while developing it, and such a textbook project could become widespread when there are future peace agreements'.[427] This collaborative initiative reflects an awareness that textbook reform is integral to reconciliation efforts[428]and should be a key strategy for dealing with the past.[429] In short, PRIME represents an important local civic attempt to challenge Israeli–Palestinian official education policy.[430]

Combatants for Peace: Soldiers

After all, he too is flesh and blood – just like you
And he can be your friend
If you extend your hand... – (Just Like You, Shalom Hanoch)

Another notable group is Combatants for Peace. Founded in 2006, Combatants for Peace is an Israeli–Palestinian NGO which brings together former Israeli soldiers and former Palestinian militants who renounce violence.[431] Describing itself as an

---

422 In 2004, after an article was published about the project, Ministry of Education officials announced that educators were forbidden to use the booklet. Steinberg and Bar-On, above n 420, 110.

423 Although the Palestinian teachers have less freedom of choice, they also found opportunities to teach the two narratives. Ibid.

424 For example, PRIME's project received some ten Israeli and mostly international peace awards, its booklet was translated into eight languages. Rafi Nets, 'Palestinians and Israelis Collaborate in Addressing the Historical Narratives of their Conflict' (2013) 5 *Focus* 232, 249.

425 'We observed that the teachers from both sides had a general feeling of ownership and accomplishment, in spite of the deteriorating external situation'. Adwan and Bar-On, above n 415, 519.

426 Ibid 517.

427 Ibid 514.

428 'This project is a good example of the role even a small group of teachers can play in violent political conflicts'. Steinberg and Bar-On, above n 420, 112.

429 Elizabeth Cole, 'Transitional Justice and the Reform of History Education' (2007) 1(1) *International Journal of Transitional Justice* 115; Dudai, 'Deviant Commemorations', above n 35, 2.

430 Eyal Naveh, 'Recognition as Preamble to Reconciliation: A Two Narratives Approach in a Palestinian-Israeli History Textbook' (2007) 3(4) *Horizons Universitaires* 173.

431 See the group's website at http://www.combatantsforpeace.org.

'egalitarian bi-national, grassroots movement', it was formed by those who actively participated in the hostilities.[432] Originally, the activists were solely ex-combatants, but today, membership is broader. The group holds public meetings of a semi-confessional nature, in which both Palestinians and Israelis share personal stories of their involvement in atrocities, and their paths to non-violence.[433] Today, ten bi-national groups operate region-wide across Israel and the Palestinian territories.[434] Many of the Palestinians involved are members of the Fateh Movement and maintain good relations with the PA. Accordingly, some Palestinian officials participate in and support the activity of this group.[435] Combatants for Peace also participates in humanitarian aid, which includes rebuilding demolished homes and schools in the West Bank. The NGO is a rare example of reconciliation efforts between ex-combatants on both the sides of an ongoing conflict.[436]

Israeli–Palestinian Bereaved Families (Parents Circle Families Forum) (PCFF)

> *The colour of our blood is red, the suffering that each of us experienced is enormous, all of our tears are equally bitter. If we can talk to each other everyone can.* (PCFF website)

PCFF is an Israeli–Palestinian NGO of over 600 Israeli and Palestinian bereaved families, all of whom have lost a family member to the conflict. As a victim group, it uses dialogue and shared narrative to advance reconciliation.[437] Bereaved Israeli parents founded the group in 1995 to support the peace process and to promote nonviolence after their children were killed in Hamas attacks.[438] Today, Israeli and Palestinian PCFF members regularly meet with youth and adults to share their personal stories and explain their decision to work through dialogue rather than revenge.

PCFF members also jointly facilitate The 'History through the Human Eye"'(HTHE) project for Israeli and Palestinian groups. Over a period of several months, participants engage in multiple dialogue sessions, share personal stories and hear first-hand testimonies of Holocaust survivors and Palestinian refugees. Workshops include lectures by Israeli and Palestinian historians and visits to

---

432 Ibid.

433 Dudai, 'Deviant Commemorations', above n 35, 2.

434 They operate between Tulkarm-Tel Aviv, Nablus-Tel Aviv, Ramallah-Tel Aviv, Jerusalem-Jericho, Jerusalem-Bethlehem, Beersheva-Hebron, and in the North.

435 The group is far from an uncontested consensus among Palestinians, but generally Palestinian participants maintain contacts with Israelis, recognise Israel, and support nonviolence. Dudai and Cohen, above n 110, 238.

436 Generally, joint veteran-based peace initiatives in other national contexts are co-founded only after peaceful resolution to their conflict has been achieved. 'Vision and Mission - Combatants For Peace'. Combatants For Peace website, above n 431.

437 'The PCFF has concluded that the process of reconciliation between nations is a prerequisite to achieving a sustainable peace'. See the group's website at http://www.theparentscircle.com.

438 Lazarus, above n 186, 35.

meaningful sites. The project concludes with an exercise encouraging participants to represent the other's perspective empathically. To date, a total of 700 people have participated in the program.[439] External research has proven that more than 80% of participants demonstrated a positive change in their perception of the other as a result of participating in the HTHE project.[440]

A key PCFF annual event is the Israeli–Palestinian Alternative Memorial Service. Together with Combatants for Peace, bereaved families and former soldiers commemorate loss on both the sides of the conflict. Participating guests include leading intellectuals, musicians, singers, and authors. The choice to hold the event on the same day as Israel's Memorial Day is significant.[441] For Israelis, Memorial Day is a sacred occasion, one traditionally focused exclusively on mourning the country's fallen soldiers and victims of terror. Thus, the very notion of Israelis and Palestinians marking the day together, and acknowledging each other's pain, is meaningful. It sends a message to both the sides about the collaborative power of truth-telling and reconciliation.[442] Indeed, the number of attendees has grown exponentially since 2006, and today counts thousands of bereaved Israeli and Palestinian family members. The event also commands more media exposure because of vigorous right-wing demonstrations and disruptions. In 2018, despite efforts by the Israeli Minister of Defence to block Palestinians entry to attend the ceremony, a record number of 8000 people attended (almost double the previous year). The Israeli HCJ ruled to allow the group of 110 bereaved Palestinians to travel for the ceremony from the West Bank.[443] Such institutional support and growing attendance bodes well for collaborative civic projects.

Unofficial Diplomatic Collaboration

> *In fact, it went even further, by offering a complete alternative game with different assumptions, different rules, and perhaps even different players.* (Jacob Shamir on the Geneva Initiative[444])

---

[439] More than 180 Palestinian and Israeli change agents participated in 2014–2015 in the program, including journalists, social workers, educators, artists, and social activists. Ibid 48.

[440] The HTHE project has been accompanied by evaluators, who have consistently recorded positive impacts among the vast majority of participants against a series of attitudinal indicators. Ibid.

[441] The ceremony was initiated by an Israeli mother, whose son was killed in Lebanon in 1995.

[442] Dina Kraft, 'Bereaved Israelis and Palestinians Join in Shared Grief at Alternative Memorial Day Event', *Haaretz* (Tel Aviv), 17 April 2018.

[443] In a strongly worded ruling, the judges said that 'the defence minister's judgment is completely devoid of sensitivity to the bereaved families' considerations, who want to hold a ceremony with Israelis and Palestinians'. Ibid.

[444] Jacob Shamir, United States Institute of Peace, *Public Opinion in the Israeli-Palestinian Conflict: From Geneva to Disengagement to Kadima and Hamas* (2007) 27.

After the collapse of Oslo, a series of collaborative 'Track Two' projects brought together Israeli and Palestinian policy figures.[445] They engaged in lobbying and popular advocacy campaigns to inform peace talks and reboot negotiations. Indeed, unofficial diplomacy helped establish joint political platforms and set common strategies for ending the conflict.[446] Most notably in 2003, the Geneva Initiative (also known as the Geneva Accord) proposed a comprehensive Israeli–Palestinian peace agreement.[447] Its creators, former Israeli minister Yossi Beilin and former PA minister Yasser Abed Rabbo, were able to demonstrate substantial common ground on pending final status issues.[448] Despite mixed reactions, the initiative exerted substantial political pressure and gained support abroad.[449] Indeed, the Geneva Accords are widely credited with prompting Ariel Sharon to withdraw Israeli settlements from Gaza in 2005.[450] In short, the Geneva Accords are a bold and innovative example of Israeli–Palestinian collaboration on conflict resolution.[451]

Overall, the Track-Two civic efforts provided formal negotiators with concepts, experience, and basic familiarity with positions of the other side.[452] For example, the Geneva Initiative's 'Dealing with the Past' project was a tool for negotiators to agree in advance on sensitive historical issues that could be embedded into the formal agreement.[453] Until today, the Geneva Initiative, through its NGOs, educate and campaign, both locally and internationally, for both sides to negotiate directly.[454] Almost 15 years later, the Geneva Initiative still survives.[455] 'Yet the very fact that it

---

[445] Influential mainstream figures from the Labor and Likud parties became engaged in intensive 'Track Two' dialogues with PLO figures. Previously the province of radical Left intellectuals, these became a mainstay of mainstream diplomacy, providing back channels for negotiation and a generation of policy options. Lazarus, above n 186, 36.

[446] Hassassian, above n 168, 82.

[447] The Accord was prepared in secret for over 2 years before the 50-page document was officially launched on 1 December 2003, at a ceremony in Geneva, Switzerland. Christine Hauser, 'Powell Meets with Framers of Symbolic Mideast Accord', *The New York Times* (New York), 5 December 2003.

[448] It was based on previous official negotiations, international resolutions, the Quartet Roadmap, the Clinton Parameters, and the Arab Peace Initiative. See the initiative's website http://www.geneva-accord.org/

[449] 'A Welcome and Legitimate Initiative', *Haaretz* (Tel Aviv) 12 October 2003.

[450] Yair Hirschfeld, *Track-Two Diplomacy Toward an Israeli-Palestinian Solution* 1978–2014 (Johns Hopkins University Press, 2014); According to Shamir, it is no coincidence that Sharon's disengagement plan was announced in December 2003, 2 months after the Geneva initiative. Jacob Shamir, above n 444, 27.

[451] Hassassian, above n 168, 82.

[452] Lazarus, above n 186, 34.

[453] 'Proceedings of an International Law Workshop', above n 332, 108.

[454] Since the writing of the Geneva Accord, the Geneva Initiative developed two cooperating NGOs, Heskem on the Israeli side, and their Palestinian counterpart Palestine Peace Coalition/Geneva Initiative (PPC/GI).

[455] Most recently on 10 May 2018, supporters of the Geneva Initiative organised a 'Palestinian-Israel Dialogue' conference in Tel Aviv. They came to discuss the Israeli–Palestinian peace process in the wake of the US Embassy moving to Jerusalem and the security situation in Gaza.

survives is worthy of respect'.[456] Other Track-Two forums, such as the Economic Cooperation Foundation and the Israel–Palestine Center for Research and Information, remain a crucial 'touchpoint' of Israeli–Palestinian interface.[457] These civil society projects help fuel the capacity and motivation in both societies to resolve the conflict.

Challenges and Opportunities for Israeli–Palestinian Transitional Justice Projects

Not surprisingly, transitional justice initiatives face similar obstacles to those met by the human rights and peacebuilding movement as discussed above in Sect. 7.4. The field is a small and embattled one, which remains oppositional not only to the official leadership but also to dominant mainstream opinion in the region. The Israeli–Palestinian transitional justice projects identified in this research lack broad-based support.[458] Arguably, some of them only target the 'converted' elites with limited impact on wider society.[459] The collapse of the peace process has all but paralysed the forces of moderation in both nations, which has weakened the efficacy and reach of non-state actors.[460] In addition, the current violence and the restrictions on movement pose great difficulties. Fragmented social structures and frozen political prejudices may also prevent such efforts from making any more than a symbolic impact.[461] Some go as far as to suggest that collaborative projects are unsuccessful because of limited time duration, inequality, and differing expectations between Israelis and Palestinians.[462] From this standpoint, transitional justice efforts are fraught.

---

[456] Hirschfeld, above n 450.

[457] Ibid.

[458] For example, by contrast, in Northern Ireland, the Ardoyne Commemoration Project enjoyed wide support within the nationalist/Catholic community. Dudai, 'Deviant Commemorations', above n 35, 2.

[459] Dajani and Baskin, above n 223, 96–7.

[460] For example, even an organisation like the Palestinian Rapprochement Centre (historically enjoying success with joint discussion) has more recently avoided popularising these meetings, instead focusing its energy within the Palestinian community rather than in trying to build any bridges to the other side. Hassassian, above n 168, 71.

[461] Dajani and Baskin, above n 223, 96–7.

[462] Kelman, 'Creating the Conditions for Israeli-Palestinian Negotiations', above n 405; Haviva Bar and Elias Eady. 'Education to Cope with Conflicts: Encounters between Jews and Palestinians' in E Weiner (ed), *The Handbook of Interethnic Coexistence* (Continuum, 1998) 514–534.

Transitional Justice as Political Activism

Nevertheless, one cannot easily discount the political value elicited by these projects precisely because of their oppositional nature.[463] As long as the conflict is active, these initiatives are by their nature 'deviant'[464] and are not intended to be a mainstream activity. It is unreasonable to expect that hundreds of thousands of people would participate in tours of Breaking the Silence or attend an alternative Israeli–Palestinian memorial service.[465] Many of the groups are keenly aware of their role as spoilers of official policy and memory and of their own power to construct new cultural identities. Thus, they have produced 'new' information on 1948, critically assessed history, offered an alternative shared narrative, and have begun to envision practical solutions for the Palestinian refugees.

In this sense, these local transitional justice efforts have armed both Israeli and Palestinian civil actors with new language to challenge the hegemonic narratives of the past. Unlike depoliticised peacebuilding and the legal discourse of human rights litigation, these unofficial measures are consciously using truth-telling, dialogue, and reconciliation to advance their goals. Whether it is former combatants admitting to their abuses, or an alternative memorial service, non-state actors are boldly confronting the Nakba, the legitimacy of the occupation, and creating space to engage with the suffering of the 'other'. By provoking wider audiences, even if they elicit negative and hostile responses, these projects are at least turning the official narrative of the past into a question that must be answered, rather than one to be simply ignored.[466] In this regard, these transitional justice projects serve the parties as a platform for political mobilisation and identity re-negotiation.

Historically Sensitive Collective Rights

Moreover, the goals of transitional justice are promoting a more historically sensitive collective rights-based approach to the conflict. Unlike mainstream human rights groups, these projects do not conform to legal discourse that pitches the rights of Israelis as 'security interests' against the 'individual rights' of Palestinians. This framing often justifies limiting human rights in the name of Israel's national security.[467] Rather, by engaging Palestinians as a 'people' with a parallel historical

---

[463] One of the strategies for truth-telling is producing oppositional knowledge and claims against the dominant knowledge for political ends. Patrick G Coy, Lynne M Woehrle and Gregory M Maney, 'A Typology of Oppositional Knowledge: Democracy and the US Peace Movement' (2008) 13(4) *Sociological Research Online* 1.

[464] Dudai, 'Deviant Commemorations', above n 35, 7.

[465] Ibid.

[466] Ibid.

[467] This is because legalistic proportionality analysis justifies limiting human rights in the name of security. Aeyal Gross, 'Human Proportions: Are Human Rights the Emperor's New Clothes of the International Law of Occupation?' (2007) 18(1) *The European Journal of International Law* 1, 8.

narrative, collaborative activity has provided space for Israelis to identify with the collective rights and aspirations of Palestinians.[468] Joint truth-telling also means that Palestinians have had the chance to regard Israelis not just as an 'occupier', but as traumatised neighbours. Whilst many programme participants could be described as 'the converted', most have still not had the opportunity to engage in meaningful discussion with the other side about the wounds, the fears, the narratives, and traumas of the past. It is also important to strengthen the beliefs, knowledge and understanding of the 'converted'.[469]

Setting the Stage

At present, it seems premature to evaluate the impact of Israeli/Palestinian unilateral and/or collaborative transitional justice measures. None of these isolated initiatives can radically transform the conflict in the short-term. Clearly, transitional justice activities will not bring about peace all by themselves.[470] It is also unrealistic to expect that local Israeli and/or Palestinian actors could mobilise many beyond their immediate circles or directly influence political elites.[471] However, as concluded in earlier chapters, truth-telling and reconciliation are gradual and fragmented processes, which cultivate conflict resolution over time.[472] They may not change specific policies or decisions overnight, but they are '…much better at laying the groundwork for cognitive changes and introducing new options for the national repertoire'.[473] As demonstrated in Sect. 7.4, unofficial projects in various settings have had a positive incremental impact on the socio-psychological dynamics of parties.

The long-term value of these kinds of pre-resolution efforts is also significant to promote a reduction of negative stereotyping and prejudice, foster empathy towards the rival, and enhance critical reflection of one's own in-group.[474] Accordingly, Israeli/Palestinian transitional justice actors can with time affect public opinion,

---

468 Daniel Bar-Tal et al., 'Psychological Legitimization- Views of the Israeli Occupation by Jews in Israel: Data and Implications' in Daniel Bar-Tal and Izhak Schnell, *The Impacts of Lasting Occupation: Lessons from Israeli Society* (Oxford University Press, 2012) 175.

469 Dajani and Baskin, above n 223, 98.

470 Adwan and Bar-On, above n 415, 514.

471 According to Dudai, the term 'bottom-up' used so often in the literature, can be misleading and is often an aspiration rather than an accurate description of many of these projects. Dudai, 'Deviant Commemorations', above n 35, 7.

472 'Our research suggests that national reconciliation does not automatically transform communities, but that does not mean the value of national processes should be underestimated'. Brandon Hamber and Grainne Kelly, 'Beyond Coexistence: Towards a Working Definition of Reconciliation' in Joanna R Quinn (ed), *Reconciliation(s): Transitional Justice in Postconflict Societies* (McGill-Queen's University Press, 2009) 302.

473 Tamara Hermann, 'Civil Society and NGOs Building Peace in Israel' in Edy Kaufman, Walid Salem and Juliette Verhoeven, *Bridging the Divide: Peacebuilding in the Israeli-Palestinian Conflict* (Lynne Rienner, 2006).

474 Nets-Zehngut, above n 404, 244.

policymakers, and inform negotiations. The gradual influence of Israeli scholarship in the 1990s and the Geneva Initiative in the 2000s[475] are cases in point. Ultimately, unofficial projects can also serve as catalysts for establishing formal mechanisms at later stages of the conflict.[476]As discussed, the Brazilian and South African[477] civil society efforts laid the foundations for national engagement with the past.

'Islands of Sanity'

In practical terms, a process of conflict transformation and confronting the past has already begun within these groups. Collaboration has built trust and kept lines of communication open during ongoing conflict. It has increased the exposure of participants to the narratives of the other side.[478] Further, because many of the projects are educational in nature, they have involved touring or teaching[479] thousands more and have had a cumulative effect on both nations. It is notable that these projects have been conducted almost exclusively by Palestinians and Israeli–Jews themselves, rather than those extrinsic to the conflict.

At the very least, unofficial efforts demonstrate the civic capacity to engage with transitional justice concepts even during hostilities. It is no small feat that so many initiatives dealing with the past already exist at this stage of the conflict. Given the challenges discussed above, they send an important signal that it is indeed feasible for the parties to confront their past abuses together. 'Among other things, they give all those people who are ready to hear the "other" voice in an open dialogue an opportunity to do so—which the state does not'.[480] Whether it is Zochrot's truth commission, or the joint Israeli–Palestinian memorial service, they serve as a counterweight to the denial, militarism, and animosity. In short, they have created what might be described as 'an island sanity' in the present landscape.[481]

[475] Jacob Shamir, above n 444.

[476] Dudai, 'Does Any Of This Matter', above n 158, 347.

[477] As discussed, the agreement of the SATRC in the 1990s did not take place in a vacuum. Black and white cadres were prepared for more than 30 years, in isolated, mostly Christian refuges, which served as 'islands of sanity' under the most severe external conditions. Adwan and Bar-On, above n 415, 514.

[478] Nets-Zehngut, above n 325, 20.

[479] For example, the PRIME educational products have continued to positively influence students year after year. Nets-Zehngut, above n 404, 250.

[480] 'They also give those from both sides who wish to air their feelings, to "confess," to publicise their regret, or to acknowledge wrong-doing by their society, a space in which it is legitimate and desirable to do so'. Ibid 7.

[481] Adwan and Bar-On, above n 415, 514.

7.7 Conclusion

This chapter explored the significant role of civil society in transitional justice and its relevance to the Israeli–Palestinian conflict. In particular, the discussion focused on unofficial truth projects to address situations where violence is endemic, and no political appetite exists for formal transitional justice mechanisms. It was concluded that there is both intrinsic and instrumental value to supporting local truth, justice, and reconciliation processes in ongoing conflict. Such efforts are likely to arise from civil society, which has made a significant contribution in various countries calling for designing and establishing transitional justice measures. As will be discussed in the final chapter, an unofficial Israeli–Palestinian truth commission could become the primary agent charged with documenting past abuses and addressing the conflict narrative in this region.

This chapter also provided an overview of the contemporary Israeli–Palestinian peacebuilding and human rights field. At the international level, there is already increasing recognition of the critical bridging role of Israeli and Palestinian civil society during the current diplomatic impasse.[482] The emphasis on civil society echoes the Quartet's July 2016 recommendation of 'increasing interaction and cooperation in a variety of fields—economic, professional, educational, cultural—that strengthen the foundations for peace and countering extremism'.[483] Having outlined the landscape of the peacebuilding and human rights field, it was concluded that Israeli–Palestinian NGOs are limited and yet remain the only actors capable of beginning a transitional justice process. Despite the challenges, Israeli and Palestinian civic actors are uniquely placed to change negative social dynamics, inform negotiations, and foster bi-lateral reconciliation.

At the same time, the disconnect of human rights and peacebuilding from the past and the 'political' seems to have created a double-edged sword. On the one hand, the NGOs' 'apolitical' activities represent a faithful attempt to adhere to the universality of human rights. On the other hand, this distance limits civil society, because it is unable to challenge the government and its narratives in any manner that might be seen as political. The ability to address both 'the legal' and 'the political' is arguably a site of struggle that transitional justice is helping to resolve.

In this regard, unofficial projects have been a significant strategy for cross-conflict engagement. They have expanded the repertoire of Israeli–Palestinian civil society from the classic models of legal advocacy and peacebuilding to the eclecticism of joint dialogue, revisionist education, truth-telling, reconciliation, and social protest. However, transitional justice as a tool of conflict transformation remains far

---

[482] In 2006, France launched an initiative to revive the Middle-East peace process. The 'French Initiative' named civil society one of three priority domains for international support, and it consulted repeatedly with Israeli and Palestinian peacebuilding NGOs in advance of the 15th January 2017 Paris Peace Conference. See Rina Bassist, 'What's in Store at Paris Peace Conference?', *Al-Monitor*, 3 January 2017, cited in Ned Lazarus, above n 186, 14–15.

[483] Middle East Quartet, 2016. See ibid.

from achieving its full potential in the region. There is scope for civil society to take up the task of tackling the past in a more comprehensive and bi-national way and to devise a mechanism that involves wider elements of both societies. The next chapter devises an Israeli–Palestinian Truth and Empathy Commission spearheaded by local academics, policy, and religious leaders, and which covers a broader trajectory of the past.

Chapter 8
Architecture of an Israeli-Palestinian Truth and Empathy Commission: Design, Goals, and Challenges

8.1 Introduction

This chapter explores the architecture and institutional design of an unofficial Israeli–Palestinian Truth and Empathy Commission (IPTEC). Given the historical dimension of the conflict (Chap. 1) and the legacy of abuses (Chap. 2), this mechanism is premised on the value of truth-telling, justice, and reconciliation to conflict resolution (Chap. 3). It also assumes the desirability of reckoning with the past to Israelis and Palestinians (Chap. 4). Arguably, the best hope for conflict transformation lies not in the traditional prosecutorial paradigm (Chap. 5), but in adopting a broader victim-centred restorative approach to the region. Specifically, the truth commission model (Chap. 6) seems well equipped to meet the discursive and justice demands of both the parties.

At present however, there is little likelihood that a truth commission could be formally established. Even in the most optimistic future scenarios, it is very hard to imagine that an Israeli or Palestinian government would sponsor, finance, and/or promote an investigation into its human rights abuses. Indeed, civic involvement may be the only way to feasibly engage the Israeli–Palestinian past. Accordingly, the IPTEC is informed by unofficial transitional justice practices promoted during active conflict (Chap. 7). It might seem counter-intuitive, against the current backdrop, to conceive of such an institution. Yet just as critical scholarship of 1948 influenced diplomats in the 1990s, and the Geneva Initiative redrew the political map in the 2000s, so too this project could break taboos, propose counter-narratives, and carve out an 'island of sanity' for the Middle East. Indeed, the IPTEC builds on the foundations of various truth-telling attempts in the region, and their valuable efforts to reframe public debate and to project a new resolution for the future.

J. Bracka, *Transitional Justice for Israel/Palestine*, Springer Series in Transitional Justice, https://doi.org/10.1007/978-3-030-89435-1_8

A small chorus of Israeli and Palestinian academics has already championed a truth commission.[1] However, with few exceptions, there has been little attention devoted to the actual infrastructure of such a body, let alone an unofficial one, created during conflict, or one seeking to investigate events beyond 1948, as well as Palestinian abuses. This chapter therefore attempts to expand the existing truth commission proposals for the region. Ultimately, it envisages a grassroot project, in which an IPTEC is jointly formulated by local academics, civil society players, lawyers, historians, and moderate religious and political leaders.

To be sure, conceiving an institution such as this one requires resolving difficult dilemmas. Thus, Part One of this chapter addresses the threshold questions of building a truth commission, such as who should be the IPTEC's commissioners and what are their credentials? Which groups are consulted? How should the IPTEC be funded? What are the institution's appropriate temporal and legal parameters? This part also sets out the proposed institutional design of the IPTEC, all of which draw from earlier comparative research. As will be discussed, the structural features of the IPTEC reflect broader debates and tensions between history, law, politics, truth-telling, justice and reconciliation. Part Two of this chapter will outline the fundamental goals of the initiative. Ultimately, the three normative pillars of transitional justice: truth-telling, justice, and reconciliation (as defined in Chaps. 3 and 4) lay the foundations for the IPTEC's mandate. Finally, Part Three examines the most pressing obstacles facing the IPTEC, from its timing to the unequal power relations between the two nations. No doubt, the work of an IPTEC would be contingent, ambitious, and inevitably precarious. However, any contribution towards reconciling the past at present would be a leap forward for Israelis and Palestinians.

8.2 Part One: IPTEC Institutional Design

Introduction and Guiding Principles

As noted above, some academics have already advocated for a truth commission in the region. In 1998, prominent Palestinian academic Said claimed that Israeli and Palestinian scholars should collaborate in addressing the history of the conflict, because their official institutions are unlikely to do so.[2] More recently, Bassiouni recommended that Israel, and the PA, establish a joint fact-finding commission

[1] Zinaida Miller, 'Settling with History: A Hybrid Commission of Inquiry for Israel/Palestine' (2007) 20 *Harvard Human Rights Journal* 293; See also Adrien Wing, 'A Truth and Reconciliation Commission for Palestine/Israel: Healing Spirit Injuries?' (2008) 17(1) *Transnational Law & Contemporary Problems* 139; Ariel Meyerstein, 'On the Advantage and Disadvantage of Truth Commission for Life: Dreaming an Israeli-Palestinian Truth Commission' (2003) 45 *Journal of Church and State* 457 ('Dreaming an Israeli-Palestinian Truth Commission').

[2] Edward Said, 'New History, Old Ideas', *Al-Ahram Weekly*, May 21–27 1998.

modelled in part on the SATRC.[3] Some Israeli practitioners have also supported this idea.[4] However, with few exceptions, there has been little academic attention devoted to the actual detail of a such an institution. Indeed, in creating a truth commission, there are a myriad of political and legal factors to consider and a wealth of comparative experiences from which to draw, such as those examples of effective civil society efforts that have operated despite hostile conditions discussed in the previous chapter.[5] In particular, two over-arching principles will guide the IPTEC design. The first one is that every truth commission is inherently unique and therefore demands a tailored response.[6] The second principle is the need for transitional justice practices to be perceived as legitimate. Perhaps the most valuable resource of any commission is its credibility. This is particularly true for unofficial projects operating in hostile political climates. Accordingly, the design elements of the IPTEC discussed below decisively promote these two principles.

Uniqueness

> *Every truth commission, just like every past it claims to represent, and every present it finds itself in, is unique.*[7]

As concluded in Chap. 4, there is no 'one-size-fits-all' solution to transitional justice.[8] More than ever before, the field is calling for locally adapted truth, justice, and reconciliation practices.[9] Indeed, to analogise Israel/Palestine to other conflicts has

---

[3] Mahmoud Cherif Bassiouni, 'Israel and Palestine Need a Joint Truth Commission', *Ha'aretz*, July 142,015. See https://www.haaretz.com/opinion/.premium-israel-palestine-need-joint-truth-commission-1.5304657.

[4] Ron Dudai and Hillel Cohen, 'Triangle of Betrayal: Collaborators and Transitional Justice in the Israeli-Palestinian Conflict' (2007) 6(1) *Journal of Human Rights* 37, 54 ('Triangle of Betrayal'); Daphna Shraga, '1948 Refugees Proceedings of an International workshop, Hebrew University of Jerusalem Faculty of Law, 14–15 December 2016' 51(1) (2018) *Israel Law Review* 47, 106.

[5] Priscilla B. Hayner, *Unspeakable Truths: Confronting State Terror and Atrocity* (Routledge, 2001) ('Confronting State Terror'); See also Neil Kritz, *Transitional Justice: How Emerging Democracies Reckon with Former Regimes* (United States Institute of Peace Press, 1995), vols. 1–3. A useful website, www.truthcommission.org, offers an in-depth, interactive study of design factors to consider in creating a truth commission.

[6] Ariel Meyerstein, 'Transitional Justice and Post-conflict Israel/Palestine: Assessing the Applicability of the Truth Commission Paradigm' (2006–2007) 38 *Case Western Reserve Journal of International Law* 281, 325 ('Transitional Justice and Post-conflict Israel/Palestine').

[7] Onur Bakiner, 'Chapter Six: Explaining Variation in Truth Commissions (II) Evidence from Thirteen Countries' in Onur Bakiner, *Truth Commissions: Memory, Power, and Legitimacy* (University of Pennsylvania Press, 2016), 183.

[8] Diane Orentlicher, 'Settling Accounts Revisited: Reconciling Global Norms with Local Agency' (2007) 1 *International Journal of Transitional Justice* 18.

[9] See Laura Arriaza and Naomi Roht-Arriaza, 'Social reconstruction as a Local Process' (2008) 2(2) *International Journal of Transitional Justice* 157–172; Kieran McEvoy and Lorna McGregor, *Transitional justice from below: grassroots activism and the struggle for change* (Hart, 2008); Patricia Lundy, 'Exploring Home-Grown Transitional Justice and its Dilemmas: A Case Study of

always been perilous and politically charged; the concerns of the region reflect the particular history of the parties, narratives, and events.[10] It is important to recall that any transitional justice mechanism emerges from the unique combination of political resources, religious traditions, and civic landscape of the parties. Only by adapting to the conflict can the IPTEC seek to transform the culture in which it operates. This feature has been described as contextuality and is often ascribed to the uniqueness of the underlying human rights abuse.[11]

On the other hand, assuming that no comparison can productively be made or that no precedents apply to the region leads to the trap of exceptionalism, which only perpetuates the violence in the Middle East (Chap. 4). Indeed, a comparative analysis of truth commission experiences reveals clear patterns.[12] One of the best lessons learned from past commissions is that their strength lies in the diversity and flexibility of the model.[13] Comparisons with other national settings are therefore worthwhile in terms of lessons learned and best practices. Throughout this chapter, a combination of comparative models will be drawn upon in designing an IPTEC.[14]

Legitimacy

Legitimacy also lies in its mythical quality: that of the imagined community....[15]

The second principle is the dimension of legitimacy when devising the procedural and substantive elements of any commission. As will be discussed in detail below, legitimacy is the core feature linking transitional institutions to sustainable peace and influencing people's perceptions of them.[16] It is also about building local ownership, in terms of what causes the institution concerned to be perceived as 'our commission'.[17] Indeed, truth commissions live and die by their moral capital.

---

the Historical Enquiries Team, Northern Ireland' (2009) 3(3) *International Journal of Transitional Justice* 1 (2009).

[10] Miller, above n 1, 323.

[11] Erin Daly, 'Transformative Justice: Charting a Path to Reconciliation' (2001–2) 12(1 & 2) *International Legal Perspectives* 73, 95; See also Mark Drumbl, *Punishment, Post-genocide: From Guilt to Shame to Civis in Rwanda* (New York University School of Law, 2000) (arguing that since each disaster is unique, so must each recovery program be unique).

[12] Bakiner, above n 7, 183.

[13] Miller, above n 1, 323.

[14] The exact shape of the commission and its specific structure will flow from consultative decisions regarding the commission's mandate, the scope of its inquiry, the resources available for its operating budget, and its life-span.

[15] Barabara Oomen, 'Justice Mechanisms and the Question of Legitimacy: The Example of Rwanda's Multi-layered Justice Mechanisms' in Kai Ambos, Judith Large and Marieke Wierda (eds.) *Building a Future on Peace and Justice: Studies on Transitional Justice, Peace and Development, The Nuremberg Declaration on Peace and Justice* (Springer, 2009) 181.

[16] Ibid,195.

[17] Ibid, 181.

Legitimacy is therefore vital to the IPTEC. Unlike a state-sponsored commission established by executive or legislative action, the IPTEC will exist outside a formal legal framework tailored to its specific operation. As will also be discussed below, the strength of this institution, as well as its greatest challenge, lies in its unofficial status. From the moment of its establishment until submission of the final report, the commission will need to secure local support and input.[18] Every element of the commission's structural design; from consultation, commissioners to its mandate should therefore seek to account for institutional legitimacy.

IPTEC Bodies

New NGO and Three Committees

An ambitious project such as this one, which also promotes an alternative model for conflict resolution, requires the creation of a new Israeli–Palestinian NGO. Whist the IPTEC would depend on and involve many existing NGOs and players, it is vital that a new civic body and space be established to pioneer the project. This is because many negative biases exist in relation to the current peacebuilding and human rights community in Israel–Palestine (Chap. 7). It is also because existing NGO initiatives tend to be directed towards documenting and monitoring individual human rights abuse and only primarily towards tackling Israeli abuses. The NGO that pioneers the IPTEC must ambitiously seek to turn a new page, untainted by past controversy and peace 'business' as usual. Moreover, it is not uncommon for truth commissions to assign different tasks to separate committees. For example, the SATRC devised three separate committees to advance the various complementary goals of the commission, which ultimately improved its overall work and efficacy.[19] A benefit of this approach is that each distinct branch of the institution could draw upon the disciplines, expertise, and methodologies best suited to its goals, avoiding the potential of strict legalism to drown out other approaches. A diagrammatic overview of the IPTEC Committees is located in the Appendix.

It is therefore proposed that the IPTEC pursue its central goals (truth-telling, justice, and reconciliation) through three independent yet inter-related sub-groups: the historical clarification committee (Historical Committee), the human rights law committee (Human Rights Committee), and the victims' testimony committee (Victims Committee). The IPTEC could also use its three committees to combine

[18] Shraga, above n 4, 105.

[19] The SATRC consisted of three committees: the Human Rights Committee, which conducted public hearing for victims and survivors; the Reparation and Rehabilitation Committee, charged with developing a policy for long-term reparations as well as urgent relief; and the Amnesty Committee, which reviewed and held hearings for amnesty applications. For more detail see Paul Van Zyl, 'Dilemmas of Transitional Justice: The Case of the South African Truth and Reconciliation Commission' (1999) 52 (2) *Journal of International Affairs* 647. ('Dilemmas of Transitional Justice').

academic, legal, and historical work with direct testimony from Israeli and Palestinian victims. As a truth-telling endeavour, the Committees should focus on Israeli and Palestinian legacies of abuse and avoid being drawn into broader debates over the present rights of refugees, demarcation of borders, self-determination claims, the division of Jerusalem and Palestinian statehood. The reality is that no unofficial truth commission could meaningfully resolve such issues, which ultimately require negotiations at the governmental level. Importantly, a broad-based consultation process as detailed below could help inform and shape the appropriate structure and scope of the IPTEC.

IPTEC Historical Committee

> *Might it not make sense for a group of respected historians..., composed equally of Palestinians and Israelis...to try to agree on a modicum of truth about this conflict?* (Edward Said, January 1999)[20]

A collaboration of Israeli and Palestinian academics, the IPTEC Historical Committee would provide a forensic as well as narrative account of the conflict. It can involve an academic exchange between local expert historians to address the historical factors that have caused gross human rights abuse, as well as hear direct individual testimony from surviving witnesses (coordinated by the Victims Committee). Drawing on Guatemala's historical clarification commission, the goal is not to judge the past but to clarify history with 'objectivity, equity and impartiality'.[21] Ultimately, the committee would seek to produce a nuanced bi-national account of the Palestinian displacement in 1948, the Israeli military occupation (1967) and the Second Intifada (2000–2005) (Chap. 1). The Historical Committee can build on the 'Shared Histories' project (Chap. 7), which brought Israeli–Jewish and Palestinian academics together to increase mutual understanding of their respective history. The Historical Committee might similarly be grounded in cultural context and inter-subjective interaction.

The involvement of expert historians would be crucial to the IPTEC. They could lend their skills to investigating archival materials, reading documents, and offering an authoritative bi-national account of the conflict. Academic collaboration could also provide the context and framework for victim testimony, demonstrating that the IPTEC seeks not to establish a singular truth, but rather to comprehend the complexity of events, and the national identity claims that arise from national

---

[20] Daphna Golan-Agnon, 'Between Human Rights and Hope - What Israelis Might Learn from the Truth and Reconciliation Process in South Africa' (2010) 17 *International Review of Victimology* 31, 31.

[21] Patrick Ball and Audrey Chapman, 'The Truth of Truth Commissions: Comparative Lessons from Haiti, South Africa and Guatemala' (2001) 23 *Human Rights Quarterly* 1, 17.

experience.[22] It could also place oral testimony on an grassroots as well as 'elite' level, permeating both in a multiplicity of ways.[23]

IPTEC Human Rights Committee

Staffed by legal practitioners, the basic task of the Human Rights Committee would consist of investigating the legal dimensions of the violence (Chap. 2), and ultimately producing a comprehensive report on the most characteristic and gross human rights abuses committed during the Israeli–Palestinian conflict. Many aspects of human rights law and IHL could be dealt with; the demands of Israeli national security, the involvement of external actors in 1948, the abuses by Hamas and other Palestinian non-state groups, and the responsibility of both the Israeli and Palestinian governments.

Consistent with the IPTEC's legal mandate discussed in detail below, the Human Rights Committee would be first tasked with formally determining the applicable legal framework to the parties. As discussed in Chap. 2, debate over which legal norms apply to the territories, and the legitimacy of legal claims is itself a central part of the conflict. Such collaborative legal work could be indispensable to the advocacy of justice for bringing pressure to bear on the parties and adding a human rights dimension to conflict resolution. Once the Committee clarifies the applicable IHL and human rights law, it could use those norms as a basis to ascertain the major violations that were committed in the relevant periods. The Committee would then seek to identify institutions, parties, structures, and ideologies that permitted, enabled, encouraged, or caused gross human rights violations.[24]

IPTEC Victims Committee

The IPTEC Victims' Committee is an auxiliary committee to the Historical and Human Rights Committees. Its primary task is to provide logistical and emotional support for victim testimony. The Committee's most critical function is to gather information from those directly affected by human rights violations. The local team will interview victims, record their stories, and prepare public hearings. To perform this function effectively, the Victims Committee would need to prepare detailed procedures and protocols for interviews and databases to record, store, and report incidents of abuse.[25]

[22] Miller, above n 1, 315.

[23] Ibid.

[24] Ball and Chapman, above n 21, 43.

[25] Eduardo González and Howard Varney (eds.), *'Truth-Seeking' Elements of Creating an Effective Truth Commission* (Amnesty Commission of the Ministry of Justice of Brazil; International Center for Transitional Justice 2013), 23.

Collaborating with the other committees, the IPTEC Victims Committee will be able to convene public hearings to expose individual as well as institutional abuses in order to foster empathy between the two sides. For example, in South Africa, separate hearings were held on institutions, such as the legal system, the business, labour and health sectors, and the armed forces. Special hearings were also held to examine the experiences of particular groups during apartheid, such as women and children. Similarly, the IPTEC Victims Committee could hold special hearings to focus on groups like the 1948 Palestinian refugees, Israeli bereaved families, as well as abuses perpetrated by specific sectors of Israeli and Palestinian societies. Having this Committee function somewhat independently from the other two would allow the team to focus all of its attention on the victims, without scholarly historical or legal debate interfering with personal narratives of human suffering.[26] It would also have the benefit of adopting methodologies and seeking experts best suited to victim testimony rather than legal or historical analysis.

Local Ownership and International Support

An important design element of any truth commission is the degree of international and/or local involvement. There is enormous variation on the role of international actors in transitional justice mechanisms. For example, South Africa's TRC was a complete national grassroot initiative, as opposed to the distinctly international character of the UN sponsored El Salvadorian Commission.[27] The UN has also been a central actor in several truth commissions, notably El Salvador, Guatemala, and Sierra Leone, and might lend its official support to an IPTEC.

Given hostilities between Israelis and Palestinians, it might be assumed that international actors could play an essential and constructive role in the formation of any transitional justice mechanism. On the diplomatic front, the Middle East Quartet[28] and, until recently, the US, have long served as third-party intermediaries. The region's peacebuilding projects are commonly pioneered and supported by external donors. Arguably, an internationally driven IPTEC would link local activists with the global community, enabling them to draw on shared values and to apply

[26] Meyerstein, '*Dreaming an Israeli-Palestinian Truth Commission*', above n 1, 472.

[27] In El Salvador, a series of six accords negotiated by the UN between 1990 and 1992, included the mandate for *La Comision de la Verdad* which constituted the first such commission ever to be completely international in nature—both in terms of its mandate and in terms of its composition. Thomas Buergenthal, 'The United Nations Truth Commission for El Salvador' (1994) 27 *Vanderbilt Journal of Transnational law* 497, 501

[28] The Quartet, set up in 2002, consists of the UN, the EU, the US, and Russia. It meets regularly and its mandate is to help mediate Middle East peace negotiations and to support Palestinian economic development and institution-building in preparation for eventual statehood.

universal human rights norms.[29] Given this initiative would begin in the margins of Israeli/Palestinian society, an international framework could lend the IPTEC support and reduce some of its isolation.

Nevertheless, there are several reasons why the IPTEC should principally remain locally operated and created. Firstly, Israeli/Palestinian civil society is best placed to devise community-based processes that accommodate the specific context and culture of the parties. Local historians, lawyers, and policy figures have long played a significant role in the Israeli and Palestinian societies, and along with academics can build the institutional and psychological rigging of the IPTEC. As discussed, non-state Israeli and Palestinian actors have already succeeded in developing transitional justice projects together. Most of the initiatives examined in the previous chapter were conducted exclusively by Palestinians and Israeli–Jews without intermediaries.[30]

Indeed, the parties themselves typically objected to the substantive intervention of third parties.[31] Even the most well-meaning international actors may not have sufficient understanding of the psychological particularities of the conflict. External donors and/or advisors may be well-versed in transitional justice, but they are less familiar with the collective memory of the rivals, or the ways in which local narratives inform explosive issues such as the Palestinian right of return. It would be concerning if to secure funding for example, the IPTEC had to conform to pre-established frameworks or adopt more conventional terminology.[32]

At any rate, local ownership is vital to the legitimacy of the IPTEC. Arguably international credentials do not equate to popular legitimacy.[33] Accordingly, historical scholarship, interviews with victims and legal investigation should be conducted primarily by Israelis and Palestinians through the three IPTEC Committees. Narratives and legal findings presented by members of the communities themselves

---

[29] Ron Dudai and Hillel Cohen 'Dealing with the Past when the Conflict is Still Present' in Rosalind Shaw and Lars Waldorf, with Pierre Hazan (eds), *Localizing Transitional Justice: Interventions and Priorities After Mass Violence* (Stanford University Press, 2010) 246, 248 ('Dealing With the Past').

[30] Rafi Nets-Zehngut, 'Palestinians and Israelis Collaborate in Addressing the Historical Narratives of their Conflict' (2013) 5 *Quest: Issues in Contemporary Jewish History* 232, 250–1 ('Palestinians and Israelis Collaborate').

[31] 'They agreed to get financial and logistical aid from third parties, but not intervention in the content of the publications. This was an outcome of a feeling that they, the third parties not understand the complexity and emotional particularities of the conflict for us, the involved parties'. Ibid, 251.

[32] For example, if the commission were forced to replace its focus on empathy with the term 'reconciliation', which has more resonance abroad. Dudai and Cohen, *'Dealing with the Past'*, above n 29, 248.

[33] For example, there was a relative lack of support for the ICTR amongst Bosnians, Croats, and Serbs, for whom many feel that 'The Hague Tribunal was a big mockery' Corkalo et al., 'Attitudes Towards Justice and Social Reconstruction in Bosnia and Herzegovina and Croatia' in Eric Stover and Harvey Weinstein (Eds.*), My neighbor, My Enemy: Justice and Community in the aftermath of Mass Atrocity (Cambridge University Press, 2004)*, 147; See also Oomen, above n 15, 82.

are far more likely to be received as credible.[34] This is especially true when sensitive counter-narratives are likely to emerge around polarising events, like 1948, which undermine official history. Indeed, as discussed in Chap. 7, the central role played by Israeli and Palestinian combatants and bereaved families in existing projects lent those initiatives moral authority.[35]

Further, there exists growing suspicion in the region concerning international actors.[36] As mentioned in Chap. 7, the Israeli Knesset passed the 'NGO Transparency Law' in 2016, requiring civil society groups to disclose their degree of funding from foreign entities in order to discredit them.[37] Israel has long argued that the UN is biased against it (as discussed in Chap. 5), whilst many Palestinians claim the UN has failed to protect them from human rights violations.[38] Recent moves by the Trump administration have also eroded a brokering role for the US in the Middle East. Moving the US Embassy to Jerusalem (2018) and recognising Israeli sovereignty over the Golan Heights (2019) have deeply alienated Palestinians. The Trump administration has also sided with Israel in its response to the deadly violence on the Gaza border in 2018.

Finally, transitional justice measures are most sustainable when they are independently created and embedded within the conflicting communities (as discussed in Chap. 7).[39] Sometimes international actors try to control a truth commission's mandate and composition.[40] The cases of Haiti and El Salvador serve as cautionary tales against structuring commissions through international intervention. The Haitian commission[41] was largely initiated and supported by North American–based diaspora communities. However, it lacked the popular support of Haitians in the country, ignored the domestic human rights community,[42] and failed to engage local

---

[34] Anita Shapira, 'Hirbet Hiza – Zikaron Veshchecha' ['Hirbet Hiza – Remembrance and Forgetfulness'], (2002) 21 *Alpaim* 9–53, (Hebrew) cited in Nets-Zehngut, *'Palestinians and Israelis Collaborate'*, above n 30, 251.

[35] Ibid.

[36] 'One of the main debates in Israeli and Palestinian societies concerns giving up "authentic values" and adopting "foreign" ones instead'. Dudai and Cohen, *'Dealing with the Past'*, above n 29, 248.

[37] The law requires Israeli NGOs to report more than 50% of funding received from foreign public sources and to indicate on all publications that they are funded by 'foreign agents'. Failing to abide by these rules will be considered a criminal offence.

[38] See Antidefamation League, Anti-Israel Bias at the U.N., available at http://www.adl.org/international/Israel-UN-1-introduction.asp cited in Wing above n 1, 156.

[39] Lundy, above n 9, 326–7.

[40] Bakiner, above n 7, 183.

[41] Haitian *Commission nationale de vérité et de justice* (CNVJ). The Commission was established to investigate the gravest violations of human rights in the aftermath of the military coup during 1991–1994 and to aid in the reconciliation of all Haitians. Joanna Quinn, 'Haiti's Failed Truth Commission: Lessons in Transitional Justice', (2009) 8 (3) *Journal of Human Rights*, 265–281.

[42] 'In Haiti a relatively high-quality commission, established under the guidance of diaspora groups, was left to oblivion, as the domestic human rights community felt left out of the commission creation process'. Bakiner, above n 7, 183.

media.[43] In El Salvador, the UN established an investigative body singlehandedly in the context of a peace agreement.[44] Most Salvadorans did not trust this body because it was formed at a diplomatic level and developed without public participation.[45] Overall, both the commissions were made vulnerable because of their complete dependence on international involvement.[46] Many truth commission experiences demonstrate that overseas actors do not invariably produce high-autonomy and high-capacity commissions.[47]

Local ownership and independence are therefore crucial to the viability of the IPTEC. In this respect, Hayner emphasises the normative value of public participation in the institutional design of a commission, both in terms of creation and effective implementation.[48] In examples such as Ghana[49] and Sierra Leone,[50] NGOs and victim associations have been at the forefront of successfully conceiving truth-telling endeavours.[51] In South Africa, intensive social debate as to the structure of a possible commission preceded the eventual creation of the SATRC.[52] The NGO sector worked directly with the public and political parties through a series of conferences.[53] In Brazil, the National Truth Commission was the direct result of civil society activities at the National Conference on Human Rights.[54] The extended dialogue and broad involvement of different social sectors were instrumental to the

---

[43] Quinn, above n 41, 265–281.

[44] The commission was established under the UN mediated Mexico Agreement of 1991, assigned to investigate 'serious acts of violence that had occurred between January 1980 and July 1991' that required 'public knowledge of the truth'.

[45] Buergenthal, above n 27, 501.

[46] Bakiner, above n 7, 151.

[47] Ibid, 8.3.

[48] Priscilia Hayner, 'International Guidelines for the Creation and Operation of Truth Commissions: A Preliminary Proposal' (1996) 4 *Law and Contemporary Problems* 173, 178.

[49] In Ghana, the Civil Society Coalition on National Reconciliation played a crucial role in developing the national commission. See International Center for Transitional Justice, *Truth Commissions and NGOs: The Essential Relationship. The 'Frati-Guidelines' for NGOs Engaging With Truth Commissions* (Occasional Paper Series, April 2004), 14 ('ICTJ Frati-Guidelines').

[50] In Sierra Leone, the NGO Working Group became a clearinghouse for information, generating civil society input and ensuring that the voice and wishes of Sierra Leoneans would be incorporated in the formation of a commission. See Paul James-Allen, 'Case Study: The Role of NGOs in the formation of the Sierra Leone Truth Commission' in Ibid, 11.

[51] Ibid 30.

[52] The SATRC was formed after an extensive consultation process carried out by parliament, which included public discussions on draft legislation. Public participation in the legislative debate helped to increase popular interest and understanding of SATRC-related policies when they were finally implemented. González and Varney, above n 25, 15.

[53] Hugo Van der Merwe, Polly Dewhirst, and Brandon Hamber, 'Non-Governmental Associations and the Truth and Reconciliation Commission: An Impact Assessment', 26 (1) (1999) *Politikon: South African Journal of Political Studies* 55, 61.

[54] See 11th National Conference on Human Rights, Brasilia, Brazil, December 15–18, 2008. http://portal.mj.gov.br/sedh/11cndh/site/_index.html.

conception of the truth commission.[55] As discussed in Chap. 7, the Catholic Church's unofficial truth commission in Guatemala (REHMI) also exemplified strong civil society participation. Various community groups and religious leaders exerted significant influence over the project's creation.[56]

Local Consultation: IPTEC Working Group

Accordingly, the formation of the IPTEC must be preceded by broad-based consultation with the public, a necessary preliminary step according to the OHCHR transitional justice toolkit.[57] The process of consultation could be led by an IPTEC Working Group with the purpose of informing both the societies about the proposed commission and seeking their views on its mandate, composition, and expected outcome.[58] Established Israeli and Palestinian NGO network forums already exist and could provide the support needed for this endeavour.[59] Although the IPTEC is presently fleshed out, it is conceivable that consultation would profoundly shape and change the structure and mandate of the three-tiered institution. For example, civic groups might decide that creating three committees is presently too ambitious and opt instead to focus all efforts on one aspect of the truth-telling enterprise. A conference or series of conferences, for example, could bring together different representatives in a shared platform to guide this process and the architecture.[60] As in Sierra Leone, an informal NGO coalition is best placed to develop a vision of engagement through discussion of the guiding goals and purposes of the commission.[61] It can also contribute to sensitising the public, mapping the conflict,

---

[55] González and Varney, above n 25, 15.

[56] For example, the Guatemalan Civil Society Assembly which helped inform REHMI included political parties, religious groups, trade unions, women's organisations, and Mayan organisations. See Celia McKeon, 'Public Participation in Peace Processes: Comparative Experience and Relevant Principles' in Terry Rempel (ed.), *Rights in Principle - Rights in Practice Revisiting the Role of International Law in Crafting Durable Solutions for Palestinian Refugees* (BADIL Resource Center, 2009) 344.

[57] Office of the United Nations High Commissioner for Human Rights, Rule-of-Law Tools for Post-Conflict States: National Consultations on Transitional Justice by the United Nations Office of the High Commissioner for Human Rights, 2009, http://www.ohchr.org/Documents/Publications/NationalConsultationsTJ_EN.pdf.

[58] *ICTJ Frati-Guidelines*, above n 49, 16.

[59] For example, the Alliance for Middle East Peace (ALLMEP) is an established network of organisations that conduct civil society work in conflict transformation, development, coexistence, and cooperative activities on the ground in the Middle East among Israelis, Palestinians, Arabs, and Jews. The Palestinian NGO network is another such forum http://www.pngo.net/.

[60] Most recently, the Israeli Peace NGO Forum met in Ramallah with the PLO Committee on Interaction with Israeli Society ICTJ. See also Ibid.

[61] James-Allen, above n 50, 11.

researching violations, integrating local practices, and enhancing participation of Israeli/Palestinian victims and former combatants in the IPTEC's efforts.[62]

Above all, consultation with victims' groups should be a priority during the creation of the IPTEC.[63] For example, NGOs devoted to Israeli and Palestinian bereaved families (PCFF),[64] Israeli victims of terror attacks (OneFamily[65] and NATAL),[66] Palestinian refugee rights (BADIL),[67] and Palestinian victims of torture (TRC)[68] should contribute information and prepare policy recommendations. Without their direct involvement and input, the IPTEC cannot credibly integrate their needs and narratives.[69] Submissions from experts and other community representatives can also be solicited orally, or in writing, or through workshops.[70] Indeed, the more victims who participate in the consultation process, the greater sense of that ownership over the IPTEC, and the greater the social pressure for its acceptance. Ultimately, truth commissions are designed over time. For example, it was, in fact, largely based on a 2-year public consultation process that the commissions in South Africa and Sierra Leone were developed.[71]

Local Representation: 'Many Hands'

To earn the respect of both the societies, the IPTEC coalition should involve a wide variety of social, religious, and political agents.[72] Effective truth commissions require the input of many stakeholders.[73] In various contexts, truth commissions

---

[62] Ibid.

[63] González and Varney, above n 25, 15.

[64] PCFF is an Israeli-Palestinian NGO of over 600 Israeli and Palestinian bereaved families, all of whom have lost a family member to the conflict. As a victim group, it uses dialogue and shared narrative to advance reconciliation. See the group's website at http://www.theparentscircle.com.

[65] OneFamily is an NGO devoted to Israeli victims of terror attacks—those who have been bereaved, those who have been maimed, and those suffering from post-trauma as a result of terrorist attacks since 2001. https://www.onefamilytogether.org/about-us/.

[66] NATAL is an apolitical non-profit organisation that provides Israelis with nationwide treatment and support for psychological trauma due to terror and war https://www.natal.org.il/en/.

[67] BADIL Resource Center for Palestinian Residency and Refugee Rights is an independent, human rights NGO committed to protect and promote the rights of Palestinian refugees and internally displaced persons. BADIL is registered with the PA and one of the leading refugee community groups. http://www.badil.org/en/.

[68] The Treatment & Rehabilitation Center for Victims of Torture (TRC) is a non-profit human rights group and mental health service provider which treats direct and indirect victims of torture through individual, group and family therapy, conducts advocacy for policy reforms and raises awareness across all sectors of Palestinian society. See the group's website: www.trc-pal.org.

[69] González and Varney, above n 25, 15.

[70] Ibid.

[71] Shraga, above n 4, 105.

[72] *ICTJ Frati-Guidelines*, above n 49, 9.

[73] Oomen, above n 15, 196.

have used participatory mechanisms to widen the range of issues they addressed and to generate social consensus. In Ghana, for example, an NGO coalition created an all-inclusive process that brought disparate political groups together to deliberate and design an appropriate truth commission.[74] Bakiner demonstrates that truth commissions created from these kinds of participatory processes are best placed to achieve successful outcomes throughout the commission process.[75]

It is therefore incumbent on the IPTEC Working Group to construct a commission that is representative. Indeed, truth commissions that exclude major stakeholders, whether they are perpetrators, victims, or diverse political players, risk being considered illegitimate by these stakeholders from the beginning.[76] In Israel, human rights issues tend to be perceived as 'left-wing', and human rights activists rarely affiliate with the political 'right'.[77] Indeed, one of the failings of Zochrot's truth commission (as discussed in Chap. 7) was that by associating with the radical Israeli political-left, the project lacked wider appeal, and was therefore too easily dismissed as a partisan effort. In this regard, representation is also crucial to the question of legitimacy.

Accordingly, it is proposed that Israeli–Jewish religious groups become active agents in the IPTEC consultation process. Indeed, there is a growing trend of engaging conservative religious constituencies beyond the secular elite classically associated with the 'peace camp'.[78] The Interfaith Encounter,[79] the Abrahamic Reunion,[80] and Roots[81] are just three of the many groups pursuing inter-faith peacebuilding between Israelis and Palestinians. Such groups could be recruited by the IPTEC Working Group. It is precisely those Israeli–Jews with strong faith-based identities who have a great deal to offer a truth commission. They are deeply invested in

[74] Franklin Oduro 'Case Study: NGO Relationships with Truth Commissions in Ghana' in *ICTJ Frati-Guidelines*, above n 49, 17.

[75] According to Bakiner's research, diverse and local civic participation are instrumental to truth commission outcomes. He conducted case histories for all truth commissions that completed their work as of 2014. Bakiner, above n 7, 183.

[76] Oomen, above n 15, 196.

[77] Andre du Toit quoted in '*Truth Commissions: A Comparative Assessment.*' Inter-disciplinary Discussion Held at Harvard Law School, (Harvard Law School, May 1996) 20. ('Harvard Law Discussion').

[78] Ned Lazarus, 'Heshbon Nefesh: Civil Society Seeking a Two-State Majority' in Yair Hirschfeld (ed.), *Developing an Israeli Grand Strategy toward a Peaceful Two-State Solution* (S. Daniel Abraham Center for Strategic Dialogue/Friedrich Ebert Stiftung, 2016) 82–97; Ned Lazarus, *A future for Israeli-Palestinian peacebuilding*, Britain Israel Communications and Research Centre (2017) 23. ('BICOM Report 2017').

[79] http://interfaith-encounter.org/

[80] https://www.abrahamicreunion.org/

[81] According to the website: 'Roots is a unique network of local Palestinians and Israelis who have come to see each other as the partners we both need to make changes to end our conflict. Based on a mutual recognition of each People's connection to the Land, we are developing understanding and solidarity despite our ideological differences'. https://www.friendsofroots.net/.

historical narratives and are driven by a moral imperative to end the violence.[82] It is also they for whom disclosing violations might be most valuable as many of them live on the front lines. In recent years, Israeli-religious Jews have been most affected by Palestinian terrorist attacks against Israelis.[83]

Politically centrist organisations are also worthy of engagement. For example, Darkeinu is the largest non-partisan group in Israel working to amplify moderate voices and push back against extremism.[84] As a grassroot movement committed to social justice and peace diplomacy, they could help broaden the base of support.[85] The mobilising power and input of a gendered coalition is also valuable. 'Women Wage Peace' (WWP)[86] is a new NGO, which has managed to unite many women in the region across the political spectrum. In October 2016, tens of thousands of women, Arab and Jewish, Israeli, and Palestinian, marched together throughout Israel to demand the renewal of peace negotiations.[87] Their public rallies demonstrate how representative activism and collaboration cut across traditional lines and sub-groups.[88] Ultimately, a representative consultative process can influence and encourage NGOs that did not anticipate the IPTEC to positively engage with the process.[89] It could be an invaluable aid to expand support for the IPTEC, provide valuable input, and garner sympathetic coverage in an otherwise sceptical media.[90]

---

[82] '...[J]ust as religious ethnic identities have the power to divide, so too they have the power to unite'. Yakov Nagen, 'The Abrahamic Union: A Confederate Solution to the Israeli Palestinian Conflict', *Times of Israel Blogs*, 29 May, 2017, http://blogs.timesofisrael.com/the-abrahamic-union-a-confederate-solution-to-the-israeli-palestinian-conflict.

[83] Over the past 10 years, Palestinians have carried out stabbings, car ramming, shootings, and other attacks primarily against Israelis in the West Bank and in Jerusalem.

[84] https://darkenu.org.il/en/

[85] 'As a grassroots movement, we work daily across Israel—door by door, town by town—setting up stalls in public centers, organizing house meetings, events, demonstrations, and protest vigils. We believe in the importance of an engaged civil society'. https://darkenu.org.il/en/.

[86] WWP is a broad grassroot movement founded in the summer of 2014 following Operation Protective Edge. It has tens of thousands of members from the right, the centre and the left of the political spectrum, Jews and Arabs, religious and secular, women from kibbutzim and from settlements, all of whom are united in a demand for a mutually binding non-violent accord, agreeable to both sides. http://womenwagepeace.org.il/en/about-eng/.

[87] WWP orchestrated a remarkable 2-week series of marches and public rallies in dozens of towns throughout the country, culminating in approximately 4000 Israeli and Palestinian women ascending the ancient desert road together from Jericho to Jerusalem, where they joined 20,000 protestors outside the Prime Minister's residence. See Lazarus, above n 78, *BICOM Report 2017,* 13.

[88] WWP began the series of marches in cities on Israel's geographic and socioeconomic 'periphery', signalling their intention to expand beyond the traditional 'peace camp' elite and to draw leaders from diverse communities. Anat Negev, (31 October, 2016, Ned Lazarus, Interviewer) cited in Ibid, 14.

[89] *ICTJ Frati-Guidelines*, above n 49, 16.

[90] For example, social media for WWP amplified their audience within and beyond the region. A news clip featuring evocative footage of jubilant Arab and Jewish women clad in white, striding together through a barren biblical landscape, drew more than 19 million views (Negev, 2016). Lazarus, above n 78, *BICOM Report 2017,* 13.

At the same time, the creation of a constructive transitional justice process will need to exclude some civic and political actors. As discussed in Chap. 7, civil society is a contested term, which could theoretically include a wider range of Israeli and Palestinian players from Hamas to the Israeli settler's Price Tag Movement. It is submitted that for both symbolic and practical purposes, illiberal, extremist, or violent groups, as well as those directly implicated in gross human rights abuses are not stakeholders in the IPTEC.

International Support

> *What we need to do internationally is try to create the conditions to help Israelis and Palestinians, not seek to substitute for them.* (John Lyndon, 2018)[91]

Most truth commissions, including unofficial ones, have relationships with international organisations based in other countries.[92] Many European and Scandinavian countries, as well as North American NGOs, have a keen interest in transitional justice[93] and would be drawn to such activities in the Middle East. International actors have long played a crucial and constructive role in the development of truth commissions. Indeed, all the high-capacity truth commissions that have operated to date have received some kind of international and/or transnational assistance.[94] In Timor-Leste sustained support from the UN and external NGOs, especially the International Center for Transitional Justice (ICTJ), created the conditions under which the commission adopted novel procedures, produced a comprehensive final report, and made broad recommendations.[95] The Sierra Leonean commission received much needed aid from a network of international human rights organisations.[96]

International aid will likely increase the capacity and efficacy of a truth commission, especially an unofficial one.[97] Accordingly, international NGOs and interested states could form support networks to advise, host and offer technical assistance to the IPTEC Working Group. The international academic and research community

---

[91] Joel Branold and John Lyndon, 'Opinion amongst the young is drifting: An International Fund for Israeli-Palestinian Peace is urgently needed', *Fathom Online Journal* 2018 http://journal.org/opinion-amongst-the-young-is-drifting-an-international-fund-for-israeli-palestinian-peace-is-urgently-needed/.

[92] *ICTJ Frati-Guidelines*, above n 49, 26.

[93] Since the mid-1990s, foreign governments and international organisations like the UN, nongovernmental funding agencies like the Ford Foundation and numerous civil society activists have been lobbying for funding and offering technical expertise to truth commissions around the globe. See Bakiner, above n 7, 183; Ibid, 26.

[94] Bakiner, above n 7, 183.

[95] Catherine Jenkins, 'A Truth Commission for East Timor: Lessons from South Africa?' (2002) 7 (2) *Journal of Conflict and Security Law* 233–252.

[96] González and Varney, above n 25, 34.

[97] Bakiner, above n 7, 183.

would provide essential resources, research and conference space, information preservation, and testimony collection.[98] Specialised NGOs like the ICTJ and the Center for the Study of Violence and Reconciliation (Johannesburg) may share their knowledge and expertise based on comparative experience.[99] Ideally, a degree of international input and support would stabilise the commission by bolstering confidence in the process. For example, internationally regarded legal experts could sit alongside local ones on the IPTEC Human Rights Committee. International actors could use their leverage to encourage Israelis, Palestinians, and their governments, to support the IPTEC process. In Sierra Leone, the truth commission managed to generate considerable civic mobilisation, partly due to constant international pressure.[100]

International financial support is also essential. Over the past decade, the EU Peacebuilding Initiative and USAID/Conflict Management and Mitigation (CMM) grant programme[101] have funded hundreds of Israeli–Palestinian peacebuilding projects.[102] Alongside international foundations,[103] they could provide vital seed-funding and monetary support to the IPTEC. Many such donors however are 'usual suspects' and have already been stretched by existing programs. These funding bodies are also likely to require evidence of strong domestic support for the IPTEC, which would be challenging for an unofficial project. Accordingly, the newly established International Fund for Israeli–Palestinian Peace offers hope to projects like the IPTEC. Developed by ALLMEP, this $200 million per year fund will leverage and increase the support for people-to-people activities from governments and private sector sources worldwide.[104] As recently as June 2018, the US portion of the International Fund has now been unlocked.[105] The idea of a consistent and central

[98] *ICTJ Frati-Guidelines*, above n 49, 26.

[99] Ibid.

[100] Michael O'Flaherty, 'Sierra Leone's Peace Process: The Role of the Human Rights Community'. (2004) 26(1) *Human Rights Quarterly* 29–62.

[101] More recently, ALLMEP has helped to secure an additional 20% in funding for the USAID/CMM grant program, with $12 M reserved for Israeli–Palestinian peacebuilding programs from 2017. http://www.allmep.org/in-bipartisan-move-us-senate-earmarks-funds-for-the-international-fund-for-israeli-palestinian-peace/.

[102] Lazarus, above n 78, *BICOM Report 2017,* 35.

[103] For example, the Ford Foundation, the Open Society Institute and the Rockefeller Foundation have all provided financial and other important forms of support, especially for NGOs, during truth commission processes. 'Truth Commissions and NGOs' the Essential Relationship. *ICTJ Frati-Guidelines,* above n 49, 26.

[104] ALLMEP has been advocating for the creation of an International Fund for Israeli–Palestinian Peace since 2009. http://www.allmep.org/in-bipartisan-move-us-senate-earmarks-funds-for-the-international-fund-for-israeli-palestinian-peace/.

[105] In June 2018, the US Senate Committee on Appropriations voted to fund a new Palestinian Partnership Fund as part of the FY19 State and Foreign Operations Bill. This fund will allocate $50 million to support exchange, cooperation, shared community-building, and reconciliation between Palestinians and Israelis. http://www.allmep.org/in-bipartisan-move-us-senate-earmarks-funds-for-the-international-fund-for-israeli-palestinian-peace/.

funding source for Israel/Palestine was inspired by the International Fund for Northern Ireland created over 20 years ago.[106]

Bi-national IPTEC

> *...[B]efore we can even talk about 'ownership,' there has to be 'buy-in' on the part of the relevant parties. In other words, if you don't buy it, you don't own it.*[107]

From the outset, it is contended that the design, implementation, and work of the IPTEC involve bi-partisan collaboration between Israelis and Palestinians as equal owners, participants, and architects in the process. There is limited precedence for a bi-national truth commission. Nevertheless, without ownership on both sides, it seems likely that any effort at truth-letting, justice, or reconciliation '...will again be lost to the continuing morass of the conflict'.[108] The bilateral character of the IPTEC is therefore grounded in boosting the credibility of the IPTEC and empowering Palestinians as a traditionally marginalised group.

Credibility of IPTEC

A commission conceived and composed solely of Israeli or solely Palestinian representatives would lack moral authority, with its findings undermined if not outright dismissed. For South Africa, it was crucial that the SATRC not be construed as a mere 'witch-hunt' against whites.[109] The involvement of both white and black South Africans in the commission process, as participants, architects, victims, and perpetrators bolstered its legitimacy.[110]

Notably, the Commission on Truth and Friendship of Timor-Leste (East Timor) and Indonesia (CTF) was the first modern bilateral truth commission created by two countries. It was jointly established by Indonesia and East Timor in August 2005.

---

[106] The International Fund for Ireland was a major source of support for inter-communal civil society engagement on a mass scale since 1986. It contributed to the support of large majorities for the Good Friday Agreement of 1998. Mari Fitzduff, *Beyond Violence: Conflict Resolution Processes in Northern Ireland.* (United Nations University Press, 2002). The BICOM Report (2017) is very supportive of a similar funding instrument for Israel/Palestine. Lazarus, above n 78, *BICOM Report 2017,* 14.

[107] Rapoza makes this comment about the hybrid East Timor tribunal (200–2006) where neither the UN nor the Timorese government ever completely 'bought in' to the process which caused significant issues. Phillip Rapoza, 'Hybrid Criminal Tribunals and the Concept of Ownership: Who owns the Process?' (2006) 4 (21) *American University International Law Review* 525, 530.

[108] Miller, above n 1, 323.

[109] Brandon Hamber and Gunnar Theissen, 'A State of Denial: White South Africans' attitudes to the Truth and Reconciliation Commission'. (1998) 15(1) *Indicator South Africa,* 8–12.

[110] Ibid.

Comprising half Indonesian and half Timor-Leste Commissioners, the CTF was responsible for finding the 'conclusive truth' about the 1999 independence referendum violence.[111] The CTF drew heavy criticism from international[112] as well as local human rights groups.[113] Some claim it was designed more to enhance bilateral diplomatic ties than to substantively contribute to truth telling, justice,[114] or even national reconciliation.[115]

Nevertheless, what is particularly notable is that its final report was fully endorsed by both East Timorese and Indonesian authorities.[116] According to the War Crimes Studies Center at Berkeley University, the CTF could be seen by each nation as '...widely acknowledged, credible and far-reaching'.[117] In fact, the CTF elicited the first official acknowledgement by Indonesia of its human rights violations in East Timor.[118] There was also credible evidence of Timorese institutional responsibility for illegal detentions and other crimes.[119] Affirmation of the commission's findings by both the nations is significant. It is particularly impressive given the range of serious transitional justice measures which proceeded the CTF.[120] Arguably, the

[111] The CTF involved an inquiry into 'the perpetration of gross human rights violations and institutional responsibility' and 'arriving at recommendations and lessons learned'. See *Commission of Truth and Friendship, From Memory to Hope: Final Report of the Commission of Truth and Friendship Indonesia-Timor-Leste* (Denpasar, 31 March 2008) ('CTF Final Report').

[112] According to the ICTJ, many aspects of the CTF were deeply flawed. 'With a creation process conducted behind closed doors with minimal consultation... the CTF fell short of international standards and local transitional justice needs...'. Megan Hirst, *Too Much Friendship, Too Little Truth: Monitoring Report on the Commission of Truth and Friendship in Indonesia and Timor-Leste*, (ICTJ Occasional Paper Series, January 2008), 37.

[113] The Timorese NGO Timor-Leste National Alliance for International Tribunal wrote an open letter in response to the commission's findings with several criticisms, including the lack of public consultation with victims. See Timor-Leste National Alliance for International Tribunal, 15 July 2008 http://www.laohamutuk.org/Justice/TFC/ANTIonCTFEn.pdf.

[114] Rebecca Strating, 'The Indonesia-Timor-Leste Commission of Truth and Friendship: Enhancing Bilateral Relations at the Expense of Justice'. (2014) 36 (2) *Contemporary Southeast Asia* 34; See also Lia Kent, 'Local Memory Practices in East Timor: Disrupting Transitional Justice Narratives'. (2011) 5(3) *International Journal of Transitional Justice* 434, 435.

[115] Hirst, above n 112, 37.

[116] Operating over 3 years, the commission handed its final report on 15 July 2008 and presented it to the Presidents of Indonesia and East Timor.

[117] War Crimes Studies Center, *East Timor Truth Commission: The Commission on Truth and Friendship* (University of California, 2014). Available at: http://wcsc.berkeley.edu/east-timor/east-timor-truth-commission/.

[118] Priscilla Hayner, *Unspeakable Truths: Transitional Justice and the Challenge of Truth Commissions* (Routledge, 2011) 65. ('Transitional Justice and the Challenge of Truth Commissions').

[119] War Crimes Studies Center, above n 117.

[120] The CTF was preceded by prosecutions in Timor Leste before the UN Special Panels for Serious Crimes. In addition, the Commission of Reception, Truth and Reconciliation of Timor-Leste (a Timorese national truth commission) previously published a massive report, and there had also been an investigation and report by the Indonesia National Human Rights Commission (Komnas HAM) and by a UN Commission of Experts.

willingness of Indonesia (the stronger party) to recognise its complicity in the violence was largely due to the bi-national nature of the commission. The Indonesians 'bought into' the process and were partial to its findings. Similarly, a joint Israeli–Palestinian commission could make it easier for Israelis to accept the outcomes of such a body.

Empowering Palestinians: From 'Objects' to 'Co-owners'

One of the goals of a bi-national IPTEC should be to empower Palestinians as equal partners in the process. As discussed in Chap. 7, the practice of excluding traditionally disenfranchised groups from transitional justice raises questions about legitimacy, local ownership, and sustainability.[121] For Palestinian society, now in its fourth generation of refugees, national identity has been shaped by a denial of collective and political rights. The Israeli occupation encroaches on the daily lives of millions of Palestinians. Ordinary Palestinians frequently feel marginalised by peace talks conducted by political elites behind closed doors.[122] Accordingly, many Palestinians exhibit feelings of 'learned helplessness'[123] arising from their perceived lack of control over their own fate. This sense of disempowerment may be found across all elements of Palestinian society including older Palestinians,[124] the refugees,[125] and increasingly the youth.[126]

Many NGOs have been unable to make any serious inroads into this despair, so long as external powers and Israeli activists are making all the decisions.[127] The lack of autonomous Palestinian voices in human rights protection and peacebuilding may inhibit the positive effect of transitional justice efforts. This creates distance,

---

[121] Lundy, above n 9, 325.

[122] Leila Hilal, *Transitional Justice Responses to Palestinian Dispossession: Focus on Restitution* (International Center for Transitional Justice (ICTJ) and the Brookings-LSE Project on Internal Displacement, August 2012) 5.

[123] Zeynep Cemalcilar, Resit Canbeyli and Diane Sunar, 'Learned Helplessness, Therapy and Personality Traits: An Experimental Study' (2003) 14 *Journal of Social Psychology* 65–81.

[124] Dan Rabinovitch and Khaula Abu-Baker, *The Upright Generation* (Keter, 2002) (Hebrew); Khalil Rinnawi, *Haevra Ha'aravit Bisrael: Seder Yom Ambivalenty/The Arabic Society in Israel: An Ambivalent Agenda* (The Management College, 2003), (Hebrew) cited in Nets-Zehngut, *'Palestinians and Israelis Collaborate'*, above n 30, 249.

[125] Joint Parliamentary Middle East Councils Commission of Enquiry—*Palestinian Refugees, Right of Return* (Labour Middle East Council, 2001).

[126] According to Khalidi, over the past decade physical separation has seen an entire new generation of Palestinians grow up '...in the archipelago of large open-air prisons...'. Rashid Khalidi 'Introduction to 2010 reissue' in *Palestinian Identity: The Construction of Modern National Consciousness* (Columbia University Press, 1997), xxv. ('Palestinian Identity').

[127] Manuel Hassassian, 'Chapter 3: Civil Society and NGO's Building Peace in Palestine' in Walid Salem, Juliette Verhoeven and Edy Kaufman (eds.) *Bridging the Divide: Peacebuilding in the Israeli-Palestinian Conflict.* (Lynne Rienner. 2006) 80–81.

defamiliarisation, and entrenches unequal power relations.[128] From this standpoint, the bi-national element of the IPTEC is essential to reverse this trend, or at least to raise the profile of Palestinian voices in conflict resolution. Shoughry-Badarne notes the challenges faced by Israeli activists when 'translating' for Palestinians whose rights have been violated. She has stated: 'Whoever does the fieldwork has to know not only Arabic, but also be culturally close to the people'.[129] As co-owners in such activities, those Palestinians involved could improve their self-efficacy[130] and feel empowered to challenge the status quo. Indeed, joint Israeli–Palestinian truth-telling projects have already enabled Palestinian organisers to take control over their own narratives. The IPTEC is therefore wedded to a bilateral framework of truth-telling, building on these ideas as well as the desire to empower Palestinians to overcome exclusion and marginalisation.

Commissioner Selection

The IPTEC will need visible commissioners as well as a wide array of professional, academic, and support staff to work in its three committees. Consistent with a consultative approach, commissioners should be selected in a transparent and participatory manner.[131] In South Africa, NGOs designed the commissioner selection process and had a strong influence in ensuring significant public and NGO participation.[132] Commissioner selection in East Timor was also undertaken with notable public civic engagement.[133] Similarly, the IPTEC Working Group could create an inclusive selection process with input from different sectors of Israeli and Palestinian societies. Given that the IPTEC Working Group is itself local and representative, it would be well placed to nominate, screen, and oversee candidates.[134] Akin to South Africa

[128] Daphna Golan and Zvika Orr, 'Translating Human Rights of the Enemy: The Case of Israeli NGOs Defending Palestinian Rights' (2012) 46 *Law and Society Review* 781, 800.

[129] Bana Shoughry-Badarne was the former Director and Legal Advisor of the Public Committee against Torture in Israel (PCATI). Her comments are from an interview with the authors in Ibid.

[130] Nets-Zehngut, *'Palestinians and Israelis Collaborate',* above n 30, 249.

[131] González and Varney, above n 25, 17–19.

[132] The SATRC was the first to design a process based on an independent selection panel and public interviews of finalists. See Hayner, *'Transitional Justice and the Challenge of Truth Commissions',* above n 118, 212.

[133] The Commission for Reception, Truth and Reconciliation in East Timor appointed commissioners on the advice of a selection panel. In calling for public nominations, the panel was required to consult broadly with civil society and give special consideration to diversity issues, including regional and gender representation UNTAET Regulation No. 2001/10 on the Establishment of a Commission for Reception, Truth and Reconciliation in East Timor, UNTAET/REG/2001/10. Section 4.

[134] González and Varney, above n 25, 17–19.

and East Timor, the IPTEC could also call for public nominations of potential commissioners.[135]

In some contexts, foreign commissioners preside over truth commissions. In El Salvador, the UN appointed three international commissioners,[136] who in turn hired an entirely non-Salvadoran staff.[137] Apparently, the violence was so polarising that no Salvadoran could be entrusted to fairly assess what occurred.[138] Nevertheless, as discussed earlier, most Salvadorans did not trust this body because it was diplomatically imposed without local input.[139] In other cases, both locals and foreigners worked together in order to boost the credibility and comparative expertise of the body. Examples of 'hybrid commissions' include Guatemala, Solomon Islands, and Kenya.[140] In Sierra Leone, the inclusion of foreign commissioners was particularly important to gain national support for the truth commission process.[141]

However, as contended above, the legitimacy of an unofficial IPTEC will largely depend on its local ownership. Moreover, having fellow Israeli and Palestinian nationals sitting on the commission could offer a supportive and affirming environment for victims. Indeed, seven commissioners, Israeli–Jews and Palestinians, all active in civil society and academia, were appointed to Zochrot's unofficial commission.[142] Their presence helped elicit testimonies from displaced Palestinians, as well as from Israeli–Jews who lived in the south and Jewish fighters who participated in military operations at the time.[143] Whilst perhaps some experienced international experts, whose objectivity both sides can accept, may join the IPTEC committees, official commissioners should remain local. As discussed above, both Haiti and El Salvador serve as cautionary tales against overseas interference with national truth-telling. There may be a profound disjuncture between the experience of international involvement and domestic 'truths', especially when the parties themselves are not the prime actors in the transitional justice process.

'Hybrid Commissions' are generally established when local investigative skills and expertise are lacking. This is not the case in Israel/Palestine. Individuals on both the sides are well-versed and experienced in addressing human rights abuse. Under

---

[135] In South Africa and East Timor, the selection process began with nominations from the public. See González and Varney, above n 25, 17–19; *ICTJ Frati-Guidelines*, above n 49, 14.

[136] The UN Secretary-General selected a former Colombian president, a former Venezuelan foreign minister, and a former president of the Inter-American Court of Human Rights to conduct the truth commission. Eric Brahm, *Truth Commissions* (Beyond Intractability Online, June 2004), available at http://www.beyondintractability.org/essay/truth-commissions/ ('Truth Commissions').

[137] Buergenthal, above n 27, 504 cited in Miller, above n 1.

[138] Brahm, *Truth Commissions*, above n 136.

[139] Buergenthal, above n 27.

[140] González and Varney, above n 25, 17–19.

[141] Hayner, '*Transitional Justice and the Challenge of Truth Commissions*', above n 118, 212.

[142] Huda Abu-Obaid, Prof. Avner Ben-Amos, Wasim Biroumi, Adv. Shahda Ibn Bari, Dr. Munir Nuseibah, Dr. Nura Resh, and Dr. Erella Shadmi.

[143] Zochrot, '*Truth Commission on the Responsibility of Israeli Society for the Events of 1948–1960 in the South*' (Final Report: English Digest, March 2016) 5 ('Zochrot Report').

the Commissions of Inquiry Law of 1968,[144] prominent Israelis have conducted several official investigations into past violence over the course of the conflict.[145] Many credible Palestinians have supported the national human rights institution of Palestine, the Independent Commission for Human Rights (ICHR). Established in 1993,[146] it receives complaints from Palestinian citizens regarding human rights violation and handles them with official bodies.[147] A 19-member board of Palestinian commissioners currently runs the ICHR in Ramallah, and it includes an impressive cohort of Palestinian intellectuals, academics, lawyers, political figures, and human rights activists.[148] From this standpoint, the IPTEC could be reliably constituted by well-respected and competent commissioners from both societies.

Composition of Commission

The IPTEC Working Group must give due consideration to the profile of commissioners.[149] Selecting appropriate members is vital, as they end up determining the policies, methods of investigation, and content of the final report.[150] Commissioners are also often involved in investigations, research, and hearing testimony. In many countries, the most successful commissions have combined the appointment of credible leaders with those of diverse backgrounds.[151] Thus, South Africa appointed commissioners based on proven integrity, capacity for impartiality,[152] as well as race, gender, region, and profession.[153] The Chilean commissioners were generally regarded as individuals of high moral standing who, together, represented a broad

[144] The 1968 law provides for the establishment of commissions to review issues of vital public interest that demand clarification and that are at the center of the public agenda, including past events that may generate public unrest.

[145] These include the 1982 Kahan Commission investigating the Sabra and Shatila massacre in Lebanon, the 2000 Orr Commission addressing the killing of 13 Arab–Israelis during the second Intifada, and the investigations by the IDF military justice office regarding the 2008–2009 events in Gaza, and the 2014 Gaza violence.

[146] The ICHR was established upon a presidential decree issued by President Yasser Arafat on 30 September 1993, in compliance with Article 31 of the Palestinian Basic Law (1993).

[147] The ICHR has a legal mandate to report without restriction on the national human rights situation and violations of any human rights. Its mandate allows it to engage with the International human rights system and conduct public education and awareness.

[148] http://ichr.ps/en/1/1/84/About-Us.htm.

[149] *ICTJ Frati-Guidelines,* above n 49, 15.

[150] González and Varney, above n 25, 17–19.

[151] Ibid.

[152] The empowering SATRC legislation indicated only that the commissioners should be 'fit and proper persons who are impartial and who do not have a high political profile'. Hayner, '*Transitional Justice and the Challenge of Truth Commissions'*, above n 118, 212.

[153] Carrie J. Niebur Eisnaugle, 'An International Truth Commission: Utilizing Restorative Justice as an Alternative to Retribution' (2003) 36 *Vanderbilt. Journal of Transnational Law* 209, 223.

political spectrum.[154] The East Timor Commission also gave special consideration to diversity issues and public credentials.[155] Accordingly, the IPTEC should combine the criteria of public standing with social representation.

Public Standing

Historically, commissioners are selected based on personal qualifications, moral leadership, and prestige. Most truth-telling bodies in Latin American were constituted in this way.[156] In Nigeria, a retired Supreme Court judge, a highly reputed figure, chaired the truth commission.[157] The SATRC also benefitted immeasurably from two of the world's most eminent personalities, Nelson Mandela who nurtured the commission, and fellow Nobel Laureate Archbishop Desmond Tutu, who chaired it, and imbued the TRC with moral authority and gravitas.[158]

In the Middle-East however, it is unlikely that political figures of such significant stature would lend their names to an unofficial truth commission at this stage of the conflict.[159] Nevertheless, the IPTEC could still appoint low-level or former political figures, mayors, intellectuals, or religious leaders to the commission even without government sponsorship.[160] For example, despite its unofficial status, the Greensboro Truth and Community Reconciliation Project (discussed in Chap. 7) involved public figures such as a Mayor, a district court judge, and a member of the House of Representatives.[161] By involving public figures, the IPTEC could distinguish itself from a purely civic initiative that limits itself only to NGO-based staff.[162]

On the Israeli side, there exist well-respected individuals 'untainted' by NGO activism, and not presently part of the Executive.[163] Episodes of racism in Israel have motivated moderate religious and centre-right figures, beyond the 'peace camp', to become vocal advocates of human rights.[164] By way of example, a number

---

[154] Their signatures on the final report gave an added weight to the truth that the commission established. Louis Bickford, 'Unofficial Truth Projects' (2007) 29 *Human Rights Quarterly* 994, 1027.

[155] In Timor-Leste's Commission on Reception, Truth and Reconciliation (CAVR), six of the seven National Commissioners had very strong civil society or NGO backgrounds. *ICTJ Frati-Guidelines*, above n 49, 15.

[156] Bakiner, above n 7, 171.

[157] Ibid.

[158] Daly, above n 11, 181–2.

[159] Ron Dudai, 'Does any of this Matter? Transitional Justice and the Israeli-Palestinian conflict' in David Downes, et al. (eds), *Crime, Social Control and Human Rights: From Moral panics to States of denial - Essays in honour of Stanley Cohen* (Willan Publishing, 2007) 345 ('Does Any of this Matter?').

[160] Ibid.

[161] Bickford, above n 154, 1017–8.

[162] Dudai, *'Does Any of this Matter?'*, above n 159, 345.

[163] Ibid.

[164] Lazarus, above n 78, *BICOM Report 2017,* 24.

of veteran right-wing politicians, such as Benny Begin and Dan Meridor, have championed inclusive politics towards Arab citizens, respect for human rights, the rule of law and cross-border dialogue.[165] As the public face of the IPTEC, such individuals could play an important role in engaging victims, authorities, and the public.[166]

Religious figures might also lend weight to the IPTEC. Indeed, clergy played a central role in the SATRC. Of the 17 Commission members, 4 came from the religious community.[167] One example of a potential Israeli candidate is modern Orthodox Rabbi Binyamin Lau, a nephew of Israel's former Chief Rabbi who has emerged as an outspoken opponent of racism and religious extremism.[168] While maintaining his position as a congregational rabbi, Lau is also the head of the Human Rights and Judaism in Action Project at the Israel Democracy Institute.[169] In the ultra-Orthodox sector, Adina Bar-Shalom—founder of the Haredi College, and daughter of the late former Chief Rabbi Ovadia Yosef—is renowned for her advocacy of higher education for women and could be another individual for consideration. Of particular note is her integration of conflict resolution and dialogue courses into the college curriculum, and her public advocacy for peace and the humanisation of Palestinians.[170] As members of two prestigious rabbinical families, such candidates, or others with similar backgrounds, could greatly enhance the standing of the IPTEC.

On the Palestinian side, there also exist potential candidates for due consideration. The existing Board and former Commissioners of the Independent Commission for Human Rights include various public figures and highly regarded locals.[171] In particular, five new commissioners could be well suited for the IPTEC. These commissioners include Shawqi al-Iyaseh, a lawyer and former PA minister; Issam Arouri, human rights activist and Director of the Jerusalem Legal Aid and Human Rights Center,[172] Ziyad Amr, human rights activist and disability rights advocate; Assem Khalil, professor of law at Birzeit University; and Hamah Zeidan, transparency and good governance advocate. As highly respected members of Palestinian society, such individuals are examples of Palestinians with a record of promoting human rights and could add considerable value to the IPTEC.

165 Ibid, 9.

166 González and Varney, above n 25, 17–19.

167 Ball and Chapman, above n 21, 18.

168 Debra Kamin, "The Bearable Lightness of Being Rav Benny". *The Times of Israel*. (16 July, 2013) cited in Lazarus, above n 78, *BICOM Report 2017*, 25.

169 https://en.idi.org.il/centers/1157/1515.

170 Elhanan Miller, 'How Rabbi Ovadia Yosef's Daughter, Adina Bar-Shalom, Became Israel's Leading Ultra-Orthodox' *Iconoclast Tablet* (11 February, 2016). cited in Lazarus, above n 78, *BICOM Report 2017*, 25.

171 http://ichr.ps/en/1/1/84/About-Us.htm.

172 http://www.jlac.ps/english.php.

Social Representation

Commissioners are also selected as representatives, at least symbolically, of certain constituencies, such as women, races, ethnicities, or religious groups. Most truth commissions outside of Latin America have followed this approach, in order to avoid bias and discrimination.[173] For example, the commissioner selection process in South Africa reflected a clear effort to achieve a high degree of representativity in terms of race, gender, and political affiliation.[174] Of the 17 members selected, 7 were women, 7 were Africans, 6 were whites, 2 were mixed race, and 2 were of Indian descent.[175] The Commission for Reception, Truth, and Reconciliation in East Timor included one member appointed by each of several civil society organisations and political parties.[176]

Given the bi-national character of the IPTEC, commissioners must also be appointed to represent both Israeli–Jews and Palestinians. As discussed above, a failure to do so would be fatal to its legitimacy. For example, in Nigeria, biases with respect to religious and demographic representation, undermined the public credibility of the seven-member panel. Yusuf notes that five members, including the Chair, were Christians in a country where more than half the population is Muslim and the religious divide was politically salient.[177] Conversely, the commissioner selection process in South Africa reflected a clear effort to achieve a high degree of representativity in terms of race, gender, and political affiliation.[178] Accordingly the IPTEC could consider the geographic origin, religion, language, class, and ethnicity of candidates, among other factors.

Recruitment of IPTEC commissioners should also include a search for professional expertise in a range of relevant disciplines.[179] These include law, in particular human rights and IHL for the Human Rights Committee, history and social anthropology for the Historical Committee, psychology, religion, journalism, gender studies, and social work for the Victims Committee.[180] This diversity has been beneficial in various past truth commission experiences. In Guatemala's Commission for Historical Clarification (1994), for example, the collaboration between lawyers and social scientists among the commissioners enhanced the body's expertise.[181]

---

[173] González and Varney, above n 25, 17–19.

[174] Dorothy Shea (ed.), *The South African Truth Commission, The Politics of Reconciliation* (United States Institute of Peace, 2000) 25.

[175] *ICTJ Frati-Guidelines*, above n 49, 14.

[176] González and Varney, above n 25, 17–19.

[177] Hakeem O Yusuf, 'Travails of Truth: Achieving Justice for Victims of Impunity in Nigeria' (2007) 1(2) *International Journal of Transitional Justice*, 268.

[178] Shea, above n 174.

[179] This is considered best practice by the ICTJ. González and Varney, above n 25, 17–19.

[180] Ibid.

[181] The commission employed three commissioner: two lawyers and a social scientist, one Guatemalan man, one male non-national, and one Mayan woman. Ball and Chapman, above n 21, 17.

According to Ball and Chapman, '...the clash of perspectives proved fruitful at the [Guatemalan] CEH'.[182] The SATRC also prided itself on the diversity of its commissioners' professional backgrounds. Of the 17 members, 4 came from the religious community; 5 from medicine, psychology, and nursing; 7 from the law; 3 from politics; and 3 from NGOs.[183] This approach was '...arguably the most ambitious to date...and here, the pursuit of truth was constructed as a multi-purpose exercise'.[184] Given that the IPTEC is a broad sociological project rather than simply a search for legal or forensic truth, the composition of the commission might favour members with diverse backgrounds and professional training.[185]

Commission Size

The number of IPTEC commissioners must be large enough to represent both Israeli–Jewish and Palestinian society fairly, but small enough to constitute a manageable and sustainable group.[186] Although commissioners should be expected to work by consensus, an uneven number of commissioners should be appointed to ensure democratic decision-making (by vote).[187] Most truth commissions have selected between 3 and 17 members.[188] In Guatemala, the narrowly drawn historical clarification commission had only three commissioners, all of whom served on a part-time basis. In contrast, South Africa appointed 17 full-time commissioners to manage 3 committees.[189] Whilst the SATRC was an ambitious enterprise, it was exceedingly difficult '...for such a large and deliberately diverse group to reach consensus on specific issues or collectively coordinate the TRC'.[190]

Given the unofficial and more discreet tasks of the IPTEC, a smaller number of between seven and nine part-time IPTEC commissioners seems the most appropriate and manageable amount to agree on policy, represent the body in public for a, and make strategic decisions. Senior IPTEC NGO staff should have the responsibility for administering the daily activities of the commission and dealing with more

---

182 Ibid.

183 Ibid 18.

184 Deborah Posel and Graeme Simpson (eds.), *Commissioning the Past: Understanding South Africa's Truth and Reconciliation Commission* (Wits University Press, 2002), 2.

185 Because human rights violations have been largely understood as violations of law, the composition of most truth commissions favors commissioners with legal training. Ball and Chapman, above n 21, 17.

186 González and Varney, above n 17–19.

187 Ibid.

188 Ibid.

189 Shea, above n 174, 25.

190 For example, one commissioner resigned for substantive reasons and another issued a minority report. See SATRC Final Report, Volume One, 227–29 (1999), 435–56. http://www.justice.gov.za/trc/report/ ('SATRC Report'); Ball and Chapman, above n 21, 18–19.

'tactical' concerns.[191] Above all, they must be highly respected locals with impeccable human rights records, with a variety of political, religious, and professional backgrounds and partial to Israeli–Palestinian reconciliation.

Temporal Parameters

A threshold dilemma for any truth commission is the scope of its historical inquiry, which is invariably the source of contention and political debate. Some commissions have dealt with violations covering multiple decades including a colonial past. For example, the SATRC examined the years between 1960 and 1994, and Ghana's National Reconciliation commission covered independence from 1957 until 1993.[192] Other truth-telling bodies have had mandates focussed on the more recent past. The Argentine commission, for example, established in 1984, focused on the period of authoritarian rule between 1976 and 1983. The Sierra Leone truth commission examined the phase of conflict from 1991 until the peace agreement in 1999, and the Greensboro Truth and Community Reconciliation Project was honed to only a few weeks in November 1979.[193] Regardless of the specific time period demarcated, it is worth recalling that a temporal limitation is both necessary and controversial at the same time.

Complex and Long History

In the Israeli–Palestinian context, the complex origins of the conflict make selecting the appropriate time-period challenging. Any temporal limitations are likely to prioritise some historical claims over others and reflect contention between the parties. According to Hayner: '[T]he mandate of a commission should be both appropriate to the context and flexible enough that commissioners may exercise a degree of discretion in their interpretation of their investigative parameters'.[194]

As discussed in Chap. 1, Israeli–Jews and Palestinians have radically different experiences of history. The Palestinian view of the conflict tends to deal with the more distant past.[195] For many Palestinians, their troubles did not begin with 1948,

---

[191] Ball and Chapman, above n 21, 43.

[192] González and Varney, above n 25, 25.

[193] Bickford, above n. 154, 999–1000.

[194] See Hayner, '*Confronting State Terror*' above n 5, (discussing the design of truth commissions).

[195] Ilan Pappe, 'The Visible and Invisible in the Israeli-Palestinian Conflict' in Ian S Lustick and Ann M. Lesch (eds.) *Exile and Return: predicaments of Palestinians and Jews* (University of Pennsylvania Press, 2005) 279–296, 279; See also Yaacov Bar -Siman-Tov, 'Introduction: Barriers to Conflict Resolution' in Yaacov Bar-Siman-Tov (ed) *Barriers to Peace in the Israeli-Palestinian Conflict* (Jerusalem Institute for Israel Studies, 2011) 15, 26.

but rather, in 1882, with Jewish settlement in Palestine.[196] Similarly, for Israelis, the history of Zionism is more complex than the immediate conflict with the Palestinians. Rather, it is located within a regional dynamic of Arab hostility and a historical mission to ensure the survival of the Jewish people.[197] From this vantage point, Israeli negotiators have sought to limit the chronology of the conflict to violations post 1967, consistent with the Oslo paradigm discussed in Chap. 4.[198]

Given that hostilities in the region have spanned for over a century and involved multiple external actors, there may be a temptation for the IPTEC to take a wider view of the inquiry. Indeed, numerous historical variables from the British mandate (1920–1948), the Holocaust, and the Arab expulsion of Jewish refugees[199] to the Arab–Israeli wars have all intersected as both causes and symptoms of the Israeli–Palestinian dispute. There is no shortage of violent clashes from pre-state violence in the 1920s, to more recent hostilities such as the Lebanon War of 1982, the First intifada and the Gaza incursions.[200] In short, the Israeli–Palestinian past is like a bottomless pit.

Narrowing the Narrative

> *Too wide a mandate, would no doubt, drown the commission in a sea of history...* (Ariel Meyerstein)[201]

In defining the breadth of a commission investigation, it may sometimes be '...necessary and appropriate to narrow the historical mandate'.[202] Accordingly, it is submitted that the IPTEC avoids contending with factors and events extrinsic to the central Israeli–Palestinian struggle. For example, concerns about the expulsion of Jews from various Arab countries, though historically valid,[203] are not directly relevant to abuses committed by Palestinians against Israelis. In a similar vein, whilst it might be tempting to address intra-societal issues between Israeli–Jews and

---

[196] Meyerstein, *'Transitional Justice and Post-conflict Israel/Palestine'*, above n 6, 328–9.

[197] Ibid.

[198] Asima Ghazi-Bouillon, *Understanding the Middle East Peace Process: Israeli Academia and the Struggle for Identity* (Routledge, 2009) 78.

[199] According to Justus Weiner, the losses incurred by Jewish refugees from Arab countries deserve to be addressed. 'Failure to resolve these claims may jeopardise the entire peace process'. See Justus Weiner, 'The Palestinian Refugees Right to Return and the Peace Process'. (1997) 20(1), *Boston College International and Comparative Law Review* 1, 52.

[200] Meyerstein, *'Transitional Justice and Post-conflict Israel/Palestine'*, above n 6, 329.

[201] Ibid.

[202] See Hayner, *'Transitional Justice and the Challenge of Truth Commissions'*, above n 118, (Appendix 1, Chart 8: What Works Best?) 335–336.

[203] Historically, the Israeli government sought to link the Palestinian displacement in 1948 with the creation of approximately 850,000 Jewish refugees from Arab countries, mainly during the 1950s. Today, almost half of the Jewish citizens of Israel (together with their descendants) are from Arab countries.

Palestinians within Israel,[204] such an approach risks de-railing the IPTEC from its primary focus on truth-telling between two geo-politically divided nations.

Arguably, a truth commission should not be the venue to try to explain the whole chain of historical factors that caused human rights abuses.[205] Practically speaking, longer time periods can make investigations too complex and time-consuming.[206] They could also impede the forward-looking and reconciliatory aspects of the work.[207] Notably, the Guatemalan Historical Clarification commission stands out for its powerful historical narrative '...that was broad yet to the point'.[208] The report's tremendous strength came from its ability to clarify abuses from the 36-year civil war (1960–1996), without being encumbered by all the root causes of violence from the proceeding century.[209]

In this light, narrow temporal parameters are suggested for the IPTEC. Attempts to investigate the conflict's entire chronology in one institution would encumber bi-national dialogue and reduce common ground. By digging up more of the Israeli–Palestinian past than necessary, the IPTEC would risk antagonising the parties. The commission should not be the forum for rehashing all the old 'moot points' about who was where first. Whilst the Historical Committee is capable of examining the background and context of human rights abuses, it cannot be expected to deal with the whole history of Zionism in the region. For practical and discursive purposes, the IPTEC will begin with 1948, and thereby avoid the earlier period of Jewish–Arab tensions, the Palestinian experience during the British Mandate, and the impact of European anti-Semitism on the conflict.

Beyond 1948

On the other hand, an exceedingly narrow approach to history might also prove problematic. Given the resonance of 1948 and the legacy of Palestinian displacement, virtually every academic in the field envisions an Israeli–Palestinian truth commission which solely examines this event.[210] For Miller, the historical focus is

---

[204] From an internal-Israeli standpoint, the central debate is over Jewish–Arab relations within Israel. For Palestinians, the internal violence between Palestinian factions and human rights violations of Palestinians by the PA is significant. According to Wing: '[t]he TRC could be used on a bi-national basis by both Palestine and Israel to heal internal injuries as well as injuries between the two peoples'. Wing, above n 1, 141.

[205] *'Harvard Law Discussion'*, above n 77.

[206] González and Varney, above n 25, 25.

[207] Meyerstein, *'Transitional Justice and Post-conflict Israel/Palestine'*, above n 6, 329.

[208] Bakiner, above n 7, 174.

[209] Ibid.

[210] Miller, above n 1, 307; Yoav Peled and Nadim Rouhana, 'Transitional Justice and the Right of Return of the Palestinian Refugees' (2004) 5 *Theoretical Inquiry Law* 317–18; Shraga, above n 4105.

squarely on the Palestinian refugees.[211] Similarly, Peled and Rouhana contemplate transitional justice for the Palestinian right of return.[212] Shraga also recommends a 1948 historical truth commission to investigate the War of Independence for the Jews and the Nakba for the Palestinians.[213] In October 2014, Zochrot established an unofficial truth commission to address Israeli responsibility for the displacement of Negev Bedouins during 1948–1960.[214]

No doubt, 1948 must be a central focus for the IPTEC as discussed in Chap. 1. Nevertheless, limiting the IPTEC to 1948, and to the 'original sin' of the conflict, raises serious concerns. Firstly, focusing on one isolated event risks the criticism made of South Africa's TRC, that by confining its mandate to the period of 1960–1994, '…the TRC looked at history through overly legalistic "narrow lenses", missing the bigger picture of apartheid, i.e. its historical foundations in colonisation'.[215] One could easily imagine similar criticisms of the IPTEC if it were to ignore the 'bigger picture' of the ongoing Israeli occupation and decades of Palestinian terrorism against Israeli civilians. Secondly, any meaningful reckoning with the past must contend with recent history as well as other central events that perpetuate the conflict. Failing to do so is likely to compromise the relevance and cathartic potential of the IPTEC, particularly as an instrument in moving the two communities closer towards conflict resolution.

Three Constituent Events: 1948, 1967, and the Second Intifada

From this standpoint, the IPTEC should address the three constituent events of the conflict (Chap. 1). As contended, the emotional orientation of fear and ethos of conflict borne out by these three periods continue to define both societies. Thus, the IPTEC would address the events of 1948 to resolve the taboo of Palestinian displacement and the right of return. In particular, the IPTEC would enable marginalised and older Palestinian refugee voices to be heard from this period.[216] The temporal jurisdiction of the IPTEC would begin in 1947 and continue until the early 1950s. The term '1948' is therefore not literal but is symbolic for the events that

---

[211] Miller suggests a hybrid commission for the investigation of 1948, with a focus on the Palestinian refugees. Her commission would cover 1945 to 1950. Miller, above n 1, 307.

[212] Peled and Rouhana, above n 210, 317–18.

[213] Dr. Daphna Shraga seeks the establishment of the 1948 Commission to unveil the truth about the 1948 events. Shraga, above n 4, 105.

[214] Zochrot's Report examines testimonies by Palestinian refugees, as well as Israeli-Jews who lived in the south and Israeli–Jewish fighters involved in displacement and expulsion operations in the area. See *Zochrot Report*, above n 143.

[215] Mahmud Mamdani, 'A Diminished Truth', in James Wilmot and Linda. Van de Vijver (eds.), *After the TRC: Reflections on Truth and Reconciliation in South Africa* (Ohio University Press, 2001) 58. ('A Diminished Truth').

[216] Wing, above n 1, 158.

lead to the creation of the Israeli state and caused the Palestinian displacement.[217] As demonstrated in Chap. 1, many of the anxieties and fears permeating Israeli and Palestinian society are traceable to the conflict's genesis.

The second event of 1967 will examine the legacy of the Israeli occupation and the Jewish settlements. As discussed in Chap. 1, the 1967 war has left a lasting discursive footprint on the conflict. Its military consequences have profoundly shaped the contemporary narratives, political identity, and collective memory of both the sides. For Israelis, its military occupation has created generations of soldiers at checkpoints, a complex bureaucratic, legal, and political regime, and over half a million Israeli–Jews living beyond Israel's recognised borders. For Palestinian society, the daily humiliation of the occupation, denial of collective political rights, and its lack of territorial sovereignty have played an instrumental role in Palestinian nationalism. Accordingly, the IPTEC will need to address 1967, not only because of its discursive imprint, but also because of the culture of impunity, asymmetry of power and human rights abuse it entrenches.

Finally, any engagement with history must contend with the legacy of bloodshed and discursive shifts heralded by the period between 2000 and 2005. The Second Intifada, coupled with the failure of Oslo, marked a significant narrative transition from conflict resolution to the resumption of violence. Beyond the thousands of Israelis and Palestinians killed, there is also the unquantifiable toll taken on the collective psyche. Until today, its radicalising effect clouds mutual perceptions and post-Oslo policy. It is therefore important for the IPTEC to address the major human rights violations committed during the period, specifically the killing of civilians by both the sides. The commission would need to limit itself to events in the past, probably ending with the withdrawal from Gaza in 2005.

Legal Mandate

Comparative Context

Truth commissions vary in terms of the legal subject matter and abuses they investigate. Some examine only a limited range of human rights violations. For example, the Sri Lankan[218] and Uruguayan[219] commissions looked at the single issue of political disappearances. The Chilean Truth and Reconciliation Commission (1991) focused only on political executions, kidnappings, and torture leading to death.[220]

[217] Shraga, above n 4, 105.

[218] https://www.ictj.org/news/sri-lanka%E2%80%99s-wavering-commitment-accountability-enforced-disappearances

[219] In 2000, Uruguayan President Jorge established *La Comisión para la Paz* (The Commission for Peace) to investigate the fate of the disappeared during the military regime from 1973 to 1985.

[220] Accordingly, torture in general and its survivors were excluded from investigations. This was later remedied by a second truth commission, namely the *National Commission on Political Imprisonment and Torture* (29 November, 2004). See Brahm, *Truth Commissions*, above n 136.

Other commissions considered broader human rights abuses, but limited their mandates temporally and substantively.[221] The SATRC mandate was directed to examine the 'nature…and extent' of gross human rights abuses, looking at the 'context, motives, and perspectives which led to such violation', and then identifying 'systematic pattern[s] of abuse'.[222] The SATRC intended to tell the story of apartheid through an extraordinary amount of testimony, but was criticised for excluding important categories of victims such as those who suffered under routine physical violence.[223] More recently, Libera is an example of a truth commission that examined both civil political and economic crimes.[224] One of its explicit goals was to dispel falsifications of the country's past socioeconomic and political development.[225] Ultimately, a truth commission's legal mandate should be robust, but flexible enough to define the types of violations and issues under examination in terms that are not exhaustive.[226]

Multiple Legacies and Legal Scope

Characterising the legal scope of the IPTEC is therefore no small task. Just as it is difficult to capture the historical causes of violence in the Middle East, it is similarly challenging, to account for the wide array of human rights abuses.[227] Both the sides could demand investigations of numerous violations throughout the conflict. As demonstrated in Chap. 2, there are credible accounts of deliberate and/or

[221] For example, the commission in El Salvador was restricted to 'investigating serious acts of violence that have occurred since 1980, and whose impact on society urgently demands that the public should know the truth'. *Commission on the Truth for El Salvador, From Madness to Hope: The 12-Year War in El Salvador* (1993) cited in Miller, above n 1, 300.

[222] See SATRC Act [4]; *SATRC Report*, above n 190, 158–64 (for a more detailed analysis of the TRC's methodological needs) cited in Ball and Chapman, above n 21, 20.

[223] For example, black South Africans forcibly removed or detained under provisions of the state of emergency. De Grieff argues that none of these victims were eligible for reparations as a class, and arguments can be made that they should have been. Pablo De Grieff ed., *The Handbook of Reparations* (Oxford University Press, 2008), 8.

[224] The Liberian Truth and Reconciliation Commission (TRC) was a Parliament-enacted organisation created in May 2005 under the Transitional Government. The Liberian TRC's mandate was to investigate more than 20 years of civil conflict in the country and to report on gross human rights violations that occurred in Liberia between January 1979 and 14 October 2003.

[225] Paul James-Allen, Aaron Weah, and Lizzie Goodfriend, *Beyond the Truth and Reconciliation Commission: Transitional Justice Options in Liberia* (International Centre for Transitional Justice, May 2010) http://ictj.org/sites/default/files/ICTJ-Liberia-Beyond-TRC-2010-English.pdf.

[226] For example, the mandate of the Peruvian commission used the terms 'torture and other serious injuries', allowing the body to investigate sexual violence without the conduct being specifically named in the mandate. *Truth and Reconciliation Commission of Peru* (Comisión de la Verdad y Reconciliación), created by Supreme Decree N° 065–2001-PCM [Peru], 4 June 2001 cited in González and Varney, above n 25, 25.

[227] Meyerstein, '*Transitional Justice and Post-conflict Israel/Palestine*', above n 6, 331.

indiscriminate attacks on both the civilian populations. Moreover, where military occupation and structural violence are part of the conflict, there exist a litany of social, cultural, and economic injuries that may be just as important as criminal ones. For example, Mamdani has been critical of South Africa's 'over-individualisation' of the apartheid narrative, whereby the SATRC ignored more routine violations, such as the social and economic violence committed against black South Africans.[228] For example, would the IPTEC investigate the economic effects of the occupation as a result of curfews, house demolitions, and road closures? What about the social impact of terrorist attacks on Israeli bereaved families, the role of Palestinian corruption, or interference with religious worship at the Temple Mount? Clearly, most daily encounters with the Israeli military or Palestinian terrorism do not rise to the level of gross human rights abuse.[229]

Despite the multiple legacies of abuse, it is contended that an overly broad legal mandate is impractical and ill-suited to the IPTEC. Even official commissions could only ever focus on a small subset of all conceivable forms of abuse. Perhaps for this reason, most truth-telling inquiries have tended not to examine issues like corruption, economic crimes, and other social and cultural misconduct.[230] Generally, truth commissions avoid getting entangled within the broader play of social and economic commentary about a conflict.[231] Should the IPTEC focus on the socio-economic dimensions of the violence as well, it could '…risk being viewed as but another voice in a world of disputed opinions and theories about justice, development, whatever. [Its] reports might lose distinctiveness and a sense of [legal] objectivity…'.[232] The IPTEC would also risk stretching itself beyond its institutional capacity and life-span.

Moreover, it is worth recalling that not all violations are equally grave. For example, the denial of a family reunification application, the loss of work inside Israel, or the destruction of an olive grove is drastically different from Palestinian civilians killed as a result of military incursions into the territories.[233] Similarly, throwing rocks at an Israeli checkpoint is distinguishable from blowing up a bus in central Tel Aviv and maiming unarmed bystanders.[234] In short, the IPTEC cannot dress every wound.[235] It also cannot address every international legal debate or institutional abuse arising out of the Israeli–Palestinian conflict. Thus, systematic structural discrimination against Palestinians is beyond the scope of the legal inquiry. As an

[228] Mamdani, '*A Diminished Truth*', above n 215, 58–61.

[229] Restrictions on Palestinian freedom of movement, destruction of personal property, discriminatory laws or Israelis too fearful of boarding a bus and experiencing post-traumatic stress are examples of less severe violations.

[230] See Mahmud Mamdani, *Citizen and Subject: Contemporary Africa and the Legacy of Late Colonialism* (Princeton University Press, 1996).

[231] Henry Steiner quoted in '*Harvard Law Discussion*', above n 77, 18.

[232] Ibid.

[233] Meyerstein, '*Dreaming an Israeli-Palestinian Truth Commission*', above n 1, 475.

[234] Ibid.

[235] Ibid.

unofficial truth-telling project, the legal focus of the IPTEC should be self-consciously selective for both practical and institutional purposes.

From this standpoint, the IPTEC Human Rights Committee should seek to confine its legal inquiry to the most extreme as well as characteristic and symbolic cases of human rights abuse from the conflict as outlined in Chap. 2. Given the symbolic resonance of 1948, this would include the Palestinian claim of return to Israel based on the freedom of movement provisions. Regarding the Second Intifada, the mandate should focus on war crimes, crimes against humanity and severe violations of civil and political rights, such as targeted killings and torture.[236]

The IPTEC Historical and Victims Committees could engage more freely with the broader, structural and socio-economic phenomena underlying abuses. Through events hearings and victim testimony, these two Committees should also be capable of addressing incidents of violence that occurred outside the temporal mandate of the IPTEC. Notably, the current ICC preliminary examination investigates ongoing international crimes allegedly committed in Israel/Palestine since June 2014 until the present. A measure of accountability and legal scrutiny therefore exists for human rights abuses committed by the parties during this recent time frame. In this light, there is temporal relevance to the IPTEC focusing on historical events that are beyond the reach of the ICC and for which there has been no reckoning with the past.

Individual Stories and Thematic Events

The IPTEC should seek to strike a balance between a narrowly framed mandate and an inclusive approach that can also address the traumas and wrongs suffered by Israeli and Palestinian victims. Indeed, if the IPTEC's overall focus were too restrictive, it could be criticised as lacking in relevance, unnecessarily arbitrary, or just being removed from the daily experiences of average Israelis and Palestinians. Accordingly, it is essential that the IPTEC Victims Committee hear as many individual stories of suffering as possible, beyond the narrow legal class investigated by the IPTEC Human Rights Committee. Many violations discussed in Chap. 2, such as restrictions on freedom of movement, destruction of property, and other discriminatory practices, do not rise to the level of gross abuses.[237] Whilst specific extreme incidents could be explored by the Human Rights Committee, the more systemic daily violations should be dealt with by the Victims Committee through oral testimony. In order to tell the 'whole story', it would help to combine personal narrative alongside legal analysis at IPTEC hearings and in the Final Report. Allowing the two committees to work in tandem is one way of avoiding the pitfalls of a relatively narrow legal inquiry.

Notably, there would be countless experiences of trauma over the three historical periods identified in this work. Thus, the IPTEC Victims Committee could look for

[236] Bickford, above n 154, 998.

[237] Meyerstein, *'Transitional Justice and Post-conflict Israel/Palestine'*, above n 6, 331.

patterns of abuse.[238] Indeed, a more thematic approach to public hearings could group together incidents or repetitive violations, akin to Sierra Leone Commission's 'events hearing' which focused on particularly significant events of the conflict.[239] 'Rather than holding individual hearings for every house demolition or suicide attack, similarly affected individuals could testify or participate in some way at a collective hearing addressing the shared violation'.[240] In this way, the Victims Committee's purview (as distinct from the narrower mandate of the Human Rights Committee) could give expression both to individual suffering and to the more systemic violations of the conflict.

Settling the Legal Regime

Firstly, the mandate of the IPTEC should address the very legal regime applicable to the conflict. As discussed in Chap. 2, debate over which international norms apply to the territories, and the legitimacy of Palestinian 'resistance' is itself a central part of the conflict. Indeed, over-arching legal themes such as the applicability of international occupation law and the Geneva Conventions demand inquiry. As discussed in Chap. 2, debate still exists over which rules of engagement apply. The IPTEC mandate should therefore include a reference to 'clarifying the legal regime applicable to the Palestinian territories from 1967, and the lawful rules of engagement'. The Human Rights Committee could establish a set of legal definitions about what constitutes a violation of a given norm from domestic law, international human rights law, or IHL. It may then seek examples, in the form of particular cases, which demonstrate the violation of the norm in question.[241] Regarding 1948, an assessment of the Palestinian right of return is also worthy of inclusion in the legal inquiry as discussed above.

Institutional Accountability

As contended in Chaps. 5 and 6, the involvement of Israeli and Palestinian institutions in human rights abuse is also essential to understanding and resolving the conflict.[242] National truth-telling often involves examining the role of social, political, and cultural institutions in historical violence. Thus, East Timor's CTF stated its intent to focus on the '...historical background, political dynamics, and *institutional*

---

[238] Wing above n 1, 158.

[239] Ibid 332.

[240] Meyerstein, *'Transitional Justice and Post-conflict Israel/Palestine'*, above n 6, 331.

[241] Ball and Chapman, above n 21, 19.

[242] As discussed, the violence in the Israeli–Palestinian conflict is more institutional and political, rather than interpersonal.

structures [and practices] that shaped events before and during 1999'.[243] Similarly, the SATRC mandate did not limit the attribution of responsibility to individuals, but where possible '…ascribed responsibility to *institutions or structures*, such as the government or the cabinet'.[244] In particular, public hearings examined the roles played by various professions and institutions in resisting or facilitating human rights abuse.[245] In Guatemala as well, the CEH interpreted its mandate to require an 'examination of the causes and origins of the internal armed confrontation, *the strategies and mechanisms* of the violence and its consequences and effects'.[246]

Accordingly, the legal mandate of the IPTEC must address the institutions, parties, structures, and ideologies that permitted, enabled, encouraged, or caused gross human rights violations. By focusing on the administration of the occupation and the infrastructure of terrorism, the Human Rights Committee can better account for past violations, from suicide-bombing to the construction of Israeli–Jewish settlements. Only secondarily should the IPTEC identify particular individuals who played roles in the abuses.[247] Beyond a small number of illustrative cases on events or institutions, individual criminal legal investigations would be better left to the ICC or some other court. As concluded in Chaps. 5 and 6, truth commissions and individual criminal justice are not mutually exclusive endeavours, and the ICC, despite its limitations, might have jurisdiction to investigate Israeli and Palestinian violations committed from 2014.

Ultimately, widening the net of accountability is important for the IPTEC to withstand the critique of narrow legalism levelled at international trials. As a non-judicial body, it is worth recalling that the IPTEC need not be constrained by principles regarding individual criminal liability. Moreover, as an unofficial truth project, the IPTEC should remain sensitive to finding ways that incentivise voluntary testimony from victims and perpetrators alike. A purely individualised approach to human rights abuses that names the names of individual wrongdoers might inhibits truth-telling by dissuading witnesses from coming forward, and/or preventing victims from telling their stories for fear of implicating themselves or others.

[243] This focus was to 'inform its conclusions with a broader understanding of the way in which the causes of the violence in 1999 were connected to previously established *institutional structures* and practices'. See 'CTF Final Report', above n 111.

[244] Paul Van Zyl, 'Unfinished Business: The Truth and Reconciliation Commission's Contribution to Justice in Post-Apartheid South Africa', in Mahmoud Cherif Bassiouni, (ed.), *Post-Conflict Justice* (Transnational Publishers, 2002), 751 ('Unfinished Business').

[245] In the midst of the TRC hearings, the Commissioners found that institutional involvement had not been appropriately addressed and so included a series of institutional hearings, receiving testimony and submissions from the business community, the military, and other sectors of apartheid society. *SATRC Report*, above n 190; Miller, above n 1, p.315; See also Van Zyl, *'Dilemmas of Transitional Justice'*, above n 19, 657.

[246] CEH, Guatemala Recommendations and Conclusions, Introduction cited in Ball and Chapman, above n 21, 20.

[247] Ball and Chapman, above n 21, 42.

Joint Accountability

Most advocates of a transitional justice mechanism for the Middle East envisage an institution which solely examines Israeli accountability for human rights abuse.[248] For example, in October 2014, Zochrot established an unofficial truth commission to address Israeli responsibility for the displacement of Negev Bedouins during 1948–1960.[249] The Commission's report encouraged Israeli–Jewish society to accept responsibility for past injustices, with reference to the current violations as part of an 'ongoing Nakba'.[250] Zochrot's Commission seems to ascribe responsibility for Palestinian refugees and the events of 1948 period entirely to Israel. As discussed in Chap. 5, the Russel Tribunal was also distinctly one-sided by exclusively investigating alleged Israeli abuses. In a similar vein, a UN transitional justice civil society conference discussed '...holding Israel accountable for its responsibilities under international law'.[251] The conference was organised by the 'Division for Palestinian Rights'. As Waters notes: 'one will look in vain for an equivalent division to protect Israelis; but this is to the point: there is no neutral [Middle-East] transitional justice position [on accountability]'.[252]

Beyond Victims and Perpetrators

For this reason, the IPTEC must avoid the pitfall of simplistically portraying one group as victims and the other as perpetrators. A one-sided IPTEC would lack legitimacy in the eyes of Israelis, and even the international community.[253] The question of legitimacy is indeed crucial, and that's why lessons from Zochrot and the initiatives noted above are so important. As discussed earlier, the bilateral dimension of the Indonesian-East Timor CTF boosted its legitimacy and capacity for Indonesia (the stronger party) to take responsibility for its abuses. On the other hand, the Special Court's inability to look into Indonesia's central role in the atrocities

[248] See Miller, above n 1, 203; Peled and Rouhana, above n 210, 317–18.

[249] Zochrot's Report examines testimonies by Palestinian refugees, as well as Jews who lived in the south and Jewish fighters involved in displacement and expulsion operations in the area. *Zochrot Report*, above n 143.

[250] 'When the Israeli society and state acknowledge the crimes and injustices involved in the ongoing Nakba and when the state is ready to redress the victims of human rights violations according to international human rights standards, peace will be possible'. See *Zochrot Report*, above n 143, 5.

[251] United Nations (UN), Division for Palestinian Rights, UN International Conference of Civil Society in Support of Israeli-Palestinian Peace, Brussels (Belgium), 30–31 August 2007, 39.

[252] Timothy Waters, 'Clearing the Path: the perils of positing Civil Society in Conflict and Transition'. (2015) 48 *Israel Law Review* 165, 180.

[253] For example, as discussed in Chap. 5, the Russell Tribunal on Palestine (March 2009) was roundly dismissed as lacking in credibility because it was one-sided and lusively critical of Israel. See Richard Goldstone, 'Israel and the Apartheid Slander', *The New York Times*, 31 October 2011.

delegitimised the tribunal in the eyes of many Timorese from the outset.[254] Similarly, in Rwanda, the hearing of a Belgian priest played an important role in legitimising the Gacaca in the eyes of local actors, while the impossibility of looking into RPF crimes remained a crucial flaw.[255]

Any truth-telling inquiry that deals exclusively with Israeli abuses would diminish the IPTEC's reconciliatory and justice-seeking capacity. Indeed, meaningful truth-telling '…requires openness on the whole messy political reality of the past'.[256] It means investigating all those responsible for gross human rights abuses whether they are members of the Israeli government, the PA, or Hamas. It also means adopting a nuanced view of historical accountability. As discussed in Chaps. 1, 4, and 5, the multi-dimensional aspects of responsibility for every event of the conflict, from 1948 to the Second Intifada, terrorism to military occupation, defies the unilateral allocation of culpability. The IPTEC must strive to set in motion accountability processes that address both societies and offer a more complex account of the conflict.

Mandates of many other truth commissions also sought to be 'balanced', covering all actors involved, and all atrocities committed, including those committed by non-state agents.[257] For example, Peru's truth commission not only examined guerrilla groups but actually attributed the majority of abuses to them.[258] The South African TRC investigated violations of the opposition forces as well as those of the apartheid regime. Indeed, the SATRC found liberation movements responsible for many gross human rights violations. The CTF concluded that 'gross human rights violations in the form of crimes against humanity did occur in East Timor in 1999' and that 'pro-autonomy militia groups, TNI, the Indonesian civil government, and Polri must all bear institutional responsibility'.[259] From this standpoint, there is sound precedent for the IPTEC to examine broad patterns of specific and systemic violations of both nations. In particular, the IPTEC will examine the conduct of the PA as well as of Palestinian militant groups. It must be able to tackle the injuries and fatalities inflicted upon Israeli civilians including Israeli–Jewish settlers, Israeli soldiers stationed in the territories, Israeli civilians or soldiers in Israel proper.[260]

---

[254] Oomen, above n 15, 196.

[255] Ibid 197.

[256] Ibid.

[257] Ibid 181.

[258] Bickford, above n 154, 998.

[259] This involved conducting an inquiry about 'the perpetration of gross human rights violations and institutional responsibility' and 'arriving at recommendations and lessons learned' See 'CTF Final Report', above n 111.

[260] Wing, above n 1, 151.

Symmetrical Violence?

Many Palestinian commentators, however, would insist that the violence of the conflict is deeply asymmetrical.[261] Some would flatly reject any inquiry covering Palestinian abuses since they would feel all actions against Israelis were justified in the name of national liberation.[262] Even merely representing both narratives of suffering as valid could be refuted on the grounds that balance is illusory under conditions of occupation. Indeed, the experience of the occupied is more intense than that of the occupier.[263]

It is worth recalling that in South Africa too, many also criticised the SATRC's contentious even-handedness. Thus, it has been argued that the legal mandate did not adequately distinguish between human rights abuses committed to support apartheid and those committed to resist it.[264] For example, '…when it came to granting amnesty, no distinction was made between those who enforced apartheid and those who fought against it'.[265] Arguably, 'there was no moral equivalence between the two, so there should never have been a legal one'.[266] Others, however, maintain that nothing in the SATRC experience precluded moral judgment or understanding the difference between apartheid and opposition to it.[267]

This debate is relevant to the IPTEC. Despite quantitative disparities in Israeli and Palestinian casualties, it is argued that psychologically each nation is collectively traumatised.[268] Despite the power asymmetries, both Israeli and Palestinian civilian populations live under chronic threats of violence,[269] and the lived

261 Ramzy Baroud, 'World Refugee Day: Palestinians Keep Their Right of Return Alive Through Hope, Resistance' *Middle East Monitor Online,* 19 June 2019. https://www.middleeastmonitor.com/20190619-world-refugee-day-palestinians-keep-their-right-of-return-alive-through-hope-resistance/; Khalidi, *'Palestinian Identity'*, above n 126.

262 Wing, above n 1, 151.

263 Waters, above n 252, 183.

264 Claudie Barude and Derek Spitz, 'Memory and the Spectre of International Justice: A Comment on Azapo' (1997) 13 *South Africa Journal of Human Rights* 269, 273. For a detailed discussion of the debate see Daly, above n 11, 155–56.

265 'The conflation of race and victimhood still permeates [South African] society, even though the commission sought a contentious evenhandedness'. Columnist Franny Rabkin quoted in Alan Cowell, 'Truth, Reconciliation and Now, a Prosecution in South Africa', *New York Times*, 19 February, 2016.

266 Ibid.

267 Kader Asmal, Louise Asmal, and Ronald Suresh Roberts, 'When The Assassin Cries Foul', in Charles Villa Vicencio and Wilhelm Verwoerd (eds.), *Looking Back, Reaching Forward: Reflections on the TRC of South Africa* (UCT Press 2000), 14.

268 'While a suicide bomber may kill only a handful of civilians and perhaps injure dozens more, the real violence done is psychological.' See Meyerstein, *'Transitional Justice and Post-conflict Israel/Palestine'*, above n 6, 301.

269 'But counting fatalities from terrorist attacks is the crudest and most simplistic way to measure the impact of terrorism'.

See Dov Waxman, 'Living with Terror, not Living in Terror: The Impact of Chronic Terrorism on Israeli Society' (2011) 5(6) *Perspectives on Terrorism* 4, 8.

experience of both peoples is characterised by existential fear and victimisation.[270] There exists a mutual vulnerability that could justify a bi-national legal framework for accountability. This is not to morally equate one with the other, or to over-simplify the cycles of conflict, but to acknowledge the need to avoid framing accountability in zero-sum terms. Without a suitably nuanced view of responsibility, Israel–Palestinian society would risk scapegoating and social amnesia at the expense of self-reflection.[271]

Moreover, an IPTEC that only examines Israeli abuses diminishes its ability to affect Palestinian society[272] and transcend reductionist history.[273] It would also deprive the Palestinian polity of the chance to address its own conflict culture that once legitimated suicide bombing[274] and which continues to support violence. For example, according to a statistic from February 2016, 73% of Palestinians between 18 and 22 support the legitimacy of stabbing civilians.[275] Ultimately, any reckoning with the past must be honest and complete and cannot ignore the various abuses committed by Palestinians during their own struggle, as discussed in Chap. 2.[276]

8.3 Part Two: Goals of the IPTEC

The IPTEC should develop a vision of engagement with Israeli–Palestinian society through its guiding goals. As concluded in Chap. 3, the three normative pillars of transitional justice; truth-telling, justice, and reconciliation are all relevant and desirable to conflict resolution efforts. They lay the foundation for the IPTEC's

---

[270] Daniel Bar-Tal, 'Sociopsychological Foundations of Intractable Conflicts' (2007) 50(11) *American Behavioral Scientist,* 1430–1453.

[271] David A Crocker, 'Reckoning with Past Wrongs: A Normative Framework' (March 1999) 13(1) *Ethics and International Affairs* 43, 54.

[272] Nets-Zehngut demonstrates how since the late 1990s, Israeli and Palestinian collaborative projects on the history of the conflict have positively impacted Palestinian society. '…[T]hrough the collaborative mechanism, Palestinians took control over their own destiny and thereby influenced it.' See Rafi, Nets-Zehngut, 'Transitional Justice and Addressing the History of Active Conflicts: The Case of the Israeli-Palestinian Conflict' (2011) *Hebrew University of Jerusalem,* Conference Paper (unpublished), 1, 16. ('Transitional Justice').

[273] Khalidi exposes the tendency in Palestinian historiography to focus on causes external to Palestinian society and even produce a narrative that denies any agency or responsibility for its own fate. Rashid Khalidi, 'The Palestinians and 1948: The Underlying Causes of Failure' in Rogan and Shlaim (eds), 'The War for Palestine' 12, 14; See also Eugene Rogan and Avi Shlaim, 'Introduction' in Eugene Rogan and Avi Shlaim, (eds.) *The War for Palestine, Rewriting The History of 1948* (Cambridge: Cambridge University Press, 2001) 2.

[274] The infiltration of Palestinian school curricula and children televisions programming with messages of martyrdom to liberate the homeland are well documented by Palestinian Media Watch. Many squares in the Palestinian territories continue to honor suicide bombers.

[275] Seventy per cent of the same cohort believes that an Intifada is a more effective mechanism of achieving national rights than negotiations. Branold and Lyndon, above n 91.

[276] Dudai and Cohen '*Dealing with the Past*', above n 29, 246.

mandate. This ensuing section therefore considers the distinctive elements and features of these goals. Overall, the aims include giving victims a voice, documenting past abuse, countering denial or 'narrowing the range of permissible lies', establishing a bi-national and reconciliatory narrative, establishing institutional responsibility, building or restoring relationships of trust, and generally furthering reconciliation through civic collaboration and narrative empathy.[277]

Notably, the goals of the IPTEC, like all transitional justice measures, are interrelated (Chap. 4). For example, the pursuit of truth-telling, or the production of knowledge about the past, is essential both to restorative justice and to historical reconciliation between Israelis and Palestinians.[278] In South Africa, the Commission handled several purposes in three distinct committees.[279] Similarly, the IPTEC should draw on its committees to pursue fundamental goals simultaneously. For example, the IPTEC Human Rights Committee can at once pursue truth telling, foster accountability and seek reconciliation through legal collaboration.

IPTEC and Truth-Telling

As discussed in Chap. 3 one of the central premises of transitional justice is that truth-telling and setting the historical record straight are essential responses to political violence. Accordingly, the IPTEC should be grounded in the desirability of truth-telling to Israelis and Palestinians (Chap. 4) and the centrality of historical narratives to ongoing human rights abuses (Chaps. 1 and 2). All the three IPTEC Committees could pursue truth-telling in its various forms around the key events of 1948, 1967, and the Second Intifada, so as to assist in the reduction, de-escalation, and potential resolution of the conflict.

'Truth-Seeking': Historical and Legal Clarification

The IPTEC might play an expert fact-finding role in establishing a new baseline of 'truths' about the conflict. As discussed in Chap. 6, truth commissions can clarify the history and law that inform legacies of violence.[280] They should establish the facts about violent events that remain disputed or denied.[281] For example, the SATRC aimed to establish 'as complete a picture as possible of the nature, causes,

---

[277] González and Varney, above n 25, 12.

[278] Yifat Gutman, 'Transcultural Memory in Conflict: Israeli-Palestinian Truth and Reconciliation' (2011) 17 (4) *Parallax*, 61, 62 ('Transcultural Memory').

[279] The SATRC consisted of the Human rights Committee, Reparations Committee, and one committee that could grant amnesty in exchange for testimony.

[280] Hayner, '*Confronting State Terror*', above n 5, 24.

[281] González and Varney, above n 25, 9.

and extent' of gross abuses under apartheid.[282] Similarly in Guatemala, the commission was mandated to clarify the brutal past with 'objectivity, equity and impartiality'.[283]

The IPTEC Historical and Human Rights Committees could therefore address the causes of violence and help to identify the institutions and national narratives that sustained abuses. The involvement of respected local historians and legal practitioners is crucial to fact-finding. These experts can lend their skills to investigating archival material, reading documents, assessing hypotheses, and tracking overall patterns of violations. Ideally, the committees could be able to establish some baseline 'truths', so that debates about the Israeli–Palestinian past can be resolved more constructively.[284] Given the unfeasibility of an official commission at present, the IPTEC might represent a viable alternative to official truth-telling and could even be a more legitimate tool for the task of clarifying the past (Chap. 7).

'Truth-Telling': Revealing as Healing

> *Telling their stories of trauma and defeat provided them with a feeling of relief, some form of partial healing.*[285] (Zochrot)

A key goal of the IPTEC should be to provide a platform for victims. As discussed in Chap. 6, many academics champion the idea that eliciting narrative or personal 'truths' about the past are vital to truth commissions.[286] Overall, many survivors and relatives find such processes psychologically beneficial.[287] Oral testimony and interviews have the potential to satisfy victims' desires to share trauma in an empathetic environment.[288] For example, many of those who testified at the SATRC '...did not so much as disclose new information, as they seized the opportunity to tell their own stories'.[289] Similar experiences were recorded by the Chilean TRC and Ghana's National Reconciliation Commission.[290]

---

[282] This was set out in the Promotion of National Unity and Reconciliation Act 34 of 1995.

[283] Ball and Chapman, above n 21, 17.

[284] Ibid, 23.

[285] Nets-Zehngut, *'Palestinians and Israelis Collaborate'*, above n 30, 249.

[286] Ball and Chapman, above n 21, 12; Peled and Rouhana, above n 210, 328; See also Eric Brahm, 'Uncovering the Truth: Examining Truth Commission Success and Impact' (2007) 8 *International Studies Perspectives* 16, 20.

[287] Brandon Hamber, 'The Burdens of Truth: An Evaluation of the Psychological Support Services and Initiatives undertaken by the SATRC', (1998). 55 (1), A*merican Imago* 9–28.

[288] Jonathan D. Tepperman, 'Truth and Consequences', (March/April 2002) 81(2) *Foreign Affairs* 128, 130; Judith Herman, *Trauma and Recovery: The Aftermath of Violence--From Domestic Abuse to Political Terror* (Basic Books, 1997).

[289] Andre Du Toit in *'Harvard Law Discussion'*, above n 77, 27.

[290] Ame and Alidu claim that Ghana's NRC offered victims the opportunity to be acknowledged and their stories validated. R.K See 1 Report of the Chilean National Commission at 16–17; Robert Ame and Seldu Alidu, 'Truth and Reconciliation Commissions, Restorative Justice, Peacemaking Criminology and Development' (2010) 23(3) C*riminal Justice Studies* 253, 258–9.

A greater goal of unofficial truth-telling is hearing and recording stories and voices denied or excluded from mainstream discourse.[291] As discussed, civic projects are often created because victims have not been adequately heard, especially by the rival side (Chap. 7). For many Israeli and Palestinian victims, the IPTEC could be the first occasion to formally narrate their experiences both to their respective societies and to each other. By validating testimony, the IPTEC seeks to contribute to recovery from trauma.[292] For example, by systematically collecting and documenting Palestinian oral history, Zochrot empowered many Palestinian interviewees (Chap. 7).[293] 'They felt that their personal stories were valuable since others were interested in hearing it...many of them had not told their stories about 1948...because of psychological difficulties such as shame, fear, trauma, lack of hope...'.[294]

Given the centrality of personal and social narratives to victims, the IPTEC should be committed to truth-telling beyond mere academic inquiry. This is particularly important given that forensic and legal 'truths' are often privileged in the framing of the conflict.[295] Nets-Zehngut demonstrates how Palestinian oral history is equally valuable as a scholarly source.[296] Indeed, with the passage of time, there will be fewer living testimonies from the 1948 period.[297] Testimony from the Victims Committee can add to the historical record of the conflict. Thus, the IPTEC process of collecting and hearing testimony could serve as an equalising step in the pursuit of 'truth' and memory recovery.

Multiple 'Truths': Pluralising the Past

> *Any history that has politics or conflict at its core, that seeks to encompass the story of a society... must work to achieve a contrapuntal narrative.* (Charles Maier)[298]

---

[291] Bickford, above n 154, 1000.

[292] Ball, above n 3; See also Crocker, above n 271, 52.

[293] Nets-Zehngut, *'Palestinians and Israelis Collaborate'*, above n 30, 249.

[294] Ibid 249.

[295] Gutman observes that state documents became representative of Israeli historiography, while oral history represented Palestinian history writing, reproducing the social hierarchy in the hierarchy of knowledge production of 1948. Gutman, *Transcultural Memory,* above n 278, 66.

[296] Rafi Nets-Zehngut, 'Palestinian Autobiographical Memory regarding the 1948 Palestinian Exodus' (2011) 32(2) *Political Psychology*, 271, 277.

[297] As discussed in Chap. 1, Palestinian scholars rely almost totally on Palestinians' oral history with regard to the conflict in general, and the 1948 exodus in particular as documents were destroyed. See also Ibid, 292.

[298] Charles Maier, 'Doing History, Doing Justice' in Robert Rotberg and Dennis Thompson (eds.) *Truth v. Justice: The Morality of Truth Commissions*, (Princeton University Press, 2000) 261.

The IPTEC should promote a multifaceted approach to truth-seeking. Given the burden of polarised history, the IPTEC could revisit the past as a site of contestation.[299] Indeed, a key lesson from Northern Ireland was developing respect for counter-narratives and accepting the existence of multiple 'truths', beyond forensic 'objective' evidence.[300] The SATRC also adopted a broad and nuanced concept of truth-telling.[301] Its final report distinguished between four versions of truth: 'forensic', 'personal', 'social,' and 'restorative', which helped South Africans gain a deeper understanding of their apartheid past.[302] The distinctions made by the SATRC illustrate that not only the factuality of truth, but above all, the interactive process of finding the truth can contribute to an improvement of social relationships.[303]

Accordingly, a pluralism of historical accounts should be pursued the IPTEC. By engaging with national narratives, the Historical Committee could consider both the objective and the subjective dimensions of truth-telling.[304] For example, the IPTEC Final Report might innovatively present Israeli and Palestinian narratives on key events of the conflict alongside one another, as well as some baseline facts agreed by the historians.[305] Applying the concept of 'narrative' itself also implies the existence of multiple 'truths'.[306] The IPTEC Victims Committee could enable individual Israelis and Palestinians to narrate their personal 'truths'. Testimony at the Victim's Committee might complement the academic framework, demonstrating that the IPTEC seeks not to establish one singular forensic truth, but rather to recognise the poly-vocal experiences of past events, and the national identity claims that spring from those experiences.[307] Ideally, the social science and legal work produced by the

---

[299] 'Although there is a degree of cognitive dissonance in the notion of simultaneously recognizing contradictory histories, the understanding of history as a collection of subjective experiences encourages the teaching of history in a poly-vocal manner rather than presenting the illusion of a unified narrative'. Miller, above n 1, 321.

[300] Zochrot, Christian Aid, Ulster University, and Transitional Justice Institute, *Toward a Framework of Transitional Justice in Israel/Palestine* (Lesson Summary from Workshop, November 2015). ('Zochrot Workshop').

[301] Of all the truth commissions, the SATRC was the most self-conscious and intentional about its conception of truth. Of these four approaches, only 'factual' truth refers to the impartial and objective evidence that most truth commissions have understood as their mandate. *SATRC Report*, above n 190, 227–29.

[302] See Van Zyl, '*Dilemmas of Transitional Justice*', above n 19.

[303] Susanne Buckey-Zistel, 'Transitional Justice in Divided societies – Potentials and Limits' (September 2009) Paper presented at the Fifth European Consortium for Political Research General Conference, Potsdam Universität 14.

[304] Conversely, some commentators believe that truth commissions should only focus on the 'objective' dimensions of truth. See Ball, above n. 8; Jack Snyder and Leslie Vinjamuri 'Trials and Errors: Principle and Pragmatism in Strategies of International Justice' (2003) 28 (5) *International Security* 44; Tepperman, above n 288, 140.

[305] Sami Adwan and Dan Bar-On, 'Shared History Project: A PRIME Example of Peace-Building under Fire' (2004) 17 (3) *International Journal of Politics, Culture, and Society*, 513, 516.

[306] Paul Scham, Walid Salem and Benjamin Pogrund (eds.), *Shared Histories – A Palestinian-Israeli Dialogue* (Left Coast Press, 2005).

[307] Miller, above n 1, 315.

IPTEC Historical and Human Rights Committees, combined with the testimony of the IPTEC Victims Committee, would place truth-telling on an grassroots as well as 'elite' level, permeating both simultaneously in a multiplicity of ways.[308]

National 'Truths': Public Engagement

Finally, the IPTEC could engage directly with the Israeli and Palestinian public. Given the psychological dimensions of the conflict, civic participation in national truth-telling is essential to the process of conflict resolution. For example, in South Africa, Chile, and Ghana, public hearings were a significant feature of national truth-seeking. In particular, the SATRC hearings were widely publicised on television and radio and became tremendously successful at generating public debate.[309] In a similar vein, the IPTEC Victims Committee could directly engage with the public through its event hearings about past abuse. The IPTEC might seek to use victim testimony to challenge official narrative and stimulate public debate. In particular, the IPTEC should seek to transcend the narrow legal and political rhetoric around 1948, 1967, and the Second Intifada. At the very least, bi-national truth-telling efforts could expose Israelis and Palestinians to hearing the 'other' in an inclusive forum. 'They also give those from both sides who wish to air their feelings…to publicize their regret, or to acknowledge wrong-doing by their society, a space in which it is legitimate and desirable to do so'.[310] Whilst it would be naive to expect the IPTEC to reconfigure the past, a 'contrapuntal'[311] narrative might generate more meaningful public discourse.

IPTEC and Justice

The IPTEC should promote restorative justice as a platform to educate and account for past abuses against both the nations. As discussed, one of the central premises of transitional justice is that a discourse of justice and human rights law is linked to peace and conflict transformation.[312] For both Israelis and Palestinians, justice

---

[308] Ibid.

[309] Ball and Chapman, above n 21, 23; Miller, above n 1, 316; Alex Boraine, *A Country Unmasked: Inside South Africa's Truth and Reconciliation Commission* (Oxford University Press, 2000) 99.

[310] Ron Dudai, 'Deviant Commemorations: Civil Society and Dealing with the Past in Active Conflicts' (Paper presented at the The Potential Role of Transitional Justice in Active Conflicts, Hebrew University Jerusalem), 7 ('Deviant Commemorations').

[311] To conceptualise the interplay between truth commissions and history, historian Charles Maier provides a musical analogy, whereby history must strive not to be 'harmonic' but 'contrapuntal'. See Maier, above n 298, 274–275.

[312] Mark Freeman, 'Transitional Justice: Fundamental Goals and Unavoidable Complications' (2000–2002) 28 *Manitoba Law Journal* 113, 114.

claims, acknowledgement, and accountability for human rights abuse are significant. Accordingly, consistent with transitional justice measures pursued in other ongoing conflicts,[313] the IPTEC should be grounded in the desirability of human rights discourse for Israelis and Palestinians. The IPTEC might potentially contribute to restorative justice through its legal findings and victims' hearings, as well as by ascribing institutional responsibility to past violations.[314]

Formal Recognition of Past Harm

By investigating systematic abuses across three periods (IPTEC Human Rights Committees), identifying victims (IPTEC Victims Committee), and establishing a complete and expert record of the past (IPTEC Historical Committee), the IPTEC could formally acknowledge violations through a restorative justice framework. Any lasting legacy of the commission requires crucial insights into the institutions, parties, structures, and ideologies that permitted or committed gross violations.[315] For example, the SATRC helped to uncover the fate of hundreds of victims and identified widespread patterns of abuse.[316] In Argentina, the National Commission on the Disappeared effectively documented the systemic nature of the junta repression.[317]

Similarly, the IPTEC could provide an essential service by presenting concrete evidence about the nature and causes of human rights abuse during the three periods. Without such evidence, Israelis and Palestinians may be less inclined to accept responsibility for the roles their military and ideologies played in the violence. A final report is also an essential product of a truth commission. Jointly published and publicly available, the IPTEC Report could seek to become a valuable formal justice-seeking document[318] and might help to create an authoritative written, audio, and video record of human rights abuses.[319] As a comparative example, the Report of the Argentine National Commission on the Disappeared[320]continues to be widely used for civic education and is reprinted regularly.[321] It is hoped that, akin to the SATRC and Guatemalan commission Reports, revelations made by the IPTEC

[313] Thomas Unger and Marieke Wierda 'Pursuing Justice in Ongoing Conflict: A Discussion of Current Practice' in Ambos et al., above n 15.

[314] González and Varney, above n 25, 9.

[315] Ball and Chapman, above n 21, 43.

[316] Van Zyl, *'Dilemmas of Transitional Justice,'* above n 19, 657.

[317] *Never Again: The Report of the Argentine National Commission on the Disappeared* (Nunca Más: Informe de la Comision Nacional sobre la Desaparicion de Personas), (Strauss and Giroux, 1986).

[318] González and Varney, above n 25, 23.

[319] Wing, above n 1.

[320] Never Again: The Report of the Argentine National Commission, above n 317.

[321] González and Varney, above n 25, 23.

might also strengthen the hand of Israeli and Palestinian reformers.[322] Such findings could be indispensable to legal advocacy, publicly vindicating the rights of victims and adding a human rights dimension to conflict resolution efforts.

Challenging Denial and Fostering Accountability

> *There are latent hypocrisies among the masses of both populations, that seem willing to turn a blind eye to human rights abuse, if it originates from the wrong ideological pole.*[323]
> (Manuel Hassassian)

One of the goals of the IPTEC is to raise public awareness about mutual legacies of abuse and joint wrongdoing.[324] As discussed in Chap. 6, truth commissions pursue accountability by making demands on collective memory and by re-examining past violations.[325] The IPTEC could help institutionalise a shared record of Israeli and Palestinian involvement in the conflict.[326] At present, there is little awareness of the international illegality and/or immorality of past conduct in either society. As the weaker party, Palestinian society does not demonstrate a popular consciousness of its own human rights violations. An assortment of reasons leads to the majority of Palestinians to keep silent about Palestinian abuses; the need to show national unity behind the PA, and genuine fear from reprisal by the authority, all compounded with an overall ignorance of human rights discourse.[327] For Israelis, the facts of the past are more commonly known; but the problem lies in the intricate ways in which wrongdoing is denied or justified in practice.[328] Whereas Palestinians sanctify attacks on civilians as legitimate resistance, Israelis dismiss military excesses and abuses as unavoidable security measures.

Unlike the archives of Eastern Europe, secret death squads in South Africa[329] or disappearances in Latin America, most abuses in the region are relatively transparent and well-documented.[330] Both sides are generally clear about what abuses took

---

[322] Van Zyl, '*Unfinished Business*', above n 244, 758–9.

[323] Hassassian, above n 127, 80.

[324] Dudai contends that the core transitional problem is the denial of human rights violations, and consequently the common purpose of all transitional justice mechanisms is to reclassify the past. Ron Dudai, 'Transitional justice as social control: political transitions, human rights norms and the reclassification of the past'. *The British Journal of Sociology* (2017) 1–21 ('Transitional Justice as Social Control').

[325] Brian Hehir in '*Harvard Law Discussion*', above n 77, 14.

[326] Ibid.

[327] Hassassian, above n 127, 80.

[328] Stanley Cohen, *States of Denial: Knowing about Atrocities and Suffering* (Polity, 2001), 223–248.

[329] Literal denials were also common in South Africa. The apartheid regime employed secret death squads, activists were killed, and their bodies were thrown into secret graves. Dudai, '*Does Any of this Matter?*', above n 159, 344.

[330] For example, a full and updated list of the names of Jewish and Arab casualties of the conflict already appears on the website of B'Tselem. Blunt literal denial is rare in Israel, and so is denial of

place and '...[m]ost violations (the collective punishment of house demolitions for example) are lawful under Israeli law...'.[331] Accordingly, by way of accountability, what Israelis and Palestinian need is not just access to the historical record, or positive assertions of fact, but a discursive assault on the very psychological foundations of the conflict.

Accordingly, the IPTEC could lessen the deniability that Israeli and Palestinian victims were abused and that both the groups participated in human rights violations. As an unofficial body, the IPTEC might be arguably better placed to challenge official narratives that deny abuses across the three major events of the conflict. As discussed, civic transitional justice projects have been advocated to counter misconceptions and myths often used by the state for their own agenda.[332] Akin to the History through the Human Eye Initiative, or the joint Israeli–Palestinian memorial service (Chap. 7), the IPTEC could serve as a counterweight to pervasive denial, militarism, and self-righteousness.[333] In this regard, the IPTEC might help to force an awareness of joint wrongdoing into the national discourse. Hearing personal narratives through the IPTEC Victims Committee could help erode blanket support for human suffering caused to the other side. For example, Palestinian testimony at the IPTEC could help Israelis confront the legacy of harm caused by the occupation.[334] By hearing victims from both the sides, the IPTEC should strive to generate a process of collective accounting, requiring everyone, from Israeli soldiers to Palestinian civilians, to examine their role in past abuses.[335]

---

responsibility. For example, Israel's government has an open policy on assassinations. That is also true for Palestinian atrocities: they do not deny the existence of suicide bombers, nor do they lay blame on foreign or unknown actors.

[331] Most of the gross violations that the SATRC investigated were officially illegal under South African domestic law during apartheid. Dudai, *'Does Any of this Matter?'*, above n 159, 344.

[332] David Androff, 'Can Civil Society Reclaim Truth? Results from a Community-Based Truth and Reconciliation Commission' (2012) 6 *The International Journal of Transitional Justice* 3.

[333] For example, Zochrot has raised mainstream Israeli awareness of the Palestinian catastrophe of 1948. 'What is remarkable about Zochrot is not its size or impact, but rather the fact that it openly offers an explicit and direct antithesis to the Israeli regime of forgetting...and proposes a new regime of re-memorizing'. Uri Ram, 'Ways of Forgetting: Israel and the obliterated Memory of the Palestinian Nakba' (2009) 22(3) *Journal of Historical Sociology* 366, 389; According to Gutman, Zochrot uses a contested and silenced past and commemorative practices to create a new vision for the future. See Yifat Gutman, 'Looking Back to the Future: Counter-Memory as oppositional knowledge-production in the Israeli-Palestinian conflict'. (2005) 65(1) *Current Sociology* 1, 2 ('Looking Back').

[334] See Nadim N. Rouhana 'Zionism's Encounter with the Palestinians: The Dynamics of Force, Fear, and Extremism' in Robert Rotberg (ed) *Israeli-Palestinian Narratives of Conflict: History's Double Helix* (Indiana University Press, 2006),133.

[335] According to Dudai and Cohen, a bilateral truth commission could trigger a broad national process of 'coming to terms' with the past. This includes dealing with the nuanced phenomena of collaboration in the Israeli–Palestinian conflict. Dudai and Cohen *'Dealing with the Past'*, above n 29; Dudai and Cohen, *'Triangles of Betrayal'* above n 4, 52.

Human Rights Norms as 'Justice'

The IPTEC might introduce a new moral framework for justice by applying universal human rights standards to the conflict. As discussed, progress towards ceasing hostilities, ending violations, and reconciling the past have been closely associated with linking justice to human rights law (Chap. 3). In particular, human rights norms can support the negotiating process, as well as provide a universal yardstick to assess past conduct. As noted, the omission of international human rights law standards from Middle East peace efforts was a source of the Oslo Accord's weakness.[336]

Establishing a common paradigm for justice is particularly important to the region. Some form of blind spot clearly exists in each nation's campaign for justice and human rights. From Zionism to Palestinian resistance, the meta-narratives of justice are ideological and often irreconcilable. For example, Palestinian claims for justice are part of the broader liberation struggle, which do not square easily with Israeli–Jewish frameworks about that same struggle. Arguably, on the Israeli side, the entire project of Zionism can be understood as a counterclaim for justice.[337] As discussed in Chap. 4, the term 'historical justice' is widely used by Israelis and Palestinians. It generates inflated expectations, when actually justice goals may need to be more modest following mass atrocity.[338] On both the sides, civil society is instrumentalised to advance a parochial definition of justice, that, seen from the other side, is an obstacle to peace.[339] For example, Zochrot calls for implementing the Palestinian right to return as a justice-seeking measure.[340] Historical justice is thus an influential paradigm in the Middle East, but has a paucity of vocabulary for joint accountability and reconciliation.

In this light, the IPTEC Human rights Committee might draw on universal human rights norms to transcend the discursive idiosyncrasies of 'historical justice'. Through a bilateral framework, Israelis and Palestinians can both equally pursue transitional justice and procedural fairness (Chap. 4).[341] By widening agreement on the universality of human rights law, the IPTEC legal experts could agree on some basic international legal standards that targeting civilians, unlawful detention, and expulsions are unjust or that mutual respect for self-determination and IHL is a

---

[336] Ibrahim Bisharat and Edward Kaufman, 'Introducing human rights into conflict resolution: the relevance for the Israeli-Palestinian peace process' (2002) 1(1) *Journal of Human Rights* 71, 81.

[337] Waters, above n 252, 183.

[338] Kimberly Theidon, 'Justice in Transition: The Micro-Politics of Reconciliation in Post-War Peru' (2006) 50(3) *Journal of Conflict Resolution* 433–457.

[339] Waters, above n 252, 184; 'Unconditional solidarity with Palestinians by Israelis does not seem a fruitful way to engage with the past'. Dudai and Cohen '*Dealing with the Past*', above n 29, 247.

[340] Tom Hill, '1948 After Oslo: Truth and reconciliation in Palestinian discourse' (2008) 13(2) *Mediterranean Politics* 151–170; Gutman, '*Looking Back*', above n 333, 7.

[341] As discussed in Chap. 4, deference to universal human rights norms might ameliorate the power imbalance between the parties, which have hampered negotiations.

virtue.[342] The IPTEC could also help confer international norms with greater moral authority.[343] Given elements within Israel are suspicious of human rights discourse, it is essential to challenge the assumption that human rights claims only apply to Palestinians. Whilst Israelis are indeed the stronger party, human rights standards remain equally relevant to Israelis as victims of Palestinian abuses.[344] In this light, human rights and 'justice' may be reciprocal demands based on shared interests and national concerns through the IPTEC.

Truth-Telling as Justice

> *The truth itself can also be understood as a form of justice and reparation. When the silence is broken…the injury caused by past abuse may begin to be repaired.*[345]

As discussed in Chap. 4, Israeli and Palestinian calls for justice are not just about criminal law, established rules, and retribution; they also involve social and reparative dimensions. For victims and the public, testimony and recognition will be critical to remedying the harms and injustices suffered. 'Due recognition', writes Taylor, 'is not just a courtesy we owe people. It is a vital human need'.[346] Palestinian advocates have long urged acknowledgement of past injustices to restoring the national dignity of the refugees.[347] Similarly, Israelis have demanded recognition of Israeli casualties, and acceptance of their own collective right to exist as a nation-state. The IPTEC therefore pursues justice by facilitating the production of personal and social truths through its three committees.[348]

Indeed, formal truth-telling measures could serve a reparative function.[349] By giving special attention to testimonies, they provide victims with recognition, often after prolonged periods of trauma.[350] Ultimately, the IPTEC seeks to establish a

---

342 Rouhana affirms the possibility of broad Israeli/Palestinian agreements on basic principles of justice. Nadim Rouhana, 'Group Identity and Power Asymmetry in Reconciliation Processes: The Israeli Palestinian Case' (2004) 10(1) *Journal of Peace Psychology* 33, 47.

343 See Colin Campbell, 'Peace and the Laws of war: The Role of International Humanitarian Law in the Post-Conflict Environment', (2000) 82 (839), *Review of the International Committee of the Red Cross*, Geneva, ICRC 627–651, 628–631; Christine Bell, *Human rights and Peace Agreements,* (Oxford University Press, 2000) 4.

344 'It is crucial to remind ourselves that universal rights apply to any individual, be they a terrorist, a refugee or a settler'. Edward Kaufman, 'Human rights dimensions in Peace-making' in Elizabeth G Mathews (ed.), *The Israel-Palestine Conflict Parallel Discourses* (Routledge, 2011) 189.

345 Aukerman, above n 79.

346 Charles Taylor 'The Politics of Recognition' in Amy Gutmann, (ed.) *Multiculturalism: Examining The Politics of Recognition* (Princeton University Press, 1994) 25–26.

347 Rashid Khalidi, 'Towards a Solution', in *Palestinian Refugees: Their Problem and Future* (Center for Policy Analysis on Palestine, October 1994) 24–25.

348 Dudai, *'Deviant Commemorations'*, above n 311, 4.

349 For Hayner, one of the fundamental goals of a commission is to formally acknowledge past abuses. Hayner, '*Confronting State Terror'*, above n 5, 24.

350 González and Varney, above n 25, 9.

relationship with Israeli and Palestinian victims not only as witnesses, but also as rights-holders and partners to the process whose experiences deserve recognition.[351] In this light, a broad notion of reparations[352] could offer both the sides the ability to more adequately address the psychological harm. Given the emotional resonance of history, meaningful measures like formal acknowledgment, the Final Report and narration itself might be as desirable as direct payments to victims.[353] The reconciliatory role of symbolic gestures will be discussed below. Ultimately, the IPTEC seeks to provide the space to hear victim testimonies, acknowledge the past, and open the possibility for a formal transitional apology. In short, truth-telling could be the IPTEC's primary reparative measure.

IPTEC and Reconciliation

The IPTEC should be grounded in the desirability of reconciliation discourse to Israelis and Palestinians (Chap. 4) and as an essential process to long-term conflict. As discussed in previous chapters, the need to reconcile historical and legal narratives and the value of grassroots inclusive transitional justice processes are a priority for the region. At the same time, the IPTEC might theoretically undermine some of the goals of reconciliation by challenging popular and official memory. However, as will be discussed below, by drawing on the contact hypothesis, notions of empathy and traditional practices, it is submitted that an 'oppositional' project could still meaningfully pursue reconciliation. As Dudai notes, unofficial transitional justice initiatives are by their nature 'oppositional', and therefore intended to be spoilers of official policy and memory.[354]

Collaboration: 'The Contact Hypothesis'

> *The best people to convince Israelis that Palestinians are not monsters, and to show the Palestinians that Israelis are not monsters, are the respective populations.* (Joel Braunold, 2015)[355]

---

[351] Ibid.

[352] Magarell makes a persuasive case for a broad notion of reparations that includes disclosure and acknowledgement of the truth about violations, victims, and responsibilities. See Lisa Magarrell, 'Reparations for Massive or Widespread Human Rights Violations: Sorting Out Claims For Reparations And the Struggle for Social Justice' (2003) 22 *Windsor Yearbook of Access to Justice* 85 at 89.

[353] 'In many cases, recognition...of the injustice that was committed, and validation of their experiences, memories and identity are the primary objective sought by victims of historic injustice.' Peled and Rouhana, above n 210, 321.

[354] Dudai, *'Deviant Commemorations'*, above n 311.

[355] On 30 June 2015, Joel Braunold, US Director of the Alliance for Middle East Peace (ALLMEP), spoke to Fathom Forum on the value of people-to-people movements to any resolution of the Israeli–Palestinian conflict. See Branold and Lyndon, above n 91.

By involving both Israelis and Palestinians in the IPTEC process, the IPTEC seeks to forge new mutual cross-border relationships, deepen existing ones, and build trust. The lack of direct contact between Israelis and Palestinians entrenches mutual fears and stigmas. Human rights and peace activism has also become constrained by the separation agendas of political elites.[356] The intent is that the very participation in the IPTEC process will attenuate the level of hostility among participants.[357] Indeed, many scholars have lauded the capacity of collaboration and dialogue[358] between rivals to reconfigure the psychological dynamics of conflict.[359] Grounded in conflict resolution theory, the contact hypothesis posits that under certain conditions intergroup contact can reduce prejudice.[360] Arguably, transformative practices remain effective, and possibly even more relevant, in the harsh context of a violent conflictual socio-political reality.[361] Notably, the contact hypothesis has been subjected to criticism, both in general[362] and in the Israeli–Palestinian context in particular.[363]

However, the research record validates the overall effectiveness of dialogue encounters.[364] As discussed, many collaborative Israeli–Palestinian projects have

---

[356] This has made it more difficult to formulate mandates and coordinate strategies among NGOs. Lisa Hajjar, 'Human Rights in Israel-Palestine: The History and Politics of a Movement' (2001) 30(4) *Journal of Palestine Studies* 21, 25.

[357] Adwan and Bar-On, above n 305, 516.

[358] According to Arendt, dialogue between rivals and dialogical collaboration are political acts that acknowledge plurality and humanity. See Hannah Arendt, *Vita activa oder Vom tätigen Leben* (Piper 2007).

[359] Norman Miller, 'Personalization and the Promise of Contact Theory' (2002) 58(2) *Journal of Social Issues,* 387–410; Marilynn Brewer and Samuel Gaertner, 'Toward reduction of prejudice: Intergroup contact and Social categorization' in Abraham Tesser, et al. (eds.), *Blackwell Handbook of Social Psychology: Intergroup processes* (Basil Blackwell, 2001) 451–472.

[360] Herbert Kelman, 'Creating the Conditions for Israeli-Palestinian Negotiations' (1982) 26(1) *Journal of Conflict Resolution* 39–75; Ronald. Fisher, *Interactive Conflict Resolution* (Syracuse University Press, 1997).

[361] Ifat Maoz, 'An Experiment in Peace: Reconciliation-Aimed Workshops of Jewish-Israeli and Palestinian Youth' (2000) 37 (6) *Journal of Peace Research* 722, 733.

[362] See Stefania Paolini, Jake Harwood, and Mark Rubin 'Negative intergroup contact makes group memberships salient: Explaining why intergroup conflict endures' (2010) 36 (12) *Personality and Social Psychology Bulletin* 1723–173; Elizabeth Levy Paluck, Seth Ariel Green, and Donald Green, 'The Contact Hypothesis Re-Evaluated' (2018) *Behavioural Public Policy* 1–30; Shelly McKeown and John Dixon, 'The "Contact Hypothesis": Critical reflections and future directions' (2017). 11(1) *Social and Personality Psychology Compass,* 1–32.

[363] Iftat Maoz, 'Does contact work in protracted asymmetrical conflict? Appraising 20 years of reconciliation-aimed encounters between Israeli Jews and Palestinians' (2011) 48 *Journal of Peace Research,* 115–125; See also Chuck Thiessen and Marwan Darweish, 'Conflict resolution and Asymmetric Conflict: The contradictions of planned contact interventions in Israel and Palestine' (2018) 66 *International Journal of Intercultural Relations* 73–84.

[364] Multiple long-term and shorter-term studies have found such peace education interventions to be successful. Ned Lazarus and Karen Ross, 'Tracing the Long-Term Impacts of a Generation of Israeli-Palestinian Encounters' (2015) 3(2) *International Journal of Conflict Engagement and Resolution*; Gavriel Salomon, 'Does Peace Education Make a Difference in a Context of Intractable

already documented positive attitudinal shifts (Chap. 7). For example, as a result of the 'History through the Human Eye"(HTHE) project with Israeli and Palestinian groups,[365] 80% of participants demonstrated a positive change in their perception of 'the other'.[366] Recent studies show that participants in intragroup dialogue develop an increased capacity for acceptance of both Israeli and Palestinian collective narratives and demonstrate a greater willingness toward reconciliation.[367] It manifested in a greater readiness to acknowledge responsibility and apologise for past transgressions.[368]

Similar outcomes are hoped for the IPTEC. Building on this success, a bi-national commission could provide Israeli and Palestinian participants in the process (lawyers, religious figures, academics for example) the type of inter-group contact which reduces prejudice and improves relations between the two sides. Precisely because the gap between national claims and experience is so vast, the IPTEC might meaningfully contribute to reconciliation. In other words, the creation of a joint transitional mechanism may itself help to foster transition and reconciliation.[369]

Empathy

> *Reconciliation is not possible unless Israelis hear the testimonies of the Palestinians who were expelled from their homes, homes that today house Israelis, and Palestinians hear Israeli victims of terror.*[370]

Given the pervasive denial of suffering on both the sides,[371] fostering empathy is instrumental to reconciliation. By providing Israeli and Palestinian victims with a space to recount their suffering, it is hoped the IPTEC could sensitise both publics to the human dimensions of conflict as discussed in Chap. 6. The fences, walls, checkpoints, and prohibitions make it exceedingly difficult for Israelis and Palestinians to humanise one another. To advance reconciliation, it is instrumental

---

Conflict?' (2004) 10(3) *Peace and Conflict: Journal of Peace Psychology* 257–274. cited in Ibid, 9–10.

[365] The HTHE project is facilitated by the Parents Circle Family Forum (PCFF) discussed in Chap. 7. It has been accompanied by external evaluators, who have consistently recorded positive impacts among the vast majority of participants against a series of attitudinal indicators. Maya Kahanoff and Nabil Shibly, *Evaluation of the History through the Human Eye Project* (Office of Conflict Management and Mitigation (CMM) at USAID, 2014) ('USAID/CMM Field Study 2014') cited in Lazarus, above n 78, BICOM Report 2017, 48.

[366] Ibid, 35.

[367] Yael Ben David et al., 'Exploring Ourselves Within Intergroup Conflict: The Role of Intragroup Dialogue in Promoting Acceptance of Collective Narratives and Willingness Toward Reconciliation' (2016) 23 (3) *Peace and Conflict Journal of Peace Psychology* 269–277.

[368] Ibid.

[369] Miller, above n 1, 307.

[370] Golan-Agnon, above n 20, 45.

[371] Stanley Cohen, above n 328, 223–248.

to use vocabularies of emotion as well as those of law.[372] As Van-Zyl writes of the SATRC: 'Often people from one side come to realize that mothers and children…feel the same pain and suffer the same loss. They come to learn that ordinary people, not leaders and demagogues, pay the price...'.[373]

Arguably, the key to reconciliation between Israelis and Palestinians is to expose each side to the other's pain. As novelist Grossman writes:

> So much of our tragedy in the Middle East is because we absolutely forbid ourselves from listening to the suffering of the other…We are totally deaf and blind to the stories of the other…only if you open yourself up…to the tragedy of the other, to his justice…then suddenly reality is no longer the projection of your nightmares….[374]

In this light, the IPTEC hearings will require both Israelis and Palestinians to view their actions '..from the outside, from the other side's perspective'.[375] Research shows that mechanisms at the most basic human level make it possible for people to empathise with others, to understand them, if they can narrate from their perspective.[376] 'Empathy encompasses much more than just compassion. Through empathy observers shape the story, give it meaning and become part of it'.[377]

As discussed, narrative projects have already enhanced the empathy between Israelis and Palestinians (Chap. 7).[378] According to empirical research, for most Israeli subjects, listening to Palestinians tell personal stories of suffering inspired them to feel increased empathy toward Palestinians as a group.[379] Many Palestinian subjects also experienced empathy for Israelis after telling their own stories to an Israeli listener, and eliciting an empathetic response.[380] Ultimately, the IPTEC hopes to enable Palestinians to view Israelis as ordinary people, and not just their occupi-

---

[372] For example, the Madres de Plaza de Mayo famously used a public space in Buenos Aires to remember their children disappeared by the Argentinian junta. The mothers' weekly marches drew on an 'emotive' vocabulary (as well as legal one) to mobilise collective action and transitional justice. Paul Gready and Simon Robins, 'Rethinking Civil society and Transitional Justice: Lessons from Social Movements and 'New' civil society,' (2017) 21 (7) *The International Journal of Human Rights*, 956, 963.

[373] Van Zyl, '*Dilemmas of Transitional Justice*', above n 19, 663.

[374] David Grossman quoted in Dudai, *'Deviant Commemorations'*, above n 31.

[375] Daly, above n 11, 86.

[376] Shelly Berlowitz, 'Unequal Equals: How Politics Can Block Empathy' in Aleida Assmann and Ines Detmers (eds). *Empathy and its Limits* (Palgrave Macmillan, 2015) 40, 50.

[377] According to Breithaupt, the ability of human beings to narrate and to think in narration is what enables and promotes empathy. Fritz Breithaupt *Kulturen der Empathie* (Suhrkamp, 2009) 114 cited in Ibid; See also Fritz Breithaupt, 'Empathy for Empathy's Sake: Aesthetics and Everyday Empathic Sadism' in Assmann and Detmers, above n 372, 151.

[378] In terms of visceral responses to dialogue, a Massachusetts Institute of Technology study found that a dialogical, or two way interaction enhanced empathy between Israelis and Palestinians, albeit through divergent mechanisms. Lazarus, above n 78, *BICOM Report 2017*, 56.

[379] Emile Bruneau and Rebecca Saxe, 'The Power of Being Heard: The Benefits of 'Perspective-Giving' in the Context of Intergroup Conflict' (2012) 48 *Journal of Experimental Psychology* 855–866.

[380] Ibid.

ers and oppressors. Similarly, Israelis may come to see Palestinians as a people who are fighting for their national rights, and not just a group predisposed to 'killing Jews' or seeking the destruction of the Jewish state.

Reconciling the Past: Mutual Recognition

> *A greater appreciation of the separate 'truths' that drive Israelis and Palestinians could plausibly contribute to conflict reduction.* (Robert Rotberg)[381]

The pursuit of reconciliatory truth-telling should be crucial to the IPTEC. As discussed in Chap. 3, one of the hallmarks of transitional justice is the invocation of a new shared past.[382] One of the foremost goals of the IPTEC would be to establish some form of 'bridging narrative' between the two societies, around the highly politicised events of the conflict. Ultimately, the IPTEC can seek to facilitate a shift from competing monologues to 'shared truths' about the past. For example, the IPTEC Historical Committee might produce a common factual account of the origins of the Palestinian refugee issue, as well as offer a critical history of 1948. Encouraging victim testimony and seeking a means of narrowing the differences between the parties, should be important elements of the commission and its process.[383]

Notably, the IPTEC might not seek to convert one side to the other, nor to create one authoritative joint narrative,[384] but rather to facilitate acceptance of at least some aspects of the other's national experience.[385] Exposing Israelis and Palestinian to their rival's narrative as legitimate and reducing gaps between them may be the key to reconciliation.[386] As long as one nation's 'freedom fighter' is another's 'terrorist', it seems unrealistic to arrive at one singular account of the Israeli–Palestinian conflict.[387] Rather, the IPTEC could focus on raising awareness of each nation's respective history through a 'bridging narrative' that accounts for both the versions of the past. This approach can build on the PRIME teacher's shared history project (Chap.

---

[381] Rotberg, above n 334, 2.

[382] Daniel Bar-Tal and Gemma Bennink, 'The Nature of Reconciliation as an Outcome and as a Process' in Yaacov Bar-Siman-Tov (ed) *From Conflict Resolution to Reconciliation*, (Oxford University Press, 2004).

[383] Judy Barsalou, 'Trauma and Transitional Justice in Divided Societies' (April 2005, Special Report), 135 *US Institute of Peace*, 7.

[384] According to Kelman, writing a joint consensual history is not a precondition of reconciliation. Herbert Kelman, 'Reconciliation as Identity Change: A Social-Psychological Perspective' in Bar-Siman-Tov, above n 382.

[385] Dudai, *'Deviant Commemorations'*, above n 311, 4.

[386] Nets-Zehngut, *'Palestinians and Israelis Collaborate'*, above n 30, 247; Dudai and Cohen also affirm: '...the goal should be to acknowledge both narratives to make each legitimate in the eyes of the other...' Dudai and Cohen, *'Dealing with the Past'*, above n 29, 247.

[387] According to Miller, the naive expectation of a fully unified history could set a standard so high that it impedes the work of any Israeli–Palestinian truth commission. Miller, above n 1, 321.

7), which innovatively presented both Israeli and Palestinian narratives around key events of the conflict side by side.[388]

The mere acknowledgement that the other side has a historical narrative itself paves the way to some mutual recognition.[389] For example, the IPTEC Historical Committee could recognise and legitimate the inherent plurality of the past, engage in self-criticism, focus on historical accuracy and make efforts to 'deconstruct perceptions and notions of the past that tend to encourage conflict and make reconciliation harder'.[390] Ultimately, the IPTEC could narrow, not eliminate, the chasms that divide national experiences. One does not have to accept the other side's history as authoritative in order to empathise.[391] An Israeli might appreciate the pain suffered by a Palestinian mother without necessarily accepting the Palestinian version of events that led to that suffering.[392] As Alexander writes: 'The solution is to study history but not focus on the past. You have your narrative, I have mine. Yours might clash with mine, but in order to move on, you respect my narrative and I respect yours'.[393]

Traditional Practices

The IPTEC could draw on Israeli–Jewish and Palestinian traditions to advance its reconciliation discourse. As discussed, growing recognition exists for more culturally aware transitional justice measures (Chap. 3).[394] For example, the African concept 'Ubuntu', meaning both 'compassion' and 'humanity', was invoked by the SATRC to support the reconciliation process.[395] Local traditional processes have

---

[388] Adwan and Bar-On, above n 305, 516.

[389] The logic of the two-narratives approach is based on the assumption that recognition precedes reconciliation. Eyal Naveh, 'Recognition as preamble to reconciliation: A two narrative approach in a Palestinian-Israeli history textbook' (2007) 3 (4) *Horizons Universities* 173–188; Dan Bar-On and Shoshana Steinberg, 'The Other Side of the Story: Israeli and Palestinian Teachers Write a History Textbook Together' (2009) 79 (1) *Harvard Educational Review* 106.

[390] Mordechai Bar-On, 'Conflicting Narratives or Narratives of a Conflict: Can the Zionist and Palestinian Narratives of the 1948 War Be Bridged?' in Rotberg, above n 334, 144, 153.

[391] Dudai and Cohen, *'Dealing with the Past'*, above n 29, 247.

[392] Charles Maeier has argued that an important form of acknowledgment is one party appreciating the pain the other has experienced. See *'Harvard Law Discussion'*, above n 77; Dudai, *'Does Any of this Matter?'*, above n 159.

[393] Neta Alexander, 'All in the Mind' *Haaretz*, 15 September, 2016. https://www.haaretz.com/israel-news/.premium.MAGAZINE-the-palestinian-who-leads-tours-through-auschwitz-1.5435444.

[394] See Arriaza and Roht-Arriaza, above n 9, 157–172; McEvoy and McGregor, above n 9; Lundy, above n 9.

[395] In his judgement against the death penalty, Justice Langa assigned special weight to 'Ubuntu' as representing a culture that emphasises communality and interdependence and recognises the person's status as a human being entitled to unconditional respect, dignity, value, and acceptance. *CCT 3/94 S. v. Makwanyane and Another* 1995 (3) SALR 391, 480–81 (CC) quoted in Aeyal

helped enable victims, perpetrators and affected communities to engage directly with one another and to reconcile. For example, in Rwanda, the use of village-level Gacaca courts[396] played a significant role in post-conflict reconciliation.[397] Timor-Leste's Commission for Reception, Truth, and Reconciliation (2001),[398] urged low-level perpetrators to participate in a 'Community Reconciliation Process', which was a form of mediation based on local customary law.[399] As a woman in East Timor said about the process, '...it is because we also involve the traditional leaders, and swear oaths as in our tradition, that reconciliation becomes true'.[400]

Similarly, IPTEC's involvement of religious figures could lend weight to reconciliation. From a religious standpoint, the values of compassion and peacebuilding are deeply embedded within Islamic and Judaic traditions. For example, customary Palestinian mediation leans on the principles of truce (*sulha*)[401] and traditional forms of peacemaking to settle disputes outside the formal judicial system.[402] Whilst sulha is carried out within local Arab-Israeli communities, it also exists within the

Gross, 'The Constitution, Reconciliation and Transitional Justice: Lessons from South Africa and Israel' (2004) 40 *Stanford Journal of International Law* 47.

[396] Gacaca is derived from the word for 'lawn', referring to members of the Gacaca sitting on the grass when listening to and considering matters before them'. It was an ancient dispute resolution method used at the local level. Jeremy Sarkin, 'The Tension Between Justice and Reconciliation in Rwanda: Politics, Human Rights, Due Process and the Role of the Gacaca Courts in Dealing with the Genocide' (2001) 45 *Journal of African Law* 143, 159.

[397] Faced with an overflowing caseload, Rwandan authorities adapted local indigenous traditions to process lower-level perpetrators of genocide. See William Schabas, 'Genocide trials and Gacaca courts', (2005) 3 *Journal of International Criminal Justice* 879–895.

[398] The Commission for Reception, Truth and Reconciliation in East Timor was established by the U.N. Transitional Administration, Final Report. Available at http://www.ictj.org/en/news/features/846.html. For appraisals see Laura Grenfell, 'Legal Pluralism and the Rule of Law in Timor Leste' (2006) 19 *Leiden Journal of International Law* 305–337; Jeffrey Kingston, 'Regaining Dignity: Justice and Reconciliation in East Timor', (2006) 13 *Brown Journal of World Affairs* 227–240; Cheah Wui Ling, 'Forgiveness and Punishment in Post-Conflict Timor', (2005) 10 UCLA *Journal of International Law and Foreign Affairs* 297–359.

[399] It permitted perpetrators of 'less serious crimes' who gave full confessions to avoid prosecution. Unlike elsewhere, perpetrators had the opportunity to issue direct apologies and make direct offers of reparation to their victims.

[400] Michael S Scheeringa (2005) 'Transitional justice: the local legitimacy of the Commission for Truth, Reception and Reconciliation in East Timor'. MA Thesis, University of Amsterdam, 48 cited in Oomen, above n 15, 181.

[401] For Palestinians, the roots of *sulha* can be found in pre-Islamic and Islamic text. It is widely accepted as a means of promoting peace and tranquility between the offended and the offender, whether they are individuals, families, tribes or towns. Indeed, before the establishment of Israel, *sulha* was used to resolve disputes between local inhabitants of Arab and Jewish decent. See Elias J. Jabbour, *Sulha: Palestinian Traditional Peacemaking Process* (House of Hope Publications, 1996).

[402] Wing, above n 1, 148.

context of Israeli institutions (i.e., local councils, courts, police, elections).[403] The combination of a 'communal sulha' with the (mainly) Islamic concept of repentance is a potential key for involving Palestinian society.[404] It is particularly important given the monopoly of fundamentalist movements like Hamas on religious discourse.[405] According to Lang, a modified process of *sulha* could be a relevant basis for an Israeli–Palestinian community justice initiative.[406] In this way, the IPTEC could seek to imbue reconciliation with elements of the parties' religious and cultural practices.

Political Reconciliation and Symbolic Gestures

Finally, a bilateral IPTEC could positively inform political reconciliation between Israelis and Palestinians. As discussed, overcoming polarised narratives poses a great challenge to the diplomatic enterprise. Whilst any formal peace settlement must ultimately be reached through negotiations, 'the official setting, in which instructed interlocutors, exposed to public scrutiny of every step of the process, must hammer out an agreement, is not an ideal setting for the negotiation of identity'.[407] There is therefore a need for unofficial efforts like the IPTEC to pursue grassroot reconciliation and to complement the diplomatic process at all of its stages.[408]

In practical terms, the IPTEC could also help to reframe negotiations by including additional negotiating partners (like refugee groups and religious figures) or reconciliatory gestures so that new solutions become more plausible. Informed by the IPTEC's work, the parties could negotiate, based on knowledge and not, as has been the case, on the basis of mythology and denial.[409] For example, the IPTEC's well-researched report could provide a basis for reconsideration of Israel' s role in the Palestinian displacement and of its readiness to offer an apology or expression

---

403 Notably, Israeli state authorities usually cooperate and support the process and the elders who facilitate it. For example, in one case that took place in a Druze village in the Galilee, the Israeli foreign minister, the minister of the police, the chair of the Knesset, and the director to the Prime Minister's Office all attended and took part in the *sulha* ceremony. Sharon Lang, 'Sulha peacemaking and the Politics of Persuasion'. (2002) 31(3), *Journal of Palestinian Studies,* 61.

404 Dudai and Cohen, *'Triangles of Betrayal'* above n 4, 52.

405 Mohammed Abu-Nimer, 'Conflict resolution in an Islamic context' (1996) 21 (1) *Peace and Change* 22.

406 Lang, above n 403, 52–66.

407 Herbert Kelman, 'The Interdependence of Israeli and Palestinian National Identities: The Role of the other in Existential Conflicts' (1999) 55(3) *Journal of Social Issues* 581, 596.

408 Ibid, 596.

409 Shraga, above n 4105.

of regret.[410] As discussed, unofficial diplomacy and critical history[411] have positively informed peace talks in the past.[412]

The IPTEC could also engender good-faith measures that build trust. As discussed in Chap. 3, academic research stresses the role of symbolic gestures, such as historical acknowledgement and identity recognition in pursuing reconciliation.[413] For both the nations, there is a perception that one side shows more grassroots support for peace than the other.[414] For example, Israelis often complain that Palestinian civil society is more concerned with boycotting Israel than with fostering peace.[415] From this standpoint, the IPTEC might be able to send an important message that both nations are committed to peacebuilding and that it is indeed feasible for them to confront and recognise their past together. Both Israelis and Palestinians could directly witness a respectful and well-meaning exchange at the academic, legal, and grassroot level. In particular, the production of knowledge on the Palestinian experience of 1948 could be framed as a gesture of regret, an act of acknowledgement, or a first step towards future resolution and reconciliation.[416]

8.4 Part Three: Overcoming Objections

Finally, it is worth considering the practical obstacles and objections facing the IPTEC. Unofficial projects are often dogged by an 'ethos of conflict' that obstructs creative thinking. No doubt, the situation on the ground is particularly desperate.

---

[410] Ibid.

[411] For example, at the 2000 Camp David peace summit the critical narrative of 1948 was so accepted in Israel that it was hard for Israeli negotiators to ignore it. Therefore, they expressed in the summits a basic willingness to publicly acknowledge the Palestinian 1948 tragedy, implicitly, and indirectly accepting Israel's shared responsibility for it as well. See Rafi Nets-Zehngut and Daniel Bar-Tal, 'Transformation of the Official Memory of Conflict: A Tentative Model and the Israeli Memory of the 1948 Palestinian Exodus'. (2014) 27 *International Journal of Political Cultural Society* 67, 86; Michal Ben-Josef Hirsch, 'From Taboo to the Negotiable: The Israeli New Historians and the Changing Representation of the Palestinian Refugee Problem' (2007) 5 *Perspectives on Politics* 241; Ian Lustick, 'Negotiating Truth: The Holocaust, Lehavdil, and al-Nakba', (2006) 60 *Journal of International Affairs*, 52–77.

[412] Hassassian, above n 127, 82.

[413] Jacob Shamir and Khalil Shikaki, 'Determinants of Reconciliation and Compromise Among Israelis and Palestinians' (2002) 39 *Journal of Peace Research* 185, 198; Jacob Shamir, *Public Opinion in the Israeli-Palestinian Conflict: From Geneva to Disengagement to Kadima and Hamas* (United States Institute of Peace, 2007) 16; See also Oded Adomi Leshem, Yechiel Klar and Thomas Edward Flores, 'Instilling Hope for Peace During Intractable Conflicts' (2016) 7 (4) *Social Psychological and Personality Science* 303–311.

[414] Dalia Scheindlin, 'Lessons from Cyprus for Israel-Palestine: Can Negotiations Still Work?' (Mitvim, 2016) 3 https://www.mitvim.org.il/images/Lessons_from_Cyprus_for_Israel-Palestine_-_Dr._Dahlia_Scheindlin_-_September_2016.pdf.

[415] Ibid.

[416] Gutman, '*Looking Back*', above n 333, 7.

Almost every meta-study of the Middle East peacebuilding field emphasises the asymmetry of power, political volatility, and the lack of social legitimacy.[417] However, it will be contended that many of these practical challenges are surmountable based on comparative experience and the existing transitional justice projects canvassed in the previous chapter. Above all else, the decision to initiate a comprehensive transitional mechanism is to engage in a process, requiring patience, vision, and a long-term commitment to transcend the past.

Asymmetry of Power

> *...Inside the encounter, they face each other armed only with powers of communication. Outside the encounter, lethal violence is an everyday expectation, Inside the encounter, discussion leaders mandate equality between participants...Outside the encounter, power structures dictate that they live in separate, unequal societies....*[418]

Clearly, ongoing conflict and vast power asymmetries between Israelis and Palestinians pose formidable obstacles to creating and implementing an IPTEC. Many of the theoretical conditions of the contact hypothesis, such as equal group status, supportive social norms, and intimate contact, are wanting. One cannot ignore the separation barrier and Israeli laws restricting freedom of movement across the border. It is difficult to dismiss the asymmetry between the '...democratically governed and militarily powerful State of Israel, and the Palestinians living in semi-autonomous enclaves of territory surrounded by Israeli security barriers, military camps and settlements...'.[419] Asymmetry also informs different motivations and expectations in peacebuilding initiatives. For example, Palestinian participants may be drawn to structural change or political mobilisation, while Israelis may be seeking to enhance their sense of acceptance and security.[420]

Each side also seeks validation from the other, albeit in different forms: Israelis in terms of Palestinian acceptance of a Jewish state; Palestinians in terms of Israeli acknowledgement of the imbalance of power and of Palestinian rights.[421] It is therefore worth questioning the extent to which the IPTEC could shift power relations, or merely serve to entrench them. Indeed, many 'people to people' peace projects

---

[417] Lazarus, above n 78, *BICOM Report 2017,* 53.

[418] Mohammed Abu-Nimer and Ned Lazarus, 'The Peacebuilder's Paradox and the Dynamics of Dialogue: A Psychosocial Portrait of Israeli-Palestinian encounters' in Judy Kuriansky (ed.), *Beyond Bullets and Bombs: Grassroots Peacebuilding Between Israelis and Palestinians* (Praeger, 2008), 19; Lazarus, *BICOM Report 2017*, above n 78, 53.

[419] 'USAID/CMM Field Study 2014' above n 361 cited in Lazarus, *BICOM Report 2017*, above n 78, 55–56.

[420] Rabah Halabi and Nava Sonnenschein, 'The Jewish-Palestinian Encounter in a Time of Crisis' (2004)0.60(2) *Journal of Social Issues* 373–387; See also Nadim Rouhana and Susan Korper, 'Power Asymmetry and Goals of Unofficial Third Party Intervention in Protracted Intergroup Conflict: Peace and Conflict' (1997) 1(3) *The Journal of Peace Psychology* 1–17.

[421] Maoz, above n 363.

have been criticised for failing to recognise existing patterns of inequality, or even reproducing them.[422] A focus on 'dialogue' as an event, rather than as an unfolding process, could lead to the false assumption that 'mere talking' can solve the conflict, when structural patterns of relationships, resource distribution, laws, and local practices are sustaining the conflict.[423]

Nevertheless, the asymmetrical relations between Israelis and Palestinians are hardly unique to the Middle East; it is a common feature of intractable conflict.[424] Veterans of Israel–Palestinian peacebuilding are keenly aware of this challenge and have designed various strategies to mitigate its effects.[425] For example, the Parents Circle Families Forum (PCFF) has reformed organisational structure and practice to enhance equality with 'two signatures on every check'.[426] According to Co-Director Faraj: 'All the reports were [previously] written in the Israeli office...Since that time [2013], we are in full partnership in writing the reports, in management, in proposals, in budgeting, and in the joint board'.[427] Moreover, the empirical record demonstrates that Israelis and Palestinians are capable of humanising one another in the current circumstances.[428] Dialogical collaboration creates space in which differences as well as equality are acknowledged.[429]

Rather than entrenching asymmetry, the IPTEC could potentially disrupt existing power relations. As discussed, justice has a qualitative value to counter an asymmetry of power with a discourse of reciprocity (Chap. 4).[430] For example, the IPTEC Victim hearings could help cultivate symmetry in psychological and human terms. In the words of Dajani: 'A parent who loses a child is a parent who loses a child, no

---

422 Mohammed Abu-Nimer, *Dialogue, Conflict Resolution, and Change* (State University of New York Press, 1999).

423 Mohammed, Abu-Nimer, *Dialogue, Conflict Resolution, and Change* (State University of New York Press, 1999); Gershon Baskin et al., *Yes PM: Years of Experience in Strategies for Peace Making: Looking at Israeli-Palestinian people to people activities,1993–2000* (Jerusalem, Israel/ Palestine Center for Research and Information, 2002).

424 Conflict-resolution scholars acknowledge that asymmetry of power is inherent to any cross-conflict endeavour. It is not unique to the Middle East. See for example, Daniel Bar-Tal and Izhak Schnell, *The Impacts of Lasting Occupation: Lessons from Israeli Society* (Oxford University Press, 2012).

425 Lazarus, above n 78, *BICOM Report 2017,* 57.

426 Ibid; Ned Lazarus, *Intractable Peacebuilding: Innovation and Perseverance in the Israeli-Palestinian Context.* (George Mason University, School for Conflict Analysis and Resolution, 2015).

427 Ned Lazarus, Interview with Mazen Faraj (Beit Jalla, 21 July, 2016) in Lazarus, above n 78, *BICOM Report 2017,* 57.

428 Bar-Tal and the late Gavriel Salomon, after years of research on conflict psychology and peace education, conclude that Israeli and Palestinian dialogue participants are equally able to 'humanise the other'. Daniel Bar-Tal and Gavriel Salomon, 'Israeli-Jewish Narratives of the Israeli-Palestinian Conflict: Evolution, Contents, Functions and Consequences' in Rotberg, above n 334, 38.

429 As discussed in Chap. 7, dialogical cooperation opened a space of mutual humanisation in which Jewish-Israeli and Palestinian dialogue partners could see themselves as equals. See also Berlowitz, above n 376, 40 and 50.

430 Kaufman, above n 344, 180.

matter his national or religious affiliation'.[431] At a practical level, the concrete, shared benefits of collaborative projects can outweigh different motivations for participation.[432] As the Director of the Olive Oil Without Borders explained: 'Different starting points led people to a similar place...They might have had different issues, but there was value for both nations'.[433]

Ultimately, the IPTEC is capable of accounting for the asymmetries. For example, akin to the PCFF, the IPTEC could establish parallel Israeli and Palestinian offices and internal governing bodies and structures.[434] Sequencing the IPTEC meetings between intra-group and inter-group encounters may improve perceptions and needs.[435] Many existing initiatives have surpassed the physical barriers by bringing groups of experts, academics, and participants to a neutral third location for common activities. There also exist virtual spaces, from live streaming to websites, that could accommodate victims who are unable to testify in person.

Timing and Political Feasibility

> *It might seem strange to contemplate transitional justice in times like these, when transition seems a remote possibility and justice is so patently absent from Israel and Palestine.* (Daphna Gola-Agnon)[436]

The present creation of an Israeli–Palestinian truth commission is arguably premature and unrealistic. As discussed, transitional justice classically entails post-conflict state-sanctioned practices (Chap. 4). Thus, for Meyerstein, an Israeli–Palestinian truth commission remains conditional on a future peace agreement.[437] Even a roundtable on truth commissions at Harvard Law School during the Oslo period dismissed

---

[431] Alexander, above n 390.

[432] For example, a major evaluative study of Seeds of Peace identified experiential differences between Israeli and Palestinian participants—but, crucially, find consistently positive outcomes and assessments of encounter participation among majorities of both groups. Julianna Schroeder and Jane Risen, 'Befriending the Enemy: Outgroup Friendship Longitudinally Predicts Intergroup Attitudes in a Coexistence Program for Israelis and Palestinians', (2016) 19 (1) *Group Processes and Intergroup Relations* 42, 70–73.

[433] For example, the Olive Oil Without Borders project, generated a trade agreement, increased production capacity, and opened up new markets for sale of surplus harvest. It received enthusiastic evaluations from both sides. *Near East Foundation Annual Report* (2014), 16. https://www.ngoadvisor.net/wp-content/uploads/2016/06/NEF-2014-Annual-Report.pdf cited in Lazarus, above n 78, *BICOM Report 2017,* 57–58.

[434] For example, some of the workshops of the Shared Histories project were conducted in Cyprus. Ibid 57.

[435] Unilateral approaches aimed at building peace constituencies within each conflict party as a preparatory phase to joint work may help the IPTEC. See Lazarus, above n 78, *BICOM Report 2017,* 57; '*USAID/ CMM Field Study 2014*', above n 365, 135.

[436] Golan-Agnon, above n 20, 32.

[437] Meyerstein, '*Transitional Justice and Post-conflict Israel/Palestine*', above n 6, 307.

the idea of a truth commission for Israel/Palestine as fanciful.[438] Clearly, ongoing violence and barren diplomacy compound the difficulties around any genuine steps towards conflict transformation.[439] Early mandates to impose transitional justice, especially by non-state actors, may ignore political, social, and budgetary realities.[440] The urge to act quickly could overshadow the need to invest in broad consultation process, on securing resources, or developing sound mechanisms.[441] No doubt, an IPTEC would benefit from a more hospitable political climate.

Nevertheless, the possibilities for unofficial truth and justice measures have expanded with the growing role of transitional justice in active conflicts (Chap. 4). As discussed, truth commissions and other measures are now conceived for periods of profound violence and extreme political instability. In particular, the IPTEC is informed by various civil society initiatives promoted successfully before a conflict has ended—as in Guatemala, Brazil, and more recently Colombia. Many activists around the world have demonstrated, time and again, that silencing and ignoring the past prevent conflict resolution, and the attainment of truth-telling, Justice, and reconciliation. Accordingly, even in situations of seemingly intractable conflict, transitional justice projects have acted without government backing to bring resolve to violent conflicts. The Israeli–Palestinian setting is no exception, and the IPTEC should build on the experiences of other countries.

Conflict Transformation Tool

> *It is clear that the new society will not come about just by thinking about it. But there is no doubt that one must begin by setting forth what is important; because, if we do not, we will never achieve it.*[442] (Costa Rican philosopher, Manuel Formosa)

Far from being premature, the IPTEC offers significant potential as a pre-resolution project. From Latin America to South Africa, progress toward political resolution is closely connected with early transitional justice measures (Chap. 4).[443] Practice shows that political transitions are only successful when certain measures are taken in the pre-transition phase. For example, long before transitional justice entered the lexicon in Northern Ireland, families held unofficial inquiries on the deaths of their beloved ones.[444] These civic steps created an environment in which accountability

[438] In particular, Palestinian political scientist Fateh Azzam expressed little confidence in the idea of a truth commission given the political circumstances and diplomatic fissures. See *'Harvard Law Discussion'*, above n 77.

[439] Louis Kriesberg, 'The Relevance of Reconciliation Actions in the Breakdown of Israeli-Palestinian Negotiations 2000' (2002) 27(4) *Peace and Change* 546, 566.

[440] Barsalou, above n 383, 5.

[441] Ibid.

[442] Manuel Formosa, "La alternative: Repensar a revolucion," *Seminario Universidad,* Universidad de Costa Rica, (23 October, 1987) 5 cited in Crocker, above n 271, 60.

[443] Bisharat and Kaufman, above n 336, 72.

[444] *'Zochrot Workshop'*, above n 300.

was sought and expected and changed the terms of the wider political debate.[445] The experience of past commissions demonstrates the benefits of early policy discussions, academic engagement and grassroot participation prior to negotiations (Chap. 7).

Similarly, the Israeli–Palestinian conflict can profit from '…planning for the moment of transition in advance, rather than awaiting its arrival'.[446] This is particularly valuable since human rights groups are currently not involved in determining the answers to the basic questions of the conflict, including those of the Palestinian refugee question, or how to comprehensively deal with legacies of historic abuse (Chap. 7).[447] In short, the IPTEC might result in a paradigm shift and should open new avenues for imaginative and creative political solutions.[448]

In particular, the IPTEC could offer a pre-figurative politics that creates spaces to re-imagine and model alternative approaches for rights and justice in the Middle East.[449] 'Pre-figuring' modalities of transition are crucial during conflict as demonstrated by the unofficial truth projects detailed in Chap. 7.[450] As discussed above, the IPTEC may play an active role in constructing contextualised visions of justice, and collective rights that positively benefit the peace process.[451] The IPTEC is also about acting out a vision of the future in which transitional justice would become formal policy.[452] This is particularly valuable since human rights groups are currently not involved in determining the answers to the basic questions arising from the conflict, including those of the Palestinian refugee question, or how to comprehensively deal with legacies of historic abuse.[453] As discussed in Chap. 7, Israeli and Palestinian human rights NGOs are more about protecting Palestinians human rights in the territories for the interim, 'until the politicians find a solution'.[454] In short, the IPTEC may result in a paradigm shift and open new avenues for imaginative and creative political solutions.[455]

---

445 Ibid.

446 Miller, above n 1, 294.

447 Golan-Agnon, above n 20, 39.

448 Kaufman, above n 344.

449 Darcy K. Leach, 'Prefigurative Politics', in David A. Snow et al. (eds.) *The Wiley-Blackwell Encyclopedia of Social and Political Movements* (Wiley and Sons, 2013), 1004–6 cited in Gready and Robins, above n 372.

450 *'Zochrot Workshop'*, above n 300; Dudai, *'Transitional Justice as Social Control'*, above n 325, 13.

451 Ibid.

452 Adam and Moodley also propose that truth seeking in Israel and Palestine can lead to future official mechanisms or can also act as a conflict transformation tool. See Heribert Adam and Kogila Moodley, *Seeking Mandela: Peacemaking Between Israelis and Palestinians* (Temple University Press, 2005).

453 Golan-Agnon, above n 20, 39.

454 Ibid.

455 Kaufman, above n 344, 184.

Whilst the current climate may not support an official truth commission, the viability of an unofficial one need not depend on a diplomatic accord. Even despite the violence, there are signs that an Israeli–Palestinian conflict transformation yet may be advanced.[456] Merely a decade ago, the Israeli state had virtually no challenge from civil society, and public discourse on the Palestinian side was exceedingly limited.[457] Today, collaborative projects between Israelis and Palestinians achieve meaningful policy change and continue to document positive discursive shifts (Chap. 7).[458] The IPTEC could build on these initiatives, as knowledge and memory-based strategies for political change.[459] Thus, despite official hostility, civic capacity exists to advance a new framework for transitional justice.

Public Support and Civic Capacity

Many would challenge the IPTEC's ability to command public support and secure participation from either side. As discussed, peacebuilding and human rights groups struggle against a tide of largely hostile public opinion (Chap. 7). Arguably, some Israelis identify with the Zionist ethos and the army too closely to support any investigation into wrongdoing.[460] Indeed, there has been a harsh backlash against unofficial truth-telling projects like Breaking the Silence and alternative memorials in Israel. Similarly, for Palestinians, those engaged in such civic activity may be seen as collaborators and/or abettors of the occupation. As discussed, many Palestinians are wedded to idealised notions of historical justice (Chaps. 1 and 4). It would also be unrealistic to expect a group like Hamas to retreat from its core ideology, which flatly rejects Israel's right to exist.

Arguably, both the sides are unprepared for the profound changes needed to moderate their national narratives. Indeed, anyone advocating such ideas risks severe social and political sanctions in the PA and to a lesser extent in Israel. As Grossman writes: '[i]n today's Israel, the self-evident has become subversive. To identify with the mourning of the other side is to immediately become a public enemy'.[461] Members of both the nations may believe that reconciliatory gestures

---

[456] Kriesberg, above n, 439.

[457] Hassassian, above n 127, 65.

[458] After the Olive Oil Without Borders project, 90% of participants reported increased trust in 'the other' and 77% indicated intention to continue cross-border cooperation. Interview with Near East Foundation (NEF) Director Charles Benjamin cited in Lazarus, *BICOM Report 2017,* above n 78, 10.

[459] Gutman, '*Looking Back*', above n 333, 12–13 .

[460] Yael Tadmir quoted in *'Harvard Law Discussion'*, above n 77.

[461] Nissan Shor, 'Not a Home? Israel Was Tailor-made for David Grossman' *Ha'aretz* (Online, 27 April, 2018) https://www.haaretz.com/israel-news/.premium-not-a-home-israel-was-tailor-made-for-david-grossman-1.6032805.

will be misunderstood and/or prove counterproductive.[462] Whilst Israelis fear that responsibility for creating the Palestinian refugees could delegitimise the state, '…Palestinians fear that a commission will be another placatory measure that does not bring concrete improvements'.[463]

Greater support may nevertheless exist for unofficial truth-telling than commonly assumed. As discussed, Israeli scholarship has subverted traditional Zionist premises on the creation of the Palestinian refugees (Chap. 1). Over the past two decades, these post-Zionist debates have filtered wider circles in Israeli society (Chap. 7).[464] Significant shifts have led to increased political tolerance and acceptance of critical narratives.[465] Despite a political shift to the right, Israeli popular culture (particularly through films and documentaries) continues to directly and critically engage with the occupation, the Palestinians, and human rights concerns.[466] In terms of Israeli participation in the IPTEC, it is notable that the Zochrot Truth Commission (2015) successfully gathered dozens of testimonies from veteran Israeli soldiers who participated in the 1948 hostilities.[467] A few of them also voluntarily agreed to publicly testify and provide evidence despite the fact that, as an unofficial commission, Zochrot had no authority to summon witnesses nor access classified documents about the events in question. If this is the track-record of former Israeli fighters, solid prospects exist that Israeli victims would feel comfortable to speak to an IPTEC Victims Committee and share their experience of abuses.

Many factors have also made Palestinian society more conducive to human rights norms and civil society. A tolerance for divergent opinions has evolved into an intrinsic value and tradition among Palestinians.[468] In recent years, a more participatory political culture has taken root.[469] A good example is the active political participation of women, which is an essential part of Palestinian civil society today and has a crucial impact on the establishment and consolidation of pluralist thinking and democratic rule.[470] In particular, well-developed ideas about civic action and resistance to official discourse exist among younger Palestinians.[471] In recent years, the enthusiasm of Palestinian civil society for popular non-violent activities[472] has

---

[462] Kriesberg, above n, 439.

[463] Miller, above n 1, 311

[464] Maoz Bar-On, 'Historiography as an Educational Project: The Historian's Debate in Israel and the Middle East Peace Process' in Ilan, Peleg (ed.), *The Middle East Peace Process: Interdisciplinary Prospectives,* (SUNY Press, 1998) 21.

[465] Nets-Zehngut, '*Transitional Justice*', above n 272, 18.

[466] *Advocate (2019), The Law in These Parts (2011), Waltz with Bashir (2008), The Gatekeepers (2012),* and *Bethlehem* (2013) are just some notable examples.

[467] See Zochrot website: https://www.zochrot.org/en/press/56178.

[468] Hassassian, above n 127, 65.

[469] Ibid.

[470] Ibid.

[471] Branold and Lyndon, above n 91.

[472] For example, since 2007, the Palestinian village of Bil'in in the West Bank has become a symbol of Palestinian non-violent resistance to Israeli occupation, Israeli settlements, and the separation wall/barrier. It has been the site of peaceful weekly Friday demonstrations.

demonstrated its organisational capacity for grassroot action. Though the space is far smaller than in Israel, national memory and history remain a platform for identity reconstruction.

'The Fringe Factor'

Ultimately, the IPTEC is far from becoming a mainstream endeavour. Israeli and Palestinian public opinion remains too entrenched in conflict for transitional justice to engender macro-change. One must recall that a project like the IPTEC does not expect to make normative inroads overnight. Rather, it would play an integral part in a longer-term transitional process. The creation of such a platform is one of the fundamental building blocks for supporting constructive social change over time.[473] IPTEC hearings may be effective in raising public awareness of potential cooperation and creating viable policy options.[474]

Attaining the support of an Israeli–Palestinian majority is unrealistic,[475] but the IPTEC could serve as a positive counterweight to the current culture of conflict and hopelessness. It could create 'zones of civility' where collaboration between Israelis and Palestinians builds solidarities between survivors that overcome, and even replace antagonistic nationalist narratives.[476] As discussed, many existing transitional justice initiatives (Chap. 7) are keenly aware of their role as spoilers of official policy and memory. It is worth recalling that resistance to transitional justice activity 'is itself an intervention in debates about memory, remembrance and memorialisation—which is to say, it is itself transitional justice'.[477]

Concluding Remarks: Expectations, Risks, and Impact

Finally, the IPTEC's ability to be regarded positively will challenge its advocates. Assessing the impact and managing expectations of transitional justice tools is no small task. From Latin America to South Africa, such measures disappoint those who expect them to deliver more than they can achieve.[478] By undertaking a wide

[473] This idea reflects John Paul Lederach's paradigm of conflict transformation—efforts to build cross-conflict networks and strengthen 'capacities for peace,' within an assumed context of ongoing conflict. John Paul Lederach, *Moral Imagination: The Art and Soul of Building Peace* (Oxford University Press, 2005) 47.

[474] Shamir, above n 413, 45.

[475] As Dudai notes, unofficial initiatives are by their nature 'deviant', and are not intended as a mainstream activity. Dudai, *'Deviant Commemorations'*, above n 311.

[476] Gready and Robins, above n 372, 963.

[477] Waters, above n 252, 178.

[478] Barsalou, above n 383, 5.

range of functions, truth commissions tend to over-promise and under-deliver (Chap. 6). Indeed, lofty claims and idealistic theory may increase the temptation to 'over-mandate' the IPTEC. After all, as an unofficial contested body, the IPTEC could risk falling short of its stated goals.

In this regard, some caution against the very creation of an Israeli–Palestinian truth commission. King-Irani argues that this measure '...is not sufficient for addressing or resolving the roots of the blood drenched crises of the Middle East. Assuming that...is cynical as well as dangerous'.[479] In the Northern Irish context, negotiators regarded a truth commission as a destabilising factor that could elevate tensions and even threaten the progress of the entire peace process.[480] Unsupported by the most powerful and mistrusted by the mainstream, the IPTEC might be accused of doing more harm than good as an oppositional project. Moreover, both Israeli and Palestinian victims are vulnerable groups that risk being re-traumatised through their participation. The IPTEC must therefore manage the expectations of both the Jewish and Palestinian communities and set clear standards by which success is measured and various counter-productive effects can be avoided.[481]

Modest by Design

It is worth recalling the disclaimer that truth commissions can only ever make a partial contribution to reckoning with the past (Chap. 6).[482] 'Truth commissions never should be seen as a panacea for the complex ills of any society. A truth commission is simply a tool...'.[483] Even a four-year process in South Africa did not begin to address the broad range of abuse and harm endured by apartheid's victims.[484] In this light, the IPTEC should not be expected to wave the magic wand of harmony after decades of violence. As with other active conflicts, transitional justice measures require modest expectations. In the words of Miller: 'If anything, this conflict now requires broadly optimistic ideas tempered by narrowly drawn expectations'.[485] Neither the conception, institutional design, nor implementation of the project is meant to fulfil every expectation or objective.

---

[479] According to King-Irani attempts to police the Israeli-Palestinian past are too controversial to be realised by an official truth commission. Lawrie King-Irani, 'To Reconcile or be Reconciled?: Agency, Accountability and Law in Middle-Eastern Conflicts (2004–2005) 28 *Hastings and International and Comparative Law Review* 369, 373.

[480] Patricia Lundy and Mark McGovern raised important considerations for why a truth commission was not the most appropriate mechanism for truth recovery and justice in the Irish post-conflict situation. See Patricia Lundy and Mark McGovern, 'The Politics of Memory in Post-Conflict Northern Ireland' (2001) 13(1) *Peace Review* 27–33.

[481] Shraga, above n 4, 105.

[482] Van Zyl, '*Unfinished Business',* above n 244, 745.

[483] González and Varney, above n 25, 37.

[484] Wing, above n 1, 147.

[485] Miller, above n 1, 308.

To this end, the normative goals of the IPTEC have been consciously constrained. For example, the commission is not mandated to create one joint history, but rather to provide a platform for recognition of both narratives, and in so doing, narrow the gap.[486] Thicker concepts of reconciliation, like forgiveness[487] and healing, are premature and will not be pursued. A key lesson from Northern Ireland is that we should not force victims into artificial relationships with one another.[488] Indeed, the term 'reconciliation' itself is too ambitious for the Middle East at present. It suggests an advanced stage of peace and conflict transformation.[489] For this reason, the IPTEC appropriates the term 'empathy' to calibrate expectations, and to more modestly pursue its grassroot reconciliatory goals. This does not suggest national hugs, or tears, or even personal catharsis. It simply means that reconciliation involves some measure of affective change or discursive shift towards peace.

Long-Term Process

It is difficult to reliably predict or measure the impact of a tool like the IPTEC. There is no easy way to quantify changes that might take place, let alone tangibly attribute positive outcomes to the project.[490] After all, the goals of the IPTEC do not target one specific state policy or decision, but challenge deeply held and broad cultural perceptions and narratives.[491] No one could expect an unofficial project to transform national mindsets in any short period of time.[492] Rather, truth and justice activities evolve in a gradual and fragmented way. '[They]…are not linear and need a long-term commitment of the peace builders rather than momentary conjectural optimism...'.[493]

From this standpoint, the IPTEC should be understood as an instrumental tool in a long-term social process. As discussed, many Israeli–Palestinian civic groups have managed to persevere through volatile conditions due to their resilience and future vision.[494] The recent Women Wage Peace movement is an example of

---

[486] Shraga, above n 4, 105.

[487] As discussed in Chap. 6, many academics have criticised the SATRC for imbuing 'reconciliation' with very Christian notions of inter-personal forgiveness. See Ball and Chapman, above n 21, 18.

[488] *'Zochrot Workshop'*, above n 300.

[489] Yaacov Bar-Siman-Tov, 'Chapter 5: Justice and Fairness as Barriers to the Resolution of the Israeli-Palestinian Conflict' in Yaacov Bar -Siman-Tov (ed) *Barriers to Peace in the Israeli-Palestinian Conflict* (Jerusalem Institute for Israel Studies, 2011) 178–226, 182.

[490] For example, the impact of Guatemala's truth commission was indirect. The Final Report was not incorporated into textbooks, but the Commission opened up space for public discussion and enabled instruction on political violence. Dudai, 'Deviant Commemoration', above n 311, 5–6.

[491] Ibid.

[492] Ibid.

[493] Adwan and Bar-On, above n 305, 514.

[494] Lazarus, *BICOM Report 2017,* above n 78, 36.

long-term investment in civil society for mobilisation and social change (Chap. 7).[495] The positive experience of bereaved Israeli–Palestinian parents and former combatants attests to the capacity of vulnerable groups to feel empowered by such measures over time (Chap. 7). In any event, the IPTEC could create a victim support group to offer trauma counselling and other psychological services to those testifying at the IPTEC in order to mitigate potential risks.

No doubt, the work of the IPTEC would be challenging. Clearly, even the most optimal design is prone to pitfalls. Thus, it is expected that not all the institutional best practices discussed above may be practically achieved. For example, it is possible that international support could be equivocal or that the project might fail to recruit all the civic actors identified as representative. However, working out the details and the difficulties that are bound to arise is in fact how the two nations begin engaging with one another and can become invested in overcoming conflict.[496] At best, the IPTEC could help to create better conditions for truth, justice, and reconciliation by encouraging shifts in the political culture and debate and by restoring dignity to those most affected by violence.[497] Even if that is all the IPTEC can achieve, this would already be considerable.

Moral and Political Imperative

While some can foresee no transitional justice for the region, many appreciate the absence of an alternative. Thus, Palestinian academic Dajani writes: 'This situation is exactly the reason why we should put more effort into reconciliation…The enmity prevalent today only means we have to try harder to move away from hatred, towards peace and empathy...'.[498] The perception that the Middle East conflict is impossible to resolve should not create a self-perpetuating refusal to consider solutions.[499] In the South African context, Du Toit called this 'loaded realism' as a way of only anticipating problems, so that a commission's infeasibility becomes a foregone conclusion.[500] While there is a clear need to avoid utopian thinking, one should also avoid approaching the IPTEC in a myopic way, only seeing it through the prism of the current stalemate.

In the final analysis, refusing to address the past is simply not the answer to an impossible present. Indeed, when despair prevails, when despite talks and

---

495 'The consciousness, the leadership, the motivation, the connections, and the strategy of WWP were all incubated over decades—through myriad campaigns, forums and projects that built networks able to leverage years of experience at a critical moment'. Ibid, 13.

496 Meyerstein *'Dreaming an Israeli-Palestinian Truth Commission'*, above n 1, 469–470.

497 González and Varney, above n 25, 12.

498 Mahmoud Dajani quoted in Alexander, above n 393.

499 Miller, above n 1, 308.

500 André du Toit, 'The South African Truth and Reconciliation Commission (TRC), Local History, Global Accounting' (2003) 92 *Politique Africaine* quoted in Dudai, *'Does Any of this Matter?'*, above n 159.

conferences, there is scant hope of a comprehensive solution, it is incumbent on practitioners to examine whether something akin to an IPTEC is possible. Certain factors can determine the relative 'success' of an IPTEC, but perhaps the decision to have one at all is the most important.[501] As the Northern Ireland, South African, and Latin American cases demonstrate, building civic bridges across the past is not the luxury of idealistic dreamers, but rather a task of political necessity awaiting all those entrapped by intractable conflict.

[501] Meyerstein, *'Dreaming an Israeli-Palestinian Truth Commission'*, above n 1, 469–470.

Appendix: The Israeli-Palestinian Truth and Empathy Commission (IPTEC) Functional Structure

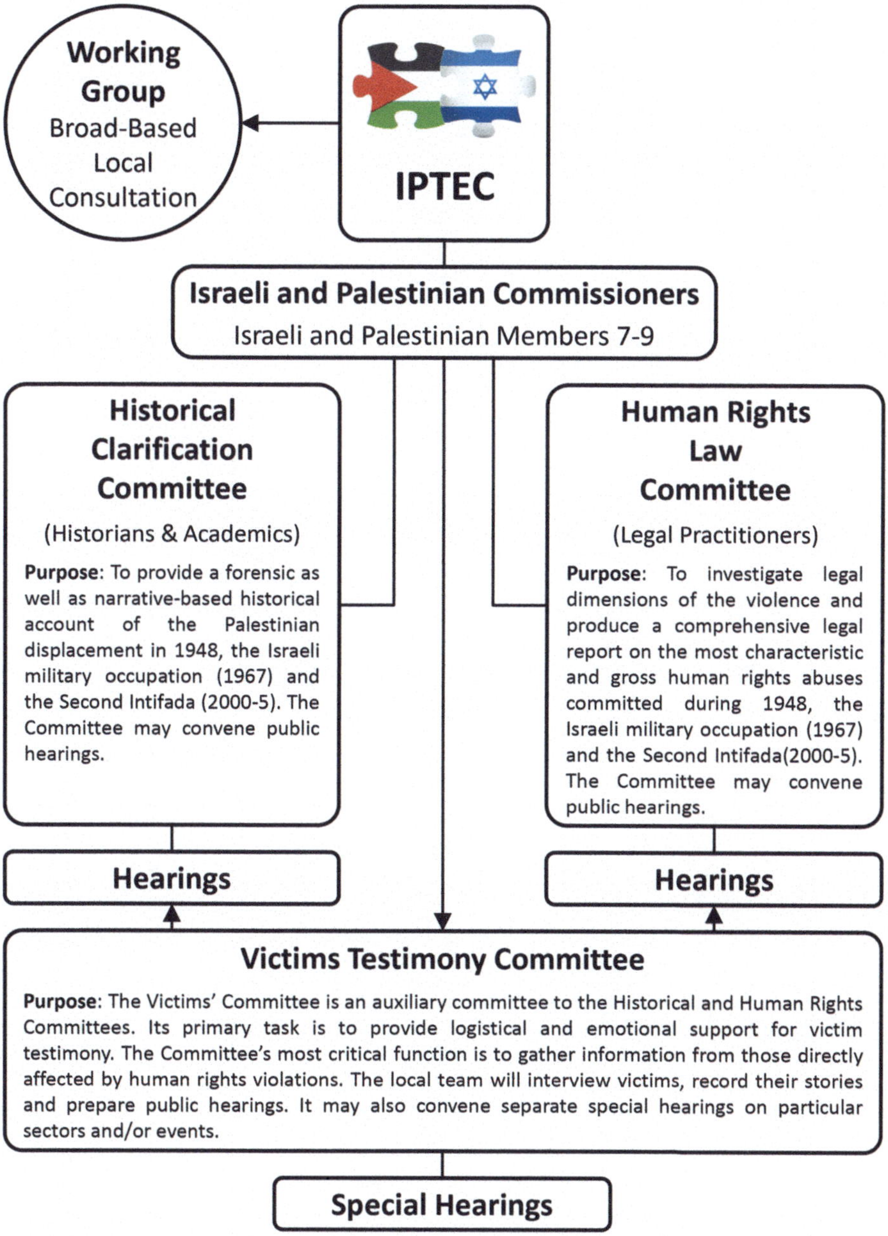

Index

J. Bracka, *Transitional Justice for Israel/Palestine*, Springer Series in Transitional Justice, https://doi.org/10.1007/978-3-030-89435-1

J

The manufacturer's authorised representative in the EU is Springer Nature Customer Service Centre GmbH, Europaplatz 3, 69115 Heidelberg, Germany. If you have any concerns regarding our products, please contact ProductSafety@springernature.com

Printed and bound by CPI Group (UK) Ltd, Croydon, CR0 4YY
30/09/2026
02225687-0007